"All who knew, loved, and learned from 'Chappo' will be enormously grateful for Stace's thorough and excellent study of the life, ministry, and influence of John Charles Chapman. Those who missed that privilege will discover in this careful work much about why and how this outstanding man had such an impact on his generation. Thanks to Baden's labors we can appreciate more deeply the richness of what God gave us in this faithful servant."

—**John Woodhouse**, former principal, Moore Theological College

"'To each is given the manifestation of the Spirit for the common good,' wrote St. Paul. This is on display here in both author and subject. Stace demonstrates impressive diligence and skill. His subject, John Chapman, appears in his far-reaching influence and service. Thank you God for Baden and John."

—**R. Harry Goodhew**, former archbishop, Anglican Diocese of Sydney

Sydney's One Special Evangelist

Australian College of Theology Monograph Series

SERIES EDITOR GRAEME R. CHATFIELD

The ACT Monograph Series, generously supported by the Board of Directors of the Australian College of Theology, provides a forum for publishing quality research theses and studies by its graduates and affiliated college staff in the broad fields of Biblical Studies, Christian Thought and History, and Practical Theology with Wipf and Stock Publishers of Eugene, Oregon. The ACT selects the best of its doctoral and research masters theses as well as monographs that offer the academic community, scholars, church leaders and the wider community uniquely Australian and New Zealand perspectives on significant research topics and topics of current debate. The ACT also provides opportunity for contributors beyond its graduates and affiliated college staff to publish monographs which support the mission and values of the ACT.

Rev. Dr. Graeme Chatfield
Series Editor and Associate Dean

Sydney's One Special Evangelist

John C. Chapman and the Shaping of
Anglican Evangelicalism and Australian
Religious Life, 1968–2001

BADEN P. STACE

WIPF & STOCK · Eugene, Oregon

SYDNEY'S ONE SPECIAL EVANGELIST
John C. Chapman and the Shaping of Anglican Evangelicalism and Australian Religious Life, 1968–2001

Australian College of Theology Monograph Series

Copyright © 2022 Baden P. Stace. All rights reserved. Except for brief quotations in critical publications or reviews, no part of this book may be reproduced in any manner without prior written permission from the publisher. Write: Permissions, Wipf and Stock Publishers, 199 W. 8th Ave., Suite 3, Eugene, OR 97401.

Wipf & Stock
An Imprint of Wipf and Stock Publishers
199 W. 8th Ave., Suite 3
Eugene, OR 97401

www.wipfandstock.com

PAPERBACK ISBN: 978-1-6667-4908-3
HARDCOVER ISBN: 978-1-6667-4909-0
EBOOK ISBN: 978-1-6667-4910-6

07/19/22

Dedicated to Karin, Caleb, Huntley, and Abigail.
My delight, my strength, and my joy.
Partners in the gospel.
Coheirs of the grace of life.

Contents

Preface | ix
Acknowledgements | xi
Abbreviations | xiv
Pictures of John Charles Chapman (1930–2012) | xvi

Part I: Prolegomena

1   Introduction: Sydney's One Special Evangelist | 3
2   John Charles Chapman: Life Contours | 38

Part II: Preacher

3   Australian Evangelical Homiletics | 73
4   The Preaching of a Theologian-Evangelist | 125

Part III: Evangelist

5   Public Witness and a Changing Nation | 157
6   The Gospel and Social Reform | 216
7   Evangelism and the Church | 251

Part IV: Pugilist and Pioneer

8   Semper Reformanda: The Gospel, the Church, and a Changing World | 283
9   The Spirit, the Word, and the Christian Life | 326
10 Conclusion: The Shaping of Anglican Evangelicalism | 355

Appendices | 365
Bibliography | 475

Preface

THIS IS THE FIRST academic historical study of a figure who came to play a defining role in the Australian evangelical movement of the late twentieth century—the inimitable preacher, evangelist, and churchman—John Charles Chapman. The study situates Chapman's career within a period marked by momentous changes to the social and religious fabric of Western society. By the end of the 1960s, such realities contributed to a statistical decline across historic Christian denominations and marked a sudden end to the social and religious contract that had regulated Western society. At the same time, global Evangelicalism was reviving, bringing vitality to large swathes in the Global South and creating a rebalancing in Western societies as conservative religious movements experienced growth and even renewal amidst wider secularizing trends.

The study examines Chapman's contribution as a leading figure in the Australian evangelical response to this period of challenge and opportunity. In his expansive ministry as director of Sydney's Anglican Department of Evangelism (1969–93) Chapman stood at the vanguard of the growing Australian evangelical movement for a generation, while playing a significant role in the development of the movement in prominent pockets of the English-speaking world. To this end, the study examines Chapman's contribution along three distinct yet interrelated lines: in homiletics, missiology, and as a vigorous advocate for the tenets of Reformed evangelical faith. As a preacher, Chapman played a defining role in the revival of a classically Reformed Protestant expository preaching model, becoming one of the leading Australian preachers to exemplify, popularize, and adapt this model for use in congregational and evangelistic settings. Chapman preached an estimated 7,500 sermons across five continents to audiences of three quarters of a million people. Few Australians may lay claim to such a legacy, ensuring his homiletic theory and praxis became an influential model in the formation of other Australian and international practitioners. Chapman's contribution as an evangelist was also highly significant. In the changing environment of the post-1960s era, Chapman emerged as a key figure in the development of new missiological tools, successfully differentiating evangelical modes-of-witness from the institutional and revivalist modes of the past. Chapman's development of a first generation of postwar theologically oriented and popular evangelistic works, alongside his insightful missional advocacy (given in seminaries, conventions, churches, and other civic forums) also supplied motivation as well as a framework and vocabulary for a generation of Christians to reengage their culture with the claims of Christ. Chapman's vigorous advocacy for the tenets of Reformed evangelical faith was also significant. The study explores the way in which, across a wide array of domestic and international fora, Chapman contended for the soteriological priority of the gospel in Christian life, mission, and thought. While highly polemical at times, the result was a stimulating history of public advocacy that sought a revival of confidence in Evangelicalism's message, and a constantly reforming vision of Evangelicalism's method. Such a legacy marks Chapman as a key figure within the generation of postwar leaders whose work coalesced to give Australian Evangelicalism its contemporary shape and dynamism. Moreover, in its analysis of this period of Australian religious history, the study contributes to a growing, yet surprising, dynamic within the twentieth-century historiographical storyline—the presence of resurgent religious, and particularly evangelical, Christian faith.

Acknowledgements

THE COMPLETION OF THIS research was an immense privilege. It involved the study of a stimulating period of evangelical history and of a network of Christian statespersons—and a key figure within this network—who contended admirably for Christian truth in fast-changing times. The process was exhilarating and fascinating, and there are many to whom I am indebted.

Sincere thanks are due to the faculty and staff of St. Mark's National Theological Centre and the Centre for Public and Contextual Theology in Canberra. This community of scholars and professionals provided an environment of support, scholarly rigor, and collegiality throughout the process of research. It was a great privilege to learn from my doctoral supervisor Dr. Michael Gladwin. His exhaustive grasp of Anglican and evangelical history, his keen scholarly mind, judicious historiographical judgments, generosity in the giving of his time, and unfailing support and enthusiasm for the project strengthened the study immeasurably. I am also greatly indebted to my co-supervisor Rev. Dr. Geoff Broughton, another model scholar in his field, who brought a wealth of theological and practical reflection to the study, and whose knowledge of the context of study sharpened many aspects of the present work. I am grateful to Professor Stephen Pickard and the Centre for Public and Contextual Theology for the provision of scholarship funds, without which the research could not have been done. My sincere thanks also to the Rev. Professor Andrew Cameron, whose enthusiasm for the study and whose generous spirit and rigorous scholarly leadership of the St. Mark's environment greatly enriched the period of research.

I am also much indebted to Greta Morris for her patient and highly professional editorial work in the preparation of this manuscript for publication. Thanks also to Megan Powell du Toit and the publishing team at the Australian College of Theology and Wipf and Stock. It is a privilege to make a contribution to the ACT Monograph Series, as it seeks to offer the academic community, church leaders, and the wider community uniquely Australian perspectives on significant research topics.

Thanks are due to the staff and archivists of numerous libraries and historical collections. My thanks to Erin Mollenhauer and Adam Tierney at the Donald Robinson Library, Moore College, whose patience in fulfilling countless requests for archived books and historic material knew no limit. I am also grateful to members of the faculty of Moore College: Dr. Philip Kern, the Rev. Dr. George Athas, and Dr. Peter Orr, who provided encouragement and critical reflection at various points during the research period. Thanks are also due to Dr. Louise Trott at the Sydney Diocesan Archives, and to the staff at the State Library of NSW and the Armidale Diocesan Registry. The helpful and immensely knowledgeable staff at the Billy Graham Center Archives in Wheaton, Illinois: Paul Ericksen, Katherine Graber, and Bob Shuster also ensured my time spent sifting through the treasures of their many collections was productive and enjoyable. Thanks also to the staff of Wheaton College's Harbor House, who provided accommodation in Chicago. I am also indebted to Rev. Adrian Lane and Rev. David Mansfield, whose enthusiasm for the research and provision of a wealth of historic material pertinent to the subject greatly enriched the study.

Sincere thanks are also due to the network of clergy and Christian leaders in Australia, North America, England, and South Africa who lived the period of study and who generously provided their reflections during the interview phase of the research (see bibliography). The time spent hearing their recollections was both enormously enriching from a research perspective as well as a great personal privilege. Their courageous advocacy for Christian truth is undoubtedly the spring from which much contemporary blessing has continued to flow. I hope they might feel that this published study accords them and their contemporaries with respect and critical sympathy. Sincere thanks to the staff at St. Helen's Bishopsgate and All Soul's Langham Place in London, who were instrumental in making my time in the United Kingdom so productive. Sincere thanks are also due to the staff at the Sydney Department of Evangelism and New Churches: Rev. Phil Wheeler, Rev. Bruce Hall, Sophie Lin, and Nola Budd, who aided the research in countless practical ways.

Sincere thanks also to the people of St. Stephen's Anglican Church Normanhurst, in Sydney. Beginning a new ministry there as shepherd and overseer of the parish and staff team in the final stages of research was a great joy. The sincerity of your faith, the warmth of your fellowship, and your passion to see Christ honored and proclaimed is a source of great pride, satisfaction, and joy.

Finally, I owe an unpayable debt to my family. I am grateful to Lea Collocott (a co-traveller in the love of learning) and Deric Collocott (who did not live to see this research completed). Their interest and support was a constant encouragement. Thanks also to Matt and Lyndal Stace, Doug and Heidi Parker, and Nicola Batten (siblings and siblings-in-law) for their interest and support.

To my parents, Dr. Doug and Nitia Stace, I owe so much. Their belief in the value of this research was a source of constant encouragement. Their generosity in funding numerous costs associated with the study also aided in its completion. Most importantly, it is their sustained witness to the Savior who stands behind all of the human actors in this story, that I thank them for. It is undoubtedly the wellspring from which so much of my own Christian faith and strength derives.

Preeminently, it is to my wife Karin and our children Caleb, Huntley, and Abby that I owe the greatest debt of thanks. The undertaking of a project of this size is undoubtedly a shared burden. The children patiently shared my attention while I juggled competing life, ministry, and research demands. I am so proud of this high-spirited trio. My hope is that this research may in some way be an encouragement to their future Christian life. However, my most special thanks go to Karin, who shared the burden of this season with patience and grace. She was brave enough to embark on this venture with me. And without her countless sacrifices, love, and support this project would not have begun, let alone seen completion. To this woman of noble character, I offer profound thanks, and consider it a sweet privilege to journey with her in the service of our Lord Jesus Christ.

B. P. S. 2022
Soli Deo gloria

Abbreviations

AAPB	An Australian Prayer Book
APBA	A Prayer Book for Australia
ADEB	Australian Evangelical Dictionary of Biography
AEA	Australian Evangelical Alliance
AFES	Australian Fellowship of Evangelical Students
ANZAC	Australian and New Zealand Army Corps
BDM	Sydney Anglican Board of Diocesan Mission
BCP	Book of Common Prayer
BGCA	Billy Graham Centre Archives
BGEA	Billy Graham Evangelistic Association
CICCU	Cambridge Intercollegiate Christian Union
CMS	Church Missionary Society
DOE	Sydney Anglican Department of Evangelism
EA	Evangelical Alliance
GAFCON	Global Anglican Future Conference
ICOWE	International Congress on World Evangelisation (Lausanne Congress)
IVF	Inter Varsity Fellowship

KCC	Katoomba Christian Convention
LCWE	Lausanne Committee on World Evangelisation
MTC	Moore Theological College
NCLS	National Church Life Survey
NSW	New South Wales
OICCU	Oxford Intercollegiate Christian Union
SC	Southern Cross Magazine
SDA	Sydney Anglican Diocesan Archives
SMBC	Sydney Missionary Bible College
SMH	Sydney Morning Herald
SUEU	Sydney University Evangelical Union
UK	United Kingdom
UNSW	University of New South Wales
WCC	World Council of Churches

John Charles Chapman (1930–2012)

Evangelical statesman

Conference speaker

Soul winner

Part I

Prolegomena and Life Contours

1

Introduction: Sydney's One Special Evangelist

Framing Chapman's Contribution

"In evangelism, like every other part of the Christian life, there is a maxim to be learned which if you learn you won't become too discouraged . . . 'The First Fifty Years are the Hardest.'"—John Charles Chapman[1]

"GOOD HEAVENS," CRIED THE elderly English gentlemen, aghast at the signage outside the London Street United Reformed Church, "the Aussies have already taken over *The Times* and *Courage*, now they're after our congregations!" "Fosters Lounge Bar Inside!" blared another sign on the building, comically marked on its apex with a "Halo of St Bruce." "Australian Evangelist John Chapman is really worth listening to!" roared the main street signage. "A Fresh Start all this week. Congregation wanted. No experience necessary. All new sermons. Unlike TV. No Repeats!"[2]

This playful cartoon parody in the Basingstoke Gazette captures the reaction of an English public to the "Fresh Start 86" campaign in Southampton, England. It hints at a quiet irony the public were enjoying at a spiritual renaissance they perceived arising within the very churches they had come to consider as both dour and dormant—a renaissance fronted of all people by an Australian! Publicity for this regional campaign was organized and

1. J. C. Chapman, *Evangelism Conference St. Helen's Bishopsgate*, January 6, 1996.
2. *The Basingstoke Gazette*, cited in Department of Evangelism Prayer Letter, no. 1 (February–April 1987).

extensive. Images of John Chapman, the veteran Australian evangelist, appeared on the back of buses and on posters in shop windows. In most towns it appeared almost as if an aggressive real estate agent had commenced business nearby. Crusade signs bearing Chapman's image multiplied on lawns and outside houses, declaring "Whatever you think . . . John Chapman is worth listening to!" The results of the campaign spoke equally loudly. A combined audience of nineteen thousand were addressed by the Australian preacher during the campaign, in cathedrals, rugby clubs, coffee shops, and civic halls. Thousands of Bible tracts and Gospels were distributed, with as many copies of Chapman's evangelistic material given away. Crucially, to the delight of campaign organizers and church leadership, eight hundred and fifty souls asked for help to make a fresh start with Jesus Christ.[3]

This portrait of a passionate Australian evangelist declaring Christ with Bible in hand, in the twilight of a century of contest and tumult over religious belief, captures a story line that is fast becoming one of the surprising features of twentieth-century religious historiography—the story of resurgent, even buoyant world Evangelicalism.[4] The strength of this movement in the English-speaking world of the twentieth century remained the historic transatlantic axis of English and American Evangelicalism. These historic wellsprings of evangelical fervor would again, in the twentieth century, supply their share of luminaries to shape the developing movement. A confident evangelical scholarship emerged. The homiletic legacy which fired and energized the movement was further sharpened. An adaptable yet theologically conservative agenda was pursued, offering the historic gospel in a new cultural husk. Such an approach bore all of the hallmarks of historic Evangelicalism and accelerated the movement's transition from the margins to occupying an increasingly influential role within the historic denominations by the close of the century. However, in the late twentieth

---

3. DOE Prayer Letter, no. 1 (February–April 1987); Interview with David Jackman, January 16, 2017.

4. The term "evangelical" describes a transnational and transdenominational Christian movement. Various taxonomies have endeavoured to capture the essence of Evangelicalism. Examining a broad sweep from the 1730s to the late twentieth century, evangelical historian David Bebbington identifies instead *four emphases* in what has become the most widely accepted scholarly definition of Evangelicalism, evidenced across its various denominational allegiances, namely (1) biblicism: a strong devotion to the Bible; (2) conversionism: the importance of a personal conversion to Christ; (3) crucicentrism: preaching and piety centered on the substitutionary sacrifice of Christ; and (4) activism: a belief that faith must be constantly expressed in word and deed. This definition, known as the Bebbington "quadrilateral," has yet to be bettered for its comprehensiveness and flexibility in both doctrinal and practical emphases. See Bebbington, *Evangelicalism*, 2, 4–17; Barclay, *Evangelicalism in Britain*, 9–14; Stanley, *Global Diffusion*, 11; Hutchinson and Wolffe, *Short History*, 16–18; Lewis, "Introduction," 1–8.

INTRODUCTION: SYDNEY'S ONE SPECIAL EVANGELIST   5

century, a new chorus of voices with a distinctly sharper accent would also come to play an increasingly spirited role within this international confederacy. As Australian Evangelicalism emerged from infancy to a self-assured adolescence, a coterie of Australian leaders began to offer the movement fresh insights, determination, and a dash of Australian impertinence as well.[5] This historical study charts something of that story. More specifically it examines the contribution to Australian and international Evangelicalism of a figure within the Australian story around whom many of the key lines converge—the inimitable preacher, evangelist, and churchman, Canon John Charles Chapman, "Chappo," Sydney's "one special evangelist."[6]

Orientation to the Study

John Charles Chapman (1930–2012) was a leading clergyman in the Sydney Anglican Diocese for over fifty years. In his expansive ministry as director of Sydney's Department of Evangelism (1969–1993) Chapman gave leadership and expression to a movement that saw significant development in homiletic, missiological, and ecclesiological theory and practice within the Sydney diocese. In turn, this leadership provided further stimulus and impetus to other Australian and international evangelical movements. Chapman's legacy within the Sydney diocese and related movements became almost proverbial. His quintessentially Australian style, jocular demeanor, and relatively modest formal theological education, belied a sharp theological acumen that issued assessments of him by contemporaries as a "theologian-evangelist . . . indeed, perhaps the first in modern times to exercise a ministry of evangelism in terms of such carefully considered theology."[7] As a preacher, some judged Chapman to be "the best evangelist the Anglican Church in Australia has ever produced"[8]—the "Australian Billy Graham."[9] With a unique ability to "poke fun at the human

---

5. On the place of Evangelicalism within historic denominationalism, see Stanley, *Global Diffusion*, 235–47. On the growing strength of its international representation by Australian leadership see Jupp, "Social Role," 32–33.

6. Manchester, "Preaching of John Chapman."

7. Appendix 4, JCCPP/BIO#5 records the text of an address in 1995 by the Rev. Dr. Paul Barnett (then Bishop of North Sydney) at the launch of Chapman's biography in which he reflects on Chapman's legacy. Access to appendices 1–5 is available through the Digital Repository and Archive of Moore College (the Ark). http://johnchapman.moore.edu.au.

8. Rev. Geoff Fletcher, Director, Sydney Department of Evangelism, 1966–69, cited in Appendix 4 JCCPP/BIO#4.

9. Poole, ACL Presidential Address, August 2013.

condition"[10] and heralding an "anointed declaration of the Word of God,"[11] Chapman opened "many a locked-door to the truth of the gospel."[12] As a thought leader, others judged him as a man of "tenacity of vision in the whole field of evangelism"[13] whose "contributions to the understanding of evangelism and how it ought to be done in modern culture are of greatest value."[14] Indeed, so influential was Chapman's contribution in an array of evangelical fora that former Sydney Archbishop Peter Jensen stated, "it is impossible to understand or explain present-day Sydney Anglicanism without reference to the titanic contribution of John Charles Chapman."[15]

Chapman's public ministry took shape at a time of conflicting religious and social trajectories. By the end of the 1960s, Protestant churches across the denominational spectrum no longer enjoyed the fruits of their historic ascendency in secular or religious life. They were confronted in the 1960s with a social and religious revolution that many now assess as epochal, and by a culture that had come to see the keys to progress and personal freedom in the natural and social sciences and in a secular humanism free from the encumbrance of religion.[16] Such forces saw a statistical decline in many Australian Christian denominations from which they have not today recovered.[17] At the same time, however, global Evan-

10. Rev. Dr. John Stott, then Rector Emeritus of All Souls Langham Place in London, and Director of the Christian Institute for Contemporary Christianity, cited in Appendix 4, JCCPP/BIO#4.

11. Rev. Joe Bell, Bishop, Church of England in South Africa, 1989–2000, cited in Appendix 4, JCCPP/BIO#4.

12. Lucas, St. Helen's Bishopsgate, March 1, 2013.

13. Rev. Richard Bewes, Rector, All Souls Langham Place, London 1983–2004, cited in Appendix 4 JCCPP/BIO#4.

14. R. Kent Hughes, Senior Pastor, College Church, Wheaton Illinois 1979–2006, cited in Appendix 4, JCCPP/BIO#4.

15. Rev. Dr. Peter F. Jensen, St. Andrew's Cathedral, November 2012, cited in Payne, "Magic Potion."

16. McLeod, *Religious Crisis*, 1; Frame, *Losing My Religion*, vi–xiv, 4.

17. Statistical evidence indicates an erosion of religious belief and a drift from involvement in religious institutions since this time. The proportion of Australians who described themselves as Christians declined from 88 percent in 1961 to 52 percent in 2016. The three major denominations derived from the United Kingdom (Anglican, Presbyterian, and Methodist) held their followings well until 1947, before seeing precipitous decline from 1961. Anglicans as a percentage of population (while peaking in 1921 at 43.7 percent) fell from 34.9 percent in 1961 to 13.3 percent in 2016; Presbyterians from 9.2 percent to 2.3 percent; and Methodist from 10.2 percent to 3.7 percent. See Hilliard, "Australia," 83; Australian Bureau of Statistics, "Population and Housing 2016"; "Census of Population and Housing 2006," cited in Jupp, "Social Status," 42. Such figures may be tempered by observing that the Christian portion of the population merely grew at a slower rate than the nation's population (1.44 percent compared with

gelicalism was reviving, bringing vitality to large swathes in the Global South and creating a rebalancing within Western societies as conservative religious movements continued to grow in marked contrast to their more liberal counterparts.[18] There is now little question that in the second half of the twentieth century, conservative churches—with defined standards of membership, belief, and moral conduct, along with a widening range of programs to increase and multiply faith via a definite evangelical message—saw higher retention rates and even renewal amidst broader secularizing trends. In most urban Australian dioceses the churches with the largest congregations and the highest income from direct giving were strongly evangelical in their theology and formed a larger proportion of Anglican churchgoers than ever before.[19] Indeed, in the last twenty years of the twentieth century, for example, attendances at Sydney Anglican churches grew in line with population growth and increased their retention of young people.[20] Given that these shifts framed Chapman's career

the wider population growth of 5.7 percent), and partly by observing the rapid growth of other religious groups via rising migration during this same period. However, these figures represent significant overall percentage decline on any assessment. See Bouma, *Australian Soul*, 67.

18. Following the practice of many scholars of world Christianity, the terms "Majority World" and "Global South" are both used to denote the majority of the world's population who live in the continents of Africa, Asia, Latin America, and the less developed islands of Australasia. The mid- and late twentieth century witnessed "church growth in large parts of the majority world on a scale unparalleled in any previous period in history." See Stanley, *Global Diffusion*, 14–15. The number of evangelicals in the world grew from 71.8m in 1910 to 210.5m by 2000. If one includes Pentecostals, the number in 2000 was 733.3m. Furthermore, the distribution of Christians between the different regions of the world shifted dramatically during this same period. At the beginning of the twentieth century 80 percent of the world's Christians lived in Europe and North America, and a mere 5 percent lived in Asia and Africa. By 2000, the proportion living in Europe and North America had dropped to 40 percent, while the proportion living in Asia and Africa had risen to 32 percent. See Barrett et al., *World Christian Encyclopaedia*, 22. For similar assessments, see McLeod, "Introduction," 1–2; Jenkins, *Next Christendom*, 1–3; Noll, *New Shape*, 9–10; Hutchinson and Wolffe, *Short History*, 221–30; Lewis, "Introduction," 4.

19. So Hilliard, "Pluralism," 133.

20. See Castle et. al., *National Church Life Survey*, 13, 20, 57–63; Kaldor et al., *Taking Stock*, 13–15, 129–31; Bellamy and Kaldor, *National Church Life Survey*, 7; Forsyth, "Sydney Anglicans," 67; Piggin, "Concrete," 184–93; Frame, *Anglicans in Australia*, 135. On the strength of conservative Australian churches in the late twentieth century, see Carey, "Historical Outline," 21; Bouma, *Australian Soul*, 83–84; Hilliard, "Australia," 86–88. For discussion of similar trends in the British and American contexts, see Atherstone and Maiden, "Anglican Evangelicalism," 18; Hutchinson and Wolffe, *Short History*, 213–20; Smith, *American Evangelicalism*, 121–25. For discussion of these divergent religious narratives see McLeod, "Being a Christian," 645–46; Davie, "Thinking Broadly," 221–31.

and that his ministry and contribution took shape amidst such conflicting trajectories, a study of this legacy is therefore all the more significant for its capacity to illuminate this period and its substantial developments.

Chapman stood at the forefront of the growing evangelical movement in Australia for a generation, while also playing an important role in the development of the movement in prominent pockets of the international evangelical world. His contribution to theological discourse on evangelistic engagement and the nexus between theology and ministry was significant. It provided a body of thought during the 1970s, 80s, and 90s that still shapes conceptions of Christian engagement and ministry strategy today. Chapman's contribution to the revival of a classically Reformed Protestant expository preaching model is also highly significant. Furthermore, on account of his persuasive advocacy for conservative faith in pulpit and publication, his extensive teaching in Sydney theological colleges, his widespread and active mentoring of a subsequent generation of evangelical leaders, and his delivery of as many as 7,500 public addresses to combined audiences of over three quarters of a million people across five continents, and spanning a career of over fifty years,[21] Chapman is said to have brought a clarity and energy to the evangelical movement of this time, both domestically and abroad.[22] However, while shorter, largely popular reflections on Chapman's work have been offered, no extended scholarly analysis has distilled his significant contribution. Furthermore, in recent literature assessing the Sydney diocese and Australian Anglicanism, Chapman's contribution has seen no substantial appraisal.[23] Given the influence of Chapman's work upon other

---

21. See Appendix 5, *Historical Speaking Engagements*.

22. Recent scholarship, for example, has highlighted the links from the 1980s between Reformed Anglicans in England and the Diocese of Sydney. They highlight the instrumentality of John Chapman "who became a celebrated evangelist," and of other notable Sydney evangelicals, in playing an important role in the movement for English and global Anglican renewal during this period, in "the founding of the Reform movement" and in encouraging a "strongly biblical approach" to theology. So, Atherstone and Maiden, "Anglican Evangelicalism," 45–46; Chapman, "Anglican Evangelicals," 263–64.

23. Mansfield's *Chappo Collection*, provides a compendium of professional and biographical reflections on Chapman by colleagues and friends from across the world. Yet, it self-consciously resists analysis of the significance of Chapman's ministry to the Sydney Diocese and to wider Evangelicalism. Mansfield, *Chappo Collection*, 15. Orpwood's *Chappo* also chronicles aspects of Chapman's life and ministry. Yet, its paucity of critical analysis, coupled with its lack of scholarly and chronological distance from its subject limits the work's scholarly significance. Other populist works on Sydney Diocese like Michael Jensen's, *Sydney Anglicanism*, acknowledges Chapman's contribution yet dwells little upon it. Jensen, *Sydney Anglicanism*, 59; Edwards, "Romance," 39, laments Jensen's under-examination of Chapman; Payne, "Magic Potion," critiques Jensen on this account. Other studies on Sydney and Australian Evangelicalism refer to Chapman's ministry yet resist substantive analysis. See Judd and Cable, *Sydney Anglicans*, 301n18;

strands of Australian and international Evangelicalism, to overlook this contribution is to overlook a serious and sustained strand of Anglican, evangelical, and Australian religious history. Consequently, by examining key facets of the life and ministry of this significant leader, this study seeks to throw new light on one of Australia's most influential religious movements and contribute to a growing literature on the intersection of Australian religious and cultural life. It also seeks to illuminate a vital Australian contribution to a global movement that has proven itself capable of reform, resistance to external threat, and authentic spiritual renewal within the complex dynamics of a century of change and opportunity.[24]

Literature Review

The present study crosses the boundaries of three distinct but overlapping literatures that both frame Chapman's contribution and invite further scholarly research. The first literature concerns *Australian Anglicanism*—its history, corporate life, and late twentieth-century character. The second concerns *Australian religious and cultural life*, particularly in light of the seismic shifts and secularizing tendencies of the twentieth century and the need to resituate Christianity within a fast changing and globalizing world. The third concerns *historic modes of Christian ministry and mission*, including the methods by which the Australian and international church has both nourished its members spiritually and facilitated an ongoing engagement with its surrounding society and culture.

Australian Anglicanism

The first of these literatures relates to Australian Anglicanism—its history, corporate life, and late twentieth-century character.[25] In this regard, the present study comes at a time of renewed interest and scholarship. Master mappers of the Australian religious scene have charted the broad contours of Australian religious life, and have called for more detailed studies to fill

---

Piggin and Linder, *National Soul*, 290, 362, 441; Chilton, "Christian Australia," 326–27.

24. Atherstone and Maiden, "Anglican Evangelicalism," 1–47; Stanley, *Global Diffusion*, 238.

25. Although the term "Anglican" was not used until 1838, this study follows David Hilliard in employing "Anglican" to denote "that branch of the Christian Church, and its system of doctrines and practices, that derives from the Church of England." Hilliard, "Anglicans," 128.

out the as yet empty places on the map.[26] In the last fifty years Anglicanism itself has produced numerous diocesan histories and studies of its notable leaders,[27] although analysis of its national vision has emerged rather more slowly.[28] This older biographical and diocesan historical strand has more recently been supplemented with histories exploring other issues such as lay piety; Anglican engagement with society, culture, and the arts; and issues relating to Indigenous mission, class, gender, and identity.[29]

Resurgent interest in the history, politics, and theology of the Sydney Anglican diocese is of particular importance for this study. Recent assessments of the diocese within the context of a variegated Australian Anglican church have been marked by considerable reserve and, often, substantial critique. Some have portrayed the diocese in largely puritanical and fundamentalist tones.[30] They also express concern at how the diocese has become so "militantly evangelical and obstructive to the mission of Anglicanism in the world" and remain confident that without its

---

26. Breward, *Australian Churches*; Thompson, *Religion in Australia*; Carey, *Believing in Australia*; Jackson, *Christian God*; Massam, "Christian Churches," 251–84; Jupp, *Encyclopaedia of Religion*. Note Ian Breward's entreaty for the completion of further research. Breward, "Learning to Write History," 47–53.

27. Key diocesan studies include Porter, *Melbourne Anglicans*; Holden, *People of the Past?*; Frame, *Church for a Nation*; Grant, *Episcopally Led*; Rayner, *Church of England*; Le Couteur, "Brisbane Anglicans"; Bayton, *Cross Over Carpentaria*; Cole, *Diocese of Bendigo*; Judd and Cable, *Sydney Anglicans*; Elkin, *Diocese of Newcastle*; Hilliard, *Godliness and Good Order*; Spooner, *Golden See*; Stephens, *Anglican Church in Tasmania*; Williams, *West Anglican Way*. Prominent biographies include: Alexander, *Four Bishops*; Brown, *Augustus Short*; Loane, *Archbishop Mowll*; Macintosh, *Richard Johnson*; Nichols, *David Penman*; Robin, *Charles Perry*; Shaw, *Patriarch and Prophet*; Yarwood, *Samuel Marsden*; Bolt, *William Cowper*; *Thomas Moore*.

28. Note the national histories offered by Kaye, *Church Without Walls*; *Anglicanism in Australia*; Frame, *Anglicans in Australia*.

29. See Fletcher, "Free Society," 93–113; Hilliard, "Anglicanism," 15–32; Fletcher, "Anglicanism and Nationalism," 215–33; Moses, "Canon," 12–21; Ely, "'Anglican' Religious Culture," 83–85; Loos, "Australian Board of Missions," 194–209; Lake, "Samuel Marsden," 1–23; Gladwin, "Journalist," 1–28; O'Brien, *God's Willing Workers*, 23–52.

30. The term "Puritan" was first used in 1573 to mark those advocating for far-reaching reforms in the Church of England. The term has taken on a pejorative connotation, synonymous with a life-denying approach to Christian faith. See Frame, "Anglican History," 123. The term "fundamentalist" arose in early twentieth-century usage in response to theological modernism. Leading international and Australian evangelicals were careful to disavow its usage in relation to orthodox evangelical thought. The term has since become employed to denote any religious position that appears conservative, anti-modern, and thus a threat to the values of a progressive society. See Cox, "Master Narrative," 202. On the term's history, see Bebbington and Jones, *Evangelicalism and Fundamentalism*. On the term's application to Sydney Diocese, see Porter, *Sydney Anglicanism*, 10–20; Atherstone, "Fundamentalists?," 1–12.

overbearing and "relentless negative influence," the national church would have "released enormous energy for growth and renewal" in other dioceses.[31] The more popular contributions of Caroline Miley, Peter Carnley, Chris McGillion, and Muriel Porter are consistent with such an appraisal of Sydney Anglicanism, advocating an approach more in sympathy with progressive modern cultural values as the panacea for stemming broader church decline and limited civic engagement.[32]

Another group of commentators, largely professional church historians, have been more measured in their criticisms. Tom Frame offers a more positive appraisal. He reckons honestly with the realities of national Anglican decline and the strengths of an articulate Evangelicalism which he sees emanating from Sydney diocese. However, he also cautions against an approach that leaves little in church life that is distinctly Anglican.[33] Stuart Piggin assesses the broader mood of Australian Evangelicalism, of which Sydney diocese is a crucial part, as buoyant and confident, even while noting a perceived doctrinal inelasticity within Sydney and a sterile "head over heart" Christianity.[34] Brian Fletcher, noting Sydney's often ungainly negotiation of

---

31. Porter, *Sydney Anglicanism*, 10; Moses, "Sydney Anglicanism," 627–28.

32. Miley advocates not a theological, but structural, hierarchical, and value-attitudinal correction to stem broader church decline. She implicates the fundamentalist and financially powerful Sydney diocese in the unequal distribution of the church's collective wealth. She also questions how a group whose beliefs, she holds, "conflict so extensively with accepted Anglican beliefs that the persons who hold them cannot be Anglicans," and laments their inclusion in national church life at all. Miley, *Suicidal Church*, 121. Archbishop Carnley, *Reflections in Glass*, whose antipathy to the Sydney diocese extends some way (having received strong rebuttal from Sydney clergy for his published views) advocates for an articulate and progressive theological and social repositioning as the vehicle for new dialogue with modern Australia. McGillion, *Chosen Ones*, sees the conservatism of the Sydney diocese as in large part a product of a conservative reaction to the exhaustion of governmental and societal reform of the 1980s, and the desire for certainty and clearly defined identity. Porter, *Sydney Anglicanism*, provides sustained critique. Noting the growing influence of the Sydney diocese in national and international Anglican life, she regrets that the Australian church did not allow Sydney to go its own way in the 1950s when potentially irreconcilable differences began to emerge. Cf. Warner, *Secularization*, 4, who notes that such approaches are common amongst more "liberal expressions" of Protestantism in "blaming the uncompromising fundamentalists for alienating sophisticated unbelievers."

33. Frame, *Anglicans in Australia*, 266.

34. Piggin, *Evangelical Christianity*; Piggin, "Concrete," 189. Note the impressive history of Australian Evangelicalism by Piggin and Linder which judges Sydney Anglicans as one of the "most powerful movements within the Protestant churches in Australia" and provides substantial appraisal laced with respectful critique. Piggin and Linder, *National Soul*, 24.

its relationship with the national church, yet affirms its constant missionary impulse and strong national contribution.[35]

A third group of commentators, writing largely from an insider's vantage point on the diocese, have recently offered critical though sympathetic analysis of the Sydney diocese. This work has occasioned renewed and constructive dialogue by re-examining aspects of the dioceses' theological character; its polity and organizational complexity; its distinctive ecclesiology, preaching, and biblical theology; and the role of certain of its leading figures in key twentieth-century evangelical movements, such as the Billy Graham Crusades and the 1974 Lausanne Congress.[36]

This recent literature has argued that the more strident critique of Sydney Anglicanism has struggled to recognize the spiritual piety that energizes the movement as it has sought to articulate a faithful adherence to Scripture, develop an intellectually vigorous faith, fulfill the apostolic mandate for mission and societal flourishing, and do so in a manner which is conservative in content and flexible in form.[37] Conservative Evangelicalism traces its roots to the eighteenth-century Evangelical Revival, the teachings of leading Protestant reformers, and the evangelical councils of the early church, securing it a historically and theologically legitimate place within Anglicanism.[38] Moreover, as a movement, Evangelicalism has exhibited qualities that have seen it survive and flourish across national and denominational boundaries, contributing strongly to international and Australian church and societal life for centuries.[39] Given the historic strengths of this

---

35. Fletcher, "Diocese of Sydney," 111–32. Note also Frame and Treloar, *Agendas* which seeks renewed national Anglican dialogue, laced with implied and often direct critique of Sydney, though contributions from Sydney figures are notably absent from this volume.

36. See McIntosh, "Anglican Evangelicalism"; Kuhn, "Ecclesiology"; Reid, "Evangelical Hermeneutics"; Ballantine-Jones, "Political Factor"; Cameron, *Phenomenal Sydney*; Chilton, "Christian Australia," esp. chs. 5, 6, and 8; Shiner, "Reading the New Testament." Michael P. Jensen's, *Sydney Anglicanism* offers an explanation of Sydney diocese to its critics and seeks to establish its continuity with Reformation Anglicanism. This work has occasioned wide dialogue from other scholars such as Atherstone, "Fundamentalists?," 1–12; Broughton, "Biblical Theology," 13–24; Giles, "Michael Jensen," 25–35; Edwards, "Romance," 36–47; Loane, "Church," 48–58; Forsyth, "Sydney Anglicans," 59–70; Judd, "Church Politics," 102–11; with M. Jensen's reply, "Sydney Anglicanism," 112–26, all in *St Mark's Review* 226 (November 2013). These works examine aspects of Jensen's defense in relation to Sydney's theology, polity, preaching, and ecclesiology.

37. See, for example, Piggin, "Concrete," 190.

38. McGrath, "Evangelical Anglicanism," 12–13.

39. Turnbull, *Anglican and Evangelical?*, 165 emphasizes the flexibility of evangelical DNA, noting: (1) the spectrum of tradition which Evangelicalism draws from, being influenced by Reformed, Pietistic, and Holiness traditions; (2) its possession of key

principally evangelical diocese and its prominent, albeit contested, place within Australian Anglicanism, an opportunity exists to contribute to this literature by critically re-examining aspects of its life through the lens of one of its most significant recent leaders. In this way, the study offers new insight into the manner in which this movement, via aspects of Chapman's contribution, adapted to large-scale societal and theological change, while remaining distinctively Anglican and methodologically progressive. Moreover, in pursuing a biographical approach, the study affords an opportunity to penetrate more deeply into the motivations and rationale that have underpinned key tenets of Sydney Anglicanism. Given that an analysis of Chapman's ministry does not feature prominently in the three noted sub-literatures on this movement, further examination is required.

Australian Religious and Cultural Life

The second literature to which this study contributes is concerned with the intersection of *Australian religious and cultural life*. In this vein, during the last third of the twentieth century it seemed obvious to some observers that religion scarcely mattered in modern Australia. Older Australian histories had tended to treat the churches with marginal interest, depicting religion as a private matter, peripheral to the main concerns of Australian life.[40] Similar commentary employed familiar tropes of the colonial Church and clergy as

---

marks in the areas of authority (the Bible), doctrine (atonement), spirituality (a personal relationship with Christ), transformation (moral and spiritual renewal); and (3) the manner in which Evangelicalism differs in expression according to the differing weight attached to these antecedents. Atherstone and Maiden, "Anglican Evangelicalism," 2 note that the "cultural flexibility . . . diversity and fluidity" of Anglican Evangelicalism is central to its vitality, suggesting its three tendencies of: *resistance* toward external threats to the gospel and ethical clarity; *reform* via thoughtful engagement with church and society; and *renewal*, via an emphasis on personal holiness and spiritual vitality, are central to its later twentieth-century strength. Cf. also Warner, *Reinventing*, 136–37; Packer, "Anglican Identity Problem," 25–72.

40. Macintyre, *Concise History*; Grimshaw et al., *Creating a Nation*; Hudson, *Australian Religious Thought*, xviii, suggests that the neglect of religion's contribution in Australia stems from left-wing historiography of the mid-twentieth century. Others, such as Carey, "Secularism Versus Christianity," 17 suggest the myth that the Australian colonies were "born modern" and thus bypassed the older history of religious oppression and church establishment, has seen a tendency in secular histories of Australia to omit discussion of religion. Coffey, "Quentin Skinner," 46–74 and Bebbington, "Discipline of History," 20–24 also suggest that the dynamic whereby religion was minimized as a factor in the past and marginalized in major historical works was also an international phenomenon driven by a confluence of mid-twentieth century Marxist and scientific rationalist thought.

agents of social control and promoters of moral and judicial severity, to serve a secular narrative.[41] Other work crafted stories of flawed and lonely clerics who struggled to replant Christianity in Australia.[42] Still others portrayed Australian history as a confrontation between Christianity and secularist philosophies, describing Australia as the first genuinely "post-Christian society,"[43] dominated by white fellas "who got no dreaming."[44]

However, the historiography of religion in Australia began to flourish even as others declared the death of Christian belief.[45] In the face of this older secularist tradition, a growing chorus of scholarship began to amplify a more positive note, redressing a definite historiographical imbalance and demonstrating that the relationship between the secular and religious in Australian history has not been a relationship of mutual exclusivity, but has been far more porous and reciprocal.[46] Two strands of this literature press upon the present study, in particular, in providing an orientation to the intersection of religion and Australian life, and the work of a figure like Chapman. These are the related literatures on secularization and the response of denominational Christianity to this phenomenon. The second concerns

---

41. Clark, "Faith," 78–79 and Maxwell-Stewart and Duffield, "Skin Deep Devotions," 129–31 depict colonial Anglican clergymen as agents of state control with a "denigrating" and "puritanical" agenda. Of such narratives, Breward, *Churches in Australasia*, 11 observes the "brutalizing" that Christianity has received in some Australian histories by its perceived colonial "links with unjust laws and cruel punishments."

42. Carey, *Oscar and Lucinda*, 300.

43. O'Farrell, "General History," 66.

44. Jackson, "White Man," 1–11.

45. Reviews of this historiography include Bollen et al., "Australian Religious History," 8–44; Carey et al., "Australian Religion Review, Part 1," 296–313; Carey et al., "Australian Religion Review, Part 2," 56–82.

46. Manning Clark was perhaps the first to give substantive emphasis to the role played by Christianity in the formation of Australian society. Clark, *History of Australia, Vol. 1* and *History of Australia, Vol. 6*, 104; Gascoigne, *Enlightenment*, 6, 20 suggests that Australia's "intellectually pluralist beginnings meant there was room for different blooms to grow: both the seed of the Enlightenment and those of the varying forms of Christianity," and indeed, what is striking about the Australian context is the extent to which the two impulses coalesced. Note also the redress given to the place of religion in Australia's history by Atkinson, *Europeans in Australia: Vol. One*, 15–17, 40, 165–80, 270; *Europeans in Australia: Vol. Two*, 175–80, 192–93; *Europeans in Australia: Vol. Three*, 264–98. See also the substantial redress given in Piggin and Linder, *Fountain of Public Prosperity* and *National Soul*; also Damousi, *Colonial Voices*; Gladwin, *Anglican Clergy*; Lake, "Such Spiritual Acres"; O'Brien, "Religion," 414–37. Note the persistence of sacral tendencies even in secular Australian ritual, see Davison, *Narrating the Nation*, 2. Note also religious themes in recent "secular" histories, in Carey et. al., "Australian Religion Review," 302–6; Ely, "Secularization," 553–56.

the literature on contextualization and the need to reconfigure Christianity within the changing context of late twentieth-century Australia.

Secularization and the Twentieth Century

There is little doubt that the twentieth century saw widespread social and religious change across Western society. What remains in contention within this historiography, however, has been the appropriateness of secularization theory as a metathesis for explaining such widespread cultural and religious change. The timing, causes, and extent of such processes are also contested. The scholarship that led to present-day analysis arose between the late 1950s and mid-1990s. Historians and sociologists of religion like Bryan Wilson, David Martin, and more recently, Steve Bruce, joined Peter Berger and Rodney Stark in conceptualizing the changing nature of religion in society.[47]

For many of these early theorists, secularization was seen as a necessary corollary of the much larger processes of modernization—itself a conglomerate of urbanization, industrialization, and the impact of the Enlightenment.[48] Religion, they suggested, had been previously strong when it held the community together with a transcendent vision, expressed through joint worship in a universal church.[49] The process of secularization, however, saw the breakdown of this worldview. Religious pluralism, individualism, diversity, and egalitarianism combined with liberal democracy to undermine the authority of shared religious beliefs, effectively privatizing religion.[50] Social discipline became decoupled from religious discipline. The miraculous was also undermined by scientific rationalism, while sacred texts increasingly lost their influence in personal decision-making and collective lawmaking. The Western world began careering rapidly toward a uniform decline in the significance of religion.[51] Moreover, it was argued, secularization would necessarily accompany modernization whenever and wherever the process

---

47. Key studies include: Wilson, *Secular Society*; Berger, *Sacred Canopy*; Wilson, *Sociological Perspective*; Martin, *General Theory*; Bruce, *Religion and Modernization*; Fenn, *Beyond Idols*; Davie, *Europe*; Beckford, *Social Theory*; Martin, *On Secularization*; Stark, "Secularization RIP," 249–73; Berger et al., *Religious America?*

48. Mid-twentieth century secularization theory was profoundly shaped by the early-century work of Max Weber, one of the most important theorists of the economic and religious development of modern Western society. See Frame, *Losing My Religion*, 9; Chavura and Tregenza, "Introduction," 299–306.

49. Taylor, *Secular Age*, 25.

50. Bruce, *God is Dead*, 30; *Unfashionable Theory*; "History, Sociology," 190–213.

51. Frame, *Losing My Religion*, 9.

of modernization occurred.[52] Scholars were also agreed that secularization constituted a longer-term process which had begun in the eighteenth century and accelerated rapidly in the nineteenth and twentieth centuries.[53]

With the development of this uniform theory, however, came a host of other regionally derived studies which challenged its veracity, particularly in relation to transatlantic religious disparities.[54] These observations, together with the rapid growth of Christianity in the Global South, the widespread growth of Pentecostalism in the Majority World, the re-emergence of Islam in global affairs, and increasingly heated debates around religious proselytism, prompted many scholars to rethink the secularization paradigm altogether.[55] Others concluded, on the strength of such disparities, that secularization as a uniform theory has been empirically shown to be false.[56] Some contemporary scholars of religion like Hugh McLeod and Callum G. Brown have more recently responded by nuancing this historiography with more considered commentary around the timing and causes of secularization. They have highlighted the 1960s in particular as the catalytic period of change and suggested that in the religious history of the West, the "long sixties"—from 1959 to 1974—might come to be seen as marking a rupture

---

52. Warner, *Secularization*, 2; Tregenza, "Secularism," 175.

53. Brown and Snape, "Introduction," 1–12.

54. On transatlantic religious disparities, see Christie and Gauvreau, *Sixties and Beyond*; Berger et. al, *Religious America?*, 10; Bruce, "UK and USA," 205–18; Hempton, "Protestant Migrations," 41–56; L. Hölscher, "Age of Secularization," 197–204; Sidenvall, "Classic Case," 110–30, all in *Secularization in the Christian World*. Note the "supply-side" theories of religion advanced by Rodney Stark and others who have sought to reconcile transatlantic religious disparities by contrasting the voluntarist and diversified religious markets of the United States with the rigid national churches of Europe. In this religious version of Adam Smith's *Wealth of Nations*, American religion is assessed as more vibrant than European religion because of the separation of church and state, the democratization of Christianity, the spread of markets and liberal capitalism, the durability of the evangelical impulse, the importance of voluntary associations, and the ubiquity of the congregational model—each affording American churches greater agility in adapting to changing "demand-side" factors like increasing secularity and religious diversity in America. Many of the most influential books on American religious history in the past quarter of a century either articulate or self-consciously contest some or all of the above propositions, and provide a salient, though still contested social-scientific rationale for American religious exceptionalism and strength. See Finke and Stark, *Churching of America*; Stark and Finke, *Acts of Faith*.

55. Calhoun et al., *Rethinking Secularism*. Compare Peter Berger's earlier support for the theory in *Sacred Canopy* with his renunciation of the secularization thesis in "Desecularization," 1–19. Berger states in this later work: "the world today is massively religious, is *anything but* the secularized world that had been predicted (whether joyfully or despondently) by so many analysts of modernity." Berger, "Desecularization," 9.

56. Cox, "Towards Eliminating," 13–26.

as profound as that brought about by the Protestant Reformation itself.[57] With regard to causes, a key finding of McLeod and others has been to suggest that it is not purely the external threats to Christianity that demand attention in any analysis of this defining period. Rather, they suggest, the crisis was as much an internal crisis precipitated by the loss of traditional belief structures within many wings of Protestantism itself.[58]

The relevance of this debate for the present study is that while most scholars today acknowledge that the secularization theory falls far short of being an irrefutable scientific thesis, they nevertheless concede its worth as a theory of "general orientation" providing a window into the changed "social imaginary"[59] and "plausibility structures"[60] of modern Western societies (not least Australia's).[61] Such scholarship also provides a rich contextual chronology which situates Chapman's career and contribution (beginning in the 1960s) at a pivotal moment in Western religious history.[62] And yet, when applied without sufficient nuance, a secularizing narrative crafts a picture of religious change in twentieth-century Western societies that is incomplete,[63]

---

57. McLeod considered data across numerous Western societies highlighting the impact of the rise of affluence and leisure, the radical ideas which reached a culmination in 1968, the impact of sexual and gender change, and the rise of civil societies based on a secular national ethos. So McLeod, *Religious Crisis*; "Crisis of Christianity," 327–40. Callum G. Brown contended not the extent, but the timing of secularization. Resonating with McLeod on the role of 1960s permissive society, Brown offered 1963 as a moment of rupture when Christian culture, as a hegemonic feature of British society, died and instigated sharpened gradients of decline in virtually all statistical indicators of religiosity and conservatism. So Brown, *Death of Christian Britain*, 1, 190–91; "Religious Crisis," 471; "Revisionist Approach," 31–58.

58. McLeod, *Religious Crisis*, 14, 208; Brown, "Religious Crisis," 473–79; Atherstone and Maiden, "Anglican Evangelicalism," 14–16; Bruce, "UK and USA," 10; Martin, *On Secularization*, 5, 187–88; Martin, *English Religion*; Hudson, *Australian Religious Thought*, 130; Frame, *Losing My Religion*, 152–67; Stanley, *Global Diffusion*, 13–14; Christie and Gauvreau, "Introduction," 5; Breward, *Churches in Australasia*, 377.

59. Taylor, "Afterward," 308.

60. Berger, *Heretical Imperative*, 17.

61. Even Charles Taylor's nuanced taxonomy of secularization, which offers some challenge to the prevailing secularization literature (cf. Taylor's "Secularism 2" versus "Secularism 3" definitions in *Secular Age*, 1–4) is in agreement on secularism's effects. Taylor describes the onset of an entirely new "social imaginary" which pervades Western thought—a way of constructing societal meaning without any reference to the divine or transcendent. "For the first time in history" he asserts "a purely self-sufficient humanism came to be a widely available option . . . accepting no final goals beyond human flourishing, nor any allegiance to anything else beyond this flourishing. Of no previous society was this true," *Secular Age*, 18.

62. Cox, "Progress Report," 17.

63. Chapman, "Intellectual History," 228.

for it emphasizes only decline at a time when religious renewal or reconfiguration in many contexts has also become apparent.[64] Given this reality, a growing chorus of scholars have called for more locally oriented studies to illuminate the diverse picture of religious change in the twentieth century.[65] Moreover, given that most previous work has centered on the transatlantic religious context, scholars have also called for "an important gap" to be filled in relation to the "New Britains" of the former British World, including Australia, New Zealand, and Southern Africa.[66]

Concerning research into the Australian context itself, scholars have noted the parallels between the Australian experience and other Western nations, particularly in the timing and causes of religious change and the importance of the 1960s.[67] A growing scholarship has also reappraised aspects of secularization in relation to Australian politics, education, and spirituality; the sacral tendencies present even in modern Australian culture; and the resilience shown by some sectors of Australian religious life, largely within its more conservative wings.[68] However, further work is needed to provide

---

64. Davie, "Thinking Broadly," 220; Stanley, *Global Diffusion*, 14–15.

65. Brown and Snape, "Introduction," 5; Cox, "Progress Report," 17; Bouma, "Religion," 212; Bruce, "History, Sociology," 199–200 suggests "It is often the case that theoretical generalisations are properly challenged by detailed historical research . . . we need further case studies"; Stanley, *Global Diffusion*, 15 suggests "the necessary regional . . . church histories" required to complete the postwar Christian story "are still in the making . . . with much of the requisite primary documentary and oral research still awaiting the attention of scholars"; McLeod, "Reflections and New Perspectives," notes that given the "coexistence of and interaction between divergent, and maybe contradictory, tendencies" (465), the analysis of religious change in post-1960s Western societies, entreats further study "approached on a case-by-case basis" (459).

66. Carey, "Secularism Versus Christianity," 13; Erdozain, "Return of Secularization," 389; Gascoigne and Carey, "Introduction," 1–30 also suggest that too little focus on these "new Britains" has created a significant gap in the broader narrative.

67. See Frame, *Losing My Religion*, 61–84, 125–70, 290–94; Hilliard, "Secularization," 78; Hilliard, "Religious Crisis," 209–27; Hudson, *Australian Religious Thought*, 62–63; Chavura and Tregenza, "Introduction," 299–306. Varying stress is also placed within this literature on the postwar religious revival, before the 1960s divergences. See Breward, *Churches in Australasia*, 361–420; Hilliard, "Religious Crisis"; McLeod, *Religious Crisis*, 34; Massam, "Christian Churches," 259–60; Piggin, *Spirit*, 125–26; Frappell, "Post-War Revivalism," 249–61; Frame, *Anglicans*, 103–5; Frame, *Losing My Religion*, 64.

68. Note the case studies developed concerning the Australian context: 1) on the longer history of the relationship between Christian and Western thought and its impact on Australian society. Judge, "Religion of the Secularists," 307–19; 2) the extent of secularism in Australia's political history. Piggin, "Power and Religion," 320–40; 3) motivations in the development of religious pluralism and the 1836 Church Act. Stoneman, "Richard Bourke," 341–55; 4) the manner in which enlightened and religious thought entered into dialogue around the question of education in Australia. Chavura,

a more complete picture. Accordingly, by examining the process of change and renewal experienced by Australian evangelicals and the role that figures like Chapman played in the Sydney diocese and wider evangelical movement, this study contributes a critical Australian perspective to the emerging picture of religious change within secularizing societies of this period. In so doing, it sheds new light on the creative response of Evangelicalism to these societal trends; and it answers the call of scholars to offer further microlevel analysis with which to sensitively nuance the complex and surprising macro-level picture of religious change in the modern world.[69]

Contextualisation and Australian Culture

Turning to the second of these literatures, this study is also relevant to the growing literature on the contextualization of Christianity within different cultural contexts. This literature has arisen within the modern history of Christian mission and missiology. It seeks to reckon with the reality that, with the emergence of Christianity as a global religion in the twentieth century, there came a corresponding need to conceptualize the way in which Christianity has related to the cultural and religious backgrounds of the people groups into which it has spread.[70] The related concept of "contextualization" subsequently entered the vocabulary of missiology in 1972 via a publication of the Theological Education Fund of the World Council of Churches.[71] This publication affirmed the older formulations of the "indigenous church" movement which had urged missionaries to assist churches in receptor cultures to become "self-supporting, self-governing . . . self-propagating" and "self-theologizing" entities as quickly as possible.[72] It also observed that

---

"Australia's Secular Heritage," 356–76; Ely, "Now You See It," 377–97; 5) the manner in which moral commitments and sacral concepts have been "smuggled" into Australia's modern "secular" culture from a deeply religious past. Melleuish, "Secular Australia?" 398–412; Hartney, "States of Ultimacy," 214–50; 6) the rise of diverse spiritualities in Australia in secularism's wake. Bouma, *Australian Soul*, xiii, 5, 18, 47–63; Frame, *Religion*, vi–xiv, 26–37; Gaden, "Australian Theology?," 22–23; and 7) case studies of resistance to secularism. Wallace, *Realising Secularism* collates papers that acknowledge the ongoing decline of mainline Christian denominations, but the resilience in some sectors of Australian religious life; also Hein, "Good Order," 58–67; Le Couteur, "An Attempt," 68–89.

69. Davie, "Thinking Broadly," 220.

70. Robert, *Christian Mission*, 3; Hesselgrave and Rommen, *Contextualization*, xi; Whiteman, "Contextualization," 2–7.

71. Coe, *Ministry in Context*; "In Search of Renewal," 237.

72. Warren, *To Apply the Gospel*; Moreau, "Evangelical Models," 165–95.

colonial missionary movements had bequeathed *forms* of church ministry to Christian leaders within receptor cultures that were unalterably Western. The publication therefore suggested that the transmission of such forms had not encouraged national church leaders to think creatively about how to communicate the gospel *to* and embed the gospel *within* their own culture. Consequently, the taxonomy of "contextualization" was proposed as one which could encompass both the process of embedding the gospel within such traditional receptor cultures *and* of how the same process might proceed within Western societies that were experiencing rapid cultural change of their own and in which new forms were also required.[73] Evangelical leaders initially responded with some caution to these proposals, recognizing the inherent and corrosive dangers of religious syncretism within this process.[74] However, from the late 1970s, the concept of "contextualization" became an important paradigm within evangelical missiology and a substantial literature has developed around it.[75]

The relevance of this history to the Australian church and to an analysis of Chapman's contribution concerns the fact that, prior to the Second World War, Australian Christianity was an almost entirely derivative religious culture. The period after the Second World War subsequently marked the successive withdrawal of British governments from its colonies and a

---

73. Coe, *Ministry in Context*, 20. In scholarly discussions on contextualization many words have been infused with technical meaning by various writers. The words adaptation, indigenization, translation, inculturation, and contextualization are all given distinct meanings. There is now general consensus, however, on the use of *contextualization* as a term that is descriptive of the general process of adapting the communication and ministry of the gospel to a particular culture without compromising the essence of the gospel itself. So Moreau, "Evangelical Models," 165–95. For the background of this history, see Conn, "Contextualization," 90–119.

74. Kato, "Gospel," 1216–224; Nicholls, *Contextualization*, 26–36; Gilliland, *Word Among Us*, vii; Walls, *Missionary Movement*, 7–8.

75. Moreau, "Evangelical Models," 25–26 estimates a universe of roughly five thousand English contextualization resources in circulation. See also Hesselgrave, "Contextualization Continuum," 4–11; Gilliland, "Appendix"; Newbigin, *Pluralistic Society*. Note the evaluation of the strengths and weaknesses of various contextualization models in Schreiter, *Local Theologies*; Bevans, "Models of Contextual Theology," 185–202; *Models of Contextual Theology*; Van Engen, "Five Perspectives," 183–202. See also the recent contributions of Julian, "Ground Level," 57–75; Moreau, "Comprehensive," 325; Wells, *Above All Earthly Powers*; Carson and Keller, "Gospel-Centered Ministry," 11–23; Carson, *Christ and Culture*. Note also the "theological vision for ministry" of the Gospel Coalition, a leading international network of evangelical leaders and practitioners which articulates, alongside a confessional statement of belief, a vision for ministry which commits evangelicals to serious reflection upon modern culture in order to produce patterns of gospel-shaped ministry which engage and connect with contemporary culture. See Gospel Coalition, "Theological Vision."

movement within receptor cultures like Australia towards establishing a truly local church leadership.[76] Perhaps the most significant dynamic during this period, however, was the growing recognition that considerable work was also required to enable Australian Christians to be more effective in reaching a changing culture while at the same time not compromising biblical integrity. Within the Sydney diocese, following a series of notable synodical addresses by Archbishop Marcus Loane in the late 1960s, a *Commission of Enquiry* was established and charged with the task of investigating the "whole problem of modern communication of the gospel" within the "prevailing intellectual outlook."[77] The members of the commission (of which Chapman played a leading role as secretary and theological consultant) spent three years in intensive deliberation. The resulting report, entitled *Move in For Action*, was made publicly available with the aim of stimulating both the Sydney diocese and "the whole of the Australian church to assess accurately its present outreach."[78] The report concluded that "the church in Australia conducts itself largely on patterns inherited from the past [which] need reassessment and change."[79] Anglicanism in Australia, they recognized, had remained "a potted plant rather than taking root in Australian soil."[80] This report was succeeded in the 1980s and 1990s with further reviews of diocesan practice (again under the strong input and leadership of figures like Chapman) to develop culturally sensitive ministry patterns for a changing Australia.[81] Over time, in response to such calls, the adoption of new clerical attire, service forms, and music became commonplace in Sydney churches and the outward expression of conservative faith in corporate worship took on forms very different from that of a previous generation. Many similar changes occurred across the spectrum of other Australian Protestant denominations as well.[82] However, the agency

---

76. O'Farrell, "General History," 66; Ward, "Christianity," 86; Chapman, "International Relations," 355–68. Within the Sydney diocese, this period marked the emergence of the first generation of Australian-born leadership, with the election of Archbishop Marcus Loane. Blanch, *Strength to Strength*, 213.

77. Archbishop Marcus Loane, 1967 Presidential Address, 1968 *Sydney Diocesan Yearbook*, 354; *Move in For Action*, 7.

78. *Move in For Action*, 8.

79. *Move in For Action*, 11.

80. Milikan, "Australian Identity," 30; Cf. O'Farrell, "Cultural Ambivalence," 7–14.

81. Central to this process was the conviction that Anglicanism was a constantly reforming religious tradition and, via careful attention both to culture and a view of ministry deduced from scriptural principles, change in liturgical and ministry practice was urged. Resolution 11/88: "Committee Re Church Growth," *Sydney Diocesan Yearbook 1990*, 373–83.

82. The influence of the charismatic movement and the arrival on the Sydney

of leaders like Chapman in facilitating such changes in an Anglican setting ought not to be underestimated, for it saw the adaptation of forms of Anglican expression which had stood more or less unaltered within Britain and her colonies for over three hundred years.[83]

In important ways, therefore, the processes of secularization and contextualization may be conceptualized as two sides of the same reformist coin. Secularization forged the emerging culture into which the churches were required to adapt and within which they subsequently embedded new forms of Christian ministry.[84] Chapman's own practice of non-liturgical attire, plain speech, and a larrikin demeanor meshed well with the spirit of his generation.[85] He sought to meet Australians on their own turf, desiring all offence caused in the preaching of the gospel to emanate only from its content and not from the form of its transmission. This, it was held, was nothing less than the apostolic imperative (1 Cor 9:19–22).[86] For its time, however, it sounded a distinctly pioneering note. And given its influence over subsequent generations of evangelical leaders in Sydney and other centers, this marks Chapman as a key figure in the growth of a contextualized Australian religious culture and in the development of a missional Evangelicalism responding to a secular culture that was pressing it from the center to the margins.[87] Moreover, while there is a body of current Australian literature reflecting a commitment to contextualized ministry practice by leading practitioners and missiologists,[88] there has been a relative paucity

---

conference scene of the Willow Creek and Saddleback models, alongside a revolution in Christian music by the likes of Hillsong, each played a role in shaping the emerging Australian and Sydney diocesan practice. On the influence of the Christian protest movement described as "The Jesus People" on wider evangelical attitudes to culture and social policy, see Chilton, "Christian Australia," 260–98.

83. Spinks, "Liturgy," 471.

84. For a stimulating analysis of Evangelicalism's relationship to and appropriation of modern cultural change in the latter century, see Bebbington, "Modernism," 2–9.

85. Moore, "Baptism in Australia" notes the Australian preference for down-to-earth and direct speech with an undercurrent of irony; Milikan, *Sunburnt Soul*, 106–11 reflects on the Australian propensity for iconoclasm, laconic humour, and self-effacing reserve.

86. Whiteman, "Contextualization," 3.

87. Murray, *Post-Christendom*, 20.

88. Note the Sydney publication, "The Briefing," which has distilled work on contextualized ministry practice since 1988. Matthias Media, *Briefing*. See other Australian evangelical work reflecting a commitment to contextualized thought and practice in Smart, *Public Christianity*; Foster; *Suburban Captivity*; and the "Social Issues Committee" of the Sydney Diocese. Anglican Diocese of Sydney, "Social Issues." This committee advances conservative theology on issues of public ethics and Christian living; note also work advanced within the Anglican tradition by the Centre for Public and Contextual

of historical analysis to show *how* this process unfolded in the Australian churches. This study thus offers an important perspective on attempts to contextualize late twentieth-century Australian religious culture.

Historic Modes of Christian Ministry and Mission

The Christian Homiletic Tradition

The third literature to which this study contributes is the literature concerning *historic modes of Christian ministry and mission*, namely the way in which the historic Christian church has nourished its members spiritually and facilitated its engagement with society.[89] Within this scholarship there are two further sub-literatures. The first relates to the sermon as the primary platform for Christian public speech. In this regard, the Christian sermonic tradition, arising out of the world of the Jewish synagogue and the early church, has always borne a close resemblance to its secular counterpart—the art of rhetoric—while early church leaders also sought to nuance carefully the ways in which it differed.[90] The application of rhetorical tools and forms to Christian preaching has been common throughout much of Christian history. However, by the eighteenth and nineteenth centuries the use of rhetoric as a conceptual tool fell into disuse in the Christian tradition as a result of the rise of critical and scientific Christian scholarship, and, in the discipline of biblical studies, the fragmentation of

---

Theology (PaCT) at Charles Sturt University, concerned to explore "the public relevance of the diverse religious traditions of today's world." Charles Sturt University, "PaCT"; also Neville, *Public Theology* addresses matters of public concern in theological perspective with the view to advancing Christian policy and thought in the public sphere.

89. While there may appear to be a degree of conceptual overlap between these second and third literatures, the third literature represents primarily the intentional and particularly verbal *modes of communication* employed by the historic church as it has contended for and represented Christian faith within its host culture and amongst its own members. The second literature, however, concerns the broader *interrelationship between Christianity and its host culture*, and the manner in which the host culture's values, norms, and practices have both *shaped* and, in turn, *are shaped by* historic Christianity.

90. Note the key historical surveys of rhetoric by Kennedy: *Classical Rhetoric*, 1–2; "Historical Survey," 3–41; *Art of Persuasion*, 7. Note the survey of the rhetorical aptitude of early church leaders such as Origen, Eusebius, Gregory of Nazianzus, John Chrysostom, the Latin fathers, Lactantius, and Augustine, in Kennedy, *Classical Rhetoric*, 157–80. For other discussion on the appropriation of rhetoric by early Christian leaders, see Judge, "Paul's Boasting," 37–50; Betz, "Problem of Rhetoric," 127–31; Anderson, *Ancient Rhetorical Theory*, 13–17; Kinzig, "Greek Christian Writers," 633–70; Satterthwaite, "Latin Church Fathers," 671–94; cf. also Augustine's work as the first systematic Christian application of the art of rhetoric in, *De Doctrina Christiana*, 4.2.3, 4.12.7.11.

exegesis into sub-topics of specialization.[91] The last third of the twentieth century, however, has seen a reversal of this trend. The study of rhetoric as a discipline in its own right revived during this period—from which has flowed its renewed application in the realm of biblical studies and in Christian homiletical production and analysis.[92]

Related to these developments has been the revival, in the early twenty-first century, of interest in the sermon as a historical artefact and as a bellwether indicator of changes in the character of societal life.[93] Within this field, an efflorescence of scholarship now considers that sermons (both oral and printed)[94] formed the dominant literary output within British society during the eighteenth and nineteenth centuries. Indeed, if a single cultural experience can be said to have been shared by all classes and conditions of people in Britain and throughout her empire, it was the experience of sitting below a pulpit hearing a sermon.[95] Alan Atkinson describes this abundance of public speech via Australian pulpits, in particular, as a "commonwealth of speech" grounded in "common conversation."[96] Joy Damousi similarly suggests pulpit oratory as being of first order significance in Australian cultural history, providing the main source of moral

---

91. So Amador, *Academic Constraints*, 13–14. For review of this history, see Kennedy, *Classical Rhetoric*, 138; Wuellner, "Rhetorical Criticism," 448–63; "Biblical Exegesis," 493.

92. Recent works on the *production of* Christian homiletics, employing the rhetorical tradition, include: Chapel, *Christ-Centered Preaching*, and MacBride, *Preaching the New Testament*. Recent works on the *analysis of* Christian homiletical history, employing the rhetorical tradition, include: Cunningham and Allen, *Preacher and Audience*; Taylor, *Preachers and People*; Eijnatten, *Long Eighteenth Century*; Ellison, *New History*. For survey works on the sweep of Christian preaching, see Old, *Reading and Preaching*, 7 vols.; Edwards, *History of Preaching*. For works on the application of rhetorical analysis to biblical studies, see Malherbe, *Popular Philosophers*; Hughes, *Early Christian Rhetoric*, 19–26; Mack, *Rhetoric*; the collection of essays in Porter, *Handbook of Classical Rhetoric*; Watson, *Persuasive Artistry*; Classen, *Rhetorical Criticism*; Porter and Stamps, *Rhetorical Interpretation*; Porter and Olbricht, *Rhetorical Analysis*; Witherington, *New Testament Rhetoric*.

93. Francis, "Sermon Studies," 611.

94. Among the first to explore published sermons as cultural artefacts are: Tennant, "Missions, Slavery," 139–80; Wolffe, "British Sermons," 181–206; Sheetz-Nguyen, "Catholic Preaching," 207–32; Burstein, "Anti-Catholic Sermons," 233–68; Francis, "Nineteenth-Century," 269–308; Wagner, "Victorian Sermon Novel," 309–40.

95. Historians have estimated conservatively that in Great Britain and her colonies there were approximately a quarter of a billion sermon events between 1689 and 1901. An estimated eighty thousand of these were published. See Gladwin, "Australian Public Life," 2; cf. Sheetz-Nguyen, "Go Ye Therefore," 549; Ellison, "Introduction," 1–14.

96. Atkinson, *Commonwealth of Speech*.

and ethical instruction for millions of religious adherents.[97] The sermonic tradition is therefore a key form of public conversation—perhaps even the most widely used platform for public speech throughout much of Australian history. Yet, even with such growing recognition, the historic value of the sermon has been largely overlooked by scholars[98] and its place within Australian history has been little assessed or appreciated.[99] A stimulating beginning has been made to this Australian endeavor by Joanna Cruickshank,[100] and Michael Gladwin,[101] and a host of authors in a recent special journal issue of *St Mark's Review* on preaching in Australian history.[102] Nevertheless, there is substantial work to be done, particularly in relation to preaching in the later twentieth century, as most studies have focused on the colonial period and the earlier twentieth century.

97. Damousi, *Colonial Voices*, 70.
98. Gibson, "British Sermon," 3–31, esp. 6; Francis, "Sermons," 32.
99. Inglis, *Speechmaking*, 17, 24; Piggin, "Jesus in Australian History," 150.
100. Cruickshank, "British Colonies," 513–26 offers one of the first comprehensive studies on colonial Australian preaching, noting the collections of sermons which arrived with the First Fleet, including their spiritual pedigree and proliferation from the 1830s onwards.
101. Gladwin, "Australian Public Life," 1–14 provides a skillful overview of Australian preaching in the colonial period with particular emphasis on sermon study in illuminating cultural history. Note also the contribution within this same volume of Frame, "National Commemorations," 16–20 in which Frame addresses twenty-first-century "community homiletics" and the art of preaching on commemorative occasions.
102. In a 2014 issue of *St Mark's Review* dedicated to Australian preaching, Hilliard, "Round the Churches," 1–13 provides a masterly account of sermon reception in late nineteenth-century Adelaide; Bolt, "Thomas Moore," 14–30 offers a fascinating account of lay sermon reading practices in the earliest days of colonial Australian settlement, examining the many volumes of sermons in the personal library of Thomas Moore; Petras, "Charles Haddon Spurgeon," 31–39 analyses the impact of the London metropolitan preacher Charles Haddon Spurgeon in Australia, via the dissemination of his printed sermons; Pettett, "Sermons of Samuel Marsden," 40–50 analyses the preaching of the most famous Australian Anglican clergyman of the nineteenth century, Samuel Marsden, noting the influence of his mentor Charles Simeon and the evangelical tone of his messages; Gunson, "Preaching," 51–59 surveys congregational preaching in the first half of the twentieth century; Moses, "David John Garland," 60–71 considers the preaching of the Rev. David Garland in urging clergy to take a prophetic lead by preaching on issues of social and political significance; Holt, "Expository Preaching," 72–83 and Lane, "Learning from the Legacy," 84–102 offer an introduction to the emergence of the influential expository preaching model in Sydney Anglican churches, noting the prominent role John Chapman played in these developments and the outworking of this homiletical model in Chapman's own ministry and legacy; Olwa, "Festo Kivengere," 103–117 illuminates the Australian influence of the prominent Ugandan evangelist Festo Kivengere in the 1950s and 1970s, noting his revivalist style and links with the Billy Graham association.

Historians are also recognizing in increasing measure the efficacy of sermons and the power of the preached medium to galvanize Christian movements across international theological networks.[103] This dynamic becomes important when considering the influence of preaching in the English-speaking world during the twentieth century. In the age of Billy Graham and John Stott, the strength of global Evangelicalism owes a considerable debt to the influence of preachers and leaders such as these, who applied the insights of a revitalized postwar evangelical scholarship to large audiences via preaching. A pan-evangelical preaching network flourished in the shadow of their work, exhibiting a similar reciprocal nature to the transatlantic network evident during the eighteenth-century evangelical revival.[104] Moreover, the transmission of preaching stylistics, including the influential expository model, travelled these same pathways. This homiletical model came to particular prominence in Australia in 1965 through the preaching of John Stott and was popularized and adapted by evangelical Australian preachers like John Chapman.[105] The historic importance of preaching in energizing Evangelicalism is thus increasingly evident.[106] Nevertheless, little attention has been given by historians to the development of evangelical Australian preaching. Still less attention has been given to the relationship of the influential expository model of preaching to the longer homiletic tradition in which it stands, both in Australia and internationally.

Chapman's homiletical legacy, in particular, was forged via the exposure of many thousands of listeners to his preaching as an oral and aural occurrence. It rose in prominence by virtue of its positive reception. Furthermore, Chapman's distillation of homiletical theory and praxis via multiple teaching avenues throughout his career (in conference, church, and college contexts) became a highly influential model for the formation of Australian and international practitioners.[107] Accordingly, by examining the preaching

---

103. The eighteenth-century evangelical revival in the North American colonies was sustained through a transatlantic network of key preachers like Jonathan Edwards and Benjamin Colman of New England, Isaac Watts and George Whitefield in England, and John Erskine of Scotland, as well as other preachers, printers, and supporters. During the revivals, the sermons of Whitefield and other British evangelicals were published in the American colonies, while the sermons of American preachers were also published in Britain. So O'Brien, "Transatlantic Community," 811–32; Tennant, "Eighteenth-Century Evangelicals," 114–32.

104. Stanley, *Global Diffusion*, 61; O'Brien, "Transatlantic Community," 811–32.

105. Holt, "Expository Preaching," 72–83; Lane, "Learning from the Legacy," 84–102.

106. Gladwin, "Editorial," ix.

107. Chapman's work, *Setting Hearts on Fire* distilled the content of his accumulated teaching, and became a standard work referenced by preaching practitioners in

assumptions and practice of Chapman and the mid-twentieth-century network in which his work took shape, and by examining the genealogy of evangelical Australian preaching, this study holds promise in adding color to the somewhat opaque silhouette which currently exists on Australian preaching. Moreover, it does so through the lens of one of Australia's most esteemed homeliticians, whom many sought to emulate.[108]

Historic Christian Evangelistic Engagement

The final subliterature to which this study contributes is the literature on *historic Christian evangelistic engagement*, particularly since the time of the eighteenth-century evangelical revivals. In this regard, a growing literature on Protestant missions has highlighted the rise of a transatlantic and transpacific revivalist movement through the work of Charles Finney and D. L. Moody in the nineteenth century; and R. A. Torrey, D. G. Barnhouse, and Billy Graham in the twentieth. The Protestantism that gave rise to this emerging movement was a highly mobile and expansionist faith tradition. It embraced the modern period's emerging technologies and print media with such effect that the revivalism which emerged from these channels became a highly effective vehicle for large-scale evangelistic reach, even if becoming somewhat formulaic.[109] Concerning this expansive movement, Stuart Piggin has argued that on all indicators of historic revivalism, the 1959 Billy Graham Crusade which swept the Australian mainland capitals (and which represents a notable Australian manifestation of this tradition) was the

---

Australia and internationally.

108. Manchester, "Preaching of John Chapman."

109. For a concise taxonomy of revivalism and its transatlantic and interdenominational development from the seventeenth to twentieth centuries, see Bebbington, *Victorian Religious Revivals*, 1–19. On the revivalist styles of Moody, Sankey, Finney, and Torrey that set the mold for revivalist preaching, see Old, *Modern Age*, 449–65, 501–9, 513–14; 164; Edwards, *History of Preaching*, 507–20, 53. On the media approach pioneered by the Billy Graham Evangelistic Association, see Bebbington, *Evangelicalism*, 8, 163–65; Massam, "Christian Churches," 251–60. On the transatlantic cross-pollination of revivalism see Chapman, "Anglican Evangelicals," 250–53; Hempton, "Protestant Migrations," 41–48. On the three major revivalist waves in Australian religious history, see Piggin, *Spirit*, 59–62, 164. On the Protestant missions movement, and the "muscular" missionary vision of the late eighteenth century, see Ward and Stanley, *Church Mission Society*; Walls, "Eighteenth-Century," 30–34. On the role British colonialism played as a nursery for the development of this missions vision, providing a logistical and communications superstructure for transmission of the written and spoken word, see Gascoigne, "Introduction," 159–78; Stanley, *Bible and the Flag*; Porter, "Cultural Imperialism," 367–91; *Religion Versus Empire*, 10; Barry et al., *Evangelists of Empire?*

closest Australian society has come to a period of genuine religious awakening.[110] Indeed, rising on the tide of a postwar religious surge and continuing to enjoy a historic ascendancy in social and religious life, churches across the Western world saw widespread increases in interest and church membership during this significant era.[111]

However, following the heady days of such expansionist and revivalist vision, the 1960s came as a shock. Even the Billy Graham evangelistic machine (which in the 1950s had drawn the largest crowds ever to have heard the preaching of the gospel in Britain, America, and Australia) saw diminishing numerical success in the 1960s and 70s in Australia and overseas.[112] Assessing such shifts left many leaders wondering if the Christian world would see such ebullient days again, and, if so, how. Few went as far as to discount the divine agency underlying the success of these mid-century campaigns and the longer-term success of the Protestant missions movement, even while noting that their success should be judged strongly along sociological-contextual *as well as* theological lines. However, such an environment of expansionist success created the danger of methodological and nostalgic presumption in the Christian world—the danger of clinging to methodologies which had served well in one period but appeared largely unsuited to the next.

This study will offer an analysis of these dynamics in the Australian context. It will suggest that a significant aspect of Chapman's legacy was to offer leadership in the post-1960s Australian Christian world, both to amplify the theological foundations of the evangelistic task and to stimulate new and creative approaches to mission that were more suited to reaching a secularizing Australian public. Prior to this time, it is arguable that little sustained theology of evangelistic engagement had existed in the Australian context. For Anglicans, the day had been carried by historic formularies and varying expressions of evangelistic pragmatism. Moreover, responses to the post-1960s milieu within the global Protestantism of the period were also varied. They included the emergence of the charismatic movement with a culturally conditioned model and an emphasis on scale;[113] an

110. On Piggin's criteria for this assessment, see Piggin, *Billy Graham*, 25–26; "History of Revival," 173–93; for discussion see Hilliard, "Secularization," 82.

111. Frame, *Anglicans*, 244; Breward, *Australian Churches*, 167; McLeod, "Crisis of Christianity," 323–47, 329; Hilliard, "Secularization," 81; "God in the Suburbs," 399–419.

112. On comparative figures, see Randall, "Conservative Constructionist," 309–33; Piggin, *Spirit*, 133, 168; Chilton, "Christian Australia," 175–222.

113. Synan, "Pentecostal Movement," 153; Hutchinson and Wolffe, *Short History*, 212, 261–64; Wolffe, "Evangelicals and Pentecostals," 50.

emphasis on social reformism more characteristic of twentieth-century liberal Protestantism;[114] the maintenance of nostalgic revivalism and social isolationism; a renewed search for political influence evidenced by the emergence of certain evangelical lobby groups; and the growth of formulations emphasizing "missional" thinking and the value of growth via church planting.[115] Chapman himself articulated positions on all such responses. Although he pursued a "mixed economy" approach to changing times (maintaining involvement in campaign-style events in Australia and internationally), Chapman's work nevertheless became an early standard bearer within the post-1960s Christian world for a crucicentric and biblicist approach to evangelistic engagement.[116] This approach emphasized, *inter alia*, Reformed theological categories, a stress on the responsibility of every Christian in evangelism, and a dialogical approach which gave space to enquirers to engage at length with biblical truth.[117] In relation to the present study, however, while a growing body of work has begun to appreciate the modes of engagement adopted (often implicitly) by mainstream Protestant churches prior to the 1960s, a comparatively smaller body of work has examined the expression of such patterns within the Australian environment itself. Still fewer have surveyed the shifting patterns of evangelistic engagement employed by Australian evangelicals during the stimulating yet disorienting post-1960s era.[118] Hence, by examining key elements of Chapman's missiological thought, practice, and leadership a key contribution of this study lies in the analysis of a pioneering Australian practical theology of evangelism, articulated against a rapidly shifting social and religious milieu, and which has become highly influential in shaping gospel-communication methodologies throughout the Reformed-evangelical world.[119]

114. Sugden, "Social Gospel," 799–800.

115. Francis and Surridge, "Sermons for End Times," 374–85; Bouma, *Soul*, 101–3. Hutchinson and Wolffe, *Short History*, 246–53.

116. Note the earlier definition of these terms as two of the elements of the "Bebbington quadrilateral."

117. The importance of Chapman's dialogical methodology in the 1960s and 1970s, for example, is evident in his being asked to present this methodology on four occasions at the 1974 Lausanne Congress on World Evangelisation, the largest gathering of world evangelical leaders of its time. See Nichols, "Future World Leaders," 2–3.

118. A number of recent articles have cursorily examined such themes. See Fletcher, "Sydney," 111–32; Hilliard, "Pluralism," 124–48; Hilliard, "Secularization," 75–88; Hilliard, "Crisis," 209–27. However, the first substantive study of Australian evangelical patterns of engagement in the pre- and post-1960s era is the recent work of Chilton, "Christian Australia."

119. Chapman's *Know and Tell* had sold forty thousand copies by the 1990s and became an influential work in shaping theories of evangelism within Australia and

Methodology

Historical Biography

This study will therefore seek to further elucidate the scholarly appreciation of this decisive period in Australian evangelical history, via an analysis of Chapman's career and contribution. To achieve this, it will be guided by a primary interrogative research aim, namely, to examine the life and legacy of John Charles Chapman and its shaping influence on Anglican Evangelicalism in Sydney and Australian religious life during the period 1968–2001. These dates have been selected not only because 1968 marked the beginning of Chapman's Sydney ministry, but also because of its significance as a moment of heightened radicalism. The year 2001 is suggested as the terminus given that it marks the rise of Sydney's Archbishop Peter Jensen and a transition point from Chapman's generation. This year also marks a new shift in the religious development of Western societies via the World Trade Center attacks and their effects.[120] The study's overriding research aim will, in turn, be explored in the form of a "historical biography"—a methodological approach that is ideal for situating this influential clergyman's actions and thought in religious, social, cultural, and theological context.[121]

Historians' attitudes towards historical biography have developed in the context of changing twentieth-century theories of history. They ranged between pre-1960s positivist conceptions of history as an empirical "science" to postmodern ideas of history as an almost subjective art form.[122] Such

---

internationally. The only comparable Australian publication prior to this was Hammond's, *In Understanding Be Men* which sold 150,000 copies in thirty years. Yet, this publication was concerned largely with evangelical doctrine, not evangelism specifically. On the continuing influence of Chapman's thought, cf. Chan, *Skeptical World*, 11.

120. McLeod, "Crisis of Christianity," 337.

121. For discussion on the interrelationship between such historiographical factors, see Bradley and Muller, *Church History*, 1–9. In particular, note the relationship of "the practice of the church as well as the thought of the church" as the remit of the church historian, and of the need for a holistic approach that takes account "of the subtle social, political, and philosophical influences" in the analysis of church ideas and actions (3). Note also that while "historical theology is a subset of the broader discipline," previous approaches which conceived of church history as merely a "history of ideas" have been increasingly critiqued (4–5). On the contention of those associated with the *Annales* school who emphasized the mere social determination of an individual's intellectual life, see Chartier, *Cultural History*, 24. Recent intellectual histories by Curthoys and Docker, *Is History Fiction?* have, however, assisted in the conceptualization of ideas as capable of being formed and held separate to the holder's context.

122. For wider historiographical development and its relationship to religious history, see Bebbington, "Discipline of History," 16–33. Church history (as a subset of religious history) was influenced by such broader trends, developing from the more

latter concerns were driven by radically deconstructionist and postmodern approaches to knowledge which arose in the wake of post-structuralism and the "linguistic turn." In their more benign expressions, such approaches demanded that one position not be "privileged" over another in historical writing; while in their more radical forms, they declared all historical reflection to be "foundationless" and reduced to absolute subjectivity.[123] Such concerns, in turn, bore upon biographical genres in suggesting that biography was a medium that could too easily yield to an author's vision, culture, and ideology.[124] Historians also became conscious of the difficulties in accessing and representing a subject's inner life as a means of understanding their guiding choices and behaviors.[125] Still others suggested that in focusing on the lives of exceptional subjects, by such selectivity biography tended to play an overly editorial role in the production of history.[126] Mindful of such concerns, the majority of professional historians have nevertheless resisted embracing such critique entirely. They have preferred to discount the nihilistic claims of extreme postmodernism and have rejected the inclination to become lost in a mire of subjectivity and relativism.[127] Similarly, most historians have also acknowledged that although the past is certainly perceived through the consciousness of the historian and is mediated by the language through which it is communicated, this does not warrant the conclusion that all historiography is merely a discourse, which is no better or worse—or

---

empirically driven science of the early century, toward a providentially ordered view of history in the mid-century, to a later-century approach which saw the discipline emerging into the larger frame of world history, no longer immune "from the demands for evidence." See Ahlstrom, "History of Religion," 136; Bradley and Muller, *Church History*, 19.

123. Jenkins, *Postmodern History Reader*, 6.

124. For a stimulating review of the development of historical biography, its diminution at the hands of deconstructionists and its subsequent revival, see Sardica, "Content and Form," 383–400; Ellis, *Literary Lives*; Backsheider, *Reflections on Biography*; Tridgell, *Understanding Our Selves*; France and St. Clair, *Mapping Lives*.

125. Israel, "Place of Narrative," 8. This contrasts Collingwood's confidence in the earlier twentieth century of entering the subject's mind and "re-enacting" their thoughts. So Collingwood, *Autobiography*, 107–8. Further, confronted by Michel Foucault's radical views of the individual as a fiction produced in a matrix of power and knowledge, and with the predominance of the economic and social history of the mid-century, some historians were persuaded that the human subject "cannot provide the enduring foundation for historical method." So Hunt, "French History," 209–24; Curthoys and Docker, *Is History Fiction?*, 123–26; cf. Gordon, *Michel Foucault*; Foucault, "Nietzsche," 76–100.

126. Goldman, "Historical Biography," 16.

127. Megill, "Reception of Foucault," 117–34; Bradley and Muller, *Church History*, 47; Sardica, "Biography," 392–93; Curthoys and Docker, *Is History Fiction?*, 126–27.

more or less true—than any other.[128] David Bebbington, a leading historian of Evangelicalism, is one among many historians who have seen these developments as an opportunity—rather than merely a threat—for the historical enterprise. Postmodern perspectives, Bebbington argues, have brought caution and humility into historical analysis, forced a greater clarification of method, and highlighted the limitations of any approach to knowledge that deems all history as either arbitrary, or, alternatively, as pure scientific fact.[129] Instead, objectivity in historical writing has come to be seen not by a canon of absolute truth. Rather, it arises as a standard of the relationship between data and its careful interpretation.[130]

Furthermore, despite such theoretical challenges posed to historical scholarship by postmodern philosophy,[131] biography has nevertheless remained one of the main forms in which Christian history has been presented. Even as trained historians became increasingly responsible for the production of religious history during the 1960s to 1970s,[132] biography has remained a prominent, even prolific form.[133] Scholars have experimented

128. See Evans, *Defence of History*, 7, 81, 109, 143; also Palmer, *Descent into Discourse*, xiv, 199 who labels much postmodernist writing as a kind of "academic word-playing" which is no substitute for "historical materialism; language is not life"; also Appleby et al., *Telling the Truth*, 200, 208, 230, 236–7 who argue strongly against postmodern approaches to history, suggesting it attacks "the very foundations of historical and scientific knowledge," through denying "our ability to represent reality in any objectively true fashion." Further, they assert, critiquing the economic determinism of Marxism, such theorists have simply offered a new kind of "linguistic determinism," which reduces "the social and natural world to language" and creates a new master narrative.

129. Bebbington, "Discipline of History," 31–33; Curthoys and Docker, *Fiction?*, 206; Appleby et al., *Telling the Truth*, 246.

130. Bradley and Muller, *Church History*, 37, 47; Wood, *Purpose of the Past*, 5, 10, 60. For discussion of a "Rankean" or "reconstructionist" view of historical writing, aimed at "verisimilitude" in content and orderliness of form, see Himmelfarb, *New History*, 18–29; Sardica, *Biography*, 390; Munslow, "Biography," 2.

131. "Postmodern" is used as a summary term for post-structuralism, deconstruction, new historicism, semiotics, and the like, and for the paradigm shift in epistemology advanced by Derrida and Foucault. So Himmelfarb, *New History*, 15–16.

132. Bollen et al., "Australian Religious History," 17.

133. This is best exemplified in the publication of Dickey, *Australian Dictionary*. Also Backsheider, *Reflections on Biography*, xxi notes "readers come back and back to biography, ceaselessly seeking to understand the way human beings have lived, the shapes of life, how individuals fit into history, and the ways humankind has grappled with the advantages and obstacles that life inevitably entails." Sardica, *Historical Biography*, 385 further notes that with the re-emphasis in the late twentieth century of history "from below" via a focus on the anonymous, the excluded, the silenced and forgotten of society—following the dominance of Marxist and structuralist collective thought—historiography has subsequently seen the return of "the individual and of

with different forms of the genre, including collective biography (prosopography), partial or fragmented individual biographies, and comparative or meta-biography.[134] Furthermore, given Protestantism's historic emphasis on the importance of personal piety and spiritual self-examination, and its privileging of the dictates of the individual conscience over the decrees of the church, biography remains a particularly useful genre for the examination of Protestant thought and expression. It allows the coherence of shared human experience and spirituality to be empathetically explored.[135] Crucially for the present study, historical biography's core advantages are further appreciable if it is remembered that history is a sum of human action. Accordingly, the study of actors behind such actions allows the historian to draw close and to connect with "somebody else's present time."[136] Indeed, through historical biography a single life becomes a focal point to fully observe a past time, space, and society.[137] It concretizes the abstract, contextualizes past choices, and allows the historian seeking a global picture of a past to obtain illuminating pieces through the actions of the one whose life has been chosen for study.[138] Effective biography also recognizes the interplay of micro and macro perspectives, allowing each to reinforce the other and enabling the reader not only to learn *about a life*, but to understand the *significance of that life within an age* and the *significance of an age through a life*.[139] Such an approach is consonant with recent scholarly biographi-

---

events" and the re-entry of biography to the core of historical research. This turn has strengthened a view of history as less an aseptic science, and more as a study of mankind, and about the diversity and richness of human unpredictability; also Wood, "Purpose of the Past," 2–6.

134. For discussion of such biographical approaches, including prosopography, partial or fragmented individual biographies, and newer approaches which urge the voice of the writer to feature more prominently in biographical writing, see Keats-Rohan, *Prosopography Approaches*; Hollow, "Introducing the Historian," 43–52. For discussion of the pitfalls of collective biography, see MacLeod and Nuvolari, "Pitfalls of Prosopography," 757–76; Morley, "Re-thinking Biographical Praxis," 81–92. For discussion of the technique of comparative or metabiography, especially suited to the analysis of subjects whose lives subsisted across multiple national boundaries and cultures, see Schweiger, "Global Subjects," 249–58.

135. Hutch, *Biography*, 4; Durston and Eales, "Puritan Ethos," 9–13 suggest Puritanism provided a language and theoretical basis for the genre of spiritual autobiography that flourished in England for some generations from the mid-seventeenth century.

136. Curthoys and McGrath, *How to Write History*, 1–2; France and St. Clair, "Introduction," 1–5.

137. Sardica, *Historical Biography*, 385, 393; Holmes, "Proper Study?," 7; Curthoys and McGrath, *History*, 178.

138. Paulin, "Adding Stones," 105.

139. Snowman, "Historical Biography," 55–56.

cal studies of twentieth-century evangelical leaders Billy Graham and John Stott, and illuminates a pathway forward for this study.[140] These biographies do not examine their subjects in a strictly chronological fashion, but rather through a series of thematic lenses that allow the reader to see the "summative effect" of the elements of each leader's persona and work.[141] These biographies resist simply narrating the story of their subject's life. Instead, they critically assess each person's work as a further lens through which to examine the religious and national culture of the period.[142] In so doing, these works commend the use of historical biography in religious history and revivify the significant legacies of their subjects for an audience increasingly unaware of their subjects' importance.[143]

Sources and Structure

Chapman's contribution will be assessed by drawing on a rich vein of archival, personal, and published primary sources, locating the subject within a wider religious network of organizations, supporters, and friends. These sources include Chapman's extensive published works and numerous domestic and international archival collections. Chapman's personal papers have also been accessed with permission, among which are previously unknown works by Chapman, biographical material, as well as the handwritten notes that informed as many as 7,500 addresses. A series of oral interviews with key domestic and international figures spanning Chapman's ministry has also been undertaken, which strengthens the documentary portrait.[144] Meaning will be inferred from these historical traces in such a way that respects their context, while locating them within the composite interpretive frame established by all other primary and secondary traces.[145] The study is organized into four sections, following a thematic and broadly chronological order. It begins with an analysis of Chapman's formative influences, followed by assessments of his contribution in the areas of homiletics, missiology, theology, and ecclesial reform.

140. See Chapman, *Godly Ambition*; Wacker, *America's Pastor*.

141. Brenneman, "America's Pastor," 133; Trollinger, "Godly Ambition," 765–67.

142. The emphasis in such critical biography is on "making judgments" versus merely "supplying information." Only in this way can a subject's significance be appropriately assessed. So Chapman, *Godly Ambition*, 6–8.

143. Erdozain, "Godly Ambition," 668–69; Hansen, "Stott Life Portrait," 47–49; Brenneman, "America's Pastor," 133.

144. Note the considerations for oral history in Curthoys and McGrath, *History*, 91–99.

145. Bradley and Muller, *History*, 31, 49.

Section A: Prolegomena and Life Contours

The first section (chapter 2) examines the social and theological influences that shaped Chapman from his earliest days. This will include his family and social formation, conversion and training, early ministry, and theological development, together with the significant reciprocal ministry relationships that shaped and sustained him throughout his extensive career.

Section B: Preacher

The second section orients the study to the historical context in which the Australian evangelical preaching tradition stands, while seeking to distill the essence of Chapman's homiletic achievement. The development of the expository preaching model in particular will be traced, with a view to situating Chapman's place in the mid-century revival of this model and its subsequent influence in the Australian church (chapter 3). This will be supplemented with an analysis of what constituted Chapman's unique theological contribution to the homiletic discipline alongside a brief analysis of the rhetorical praxis of this celebrated Australian preacher (chapter 4).[146]

Section C: Evangelist

The third section of the study considers Chapman's significant legacy as an evangelist and missiological thought leader. A portrait of evangelistic engagement within Australian Evangelicalism in the pre-1960s era will first be offered, supplying a salient reference point for the subsequent analysis. Following this, Chapman's missiological contribution in key areas of the post-1960s Christian world will be assessed. This will include his involvement with and methodological innovations regarding the ubiquitous crusade movement and emerging pan-evangelical networks that influenced Australia and internationally during the 1970s to 1980s (chapter 5). The challenges

---

146. Elements of the classical rhetorical tradition will form a useful conceptual tool in analysing the shape of Christian homiletics across the eras of history. While a comprehensive analysis of this history employing such tools is impracticable, the classical "parts of speech" such as invention, arrangement, style, memory, and delivery will implicitly inform the analysis. Consideration will also be given to the Aristotelian modes of persuasion like *logos* (oratorical content), *pathos* (the emotional swaying of an audience), and *ethos* (speaker trustworthiness and reception). Such categories will form a further useful tool in assessing the qualities of the twentieth-century tradition that Chapman shaped, embodied, and taught. For recent examples of the use of such tools in homiletic analysis, see Chapel, *Christ-Centered Preaching*; 35–41; MacBride, *Criticism*.

encountered by Chapman and other leading conservatives associated with the rise of the Lausanne Congress for World Evangelization (1974) and the struggle to balance the objectives of evangelical humanitarianism with the priority of gospel proclamation will also be assessed (chapter 6). Following this, an analysis of Chapman's evangelistic formulations with reference to the scholarship of certain Australian theologian-practitioners will also be given. This will include his advocacy in promoting a widespread missional culture among evangelical churches and a view of the church's mission in which both leaders *and* members played an active role (chapter 7).[147]

Section D: Pugilist and Pioneer

The final section examines Chapman's influential contribution to key areas of ecclesiological and theological reform. This will involve the tracing of key features in the movement to contextualize worship and ministry practices in Australian (particularly Sydney) Anglicanism and Chapman's key role within this process (chapter 8).[148] This will be followed by an analysis of Chapman's advocacy, along with leading figures, in promoting a classically Reformed theological position in response to the charismatic renewal movement of the 1960s to 1980s (chapter 9).[149] The final chapter will gather the threads of this analysis together, drawing conclusions about Chapman's shaping influence on the Australian and wider evangelical movements (chapter 10).

There are places in the present study when significant historical context is supplied. This is particularly in relation to the discussions surrounding the history of Australian (and more broadly evangelical) homiletics, alongside the historic patterns of missiological advocacy pursued by Australian evangelicals in the pre-1960s era. This is not only because such an analysis more fully frames and distills the significance of Chapman's contribution in these

---

147. The influential ecclesiology of D. W. B. Robinson and D. B. Knox will bear particular mention in this analysis.

148. *Move in For Action*.

149. During the 1960s the charismatic movement gained significant momentum within Sydney Anglican circles via the advocacy of leading clergy and the growing St. Andrew's Cathedral healing ministry. Such activities raised sufficient concern within the diocese that at the 1971 session of synod a resolution was passed requesting the Standing Committee to appoint a committee to consider the charismatic movement from a scholarly and pastoral standpoint. Chapman played a leading role in establishing this committee and provided a strong counterpoint to charismatic theology across numerous other forums in his public ministry. See *Both Sides to the Question*, 3; Egan, "Healing Ministries," 73–91.

areas, but also because these areas are currently underexamined in Australian religious historiography.[150] Hence, in pursuing such extended analysis, not only does the present study more fully illuminate the shape of Chapman's contribution, but it offers greater insight into the shape of Australian and world Evangelicalism of this period. Indeed, as noted in the discussion above of the strengths of the biographical genre, in pursuing such an approach we both learn about a life and are enabled to understand the *significance of that life within an age* and the *significance of an age being examined through a life*. Both provide reflections upon and windows into one another.[151] In addition, many more aspects of Chapman's life *could* be examined through the course of this study. As such, Chapman's status as a single man, his personal prayer and piety, and the global network of connections he developed (which became important to the emerging evangelical movement) each invite considered reflection. While these aspects of Chapman's life will be considered in various places, they are not the main focus of this study.[152] Rather, consonant with recent scholarly biographies of other evangelical leaders (such as John Stott and Billy Graham) the areas of Chapman's contribution highlighted in this study relate to some of the defining issues for the Australian and world evangelical movements of this period.[153] Accordingly, by examining such key facets of Chapman's career and contribution, this study holds promise for shedding fresh light on the principles that energized one of Australia's most significant religious movements as it navigated a period of immense change via a process of reform, resistance to external threat, and authentic spiritual renewal. That such developments occurred at a time of crisis amongst world ecclesiastical movements makes the achievements of this period and its key actors all the more significant.[154]

150. Note the preceding discussion of these historiographical deficiencies.

151. Snowman, "Historical Biography," 55–56.

152. In relation to Chapman's single status, for example, there is little doubt that this was a key element in his wide impact, affording him time and liberty to invest in his ministry with its extensive travel. Recent popular works on Chapman have reflected on Chapman's motivation for remaining single for the sake of his ministry. So Mansfield, *Chappo Collection*, 93–108. However, there is also a sense in which Chapman's single status was almost incidental. Chapman spoke of it infrequently in public contexts. Nor did he wear it as a badge of "heroic act of the will" for the sake of the gospel. Rather, it was a life context that unfolded in light of his clear missiological priorities and afforded him a full and varied life. Interview with Rico Tice, January 17, 2017. Cf. the parallel with John Stott, whose singleness facilitated a wide-ranging international ministry. Chapman, *Godly Ambition*, 63–64.

153. Chapman, *Godly Ambition*; Wacker, *Pastor*; Erdozain, "Stott," 668; Brenneman, "Pastor," 133.

154. Snowman, "Biography," 56; Atherstone and Maiden, "Anglican Evangelicalism," 2.

2

John Charles Chapman: Life Contours

Intersecting Historical Contexts

"What then is the secret of the joy, help and blessing that this man has brought to so many? 'Truth through Personality.' . . . God fashions instruments to carry His Name. Tom is not Dick, nor is Dick Harry. When God chooses and sends some singular and unusual character into His harvest field, unusual ministry will result, to the glory of God who planned it all."—R. C. Lucas[1]

IN WAR-TIME SYDNEY, FEARS of a Japanese strike against the city ran high. To prepare the community, the *Sydney Morning Herald* ran a series of "community supplements" outlining what their readers should do if the air-raid sirens went off. Muriel Chapman of suburban Oatley took great care in collecting these supplements. She studied and placed them at choice spots around the Chapman home. "Fill up the bath and the tubs in case the mains were hit," was the advice. "Position the strongest table in the middle of the house and get the family under it." She prepared diligently.[2]

On May 31, 1942, the sirens went off for real and Muriel meticulously got to work. She filled the bath and the tubs. She moved the inch-thick, six-foot kitchen table and positioned it in the center of the home. She roused the boys. Yet, Albury Chapman would not be woken. "Get up, Dad," cried

1. Dick Lucas, "Foreword," in Orpwood, *Chappo*, vi.

2. Given the reality of "enemy planes over Australia" and drawing on "experience in raids over England," the Herald's advice extended to the care of pets and children, the arrangement of household goods and immediate measures to take "as soon as the sirens go off." *SMH*, Saturday May 2, 1942, 5; *SMH*, Friday May 8, 1942, 3.

Muriel once, twice, and a third time. Albury staggered into the room and the family crouched under the kitchen table. "Do we know if this one's for real?" he cried as he climbed reluctantly under the table. But Muriel had disappeared. "Mum, where are you?" cried Albury in exasperation. "I'm looking for my false teeth!" came a voice from the bedroom. "Don't worry, Toots," chirped Albury, "if the Japs start dropping anything, it won't be Sergeant's pies!!"[3]

It was into a home such as this in Oatley, Sydney, that John Charles Chapman was born on June 23, 1930, the second son of Albury and Muriel Chapman. It was a suburban world not twenty kilometers from the birthplace of European Australia in Botany Bay—a rustically Australian world of its time that would play its own unique role in shaping the figure that Chapman was to become.

Intersecting Historical Contexts

Interwar Australia

In the Australia of Chapman's birth, the guns of the Great War had not long fallen silent, yet the legacy of 60,000 sons lost in battle—out of a nation of 4.5 million—together with the 150,000 who returned wounded or impaired, still weighed heavily on the nation's soul.[4] Two different national stories jostled for ascendancy in the war's aftermath. Social despondency engulfed many servicemen as "broken comrades" caroused in public houses, occasioning new calls for temperance and a return to moral principles. Enthusiasm for the righteous struggle the war had represented gave way for many in these years to a futility that overwhelmed any vestiges of national pride. This strained a war-weary public's solidarity with the religious and political establishment that had championed the bloody conflict.[5] Alongside war's inexorable shadow, however, the 1920s offered new prosperity and hope for many. Successive governments promoted industry, investment, and rising protectionism.[6] "Men, Money and Markets" was the key to

---

3. Interview with Dr. David Seccombe, February 15, 2017; Interview with Phillip Jensen, February 16, 2017. This same story was recounted by both Seccombe and Jensen in separate interviews during the research phase of this study.

4. Bashford and Macintyre, "Introduction," 3; Garton and Stanley, "Great War," 39–63.

5. Clark, *History of Australia Vol. 6*, 80–82; Snape, "Great War," 131–50; Garton and Stanley, "Great War," 62.

6. Merrett and Ville, "Tariffs, Subsidies, and Profits," 46–70.

the limitless opportunity that lay before the nation.[7] Unions capitalized on burgeoning trade to press for improved wages and conditions.[8] Consumer durables from North America and Europe arrived with the throng of new immigration.[9] The motor car became increasingly visible on Australian streets. Household gas and electricity connections rose. Vegemite's conquest of the Australian palate enlarged, while branded confectionery, convenience foods, and packaged cereals also boomed.[10] In home entertainment the radio was king, while the sporting hero enjoyed the adoration of a resilient and proletarian public. Don Bradman's emerging batting heroics and the effortless victories of the racehorse "Pharlap" regularly transfixed the nation.[11] Sydney's "coat hanger" dominated the harbor skyline.[12] Suburbs multiplied on the edges of cities. Long suburban streets and little square bungalows proliferated, while the inner cities became the apex and visible emblem of Australian urban struggle.[13]

Economic contraction soon followed. A swollen public sector sent public debt soaring in the late 1920s, alongside the continuing and crippling strain of war repatriation costs.[14] For an economy reliant on export revenue and capital inflows, such proto-Keynesianism bit hard in the tumult of 1929-30. The stock market crash of October 1929 paralyzed global credit markets and Australian terms of trade soured with the plummeting world trade.[15] Downward pressure on wages combined with sharp unemployment to focus the crisis at the domestic level.[16] Evictions led to overcrowding in the inner-city doss houses, leaving many to sleep in parks or around railways. Breadwinners overwhelmed private charities, while governments marshalled weakened budgets to supply unemployment relief and emergency

---

7. Clark, *History of Australia Vol 6.*, 224.
8. Ville, "Economy," 378-80.
9. Greenwood, *Australia*, 319.
10. Merrett and Ville, "Tariffs, Subsidies, and Profits," 57-59.
11. Bongiorno, "Search for a Solution, 1923-39," 70.
12. The Sydney Harbour Bridge was completed in 1932 after nine years of construction. Ellmoos and Murray, "Sydney Harbour Bridge."
13. Thornhill, *Making Australia*, 83; Siriwardana, "Causes," 54.
14. Siriwardana, "Causes," 54; Clark, *History of Australia Vol 6.*, 293; Garton and Stanley, "Great War," 59-61.
15. Valentine, "Depression in Australia," 47; Siriwardana, "Causes," 53.
16. Unemployment increased sharply. It peaked at 30 percent in 1933 and remained high throughout the 1930s. Unemployment was sharpest in inner-city areas where, among adult males, it reached highs of 40 percent. So Valentine, "Depression in Australia," 44; Potts, *Myth*, 11.

sustenance rations.[17] Yet, for all the manifest turmoil of these difficult years, Australia remained a nation chastised but not broken by the Depression, under duress but not disintegrating.[18] Just as previous periods of adversity had tempered the Australian spirit, so these years brought a humility and resilience to the nation—an egalitarian tone and shared wisdom in adversity that colored the nation's self-image and its cultural life.[19]

Working-Class Suburban Family

The Chapman family were among the fortunate suburban families who weathered the Depression years diminished, yet unbroken. After making their start in Rockdale, Albury and Muriel Chapman began life in Oatley on Sydney's urban fringe with the throng of like families relocating in the 1920s.[20] Albury Chapman (b. 1889) was from country stock in Holbrook, New South Wales, the sixth child of Hume Jones Chapman and Eliza Day Crisp. Albury was apprenticed as a fitter and turner before spending time at sea as a marine engineer and in munitions manufacturing in England during the Great War. On returning to Australia after the war he began a lifelong career with the NSW Railways Department. This was an industry of strategic value in the modernization of enterprise and infrastructure to service the expanding economy.[21] Muriel Chapman (b. 1891), the middle child of James Varley and Louise Gregory, endured a childhood marked by sadness. She lost her mother at nine years of age and her stepmother at eleven years. This cast Muriel and her siblings on the care of relatives in Bexley. Muriel was a motherly and sweet woman. Her family had given rise to the famous Gregory line of sportsmen who by 1910 boasted over twenty

---

17. Bongiorno, "Search for a Solution," 77.

18. The high unemployment rate of the inner cities was offset by low unemployment in rural districts and in the outer suburbs of the cities. Three quarters of eligible wage earners held employment at any time. Those without jobs used their time producing goods at home for consumption or exchange and maintained their living standards in ways that economists could not measure. See Potts, *Myth*, 11–13. For a comparative analysis of the impact of the Depression years on Australia versus its impact on other industrializing nations, see Valentine, "Causes," 43–50.

19. Thornhill, *Making Australia*, 125–27.

20. The author is indebted in this family portrait to aspects of the earlier work of Chapman's biographer, Michael Orpwood, *Sake of the Gospel*, alongside fuller transcripts (resident in the Sydney Anglican Diocesan Archival collection) that were supplied by Chapman to Orpwood for the writing of this earlier 1990s era biography.

21. Taksa, "Matter of Timing," 1–26.

children who had represented NSW in a variety of sports including cricket, football, sailing, and athletics.[22]

For the Chapman family life in Oatley was modest, communal, and parochial. John and his older brother Jim shared the back verandah, while Grandpa Varley occupied an inside room. The iceman came twice a week and the old copper handled the washing. Neighbors subsisted in these difficult years by growing vegetables and sourcing fish and oysters from the nearby George's River. With only modest means themselves, when the home next door was razed to the ground by fire, the Chapmans took their neighbors in immediately while they regathered the threads of their fractured existence.[23] Oatley itself lay on the southernmost reach of Sydney's suburban fringe. It was, quite literally, the end of the line—notable as the terminus of the first railway electrification project in Sydney, which reached this station from central Sydney in 1926.[24] Oatley Post Office opened in 1903, giving the suburb official recognition.[25] Tom Ugly's Bridge, which crossed the George's River to the south and connected Sydney at large with the Sutherland Shire, had been in use from only 1929.[26] Thus for the young Chapman the edges of civilization lay at Hornsby in the far north and Sutherland in the south. The far west was Parramatta on a good day, otherwise it was Ashfield. And though he had heard of Wollongong, further south still, he had not been there.[27]

The Chapman home was both humorous and belligerent. They would laugh as a family and jokes and humorous stories were regularly told, though quickness in repartee and able raconteuring were considered the best form of humor.[28] Chapman's aunt made sport by sending newspaper cuttings which had tickled her, stuffed into a manila envelope until it was cylindrical. She never wrote much, just the cartoons and articles conveyed her tone. She loved misprints and wrong spellings. If a bishop appeared in a cope and miter, the cutting arrived with the caption, "Just one of the boys!"[29] Albury Chapman was a giant personality. He was strong in his

22. The Rev. Prebendary Dick Lucas, Rector Emeritus, St. Helen's Bishopsgate, Service of Thanksgiving; Orpwood, *Sake of the Gospel*, 17.

23. Interview with Phillip Jensen, February 16, 2017.

24. Brady, "Sydney's Electric Trains," 41–66.

25. Oatley was named after James Oatley, a watchmaker sent to Sydney in 1814, pardoned and put to work installing the clock at the Hyde Park Barracks. Pollon, *Book of Sydney Suburbs*, 193.

26. Roads and Traffic Authority, "Tom Ugly's Bridge."

27. Grant, "John Chapman Interview."

28. Interview with David Mansfield, November 29, 2016.

29. Chapman to Orpwood, February 1, 1994. Box 1, Board of Diocesan Mission

convictions and raised his sons Jim and John on a diet of argument and old Australian humor. Teasing and pulling your leg was the way of things.[30] Albury would fish with an old friend, and jest with his impressionable son that his mate "was the first man to row a boat over the Blue Mountains." This was a claim the young John took delight in remaking at school show-and-tell.[31] "Comedians, rather than historians," wrote the historian Manning Clark, "taught Australians who they were."[32] Indeed, few peoples have prized humor as a mode of communicating more than Australians. Their humor can be exuberant and boisterous, while dry and understated. With an air of self-mocking, it delights in an irreverence which cautions the hearer not to take oneself, nor the things most revered, too seriously.[33] Australian humor has the "sardonic savage flavor . . . of a people who knew . . . life is made bearable by being treated as a joke."[34] Such was the humor of Chapman's homelife. Albury saw the funny side in situations and was a dry humorist, with a hard edge that could often be caustic when directed at people.[35] When Albury and his sister Millie were together, one could barely eat on account of the banter between them.[36] Such room-sized personality, bequeathed subtly though surely in this way, would play a defining role in Chapman's itinerant ecclesiastical career.[37] It imbued a presence that could not be ignored,[38] an ebullience that disarmed a room, and a quick-witted sharpness of mind that was often penetrating.[39]

Belligerence also marked the Chapman home. John was raised arguing. Albury, an intelligent and avid reader, and Labor party man to the back teeth, saw in Labor the opportunity for an "enlightened and self-reliant community,

---

Files, Sydney Diocesan Archives (SDA).

30. Jensen and Freney, "Majoring on the Majors."
31. Jensen and Freney, "Majoring on the Majors."
32. Morgan, "Realism and Documentary," 238–52.
33. Thornhill, *Making Australia*, 133.
34. Wright, *Preoccupations*, 81.
35. Interview with David Mansfield, November 29, 2016.
36. Chapman to Orpwood, February 1, 1994, BDM Box 1, SDA.
37. Dick Lucas notes Chapman's humor to be "an inborn gift, inherited from his father . . . John was not a joker in any professional sense. And in a preacher, self-conscious jokiness can repel rather than commend the message. But there was a sense in which John could not help himself. Humor and wit was not an extra stuck onto his personality, it was just the man himself." So Lucas, *Service of Thanksgiving*.
38. Jensen and Freney, "Majoring on the Majors." Chapman regularly "held court" in social contexts. His presence was frequently so overshadowing that one considered themselves as "being in his company," not "he in yours." Interview with Grant Retief, August 29, 2017.
39. Interview with Tony Payne, November 29, 2016.

without an underclass, fitted to be the most progressive in the world."[40] His support for the Labor cause was therefore unwavering.[41] Even in retirement, Albury listened to the parliamentary broadcasts, giving time to the Labor speakers. When the Liberal speakers came on, however, he would turn the volume down, take the time, and turn it back up again when they were over. When asked how he knew they had nothing good to say, he simply replied, "They're Liberals, aren't they?"[42] Albury escorted his sons to hear politicians campaigning from the back of trucks in the shopping center at Oatley. It was the way they answered hecklers that he loved. If they were a politician worth hearing, they would march to Mortdale to hear the same man once more.[43] Such a practical education in the rhetoric of public disagreement was formative. Whether "throwing dust in the air" at the Sydney Synod or Standing Committee,[44] engaging in animated dialogue with his staff, or marshalling arguments with an agility that was difficult to match,[45] Chapman's homelife steeled him never to shrink from disagreement, however impressive or well-credentialed the opposition. Disconcertingly for some, Chapman was not afraid to change his mind either. Passionately arguing a case one day, he would return the next day, recognizing his error and arguing the counter case.[46] As Chapman grew in his own settled conviction, this same quality would come to place considerable strain on his paternal relationship. This was a failing not entirely of his father's own making.[47] Overreach in argumentation also presented a constant danger. This ensnared the evangelist not infrequently, for which he was known to travel inconvenient distances to reconcile and recalibrate a relationship.[48] Nevertheless, born and raised at a

40. McMullin, *Light on the Hill*, 56.

41. Interview with David Mansfield, November 29, 2016.

42. Jensen and Freney, "Majoring on the Majors."

43. Chapman to Orpwood, February 1, 1994, BDM Box 1, SDA.

44. Interview with Dick Lucas, January 20, 2017.

45. Interview with Dr. Paul Barnett, December 2, 2016; Interview with Donald Howard, February 17, 2017.

46. Jensen and Freney, "Majoring on the Majors." Ian Powell, Chapman's associate for some years notes, "I enjoyed arguing with him. It is done with vigor and totally without spite. I have never known a man more ready to declare he was wrong." Ian Powell to David Mansfield, BDM Box 1, SDA.

47. Interview with Dick Lucas, January 20, 2017.

48. Preaching one evening in Wollongong, Chapman made sport of Christian teetotalers, of which the rector of the church held settled personal convictions. Realising his offence, Chapman drove immediately the next day to apologise. Interview with David Short, February 17, 2017. Marcus Loane states, "There was at times in John an abrasive quality which upset others . . . I think this arose from his own intense conviction of what is right and where truth lay." Marcus Loane to Michael Orpwood, BDM

time when life was given to the pursuit of great causes by which nations rose and fell, Chapman's working-class and intelligent family and social world schooled him in argumentation. While eschewing unalloyed cynicism, it taught him never to be taken for a fool.

Education and Enculturation

Chapman's education took place in the shadow of another global and protracted conflict. The nation's entry into a second world war was greeted with little of the imperialist enthusiasm so evident among Australians in 1914. Twenty-five years later many families still mourned lost sons, brothers, and husbands. As Australia emerged from the Depression years with unemployment still at 9 percent in 1939, war thus presaged further years of difficulty.[49] Japanese entry into the war in 1941 transformed the Australian home front as well. While Japan's strategy toward Australia remained one of containment and isolation, fears of a Japanese landing or attack intensified.[50] Air raid precaution drills were introduced. Communal air raid shelters were erected. Shop windows were boarded up and first aid stations were introduced. Austerity measures also came abruptly into force.[51] As liberation edged closer, a landslide election victory to Labor in 1943 won a record parliamentary majority that set the stage for ambitious postwar reconstruction.[52] While the war had brought upheaval, it had also brought expansion, supercharging gross domestic product between 1939 and 1945

Box 1, SDA. Chapman would, on occasion pursue his aims in debate to the detriment of his cause. During a spirited Synod monologue, Archbishop Loane tired of Chapman's address and asked him to stop speaking. Chapman retorted reflexively, "Might I then whisper, Archbishop?" Interview with Dick Lucas, January 20, 2017.

49. Over one million Australian men and women served in uniform in a population of just over seven million. Five hundred and sixty thousand served overseas. Despite fewer losses than its counterpart in the earlier century, thirty-four thousand Australians perished in the Second World War, nine thousand were held as prisoners of war in Europe and twenty-two thousand prisoners languished in the Pacific. See Macintyre, *Concise History*, 192; Darian-Smith, "World War 2," 88.

50. The raid by Japanese midget submarines who entered Sydney Harbour on the night of May 31, 1942 (shelling suburbs and sinking the HMAS *Kuttabul*, killing nineteen sailors) sent public alarm soaring. See Stanley, *Invading Australia*; Horner, "Australia in 1942," 18, 23.

51. By mid-1942 domestic consumption was restricted. Rationing extended to tea, sugar, butter, and meat. Shortages of fruit and vegetables, pots, clothes, and matches were also frequent. Blainey, *History*, 209; Darian-Smith, "World War 2," 97.

52. Hay, "Institute of Public Affairs," 198; Darian-Smith, "World War 2," 89.

by 25 percent.[53] Under the stimulus of total war, resources which had lain idle during the 1930s were mobilized, and in the postwar period munitions capabilities were repurposed to stimulate industry. Technical schools proliferated as industry blossomed.[54] Full employment was the centerpiece of Labor's blueprint. In its 1945 White Paper, it outlined a Keynesian approach to the nation's prosperity—scheduling public works schemes to soak up labor surpluses should the war-charged demand abate.[55] The slump did not occur. Rather, the boom gathered force, giving rise to a gilded age of increasing optimism, and ambitious programs in infrastructure, health, and education.[56] The size of government, and the desire for security, growth, and employment in a technically charged age were thus key themes in the nation's recovery. Such themes would also come to strongly shape the direction of Chapman's postwar education.

Chapman was schooled at Oatley and Mortdale state schools in his primary years, at the height of the Second World War. Neither of his parents had progressed beyond primary school. They were therefore quietly determined that their sons would be better educated. Three years at Sutherland Intermediate High School followed (1943–45) alongside two years at Sydney Technology High School (a prized selective school in Sydney's Albion Street, Paddington) where Chapman completed his leaving certificate (1946–47). Entry to the school required a high pass in the Qualifying Certificate at age fourteen, and students from across the city and nation sought out the prized education for its high academic standards and extensive extracurricular program.[57] At Sutherland Intermediate High School Chapman had enjoyed "big fish" status in a comparatively smaller pond. However, at Sydney Technology Boy's High School, Chapman became a smaller fish in a considerably larger pond. New to the school and suffering the insecurities of youth, Chapman chose subjects which friends had enrolled in, over against those he naturally prized. At the close of his leaving certificate, he therefore gained a matriculation to pursue Mathematics as opposed to English

---

53. Maddison, *World Economy*, 462.
54. Macintrye, *Concise History*, 198.
55. Powell and Macintrye, *Land of Opportunity*, ch. 11.
56. Macintyre, *Concise History*, 200.
57. The school, one of the six original New South Wales selective schools, reopened on its current premises at Bexley in 1956. Academic standards at the school have remained consistently high, alongside a broad program of extracurricular activities like cadets, chess, drama performances, model and science clubs, and state debating competitions. The school has now become known simply as "Sydney Technical High School." Sydney Technical High School, "School History."

or History.[58] Nevertheless, Chapman excelled in his studies. Attaining the highest leaving certificate score of a "Six A Pass," Chapman's academic options lay wide open before him.[59]

Yet, in a turn of providence for which he would harbor inadequacies into his adult years, Chapman did not pursue a university qualification in a traditional tertiary setting. Albury Chapman, an intelligent man with limited formal education himself, would not allow his son to pursue a university education. He believed it to be elitist and unnecessary. "University is for the toffs," he opined. Moreover, John's older brother Jim had, since leaving school, secured the most prized goal of one's working life—stable government employment. Such a station, Albury insisted, would provide unerring security. Moreover, in pursuing a practical qualification, his son John would acquire skills for the betterment of his country and home.[60] The low birth rate of the 1930s as well as the raising of the minimum age for school leaving had produced a shortage of schoolteachers by the 1950s.[61] Such a career path, government funded and practical, spelled the security Albury so coveted for his family. Hence, against the backdrop of an age of deprivation and in the shadow of Keynesian big-government, Chapman enrolled at Sydney Technical College in Ultimo, for a Diploma in Manual Arts and a future in the public service. The course taught the manual arts disciplines of woodwork and metalwork alongside sketching and ceramics. An exposure to the liberal arts in psychology, English literature, ancient and modern history was also included. This gave graduates status as associates of the Sydney Technical College, a designation highly regarded in many professions.[62] Chapman, in turn, pressed the qualification into immediate service, beginning his teaching career in the manual arts at Manilla and Tamworth High Schools in 1951.[63]

Concerning his education, Chapman's native intelligence was a quality that many would come to highly esteem. They judged him to be decidedly

58. Chapman to Orpwood, January 15, 1994, BDM Box 1, SDA. The New South Wales "Leaving Certificate" was introduced in 1913, at the end of the student's high school education and was externally set and marked by a board of examiners, covering six core areas of study. NSW Government, "History."

59. Interview with Phillip Jensen, February 16, 2017.

60. "Secure advancement," whether in secular or ecclesiastical work, marked Albury's approach. On Chapman's later decision to pursue ordination, "advancement" was again heavily stressed. Albury enquired how many years of service his son would need to offer before securing ecclesiastical preferment. Interview with Phillip Jensen, February 16, 2017.

61. Barcan, *Two Centuries*.

62. Freyne, "Sydney Technical College."

63. Chapman to Orpwood, January 15, 1994, BDM Box 1, SDA.

undereducated for the gifts of natural intellect he possessed.⁶⁴ Hence, it posed some irony that an intellect befitting a higher station would begin a career teaching children to make sugar scoops and teapot stands instead.⁶⁵ Yet, in many ways, it was the disciplines of the teacher craftsman and the apprenticeship model that would prove to be Chapman's most productive.⁶⁶ Chapman's own oratory was well served by the meticulous crafting of its various elements. He devoted himself to the perfecting of his rhetorical timing and narrative skill.⁶⁷ Moreover, as Director of the Department of Evangelism and lecturer in homiletics at Sydney theological colleges, Chapman exerted wide influence over a generation of preacher practitioners via the teaching of preaching and ministry craft. A less formal and uncluttered education produced an aptitude to distill thought and praxis for wide audiences. His capacity for searching reflection on a subject's method or technique, given not from the studied distance of the academy but through the lens of the teacher practitioner, also became notorious.⁶⁸ Hence, in an era before "mentoring" became *de rigeur* in evangelical ministry pathways, Chapman's coaching of colleagues and students became a harbinger of an approach that would later gain wide currency.⁶⁹

64. Jensen and Freney, "Majoring on the Majors." In the early 1990s, Chapman was invited to become Principal of George Whitefield College in Cape Town South Africa by the outgoing Principal, D. B. Knox. Chapman declined the invitation, on the grounds he had only a ThL and a Manual Arts education. Dr. Knox replied "Chappo, you've got more theology in your little finger than the rest of the Sydney Diocese." Chapman was also offered the principalship of Sydney Missionary and Bible College, which he also declined. Interview with Dr. David Seccombe, February 16, 2017. Regarding Chapman's theological acumen, Sydney luminaries, such as Donald Robinson considered Chapman's gifts of intellect of such an order that he may, had he pursued a path of scholarship, been highly adept in such a pursuit. Interview with Archbishop Harry Goodhew, November 14, 2016.

65. Jensen and Freney, "Majoring on the Majors."

66. Chapman's making of gifts and household objects for the use of his staff displayed a practical generosity. Chapman also instructed his associate, Ian Powell, in making furniture for his home, and doll houses for his daughters. Interview with Ian Powell, March 12, 2017. Arriving for a particular preaching tour in England, Chapman also delighted his hosts in Crowborough with five handmade toy kangaroos for their children. Interview with Andrew Cornes, November 24, 2016.

67. Jensen and Freney, "Majoring on the Majors."

68. Interview with Dick Lucas, January 20, 2017.

69. The Ministry Training Strategy (MTS) was begun on the campus of NSW University and St. Matthias Anglican Church Sydney by the Rev. Phillip Jensen. The program assumes a two-year apprenticeship in a parish or student context and has seen thousands begin vocational Christian work via such an apprenticeship model. Jensen himself had spent a two-year period working as a staffer and apprentice with Chapman in 1973 to 1974 at the Department of Evangelism, prior to his ministry on the

A keen interest in sport, drama, poetry, and the arts also marked Chapman's development. In an era before television had captured the attention of Australian homes, Chapman's Saturday evening church fellowship outings involved cardplaying, communal singing, and the learning and reciting of poetry. Mixed with Chapman's own "verbatim-like memory"[70] such artistic training enabled Chapman to offer a flawless retelling of Banjo Paterson's *The Man from Iron Bark* on request many years later.[71] Chapman was also undeniably a man of culture. Having taken singing lessons at the Sydney Conservatorium of Music, he had sung to the works of Schubert and England's Roger Quilter on local radio.[72] A contemporary also recalls a sixteen-year-old Chapman singing at her wedding, reflecting, even then, a distinct stage presence and theatrical ability.[73] Significantly, Chapman had also performed the bass solo in Handel's Messiah at St. Peter's Cathedral in Armidale for three years, conducted choirs to accompany parish missions, and received acclamation for his leadership of the NSW CMS Summer School choir in the 1960s.[74] An aptitude for children's ministry and humorous storytelling was also apparent. Such performances employed the entire area of a lounge room or elevated pulpit, inviting enraptured audience engagement.[75] Indeed, ready to follow any suggestion for a visit to a garden, gallery or site of interest, Chapman possessed a wide enjoyment of life and culture that served only to enhance his pulpit appeal. A competitive zeal also impelled him constantly to seek to perform at his best.[76]

---

campus of NSW University. Jensen describes this period as formative "in every way." DOE Prayer Letter, February 1973; Interview with Phillip Jensen, February 16, 2017; MTS, "What is MTS?"

70. Peter Chiswell to Michael Orpwood, BDM Box 1, SDA.
71. Interview with David Mansfield, November 29, 2016.
72. Chapman to Orpwood, January 15, 1994, BDM Box 1, SDA.
73. Interview with David Mansfield, November 29, 2016.
74. Interview with Dick Lucas, January 20, 2017.
75. John Wheeler to Michael Orpwood, BDM Box 1, SDA.
76. Rico Tice, a notable English evangelist, who estimates Chapman to have exerted considerable influence on his own ministry, suggests it was Chapman's mature appreciation for life and culture that made him effective in winning others. Interview with Rico Tice, January 17, 2017. While enjoying competitive tennis for many years, injuries sustained in a car accident in the 1980s placed lasting restrictions on Chapman's agility. Interview with Adrian Lane, March 27, 2017.

Conversion and Christian Formation

A Church-Sending Family

Chapman's Christian formation took shape in a "church-sending," not a "churchgoing" family.[77] His homelife was warm to Christian faith, while also lacking in clarity and depth. Muriel Chapman was a prayerful woman and an avid Bible reader. She was committed to the activities of the Oatley Anglican Parish. Yet she was converted only in her forties by the witness of her two nieces, who were, in Chapman's estimation, "rip-roaring Christians . . . they evangelized everything that moved, and most things that didn't." They led Muriel to Christ before they "shot off to Colombia" to spend the rest of their lives in missionary service.[78] Still lacking assurance into her later years, Muriel made a profession of faith "under every evangelist that came to Australia." "She was a dream for the evangelist," recalled Chapman, "and kept the figures up all over Sydney for many years."[79] Albury Chapman, however, was a tougher proposition. He never attended church, save for weddings and funerals, and voiced a strong anti-clerical antagonism.[80] Yet the Chapman boys attended regularly.

Church was full of mysteries for the impressionable youths. Being the most formal experience of their young lives, Chapman wore shoes only on Sundays. He flapped around in them for some years while he grew into the shoes and a number of years while he grew out of them.[81] Church life exuded formality. The minister would announce the "feast" for the forthcoming week according to the Anglican liturgical calendar. Yet when the boys arrived, to their manifest disappointment "it was the lightest fare they'd ever seen . . . there wasn't so much as a broken biscuit to suck on."[82] When the offertory was announced, the youths would ogle the sum of money in their hands, before reluctantly "shaking it loose over a brass bowl until it dropped in and the man gave it to God."[83] Chapman

---

77. Interview with David McDonald, December 6, 2016.

78. Chapman, "Repentance and Faith."

79. Chapman, "Repentance and Faith."

80. Orpwood, *Sake of the Gospel*, 7.

81. Chapman, "Repentance and Faith."

82. Chapman, "Repentance and Faith."

83. Chapman, "Repentance and Faith." In these years, the churches within the orbit of Oatley Anglican Parish exhibited a middle-church disposition. Broadly evangelical, the style of their Sunday worship was formal and liturgical. Interview with Ray Smith, Bishop of Liverpool Region, 1990s, February 21, 2017. The Rector of St. Paul's Oatley from 1929 was the Rev. William Siddens. The Lord's Supper administered from the eastward position was commonplace, while the congregation bowed in veneration as

was baptized at St Paul's Oatley in September 1930. He could dutifully recite the Catechism from the *1662 Anglican Book of Common Prayer* at the age of seven and was confirmed by Bishop William Hilliard on April 20, 1945, aged fifteen.[84] He attended Sunday school where he learned the seasons of the church year and the appropriate colors of those seasons. Yet, for all practical purposes, by his own estimation, Chapman remained unconverted. Indeed, he later quipped, he was "as far from authentic faith as if he had grown up in Communist Russia."[85]

A more decisive Christian commitment would soon take shape. At Sutherland High School, John sat next to Dick Tischer who shared with John the message of Christ and warned him of the perils of irreligious and unspiritual churchgoing. Tischer invited Chapman to join him at the Inter School Christian Fellowship (ISCF) group and to other holiday camps with the Sutherland Congregational Church.[86] During school holidays, John would often stay with his widowed Aunt Millie and his cousins. Here, an authentic faith resounded throughout their home. Formal prayer was replaced with personal prayer around their dinner table. This was an activity which, if at first was startling, became alluring. Under firm conviction of sin, yet still lacking assurance, a moment of decision came at a Salvation Army youth camp in Collaroy, in the spring of 1946. Chapman attended the camp, intending that he would make a firm profession of faith.[87] Grasping little of authentic discipleship or the lordship of Christ, Chapman dived headlong into his newly acquired Christian faith, overwhelmed at the love of Christ. He enjoyed singing and praying, and the encouragement of being in the presence of Christians. Moreover, the promise that he would one day take his place in the new creation Christ would establish, seemed better than his best hope.[88]

Sydney Evangelical Sea Change

While initially drawn to the style of the Congregational Church and the Salvation Army, given the burst of spiritual life he had experienced there, Chapman's father insisted that John's religious energy should be directed

---

they recited the words of Christ's incarnation in the Creed. So Orpwood, *Sake of the Gospel*, 7.

84. Chapman, "Diocese of Armidale"; West, "Hilliard, William George," 165–66.
85. Grant, "John Chapman Interview."
86. Chapman to Orpwood, January 15, 1994, BDM Box 1, SDA.
87. Orpwood, *Sake of the Gospel*, 11.
88. Chapman, *Sinner's Guide*, 73; *Foot in Two Worlds*, 12–13.

within the Anglican Church. If his son was to be involved in church life at all, it should at least be in a place of orthodoxy.[89] The Anglican Parish of Oatley, moreover, was undergoing something of an evangelical sea change of its own. The influence of the Cambridge-educated and CICCU-molded[90] Howard W. K. Mowll as Archbishop of Sydney and his long episcopacy (1933–58) was now being felt keenly across the Sydney Anglican Diocese, alongside the steely and assured Irish evangelical fervor of Thomas Chatteron Hammond as Principal of Moore College (1936–53).[91] A previous period of moderate evangelical conviction under predecessors Archbishop Wright and Principal Davies was now assailed by the muscular, centrist,

---

89. Orpwood, *Sake of the Gospel*, 11.

90. Founded in 1877, the Cambridge Inter-Collegiate Christian Union (CICCU) traced its origin to the ministry of Charles Simeon, the evangelical Vicar of Holy Trinity Anglican Church in Cambridge (1782–1836) who influenced successive generations of students. The conservative scholarly strength that developed in the CICCU came to play a central role in the formation of the Inter-Varsity Fellowship (IVF) in 1928. See Chapman, *Ambition*, 27; Stanley, *Diffusion*, 89, 94.

91. Mowll's long episcopacy in Sydney began in 1933 in succession of Archbishop John C. Wright. Prior to his Sydney episcopacy, Mowll had served as a missionary bishop in a vast diocese of Western China (1922–32) and at Wycliffe College in Toronto, Canada as a professor of history and dean of studies (1913–22). Mowll studied at Cambridge at the height of the tension between the CICCU and the SCM, culminating in the formal disaffiliation of the CICCU from the SCM in 1910. As President of the CICCU for five terms between 1911 and 1912 the great event for which he was responsible while president was the R. A. Torrey mission to Cambridge University in November 1911, the most remarkable event of its kind since the missions of D. L. Moody in 1882. His tall frame (at six feet four inches), enormous energy, sound memory, and grasp of detail, and unwavering evangelical convictions precipitated twenty-five years of growth and activity in Sydney diocesan affairs. Loane, *Archbishop Mowll*; Loane, *Men to Remember*, ch. 5; Loane, "Mowll," 272–78; Judd and Cable, *Sydney Anglicans*, 227–48; Stanley, *Global Diffusion*, 57; Piggin, *Spirit*, 126–34.

Hammond arrived in Sydney in 1936 at the invitation of Archbishop Mowll. Given the college's importance in supplying theological strength to the diocese and in the light of its recent decline under Archdeacon Davies (the college's most recent principal, who had made little protest against the onset of critical scholarship) Mowll desired a conservative evangelical to put new vigor into the college. Having previously served a long and energetic ministry as Superintendent of the Irish Church Missions Society (1919–1936), Hammond was confident and assured and soon established himself. Moore College was in debt and dispirited. Hammond raised morale and academic standards, trained nearly two hundred ordinands, dispelled uncertainty and laid a durable evangelical base which was amplified throughout the twentieth century. His popularity as a speaker at conventions, reformation rallies, and houseparties alongside his Sunday evening broadcasts on radio 2CH on matters of Reformed theology, saw his work and influence soon felt keenly outside the college and diocese. Nelson, "Hammond, Thomas Chatteron," 150–52; Piggin, *Spirit*, 132–34; Stanley, *Global Diffusion*, 116; Cameron, *Phenomenal Sydney*, 32; Judd and Cable, *Sydney Anglicans*, 233.

and expansionist evangelical vision of Mowll and Hammond.[92] Ordinands began filling the revitalized Moore College and were promptly sent into Sydney parishes such that by the time of Hammond's retirement in 1953, some two hundred had been trained under his tutelage.[93] In the nineteenth century, under the soaring influence of the evangelical Bishop Frederic Barker (1855–81), a large number of the Sydney clergy had become known as "Barker's men."[94] So, now under Mowll and Hammond, a coterie of newly energized conservative clergy also began to reshape the Sydney diocese with the definitive stamp of their mentors. Conservative evangelical conviction touched by Keswick holiness piety,[95] a determination to uphold the doctrines of justification by faith and the divine authority of the Scriptures,[96] and a desire to stimulate the diocese into a visible evangelistic witness, became the key badges of clergy in their mold.[97] Mowll stirred the diocese to a fresh fervor, while Hammond supplied the clergy to him with a steady conservative resolve.[98]

In the Parish of Oatley, Noel Paddison, a young minister who was trained under Hammond, was appointed as curate-in-charge of the reorganized parish in 1946. This brought a swift change in style and tone and a desire to energize the parish youth. Promoted to a protuberant role in the youthwork and Sunday worship, Chapman developed quickly. As a zealous lay preacher, Chapman would boldly invite parishioners of all ages to seek his counsel after the meeting if they had been moved by the teenager's intrepid proclamation.[99] With his good friend Peter Chiswell, Chapman would

---

92. Archbishop J. C. Wright had promoted an Anglican order which expressed a much wider spectrum of opinion. He was convinced that evangelicals would be the poorer without variety. Hence, in his opening Synod charge in 1909 he urged "the possibility of deep spiritual unity beneath a diversity of theological standpoints" (Presidential Address 1909, *Sydney Synod Reports*, 1910). Sydney parishes multiplied by 50 percent under his leadership of twenty-five years. Continued ill-health through the 1920s limited his administrative effectiveness and blunted his reception amongst a polity calling for decisive leadership from the church militant, through the struggles of the postwar and Depression era. See Judd and Cable, *Sydney Anglicans*, 160–225; Judd and Dickey, "Wright, John Charles," 412–13. For treatment of Principal Davies' seventeen-year influence within Moore College, see Loane, *Centenary History*, 113–38; McIntosh, "Anglican Evangelicalism," 267–392.

93. Loane, *Centenary History*, 152.

94. Maple, "Barker, Frederic," 24–26; Judd and Cable, *Sydney Anglicans*, 74; Loane, *Hewn From the Rock*, 88–89.

95. McIntosh, "Anglican Evangelicalism," 145.

96. Loane, *Archbishop Mowll*, 133.

97. Judd and Cable, *Sydney Anglicans*, 245.

98. Judd and Cable, *Sydney Anglicans*, 246.

99. Orpwood, *Sake of the Gospel*, 14.

also jump the fence at Oatley station before travelling to Hurstville to preach in the open air—somewhat unaware of the incongruity in his actions.[100] Moments of theological struggle were not absent either. As he encountered the doctrine of election in the Scriptures for the first time, Chapman was infuriated and threw his Bible across an open yard. After minutes of self-recrimination, he picked his Bible up repentantly with a fresh resolve and regard for the high place of Scripture in Christian discipleship.[101] The need for clarity in personal witness also became apparent. Asked by a camper on a weekend conference how to become a Christian, Chapman floundered. Unable to offer a satisfactory response, Chapman's friend skillfully led the camper to Christ instead. Heavily chastened as he prayed alone that evening, Chapman resolved, "Lord, this will never happen to me again. I give you my word that I will become equipped to do this."[102]

In 1943, Archbishop Mowll had appointed the Rev. Graham Delbridge, a man of charismatic power and a dynamic young evangelist, as the first diocesan chaplain for youth work.[103] Mowll's vision was that inspiring leadership at the diocesan level was needed to train and support youth work in the parishes. Delbridge wasted no time in realizing this vision, beginning a burst of initiatives that deepened the spiritual lives of young people throughout the diocese.[104] The need for camp and conference sites was satisfied in 1945 when the Youth Department acquired an eleven-acre site on the shores of Port Hacking, followed by a second in the National Park in 1947. Such newly acquired infrastructure opened the way for new camps and house parties. In time, thousands of young people attended these venues to receive instruction in the Christian faith.[105] With the encouragement of his overseers at Oatley Parish, Chapman soon joined the throng of youth benefitting from this emerging movement and became quickly enmeshed in its leadership.

---

100. Interview with Ray Smith, February 21, 2017. On "open-air campaigning," which became a popular evangelistic medium of this period, see Duffecy, "Field, Edward Percy."

101. Interview with David Short, February 17, 2017.

102. Chapman, *St. Helen's School*.

103. Dickey, "Delbridge, Graham," 92–93; Loane, *Mark These Men*, 92.

104. Judd and Cable, *Sydney Anglicans*, 246; Emery et al., *Delbridge Years*, 14–15.

105. Judd and Cable, *Sydney Anglicans*, 246; Loane, *Mark These Men*, 92; Emery et al., *Delbridge Years*, 17–18; Delbridge would go on from this appointment to become Rector of Holy Trinity Adelaide, which expanded rapidly under his leadership. He later served as the Bishop of Wollongong and of the Diocese of Gippsland. Dickey, *Australian Dictionary*, 92.

The youth camps had a strong conversionist tone. Many young people were converted there while others were inspired to ordination via their formative influence. Chapman—who was now at college in Ultimo—met regularly with a band of fellow enthusiasts whom Delbridge had gathered to assist him in the work. It was a time of vision setting and capturing. Prayer was offered for the youth of their parishes alongside prayer for an array of wider concerns.[106] Camps were run on long weekends and over Christmas and New Year breaks. Delbridge expounded the Bible at these camps in the fashion of J. C. Ryle's *Expository Thoughts*. A work of classic evangelical piety, by later standards Delbridge's heavy reliance on such a text would be seen as somewhat quaint.[107] However, by the sheer force of his oratory Delbridge won the confidence of the youth leaders, who expectantly brought their peers.[108] Leadership aptitude was tested for the assistant missioners who became involved.[109] Room leaders exhorted their room groups on the state of their spiritual condition, constantly pressing for a decision.[110] Archbishop Mowll also delighted in attending these camps periodically, which undoubtedly raised their growing profile.[111] Moreover, following his attendance at the 1947 World Conference of Christian Youth in Oslo, the profile of Delbridge and the Sydney youth movement grew considerably.[112] The entire experience left an indelible imprint on Chapman and the many emerging leaders who became involved. A passion for mission and a strong vision for reaching Australia resulted, alongside a vision to work within church structures for their betterment.[113] Similarly, a vision for the

---

106. Chapman to Orpwood, January 15, 1994, BDM Box 1, SDA; Judd and Cable, *Sydney Anglicans*, 247.

107. Chapman to Orpwood, January 15, 1994, BDM Box 1, SDA. Ryle's classic work was crafted in its own day to produce "more reverent, deep-searching study of the Scriptures." See Ryle, *Expository Thoughts*, preface ii–iii.

108. Grant, "John Chapman Interview."

109. Emery et al., *Delbridge Years*, 20.

110. Chapman to Orpwood, January 15, 1994, BDM Box 1, SDA.

111. Harris, "Memories," 58.

112. The conference in Oslo was the largest of its kind at the time. Seventy-five nations were represented by 1,200 delegates. Photos of Delbridge with the Queen at a garden party at Lambeth Palace (en route to Oslo) circulated in Australia. A "Post-Oslo" conference in Sydney also bound together emerging leaders within the movement, which expanded quickly, inhabiting new offices and forming a hub for other diocesan youth work. So Harris, "Memories," 21–29.

113. *Preaching Christ Newsletter*, August–October 1990. With a political and ecclesiastical upbringing, Delbridge modelled to Chapman how to work within an ecclesiastical system to achieve change. Jensen and Freney, "Majoring on the Majors."

unvarnished preaching of Scripture in Christian life and witness became, for Chapman, an abiding central conviction.[114]

Armidale Beginnings

With the profile of the Sydney youth ministries now raised nationally and with a paucity of organized youth work occurring in many other Australian dioceses at the time, in the Easter of 1950 Delbridge was asked to send a delegation to the Anglican Diocese of Armidale to run their inaugural diocesan youth camp.[115] Chapman and a contemporary in the Sydney movement, Alan Quee, were sent as Delbridge's envoys. Sixty teenagers from the surrounding towns attended the camp in the rustic surrounds of a shearers' shed on a property in the Bingara Parish. The young Sydney preachers conducted the program and delivered the addresses. A repeat invitation was issued for the June long weekend of 1950 at a property outside of Gunnedah, where 150 teenagers attended.[116] This was followed in 1952 by another conference over the Easter weekend with an attendance of ninety.[117] Many assessed that the camps had proven of "immense value." Thus, their influence began to spread to "every corner of the Diocese."[118] This drew the attention of the senior clergy of the Armidale diocese who came with interest and enthusiasm to observe the new work.[119]

The success of these camps and the bold vision for Australia that Delbridge had conveyed began to weigh heavily upon Chapman's decision about a suitable location to begin his teaching career. With his studies nearing completion (after which he was bound to serve for a period with the Education Department, including a portion in country areas) Chapman applied to work in the Tamworth area in northern NSW.[120] He was drafted to Ma-

---

114. Grant, "John Chapman Interview."

115. The Anglican Diocese of Armidale lies in the northern inland region of New South Wales. Spanning a distance of 325 kilometres between its extremities, it comprises thirty-one parishes across the centers of Armidale, Glen Innes, Gunnedah, Inverell, Moree, Narrabri, Tamworth, and surrounding towns. Anglican Diocese of Armidale, "About the Diocese." On the concerns of a growing number of Armidale clergy who desired to raise diocesan youth ministry in importance, see "Youth for the Church," 19; Stockdale, "Youth Organisations."

116. Chapman to Orpwood, January 15, 1994, BDM Box 1, SDA.

117. Diocesan Registry Armidale, *Yearbook of the Diocese of Armidale*, 1952, 28; Diocesan Registry Armidale, *Yearbook of the Diocese of Armidale*, 1953, 32.

118. Stockdale, *Youth Organisations*.

119. Chapman to Orpwood, January 15, 1994, BDM Box 1, SDA.

120. Chapman to Orpwood, January 15, 1994, BDM Box 1, SDA.

nilla, forty-five kilometers outside of Tamworth. Throughout 1951 to 1955 he began his career in manual arts in Manilla, Tamworth, and Gunnedah, before returning to Sydney in 1956 to teach at Easthills Boys High school.[121] In these country municipalities, alongside his classroom teaching, Chapman busily engaged in church fellowships and in the wider work of diocesan youth camps and its youth council.[122] He also served as a parish councillor, choir leader, and lay reader in the Parish of Gunnedah.[123]

The episcopacy of Bishop John Stoward Moyes (1929–64) cast a striking shadow over the Armidale diocese during this era. With an exalted ecclesiastical career, statesmanlike presence and an energetic legacy applying the social implications of the gospel to Australian life, Moyes was a commanding figure.[124] Considered by some to be among a band of "prophetic churchmen" in the interwar years, Moyes acted as a force for societal unity and cohesion and wielded the authority commensurate with such a civic position. He mixed freely with governors and heads of state, winning patronage and exerting wide influence.[125] And yet, for all the immense vigor of his long episcopacy, Moyes had not achieved the same success in promoting biblical literacy or conversion growth within his country diocese. Moyes's ecclesiastical vision drew from sources as various as Christian socialism, Tractarianism, modern biblical criticism, and ecumenism.[126] Clergy from different hues thus came together during his bishopric under the umbrella of a

121. Grant, "John Chapman Interview."
122. Chapman to Orpwood, January 15, 1994, BDM Box 1, SDA.
123. Chapman, "Diocese of Armidale."
124. Moyes was a graduate of St. Barnabas's Theological College and was ordained in 1907, before serving curacies in Port Pirie in 1908–1909 and the London parish of Lewisham in 1911 to 1913. The extreme poverty he witnessed there consolidated his commitment to a social application of the gospel. Returning to South Australia in 1913, Moyes served several successful incumbencies before his consecration as Bishop of Armidale in November 1929. Moyes excelled as an author and advocate for the rights of workers; criticized banking policy during the Depression; delivered the Moorhouse lectures in 1941 in which he criticized Australian institutions for promoting societal individualism devoid of higher principle; backed the movement to reform the White Australia policy; challenged the Menzies government over its proposed Communist Party Dissolution Act of 1950; and in 1965 Moyes opposed the Vietnam War in a series of spirited written exchanges with the Australian Prime Minister, Robert Menzies. He also chaired the Anglican General Synod's social questions committee (1933–63) and the Christian Social Order Movement (1943–51). See O'Brien, "Moyes, John Stoward"; Terracini, *John Stoward Moyes*; "Vietnam War," 70–88; "Bishop JS Moyes," 106–27.
125. O'Brien, "Cultivated Man," 243.
126. O'Brien, "Cultivated Man," 244; Chavura and Tregenza, "Political History," 3–26, notes Moyes among a group of Australian churchmen in the 1920s who contributed to the Morpeth Review, which served an amalgam of intellectual and ecclesiastical traditions and sought to engage the issues of the day.

liberal-orthodox and socially oriented formal Anglicanism.[127] Formality and ritual, however, masked a more pressing need within the parishes—the need for basic instruction in the Christian faith. Neither high church nor evangelical in their ministrations, a theologically amorphous clergy gave rise to a laity only modestly formed in private conviction.[128] As a result, the arrival of a more self-assured Evangelicalism in Chapman and a rising tide of Sydney voices was met by numerous clergy and laity with a mixture of enthusiasm, alongside a degree of reservation and concern.[129]

Despite this, a warm and cordial relationship developed between Moyes and Chapman. This was aided, at least in part, by their shared sympathies for the Australian Labor Party. Chapman's abilities in youth work gained the bishop's thanks and esteem. Moreover, perceiving an aptitude for learning, Moyes encouraged Chapman to pursue further tertiary study.[130] Urbane and poised with a somewhat imperious disposition,[131] Moyes admired those who would make a spirited stand in opposition to his own.[132] Chapman therefore reputedly pressed Moyes in conversation, at times, concerning where he had found a particular assertion "in the Bible." This caused the bishop often to chortle, pause, and reexamine the statement just made.[133] After Chapman's return to Sydney (1956–57), Moyes and Chapman corresponded regularly. They exchanged encouragements, news, and confirmations of prayer.[134] Now re-engaged in frenetic lay ministry in his home parish of Oatley, Chapman soon began to shift his gaze toward the need for further theological training to complete the licentiate in theology he had begun by correspondence in

127. Peter Chiswell to Michael Orpwood, December 1994, BDM Box 1, SDA; Interview with Ray Smith, February 21, 2017. Moreover, lacking a theological college, Moyes adopted a pragmatic approach in the selection of clergy, while accepting a larger number from St. John's College Morpeth. In 1955, a special session of the Newcastle Diocese resolved to acquire the interests of the other dioceses in the college, granting Moyes some freedoms to extend invitations to graduates of other colleges. So Elkin, *Diocese of Newcastle*, 593.

128. Chapman to Orpwood, January 15, 1994, BDM Box 1, SDA.

129. Frank Elliott to Orpwood, August 1, 1994, BDM Box 1, SDA; Interview with Ray Smith, February 21, 2017.

130. Interview with Ray Smith, February 21, 2017.

131. O'Brien, "Cultivated Man," 245.

132. Peter Chiswell to Michael Orpwood, December 19, 1994, BDM Box 1.

133. Frank Elliott to Michael Orpwood, August 1, 1994, BDM Box 1, SDA.

134. John Chapman to Bishop John Moyes, June 24, 1956; John Chapman to Bishop John Moyes, July 10, 1956; Bishop John Moyes to John Chapman, January 7, 1957; John Chapman to Bishop John Moyes, March 8, 1957; Bishop John Moyes to John Chapman, April 12, 1957; John Chapman to Bishop John Moyes, October 26, 1957; Bishop John Moyes to John Chapman, October 30, 1957; John Chapman to Bishop John Moyes, November 2, 1957, *Armidale Diocesan Registry*.

1954.[135] Moreover, with a fire now burning brightly to pursue a Bible teaching ministry and with a growing desire to see a more biblically grounded pattern of ministry established in the Armidale diocese, Chapman applied to Bishop Moyes for ordination.[136] On January 7, 1957 Moyes confirmed Chapman's candidature for the Armidale diocese as well as the timely payment of his Moore College fees of £150 a year.[137]

Theological Education and Vocational Ministry

Postwar Sydney Evangelical Christianity: Equipoise and Change

Chapman's return to Sydney life came at the height of a postwar boom in society and church affairs. Socially an appetite for conservatism lingered, fueled by the threat of nuclear proliferation and a continuing unease that the postwar peace accord might not endure. The Menzies government pressed the postwar agenda of immigration and investment, mixing new nationalism with a love for all things British. It was an Indian summer for Australian production, while the rush for Australian minerals also resumed.[138] Cities expanded to accommodate migrants and postwar newlyweds, just as a building boom lifted home ownership rates to 70 percent. The Beatles received an excited local welcome, while the first television stations emerged to broadcast the 1956 Melbourne Olympics.[139] Australia was a model of social and economic vibrancy in changing times.

In ecclesiastical affairs, it was a time of confidence and change as well. New parishes were established in the expanding suburbs and church

---

135. During 1956 Chapman was active running the ISCF group at Easthill Boys High School, preaching at St. Paul's Oatley and other church camps, running weekly Bible studies, and serving as the Minister's Warden. Chapman to Orpwood, January 15, 1994, BDM Box 1, SDA. The Licentiate in Theology became the standard qualification for ordination via the Australian College of Theology, which was established by General Synod in 1891 to coordinate the Australian Anglican seminaries. So Hilliard, "Anglicans," 134.

136. In 1956 Chapman was approached by CMS to become headmaster of a school in North Borneo. He declined the invitation. Chapman, "Diocese of Armidale. Questions for Candidates for Holy Orders," *Armidale Diocesan Registry*.

137. Bishop John Moyes to John Chapman, January 7, 1957, *Armidale Diocesan Registry*. These fees (of £150) equate to $4,800 in present-day terms. For conversion see: Reserve Bank, "Pre-Decimal."

138. Macintyre, *History*, 209, 228; Blainey, *History*, 219–31; Brett, "Menzies Era," 112; Bolton, *Oxford History*, 89–109.

139. Bolton, *Oxford History*, 122; Brett, "Menzies Era," 113, 123; Blainey, *History*, 234–38.

memberships grew rapidly nationwide. It was a period of "equipoise" within Sydney evangelical Christianity, in the estimation of some, when the strands of piety, scholarship, and social engagement coalesced in a fruitful way.[140] A new generation of ecclesiastical leadership also began to emerge. After the death of Archbishop Mowll in 1958, the equally formidable figure of Marcus Loane began his long ascendancy as principal of Moore College and Archbishop of Sydney.[141] In the realm of scholarship, D. B. Knox and D. W. B. Robinson also began their steady paternal influence over Sydney Anglican polity and life—an influence that would collectively span some forty years.[142] Loane, like his mentors and former metropolitans, Mowll

---

140. Brett, "Menzies Era," 127; Hilliard, "God in the Suburbs," 399–419; Piggin, *Evangelical Christianity*, 125, 163.

141. Loane was awarded a BA (USyd) in 1932, ThL (Moore College) in 1933, MA in 1937, DD (Wycliffe College Toronto) in 1958, and KBE in 1976. After ordination in 1936, Loane served in parish ministry in England, before returning at the outbreak of war, where he was appointed Vice-Principal of Moore College. After war chaplaincy service in New Guinea, he returned to Moore College where he resumed his post as Vice-Principal, then Principal in 1953. Appointed by Mowll as Coadjutor Bishop in 1958, Loane was elected the first Australian born Archbishop of Sydney in 1966, serving until 1982. Loane had a prodigious output as a scholar of ecclesiastical history. His work on the English Reformers was formative in the thought of John Stott. A thoroughgoing evangelical, Loane was widely respected. He held firmly to Reformed convictions in a time of change, while doing so with an irenic spirit. See Blanch, *From Strength to Strength*; Cameron, *Phenomenal Sydney*, 108–41; Piggin, *Evangelical Christianity*, 112, 117; Ballantine-Jones, "Political Factor," 41–44, 149–68.

142. Knox (b. 1916) was from an ecclesiastical family, the son of David John Knox, a prominent Sydney clergyman (Dickey, "Knox, David James," 205–6). D. B. Knox was ordained in 1941 by the Bishop of Ely, after studying theology at St John's College, Highbury. Knox served two years as curate at St. Andrew's the Less in Cambridge, before shipboard service during the Normandy invasion. Returning to scholarship in 1947, he completed a London MTh and was appointed to the staff of Moore College. Taking study leave again from 1951 to 1953 he completed a doctoral study on the *Doctrine of Faith in the Reign of Henry VIII*. He succeeded Marcus Loane as Principal of Moore College in 1959, where he served until 1985. In retirement, Knox accepted a call to establish a theological college for the isolated Church of England in South Africa. See Dickey, "Knox, David Broughton," 206–7; Cameron, *Enigmatic Life*; Kuhn, "Ecclesiology"; Robinson, "Appreciation," xi–xvii; Banks, "D. B. Knox," 377–404.

Donald Robinson (b. 1922) was also from an ecclesiastical family, the son of R. B. Robinson, one of Mowll's right-hand men (Judd and Cable, *Sydney Anglicans*, 32, 236). Robinson graduated from Sydney University before war service in Newcastle and New Guinea. Formative years were spent from 1947 to 1948 in postgraduate study in Cambridge, where he was exposed to the work of the New Testament giants C. F. D. Moule and C. H. Dodd. While at Cambridge, Robinson engaged in the work of the CICCU, and was a founding member of the International Fellowship of Evangelical Students (IFES). Returning to Sydney in 1950, he was ordained and spent two years as a Curate at St. Mathew's Manly Parish, before lecturing at Moore College, where he became Vice-Principal (1959–72), Bishop Coadjutor of Sydney (1973–81), and Archbishop of

and Barker, was an evangelical pietist. His deep appreciation for evangelical history and the treasures of confessional Anglicanism stamped Loane's leadership of the college and his subsequent episcopacy.[143] Under Loane the college possessed less of the academic edge that characterized its later-century life. Holiness programs and local missions alongside instruction in preaching and pastoralia mixed seamlessly with the wider academic curriculum to round out the training of aspiring pastors.[144] Loane's objective was to produce clergy with a firm grasp of their biblical and confessional roots. Such a proclivity for history and the strengths of the Reformation inheritance resulted in a degree of antiquarianism in Loane. Preeminently, however, Loane desired to produce a generation of leaders who were Christian, Protestant, and Anglican, in that order.[145]

The emerging leadership of Knox and Robinson at Moore College also fostered continuity with Loane's legacy, combined with a subtle yet significant shift. A Reformed confessionalism continued unabated. And yet the years of their collective formation within the world of postwar English scholarship began to shape their approach to theological education in Australia. In England, the Tyndale Fellowship for Biblical Research—of which Knox was a founding member—had begun to give voice to a growing response to the higher-critical and liberal-theological ideals that had dominated the agenda of early twentieth-century biblical scholarship.[146] Many alleged that the response of English evangelicals to these early century challenges had previously displayed a degree of "irrationalism" toward the

---

Sydney (1982–92). See Cameron, *Phenomenal Sydney*, 142–78; Ballantine-Jones, "Political Factor," 169–96; Kuhn, "Ecclesiology," 64–76.

143. On Loane's affinity with Barker and Mowll, see Loane's 1969 Presidential Synod Charge, *Sydney Yearbook 1970*, 244–46. Note that the term "confessional" is used here to describe the founding statements of "doctrinal belief intended for public avowal by an individual, group, congregation, synod, or church" which characterize and demarcate the historic Christian denominations. In the case of Anglicanism, its confessional statements are expressed in the Ordinal and Thirty-Nine Articles of Religion. Lawton, "Anglican Theology," 182; Britannica, "Confession of Faith."

144. Interview with Archbishop Harry Goodhew, November 14, 2016; Lawton, "That Woman Jezebel," 4–12. For an examination of the Holiness movement, see ch. 9. This movement privileged the need for a personal experience of conversion, growth in moral perfection, and heightened religious affections. It significantly infused the spiritual diet of twentieth-century Australian movements such as the Katoomba Christian Convention. Anderson, *Introduction to Pentecostalism*, 25–28.

145. Blanch, *Strength*, 45; Loane, *Masters*, 223–300. On Loane's hierarchy of identity, Loane stated, "I am a Christian; I am a Protestant; I am an Anglican. It is of greater significance to be the first rather than the second, or to be the second rather than the third." See Loane, "True Position," 5; *Sydney Diocesan Yearbook 1981*, 224.

146. Stanley, *Global Diffusion*, 94; Noble, *Tyndale House Fellowship*, 48–57.

pursuit of intellectual endeavor and an underlying suspicion of scholarship. Hence, seeking to redress these tendencies, in 1944 the young evangelical scholar F. F. Bruce coopted the help of the IVF-UK's Biblical Research Committee to form the Tyndale Fellowship for Biblical Research. Bruce's aim was to consider how to remove "the reproach of obscurantism and anti-intellectual prejudice" from English Evangelicalism and to facilitate the revival of a "full-orbed historical Evangelical Faith."[147] Bruce stressed that for the fellowship to play the role he felt was required, its researchers must "necessarily be unfettered." Tyndale scholars, he suggested, should be free to adopt whatever conclusions they believed the evidence warranted on precisely the points that conservative evangelicals had thought necessary to resist in the past. "Evangelical Christians," Bruce insisted, "must once and for all give the lie to the common idea that they are afraid of scientific research."[148] The community of scholars that the Tyndale Fellowship nurtured were to play an unparalleled role in the intellectual rejuvenation of conservative Evangelicalism.[149] From the late 1950s, sped on by its publishing arm *The InterVarsity Press*, evangelical scholarship in this mold displayed a judicious and sophisticated rigor, combining orthodox theology with a repudiation of sectarian theological attitudes and positions.[150]

Such was the scholarship that flourished at Moore College in the late 1950s and which began to permeate the bookshelves and sermon manuscripts of emerging evangelical leaders like John Chapman. Robinson was primarily a linguist and biblical theologian. He lectured in church history alongside biblical and liturgical studies. Influenced by the world of postwar biblical research, his sharp mind pioneered a body of provocative work. He addressed topics as diverse as ecclesiology, eschatology, and evangelism alongside studies in the sacraments and Christian worship. Seeking new ways to integrate the Bible's parts and new solutions to scholarly challenges, Robinson also pioneered an integrative "promise-fulfillment" hermeneutical method that was later termed "biblical theology." Its careful contextual

---

147. Bruce, "Tyndale Fellowship," 60; Wolffe and Hutchinson, *Short History*, 192–93; Packer, *Fundamentalism*, 9–23.

148. Such positions included the composition of the Pentateuch or the book of Isaiah, the dating of Daniel, the sources of the Gospels or the authenticity of the Pastoral Epistles. See Bruce, "Tyndale Fellowship," 57–59.

149. Noll, *Between Faith and Criticism*, 102.

150. Stanley, *Global Diffusion*, 44. From the 1950s until the early 1990s the Tyndale/Inter-Varsity Fellowship scholars (together with the works of John Stott and J. I. Packer who popularized their more scholarly contributions) accounted for more books which shape the judgments of evangelical scholars than any other. So Wolffe and Hutchinson, *History*, 193–94.

handling of biblical texts promoted holistic and intertextual exegesis.[151] Robinson's overriding concern in developing such material was to begin "a journey of discovery" that allowed the Bible to speak "on its own terms, whether or not we knew what to do with it in the end."[152] If Loane had tended to seek the commonalities the contemporary Christian shared with New Testament believers, Robinson was "on a mission to make the Bible strange again." The fact that it was not immediately obvious where such a journey would land in modern Australia was all "part of the thrill."[153] Knox, on the other hand, was a systematic theologian. He possessed a powerful and original mind and the enviable gift of a teacher—the ability to create an appetite for theology in his students.[154] Significantly, Knox did not produce many theological works of an academic nature. He had little interest in scholarship for its own sake. His work was rather directed towards the formation of would-be ministers, and it lived on woven into the fabric of his students' lives.[155] Given his strong conviction that God spoke uniquely in Holy Scripture, the exposition of the Bible occupied the central role in Knox's pedagogic method.[156] Highly attuned to contemporary and confessional theology, he interacted with others for clarity and elucidation. He found support for his work in Anglican formularies yet felt at liberty to disagree.[157] For Knox, "the real text-book was Scripture . . . not the writings of others, no matter how sharp or how learned."[158] Thus, beginning with Scripture, texts would build to the examination of themes. Relating these to other doctrines and to their historical interpretation, Knox sought fidelity to the text *before* tradition, seeking a heuristic reading of the Bible rooted deeply in textual study.[159] Such an approach produced a stimulating legacy in areas as diverse as biblical and canonical

---

151. Kuhn, "Ecclesiology," 65; Blanch, *Strength to Strength*, 177; Piggin, *Evangelical Christianity*, 177–80. Robinson's "promise-fulfillment" hermeneutic was seen as a companion and complement to sound exegesis and would later be popularized by Graeme Goldsworthy. Leading scholars consider that Robinson's longitudinal biblical-theological approach to Scripture constituted a "genuine innovation" of Australian biblical studies. See Reid, *Hermeneutics*, 139–63; Goldsworthy, *Christ-Centered*, 19–26.

152. Robinson, "Origins and Unresolved Tensions," 8.

153. Shiner, *Reading the New Testament*, 58. Robinson's published works have been recently collated by Bolt and Thompson in *Donald Robinson, Vols. 1 and 2*.

154. Robinson, "Appreciation," xi–xiii.

155. Robinson, "What We Owe Him."

156. Jensen, "Training for the Ministry." Reprinted as Payne, "On Training," 21–36.

157. Robinson, "Appreciation," xii.

158. Payne, "On Training," 23.

159. Robinson, "Appreciation," xii; Judd and Cable, *Sydney Anglicans*, 288–89; Loane, "David Broughton Knox," 9.

studies, ecclesiology, and homiletics, as well as liturgiology, constitutionalism, and Christian worship.[160]

This striking shift from a settled confessionalism toward a pattern of belief that submitted all formulations to the reforming lens of Scripture illuminates latter-century Sydney Evangelicalism in its most influential and confounding sense. It began a theological revolution that would reshape modern Sydney Anglicanism—leading it into a creative period in which a narrower "sectarian Anglicanism" was eclipsed by a more "broadly Reformed theological vision."[161] Notably, Chapman himself would spend only the comparatively brief period of a year within this environment before being sequestered to return to Armidale to fill pressing clerical shortages. Yet, it was this textually driven ethos and the figures of Loane, Knox, and Robinson with whom Chapman would interact extensively as a theologian, churchman, and preacher throughout his ministry career.[162] Indeed, it was such heuristic tools of analysis that would prove foundational in framing the fresh approaches to theology, homiletics, missiology, Christian discipleship, and ecclesiastical reform that came to characterize Chapman's ministry and contribution in later years. As an avid reader and student of Scripture, Chapman worked with considerable dedication to deepen his theological vision. As such, not only during the years of his ministry in the Armidale diocese (1960–68) but long into his extensive program of speaking and public missional advocacy (1968–2012), Chapman maintained a disciplined daily program of study which engaged the emerging body of Reformed and evangelical scholarship that proliferated across the English-speaking world. This sharpened his theological judgments and exegetical proficiency and provided a reservoir of learning that shaped what would become his own defining contribution to Australian evangelical thought and expression in later years.[163] In addition to the receipt of such tools of analysis, the other

---

160. Kuhn, "Ecclesiology," 164. Knox's scholarship has been collated by Payne, Birkett, and Beilharz, in *D. Broughton Knox: Selected Works*, Volumes I–III.

161. Shiner, *Reading*, 47–48.

162. Discussion of Chapman's interaction with the thought of Knox and Robinson follows in chapters 3 and 6.

163. The contours of Chapman's homiletic, evangelistic, and discipleship-oriented theology will be discussed within the relevant chapters throughout the course of the study. However, manuscripts from the period of his Armidale ministry demonstrate the influences that bore upon him at such an early stage. Studies in a range of biblical books including Jeremiah, 1 John, 1–2 Thessalonians, and Ephesians engaged the works of Augustine, Calvin, B. F. Westcott, and C. H. Dodd alongside other leading evangelical scholars such as F. F. Bruce, Leon Morris, James Moffatt, T. C. Hammond, D. W. B. Robinson, and D. B. Knox. Such preparatory study produced a body of unpublished work in the areas of Christian ministry and Christian growth. See Appendix

significant outcome of this period for Chapman was the establishment of a collection of long-standing collegial relationships. Indeed, readying themselves for ordination at Moore College were a band of young churchmen who would themselves go on to assume positions of significant leadership within Australian Evangelicalism. As such, during this period Chapman added the figures of Harry Goodhew, Dudley Foord, Peter Chiswell, Ray Smith, and Paul Barnett to a widening network of friends, advocates, and interlocutors with whom he would work and minister in later years.[164]

Ordination and Ministry in Armidale Anglican Diocese

In November 1957 Chapman was requested by Bishop Moyes to return to the Diocese of Armidale to serve pressing rural ministry needs. He was

---

3: "Rev J. Chapman: Notes on 1 John," JCCPPB1; "Rev J. Chapman: Notes on Prayer and the Christian," JCCPPBIO#3; "Rev. J. Chapman, Jeremiah and 1 Thessalonians," JCCPPB2; "Rev J. Chapman Studies: Jeremiah, Atonement, 2 Thessalonians, Ephesians 1–6," JCCPPB3; "Rev J. Chapman: Studies in Sanctification, The Work of the Holy Spirit," JCCPPB4; JCCPPB5: Teaching Series 1—an unpublished series of preaching notes (entitled *Lord of Heaven and Earth*) was modelled on the theology of D. B. Knox and covered aspects of God's sovereignty, holiness, kingdom, and revelation in Christ. In his later career Chapman continued this pattern of daily study. In a series of correspondences (1985–89) with a colleague studying overseas he gave further insight into the influences that continued to shape him. He included quotes and "weekly thoughts" from his study of works as diverse as: Calvin (John's Gospel), Stott (*Issues Facing Christians Today*), A. Plummer (Luke's Gospel), D. Carson (Matthew's Gospel), C. H. Spurgeon (*Lectures to My Students*), L. Morris (Hebrews), D. Carson (2 Corinthians), T. C. Butler (Joshua), M. Wilcox (1–2 Chronicles: Bible Speaks Today), R. Smith (Micah-Malachi), L. C. Allen (Psalms: Word Bible Commentary). Chapman to Lane Correspondence, Box 3, Adrian Lane Papers 1973–2005.

164. After significant parish leadership in Sydney and Brisbane (1958–79) Harry Goodhew was Bishop of Wollongong (1982–93) and Archbishop of Sydney (1993–2001). *Sydney Yearbook* 2015, 280. Dudley Foord was Rector of Kingsgrove (1960–65), Dean of Students, and Senior Moore College Lecturer (1965–1973), Director of Post Ordination Training (1970–78), Rector of St. Ives (1972–78), and presiding Bishop of the Church of England in South Africa (1984–87). Ballantine-Jones, "Political Factor," 53. After parish incumbencies in Armidale, Peter Chiswell (Chapman's oldest friend) became the second longest serving bishop of Armidale. Anglican Church League, "Bishop." Ray Smith was ordained in 1958 and served in a number of parish appointments in Armidale before assuming the role of Director of Christian Education and Archdeacon (1968–86). A period as Director of Extension Ministries at Trinity Episcopal School for Ministry in Pittsburgh (1986–90) was followed by service as Rector of St. Matthew's Wanniasa and Archdeacon of Canberra (1990–93), and Bishop of Liverpool (1993–2001). *Sydney Yearbook* 2015, 230. Paul Barnett was ordained in 1963, before ministry as Rector of St. Barnabas Broadway (1967–73), Rector of Holy Trinity Adelaide (1973–79), Lecturer in History at Macquarie University (1980–87), and Bishop of North Sydney (1990–2001). *Yearbook* 2015, 256.

ordained on December 21, 1957 (St. Thomas's Day) and began general duties in the Parish of Moree during 1958 to 1959. In 1960, Chapman was appointed as Youth Director of the Diocese (and Director of Christian Education in 1966) and relocated to the Diocesan Registry in Armidale. Foreshadowing the peripatetic nature of his later work in the Sydney diocese, this role involved the training (in aspects of ministry and Christian growth) of youth and Sunday school teachers across the diocese. A connection with the University of New England's AFES group also developed.[165] Chapman became a regular speaker on campus and developed a strong presence among the students who came to value his hospitality, dramatic flair, and sound pastoral advice.[166] Maintaining a fast-paced preaching schedule in every corner of this diocese, during this formative era Chapman was drawn into a position of confidence with senior clergy, thereby exercising a degree of leadership somewhat inaccessible to clergy of similar age and experience elsewhere. This not only sharpened his political judgments but foreshadowed a peripatetic future in clergy training, mobilization, and support. Indeed, while the assessment of ecclesiastical change is neither straightforward nor linear, it is significant that on account of Chapman's influence and solicitation of other evangelical clergy to work alongside him there, by the time of Bishop Moyes's retirement in 1964 the evangelical voice in this diocese had risen to such an extent that Clive Kerle (the evangelical Bishop Coadjutor of Sydney) was elected to replace him. For a diocese with a strongly Anglo-Catholic heritage, characterized more by its ecclesial forms than its evangelical fervor, such a development was striking. Not only did such events run contrary to the prevailing liturgical and theological mood in Australian Anglicanism, but they also foreshadowed an ascendant evangelical movement that began impacting the global church both from within the historic denominations and along fresh ecclesiological pathways.[167]

---

165. Mirroring the rise of the InterVarsity Fellowship worldwide, the Australian Fellowship of Evangelical Students (AFES) developed following the 1930 visit of Dr. H. W. Guinness (the first travelling secretary of the IVF). By 1958, approximately two thousand students were involved with the Australian movement. See AFES, "History."

166. Chapman to Orpwood, January 15, 1994, BDM Box 1, SDA; Interview with Dr. David Seccombe, February 16, 2017.

167. The election of Kerle and the key role played by Chapman in these events is recounted by Orpwood, *Chappo*, 38–42; On the tone of Australian Anglicanism and the rise of an ascendant Evangelicalism, see Hilliard, "History," 130–31; Stanley, *Diffusion*, 235–46. With rural ministry struggling to stem numerical and financial losses during this period, it is also noteworthy that under the stewardship of Bishops Kerle and Peter Chiswell (who succeeded Kerle) the Armidale diocese retained considerable buoyancy and came to assume an almost uniformly evangelical character. See Hilliard, "Anglicans," 136; "Right Reverend," 5.

Director of the Sydney Anglican Department of Evangelism

In 1968, Chapman's attention was wrested back towards the Sydney diocese with an invitation from the Board of Diocesan Missions (BDM) to join their staff. The Board's Director, Geoff Fletcher, was a giant personality and a passionate orator who, upon his appointment in 1966, brought the work of Campus Crusade to Australia, popularizing their "Four Spiritual Laws" of personal evangelism.[168] Fletcher's passion to see evangelistic fervor take hold among members of the Sydney laity matched a mood in the international evangelical community to see congregations as centers of evangelism, and evangelism as the vocation of every believer.[169] Fletcher thus returned from the 1966 Berlin Congress and a tour of leading American ministries with plans to see this vision become a reality in the Australian church.[170] By this time, Chapman's own ministry in Armidale had also become recognized among Sydney leaders. The dialogical approach to evangelism he had developed there (with its emphasis on lay involvement) struck a chord with Fletcher's vision and he was invited to join the staff to implement this—and the board's other objectives—on a broad scale.[171] It was an invitation Chapman may not have given more than passing consideration to, were it not for developments in his own family life. Yet, with the death of his father in 1967, his mother suffering ill-health in 1968, and with the election of Clive Kerle securing cherished aspirations for the progress of Evangelicalism in Armidale, the way seemed clear for acceptance.[172] "The Rev. John Chapman, whose work in Armidale the Lord has singularly blessed, will be joining me as a colleague in the work," Fletcher declared to BDM supporters. "God has so wonderfully blessed the Department of Evangelism that we have desperate need of assistance."[173] Chapman commenced duties on October 1, 1968. He was paid an annual salary of $2,950, a car allowance of $850, and the provision of a residence in Sydney's south, where he

---

168. Fletcher had previously contributed as General Secretary of CMS NSW in the revival of this movement and its Summer School between 1955–64, during which enrolments at the Summer School jumped from 211 to 1200. So Cole, *Church Missionary Society*, 227–29. Campus Crusade for Christ was founded in 1951 by Bill Bright as a ministry to university students at UCLA, California. It has developed into a global network of student and outreach related ministries. See Cru, "About Us."

169. See Mueller, *Strategy of Evangelism*, 9; *Move in for Action*, 128–29.

170. BDM Prayer Letter, November 1966, 3.

171. BDM Board Minutes, Friday March 22, 1968.

172. Chapman to Orpwood, January 15, 1994, BDM Box 1, SDA.

173. *Not Ashamed of the Gospel: John Chapman and the Department of Evangelism.* Unpublished History, 6, BDM Box 1, SDA.

would reside for twenty-three years.[174] Growing tensions between Fletcher and Sydney episcopal leaders over certain emphases in the Campus Crusade material, alongside the growth of his Lay Institute for Evangelism (LIFE) on a national scale, issued in Fletcher's resignation only three months later.[175] With Chapman's schedule now "full to overflowing with activities and opportunities to preach the gospel,"[176] the Board needed little persuasion to invite Chapman to succeed Fletcher. A letter was thus promptly received "from the Archbishop duly appointing Mr Chapman to the position of Director . . . from 1 July 1969 for a period of two years."[177] Fletcher also passed the director's baton, confident that he was handing it to "the best Anglican evangelist he knew who, once he began putting a hook on his line, surprised himself and became a blessing to countless others."[178]

Chapman was commissioned at a service in St. Andrew's Cathedral on July 8, 1969, at which Bishop A. J. Dain preached. Consecrated by Bishop Barker in 1868 as the site of the diocese's significant rites of passage, the cathedral was an auspicious place to begin his tenure. "God has made known to us His world plan," Chapman wrote in his inaugural 1969 newsletter. "He is working out a plan which will in the fullness of time bring everything in heaven and earth under the Lordship of Christ. This is why we should now be calling on 'all men everywhere to repent' and believe on the Lordship of Jesus Christ."[179] This was a vision from which Chapman would not depart. Over the course of his subsequent ministry Chapman would offer the news of Christ to a strikingly wide cross section of people in Australia and across the world. He would preach in embassy receptions, student and parish missions, Bible conventions, cathedrals, synods, stadiums, parks, civic halls, high schools, business luncheons, and lecture theatres. Records of his public preaching indicate that Chapman preached an estimated 7,500 sermons across five continents to combined audiences of over three quarters

---

174. *Not Ashamed of the Gospel: John Chapman and the Department of Evangelism*. Unpublished History, 6, BDM Box 1, SDA. These annual salary and car allowance amounts were the equivalent of $37,110 ($2950) and $10,695 ($850) in present-day terms. For historic monetary conversions, see Reserve Bank, "Inflation Calculator."

175. Concern was expressed toward LIFE's evangelistic toolset on account of its relative silence on the doctrines of sin and repentance, as well as other perceived theological omissions which its more culturally stylized approach appeared to make. So Gray, "Evangelism," 128.

176. BDM Department of Evangelism, Prayer Letter, no. 3, December 1969, 1.

177. *Not Ashamed of the Gospel: John Chapman and the Department of Evangelism*, 8, BDM Box 1, SDA.

178. Geoff Fletcher, cited in Gray, "Evangelism," 130.

179. John Chapman, BDM Department of Evangelism, Prayer Letter, no. 1, June 1969, 1.

of a million people. Almost certainly this places Chapman in the elevated company of Australia's most significant and prolific preachers. He preached more frequently, to larger combined audiences and across a broader cross section of world Evangelicalism than any Australian preacher before him.[180] "Was there ever an age when men were so disillusioned with life . . . so much in need of the Savior of men?" Chapman inquired in 1969.[181] "When Jesus looked on the crowds his heart was filled with pity . . . There is a great harvest," Chapman declared, yet "there are still few workers. Today is a time for us all to beg God to send out more workers."[182] Just as Australian society stood on the precipice of pervasive cultural and religious change, there emerged a messenger gripped with a passion to "lead men and women to the One in whose knowledge, is life eternal."[183] Over the course of the next generation, by means of a blend of impassioned biblical instruction mixed with a straight-talking singularity of mind, Chapman would bring new energy, clarity, and direction to the evangelical movement.

Conclusion

John Chapman was clearly the product of a collection of powerful generational, social, and religious influences which left a defining imprint on his life, temperament, and ecclesiastical career. As a member of the "nation-building" generation who came of age between the First and Second World Wars, Chapman's generation was responsible for shaping much of the post-war religious, social, and economic compact that permeated later twentieth-century Australian life and society. An unflamboyant, hardworking, and outspoken homelife shaped Chapman's temperament. An early exposure to political and public discourse, alongside an uncluttered practical education also produced an aptitude to distill thought and praxis for wide audiences. This brought an instinctive shrewdness to his personal, political, and spiritual judgments. Such influences were balanced by a maternal sweetness in

---

180. Appendix 5: *Historic Speaking Engagements*. Of comparable ubiquity is Alan Walker, an Australian Methodist minister. Between 1953 and 1957 Walker preached a "Mission to the Nation." He visited dockyards, red-light districts and filled town halls. See Massam, "Christian Churches," 260. Other episcopal figures preached widely as well. However, little data exists with which to measure this. It is also uncertain whether they preached with such sustained breadth and frequency across such a wide cross-section of Evangelicalism.

181. John Chapman, BDM Prayer Letter, no. 3, December 1969, 1.

182. John Chapman, BDM Prayer Letter, no. 5, June 1970, 1.

183. John Chapman, BDM Prayer Letter, no. 3, December 1969, 1; cf. McLeod, *Religious Crisis*.

his homelife and a love of laughter, sport, music, culture, poetry, and the arts which deepened his personal empathy and heightened his evangelistic rapport and his effectiveness in winning others to Christian faith. Ecclesiologically, Chapman was the product of a postwar revival in evangelical piety and scholarship that took place within Sydney Anglicanism and across other significant pockets of the Western ecclesiastical world. Anchored strongly in Reformed confessionalism, this movement exhibited a theological creativity uncommon only a generation earlier. Submitting previously assumed theological and confessional certainties to the control of Scripture and to the rising wave of postwar evangelical scholarship, this period saw a narrower sectarian Anglicanism give way to a more broadly Reformed theological vision. This environment proved foundational in framing the fresh approaches to theology, missiology, and ecclesiastical reform that became characteristic not only of Chapman's ministry but also of other Sydney diocesan figures in later years. Moreover, thrust into positions of responsibility at a relatively young age, Chapman witnessed at close hand the reform of an Australian diocese via the application of evangelical ministry patterns. Such experiences proved critical in equipping Chapman for the significant roles of leadership, advocacy, and reform that he would later assume.

Part II

Preacher

3

Australian Evangelical Homiletics

A Brief History

"Let your sermons be full of Christ, from beginning to end crammed full of the gospel . . . Preach Jesus Christ, brethren, always and everywhere."—Charles Haddon Spurgeon[1]

AT TEN O'CLOCK ON Sunday February 3, 1788, on the beach at Sydney Cove, the young Cambridge educated chaplain, the Rev. Richard Johnson, lifted his voice to a large crowd of soldiers, sailors, and convicts to deliver the first sermon at a service of divine worship in the colony of New South Wales.[2] Being the first Sunday after the Fleet's arrival, careful preparations were made for the impressive occasion. Convicts were ordered to "appear as clean as circumstances will admit" and that "no man should be absent on any account."[3] Johnson chose his text with care, Psalm 116:12: "What shall I render unto the Lord for all his benefits toward me? I will take the cup of salvation and call upon the name of the Lord." The text was an appropriate one for the occasion, reflecting the experience of the psalmist who had endured severe testing and yet had survived to give thanks for God's deliverance. So too, the company gathered in the cove had much for which to be thankful. Lifting his hearers' hearts to the God who had brought them safe passage to these distant shores, Johnson exhorted them as "mortals and yet immortals" to whom the gospel "proposes a free and

1. Spurgeon, *Soul Winner*, 79.
2. Cruickshank, "Sermon," 519; Murray, *Australian Christian Life*, 3.
3. Macintosh, *Richard Johnson*, 49.

gracious pardon to the guilty, cleansing to the polluted, healing to the sick, happiness to the miserable and even life for the dead." Ranging freely in the evangelical style of the day, Johnson mixed scriptural reflection and exhortation to remind his audience of the gravity of their spiritual condition.[4] Lieutenant Ralph Clark, an observer, noted that Johnson delivered "a very good sermon . . . the behavior of the convicts was regular and attentive."[5] The Christian sermon had arrived in Australia.

Almost precisely two centuries later, at eight o'clock on the evening of Sunday February 12, 1989, the Australian evangelist, John Chapman, stood ready before a large English crowd in the Guildhall at Cambridge, for the last of a series of eight addresses as lead missioner for the Cambridge Inter-Collegiate Christian Union (CICCU).[6] This too was a notable occasion and a fitting one. Given the influence evangelical Anglicanism in Cambridge had exerted upon Richard Johnson, Australia's first chaplain, two centuries of evangelical proclamation in Australia was now reaping a return, as Chapman stood and echoed back the gospel first proclaimed on Australia's distant shores.[7] CICCU missioners stood in a distinguished line that stretched back to D. L. Moody in 1882 and R. A. Torrey and D. G. Barnhouse in the early twentieth century. The missions of John Stott and Billy Graham in the 1950s had also brought significant impetus and, with the swelling tide of postwar Evangelicalism, the ministry among students at Cambridge remained one of the brightest spots for the evangelical cause in Britain.[8] Fifty-two assistant missioners supported Chapman in

---

4. See Johnson, *Address to the Inhabitants*, 15. Cruickshank, "Sermon," 519 suggests Johnson's *Address to the Inhabitants* (which was widely considered to be a published sermon) may be reflective of his general homiletic approach. It is therefore illustrative of the likely shape, force, and evangelical content of this first colonial address.

5. Murray, *Australian Christian Life*, 4.

6. Founded in 1877, the CICCU traced its origin to the ministry of Charles Simeon, the nineteenth-century evangelical Vicar of Holy Trinity Anglican Church in Cambridge (1782–1836). Simeon exerted influence on at least two generations of Cambridge graduates and worked to increase evangelical influence in the Church of England. Chapman, *Godly Ambition*, 27.

7. Johnson had studied at Magdalene College in Cambridge, which by 1778 had come under the influence of the evangelical scholars Samuel Hey, William Farish, and Henry Jowett. Farish, a man of ardent evangelical conviction, was Johnson's tutor during his time at Magdalene. By 1782, Charles Simeon was preaching in St. Edward's church to packed assemblies. In November 1782 he began his lifelong ministry in Holy Trinity, Cambridge. Magdalene men, like Johnson and Samuel Marsden, were among those who flocked to hear Simeon. Macintosh, *Richard Johnson*, 32; Macintosh, "Richard Johnson," 188.

8. Chapman, *Godly Ambition*, 35, 38.

this weeklong, well-organized campaign,[9] supplementing the evening's preaching with apologetic seminars and organized follow-up.[10] Up to one thousand students filled the Guildhall and its overflow each night for the addresses.[11] Chapman expounded Luke's Gospel with a series entitled "This is Jesus," working sequentially through the gospel text.[12] His addresses included sermons entitled "Are You Scared of Death?" (Luke 8:40–56); "Nothing Recedes Like Success" (Luke 12:13–21); "Lost and Found" (Luke 15:1–32); "Too Good for Heaven?" (Luke 18:9–14); "A Matter of Priority" (Luke 18:18–34); and "Why Did Jesus Have to Die?" (Luke 22:14–23). On this final evening, Chapman concluded with the good news of Christ's resurrection, preaching from Luke 24:1–49, "You Can't Keep a Good Man Down."[13] The sermons employed the expository genre.[14] They combined Chapman's wit and narrative art with a studied attention to the detail and theology of each text. A composite portrait of Christ was the net effect. This invited hearers to consider the uniqueness and call of Christ through the week, and there were "many who came to Christ" and many Christians who took "heart to tell the gospel to their friends."[15] In the afterglow of the campaign, Chapman was invited to mission for the Oxford Inter-Collegiate Christian Union in February 1994, with similar effect. Teaching sixty co-missioners each morning from Colossians and preaching to a seven-hundred-strong crowd in the Sheldonian Theatre

---

9. *Preaching Christ Newsletter*, February–April 1989.

10. Specialist meetings were organized covering questions of pluralism and existentialism, such as: "Eastern Religions," "Do All Religions Lead to God?," "Islam: Forwards or Backwards from Christ?," "African Religions and the Gospel: Continuity or Discontinuity?," "Religion: The Opiate of the People?" See "Report on the Cambridge Inter-Collegiate Christian Union Mission, 12–19 February 1989," Box 3, Adrian Lane Papers 1973–2005, Mitchell Library NSW.

11. John Chapman to Peter Adam (Vicar, St. Jude's Carlton, Melbourne), February 28, 1989, BDM Box 1, SDA.

12. *Preaching Christ Newsletter*, February–April 1989.

13. Handwritten manuscripts of these addresses are located in Chapman's personal files, and annotated in Appendix 3 noting title, place and date. Likely transcriptions of several of the addresses are also found in the sermon transcription in Appendix 1. The sermons transcribed in this appendix were delivered by Chapman in other locations on the same scriptural passages, and likely bear a close resemblance to the shape of the sermons delivered to the CICCU.

14. The characteristics of the expository preaching genre will be defined and discussed in the following section.

15. *Preaching Christ Newsletter*, May–July 1989. In examining select passages from Luke's Gospel, Chapman's expositions established a progressively illustrative and informative portrait of the person of Christ as revealed in Luke's Gospel.

each night from Luke's Gospel,[16] Chapman remains the only Australian to have preached at both historic university missions.[17]

The similarities between these preachers across a substantial time period reveals a consistency in evangelical preaching that is salutary. Against the vicissitudes of Australian life (including the church's entanglement with colonialism and the challenges of nineteenth- and twentieth-century critical-scientific and secularizing thought),[18] their preaching at the bookends of this long period bears a striking harmony. Ardent evangelical fervor called their hearers to receive Christ as Lord in light of his atoning death and the coming age. Stylistically, however, their preaching sounded very different. Johnson employed a textual-thematic approach. He used his text as an anchor point, while ranging freely across the Scriptures. Chapman employed the expository style, examining the coherence of a passage and building exhortation from its unique themes. Both styles exhibit the highest regard for Scripture,[19] yet how may such differences be accounted for?

This chapter locates the preaching of John Chapman and Sydney Evangelicalism within the longer arc of Christian homiletics, observing summary developments in the various epochs. With the revival of the expository genre at points along this longer arc and with its reapplication in the twentieth century, such an examination brings valuable context to the study of historic and contemporary Australian homiletics. The analysis surveys the preaching traditions in broad terms, noting developments over time, and key lineages and trajectories.[20] By then locating Chapman's contribution within the larger tradition of twentieth-century homiletics and by appreciating the centrality of the sermon in shaping Australian evangelical life, the analysis (in this and the following chapter) contributes to a developing scholarly portrait of Australian preaching. It also supplies evidence for Chapman's reputation as a celebrated and significant Australian preacher.

---

16. Interview with Rico Tice, January 17, 2017; *Preaching Christ Newsletter*, May–July 1994.

17. Marcus Loane to Michael Orpwood, BDM Box 1, SDA; Dr. Paul Barnett, Appendix 4, JCCPP/BIO#5. See Appendix 3 for texts, titles, and sermon dates for the *Oxford Inter-Collegiate Christian Union* mission, February 1–6, 1994.

18. Maxwell-Stewart and Duffield, "Skin Deep," 129–31; Breward, *History*, 11; Carey, "Historical Outline," 18; Frame, *Anglicans*, 235; Noll, *Faith and Criticism*, 11–14, 61–90; McLeod, *Religious Crisis*, 1; Frame, *Losing My Religion*, vi–xiv, 4.

19. Greidanus, *Modern Preacher*, 11; Robinson, *Biblical Preaching*, 4–12.

20. This approach echoes that of Edwards, *History of Preaching*, xx, in his major preaching opus, and is part anthology/prosopography, while tracing major theoretical developments in the discipline.

Defining Preaching

The activity of preaching is essential to historic Christianity.[21] No attempt to understand Christianity can overlook the foundational truth that Christianity is a religion of the "word of God." Indeed, the entire Christian preaching tradition rests upon the conviction that God has spoken, and that without this historic self-revelation of God there can be no preaching ministry.[22] Such a conviction holds that, speaking through the prophets of Israel, God interpreted to them the significance of his saving activity in history and instructed them to convey his self-revelation in speech or writing.[23] Similarly, it is held that, in the New Testament, Christ spoke and embodied God's self-revelation, and instructed his apostles to be witnesses to his ministry and resurrection, public heralds of divine reconciliation, and stewards of the sacred trust God had conveyed to them.[24] Moreover, undergirding the Christian preaching tradition is the conviction that through Holy Scripture (God's word written in the various forms of biblical literature)[25] God speaks a contemporary word to humanity. He speaks today, through what was spoken then, as the apostolic witness is announced and applied by the contemporary preacher.[26] This elevated conception of preaching is captured in the Reformed tradition by John Calvin, who states that "among the many excellent gifts with which God has adorned the human race, it is a singular privilege that he deigns to consecrate to himself the mouths and tongues of men in order that his voice may resound in them."[27] Indeed, "if we come to church," Calvin suggested, "we shall not only hear a mortal speaking, but we shall feel (even by his secret power) that God is speaking to our souls, that

---

21. Siegert, "Homily," 421 notes of all religious movements "known in antiquity, only Jewish worship . . . and Christian worship which imitated it—demanded a speaker's rhetorical activity"; cf. Packer, "Why Preach?," 2.

22. Adam, *Speaking God's Words*, 15.

23. Stott, *Between Two Worlds*, 126.

24. Heb 1:1–4; Matt 28:19–20; Acts 1:8, 21–22; 2 Cor 5:18–21; 1 Tim 2:7; 2 Tim 1:11; 1 Cor 4:1, 2; 2 Tim 1:14. See Kim, "Eschatological Herald," 9–24; Stott, *Preacher's Portrait*, 17, 30.

25. Including covenant law, story, wisdom saying, apocalyptic, gospel, parable, letter, and prophecy. See Kennedy, *Classical Rhetoric*, 137–43; Childs, *New Testament*, 419–27.

26. Adam, *Speaking God's Words*, 112–19; Greidanus, *Modern Preacher*, 7–8.

27. Calvin, *Institutes*, 4.1.5. The examples highlighted here stem from figures and authorities within the Continental and English Reformations, which were so formative in shaping the Sydney Anglican tradition from which the preaching of John Chapman arose.

he is the teacher."[28] Similarly, the Westminster divines declared: "The Spirit of God maketh the reading, but especially the preaching of the word, an effectual means of convincing and converting sinners, and of building them up in holiness and comfort through faith unto salvation."[29] Evidently, the New Testament writers describe a *variety of forms* of ministry of the word of God. This is a fact that cautions a focus on preaching as representing the totality of the effective speaking ministries in the church.[30] Nevertheless, the ministry of preaching stands irreducibly at the heart of the church's mission and has energized major periods of historic Christian growth.[31]

Preaching Genres

Several genres or kinds of sermon forms have proliferated across the preaching tradition, and run parallel within various epochs, even intermingling within the work of notable homileticians.[32] The *expository sermon* genre is marked by the systematic explanation of Scripture done on a week-by-week, or even day-by-day basis at the regular meeting of the Christian congregation.[33] The expository sermon finds precedent at key points in the worship of Israel in the pre- and post-exilic periods, notably via the ministries of Moses and Ezra.[34] A twofold pattern of the reading and interpretation of the Law was established in synagogue worship by the New Testament era. In the early church, the reading of the Law and the Prophets and their exposition continued, supplementing Jewish exegesis with a Christologically informed

---

28. Calvin, *Calvin's Sermons*, 665.

29. *Westminster Shorter Catechism*, Question 88.

30. No less than thirty-three Greek verbs are used in the New Testament to capture the "speaking activity" of the church. Extended passages such as Romans 12, Ephesians 4, and 1 Corinthians 12 and 14 denote an entire category of word-ministry gifts which function in ways besides public preaching to the assembled congregation. So Kittel and Friedrich, *Theological Dictionary*, 703.

31. Old, *Biblical Period*, 7, 111; Dargan, *History of Preaching*, vol. 1, 13.

32. For other taxonomies to capture the historic homiletic activity in this survey, see Kennedy, *Rhetoric*, 155–57.

33. Kennedy, *Rhetoric*, 156 categorizes the expository genre as "homily." *Homilia*: "coming together, conversation."

34. Moses expounds the Sinaitic law, before giving it to the priests and making provision for its ongoing reading and exposition (Deut 31:9–13). Similarly, Ezra the priest "brought the law before the assembly" and "read from it." The Levitical priests also shared in this ministry, reading "from the book of the law of God, making it clear and giving the meaning so that the people understood what was being read" (Neh 8:1–8). Adam, *Speaking God's Words*, 39–40; Siegert, "Homily," 429.

hermeneutic.[35] In its purest form, expository preaching follows the *lectio continua* and makes its claim to be, at heart, "Bible-centered preaching."[36] It seeks to handle the text of Scripture in such a way that its essential meaning as it existed in the mind of the biblical writer and as it relates to the wider doctrines of Scripture, are made plain and applied to the hearer. Through a historical and literary study of the passage, the expository sermon aims to communicate what God committed to Scripture, so that it speaks a contemporary message.[37] It is noteworthy that the expository genre, which is derived from the pattern of Israel's worship, emerges as the dominant genre in major epochs of the Christian era.[38]

While expository preaching is commonly directed to the regular Christian congregation, the *evangelistic* or *missionary sermon* genre is directed to those outside, announcing the apostolic *kerygma* with focused intent.[39] While the evangelistic sermon may contain expository elements, it may also contain apologetic content, offering reasoned evidence for Christian belief.[40] The *catechetical sermon* genre is employed in the instruction of Christian believers in a particular aspect of Christian confession and theology. It is, by definition, a systematic form of preaching that outlines basic teaching by the examination of historic creeds or doctrinally rich biblical texts.[41] The *festal sermon* genre predominates in the marking of observances in the church calendar. It was originally associated with the celebration

---

35. Philo's *Hypothetica* describes Sabbath worship, whereby the "priest . . . or one of the elders reads the holy laws to them and expounds them point by point," preserved in Eus *P.E.* 8:7:12–13, cited in Siegert, "Homily," 430. On synagogue preaching, see Meyers, "Synagogue," 6:252–60; Kennedy, *Classical Rhetoric*, 144; Hengel and Denies, *Pre-Christian Paul*, 32; Neusner, *Rabbinic Traditions*, 341–76.

36. *Lectio Continua* describes the sequential reading and exposition of Scripture at regular intervals in Christian worship.

37. Greidanus, *Modern Preacher*, 11; Robinson, *Biblical Preaching*, 4–12.

38. Kennedy, *Classical Rhetoric*, 67, 72; Davies, *English Preaching*, 194–95.

39. Kennedy, *Classical Rhetoric*, 88, 155; Old, *Biblical Period*, 11.

40. The sermons of the apostles unfold the Christ-event to Israel via scriptural exposition (Acts 2:14–41; 13:13–52). However, Paul's preaching on Mars Hill (Acts 17:16–34), while containing biblical concepts and echoing Old Testament thought, adopts a method of presentation that is adapted to the intellectual climate of Athens. See Hemer, "Speeches of Acts," 239–59; Kennedy, *Rhetoric*, 88, 148, 155; Old, *Biblical Period*, 11.

41. This genre finds precedent in the interpretive preaching of the rabbis in the schools of Jerusalem and Babylon. The Sermon on the Mount (Matt 5–7) and the New Testament *Haustafeln* (1 Peter, Ephesians, and the Pastoral Epistles) also reflect similar patterns of catechesis. Catechetical preaching is often prevalent after periods of heightened evangelistic activity or following periods of reform when foundational elements of Christian faith are relaid. Old, *Biblical Period*, 13–14.

of the Jewish Passover and the reciting of Israel's sacred history. However, as the Christian calendar developed, and with the entrance of Christianity into public and civil life in the Constantinian period, traditions arose around the appropriate scriptural lessons for the various holy days. In time, the number of feasts within the Christian calendar proliferated. This made increasing claims upon the focus and practice of preachers in the post-patristic period.[42] The *prophetic sermon* reflects a quality of preaching more than a discernable genre. Found across the various epochs, it marks a fresh and even inspired word for a particular time and place. Arising within the ministry of Israel's prophets (who brought divinely sanctioned messages from within and outside of the formalized structures of Israel's national life), in the age of the Christian church such prophetic utterances might be said by some to have been abrogated. However, at certain moments in the Christian era and via the preaching of charismatically gifted preachers—the likes of Chrysostom, Luther, Calvin, Wesley, Whitefield, and Billy Graham—it may be suggested that a similar *prophetic function* has been performed via their preaching. Such preaching has applied Scripture to particular historical moments with a fresh authority and has brought the church into periods of deeper fervency, resolve, and maturity—shaping the very course of Christian history.[43]

The Arc of Historic Christian Proclamation

Two important watermarks in the development of the preeminent *expository* genre are observable, following the more catechetical and apologetically

---

42. In the *festal* sermon, the preacher constructed the oration to suit the festival celebrated, quoting from Scripture such verses as seemed to support the theme. Under the influence of Greek panegyrical oratory (a style employed on lavish public occasions, seasonal and ecclesiastical celebrations) a rhetorical extravagance (as opposed to exegetical precision) became evident in the festal sermon genre. See Allen, "Greek Homily," 201–26; Barkhuizen, "Proclus of Constantinople," 179–93; Kennedy, *Greek Rhetoric*, 23–26, 149–50; Kennedy, *New History*, 260–61.

43. Keller, *Preaching*, 30; Old, *Biblical Period*, 16. The prophetic sermon is to be distinguished from the activity of Christian prophecy. "Prophecy" represents a Holy Spirit-directed "intelligible, articulate, communicative speech-act" by a member of the Christian church for its edification. See Thiselton, *First Epistle*, 1094. For views on the nature of "prophecy" spanning the charismatic and evangelical spectrum, see Thiselton, *First Epistle*, 1074–1100. Undoubtedly, the impact of "prophetic" preaching is as much a theological judgment as it is historical. Nevertheless, the shaping of the Christian era via the preaching of notable leaders appears an inescapable observation from any study of Christian history.

oriented preaching of the early church.⁴⁴ These are the Patristic and Reformation ages, the insights of which would also shape the revival of biblical exposition in the twentieth century. The application of rhetorical methods to preaching has also proven to be a substantial influence across major epochs of the Christian era and supplies an important element in framing the following analysis of the Christian homiletical tradition.⁴⁵

The Early Church and Patristic Age

In the nascent Christian church, the biblical account of Acts furnishes substantial detail on the apostolic preaching pattern and provides indications of its centrality in the life of the church. In settled periods of ministry, Luke records the regular exposition of Scripture alongside the transmission of the apostolic tradition (*paradosis*) as being the normative teaching pattern.⁴⁶ In addition, as the early witness of the *Didache* and Justin Martyr's *Apology* attest, the focal point of the early Christian worship assemblies consisted in a daily preaching ministry involving a body of prophets, teachers, bishops, and deacons devoted to the work of preaching and teaching.⁴⁷ In the post-apostolic era, Christian proclamation necessarily adopted a more defensive tone. As the movement faced mounting resistance from Jewish and Greek auditors, and as pressure from the Roman political class intensified during the second century, Christian apologists sought to shield Christianity from repression and defend it against charges that it was only the religion of the illiterate and barbarian. These propagandists maintained, on the one hand, that to make converts the new religion must use a simple, comprehensible style, insisting that at the heart of the Christian message lay truth, not stylistic beauty. Yet, in their oral

---

44. Given the influence that the expository genre has exerted upon Australian Evangelicalism and upon major strands of world Evangelicalism, significant attention is given in this survey to an examination of its development and progression.

45. Kennedy, *Classical Rhetoric* 3–41.

46. Peterson, *Acts of the Apostles*, 565; Fitzmyer, *Acts of the Apostles*, 677; Bock, *Acts*, 448–66, 558.

47. Describing the earliest Christian gatherings, Justin Martyr reflects that the "memoirs of the Apostles and the writings of the prophets" were read, and "the ruler in a discourse instructs and exhorts to the imitation of these good things." Justin Martyr, 1 *Apol*. 67. The Didache also contains material which extends back to the earliest Jewish Christian communities and demonstrates the time devoted to preaching and teaching in the early church. Didache, *Apostolic Fathers*, 1:309–33, 4.1–2. While the dating of these sources is contested, there is broad agreement that they date from the late first or early second century (*Didache*) to the mid-second century (Justin's *Apology*). Old, *Biblical* Period, 254–67.

and written defenses, the cautious use of rhetorical technique and philosophical argument became increasingly evident, as they sought to translate the Christian faith into categories amenable to the Greek mind and pagan elite.[48] In the Constantinian period (c. 313–37) major realignments began to reshape the relationship between classical culture and the church. This gave rise to a "golden age" of Christian preaching. From a persecuted minority Christianity moved to a position of privilege and considerable influence. In their formal education many Christian leaders received a grounding in the techniques of effective speech. This, in turn, brought an eloquence to the preaching tradition it had seldom before seen.[49]

Several figures are noteworthy in setting the high-water mark for preaching in the Patristic age. Among the Cappadocian Fathers, Gregory of Nazianzus (c. 330–91) developed such an ability as an orator-preacher that he was celebrated as one of the greatest orators since Demosthenes.[50] However, notable as leading expositors during this era were Origen (c. 185–254), Chrysostom (c. 349–407), and Augustine (c. 354–430). Bringing their erudition and rhetorical training to bear upon their preaching, Origen and Chrysostom expounded the biblical text verse-by-verse in a flowing, spontaneous style. They offered a general interpretation before highlighting key points in the text (observing key words, figures of speech, and grammatical structures) and making application. The evidence of their sermon manuscripts reflects the use of a *lectio continua* model—working sequentially through the books of the Bible. Exuding a simplicity and high sense of Scripture's authority, their preaching invited the admiration of preachers in later generations who frequently utilized their manuscripts in

---

48. During this era, a defensive note toward new ideas crept into Greco-Roman society, against which the Christian religion was seen as a threat. Apologists such as Justin Martyr, Tertullian, Clement of Alexandria, and Origen attempted oral and written defences which sought to revive elements of Christianity's social standing. They utilized Attic language and style to illicit a serious reception by an educated audience. Surviving sermons like *The Second Epistle of Clement* and *Melito's Paschal Homily* also reflect the developing synthesis of homiletical method in this era. Alongside the plainer approach of exposition these demonstrate the impact of the rhetorical tradition in shaping sermons with an increasing artistry. See Satterthwaite, "Latin Church Fathers," 671–94; Kinzig, "Greek Christian Writers," 633–70.

49. Kennedy, *Greek Rhetoric*, 185–90; Kennedy, *Classical Rhetoric*, 162–63; Kinzig, "Greek Christian Writers," 633–71.

50. While examples of exposition are evident in the preaching of the Cappadocian Fathers (Basil of Caesarea, Gregory of Nyssa, and Gregory of Nazianzus), the genre for which they are noted is the panegyric. The heavy imitation of this style would lead Byzantine preaching away from exposition toward a heavily ornamented homiletic. Kennedy, *Emperors*, 216–30.

place of original sermons.[51] No less compelling as an expositor—on account of his mastery of rhetoric, vast biblical memorization, and a virtuosity that grew from the melding of form and content in the heat of the message—was Augustine of Hippo. Perhaps the key significance of Augustine's work during this era, however, was the forceful yet considered accord he developed between the secular and Christian arts of oratory.[52] In this vein, Augustine's *On Christian Doctrine* presented the first systematized Christian preaching manual (*Ars Praedicandi*), alongside an entire program for the development of the preacher in the liberal arts. Books 1–3 offered precepts for the discovery of Scripture's meaning (*hermeneutics*), while Book 4 presented a rhetorically oriented program for Scripture's effective communication (*homiletics*).[53] The exegesis of Scripture in Augustine's manual (Books 1–3) approximated to the classical categories of *invention* and *arrangement*.[54] In Book 4, Augustine then gave consideration to the duties of an orator, and how the preacher might seek to "teach, delight and move" his audience, as well as the rhetorical styles appropriate to achieve such ends.[55] In this way, Augustine recognized the essential universality of rhetoric and sought to sanctify the art of "eloquence" while also recalibrating it for Christian use.

51. By the standards of later orthodoxy Origen's theology caused significant controversy. Despite this, his homiletic influence remains noteworthy. On Origen's expository approach (including his tripartite view of Scripture: literal, moral, and allegorical) see Olivar, "Reflections and Problems," 21–32; Castagno, "Origen," 65–88. On Chrysostom's preaching and use of rhetoric, see Kelly, *Golden Mouth*, 2–20; Rylaarsdam, *John Chrysostom*, 234–60.

52. On Augustine's scholarship, including his work as a professor of rhetoric, as well as his contributions in the areas of Trinitarian theology, anthropology, ecclesiology, hermeneutics, and eschatology, see Kennedy, *Rhetoric*, 170–82; Pecknold and Toom, *T&T Clark Companion*, 3–112.

53. Augustine, *On Christian Doctrine*, 519–97; Kneidel, "Ars Praedicandi," 3–20.

54. Classical rhetoric had developed a set of precepts grouped in five "parts" that recapitulate the act of planning and delivering a speech: *invention* (planning the content and argument), *arrangement* (of the contents into logical sequence and unity), *style* (the choice and combination of words into clauses, periods, and figures), *memory* (the use of mnemonic systems to retain the contents in mind), and *delivery* (oral expression and gesture). The precepts of rhetoric were then used as the basis of the critique and interpretation of texts of all kinds, including, eventually the Christian Scriptures. So Kennedy, "Historical Survey of Rhetoric," 3–42; Kennedy, *New History*, 267; cf. Heath, "Codifications of Rhetoric," 59–76; Steel, "Divisions of Speech," 77–91.

55. The "duties" of an orator—to instruct, delight, and move—were tied by Augustine to Cicero's three kinds of style, and recast to serve preaching: teaching in the plain style, delighting in the middle style, and moving in the grand style. While teaching was most important, the preacher must also delight listeners to retain them, and move them to impel their wills. So Augustine, *De Doctrina Christiana*, 4.27, 33–58; cf. Cicero, *Brutus. Orator*, 20–24 where Cicero presents his thesis on style; Kennedy, *Rhetoric*, 179.

Few other works have exercised the same influence on the preaching tradition. In the redaction of Augustine's homilies into collections that were preached across the Latin world, Augustine's hermeneutic and homiletic influence was unequalled until the Reformation age.[56]

The Renaissance and Reformation Age

With the age of the Protestant Reformers, a second clear watermark in biblical preaching emerges. Crucially, however, in the intervening centuries a decline in classical culture across the Latin- and Greek-speaking worlds had seen a corresponding decline in the quality of Christian preaching. Beginning in the fifth-century West and sixth-century East, there was a deterioration of the conditions of civic life that had sustained all kinds of public speech, including preaching. Political and military upheaval in the Western Empire saw much that was regarded as the core of classical culture in abeyance. Latin remained the language of religion and scholarship. However, knowledge of the biblical languages became rare, as fewer clergy were educated in the literary arts. This made exposition in the patristic mold increasingly unattainable.[57] The Carolingian Renaissance in the eighth-century West envisioned a clergy with the ability to forge a revitalized Christian society via learning, and achieved modest gains toward this end.[58] Biblical exposition was also preserved, to some degree, by the monastic orders, which became oases of scholarship in the medieval desert.[59] As the foundations of modern universities were being laid via the scholasticism of the twelfth century, a host of preaching handbooks also began to reappear. Echoing the work of Augustine, these manuals adapted the parts of classical oratory to Christian preaching and foreshadowed the rise of the thematic sermon in the early modern era.[60] However, it was the preservation of the works of antiquity in

---

56. Kneidel, "Ars Praedicandi," 4; Mack, *Renaissance Rhetoric*, 259. On the contributions of other Latin fathers like Tertullian, Jerome, Cyprian, Ambrose, and Arnobius and the influence of Cicero upon them (whose work became the most studied rhetorical *techne* for a millennium), see Kennedy, *New History*, 168–70.

57. The decline in clerical learning and the growing festal calendar in the medieval period saw the dominance of the lectionary (readings for liturgical seasons) and homiliaries (collections of homilies following the lectionary) in Christian worship until the Reformation. Halsall, *Barbarian Migrations*, 5–25.

58. McKitterick, *Frankish Church*, 80–114; Kennedy, *Classical Rhetoric*, 197–208; Edwards, *History*, 158–68; Old, *Medieval Church*, 189–98.

59. Old, *Medieval Church*, xvii–xviii, 341–436; Murphy, *Rhetoric*, 311–44.

60. Murphy, *Rhetoric*, 310; Kneidel, "Ars Praedicandi," 10–18; cf. the following discussion on English preaching.

Byzantium and their rediscovery in the Renaissance West that set the stage for a reflowering of biblical exposition in the Reformation age. The Renaissance period saw the works of Greek and Latin literature (including a host of rhetorical treatises and preaching manuals) recovered in the West, alongside translations of such works in considerable numbers. The work of the Christian humanist, Erasmus (c. 1466–1536) was also crucial in the revival of Christian learning. Alongside his translation of the Greek New Testament (1516), Erasmus revived the study of the church fathers, republishing notable works of Origen, Chrysostom, and Augustine.[61]

With the availability of such ancient sources and linguistic tools, an *ad fontes* preaching school emerged in the shadow of the new Christian humanism which matched and even exceeded the wealth of the patristic age.[62] Luther sparked the movement and is surely to be regarded as its initiator.[63] Inspired by Luther and Chrysostom, Zwingli, the Reformer of Zurich, carried the prophetic zeal of Constantinople's patriarch to Swiss society.[64] In Zwingli, the Reformed preaching tradition resumed a distinctive patristic shape, replacing the now familiar rhythm of the liturgical calendar with the practice of the *lectio continua* in Protestant pulpits.[65] The same scriptural intensity gripped Zwingli's successor, Heinrich Bullinger. In his forty-four-year pastorate, Bullinger preached approximately 7,500 sermons, working through every book of Scripture.[66] Calvin, the supreme Reformation expositor, also preached his way through the bulk of Scripture and set a new high-water mark for the homiletic tradition. Like other Reformers, Calvin found in Chrysostom a concise expository model, while in Augustine's preaching and rhetorical opus (*On Christian Doctrine*) he learned to place eloquence at the disposal of exposition.[67] Enslaved to no particular method, Calvin developed his sermon as the biblical passage proceeded. He desired to conform his preaching "to that manner and order which the Holy Ghost has here set down."[68] Drawing on a store of commentary and lecture material, Calvin constructed each sermon with the original Greek and Hebrew in hand. He engaged the text phrase by phrase, drawing applications and using

61. Mack, "Classical Rhetoric," 261–77; Mack, *Renaissance*, 2–6, 28, 258–59.

62. George, *Theology of the Reformers*, 47–49; Old, *Reformation*, 67–70.

63. Meuser, *Luther the Preacher*, 37–39; Old, *Reformation*, 4–42.; Kreitzer, "Lutheran Sermon," 35–64.

64. Ford, "Reformed Tradition," 67–68.

65. Wolterstorff, "Reformed Liturgy," 294.

66. Ford, "Reformed Tradition," 67.

67. Parker, *Calvin's Preaching*, 59–64; Adam, "Lively," 14; Ford, "Reformed Tradition," 71.

68. De Koster, *Light for the City*, 81.

images from daily life to make difficult passages clear.⁶⁹ The arc of Calvin's preaching also bent strongly towards mission. Calvin's preaching was thus infused with entreaties to be engaged in that activity without which "the Church cannot but decay and perish." Hence, a key feature of his ministry was the mobilization of missionary endeavor in a crescendo from the mid-sixteenth century. This played a vital role in energizing congregations across Europe and the English-speaking world.⁷⁰

English Preaching, the *Ars Praedicandi,* and the Protestant Plain Style

Political-Ecclesiological Context and English Preaching

In contrast to the *ad fontes* homiletical model that prospered in the Continental Reformation, the preaching that developed in Britain and, in turn, gave rise to Australian Evangelicalism followed a somewhat different course. More obviously than its Continental counterpart, the Reformation in England derived from a complex confluence of theological and political causes. The English fields had been plowed for a revival of Christian faith since the days of Wyclif (c. 1330–84) and the Lollards. Enthusiasm for humanist learning and a rising anti-clericalism were also fertile ground for Lutheran theology when it began impacting Britain in the 1520s. The Cambridge "White Horse Inn" movement also supplied a cadre of leaders sympathetic to such Lutheran overtures.⁷¹ Tyndale and Coverdale first translated the Bible into English, supplying stimulus to the Protestant advance. Moreover, the exile of one thousand leading Protestants to the Continent in the Marian era delivered, on their return, a group zealous to recapture England to the Reformed faith.⁷² Ultimately, however, England's Protestantism was secured with the imprimatur of the state. The Henrician *Act of Supremacy* (1534) secured the break from papal authority and the Edwardian reforms (1547–52) gave the Reformed ideals their legal and theological base.⁷³ However, it was within the Elizabethan settlement itself (1559), reinforced by the 1563

---

69. De Koster, *Light for the City,* 84; Parker, *Calvin's Preaching,* 160–62, 165–68.

70. See Calvin, *Timothy and Titus,* 1064; Medeiros, "Reformers' Commitment," 113–60.

71. Lindberg, *European Reformations,* 310–11.

72. Trueman, "Medieval Renaissance," 57.

73. This consisted of the *Prayer Book* (1552) and the original *Forty-Two Articles of Religion* (1553). So Frame, "Anglicans," 123.

Act of Uniformity, that the seeds of an ongoing struggle for the soul of the English church were contained and would shape its subsequent life. Poised delicately between its Lutheran, Catholic, and Reformed poles, the Elizabethan settlement met with less than universal approval on numerous fronts (primarily ecclesiological, but also soteriological). This invited a culture of strong disputation in England for over a century.[74]

Such ecclesiological and political flux had definite homiletical implications. Cranmer's *Book of Homilies* (1547) was intended to harness the persuasive power of the pulpit to foster the nation's new religious beliefs. It was also designed to counteract the impact of poor clerical education and the presence of "Romish" sermon collections in circulation at the time.[75] Many scholars are agreed that by the 1580s significant progress had been made towards achieving Cranmer's reforming ideals.[76] In form, however, Cranmer's 1547 homilies were divided between *loci* describing essential Protestant doctrine and those addressing key ethical concerns. They relied as much upon grace-derived reason and patristic authority as they did on expounding Scripture.[77] Consequently, within the very process enacted to secure the Elizabethan settlement, a more catechetical and disputative preaching came to dominate in England.[78] As Reformed theology began to take firmer root, *lectio continua* expositions were not unknown among clergy who possessed the materials and confidence to preach. These were mixed with thematic series on a range of texts.[79] Likewise, as the propor-

---

74. Puritanism desired to "purify" the church of Catholic vestiges and replace Elizabeth's *via media* by a church rigorously normed by Scripture. Conversely, Richard Hooker, elaborated a theory of ecclesiastical and civil law resting on reason and natural law, and became the apologist *par excellence* for the Elizabethan Settlement. These two divergent impulses, in large measure, would determine the religious and political course of events in Britain, through the revolution of 1649, the restoration of 1660, and 1689 *Act of Toleration*. See MacCulloch, *Later Reformation*, 30; Trueman, "Renaissance," 57.

75. Null, "Tudor Homilies," 349–50.

76. With the advent of the second *Book of Homilies* (1563) the people of England heard weekly and uncompromising condemnation of essential Roman Catholic beliefs, and in the distinctly Protestant religious culture now mandated by the State, the birth-pangs of Protestant England had delivered a broadly Protestant nation. So Null, "Tudor Homilies," 365.

77. Null, "Tudor Homilies," 354; MacCullocch, *Thomas Cranmer*, 293–94.

78. Hunt, "Elizabethan Settlement," 367.

79. On the *lectio continua* series of recognized preachers such as Edward Dering in London in the 1570s, John King in York in the 1590s, Arthur Hildersham in Leicestershire between 1609 and 1611, Thomas Jackson in Canterbury Cathedral from the late 1610s to the 1630s, mixed with the thematic sequences of the conformists Anthony Higgins and Brian Walton, moderates such as Richard Sibbes and John Preston, and

tion of graduate clergy increased to almost three quarters between 1600 and 1640, sermonic capability also strengthened. Nevertheless, new editions of the homilies between 1591 and 1640 combined with a growing lectionary-driven sermon rhythm in English parish life, as well as the persistence of a "plain country divinity" (a religion of "moral progress") and the rarified preaching expectations of urbane Londoners, to stem the tide of a culture of exposition within English pulpits.[80]

Ars Praedicandi *and the Protestant Plain Style*

Such developments as these, however, ought not to obscure the influence of a form of sermon construction and delivery that would eclipse all others in English preaching, right up to the evangelical and modern eras—the influence of the Protestant-plain or textual-thematic sermon form. This form became so dominant that it deserves mention at its earliest appearance. The forerunner to this homiletic form lay in the medieval "thematic" or "school" sermon, which emerged as rhetorical studies revived in the European university schools of the thirteenth century. This period unleashed hundreds of theoretical manuals of preaching (*artes praedicandi*) and a distinct rhetorical genre.[81] While a single thematic sermon form is not identifiable (given the hundreds of *artes* that were written), its characteristic shape consisted first in the foregrounding of the *thema* (a single scriptural text) announced after an introductory prelude and followed by a brief prayer. Second, came the all-important *divisio*, which divided the *thema* into subparts filled out by various medieval proofs (scriptural interpretations, pagan or patristic authorities, allegories, moral exempla, and fables). A concluding *peroratio* recombined the original terms of the division in a unitary way.[82]

---

high Calvinists such as Robert Bolton and Thomas Hooker, see Green, *Print and Protestantism*, 36–40. On the "matey chats" of Hugh Latimer, one of the preeminent preachers of the early English Reformation, and his looseness of structure, racy anecdotes, and use of exempla more akin to medieval preaching, see Seymour-Smith, *English Sermon*, 54; Smyth, *Art of Preaching*, 107–13.

80. Green, "Parishes," 139, 145, 146; Patterson, *Making of Protestant England*, 3.

81. The medieval style of preaching is associated intimately with the method of the university schools. The composition of a learned sermon, to be preached before the university—*ad clerum*—was one of the exercises required for the degree of Master in Theology. A preacher, trained in such forms, was shaped substantially by it. Smyth, *Art of Preaching*, 19.

82. Before the thirteenth century, only four major Christian treatises on the art of preaching were known: Augustine's *De Doctrina Christiana* (c. 396, 426), Pope Gregory's *Cura pastoralis* (c. 591), Guibert of Nogent's *Liber quo ordine sermon fieri debeat*, (c. 1084), and Alain de Lille's *De arte praedictoria* (c. 1199). By the middle of

While repudiating the excesses of the medieval sermon form, subsequent humanist and Lutheran theorists like Erasmus and Melancthon also developed preaching manuals modelled on the classical art. These too stressed divisions, definitions, and argument as the means of expounding a text's doctrine.[83] However, it was in William Perkin's *Arte of Prophesying* (c. 1592) that the germ of the Puritan sermon form and the earliest handbook of the plain style emerged. Since the time of the earlier Reformation, no substantial sketch of the ideals that should inspire a parish minister had appeared from an English pen. Perkins, a powerful Cambridge preacher and scholar, thus labored to fill this gap. Perkins spent a large portion of his *Arte* uniting Reformed theology with Puritan piety to sketch a plan of study and a manual of preaching and ministry to remediate English conditions.[84] He summarized the "sacred and only methode of preaching" as being:

> 1) To read the Text distinctly out of the Canonicall Scriptures, 2) To giue the sense and vnderstanding of it being read, by the Scripture it selfe, 3) To collect a few and profitable points of doctrine out of the naturall sense, 4) To applie (if he haue the gift) the doctrines rightly collected, to the life and manners of men, in a simple and plaine speech.[85]

Hence, after following Perkin's rules for interpretation seeking the most natural and plain scriptural sense (steps 1 and 2), a preacher would then "rightly cut" the text into doctrinal divisions "whereby the word is made fit to edifie the people of God" (step 3) before applying these to the mind and the Christian life (step 4).[86] In articulating this approach, Perkin's *Arte* effectively applied the process of the patristic homily not to an entire passage but to a text, expounding its context and grammar

---

the thirteenth century, however, the thematic sermon had progressed toward a developed rhetorical genre with technical vocabulary and stabilized patterns of organization, displaying a clear debt to classical rhetoric. However, by its imitation of the features of scholastic disputation, its encouraging of ornate figures of speech to aid memorability, and given the wide latitude afforded by medieval methods of biblical interpretation, the medieval sermon form tolerated and even encouraged the introduction of countless non-scriptural proofs that played to popular taste. So Murphy, *Rhetoric*, 275, 285–355; Wenzel, "Arts of Preaching," 84–96.

83. Kreitzer, "Lutheran Sermon," 49–52; Kneidel, "Ars Praedicandi," 12–13; Dargan, *History of Preaching*, vol. 1, 142.

84. Breward, *William Perkins*, 35–36; Pipa, "William Perkins," 82–85.

85. This gives Perkin's summary of his entire work in four principles. See Perkins, *Works*, 2:673, cited in Pipa, "William Perkins," 103. Perkin's method is aptly named the "Doctrine-Use" scheme. Kneidel, "Ars Praedicandi," 13.

86. Breward, *William Perkins*, 331–49.

and collating its doctrines and applications.[87] As a prodigious preacher, Perkins also bequeathed a vast legacy of varying sermon kinds, as well as a range of expository commentaries alongside his preaching of smaller units. However, the concern for "divisions," "doctrines," and their "uses" was pervasive, even in his extended scriptural treatments.[88] This produced in the Puritan sermon form a more diffused structure. In employing this approach, the preacher constantly digressed, tracing doctrines as if limbs on a tree. Such an approach also lacked a concern for biblical philology and the effect that examining a longer passage brought to a sermon's shape and rhetorical force (the distinguishing mark of patristic and Continental preaching).[89] Nevertheless, the completeness of Perkin's work made it an influential *Arte* among preachers and the model prospered. Indeed, in the religious fervency of seventeenth-century England, a form of preaching that promoted doctrine and response, and could be used to challenge the apostles of alternative theological persuasions, became particularly apt. As historians of preaching have noted, such was the interest in religious interchange that issued from British pulpits in this turbulent era that "not only did the pulpit outdraw bearbaiting and morris-dancing, but even in sophisticated London the popular preachers attracted larger audiences ... than Shakespeare and Jonson in their prime."[90]

In the later seventeenth century, as the nation and clergy began inevitably to tire of religious controversy and as the cultural ambience became colored by the dawn of Enlightenment thought, a plainer, more judicious preaching was strongly promoted.[91] Prominent theorists and practitioners of this approach, like the influential Restoration clerics Robert South and Archbishop John Tillotson (1691–94), achieved immense prominence.

---

87. Davies, *Worship and Theology Vol. 1*, 304; Miller, *New England Mind*, 332–33.

88. For extended analysis, see Pipa, "William Perkins," 105–25.

89. Parker, *Calvin's Preaching*, 1–8. Perkin's *Arte* also reflects the influence of the French logician Pierre Ramus, who became influential among English and American Puritans. This gave to Puritan sermons an air of logic over oral persuasion. See Kneidel, "Ars Praedicandi," 13. On Perkin's indebtedness to Augustine and Erasmus, see Patterson, *Perkins*, 121–22.

90. Seventeenth-century England was *par excellence* an age of sermons. It was a century of theological and political upheaval, and the sermons of the period reflect its varying opinions and emotions in a striking manner. Besides its strictly religious function, seventeenth-century English preaching took the place of the journalistic press or modern broadcasting company. Indeed, in a time when "the whole of England became a Hyde Park corner," thousands attended sermons as a civic event, or afterwards studied them in print. See Seaver, *Puritan Lectureships*, 5; Mitchell, *English Pulpit Oratory*, 3–4; Davies, *Worship and Theology Vol. 2*, 133.

91. Ihalainen, "Enlightenment Sermon," 228–34.

While highly erudite, South was the more prominent theorist. He fused the competing styles that had absorbed the interests of previous preachers into a plainer and more harmonious whole. The net effect, reinforced by Tillotson's wide promulgation of the plain style, saw eighteenth-century English sermons characterized by division into fewer parts than the elaborate compositions of Puritan or other Stuart-era preachers. The result was the prevalence of an almost universally observed sermon pattern, exuding the ostensibly "classical" rhythm of announcing text and theme, divisions, proofs, and applications.[92] Undoubtedly, there were stark differences in the theology that issued from the pulpits of non-conformist and mainstream preachers in the shadow of the Tillotson era. Moreover, the wave of revival that swept the nation from the 1730s under the influence of George Whitefield and John Wesley brought relief to many listeners from the latitudinarianism that had descended upon it.[93] Indeed, to serve the almost limitless variety of places and people to whom they preached, in the hands of the evangelical preachers the plain style was simplified further. They preached, in effect, biblically rich evangelistic orations to revive the nation.[94] The

---

92. Tillotson became the most widely published English preacher of the eighteenth century. His "latitudinarianism" sought a compromise between deism and traditional religion. Thus, for Tillotson, the sermon became a moral essay, the vehicle of a sober prudential ethic. Stylistically, however, as the numerous eighteenth-century manuals on both sides of the Atlantic and denominational-divide attest, the Protestant plain style (following Tillotson) became virtually the "universally established" English practice. For a survey of *artes praedicandi* expounding this model, see the list of major eighteenth-century treatises in Britain by James Downey, Harry Caplan, and Henry King, cited in Deconinck-Brossard, "Art of Preaching," 95n3. Of this model's classical affinities: *Inventio* (invention) corresponded to the choice of a theme and suitable "text" by which the theme could be unfolded; *Dispositio* (arrangement) involved the announcement of text and theme and the winning of the audience (*exordium*), followed by the outlining of the main propositions drawn from the text under distinct headings (*divisio*); *Elecutio* (Style) was recommended as being of simple eloquence, as opposed to "affected Rhetorick" as well as the development of sentence, clause, and syntactical structure; *Memoria* (memory) oscillated between the two extremes of extemporisation and "book-utterance." Non-conformist preachers erred towards improvisation. In mainstream churches, the written sermon was the norm; *Pronunciatio* (delivery) involved recommendations for lively reading technique, once improvisation had been ruled out. Deconinck-Brossard, "Art of Preaching," 110–27. On Tillotson's theology and wide influence, see Aston, "Rationalism," 390–405; Old, *Moderatism*, 544–45; Davies, *Angels*; Mitchell, *Pulpit Oratory*, 24; Old, *Reformation*, 334–59; Smyth, *Art of Preaching*, 106–66, 123–29; Gibson, "British Sermon," 20.

93. For discussion of the attributes of latitudinarianism (the dominant theologically, philosophically, and politically moderate form of seventeenth-century Anglicanism), see Fitzpatrick, "Latitudinarianism," 209–27.

94. Whitefield's sermons displayed a stripped-down quality, stylistically and theologically. Yet, infused with a pietistic devotion they left audiences captivated. Whitefield

result was that by the mid-eighteenth century, the influence of the plain style from both strands supplying the preaching of the English church was dominant and the pattern was uniform. The exposition of a single Bible text proceeded with an introduction, headings, and application, before an oratorical climax. The many divisions that had characterized the English pulpit during the previous centuries had yielded to a simpler form better adapted to the capacities of the multitudes who thronged to listen to the peripatetic preachers in the vast assemblies that multiplied during the so-called age of the evangelical revival.

A Normative English Preaching Style

With few exceptions, in the ensuing eighteenth and nineteenth centuries, the plain style became the normative mode of preaching in the pulpits of Wales, the Anglican and Presbyterian pulpits of Scotland, and the non-conformist churches of the Baptists and Congregationalists, of which Charles Spurgeon was the foremost exemplar.[95] Within Anglicanism, Charles Simeon, the evangelical Vicar of Holy Trinity Church in Cambridge (1782–1836) made strides toward preaching of a more expository kind, and worked assiduously to establish evangelical piety within the denomination, both in England and abroad.[96] Simeon's preaching opus, the *Horae Homileticae*, contained 2,536 outlines from every biblical book, and was published to promote evangelical preaching across the land. The work was highly successful and went through

---

preached an estimated eighteen thousand sermons in churches and open fields. Drawing on his dramatic training, Whitefield stamped his feet, beat his breast, and choked his voice in tears, punctuating his delivery with as many as sixty questions to engage hearers. Underpinning the oration, however, lay the neoclassical outline of Tillotson. It differed only in the impassioned peroration by which he pleaded with hearers to accept Christ. So Stout, *Divine Dramatist*, 66–68; Dallimore, *George Whitefield*, 51–59.

Wesley's greatness lay not primarily in his oratory, but in his abilities as the organizational genius of the evangelical revival. Yet, as an Oxford-educated scholar, he preached the doctrines of justification to coal miners and scrub maids (travelling an estimated 250,000 miles and preaching forty thousand sermons). Wesley used his own published sermons to convey the theological system of Methodism and as a guide for the many lay preachers who formed the movement under him. These were the product of Wesley's "sermon-barrel," a collection of sermons developed in a style easily understood and which he adapted as occasion demanded. Tillotson's neoclassical form left its unmistakable stamp upon Wesleyan preaching also. So Edwards, "Varieties of Sermon," 3–57; Old, *Moderatism*, 110–34.

95. Morgan-Guy, "Sermons in Wales," 189; Morgan, "Welsh," 199–211; Matheson, "Churches of Scotland," 152–65; Old, *Modern Age*, 429–540, 936–40.

96. Bebbington, *Evangelicalism*, 31–32; Simeon, *Evangelical Preaching*, xvii.

eight editions.[97] The theory mediated in this work was that of the Reformed French text, Jean Claude's *Essay in the Composition of a Sermon*. Discovered early in his tenure, Simeon realized that Claude's theorization confirmed many of the homiletic principles he had discerned on his own. The principles related to the selection of texts in their biblical frame, rules for grammar, textual division, and explication, and securing a homiletic proposition or theme.[98] Simeon's inclusion of a second essay on the nature of the Christian message was also intended to buttress the evangelical quality and impact of his work.[99] It is unclear to what extent Simeon grasped the indebtedness of Claude's work to the classical art. Its appeal lay in its more purposeful guidelines for exegesis, even if only of a textual kind.[100] Yet the influence was unmistakable. This produced in Simeon's pulpit and those of his pupils an almost changeless neoclassical rhythm. A text's theme was announced, followed by its divisions, applications, and uses.[101] Simeon's preaching undoubtedly resounded with a clarity and sparkling oratory that placed him among England's greatest preachers. The Cambridge evangelical circle also remained a key influence on the evangelical succession that shaped the English church down the course of the nineteenth and twentieth century.[102] Nevertheless, as Victorian dust settled upon the *Horae Homileticae* and as English preachers overlooked the finer nuances of the Simeon-Claudian system in favor of a simpler and somewhat instinctive English method, this produced in English pulpits the familiar rhythm of the plain style. This model remained the prevailing English preaching custom until the revival of Continental style exegesis in the mid-twentieth century.[103]

97. Gibson, "British Sermon," 20; Stott, "Foreword," in Simeon, *Evangelical Preaching*, xv.

98. Simeon, *Horae Homileticae*, xv–xxi, 1–120. Jean Claude was the leading voice of French Protestantism during the late seventeenth century. Claude's essay became a classic Protestant preaching text. So Simeon, *Horae Homileticae*, xvi; Smyth, *Art of Preaching*, 179–81.

99. Note Simeon's inclusion of "A Sermon on the Gospel Message" in *Horae Homileticae*, 121–29.

100. Autrey, "Jean Claude," 159–75; Old, *Modern Age*, 567–69.

101. Note this pattern of theme, division, and uses across forty sermons in Simeon, *Preaching*, 3–279; Smyth, *Art of Preaching*, 184.

102. Barclay, *Evangelicalism*, 9–78; Old, *Our Own Time*, 460–92.

103. Smyth, *Art of Preaching*, 201; Old, *Our Own Time*, 447–91.

Australian Evangelical Preaching

Founding Influences

In keeping with such developments, the preaching that arrived on the tide of colonial Australia was the Protestant plain style, infused with an evangelical content and tone. With little variation, this now conventional English model marked the orations of colonial Chrysostoms well into the twentieth century. Richard Johnson and Samuel Marsden (the colony's leading early chaplains) were products of the eighteenth-century revival and provide notable examples of this model. Like other early colonial missionary leaders, Johnson and Marsden's preaching mixed a concern for world evangelization with a concern for state-sanctioned order that promoted Christian society through education and moral reform.[104] Yet, it was not a "scanty morality" to which they viewed themselves as being called, but to "publish glad tidings of a free and full salvation."[105] Indeed, longing that "God will make bare his holy arm in the conversion of the souls of men," in a form modelled on Simeon and the plain style he exemplified, Marsden (in particular) utilized Simeon's outlines almost "slavishly" at times. He matched occasion for occasion, and even tone for tone.[106]

As the colony transformed from a penal settlement to an increasingly free and commercial society, the agencies of church and state began to disentangle. Newly arrived clerics found freedom in a more wholly prophetic ministry than the coercive tone of their clerical forebears.[107] With the passing of various *Church Acts* (1836–47) the quasi-establishment status of Anglicanism also dissolved and opened the way for clerical leaders of other persuasions. Their combined voices gave rise to an ascendant Victorian religion that welcomed preaching across the nation's key rites of passage.[108] A

---

104. Indeed, Johnson despaired of the spiritual progress made in the colony and feared that without strong moral admonitions achieving reform would be like felling a "large tree with a wooden hatchet." So Bonwick, *Australia's First Preacher*, 41; cf. Strong, "Missions," 502; Le Couteur, "Churchmen," 193.

105. Samuel Marsden, Sermon 93:12, cited in Pettett, "Sermons of Samuel Marsden," 40–50, 41.

106. Pettett, "Charles Simeon's Influence," 25–37; Pettett, *Samuel Marsden*, 71–74. Johnson's journals also record his custom of English "textual" preaching. They note sermons from: Eph 2:17, 1 Cor 1:7, Matt 3:12, Prov 19:21, 1 Pet 4:18 as well as others from 2 Sam 16:17 and Jer 6:10, cited in Murray, *Australian Christian Life*, 13–15, 21–25.

107. Pettett, *Preacher*, 71; Fletcher, "Free Society," 94–96; Gladwin, *Anglican Clergy*, 14.

108. Hilliard, "Secularization," 77; Fletcher, "Free Society," 97–108; Gladwin, "Public Life," 4–9.

culture of eloquence also began to flourish from the mid-nineteenth century. This was attended by the proliferation of public lecture and debating societies.[109] Published sermon collections and the sermons of the English metropole in colonial newspapers also reinforced a sense of shared identity and sermon taste.[110] Yet, while denominational emphases varied, the English plain style remained the unassailed communicative channel. For High Church Anglican clergy, sermons were rational and decorous. They emphasized duty to God and man, mixed with practical piety. After the 1830s, colonial Anglo-Catholics shared with High Churchmen and Roman Catholics a stress on the sacraments and prayer, alongside the authoritative beauty of their various ecclesiastical forms.[111] Colonial Methodists expounded their texts and divisions, yearning earnestly for outpourings of revival.[112] So too, their Presbyterian contemporaries preached textually with a Puritan flair. "Like the bones in Ezekiel's vision," lampooned the 1862 *Presbyterian Magazine*, their "never-ending divisions and uses," were "very many and very dry" and did "duty at the head of every section."[113] For Anglican evangelical clergy the pulpit also remained a key vehicle for conversionist fervor. Indeed, urged the Irish Anglican, William Stack, "the public announcement of God's holy will is the highest duty of our ministry." No preaching is worthy of the Christian pulpit, he suggested, that does not suppose humanity to be "fallen and in need of divine grace."[114] The elevation of Frederic Barker as Bishop of Sydney (1855) saw a revitalized Evangelicalism permeate the pulpits of his Anglican diocese. Over a twenty-eight-year tenure Barker bequeathed a strong, clergy-led Evangelicalism, supported by an evangelical lay consensus. His preaching won hearers via a fervent and earnest manner, while the English plain style gave semblance to his thoughts.[115]

109. Damousi, *Colonial Voices*, 61, 71–75; Gladwin, "Public Life," 7–8.

110. Cruickshank, "Sermon," 519–20; Pedras, "Spurgeon," 34; Piggin, *Spirit*, 57; Gladwin, "Public Life," 5.

111. Gladwin, "Public Life," 5. On the convergence of the once doctrinally distinct High Church and Anglo-Catholic movements by the end of the 1800s, see Wolffe, "Religious Identities," 301–23.

112. Piggin, *Spirit*, 25; Murray, *Australian Christian Life*, 63, 146, 305–6, 314.

113. Cruickshank, "Sermon," 522.

114. Gladwin, "Public Life," 2–5; Rawlyk and Noll, *Amazing Grace*, 6.

115. Jane Barker's journal suggests a more expository practice by her husband in clergy Bible study. On June 20, 1855, she records an evening "reading Philippians 4 with an exposition and prayer." On March 29, 1856, Barker spoke at a prayer meeting on 2 Corinthians 6. In his public preaching, however, the textual plain style was more prevalent. November 11, 1855, records Barker preaching at St. Philip's "a sweet sermon . . . on 'In his favour is life.'" March 26, 1856, on Easter Sunday Barker preached at St. James's in the morning on John 11:23–24, and on John 11:25–26 at St. Philip's in the

Twentieth-Century Evangelical Australian Preaching

Within the familiar cadences now established by the plain style, the growth of revivalist and open-air preaching traditions alongside the emergence of a cosmopolitan culture combined to bring new emphases into twentieth-century Australian pulpits. Between 1863 and 1912 a host of celebrated world evangelists frequented Australasia. Gathering crowds in tents and mission halls as well as city and suburban churches, such missions revived a spirit of evangelical confidence after the confrontational environment of the Victorian era.[116] As a result, in Sydney, parish missions began to proliferate while open-air evangelists took to the streets. Simple revival-style messages in city-squares, beaches, and factories combined with emotionally charged consecration hymns and decision calls to follow Jesus.[117] In the mid-century, the figures of T. C. Hammond, H. W. K. Mowll, and Marcus Loane were also notable influences on the Sydney preaching tradition. Hammond's scholarly influence at Moore College began to displace the homely revivalism of the earlier century, supplying clarity to an Evangelicalism many believed had become sentimental and out of date. He combined gifts of intellect with experience in open-air campaigning to produce a formidable and polemical kind of preaching. Archbishop Mowll also combined open-air preaching influences with the arresting presence of an imposing frame. He toured his diocese ceaselessly and preached prolifically. The inside of Mowll's Bible was heavily annotated, containing a selection of sermon notes, textually arranged.[118] Loane also embodied a preaching that was measured and passionate. Reflecting the conventions of an emerging cosmopolitan culture and, with his own pietistic flair, Loane developed a model of preaching that carried the congregation along on a seamless "flow of logic" coupled with "passion," "imagination," and "pauses" for "silent stillness."[119] An admirer of the preaching of Ryle and Simeon, he maintained the plain style along

---

evening, cited in Murray, *Australian Christian Life*, 221, 230–41. On Barker's legacy, see Maple, "Barker, Frederic," 21–26; Judd and Cable, *Sydney Anglicans*, 70–74, 118–207.

116. Judd and Cable, *Sydney Anglicans*, 118–207; McIntosh, *Evangelicalism*, 30–64; cf. Francis, "Paley to Darwin," 445–59.

117. The impact of revivalism will be discussed in later chapters. See Piggin, *Spirit*, 56–59; Judd and Cable, *Sydney Anglicans*, 150–52.

118. Nelson, "Hammond, Thomas," 152; Braga, *Katoomba*, 173; Judd and Cable, *Sydney Anglicans*, 150–51; Piggin, *Spirit*, 128; Loane, "Mowll," 132.

119. Loane, "Art of Preaching," 11–12. The emerging cosmopolitan culture aspired to a "controlled and disciplined expression of the English language." Speeches of public figures were thus delivered carefully with attention to pitch, pace, and volume, often with a powerful peroration. So Damousi, *Colonial Voices*, 215–87.

the full course of his ministry.[120] Sermons in commercial newspapers alongside those in synodical and diocesan publications also reveal much of the mid-century Sydney evangelical preaching tradition. Addressing a range of doctrinal, moral, and existential questions, many parish sermons examined topics as varied as the place of the Bible in the life of the nation, or the worth of church attendance and moral rectitude. Others traced the lives of Old Testament heroes, or asked questions about faith and the richness of the church's sacramental heritage.[121] Still others in synodical and cathedral settings addressed questions of providence regarding world events or extolled the virtues of Reformed worship and the need for world evangelization.[122] Cranmer's 1662 lectionary readings remained a regular feature of many mid-century Anglican services, providing an important

---

120. Excerpts of Loane's preaching at the height of his episcopacy proliferate through the pages of the Sydney diocesan magazine *Southern Cross* and confirm his textual practice. Select examples include: Loane, "Everlasting Arms," 14–15, on Deut 33:27; "What Shall I Render," 14, on Ps 116:12; "Come, Drink," 15, on John 7:37; "Woe Lo Go," 16–17; "Daughter of Moab," 9, on Ruth 1:16; "Judgement," 17, on 1 Pet 4:17; "Power of God," 18–19, on 1 Pet 1:5; "Could Not Believe," 18–19, on Acts 12:5; "What the Spirit Saith," 36–37, on Rev 2:7.

121. The *Sydney Morning Herald* records a cross-section of Sydney Anglican textual-thematic preaching in the mid-century. Examples include: Edwards, "Why Go to Church?"; Pitt, "Place of the Bible"; King, "Old Testament Heroes"; Canon Arrowsmith, St. John's Darlinghurst, April 5, 10:30am, "Why the Sacraments?," 7:45pm, "Where Are Your Sins"; April 6, "Do Morals Matter?"; April 7, "Can We Trust the Bible?"; April 8, "Where Are We Heading?"; April 9, "Is Death the End?"; April 10, "How Should I Live my Life"; Lormer, "What Jesus Christ Means"; St. Peter's North Sydney, Reformation Sunday, 11am, "Faith of our Fathers."

122. The sermons of leading clergymen at the Sydney Synod illuminate further aspects of the mid-century practice. Examples include: Rev. G. K. Bell, Lord Bishop of Chichester, England. Synod Service, November 7, 1949, Text: Eph 4:16, *1950 Sydney Yearbook*. The sermon provides commentary on the destruction of materialism sweeping the world and notes the value of the human soul against the nihilism of Nazism; Most Rev. J. B. Booth, Archbishop of Melbourne, Synod Service, October 18, 1954, Text: Rom 1:16, *1955 Sydney Yearbook*. The sermon exhorts the synod in light of the Evanston WCC conference of the need to reach the world's population; Rt. Rev. W. G. Hilliard, Synod Service, Text: Luke 24:15, *1959 Sydney Yearbook*. The sermon exhorts the synod that as the risen Lord was present with his disciples on the Emmaus road, so we may "realise his presence" within our own synodical deliberations; Rev. Canon H. M. Arrowsmith, Synod Service, September 21, 1959, Text: Ps 8:3–4, *1960 Sydney Yearbook*. The sermon notes, in light of momentous world events, that "God has the first word in history, and he will have the last word too"; Rev. Canon D. B. Knox, 300th Anniversary of the Book of Common Prayer, October 8, 1962, Text: Ps 95:6, *1963 Sydney Yearbook*. Knox expounds a biblical theology of worship; Shilton, "Cathedral Sermon," 15–16. The sermon systematizes scriptural texts to suggest benefits of cathedral worship; Robinson, "Sermon Preached," 3–6. The sermon expounds the doctrine of justification by faith; Hewetson, "Not Shepherds," 12–13, Text: John 10:7.

means of buttressing evangelical thought. In many churches the clergy's mid-week Bible study also accommodated the needs of the congregation's spiritual growth. A more expository style flourished in such contexts.[123] Yet, despite the presence of such readings and weekly studies, the Sunday sermon was usually instinctive in its focus—heavily reflecting the direction of a clergyman's spiritual interests or devotional patterns. A chosen text supplied a hook or garnish from which to move swiftly on to doctrinal and moral exhortation or to a prophetic engagement with the life of a still predominantly Christian nation.[124]

Consequently, from the colonial chaplains through to the preaching of twentieth-century clerical figures, the Sydney evangelical preaching tradition maintained a conventional and strikingly consistent shape. The venerable rhythm of the Protestant plain style supplied its enduring form, while a fidelity to Evangelical and Reformed doctrines supplied its dependable, if not polemical, force. It was not the preaching of the patristic fathers or Continental Reformers. Rather, in the tradition of Perkins, Tillotson, and Simeon, its ancestry belonged to the forms that had shaped the preaching tradition across the churches and revival halls of Great Britain. Under the influence of the British Protestant missionary-movement and the Cambridge evangelical circle, this tradition had profoundly shaped the preaching assumptions and practices of the Australian Church.

Twentieth Century Expository Revival

Against the backdrop of this now long-standing tradition, Australian evangelical preaching was soon to transform. In its place there developed a mode of preaching that saw the convergence of two of the great rivers of Christian oratory, the *expository* and *textual-thematic*. The result, in an age of rapid secularization and declining religious participation, would bring the renewed preaching of Scripture to bear upon the Australian religious context of the later century. In the pre-1960s era, a widespread familiarity with the rudiments of Christian doctrine had made the preaching of the gospel accessible to a broad cross-section of Australian audiences. However, as the process of secularization took firmer hold, such assumptions could no longer be made. Indeed, loosed from the shared religious understanding of the previous era, the preaching of the mid-century rapidly embodied a world of religious authority and sacred knowledge that many Australians were actively

---

123. Old, *Moderatism*, 149–57; Judd and Cable, *Sydney Anglicans*, 294; Hewitt, "Preaching from the Platform," 81.

124. Interview with John Chapman, Gavin Perkins, *Cornhill Training College*, 2009.

leaving behind. Importantly, the homiletic revolution that emerged did not derive as a direct correlate of such changes. Its genesis lay rather in the decades preceding its appearance. Yet, its appearance proved timely. Into the maelstrom of change the deeper exegetical engagement that emerged across the pulpits of the evangelical world delivered fresh advantages. Infused with the tools made available with the renaissance of postwar evangelical biblical scholarship, such developments brought renewed confidence and rigor to the preaching of evangelical leaders as they sought to challenge the rise of secular assumptions and to buttress evangelical belief.[125]

Theological Renaissance and the Expository Pulpit

Portents of the expository revival began to appear in the Protestant world of the late nineteenth century with the renaissance of conservative biblical scholarship. In Britain, under the Cambridge trio of J. B. Lightfoot (a meticulous church historian, 1828–89), B. F. Westcott (a biblical commentator of rare insight and scholarly depth, 1816–1900) and F. J. A. Hort (an exacting textual critic, 1828–92), a tradition of careful scholarship and reasoned conservatism began to provide an alternative to the liberal skepticism that dominated academic biblical studies of this period. In their treatment of the New Testament these scholars began to sketch the beginnings of the modern exegetical discipline. Westcott and Hort's reconstruction of the New Testament text (1881) saw the revival of grammatico-historical exegetical principles established during the Reformation era and a proliferation of exegetical commentaries on the New Testament text. Their work also cast fresh doubts on the assumptions of higher-critical scholarship. It demonstrated that while questions remained, the New Testament rested on secure textual and historical foundations.[126] Heirs of the Cambridge trio in the twentieth century (including P. T. Forsyth and C. H. Dodd) continued to model an intellectually rigorous scholarship. This bolstered a growing confidence in

---

125. Stanley, *Diffusion*, 13; Hilliard, "Pluralism," 126; Noll, *Faith and Criticism*, 102; Wolffe and Hutchinson, *History*, 193.

126. Modern biblical criticism emerged in response to a confluence of factors. The influence of enlightenment and scientific ideals began to stress the "human" as opposed to "revealed" nature of Scripture. Research advances in philology, archaeology, and non-Christian world religions also challenged many previous orthodoxies regarding Scripture. The result was the rise of a scholarly discipline posing new theories of Scripture's provenance and dating (assuming it was of human origin). So Noll, *Criticism*, 12–32, 62–71. On the assumptions undergirding F. C. Baur's (c. 1792–1860) Tübingen school, including his belief that Christianity was the product of a Hegelian synthesis of religious ideas, see Bray, *Biblical Interpretation*, 322–29.

the foundations of conservative thought and biblical-exegetical study.[127] The evangelical student organizations in British universities were also important conduits for such homiletic developments. The preaching of H. C. G. Moule as Sunday evening lecturer at Holy Trinity Church and Principal of Ridley Hall College in Cambridge (1880–1901) was the most notable ministry of its kind since the days of Charles Simeon, casting an immense influence over generations of evangelical undergraduates. Moule's expositions of the Greek text and his Sunday evening sermons from Simeon's pulpit were considered "masterpieces of English prose."[128] On Sunday evenings Moule preached to packed crowds at the Round Church in Cambridge. After this, in the tradition of Simeon, students crowded Moule's study chambers for another reading from the Greek New Testament and a further half-hour exposition.[129] The conservative scholarly strength such developments imparted to the Cambridge evangelical student ministry (the CICCU) came to play a foundational role in the formation of the Inter-Varsity Fellowship (IVF) in 1928. Under the influence of the IVF, organized evangelical scholarship became a reality for the first time in Britain.[130] The revival of conservative English scholarship was also mirrored by Reformed scholarship on the European continent by Karl Barth. Arising from his study of *Der Römerbrief* (1919) and via his *Kirkliche Dogmatik* (1932–67), Barth established what was to become his enduring contribution to theology and the work of preaching. Indeed, with a growing skepticism about the optimistic view of human progress upon which much of the liberal-critical agenda rested, Barth posited that human discovery (whether philosophical, scientific, ethical, or religious) could not be relied upon to reveal divine truth. Rather, divine truth was made available by divine self-disclosure. Barth's blend of theological conservatism and critical method inspired a generation of Reformed theologians. As a result, a fresh caution toward the assumptions of old-school liberalism began to take hold in American and British theology. This was

127. Dodd's *Apostolic Preaching* was a watershed. In the face of liberal deconstructionism, Dodd's work in reconstructing the earliest preaching (or *kerygma*) of the New Testament witnesses (apostles) secured an earlier dating for and a high degree of unity in apostolic preaching content. Dodd, *Apostolic Preaching*, 13. Other heirs of the Cambridge trio were J. Denney, J. Orr, A. Robinson, C. F. D. Moule, and Charles Gore. Noll, *Criticism*, 81–82.

128. Loane, *Makers*, 81.

129. Bray, *Biblical Interpretation*, 346; Loane, *Makers*, 62–94.

130. Note the fuller discussion of the IVF Biblical Research Committee's approach to scholarship in chapter 2. In the United States, the formation of the *Evangelical Theological Society* (ETS) mirrored the IVF. Unlike the IVF, however, the ETS insisted on a more confessional stance regarding aspects of critical scholarship. Stanley, *Diffusion*, 94; Noll, *Criticism*, 82–84.

attended by calls for a more biblical understanding of God's relations with mankind that emphasized the doctrines of sin, atonement, and justification. Such developments came broadly to be referred to as the "biblical theology movement." While this movement combined a variety of positions and traditions, it nevertheless shared a reaction against abstracting theological enquiry and encouraged a closer engagement with the biblical text. Such developments were overlaid by the rise of modern literary criticism, which yielded a greater appreciation for biblical genres. New finds in archaeology (which further secured the historical veracity of the biblical text) and the rise of postwar Jewish scholarship (which yielded new insights into Old Testament study and a greater appreciation for the unity of Scripture) were also significant.[131] The net effect was the emergence of a generation of scholars who, while familiar with the assumptions of critical scholarship, resolved that however one may explain it, Scripture still exuded a demonstrable capacity to guide and enliven the global church.[132]

Expository Forerunners

A number of figures in the English and American contexts also became harbingers of the more fully developed expository discipline that matured in the mid-twentieth century. In England, the ministries of G. Campbell Morgan at Westminster Chapel in London (1904–17 and 1933–45) and his better-known successor Dr. D. Martyn Lloyd-Jones (1945–68) were significant. Morgan and Lloyd-Jones were part of the emerging transatlantic network of preachers who filled the pulpits and evangelical mission platforms of the interwar and postwar eras. Infused with Welsh revivalist and Puritan Reformed influences and stimulated by the wealth of exegetical commentaries now proliferating across the evangelical world, these pulpit giants preached prodigious sermon series across entire books of the Bible. They filled Westminster Chapel with crowds of over two thousand people per week.[133] In North America the influence of D. G. Barnhouse (1895–1960) and J. M. Boice (1938–2000), both senior ministers of Tenth Presbyterian Church in Philadelphia, was also significant. Barnhouse (pastor from 1927 to 1960) was known for his gifts as an evangelist. However, in 1949 he began his own

---

131. Bray, *Biblical Interpretation*, 376–423; Noll, *Criticism*, 90–121; Childs, *Biblical Theology*, 16.

132. Old, *Modern Age*, 763; Old, *Our Own Time*, 495; Edwards, *History*, 681; Bray, *Biblical Interpretation*, 376–423.

133. Old, *Modern Age*, 874–88; Stanley, *Diffusion*, 112–13; Chapman, "Anglican Evangelicals," 249.

expository series on Romans (broadcast on NBC radio for twelve years) while for over thirty years he conducted a Bible class in New York that drew attendances of over five hundred people per week. Before the age of television and Billy Graham, Barnhouse spoke to more hearers than any Protestant leader of his generation. Boice (pastor from 1968 to 2000) shared a passion for systematic expository preaching. Travelling widely, he preached in over thirty countries and published thirty expository commentaries on biblical books.[134] In a time when Norman Vincent Peale's therapeutic religion of *The Power of Positive Thinking* outsold every book in American homes but the Bible, and when even American preachers tired of the personality-driven preaching proliferating from coast to coast, Barnhouse and Boice's passion for biblical exposition and Reformed ideals instilled a new eagerness for biblical truth among the evangelical community.[135]

Notwithstanding the contribution of such notable practitioners, it was to the preaching of John R. W. Stott (1921–2011) that the revival of expository preaching owes its most significant debt in the postwar era. Stott was appointed Rector of All Soul's Langham Place in the heart of London in 1950. It was from here, on a single pastoral charge over several decades, that Stott's legacy emerged. Stott first made his mark as an evangelist in university missions across the world. His prolific writing in the Reformed tradition and growing leadership across the ministry platforms of world

---

134. Russell, "Donald G. Barnhouse," 33–57; Ryken et al., *Celebrating the Legacy*.

135. The history of American preaching had been varied. A form of exposition in the plain style was preserved in the Southern Baptist tradition by John Broadus (1827–95), a founding figure of the Southern Baptist Seminary (1877). Broadus published a homiletic textbook (echoing Charles Simeon) that aided in the selection and exposition of texts. It was used widely in Southern Baptist and evangelical seminaries into the mid-twentieth century. This was in marked contrast to the preaching that characterized the other major strand of American Protestantism (the "Great American School of Preaching"). Within this school, revivalists like Charles Finney (1792–1875) and D. L. Moody (1837–99) preached a simple message of conversion that gave little credence to liberal ideals. The other strand of this school was exemplified by H. W. Beecher (1813–87), P. Brooks (1835–93), H. E. Fosdick (1857–1954), and N. V. Peale (1898–1993). In an age of optimistic humanism and Romanticism, Beecher and Brooks promoted a homiletical theory that endowed the heroic personality of the preacher with an elevated status. They suggested the efficacy of Christian preaching lay not in its doctrine but in the living force of the preacher's soul brought to bear on the soul of the hearer. The preaching that followed in this tradition became culturally accommodationist and existentially positivist in tone. Such an approach characterized American preaching until it was punctuated by the likes of Barnhouse and Boice. The rise of conservative scholarship in seminaries like Westminster (Philadelphia), Gordon-Conwell (Boston), and Southern Baptist (Louisville) was also crucial in the rejuvenation of American Evangelicalism and the rise of American exposition from the 1940s. Old, *Modern Age*, 435–500, 530–79; Noll, *Criticism*, 93–97.

Evangelicalism also secured his place as the dominant intellectual and influencer for a rising generation of Christian leaders.[136] Like Lloyd-Jones, Stott favored sequential exposition as the engine of his ministry. However, Stott's preaching series were markedly shorter, more varied, and consistently evangelistic in intent. Similarly, while it was the English Puritans who so inspired Lloyd-Jones (seen in his tightly wound doctrinal-expository style) Stott's model derived from other homiletic streams. During his studies at Cambridge, Stott's involvement in the holiday camp ministry of his mentor E. J. H. Nash or "Bash" (an evangelical clergyman with the Scripture Union) was highly formative. It instilled in Stott a love for Scripture and a model of rhetorical "depth with simplicity" that endured across a long and significant ministry.[137] At Cambridge, leading figures of the Faculty of Divinity (notably C. H. Dodd and C. F. D Moule) also modelled for Stott a stimulating combination of biblical fidelity and academic rigor. However, by far the more lasting source of spiritual formation came via Stott's immersion in the CICCU. A number of elements combined to affect this influence. At Cambridge, Stott was introduced by a fellow student (Douglas Johnson, the first Secretary of the IVF) to the work of Charles Simeon. Stott later recalled that Simeon "was one of the greatest and most persuasive preachers

136. John Stott was born to the most privileged level of English society. As a boy Stott studied at Rugby (a prestigious English public school) before entering Trinity College in Cambridge. Recognizing a call to ministry, he transferred to Ridley Hall to study theology. He was ordained in 1945 and served as assistant at All Souls, Langham Place. Following the rector's (Harold Earnshaw-Smith) sudden death in 1950, Stott was appointed rector. He soon established in the middle of a city whose church attendance was lamentably poor, a large and expository ministry. Stott's initiative in reviving the "Eclectics" group of younger evangelicals was also significant. This led to the first *National Evangelical Anglican Congress* (NEAC) at Keele in 1967. In 2005 *Time Magazine* described Stott as "a touchstone of authentic biblical scholarship scarcely paralleled since the days of the 16th Century." Chapman, *Ambition*, 3–30; Dudley-Smith, *Leader*; *Global Ministry*; Old, *Own Time*, 460–80.

137. Nash's ministry among public schoolboys was motivated by a belief that such schools were the source of England's future leadership. He persevered in this ministry for thirty-five years. As a preacher Nash modelled depth with simplicity. The weekly talks at the holiday camps followed a careful rhythm. They moved from the problem of sin to the cross of Christ, seeking to sketch a simple outline of the Christian life. It was not expository preaching. They were "camp talks" in the English plain style. A Bible text adorned a three-point rhetorical structure. Then, as the week moved to a time of decision, the *ABC* of the Christian faith was implored. The camper should *Admit* their need; *Believe* Christ had died for them; and *Come*, for the remedy God provided was available for all. Among the seven thousand boys who passed through these camps were future headmasters, politicians, professionals, and numerous clergy. So Dudley-Smith, *Leader*, 137–50; Stott, "Counsellor and Friend," 57–65; Eddison, "Introduction," vii–ix; Interview with Richard Bewes, Rector Emeritus, All Soul's Langham Place, January 19, 2017.

the Church of England has ever known" whose "uncompromising commitment to Scripture captured [his] admiration and held it ever since."[138] While Stott would go on to conform Simeon's model to the preaching of passages rather than merely the preaching of texts, Simeon's practice of seeking *unity*, *perspicuity* and *simplicity* in sermon design and delivery became a hallmark of Stott's own developed approach.[139] The CICCU Saturday night Bible readings also formed the core of its spiritual life during this era. As British churches and student ministries began tasting the firstfruits of a postwar spiritual-exegetical renaissance, these weekly studies were well attended. In the 1940s these expository studies were held in colleges across the campus where a host of visiting clergy and Ridley ordinands would often speak.[140] However, by the early 1950s the Union Debating Chamber began to team with over four hundred weekly auditors for these Saturday night expositions (now centrally accommodated). Alongside the seasoned voices of Donald English (a Methodist titan), Ernest Kevin (then Principal of the London Bible College) and Alan Stibbs (then Vice Principal of Oak Hill College), many of the rising stars of British preaching filled the Union Chamber during these years of postwar buoyancy. Alongside Stott, who began preaching regularly, J. I. Packer (the future evangelical theologian), Alec Motyer (the future Old Testament scholar), Richard Bewes (the future Rector of All Soul's Langham Place), and Dick Lucas (the future Rector of St. Helen's Bishopsgate) were among the rising names apprenticed.[141] Alongside the Saturday evening "readings," Sunday evenings at Holy Trinity Cambridge also comprised the weekly evangelistic address. No less expository, these addresses were aimed to offer an exposition of the gospel to the many "unconverted" students in attendance. On behalf of the CICCU, Stott prepared a letter of invitation sent to all CICCU speakers, outlining the form of preaching they were requested to provide. While visiting preachers were given a degree of freedom to explore a range of topical or doctrinal interests (alongside the weekly *lectio continua* approach followed on Saturday evenings), a concern that the Sunday evening addresses should be evangelistic and expository was now the consistently expressed ideal.[142] Naturally, Stott and other emerging English expositors would begin to propel this expository revival beyond its nineteenth- and early twentieth-century

---

138. Dudley-Smith, *Leader*, 197–201; Stott, "Foreword," xxvii.

139. Simeon, *Horae Homileticae*, xv–xxi, 1–120.

140. Chapman, *Godly Ambition*, 25; Dudley-Smith, *Leader*, 197.

141. Interview with Richard Bewes, Rector Emeritus, All Soul's Langham Place, January 19, 2017; Dudley-Smith, *Leader*, 198.

142. Dudley-Smith, *Leader*, 199.

foundations in ways commensurate with their own unique strengths and abilities. Yet, when asked to identify the source of his own expository praxis in later years, the weekly Bible readings at the CICCU contained, for Stott, an early and significant homiletic ideal.[143]

In the exuberant postwar era, with a burgeoning air travel and communications revolution taking hold, Stott's ministry and the spread of expository preaching continued rapidly. Within this environment, leading figures like Stott were enabled to widen their influence through international preaching tours without significant disruption to the primary sphere of their ministry in the local church.[144] The rise of English as the preeminent language in world political and economic affairs was also a significant factor in the propagation of expository preaching. This smoothed the passage of proliferating IVF publishing materials and ensured a wide global readership for such exegetical and theological works. Moreover, in the climate of spiritual hunger and moral seriousness that followed in the wake of war, expository preaching (with its clear pronouncements on human nature and the explanatory power inherent in the clear unfolding of Scripture) began to resonate existentially for a generation seeking clarity and a semblance of hope in a fast-changing world. Such a mood was nowhere stronger than in the student world.[145] Consequently, as an Englishman, evangelical, and university evangelist, Stott found himself at the heart of three of the brightest spots in world Christianity. Missions in Cambridge and Oxford in 1952, 1954, and 1958 were some of the most successful in living memory. This was matched by a wave of significant university missions during the 1950s across Britain, North America, Australia, and South Africa.[146] Believing that the life of the mind and Christianity were not antithetical, Stott succeeded in offering tightly reasoned expositions of gospel truth, mixed with penetrating intellectual analysis.[147] His "plain unhurried Biblical exposition" mixed with strong gifts of concentration to forge a preaching that was considered clear

---

143. So Adam, "Fifty Years."

144. Chapman, *Godly Ambition*, 41; Stanley, *Diffusion*, 16.

145. Stanley, *Diffusion*, 19–22; Chapman, *Godly Ambition*, 33, 37–38; Judd and Cable, *Sydney Anglicans*, 262.

146. Nowhere outside Britain was Stott's influence more evident than in Australia, which he visited in 1958, 1965, 1971, 1979, 1981, 1986, and 2002. Australia became, for Stott, a context in which he felt particularly at home, on account of its evangelical rigor and close cultural correspondence. See Dudley-Smith, *Leader*, 376–419, 533; Chapman, *Ambition*, 33–35.

147. "Man with a Mission," *Varsity*, November 15, 1958, 4, cited in Chapman, *Ambition*, 34.

and arresting.[148] Indeed, combining the simplicity and conversionist ardor of the "Bash Camps" and Charles Simeon with the informed conservatism learned at Cambridge, the net effect of such influences was the development of an approach that wrapped the inner exegesis of the Continental Reformation in the congenial arrangement of the English plain style.[149]

In the 1970s, Stott's ministry shifted away from a settled pastoral charge toward the training, via the Langham Trust and the Lausanne Movement, of scholars in the Majority World.[150] This signaled a partial withdrawal from his role at the forefront of British ministry networks. Within this altered context it fell to another expositor, Dick Lucas (a preacher of no less renown), to pass the baton of expository preaching to the emerging generation of British clergy. Lucas arrived in 1961 as rector of the spacious, yet effectively empty St. Helen's Bishopsgate, in the heart of London's financial center. Through a lucid and compelling ministry of thirty-five years (1961–95), by the early 1990s St. Helen's had expanded to accommodate one thousand members across various family and student congregations. In the 1980s Lucas established a number of new instruments of evangelical communion aimed to advance biblical exposition across England. These included the Evangelical Minister's Assembly (1984), the Proclamation Trust (1986), and the Cornhill Training Course (1991). Such initiatives served to elevate Lucas to a position of preeminence in the development of expository

---

148. "Successful Week of University Missions," *Varsity*, November 15, 1952, 3, cited in Chapman, *Ambition*, 36.

149. Stott's homiletic approach condensed the theology of each passage under a lead idea, expounded within a three- or four-point rhetorical structure—including subdivisions, proofs, and a short peroration. Stott's sermons from the Keswick platform on Romans 5–8 (1965), 2 Timothy 1–4 (1969), Matthew 5–7 (1972), Ephesians 1–6 (1975), 1 Thessalonians 1–5 (1978), and 1 Corinthians 1–4 (2000) bear out this almost changeless rhetorical structure, as Stott works sequentially through the biblical sections under examination, encapsulating their ideas under a succinct rhetorical structure. Even his thematic Keswick studies "The Spirit in the Life of the Believer" and "The Lordship of Christ" display the same structure while grouping texts systematically. See Stott, *John Stott at Keswick*. Stott did not, however, confine his expositions solely to longer passages, contending that "all true Christian preaching is expository preaching ... Properly speaking, 'exposition' ... refers to the content of the sermon (biblical truth) rather than style (a running commentary). To expound Scripture is to bring out of a text what is there and expose it to view. The expositor prizes open what is closed, makes plain what is obscure, unravels what is knotted and unfolds what is tightly packed ... But the 'text' in question could be a verse, or a sentence, or even a single word. It could equally be a paragraph, or a chapter, or a whole book. Whether it is long or short, our responsibility as expositors is to open it up in such a way that it speaks its message clearly, plainly, accurately, relevantly, without addition, subtraction or falsification." Stott, *John Stott at Keswick*, 112.

150. Dudley-Smith, *Global Ministry*, 141–42, 371; Langham Partnership, "History."

preaching among a rising generation of British clergy.[151] While Lucas credited his own early preaching influences to the towering example of John Stott, Lucas himself developed a reputation for opening the Bible with prodigious skill. His preaching displayed the familiar hallmarks of English exposition. It exuded the simplicity and arrangement of Stott and Simeon's modified plain style. However, Lucas's delight in Scripture and his probing heuristic approach also produced a style that was constantly seeking for the surprises in familiar texts until the "puzzle" was "solved and the passage fell cleanly apart." Indeed, not only did Lucas's absorbing approach inspire a new generation to emulate the provocative orations of Britain's expository "Rembrandt," but the combined effect of Lucas's new preaching fellowships and forums strengthened the fellowship of evangelical clergy and preachers emerging in important pockets across the globe.[152]

The Rise of Australian Expository Preaching

The rise of expository preaching within Australian Evangelicalism owes much to these international developments. As it matured it also began to repay the investment it had received. In the postwar era the pan-evangelical preaching of Stott and Billy Graham precipitated a climate of growing pulpit confidence and a model of passionate and dignified oratory that gripped many young preaching aspirants. Graham was not an expositor in the mold of the emerging English school. Yet, in his dedication to Scripture and in the

---

151. Lucas was among the many English Christian leaders converted at the "Bash" camps. After serving with the Royal Navy during World War II and training for the ministry at Cambridge, Lucas served a curacy at St. Nicholas' Sevenoaks before a stint with the Church Pastoral Aid Society. Having developed a reputation as an effective leader of university missions and following a series of lunchtime addresses he had given in central London, Lucas was offered the incumbency of the large medieval church, St. Helen's at Bishopsgate. In an effort to reach the financial district, Lucas centered his work initially on weekday lunchtimes, when the city was busy. He hosted lunchtime services with a twenty-minute expository sermon. Soon, several lunchtime sessions had begun each week. By the 1970s St. Helen's was bursting under Lucas's preaching and that of his growing staff. Early preaching conferences developed into the *Evangelical Ministers Assembly* (1984). By the early 1990s the *EMA* had become a key rallying point for over one thousand ministers across Britain and hosted leading expositors from across the world. The founding of the *Proclamation Trust* (1986) saw the enterprise established on a firmer financial base. Noting the effect of Moore College on Australian Evangelicalism, in 1992 Lucas invited David Jackman to establish the *Cornhill Training Course* in London as an introductory theological and homiletic academy to train students from across the world. Interview with William Taylor, Rector of St. Helen's Bishopsgate, February 10, 2017; Adam, "Fifty Years"; Stott, *God's Voice*, 9–10; Green, "Preaching," 11–23.

152. Green, "Preaching," 12; Interview with Dick Lucas, January 20, 2017.

vast numbers who flocked to hear the American southerner preach, Graham lent significant strength to the rising biblical and expository mood.[153] Stott's 1958 Australian visit was also the first exposure many Australians received to the stimulating new climate of exposition and it supplied fuel for the expository flame.[154] The rise of critically aware scholarship at Moore College was also a significant catalyst for these developments. Principal D. B. Knox lamented that a rhetorical aptitude in mid-century Sydney sermons was not appreciably being matched by a corresponding depth in biblical content. Hence, he urged that a more "full-orbed" ministry that did not "shrink from declaring the whole counsel of God" should be elevated to a new prominence in the life of the church.[155] As a preacher, though lacking in oratorical finesse, Knox exuded the rigor of his own training at Oxford and Cambridge. He worked with the Greek text in hand and provided an extemporary translation and exposition. Indeed, while the college began to fill in this era with enthusiasts who had enrolled on account of the reputation of other faculty preachers, it was Knox who soon rose in their esteem to embody a preaching that was lucid and richly biblical.[156] The exegetical prowess of D. W. B. Robinson was no less significant. As an heir to the Cambridge tradition of C. H. Dodd and C. F. D. Moule, Robinson became a leading figure in the rise of critically informed exegesis in the Australian church. His stimulating approach imparted to students the disciplines of self-directed learning and a confidence in their exegetical judgments.[157] Some believed Robinson's lectures and preaching were, at times, indistinguishable. Hence, as college graduates began earthing the training they had received, they forged their own praxis, both in appreciation of and in reaction to, exemplars like Robinson.[158] Older practitioners of the plain style,

---

153. Stanley, *Diffusion*, 16; Old, *Own Time*, 61–63. Graham's ministry will be the subject of discussion in later chapters.

154. During this visit Stott briefed Moore College students on the work of *All Souls* and led missions across a host of universities. Dudley-Smith, *Leader*, 533–34; Loane, "Reaching Out," 89–91.

155. Knox, "Priority of Preaching," in Birkett, *Selected Works, Vol. II*, 239; Knox, "Let the Word Do It," in Birkett, *Selected Works, Vol. II*, 233.

156. Cameron, *Enigmatic Life*, 133; Dickey, "Knox, David Broughton," 206; Interview with Rev. Dr. P. F. Jensen, December 2, 2016.

157. Shiner, "Appreciation," 9–62; Cameron, *Enigmatic Life*, 137; Interview with Rev. Dr. P. F. Jensen, December 2, 2016.

158. Interview with Rev. Dr. Paul Barnett, December 2, 2016. Notwithstanding the perceived oratorical weaknesses of Robinson's preaching, others, like Broughton Knox (who preached on the occasion of Robinson's consecration as bishop) declared his belief that Robinson was the "greatest biblical exegete in the world." Interview with Dr. Bruce Ballantine-Jones, February 14, 2017. Others such as the Rev. Dr. Peter O'Brien,

like Marcus Loane, lamented an apparent dryness as some younger clergy made heavy work of the expository style. Their preaching became "dry as dust," he suggested, "fell flat," and was "too dull for words."[159] Nevertheless, the discipline matured rapidly.

Mirroring the growth of the expository model overseas, such developments in scholarship and exegesis soon began to be reflected in preaching across a swathe of Sydney pulpits. St. Barnabas's Anglican Church on Broadway was one of the first to practice the new model of exposition. The church's young rector and future New Testament scholar, Paul Barnett (1963–1973), set a leading example by adopting a *lectio continua* program.[160] Barnett applied formidable intellect and precision to such expositions. Moreover, as a growing student church (with links to Sydney University), St. Barnabas exercised a strong influence upon a generation of young minds, including Anglican ordinands and diocesan lay members. These, in turn, carried an appetite for exposition to other churches they later joined.[161] In the early 1960s, the future Sydney bishops John Reid and Donald Cameron also offered expository leadership in various contexts. Incorporating a *lectio continua* approach into the rhythm of their parochial ministries, they became early and admirable models of the rising homiletic school.[162] Dudley Foord, rector of Sydney's Kingsgrove Parish (1960–65) and Moore College Dean of Students (1965–72), also played a leading role. A man of gifted oratory, Foord had served as an assistant missioner at John Stott's 1958 Sydney University Mission and successfully led student missions of his own across Australia in the 1950s and 1960s. In 1963, Foord was sponsored by the Australian IVF

Vice-Principal of Moore College (1985–2000) regarded Robinson as the exegete par excellence: "He had this ability to trace a line straight through a passage to get to the very heart of it." Interview with Peter O'Brien, March 17, 2003, cited in Cameron, *Enigmatic Life*, 231; *Sydney Yearbook*, 2015, 301–2.

159. Loane, "Foreword," v.

160. Interview with Rev. Dr. Paul Barnett, December 2, 2016; Sydney Diocesan 2015 *Yearbook*, 255.

161. Interview with Rev. Dr. Peter Jensen, December 2, 2016; Cameron, *Enigmatic Life*, 231.

162. By the close of his incumbency at Sydney's Gladesville Parish (1956–69) John Reid (Bishop of South Sydney, 1969–93) had preached sequentially through a large number of biblical books. Reid later became chairman of the Katoomba Christian Convention (1971–76) where he championed expository preaching. He also played a key role in the Lausanne Movement and was a key influencer in the movement for diocesan reform. Interview with John Chapman, *Cornhill College*, 2009. Donald Cameron (Federal Secretary of CMS 1965–72 and Bishop of North Sydney 1983–90) also began to employ an expository model as Rector at Bellevue Hill (1963–65) and became a champion of exposition via the St. Andrew's House Bible Studies and College of Preachers. Interview with Donald Howard, February 17, 2017; Sydney *Yearbook 2015*, 265, 308.

(AFES) to assess other student ministries in parts of Asia. This was followed in 1966 by similar tours across Europe and the United Kingdom where he forged fresh links with Stott and the ministry of All Soul's Langham Place. These visits were formative for Foord and exposed the diocese, via his influence, to pockets of leading thought and expository practice across the world.[163] With a growing reputation as a preacher of substance and rhetorical agility, John Chapman also joined the wave of expository pioneers as a preacher at key forums on the Sydney ministry calendar. Though still serving as Youth Director of the Armidale diocese, Chapman's expositions of 1 Thessalonians at the 1963 Moore College retreat bore the fruit of intensive study. He was described by a participant as a man "anointed by the Spirit" and with "a great capacity to analyze and present the text." These studies left "an indelible impression upon all who were there."[164] Likewise, preaching at the 1963 annual service for the CMS League of Youth in St Andrew's Cathedral, Chapman's exposition was remembered as "larger than life and the impact of his presence was memorable."[165] Hence, at the dawn of the 1960s a coterie of Sydney clergy began to harness the rising expository mood. Aligned with shifts in scholarship and exegesis developing in key pockets across the globe, this produced a kind of preaching that offered a subtle departure from the rhythm of the older plain style.

An Expository Tipping Point

Notwithstanding these developments, it was the 1965 visit of John Stott to the CMS Summer School in Katoomba that represented a defining moment in the movement toward a culture of exposition and which captured the imagination of a new generation of Sydney clerical leaders.[166] Stott's exposi-

---

163. Foord had run two highly successful missions at the University of New England, in Armidale, in the early 1960s. In 1963 and 1966 (when newly appointed as Dean of Students at Moore College) Foord had investigated student work in Indonesia, India, Nepal, Afghanistan, Germany, and the United Kingdom. This was followed by missions in Perth, Adelaide, and Brisbane, and an array of missions in over thirty-five countries between 1960 and 1980, predominantly in Asia and the Middle East. Interview with Elizabeth Foord, November 11, 2016; Dudley-Smith, *Leader*, 401n66; Piggin, *Spirit*, 135.

164. Interview with Donald Howard, February 17, 2017; Howard, "Blood, Sweat and Tears," 131–41.

165. Interview with Dr. Bruce Ballantine-Jones, February 14, 2017.

166. Some conjecture exists around the dating of Stott's visit. Michael Orpwood (Chapman's biographer) records the visit as occurring in 1958. So Orpwood, *Chappo*, 79. This dating is followed by Jensen, *Apology*, 59. Dudley-Smith, *Leader*, 398 locates Stott in Australia in 1958 for the *Intervarsity Fellowship* missions in Sydney and

tions in 2 Corinthians were entitled "We Do Not Lose Heart." They had been delivered previously at *All Soul's* (subsequently published in the *Bible Speaks Today* series) and were considered by Sydney clergy to be "monumental . . . they were breathtakingly good."[167] By now a well-travelled and polished orator, Stott's "meticulous preparation . . . flawless diction [and] persuasive logic,"[168] as well as his "clear" and "moving" delivery,[169] mixed seamlessly with his gifts in arrangement, exegesis, and application to produce sermons that were considered "masterful."[170] His preaching held listeners enthralled as he "illumined the text" of Scripture in a way that "few had ever heard taught so clearly."[171] For Sydney listeners he therefore embodied an approach that had been eagerly aspired to, but was now demonstrated in an accessible and transferrable way.[172] Chapman himself noted of Stott's method: "I was so taken by the way he stuck to the text and stayed with it. He could show you the logic of the argument *in* the Scriptures and how that passage fitted into an overall argument *from* the Scriptures." The immediate effect was to inspire a fresh belief that this was the way in which all regular biblical preaching ought to be done.[173] Having heard Stott, many young clergy, including Chapman, now declared that they finally "understood what Broughton [Knox] had been talking about." So, Chapman "went home, burned all [his] sermons and started again."[174] Stott's watershed 1965 visit was soon given further currency in the Sydney context with the establishment by Synod ordinance of the *College of Preachers* (1970).[175] This was

---

Melbourne. However, the 1965 date is confirmed by Holt, "Preaching," 79, who cites minutes from the CMS NSW Summer School Committee which records the visit (and 2 Corinthians sermons) occurring in 1965. Geoff Fletcher served as CMS NSW General Secretary (1955–64) and had recently revived its Summer School. With a keen interest in congregations as centers for mission (a key focus of Stott's *All Soul's* ministry), Fletcher is likely responsible for extending the preaching invitation to Stott. See Cole, *History*, 227–29.

167. Interview with John Chapman, *Cornhill Training College*, 2009.
168. Loane, "Reaching Out," 89–91, 90.
169. Lucas, "Helpless with Laughter," 45, 47.
170. Jensen, *Apology*, 60.
171. Hunt and Hunt, "Double Portion," 99–103.
172. Holt, "Preaching," 80; Adam, "Fifty Years." Note Stott's transferable model articulated in Stott, *I Believe in Preaching*, 196–246.
173. Chapman to Orpwood, January 15, 1994, BDM Box 1, SDA; Adam, "Fifty Years."
174. This is Chapman's recollection of his response to hearing Stott in 1965. Interview with Phillip Jensen, February 16, 2017.
175. Synod Resolution 10/1970, "College of Preachers," *1972 Sydney Diocesan Yearbook*, 350.

a development in which John Chapman and Dudley Foord played a leading role.[176] Viewing with interest the recent establishment of such a college in the Anglican Communion in Britain and America, the inaugural committee were charged with establishing a parallel work in Sydney. Its purpose was to "furnish instruction, encouragement and stimulation to ministers engaged in the task of preaching," and to see that "competent and comprehensive" training was given to clergy in their formative years.[177] The first *College of Preachers* conference was held at Moore College on November 7–10, 1970. Its program consisted of a) seminars on "Getting at the Text of the Bible"; b) workshops on sermon preparation; c) a "Preacher's Laboratory" with the help of "videotape equipment"; and d) seminars on communicating with Australians today. The second *College of Preachers* conference was held at Gilbulla (a conference center in Sydney's south-west) during July 2–5, 1973. It invited experts in their field as communicators, like the Rev. Alan Walker (Central Methodist Mission), the Rev. Bruce Wilson (University of NSW), Mr. Allan Craddock (University of Sydney) and Mr. Clifford Warne (Church of England Television Society) to convey aspects of communication and preaching theory to the clergy delegates. Teaching aids included video facilities for sermon review, alongside workshops in which techniques of sermon preparation could now be applied.[178]

Chapman and Foord were leading figures in the college's early period. To assist in the development of expository practice (the committee's foremost priority) alongside the daily keynote addresses, a weekly program was

---

176. Chapman and Foord were members of the inaugural College of Preachers committee and had played a leading role in persuading the Sydney Synod of the merits of such homiletic training. Interview with Phillip Jensen, February 16, 2017.

177. The council was convened under the chairmanship of Bishop A. J. Dain (succeeded by Bishop J. R. Reid in 1973), and included the Revs. J. Chapman, D. Foord, A. Blanch, B. Burgess, R. Goodhew, D. Hewetson, G. Robinson, B. Smith, P. Watson, and D. Wilson. The college's founding ordinance stipulated: thirty men per session of the college were to be trained; i) ten men by invitation from the council, ii) the remainder in equal proportions between the third and sixth years of ordination, as well as others who may apply. See Resolution 10/1970, "College of Preachers," *Sydney Yearbook 1972*, 351. The British *College of Preachers* was established in 1960 under Donald Coggan's initiative (Archbishop of Canterbury, 1974–80, author of *Stewards of Grace*, 1958). As a conduit for the practice of exposition it had received over one thousand applications before 1970. Davies, *English Preaching*, 195–96; Stott, *Preaching*, 31. Dudley Foord's connections with English preaching networks in the 1960s likely forged the initial connection with the college. The Sydney Council were then able to request information for the purposes of establishing a similar college in Sydney. Resolution 10/1970. The *College of Preachers* in the United States was established under the Episcopalian Dr. Theodore Wedel in 1939 at the Washington Cathedral. Edwards, *History*, 682.

178. Report of the Standing Committee 1972, 4/1971 "College of Preachers," *1973 Sydney Diocesan Yearbook*.

designed to assist clergy in developing *lectio continua* series on biblical books. Every clergyman thus left the conference with an expository series well in train.[179] As the college grew, aided by the input of Sydney's own emerging expositors (like Chapman, Foord, Reid, Alan Cole, Graeme Goldsworthy, D. W. B. Robinson, and D. B. Knox), the college also welcomed such international evangelical luminaries as Don Carson, Dick Lucas, Harold Ockenga, and Stott. The keynote addresses repeatedly emphasized both the theology *and* praxis of preaching. The importance of the preacher's spiritual life and motivation was also emphasized.[180] As a result, the college fast became a yearly rallying point for clerical inspiration and an effective vehicle for the transformation of pulpit ministry.[181] Indeed, alongside the championing of the merits of exposition via diocesan media channels, after a decade of the college's influence over the Sydney Anglican and wider evangelical network, many clergy increasingly struggled to remember a time when expository preaching had not been the assumed and normative homiletic ideal.[182]

Conventions and Bible Forums

Following Stott's landmark 1965 visit and the rise of the College of Preachers, a host of other key channels influenced the expository shift in pulpit

179. Interview with John Chapman, *Cornhill Training College*, 2009.

180. Keynote papers at the college included such topics as: "Firing up the Preacher" (Denis Ryan), "Planning the Preaching Program" (Allan Blanch), "Exegesis" (Graeme Goldsworthy), "Expository Preaching" (Alan Cole), "Gospel Preaching Every Sunday" (John Chapman), and "The Theology of the Preached Word" (Donald Robinson and Dr. Don Carson). Edwards, "Romance," 39; Howard, *Preach or Perish*, ix, 1, 9, 17, 95, 131, 137, 273, 289. The 1987 *College of Preachers*, for example, covered the keynote topics of: The Preacher and His God; The Preacher and His Planning; The Preacher and the World; The Preacher and His Preparation; The Preacher in Action; Teaching through Preaching; Making Sermons Relevant; Use and Abuse of the Voice. See "1987 Report of the Standing Committee," *Sydney Yearbook* 1987, 349.

181. Edwards, "Romance," 39.

182. Interview with John Chapman, *Cornhill Training College*, 2009. Expository sermon "skeletons" began to appear in the Sydney Diocesan Magazine *Southern Cross* (SC) from the late 1960s. See: Reid, "Son's Sacrifice," 8–9, on Eph 2:11–12; "Spirit's Work," 12–13, on Eph 4:7–24, 5:15–20; "Believer's Love," 27–28, on Eph 3:14–19, 5:1–21; "Water Turned into Wine," 8, on John 2:1–11; "Boy Restored," 14, on John 4:46–54; "Romans 8," 19–20; O'Brien, "Freedom from Death," 15–17; Jensen, "Four Psalms," 13–14, on Pss 50, 55, 38, 90; Reid, "Ephesians," 13–17; Oliver, "Studies in Titus," 13–16; Turner, "Paul's Letter," 15–18; Hill, "Theological Fabric," 13–15; Woodhouse, "Gigantic Mercy," 15–17; Dawson, "Duties and Responsibilities," 13, 23; Cole, "Songs from the Heart," 14–15; Vitnell, "God's Actions," 14–15; Blake, "Letter to Jude," 14; Barnett, "2 Corinthians 4–5," 14–15; Hewetson, "Four Parables from Luke," 15–16, 21; Halls, "Advent," 13; Howell, "Isaiah," 16, 21–22; Webb, "Wisdom: Part 1," 26; "Wisdom: Part 2," 26–27.

culture. The revitalization of the Katoomba Christian Convention (KCC) under the chairmanship of John Reid (1971–76) and Phillip Jensen (1983–91) played a significant role in this process. Historically, the convention was shaped by a spiritual piety modelled on the English Keswick Convention and had welcomed a succession of international and local preachers since its founding in 1903.[183] In the familiar cadences of the plain style, Katoomba speakers had typically explored the convention's "Keswick-style" agenda of the cultivation of inner piety, and were given wide latitude to select material they believed would develop such aims.[184] However, by the early 1970s, this once successful formula began to tire. An ageing constituency and a shifting social mood saw attendances falling as even the most committed participants grew weary of the convention's seemingly "stale, tired and repetitive" approach. A review of the convention formula under the leadership of John Reid opened the way for its revitalization under Phillip Jensen in the 1970s. Influenced by the example of his own expository mentors (like Knox, Robinson, and Chapman) and the growing reception of expository practice among other contemporary ministries (such as the CMS Summer School and his own expanding ministry interests), Jensen aspired to see the word of God taught seriously for a new generation.[185]

The inaugural Katoomba Youth Convention (1974) saw the beginnings of change. Held over the Australia Day long weekend (January 25–28), six hundred delegates heard a series of compelling expositions from a trio of international and Australian figures.[186] In the pursuit of a revitalized format, the conference continued to shift from its earlier focus on the cultivation of inner piety toward the opening of Scripture for the concerns of a modern world. Speakers were allocated Bible passages or entire biblical books from which to examine a range of contemporary themes.[187] Sermon outlines were provided, and delegates were urged to avail themselves of the opportunity

---

183. See Braga, *Katoomba*, 5, 70–2; Bebbington, *Evangelicalism*, 179.

184. The convention's aim, like its parent, was to further the "deepening of spiritual life" through prayer, reverent Bible study, teaching on personal holiness, and foreign missions. Katoomba speakers organized their material around a program of Monday: The Fact of Sin in the Regenerate Life; Tuesday: The Way of Victory; Wednesday: The Fullness of the Holy Spirit; Thursday: The Call to Surrender; Friday: The Challenge for Service; Saturday: Missionary Day. Braga, *Katoomba*, 70, 81, 141.

185. Braga, *Katoomba*, 127–29, 131–33.

186. The 1974 speakers were Dick Lucas (Rector of St. Helen's Bishopsgate in London), the Rev. Dr. Stuart Barton Babbage (Master of New College, UNSW), and the Rev. Bruce Smith (Lecturer at Moore College). See Braga, *Katoomba*, 134.

187. Themes included: "Getting to Know God," "Preparing for What Future?," "Holiness: The Art of Being Different," "Top Priority—Seek First the Kingdom," and "Seeing the World God's Way." See Braga, *Katoomba*, 138–39.

for serious Bible study. So positive was the reception of the new expository format, aided by a surge of youthful energy and skillful convention planning, that by 1984 attendances had risen to more than four thousand. The 1988 Bicentennial Convention saw six thousand young people fill the largest tent in Australia. With another six thousand attending in 1989, the need to diversify the number and size of convention meetings and to expand the conference facilities became pressing.[188] Growing rapidly to become one of the largest stages available to an Australian preacher, alongside an exposure to leading international expositors, the convention also became an effective platform from which to showcase the best of Australia's expository talent.[189] Now a regular speaker across Australia's largest evangelical platforms, the familiar figure of John Chapman occupied the convention platform more than most. From 1974, Chapman was a member of the Katoomba speaker's panel twenty times.[190] Never more at home than in crowds of Katoomba's size, Chapman played to such crowds like a musician to his instrument. He was considered by conference organizers to be clear and dependable, while adaptable and engaging. With a humorous lightness of touch mixed with an unyielding spiritual seriousness, Chapman offered numerous expository sermon series that became significant turning points for many listeners and future clergy.[191] Chapman's good humor and adaptability were also important aids to his appeal. When the power went out in the Big Tent

---

188. By 2003 twenty-eight thousand annual delegates attended a range of diversified Katoomba Conventions (Men's, Women's, Youth, and Training forums) from Sydney and across the wider network of Australian Evangelicalism. See Braga, *Katoomba*, 138–52.

189. Of the speakers at the Katoomba Youth Convention from the 1970s to 2000 more than seventy-five percent were Sydney Anglicans. Prominent international speakers included Don Carson, Frank Retief, Dick Dowsett, and David Jackman. The most prominent of the Australians included: John Chapman, 1977, 1979, 1981, 1984, 1986, 1988, 1997; David Cook, 1983, 1988, 1995, 2000; John Woodhouse, 1990, 1994; Phillip Jensen, 1983, 1988, 1992, 1996, 2000; David Short, 1989, 1997; Mike Raiter, 1989, 1993, 1999; Ian Powell, 1990; Peter Jensen and Simon Manchester, 1991; Alan Stewart, 1993; Peter Adam, 1995, 2000. KCC, "Resources." Appendix 5, *Historical Speaking Engagements*.

190. Chapman had also spoken at CMS Summer School NSW in 1974, 1975, 1976, 1977, 1980, 1982, 1991; CMS Summer School Queensland in 1981, 2009; CMS Summer School Tasmania, 1978; CMS Missions Conference Paris, 2004; and Belgrave Heights Convention in 1978, 1979, 1988, 2003. Appendix 5, *Historical Speaking Engagements*; Braga, *Katoomba*, 141.

191. Mark Thompson (the future Principal of Moore College) assessed Chapman's Katoomba preaching in the 1980s as being a significant turning point in his grasp of Scripture. Similarly, Tony Payne (the future Director of Matthias Media) recalls Chapman's 1980s Katoomba addresses on "Holiness" as like tonic to a thirsty soul. So Thompson, "Reflection"; Interview with Tony Payne, November 29, 2016.

in the 1980s, with a humorous touch and by sheer force of oratory, Chapman made himself heard to a crowd of five thousand with apparent ease. This secured Chapman's place as an important fixture of the convention's revitalized approach.[192] The combined effect of the convention's renaissance was to amplify expository practice (as well as evangelical conviction) among the many clergy, churches, and student ministries from which the convention drew.[193] Indeed, leading expositors who filled the convention platform in the 1980s and 1990s (like John Woodhouse, Phillip Jensen, and Simon Manchester) had also begun to establish large and vibrant congregations in suburban Sydney, aided in large measure by the rigorous exposition of Scripture.[194] Similarly, many of those who would fill the theological colleges of Sydney to capacity in the 1990s and 2000s (especially Moore College, Sydney Missionary Bible College, and the Baptist Morling College) were, in many cases, the same participants who had eagerly thronged to fill Katoomba's enormous "Big Tent" in the 1980s.[195]

Alongside the renaissance of the Katoomba platform, the pioneering of a fresh Bible teaching ministry in the heart of the city of Sydney (the "City Lunchtime Bible Talks") was another important contributor to the growing appetite for biblical exposition. Previously, a smaller Bible study for

192. Jensen and Freney, "Majoring on the Majors"; Interview with Alan Stewart, December 7, 2016.

193. Interview with Tony Payne, November 29, 2016; Braga, *Katoomba*, 152.

194. Apprenticed under John Chapman in 1973–74, the Rev. Phillip Jensen began a significant ministry as Chaplain to the UNSW and Rector of St. Matthias' Centennial Park (1975–2003). On a diet of expository preaching and searching social analysis, by 2003 the parish had become the largest Anglican ministry in Australia. It boasted three thousand weekly congregants across multiple ethnic, family, and student congregations. Jensen also pioneered a host of supporting ministries including Matthias Media, the Ministry Training Strategy (responsible for inspiring hundreds of graduates toward vocational ministry), and supplied impetus for a church planting movement in the 1990s. *Sydney Yearbook* 2015, 288; Ballantine-Jones, "Political Factor," 54. The Rev. Dr. John Woodhouse was a lecturer in Old Testament at Moore College (1982–91), Rector of Christ Church St. Ives Anglican (1991–2002), and Principal of Moore College (2002–13). Under Woodhouse's expository ministry at St. Ives the congregation swelled to boast one of the largest youth and university ministries in the diocese. As a large "sending ministry," the suburban St. Ives congregation populated churches across Sydney's North Shore as well as Moore College with well-trained and highly biblically literate congregation members and ordinands. *Sydney Yearbook*, 2015, 324. The Rev. Simon Manchester (previously a curate under Dick Lucas at St. Helen's Bishopsgate) became Rector at St. Thomas' North Sydney in 1990. From a dispirited base the congregation grew to be the largest Anglican Church on Sydney's Lower North Shore and played a role in revitalizing numerous other ailing local churches. A committed expositor, Manchester became a regular speaker on Sydney preaching platforms and a regular preacher on Sydney Christian radio. *Sydney Yearbook*, 2015, 204.

195. Jensen, *Apology*, 63; Braga, *Katoomba*, 136.

employees of St. Andrew's House had been conducted in the 1960s by Geoff Fletcher (former director, DOE). During the 1950s, the Cathedral Luncheon Club had also been a prominent vehicle for public Christian engagement. However, it had primarily assayed current events and missionary news on its platform, as opposed to the public exposition of Scripture.[196] In 1969, Chapman and John Reid (now in prominent leadership roles at St. Andrew's House) jointly perceived an opportunity to begin an expository ministry to city workers. Inspired by the example of such ministries in other contexts (like the lunchtime ministry at St. Helen's Bishopsgate), Chapman and Reid sought to develop a series of "Lunchtime Bible Encounters" to which Christians *and* non-Christians could "Come, Eat and Enjoy."[197] The first series (July–September 1969) began in the Cathedral's lower chapter house. It showcased the preaching of John Reid (Ezekiel 1–47), Dr. John Painter (Luke 8–19), and John Chapman (Galatians 1–6) and was well received. The second lunchtime series (February–May 1970) examined Genesis 11–22, Psalms and Amos 1–8, and saw "hundreds" now enthusiastically attending.[198] Recorded and distributed by the Anglican Radio Unit, these studies grew in appeal and soon welcomed other Sydney preachers to the platform. Their popularity was such that by 1978 parallel lunchtime forums had been established in five other city locations and drew combined audiences of several hundred per week.[199] Seeing the value of the lunchtime forums in aiding Christian growth and evangelism, during the 1980s the Department of Evangelism, under Chapman, committed additional resources to the initiative. Such heightened planning and promotion saw the lunchtime "Bible Talks" further establish themselves as a popular fixture in the rhythm of evangelical city ministry.[200] In 1991, the lunchtime "Bible Talks" were incorporated under the new name of the "City Bible Forum." This grew from a partnership between Chapman's successor at the Department of Evangelism

---

196. A sample of the speakers at the Cathedral Luncheon Club included (*inter-alia*) the cricketer, Mr. W. A. Oldfield, "Last Test Series"; Dr. Howard Guinness, addressing a film on the recent "Ampol Trial"; Mr. O. D. O'Berg, "Call to Personal Service"; Rt. Rev. Alfred Stanway, "Africa Today"; Mr. B. Chaseling on "Overland to London"; Rev. Alan Walker, on "Discoveries on Both Sides"; Reid to Orpwood, BDM Box 1, SDA.

197. *Southern Cross*, October 1969, 16, 21; Reid to Orpwood, BDM Box 1; BDM Newsletter, August 1976.

198. Reid, Painter, and Chapman preached the second series of expositions as well. *Southern Cross*, October 1969, 16, 21.

199. Lunchtime Bible talks were established by 1978 at St. Andrew's Cathedral, St. James's Phillip Street, Scotts Presbyterian York Street, St. Philip's Anglican York Street, St. Thomas's North Sydney. BDM Prayer Letter, no. 3, August 1978.

200. BDM Prayer Letter, November 81–January 82; BDM Prayer Letter, May–July 1984; BDM Prayer Letter February–April 1995.

(David Mansfield) and others with a desire to reach city workers. The City Bible Forum subsequently expanded the lunchtime format into a group of ministries with a branch in every state capital across Australia. Despite such diversification, the ministry remained committed to the evangelistic-expository intentions of its earlier beginnings. It sought to make "the discussion of life's challenges and of the Bible as accessible as possible," and continued to be an effective vehicle for reaching thousands of Australians within and outside the boundaries of denominational Christianity.[201] While Chapman remained somewhat removed from these later developments, his pioneering initiative in the lunchtime Bible studies was nevertheless considered a "major contribution to the life of the city," and his engaging expositions impacted an entire generation of city workers.[202]

Student and Regional Missions

Alongside these various expository initiatives, the birth of the modern AFES movement (Australian Fellowship of Evangelical Students) and a revived culture of student missions in the late 1970s assisted the rise of expository preaching across wide segments of the Australian evangelical movement. Mirroring the rise of the InterVarsity Fellowship worldwide, the AFES had developed following the 1930 visit of Dr. H. W. Guinness (the first travelling secretary of the IVF) who energized students with a fervent gospel message and an ardent Christian enthusiasm.[203] By 1958, approximately two thousand students were involved with the Australian movement, and the celebrated 1958 mission of John Stott to various Australian universities crowned a decade of energetic student witness that echoed the growth of the movement worldwide.[204] The "long 1960s,"[205] however, were a time of intellectual and social ferment on Australian university campuses, just as they were within Australian society at large. Within this climate, the confident 1950s culture of student missions began to attenuate.[206] In the mid-1970s,

---

201. See City Bible Forum; *Preaching Christ Newsletter*, August–October 1994, 15; *Preaching Christ Newsletter*, February–April 1995.

202. John Reid to Michael Orpwood, BDM Box 1, SDA; Cook, "Chappo."

203. Braga, "Guinness, Howard Wyndham," 140–42; AFES, "History."

204. *Sydney University Evangelical Union, Member's Handbook*, 1979. Box 15, Adrian Lane Papers, 23–26; Dudley-Smith, *Leader*, 398–402.

205. See chapter 1 for definition and discussion of this defining decade. Cf. McLeod, *Religious Crisis*, 1–15.

206. Sporadic and smaller student initiatives had continued during the 1960s. However, widespread student apathy and a decline in student involvement had resulted in only limited public missions on university campuses since the halcyon era of the 1950s.

support for a revival of public-style missions gathered pace, particularly among the leadership of the Sydney University Evangelical Union (SUEU), the largest of the campus ministries. While uncertainty lingered about the most effective approach to pursue, a return to a public-style mission was agreed by the SUEU leadership, to be held in July 1977.[207] The speakers selected were the now well-known Chapman, alongside the rising New Testament scholar (and previously rector of St. Barnabas's Broadway), Paul Barnett. Energetic planning preceded the mission. This included extensive counsellor training and a wide publicity program to engage the student body.[208] A seven-session program was also envisaged in which a series of expository and apologetic addresses would develop a portrait of the person of Christ while demonstrating elements of the gospel's intellectual and historical credibility.[209] To secure maximum engagement in the marketplace of student ideas, three of the seven addresses were to be delivered on the university front lawn. Stretching before the university's historic sandstone quadrangle and beside the modern Fisher Library, the front lawn represented the university's "town square." Here students rallied and defended their cherished causes, beliefs, and ideals. The unpredictability of such a forum excited but also unsettled Chapman and Barnett.[210] However, when a crowd of more than one thousand gathered for the opening front-lawn encounter and a cordial tone attended the question time, such fears were allayed. Attendances remained heightened across the seven-day mission initiative and a detailed program of follow-up began the nurture of the many students who had newly committed to Christian faith.[211]

SUEU Handbook, 24–26; Hilliard, "Sixties," 99–117. See chapter 1 for discussion on "secularization."

207. Macintyre, *Concise History*, 231–38; "Report of the SUEU Mission. 29 June–7 July 1977," Box 1, Adrian Lane Papers, 1–2.

208. *SUEU Handbook* 1979, 28; "Report of the SUEU Mission, 1977," 1–13.

209. The mission program (themed "Go Back, You're Going the Wrong Way") was as follows: June 29, Chapman and Barnett on front lawn, "Jesus: Other than Ordinary?"; June 30, Chapman in Carslaw Lecture Theatre (CLT), "Man or God? Rediscover Jesus"; July 1, Chapman and Barnett on front lawn, "Who Does Jesus Think He Is?"; July 4, Barnett in CLT, "People in Rebellion—Where Do You Stand in Relation to God?"; July 5, "Your Chance to Speak: Are You Prepared to Stand Up for What You Think?" An opportunity to question Chapman and Barnett; July 6, Chapman in CLT, "Why Should You Go Back?" (Chapman preached from Acts 17:16–34); July 7, Barnett in CLT, "It's the Real Thing? What Being a Christian Is All About." See "Report of the SUEU Mission, 1977," 3–4, 7, 9–11; Appendix 3, JCCPPHW6, HW9.

210. Chapman to Lane, March 21, 1987. Box 3, Adrian Lane Papers; Interview with Rev. Dr. Paul Barnett, December 2, 2016.

211. "Report of the SUEU Mission. June 29–July 7, 1977," 7–10; Macintyre, *Concise History*, 226.

The unexpected success of the 1977 mission had numerous consequences. Not least was the renewal of a culture of involvement among Christian students as the mission was planned and run. The clarity of the expositions alongside an interactive mission format also imparted a renewed confidence in the gospel's ability to stand credibly in the public square. As news of the mission's success reached the 1978 AFES National Conference, other student groups were emboldened to organize and run such public missions. The net effect was a wave of student missions in Sydney and across the nation in subsequent years.[212] A mission at the University of NSW in August 1978 invited Chapman and Barnett to deliver a two-week program of expositions. Entitled "Cross-Talk," a similar mix of public events alongside seminars and dialogue forums marked the central approach.[213] In 1980, John Chapman and Phillip Jensen were invited to speak at the jubilee mission of the Sydney University EU. A slogan of "No Christ, No Life. Know Christ, Know Life" examined the double-edged nature of the Christian gospel.[214] Conducted in the largest lecture theatre on the university campus, capacity crowds created an energy in each of the mission events. Indeed, Jensen's address on "sexuality" was so enthusiastically received that a local newspaper wryly headed their bulletin "God Got More Than Gough." This was on account of the crowd which eclipsed a parallel gathering to host the former Prime Minister, Gough Whitlam, on campus that day.[215] Similar initiatives (many featuring Chapman as the lead speaker) at the University of Sydney and UNSW (1981), Macquarie University (1982, 1985), and New England University (1983) saw the fine-tuning of the student-missions approach. As a result, thousands of students were engaged with the claims of Christ during a season of heightened mission activity. This in turn gave impetus to the rise of evangelical university ministries across the nation, fed on a diet of Bible exposition.[216]

---

212. "Report of the Evangelistic Mission"; Box 1, Adrian Lane Papers; Prince and Prince, *Out of the Tower*, 65–66.

213. Chapman addressed students from: John 3, "Eternal Life, Be in It"; 1 Thess 1:9–10, "Will the True Christian Stand Up?"; Luke 12:13–20, "A Successful Life?"; Luke 9:28–36, "More Than a Carpenter"; "Jesus, Who Does He Think He Was?" Appendix 3, JCCPPHW1, HW4, HW8; HW9, HW10; BDM Prayer Letter November 1978; BDM Prayer Letter August 1978.

214. Chapman preached from John 4, "Christ and Life's Satisfaction"; John 9, "Christ and Life's Direction"; John 10, "Christ and Real Life"; John 11, "Christ and Life Forever." Jensen examined the Bible's teaching on work, sex, leisure, and death. See "Report: SUEU Mission 29 June–11 July 1980," 1–2. Box 15, Adrian Lane Papers, 1–2, 6; Appendix 3, JCCPPHW24–27.

215. "Report: SUEU Mission 29 June–July 11, 1980," 7–8; Orpwood, *Chappo*, 131.

216. Three thousand students were addressed at Sydney and NSW Universities

Inspired by the success of such initiatives, in the early 1980s the Department of Evangelism held a sequence of significant regional missions in partnership with churches across the Sydney and Illawarra area. The now experienced expositor and rector of St. Helen's Bishopsgate, Dick Lucas, was invited to speak at the first of these in July 1982. Large numbers attended Lucas's expositions of Mark's Gospel at the Sutherland Civic Centre over several evenings.[217] Seeing the potential of such an approach and believing Chapman to be the equal of any other expositor, leading clergy urged that Chapman should be appointed as lead missioner for a series of future regional campaigns. On such advice, with Chapman as the keynote preacher, extensive prayer and planning preceded an array of civic-hall-style meetings in 1984 in Sydney's southwestern corridor. These drew attendances of 9,500.[218] In November 1984, a similar campaign in Sydney's Hurstville region attracted the partnership of twenty-five local churches and saw seven thousand attend an array of similar town-hall-style meetings. The sight of consistently large crowds and overflowing auditoriums both delighted campaign organizers and strengthened a collective desire for future regional missions.[219] Indeed, on news of the success of these initial campaigns, similar initiatives were planned and run over four years in advance. As a result, amidst a rapidly expanding domestic and international schedule, between 1984 and 1992 Chapman addressed combined audiences of 77,500 across as many as twenty regional mission campaigns throughout the Sydney and Illawarra area.[220]

The combined effect of these related preaching initiatives wound key strands of a culture of confident exposition, even in the face of significant societal change. Indeed, the confident mood of exposition that emerged among

---

in 1981. At Macquarie University 1,200 were addressed in 1982 and six hundred in August 1985. Six hundred were addressed at the New England University in 1983. See Appendix 5, *Historical Speaking Engagements*. A mission at UNSW in 1982 at which Dick Lucas spoke was also considered highly successful. DOE Prayer Letter, November 1982–January 1983. Missions were also staged at Mitchell College in Bathurst in October 1982 and August 1983 (Mission Brochures, Box 1, Adrian Lane Papers, Mitchell Library), and at Sydney University in July 1984 (with lead speakers Phillip Jensen and Robert Forsyth). See *SUEU 1984 Reachout Brochure*. Box 1, Adrian Lane Papers.

217. Average attendances exceeded seven hundred. *Preaching Christ Newsletter*, August–October 1982; *Preaching Christ*, November 1982–January 1983.

218. Rev. Dr. Paul Barnett, Master Robert Menzies College, to John Chapman, April 22, 1982, BDM Box 1, SDA; *Department of Evangelism Newsletter*, May–July 1984; *Department of Evangelism Newsletter*, August–October 1984.

219. *Department of Evangelism Newsletter*, August–October 1984; *Department of Evangelism Newsletter*, November 1984–January 1985.

220. Appendix 5, *Historical Speaking Engagements*.

the churches of Sydney and the wider evangelical base began to strike the first notes of what would later be seen as something of a religious renaissance. As Brian Stanley suggests, faced with a growing crisis of religious belief in this era, the decision by a large proportion of evangelicals to eschew a revisionist presentation of Christian doctrine and to persist in an intelligent yet conservative presentation of biblical truth, proved notably successful. Likewise, as David Hilliard observes of evangelical ministry patterns in the post-1960s era, many evangelicals continued to emphasize traditional standards of belief and moral conduct along with a widening array of programs to increase and multiply faith. The result was that by the 1990s in many urban dioceses, the churches with the largest congregations and highest incomes were strongly evangelical in tone and formed a larger proportion of Australian churchgoers than ever before. The Sydney diocese, as a key example of such countervailing religious trends, was no exception.[221]

Similarly, the fruit of such initiatives for Chapman's own preaching ministry would see him continue to grow in stature and appeal. Indeed, as a now "celebrated evangelist,"[222] between 1974 and 2008 Chapman preached to estimated combined audiences of 170,000 across the United Kingdom. This included major English evangelical parish platforms as well as major missions at Cambridge and Oxford, and a wide array of clergy and undergraduate forums. During this same period in North America and South Africa, Chapman addressed audiences of 16,000 and 20,000 respectively. Across other international networks he addressed an estimated 35,000 via major clerical and student forums. Between 1969 and 2012 Chapman addressed an estimated combined audience of 580,000 Australians. This incorporated listeners across every state capital and major domestic preaching platform, including seminaries, Bible conventions, and denominational conferences, alongside an array of churches, parachurch bodies, and missionary assemblies.[223]

In 1984, through his leadership of the Department of Evangelism, Chapman began a homiletic mentoring program. This program became

---

221. Stanley, *Diffusion*, 13; Hilliard, "Pluralism," 133; cf. Castle, *NCLS*, 57–63 and Kaldor, *Taking Stock*, 13–15 which record that between 1980 and 2000 attendances at Sydney Anglican churches grew in line with population growth and increased their retention of young people. Chapman himself later identified this period and its related preaching initiatives as catalysts that marked the beginnings of a change in mood and fortune for evangelical churches following the "barren" 1960s. See J. C. Chapman to Dr. W. Smyth (Chairman, Conference for Itinerant Evangelists 1983), September 9, 1981, BDM Box 1, SDA.

222. Chapman, "Anglican Evangelicals," 263–64.

223. See Appendix 5, *Historical Speaking Engagements*, from which these combined estimates are drawn.

highly sought-after among aspiring preacher-evangelists. Many of these would go on to become significant preachers and leaders in their own right.[224] Between 1985 and 2005 Chapman also began a long-standing ministry, training successive generations of preachers in Sydney theological colleges. This involved instruction in the theology *and* praxis of preaching, as well as the development of a practical program offering homiletic instruction and critique. From 1991, Chapman was also integrally involved in the training of pre-seminarian preachers. Through his extensive involvement in the "Ministry Training Strategy" conferences (an annual recruitment conference drawing as many as 800–1,000 ministry aspirants), he developed a practical program teaching the essence of expository preaching. When distributed as a video resource, this material was received enthusiastically by preachers across the English-speaking world.[225] Ultimately, Chapman's preaching pedagogy was distilled in his popular volume *Setting Hearts on Fire*. For a generation of Australian and international preachers this work became a favored resource for homiletic instruction and critique.[226] Thus, over the course of his ministry, Chapman offered homiletic leadership through an array of key preaching forums and fellowships across the Australian and international evangelical church. Combined with a preaching ministry that was as widely sought as it was enjoyed, Chapman's preaching became integral to a movement which, in the face of defining social change, developed a culture of rigorous exposition. This, in turn, supplied impetus and strength to the pulpits of the late twentieth-century evangelical world.

Conclusion

This chapter demonstrates that historically, Australian evangelical preaching rested strongly within the English tradition of the "textual" or Protestant plain style. This model became the conventional preaching pattern in England and her colonies until the mid-twentieth century. The tradition of expository preaching, however, derived from a different ancestry. Modelled on the twofold pattern of the reading and interpretation of the Law in Jewish and early Christian worship, expository preaching seeks to examine a Bible

---

224. See Appendix 2 for a list of apprentices drawn from historic DOE/Preaching Christ Newsletters.

225. Appendix 5, *Historical Speaking Engagements*; McDonald, "Chappo's Gain"; MTS, "What is MTS?"; Appendix 4, JCCPP/PROC#5, School for Bible Teachers: Giving a Talk.

226. Interview with David McDonald, December 6, 2016; Matthias Media, "Setting Hearts on Fire."

passage such that its essential meaning as it existed in the mind of the biblical writer is made plain and applied to the hearer. This model flourished in the biblical and patristic periods. It was later revived during the Continental Reformation, as the tools of classical and biblical learning were rediscovered. However, due to the existing dominance of the "textual sermon" and various complexities of the English Reformation, such insights did not carry over into English preaching at that time. The tradition of expository preaching developed in English-speaking contexts in the mid-twentieth century as a result of the revival of conservative biblical scholarship in the prewar and postwar eras. Under the influence of leading figures such as John Stott, the insights of a pattern of rigorous textual study were combined during this time with various rhetorical features of the older plain style. Catalyzed by Stott's approach, after the 1960s Chapman subsequently became one of the leading Australian preachers to exemplify, popularize, and adapt this model for use in congregational and evangelistic settings. The biblical clarity supplied by means of the expository model also became a useful aid in evangelistic engagement against a backdrop of significant twentieth-century social change and increasing biblical illiteracy.

4

The Preaching of a Theologian-Evangelist

Servant of the Word and of the People

"Not only are preachers the servants of the word. They are to be servants of the people to whom they speak (2 Cor 4:5; 1 Thess 2:7–8). It is because we are servants of the word that we work hard at understanding the Bible. Because we are servants of the people, we work hard at presenting the message with clarity and passion, showing the relevance and the importance of it to our lives."—John Charles Chapman[1]

ON THE MORNING OF August 27, 1992, several hundred community leaders gathered at the Merlin Hotel in the center of Perth, Western Australia, for a "Community Leader's Breakfast." The breakfast was the initiative of a local Anglican Church, St. Matthew's Shenton Park, as part of a smorgasbord of mission events to engage the community. The events included a dinner at the famed Western Australian Cricket Association ground, several university outreach meetings, an indigenous cultural night, as well as a larger-scale meeting at the Perth Concert Hall. Numerous community leaders were in attendance at the Merlin Hotel. They included Sir Charles Court (Western Australian Premier during 1975–1982), his son Richard Court (who also served as Premier between 1993–2001), Chief Justice David Malcolm (1988–2006) and a range of other notable figures.[2] The keynote speaker

---

1. Chapman, *Setting Hearts on Fire*, 26.
2. Interview with Dr. David Seccombe, February 16, 2017; Appendix 5, *Historical Speaking Engagements*; Wikipedia, "Charles Court"; "Richard Court."

for the mission was the veteran evangelist, John Chapman. On the morning of the breakfast, in his customarily direct yet jovial manner, Chapman pressed the claims of Christ with an address from Luke 9:10–27. The address juxtaposed the weight of the choice to follow Christ alongside the inestimable worth of the human soul. While some listeners naturally bristled at the evangelist's directness, others found themselves strangely allured by it. Indeed, a young waitress was so entranced that she quietly forgot her morning duties and stood listening through the entire address. Later that day, the rector of Shenton Park Anglican Church received a phone call from Sir Charles Court. Finding himself also moved by the morning's address, Sir Charles had phoned to enquire after Chapman's other speaking commitments, for he was eager that he and his other family members might attend another meeting to hear the veteran evangelist speak.[3]

What constitutes the essence of such diverse homiletic appeal? That this somewhat eccentric clergyman from an ordinary Sydney suburb with limited opportunities for tertiary education should maintain an exhaustive preaching schedule for over five decades—across the smallest of rural establishments to the rarified context of the world's oldest universities[4]—poses a homiletic puzzle worthy of reflection. One observer, reflecting on Chapman's preaching, suggested that when Chapman came to preach at the height of his ministry "it was like the evangelical circus had come to town." This did not mean that his preaching constituted merely "entertainment (though it was gripping) or that there were clowns (though he was hilarious) or even that it was a spectacle (though he was larger than life)." Rather, it suggested that as a preacher Chapman seemed to possess an ability to bring together "the best blend of important information and the enjoyment of that information, making everything else look pretty ordinary."[5] Others suggest that Chapman's preaching exuded a highly democratic and populist appeal. That is, he possessed an ability to embody the Australian spirit of mateship, self-effacing humor and the rugged earthiness of "the man on the street." Still others describe his preaching as prophetic. They suggest that he possessed the courage to speak with a force and directness that others admired and would emulate, but lacked the courage and wit to do so.[6] How may such homiletic qualities be explained?

3. Interview with Dr. David Seccombe, February 16, 2017. David Seccombe was rector of Shenton Park between 1979 and 1992.

4. Interview with Alan Stewart, December 7, 2016; Appendix 4, JCCPP/BIO#5, Dr. Paul Barnett 1995 address.

5. Manchester, "Preaching of John Chapman."

6. Interview with Dr. David Seccombe, February 16, 2017; Piggin, "Culture," 154–55; Bouma, *Soul*, 45–47.

The following chapter pursues the question of what comprised the essence of Chapman's homiletic approach and achievement from the perspectives of both its theological and rhetorical characteristics. A theological assessment is important given that ultimately *all* Christian ministry is theologically driven. Indeed, on account of its public nature, such a reality is perhaps no more clearly seen than in the assumptions preachers carry with them into the pulpit. As John Stott elucidated, "the secret of preaching is not in mastering certain techniques but being mastered by certain convictions . . . theology is more important than methodology." Stott added that a preacher's convictions concerning God, Scripture, the church, and the place of preaching in the purposes of God would thus *necessarily* affect their homiletic approach.[7] Yet, such a conviction does not thereby diminish the intrinsically rhetorical nature of preaching. Rather, as George Kennedy notes of *all* ancient and modern modes of communication: "every communication is rhetorical because it uses some technique to affect the beliefs, actions or emotions of an audience." Preaching, as a persuasive medium, is not exempt.[8] Arguably, the apostolic model itself exhibits a theologically informed use of the means of persuasion, displaying a concern for "preparation, passion and clear articulation" (1 Cor 1:18—2:5; 2 Cor 4—5).[9] Similarly, for the modern preacher, a strong theology of preaching need not sanction a "half-heartedness" in preparation and delivery, but should display itself in an eagerness to unfold Scripture in an "engaging, accessible way."[10] Such a twofold conviction was undoubtedly Chapman's. Chapman was familiar with the twin homiletic task of the preacher as both a "servant of the word" (with the responsibility of teaching Scripture) *and* as a "servant of the people" (with the task of preaching in such a way that the message was clear and appealing).[11] Consequently, Chapman addressed himself to these twin responsibilities both in his own preaching and in his ministry of equipping other preachers across the world.

Given this reality, the first section of this chapter examines elements of Chapman's *theological emphases* in preaching. This will not be an attempt to distill Chapman's theology of preaching exhaustively. Numerous works from the Reformed tradition have transposed the essence of preaching to the modern movement, and Chapman shared many convictions with such

---

7. Stott, *Challenge of Preaching*, 12.

8. Kennedy, *New Testament Interpretation*, 10.

9. Carson, *Cross and Christian Ministry*, 35.

10. Taylor and Dargue, *Style or Substance*, 85. Note that a concern for the rhetorical properties of Christian preaching goes back to Augustine. See chapter 3.

11. Chapman, *Setting Hearts on Fire*, 9. See the application of these aspects of homiletics on 13–86, 89–230, cf. Luke 1:2, 2 Cor 4:5.

theorists.¹² Rather, the chapter seeks to distill the unique emphases that Chapman himself brought to the wider discipline. Following this, elements of Chapman's *rhetorical praxis* will be examined. This will be done using aspects of classical rhetorical criticism and modern homiletical theory with reference to a selection of Chapman's historic addresses. Such categories have provided a staple of conceptual tools in the analysis of speech across the classical and Christian rhetorical traditions. As such, they provide a useful framework by which to assess aspects of Chapman's preaching and its legacy.[13] In so doing, the discussion seeks to shed light on the thought and praxis of a celebrated and significant Australian preacher who rose to a position of international prominence in his art.

Servant of the Word: A Theological Analysis

Preaching is Theocentric

As an inheritor and exponent of the Reformed and mid-century evangelical homiletic tradition, Chapman's theology and practice of preaching was infused with the tradition's foundational elements. In unison with leading contemporary and historical theorists, Chapman held to the primacy of the preached word of God as the cornerstone of Christian ministry. In his written works on the subject (which evince his wider historic instruction),[14] Chapman observed that there is a contemporary word from God to be spoken, revealed definitively in Christ the Son, and which is mediated in the Scriptures of the Old and New Testaments (2 Tim 3:16–17, Heb 1:1–2).[15] Chapman examined the ministry of reconciliation that had been entrusted to the Christian minister and noted that in the faithful proclamation of this inscripturated word the minister shared in the apostolic task of heralding a word capable of bringing life and maturity to God's church (Acts 20:20–21).[16] Chapman also acknowledged the spiritual injury that could be inflicted upon the church by the neglect or misuse of this commission or by the misalignment of a life that contradicted the message proclaimed

---

12. Cf. Stott, *I Believe*; Stott, *Preacher's Portrait*; Lloyd-Jones, *Preaching*; Greidanus, *Modern Preacher*; Robinson, *Biblical Preaching*; Calvin, *Institutes*, 1.6–13.

13. Kennedy, *Interpretation*, 13–20 for a survey of such categories.

14. Chapman to Orpwood, January 15, 1994, BDM Box 1; Appendix 4, JCCPP/PROC#3, *Lectures on Preaching 2B*, 1994.

15. Chapman, *Setting Hearts on Fire*, 13–17; cf. Adam, *Speaking God's Words*, 112–19; Greidanus, *Modern Preacher*, 7–8.

16. Chapman, *Setting Hearts on Fire*, 19–23; cf. Calvin, *Institutes*, 4.1.5.

(2 Tim 2:15).[17] Consequently, noting the Pauline injunction to "preach the word" (2 Tim 4:1–4) in favorable and unfavorable conditions, Chapman urged the minister to be "comprehensive" and "persevering" in this work: "correct, rebuke and encourage with great patience and careful instruction." For "the essence of preaching," Chapman urged, "is the word of God," and so "we are to listen carefully to what God says to us through his word and take care to teach it."[18] In the promotion of such core homiletic convictions, Chapman thus shared much with the prevailing assumptions of the postwar Reformed and evangelical preaching tradition.[19]

Preaching is Theocentric in Content: Jesus is Savior and Lord

However, Chapman was at pains to promote a kind of preaching that "converts the world."[20] Of first importance in this regard was a studied clarity about what the foundational characteristics of the biblical gospel were.[21] While such a statement may strike the contemporary observer as self-evident, during the period in which Chapman formulated his initial emphases such an understanding could not be assumed. For, as will be noted in later chapters, public witness in Australian Evangelicalism had to this point relied heavily on the inherited structures of Anglo-Christian identity and a cultural familiarity with Christian thought. This combined with an evangelical culture many believed had become "subjective and sentimental," alongside the influence of liberal-theological speculation and the varied theological commitments that aggregated under the banner of pan-denominational movements (like the WCC, BGEA, and Lausanne networks) to create a climate in which clerical presentations of the gospel often lacked clarity in significant respects.[22] It was into such a context that Chapman began to offer his own correctives.

---

17. Chapman, *Setting Hearts on Fire*, 23–25; cf. Stott, *I Believe*, 248–49.

18. Chapman, *Setting Hearts on Fire*, 13–14; cf. Stott, *Preacher's Portrait*, 17, 30.

19. For a magisterial summary of the Reformed theology of preaching, see Reymond, *Systematic Theology*. Reymond begins his study with the "Knowledge of God by Revelation" (3–116), before proceeding to the "Nature and Works of God" (129–456) and the "Salvific Work of God" (461–795). This follows Calvin's treatment and order in the *Institutes*, Books 1–4. See K.S. Oliphint, "Primal and Simple Knowledge," 16–43. In attributing the preaching of Scripture as preeminent in the knowledge of God, Chapman is in agreement with such works.

20. Chapman, "Preaching that Converts," 161–74.

21. Chapman, *Setting Hearts on Fire*, 29.

22. Judd and Cable, *Sydney Anglicans*, 150–51. These themes are examined in chapters 3, 5, and 6 and will not be examined here.

Particularly influential in shaping Chapman's emerging conception of the biblical gospel was the scholarship of D. B. Knox, D. W. B Robinson, and Graeme Goldsworthy. Knox's wider project during this era had displayed a concern to address what he described as the many "man-centered" approaches that had captured the attention of theologians. Such anthropocentrism, Knox argued, were "distortions of the gospel and an assault on the Godness of God." By either supplementing, diminishing, or bypassing the study of Scripture, they had turned the study of theology into a trivial study of man. Rather, convinced that Scripture was profoundly *theocentric* and consistent with the emphasis of much postwar evangelical scholarship, Knox confronted such distortions by promoting Scripture as the foundation on which all theological reflection ought to proceed.[23] Especially influential for Chapman was a series of Knox's addresses at a 1965 CMS Regional Summer School on "The Person of God." As an early version of Knox's work *The Everlasting God* (1979) these studies developed a range of themes concerning the relationship of a sovereign, holy God to his world. By such means, Chapman suggested he came to grasp what Knox described as the "heart of all theology," that via the seeming defeat and ignominy of the cross, God displayed his victory over every barrier separating God from man.[24] Also influential was the biblical-theological scholarship of Robinson and Goldsworthy. These scholars had sought to construct an interpretive framework promoting a greater unity across the breadth of the biblical literature. It sought to reframe the Bible's story line such that it ceased to be a "mass of unconnected writings," but rather demonstrated the death and resurrection of Christ as the interpretive key to the whole. As a framework through which the preacher was able to articulate the Christological significance of each part of Scripture, this framework became, for Chapman, an important hermeneutical tool.[25]

Consequently, distilling the insights of Knox, Robinson, Goldsworthy, and others, Chapman summarized the biblical gospel to be: 1) a proclamation with its origin in God; 2) concerning God's powerful Son who is shown to be Lord and Messiah by his resurrection from the dead; 3) who calls people from among all the nations to the "obedience of faith"; and 4) toward

---

23. Jensen, "On Training," 22.

24. See Appendix 4, JCCPP/BIO#3, Chapman, *Lord of Heaven and Earth*, 2–45; cf. Payne, *D. Broughton Knox, Vol. 1*, 37–146.

25. See the discussion in chapter 2 on the chronological priority of Robinson's biblical-theological approach to Scripture (which Goldsworthy later popularized) that became an important hermeneutical tool for Chapman. See Chapman, "Preface," in Goldsworthy, *Preaching the Whole Bible*, vii–viii; Reid, *Hermeneutics*, 139–63.

whom the only appropriate response is "repentance and faith."[26] Chapman was mindful of the textured language used by the biblical writers to describe various aspects of this gospel. He juxtaposed Christ's own emphasis in speaking of "the kingdom of God" (Mark 1:15) with Paul's frequent employment of atonement motifs (1 Cor 15:1–4), as well as other passages that spoke of Christ's eschatological victory by means of the cross (Luke 11:21; Col 2:15).[27] Elsewhere, Chapman examined the gospel in terms of the promise-fulfillment motifs of biblical theology.[28] In still other places, Chapman acknowledged the different approach employed by Paul in his presentations to Jew *and* Gentile audiences (Acts 17:16–34; cf. 13:16–41).[29] However, the unifying thread in all such material was the identity of Christ as both Savior *and* Lord. As the focal point of all God's purposes, Chapman contended, Jesus is able to save *because* he is Lord. Indeed, it was the very identity of Christ *as* Lord that enabled the salvific exchange of the cross to occur. Through the cross God acted with simultaneous justice and mercy, ensuring the just requirements of his law had been met while also justifying those who had broken it (Rom 3:21–25). While the Bible may separate such aspects of Christ's person and work to describe them, Chapman contended that they are, in reality, inseparable. "That is why the true response of a person to Christ is a genuine repentance which involves recognizing Jesus to be the true king in God's world and seeking to live under his rule."[30]

As a result of this integrated approach to the soteriological themes of Scripture, Chapman therefore sought in his own preaching (particularly in his evangelistic presentations) to "look for parts of the Bible that [are] good and simple summaries of the whole" and that allowed him to speak

26. Chapman, *Know and Tell*, 16–28.

27. Chapman resolved such tensions by noting that when Paul describes his ministry as "preaching the kingdom," he explains that this involved declaring to "Jews and Greeks that they must turn to God in repentance and have faith in our Lord Jesus" (Acts 20: 21–25). Hence, the message of the "Kingdom" and "faith in Christ" were not in conflict. Chapman, *Know and Tell*, 29–40, 32.

28. Cf. chapter 2. Chapman noted the Bible's descriptions of Christ as the "seed" of the woman who would crush Satan's head (Gen 3:15), the promised Abrahamic seed (Gen 12:2–3), the promised Davidic ruler (2 Sam 7), the fulfillment of the Old Testament typologies established in the Exodus, the Law, and Temple (John 2:19–22), as well as in Israel's prophetic literature (as both Israel's promised King *and* the Isaianic suffering servant, Matt 16:16–23). Chapman, *Setting Hearts on Fire*, 29–48.

29. In such contexts, Chapman noted, the apostle emphasizes both promise-fulfillment and lordship motifs, as it appeared to suit his purpose. Chapman, "Preaching that Converts," 168.

30. Chapman, *Know and Tell*, 35–36. Not only did Christ pay for sins, Chapman contended, but he perfectly kept the law and grants his "perfect law keeping" as a gift to those who trust him. So Chapman, *Lord of Heaven and Earth*, 23–24.

explicitly about "the saving Lordship of Jesus."[31] Characteristic of Chapman's practice was a preference for preaching the Gospels. Undoubtedly, a partly apologetic motive drove this practice. Chapman was persuaded that the narrative sections of the Gospels contained, in essence, the "gospel in miniature."[32] Moreover, given the sharply diminished familiarity of modern listeners with the biblical material, Chapman was also persuaded that in preaching from the Gospels the preacher was better able to introduce listeners in an empathetic and natural way to the one they were being called to trust, and to clearly articulate his lordship and saving work. Chapman's own personal piety also undoubtedly drove his selection of such material. Indeed, for Chapman, "there was no one more impressive or wonderful than Jesus," so he rarely tired of presenting Christ in this way. In his preaching of such narratives, he would often string together a rapid-fire aural collage of Christ's miraculous signs and impressive works so that the listener could grasp Christ's greatness. To say that Chapman "preached Christ," noted a colleague and contemporary, "is not saying quite enough. He was not just faithful, he was forceful. He wanted people to come face-to-face with Jesus' life," to hear of Christ's glory, truth, and love, and to respond joyfully as Chapman had.[33] Hence, while not limiting his evangelistic preaching exclusively to the Gospels, Chapman regularly "used the gospels in order to gospel"[34] and developed a renowned proficiency in this practice.

Preaching is Theocentric in Power: God is Sovereign in Conversion

A second emphasis Chapman offered the emerging postwar homiletic tradition was an amplified conception of God's sovereignty in conversion, by the agency of his Word and Spirit. Again, Chapman's emphasis in this regard was not uncontroversial. A popular Arminian accent pervaded much of the evangelical missional culture and approach of the mid-century. One of the fruits of this popular Arminianism was the spread of revivalist models of evangelism. Infused with a higher estimation of human capacity in the process of salvation, this expansionist movement promoted a

---

31. Chapman, *Setting Hearts on Fire*, 58; "Preaching that Converts," 170.

32. Such stories had likely been selected by the biblical writers, he averred, because they so vividly portrayed and demonstrated Christ's lordship and salvific power. Grant, "John Chapman Interview."

33. Manchester, "Preaching of John Chapman."

34. Grant, "John Chapman Interview."

"decision-oriented" and "technique-driven" model of response.[35] This was supplemented after the mid-twentieth century by the rise of various mediating theological positions. "Middle Knowledge" theorists like Alvin Plantinga and later Thomas Flint and William Lane Craig sought to reconcile a high view of God's sovereignty with an equally high view of human freedom.[36] "Open Theism" theorists like Clark Pinnock and William Hasker also advanced a view that suggested that to safeguard human freedom God's control and knowledge of the future was not exhaustive. Rather, God was to be conceived as a self-limiting God who had not created a blueprint of all that will happen but who "predestined purposes and goals which God is pursuing."[37] In contrast with such positions, J. I. Packer's advocacy for an Augustinian-Reformed position was also significant. Packer promoted a compatibilist view which suggested that God ordains all that comes to pass in such a way that he is neither the author of sin nor violator of the will of his creatures, and that such realities coexisted in an indissoluble union. Far from being a disincentive to evangelism, Packer suggested, such a view of God's sovereign grace "creates the possibility—indeed the certainty—that evangelism will be fruitful."[38] Packer's work was received favorably in conservative circles. However, with the rise of other mediating positions in an increasingly libertarian age, lingering concerns about the relationship between divine sovereignty and human agency continued to fuel debate across churches, campuses, and denominational forums well into the later century.[39]

---

35. A fuller examination of revivalism follows in the next chapter. However, "Arminian" theology suggests that the destiny of individuals is based on God's foreknowledge of the way they will either freely reject or freely accept Christ. Augustinian soteriology, however, on which Reformed theology builds, rests the cause of salvation in God's pretemporal "election" irrespective of human merit or volition. So Reymond, *Systematic Theology*, 472–73. On the rise of Arminian thought between the 1830s and 1950s, see Noll, *America's God*, 293–385.

36. Middle knowledge theorists revived the view known as "Molinism" (after the Jesuit, Luis de Molina c. 1547). They held that God knows what humans will do not because he preordains their behavior but because in his eternal knowledge he knows what free creatures will do in all possible circumstances (his middle knowledge). So Perszyk, *Molinism*, 1–19; cf. Plantinga, *Nature of Necessity*; *God, Freedom, and Evil*; Craig, "Middle Knowledge," 141–64.

37. As this view intersected the question of salvation, such theorists held that while God wills that all people should be saved, God's will was not always done, for he will not force his grace upon anyone. See Pinnock, *Grace Unlimited*, 106–7; Pinnock et al., *Openness of God*, 112–24; Beilby and Eddy, *Divine Foreknowledge*, 9–12.

38. Packer, *Evangelism*, 22–23, 115–17.

39. Beilby and Eddy, *Divine Foreknowledge*, 9. On Barth's contribution to the debate, which affirmed aspects of Reformed thought while fuelling concerns regarding

Chapman's advocacy for a Reformed application of the doctrines of grace in preaching was therefore offered into this environment. As such, echoing the Augustinian-Reformed description of humanity as "blind" (2 Cor 4:4–6), "dead in spiritual matters" (Eph 2:4–5), "powerless" (Rom 5:6) and at "enmity" with God (2 Cor 5:20), Chapman observed that such descriptors confirmed the truth of humanity's inability to turn back to God without the prevenient work of God's grace. Instead, he observed, human salvation lay in the sovereign initiative of God who not only called humanity back to himself and orchestrated the program of the gospel's advance (Matt 28:18–20; 2 Cor 5:20; Acts 14:27) but who also conditioned humanity's response of repentance and faith (Acts 5:31; 11:15–18; Eph 2:8). Lest such assertions should lead to the mistaken doctrine of hyper-Calvinism (which espoused a limited view of the atonement and discouraged the pursuit of evangelism), Chapman affirmed humanity to be responsible agents whose wills were not overridden by God's power but who instead exercised real and accountable human agency.[40]

As the notion of human agency related to the activity of preaching, Chapman drew attention to preaching and prayer as the *means* by which God worked out his purposes for humanity. Indeed, in response to the idea expressed by some that preaching was of little use unless God had already regenerated the hearer, Chapman resounded with an emphatic "No!" Rather, with Paul, he affirmed that "faith comes from hearing the message, and the message is heard through the word of Christ" (Rom 10:17). Consequently, the Christian minister was not to be inactive, for preaching and prayer are "the powerful way God saves people."[41] Chapman contended that the possession of firm convictions on these matters ought to relieve the preacher from the pressure to "get results" and "free them" to pursue the work of preaching and evangelism with a settled fervor. The minister's effectiveness "must never be gauged on how many people respond" to their ministry, Chapman contended, but on their "faithfulness to the gospel and in telling it. We should rejoice when many are converted and be sad when many are not . . . [but] the response is not in our hands. *Faithfulness in preaching the gospel, and in prayer, is what God is looking for* (1 Cor 4:2)."[42] To illustrate such a conviction, Chapman was fond of likening the evangelist to "someone who runs around the orchard giving the trees a shake. If the fruit is ripe,

---

universalism, see O'Neill, "Barth's Doctrine," 311–26.

40. Chapman, *Know and Tell*, 71–78; Packer, *Evangelism*, 38–39; Erickson, *Christian Theology*, 927–33.

41. Chapman, *Know and Tell*, 80–81.

42. Chapman, *Know and Tell*, 82; Chapman, *Setting Hearts on Fire*, 74–75.

it will generally fall off. If there is no ripe fruit, then it doesn't matter how hard you shake, no fruit will fall. [However], when the fruit is *really* ripe, sometimes it will drop off even when a cow or an old horse walks by!"[43] Such a "beautifully Calvinistic conviction," observed one contemporary, not only pervaded Chapman's practice but gave a clarity and calm to many others in the pursuit of their preaching ministries.[44]

---

43. Chapman, *Setting Hearts on Fire*, 166.

44. Interview with Ian Powell, March 12, 2017. Indeed, recalling Chapman's ministry as missioner for the 1989 Cambridge Inter-Collegiate Christian Union (CICCU) and 1994 Oxford Inter-Collegiate Christian Union (OICCU) missions, Rico Tice suggests that Chapman's confidence in "just teaching the Bible" was exemplary of such a strongly Reformed approach. Crucially, while well received, Chapman's approach at the CICCU mission had also been critiqued by certain student leaders who voiced that his "Bible teaching" approach had been more pedestrian than they wished to esteem. However, returning eight years later, flying in the face of such an assessment, Tice recalled, were the numerous student-converts of the 1989 CICCU Mission who had begun study for ministry. Similarly, during the 1993 OICCU mission, Chapman's Reformed conviction was again revealing. Assembling the sixty co-missioners for teaching each morning (following the public meetings each night) the Oxford student committee had wished to "announce numbers" of those who had "professed faith" the night before. At this suggestion, however, Chapman sharply demurred. Somewhat affrontingly, Chapman retorted "I am leaving now. This has nothing to do with me. If there are many professing, we will all be driven to pride. If there are only few, we will all be driven to discouragement. Either way, the counting of numbers will have no impact on the fruitfulness of the mission." At that, Chapman left the room. Such a strong embodiment of Reformed soteriology, Tice assessed, was not only foundational for his own emerging ministry, but for many emerging preacher-leaders across the evangelical world. Interview with Rico Tice, January 17, 2017. Similarly, in an address to the *Anglican Evangelical Junior Clergy Conference*, in England, July 2011, John Richardson (an evangelical Anglican Vicar) noted Chapman's impact in English evangelical channels from the 1980s. Richardson noted that, uncomfortable with the direction taken by the wider English evangelical movement, under the leadership of Dick Lucas, the *Evangelical Minister's Assembly* and the *Proclamation Trust* aspired to a recovery of preaching, which inevitably entailed a recovery of theology. Hence, the speakers invited to address the EMA were often men of theological acumen as well as skilled communicators. Notably, most of them came from abroad. Many were from America, but some, and in the end the most influential, he alleged, were "from the diocese of Sydney in Australia." Richardson highlighted the reflections of Dick Lucas, in particular, in relation to Chapman's impact in England. Lucas stated: "When he first came to us he did a series on God and his sovereignty, and so on. I remember then being amazed at the theological nous of this man. After all, he'd come across to do evangelism and we weren't used to travelling evangelists quite like this!" Richardson, "AEJCC."

Preaching is Missiological

Preaching is Missiological in Essence: All Preaching is Evangelistic

Another area in which Chapman offered a valuable contribution to the homiletic tradition was in his stress that all preaching was, of its essence, missiological. A number of theological and pragmatic motivators drove this emphasis. On the one hand, Chapman was eager to negate a kind of preaching that was only seen as "evangelistic" in the context of guest or revival-style occasions. Such preaching, he suggested, promoted a shallow appeal to the "gospel" as something different from the rest of Scripture and detracted from an Augustinian-Reformed view of the Bible.[45] Similarly, Chapman was concerned that a wedge should not be driven between the conception of a preacher's task in shepherding Christians alongside their work in reaching the world.[46] Chief among Chapman's targets in addressing this theme was the ecclesiology of D. B. Knox and D. W. B. Robinson. Collectively, their work had proposed a view of church that saw it as largely a context for the edification of Christians and which lacked an *inherently* evangelistic function. They consequently inferred that evangelism was an activity that occurred primarily *beyond* the bounds of the local church by means of the work of specialist preachers.[47] Chapman, however, was at pains to promote a conception of preaching that saw it as inherently evangelistic. Indeed, applying the insights of postwar biblical-theological reflection, Chapman contended that when the preacher took care to demonstrate how a passage related to Scripture's grand Christological narrative, then "there [was] a sense in which *every talk will be evangelistic.*"[48] This ought not invite a ham-fisted "gear change" in which an exposition became woodenly infused with a Christocentricity.[49] Rather, Chapman averred, when it could be shown how the part of the Bible being examined took its place in the overall revelation

---

45. Chapman, "Preaching that Converts," 163. Such observations were also made by Chapman in a series of addresses at the Evangelical Minister's Assembly in London, 1991. See Chapman, "Evangelism Every Sunday" and "Repentance and Faith," Manuscripts 1 and 2 in Appendix 1. Cf. Packer, *Evangelism*, 22; Beilby and Eddy, *Divine Foreknowledge*, 161–89.

46. Chapman, "Preaching that Converts," 163–69; Chapman, "Repentance and Faith," Appendix 1.

47. This discussion is taken up at length in chapter 7. As such it will not be discussed at length here.

48. Chapman, *Setting Hearts on Fire*, 53–60, 57. Cf. also Barth's heavily christological hermeneutic in *Church Dogmatics*, 2.13, 1–44.

49. Chapman, *Setting Hearts on Fire*, 54–57.

God had made in Christ, then a congregation and preacher could expect to hear and engage in "evangelism every Sunday."[50] Additionally, Chapman appealed to Paul's description of his own twofold pattern of ministry as a template for the work of the overseer-teacher today (Acts 20:20–28). As such, Chapman noted the way Paul employed a description of his ministry as *simultaneously* one of "preaching the kingdom" (v. 25) and proclaiming "the whole will of God" (v. 27) with the work of preaching "repentance" and "faith" (v. 21).[51] Chapman concluded from this that there was no distinction in the apostle's mind between the objectives of an evangelistic or a regular preaching ministry. Moreover, Chapman concluded, there was a "sameness about the response" Paul sought from all hearers. That is, as he fulfilled his ministry of "preaching the kingdom" and declaring "the whole will of God," the apostle sought an *initial and continuing* response of "repentance" and "faith" from all people (Acts 20:21). Hence, Chapman concluded, whether a sermon was specifically evangelistic or contained more general teaching on the Christian life, if the apostle sought to illicit this dual response to the preaching of Scripture, then so too must the contemporary pastor. In every sermon, whether it was *explicitly* evangelistic or otherwise, Chapman sought to expound the centrality of Christ in all of Scripture and to promote a kind of preaching that "converts the world." Moreover, he contended that while a pulpit ministry was insufficient on its own to meet the evangelistic needs of the modern church, even so, the work of evangelism must surely *begin* there and radiate out into the life of the local church and world.[52]

Preaching is Missiological in Urgency: Eschatology and God's Plan for the World

Another distinctive note that rang from the homiletic theopraxis of John Chapman was the eschatological urgency that ought to characterize effective preaching. Such an emphasis undoubtedly arose from decades honing his craft as a public evangelist. Like all effective oratory, Chapman recognized the need for persuasion in a preacher's presentation.[53] However, aside from such rhetorical imperatives, the need for urgency in preaching was,

50. Chapman, *Setting Hearts on Fire*, 53–60; Chapman, "Preaching that Converts," 164; Chapman, *Know and Tell*, 45–46.

51. Chapman, "Repentance and Faith," Appendix 1; Chapman, "Preaching that Converts," 168.

52. Chapman, "Preaching that Converts," 168; Chapman, "Every Sunday," Appendix 1.

53. Chapman, *Setting Hearts on Fire*, 170–75.

for Chapman, a deeply *theologically derived* proposition. It found its source in an awareness of the love of Christ, the cost of redemption, and a knowledge of God's eschatological plans for his world. Consequently, Chapman was often at pains to emphasize that in light of such realities there was "no place for detached indifference on the part of the speaker."[54] For, he reasoned, if the price of humanity's redemption was the atoning blood of God's Son, then humanity's rebellion must be highly significant. Indeed, if there had been "any other way" to secure redemption "then surely it would have been found."[55] Consequently, he counselled, if the preacher "is not overwhelmed by the love of God in sending his Son," nor "horrified by the prospect that people will spend eternity . . . separated from God . . . there is something amiss."[56] On the contrary, the preacher must be acutely conscious that the message proclaimed "is a matter of life and death! We are offering forgiveness of sins. We are warning of the horror of judgment. Tears would be appropriate (Acts 20:19). Our preaching on such matters *cannot* be matter-of-fact."[57] Indeed, he reasoned, "at no stage should we give the impression, either by word or attitude, that there is plenty of time and that a person may turn to Christ whenever they [wish]. God says, 'Today if you hear my voice do not harden your heart' (Ps 95:8) . . . gospelling is *urgent*."[58] Naturally, Chapman was careful to caution the preacher against the error of rhetorical sleight of hand or manipulation. However, he averred, the bulk of Anglican evangelical preachers were not usually guilty of this indulgence. The opposite was more usually true. Hence, drawing on the example of the preaching of the first-century apostles, Chapman noted "they 'begged' people to be reconciled to God (2 Cor 5:11, 20). They didn't tell, or inform, or suggest, or even advise. They begged! It is hard to do that in a detached way. They argued, reasoned, and persuaded, sometimes with tears (Acts 20:19). It was a matter of life and death."[59]

Such was the practical edge of a deep-seated awareness of the gravity of the cross of Christ, and such was Chapman's practice. Indeed, just as weeping and preaching went hand in hand for the apostle Paul (Acts 20:31),[60] so Chapman was frequently overcome with emotion and openly

---

54. Chapman, *Setting Hearts on Fire*, 174.

55. Chapman, *Setting Hearts on Fire*, 173; J. C. Chapman, *Preaching Christ Newsletter*, August–October 1990.

56. Chapman, *Setting Hearts on Fire*, 170.

57. Chapman, "Preaching that Converts," 172.

58. Chapman, *Setting Hearts on Fire*, 177–78.

59. Interview with Alan Stewart, December 7, 2016; Chapman, *Setting Hearts on Fire*, 171; McClymond, *Issues*, 5 on manipulative revivalism.

60. Stott, *I Believe*, 261, 271; Chapman, *Setting Hearts on Fire*, 171.

wept in the pulpit as he recalled the overwhelming love of Christ and the realities of the coming judgment.[61] For, Chapman averred, "sentimentality" may lead us to believe that "all people are secure." Yet, the Bible exhorts us otherwise. It says that "'God commands all men everywhere to repent, for he has set a day when he will judge the world in righteousness.' We need to live in the world of reality [and not] allow the urgency of the gospel to slip away."[62] Rather, he added, Christ's coming has "brought us into the perpetual harvest time of the kingdom of God (John 4:34–36). 'Later on,' is inappropriate for evangelism. There is an urgency at harvest time. It calls for action. It is inappropriate to think in terms of delay regarding people being called into God's kingdom. We are to 'open our eyes and look at the fields.' Harvest is now. It is urgent. People will be lost."[63]

Servant of the People: A Rhetorical Analysis

An Expository Plain Style of Preaching

Notwithstanding the fact that Chapman saw preaching to be a primarily spiritual and eschatological activity, he also recognized it as being subject to the rules of effective human discourse.[64] Given this, in both his own pedagogy and praxis, Chapman pursued an *expository plain style* of preaching. Modelled on the approach of other leading twentieth-century evangelical preachers like John Stott and Haddon Robinson, this approach combined the strengths of postwar evangelical scholarship and exegesis with the rhetorical strengths of the English plain style. It sought to condense the theology of a biblical unit (a single text, passage or theme) under a "lead" idea, expounded using a three- or four-point rhetorical structure. While such a rhetorical formula had characterized Protestant preaching (in varying degrees) since the early modern period,[65] preachers

61. Retief, "More Thanks"; Interview with David McDonald, December 6, 2016.

62. J. C. Chapman, *Preaching Christ Newsletter*, February–April 1983.

63. J. C. Chapman, *Preaching Christ Newsletter*, February–April 1986. For illuminating discussion on the place of emotions in Christian preaching and of the regularity of weeping and tears in the preaching ministries of historical figures such as George Whitfield and D. L. Moody, see Stott, *Between Two Worlds*, 275–79.

64. See Appendix 4, JCCPP/PROC#4, *The Spoken Word: Training Course*. This document contains notes from a course Chapman attended stressing the importance of aspects of public speech like breathing, voice production, and body language. Cf. Chapman, *Setting Hearts on Fire*, 9–10, 89–91, 159–80 where Chapman teaches the importance of effective public communication.

65. As noted, classical rhetoric had developed a set of precepts grouped in five "parts" that informed the act of planning and delivering a speech. Invention (*inventio*)

like Chapman, Stott, and Robinson came to excel in the use of this formula to exposit longer biblical units.[66]

The homiletical approach Chapman taught and modelled in pursuing this rhetorical ideal was an essentially fourfold process. First, and preeminently, was detailed study of the text of Scripture. This involved the interrogation of a passage with the aid of biblical commentaries, and by means of a series of diagnostic questions to assist the preacher in gaining clarity on the text's essential meaning.[67] From this process, it was intended that a unitary theme (Chapman called this the "big idea") which encapsulated the text's essential teaching could be derived and distilled.[68] Second, in a

---

related to the process of establishing a subject or theme (the *propositio* or *thema*) by various modes of argument. Arrangement (*dispositio*) involved the announcement of a subject or theme as well as the elements of a discourse needed to unfold this theme. This included the initial winning of an audience (*exordium*), the establishment of background and factual details (*narratio*), an outline of the main propositions needed to establish a subject (*partitio*), the inclusion of various supporting facts and illustrations (*confirmatio*), and the closing exhortation designed to make all that preceded clear and compelling (*peroratio*). Style (*lexis*) related to the choice and combination of words into clauses, periods, and figures and was organized around four stylistic virtues (clarity, correctness, ornamentation, and propriety) and three kinds of style (the plain, middle, and grand). Memory (*memoria*) related to the use of various methods to help retain a speech's contents in mind. Delivery (*pronunciatio*) involved considerations for the control of voice, stance, and gesture. The Aristotelian modes of persuasion such as *logos* (oratorical content), *pathos* (the emotional swaying of an audience), and *ethos* (speaker trustworthiness and reception) also formed part of the canon of classical rhetoric. Aristotle's *Rhetoric* (4 BC) was the first systematic distillation of these categories. Cicero's *Orator* (55 BC) crystallized the classical rhetorical art and became the most closely studied *techne* for a millennium. The classical art was developed by teachers of public speaking and was transmitted to the Middle Ages, Renaissance, and modern period. First appropriated for Christian use by Augustine (*On Christian Doctrine*, c. 397 AD), the ostensibly classical rhythm of announcing text and theme, followed by divisions, proofs, and applications became the almost universal mode of English Protestant preaching well into the twentieth century. See the longer discussion of this in chapter 3. Cf. also Kennedy, "Historical Survey," 3–42; Kennedy, *New History*, 10–12; Heath, "Codifications," 59–76. The concern for a unitary "theme" expounded with the aid of divisions was present in the work of nineteenth- and early twentieth-century homileticians like Charles Simeon, Donald Miller, and J. H. Jowett and was developed in the mid-twentieth century by Haddon Robinson and John Stott. It was from the work of Robinson and Stott that Chapman developed much of his homiletic pedagogy. See Chapman, *Setting Hearts on Fire*, 89–104; Robinson, *Biblical Preaching*, 15–26; Stott, *Preaching*, 196–246; Stott, *Between Two Worlds*, 211–25.

66. While an analysis of Chapman's preaching manuscripts, titles, and their associated texts reveals the presence of thematic, textual, and doctrinal preaching, the vast majority of his sermons exposited longer biblical units. See Appendix 3.

67. Chapman, *Setting Hearts on Fire*, 89–91; cf. Chapman, *Lectures on Preaching 2B*, 1994, Appendix 4, JCCPP/PROC#3, Lecture 2.

68. Chapman, *Setting Hearts on Fire*, 91–92. The distilling of a "big idea" was a

manner resembling the classical and Puritan rhetorical traditions, Chapman proceeded to "divide" the passage into logical and manageable units.[69] These divisions and summary ideas would then be expounded following a *State, Show, Explain, Illustrate, Apply* rhetorical formula.[70] The preacher was to *state* the point or division derived from their study (distilling the text's logical units and ideas sequentially). The preacher was then to *show* biblically from where the point was derived. This invited a listener's engagement with the text and facilitated learning. The preacher was then to *explain* the point's meaning and implications in concise theological and pastoral language. The preacher would then *illustrate* the point by offering examples, analogies, and proofs to reinforce it and enhance audience comprehension. After this, the preacher was to *apply* the point to ensure its contemporary relevance to the listener was clear.[71] Third, following the "division" and exposition of the passage, the preacher then envisaged how the sermon might be introduced and concluded. This step was recommended only *after* the development of the "big idea" and main sermon body. This ensured a rhetorical unity framed the sermon as a whole by aligning its key teaching points with the ideas and rhetorical devices used to introduce and reinforce them. The conclusion aimed to reinforce the sermon's divisions and themes. Similarly, the sermon's introduction (conceived last of all) ought to set the scene for the entire address. Its purpose was to arouse audience interest, to set the congregation at ease, and to introduce the sermon's "theme" or "big idea" by the use of a question, statement, story or anecdote.[72] Fourth, to allow liberty in delivery, the preacher would spend considerable time in rhetorical and spiritual preparation. This involved attention to the use of a sermon manuscript, the use of memory aids, sermon practice, and extensive prayer.[73]

---

proposition Chapman adapted from the work of Robinson, *Biblical Preaching*, 15–26 and Stott, *Preaching*, 196–246. Stott used the terminology of "isolating the dominant thought or theme." This was a practice Stott derived from Simeon, who used the language of a "categorical proposition." So Simeon, *Horae Homileticae*, vi–vii.

69. Chapman, *Setting Hearts on Fire*, 91–92; cf. Pipa, "William Perkins," 103; Kneidel, "Ars Praedicandi," 13; Deconinck-Brossard, "Art of Preaching," 110–27.

70. See Haddon Robinson's earlier articulation of a similar process in his *Biblical Preaching*, 49–66.

71. Chapman, *Setting Hearts on Fire*, 89–115; cf. Chapman, *Lectures on Preaching 2B*, 1994, Appendix 4, JCCPP/PROC#3, Lectures 4–6. Importantly, this process was to be repeated for each subsequent "point" or "division" throughout the course of the sermon. In a thematic sermon, the same rhetorical process would be followed by the division of the topic into points of doctrine.

72. Chapman, *Setting Hearts on Fire*, 117–27; cf. *Lectures on Preaching 2B*, Appendix 4, JCCPP/PROC#3, Lectures 7–8.

73. Chapman, *Setting Hearts on Fire*, 129–38; cf. *Lectures on Preaching 2B*, Appendix

Chapman the Preacher

Chapman's own published work on preaching was written to help others gain proficiency largely in the *evangelistic* or *missionary sermon* genre.[74] Aimed at the beginner and intermediate preacher, this work was designed to help them attain "better-than-average results . . . faster."[75] However, given his own maxim that "all preaching will be evangelistic when set in its biblical theology"[76] and given the rhetorical artistry present in all preaching and homiletic instruction,[77] Chapman's work became a popular resource for preachers across the English-speaking evangelical world.[78] Like all mature homileticians, Chapman's exemplification of his own pedagogy was nuanced. He aimed to provide enough artistry to enhance sermon clarity and avoid calling attention to the homiletic bones that underlay his preaching. His goal was rather to sweep listeners up into the glory of the Spirit's revelation than to have them notice the artistic discipline being observed.[79] For as exponents of the discipline had long noted, if "unconcealed," rhetoric "would cease to be art."[80] Nevertheless, Chapman's own preaching did display sufficient artistry, uniformity, *and* variety to invite analysis.

Invention and Arrangement

Alongside the growing number of twentieth-century evangelical expositors, the goal of Chapman's preaching (as noted above) was that by means of a historical and literary study of a biblical unit he might communicate what God committed to Scripture so it spoke a contemporary message.[81]

4, JCCPP/PROC#3, Lectures 10–11.

74. See chapter 3. Cf. Kennedy, *Classical Rhetoric*, 88, 155 and Old, *Biblical Period*, 11 on the missionary sermon genre.

75. Chapman, *Setting Hearts on Fire*, 161.

76. Chapman, *Setting Hearts on Fire*, 60.

77. Kennedy, *Rhetorical Criticism*, 10; Chapel, *Preaching*, 25–41.

78. Interview with David McDonald, December 6, 2016; Matthias Media, "Setting Hearts on Fire."

79. See Chapel, *Christ-Centered Preaching*, 138–39; Stott, *Between Two Worlds*, 228–29, 265, and Robinson, *Preaching*, 92–92, 135–48 for illuminating discussion on the importance of homiletical artistry coupled with the avoidance of artifice in Christian preaching. On Chapman's theory of the need for artistic discipline coupled with homiletic experimentation, see Chapman, *Setting Hearts on Fire*, 159–80.

80. See Quintilian, *Institutio Oratoria*, 6.8.3.2. Quintilian was the greatest teacher of rhetoric in the first century. So Kennedy, *New History*, 177.

81. See the discussion in chapter 3; cf. Greidanus, *Modern Preacher*, 11; Robinson, *Biblical Preaching*, 4–12; Chapman, *Setting Hearts on Fire*, 13–17.

Consequently, in keeping with other expositor-orators, for Chapman, the process of *invention* was taken up with uncovering and distilling the meaning of a given scriptural text or theme.[82] However, once this was established and a passage *or* theme's lead idea was distilled, Chapman's *arrangement* and presentation of his material followed a conventional, yet engaging and imaginative, approach.

A particularly striking feature of Chapman's preaching was his frequent use of various kinds of inductive sermon arrangements.[83] An analysis of ten transcribed sermons preached over a ten-year period at a range of domestic and international clerical, parish, and seminary contexts makes this clear. These sermons were *thematic, evangelistic,* and *catechetical* in genre and expounded some of Chapman's most favored narrative and epistolary texts and themes. Hence, Chapman's use of such inductive arrangements in this array of contexts indicates something of a stylistic pattern.[84] In *semi-inductive arrangements*, only a subject is presented in the introduction (by way of a question or statement) which the sermon divisions then complete to form an overall proposition. In *inductive-deductive arrangements* the full proposition is stated earlier in the sermon, after which it is explained, proven, and applied with each successive point.[85] Whichever permutation is employed, in the hands of a skilled preacher sermons patterned in this

---

82. Chapman, *Setting Hearts on Fire*, 89–91.

83. For analysis of the varying kinds of sermon arrangements see Robinson, *Biblical Preaching*, 78–96.

84. See manuscripts 1 to 10 in Appendix 1. Manuscripts 1 and 2 were preached at the 1991 Evangelical Minister's Assembly in London to one thousand clergy. In these sermons Chapman thematically explores two of his most favored subjects: "Evangelism Every Sunday" and "Repentance and Faith Every Sunday." Manuscript 3 was preached at the "Club 5 Conference" (a forerunner to the modern MTS Conferences) in the early 1990s as part of a course on expository preaching. The sermon expounds Rom 3:21–26 and asks, "How Can God Declare Me Right When I'm Wrong?" Manuscripts 4 to 7 represent some of Chapman's most frequently delivered evangelistic sermons. Titled "Too Good for Heaven?" Luke 18:9–14 (#4), "A Fresh Start" John 3:1–16 (#5), "Nothing Recedes Like Success" Luke 12:13–21 (#6) and "You Can't Keep a Good Man Down" Luke 24:36–49 (#7) they are indicative of Chapman's characteristic approach to evangelistic preaching from the gospels. Manuscripts 8 to 10 were preached at the Moore College chapel in the 1990s where Chapman lectured in homiletics. Titled "Forgiven Much, Loved Much" Luke 7:36–50 (#8), "He Must Increase" John 3:22–36 (#9) and "What is at the Heart of Ministry?" 2 Tim 4:1–5 (#10) they represent Chapman's characteristic approach as a mature expositor.

85. This is in contrast to a purely *inductive* arrangement which moves toward a complete statement of the main idea only at the end of the sermon. This also contrasts a purely *deductive* arrangement in which the complete proposition is stated in the introduction after which it is taken apart and analysed in the sermon body. For analysis see Robinson, *Biblical Preaching*, 78–96.

way can produce tension, interest, and build toward a compelling rhetorical apex.[86] Chapman displayed a preference for using a *semi-inductive arrangement* in catechetical contexts, allowing him to build gradually toward a holistic teaching proposition. However, in evangelistic contexts his preference for *inductive-deductive arrangements* produced a clear statement of what he wished to convey earlier, while still retaining a degree of rhetorical suspense. Either way, by using such arrangements, Chapman invited the listener on a journey of discovery that resisted predictability while still tailoring his teaching to suit varying pedagogical needs.[87]

The components and variety within such arrangements also invites analysis. In the *exordium*, Chapman would commonly begin with prayer.[88] In both didactic and evangelistic contexts this served to heighten audience expectation of an elevated rhetorical encounter. It was also indicative of Chapman's view of the doxological function of preaching and the power of God's word to save, sanctify, and reform.[89] After this, alongside the need to introduce his subject, Chapman's goal in the *exordium* (especially in guest settings) was to win the crowd. This was often done by engaging in lighthearted repartee or relaying a humorous story that often resulted in uproarious audience laughter.[90] In potentially hostile clerical and guest environments, Chapman's use of humor served to breakdown audience tension and resistance, as well as gently "pricking the bubble" of human pretension and pride. Indeed, noted John Stott, "provided we are laughing at the human condition, and therefore at ourselves, humor helps us to see things in proportion . . . it is often through laughter that we gain glimpses of the heights from which we have fallen . . . leading to a wistful desire to be ransomed."[91] It was in this sense that, while maintaining unerring seriousness toward the gospel,[92] Chapman's inborn gift for humor in a sermon's

---

86. Robinson, *Biblical Preaching*, 85.

87. Manuscripts 1, 2, and 10 (chiefly catechetical in purpose) reflect a *semi-inductive arrangement*. Chapman states the sermon's "subject" after the exordium, which the major points "complete" to form the proposition. Manuscripts 3, 4, 5, 6, 7, 8, and 9 (chiefly evangelistic in purpose) reflect an *inductive-deductive arrangement*. Chapman states the proposition following an exploratory exordium, which is then explained, proven, and applied by each successive point. See Appendix 1.

88. Note this pattern in manuscripts 4, 5, 6, 7, 9, and 10 in Appendix 1.

89. On the doxological function of preaching, see Old, *Biblical Period*, 76–77, 132–33; Old, *Modern Age*, 421–22.

90. Note this pattern in manuscripts 1, 2, 4, 5, 6, and 7 in Appendix 1.

91. Stott, *Between Two Worlds*, 289, 291.

92. See Chapman, *Setting Hearts on Fire*, 112–13 on the appropriate use and misuse of humor.

exordium or in other places (with a punchline often at his own expense) opened "many a locked-door to the truth of the gospel."[93]

After an exploratory *exordium*, Chapman consistently moved to an announcement of his key subject. In evangelistic settings this typically involved the articulation of a proposition (by means of a statement or question) which the exposition then explained and applied.[94] After a *narratio* (which supplied necessary background to the text)[95] Chapman arrived at the first of his major divisions (the *partitio*).[96] Then followed an exposition by means of a two- or three-point structure to establish a sermon's proposition, before concluding with a *peroratio* and prayer. Chapman resisted a slavish adherence to his own stated steps in exposition and naturally developed artistic modes by which these could be expressed. Even so, his praxis of *stating, showing, explaining, illustrating,* and *applying* each sermon division was remarkably consistent.[97] Chapman's use of the technique of "narration" (especially in preaching the Gospels) often involved the melding together of these steps. This involved the re-creation of dialogue or the adding of interest to the account by vividly filling out the setting, action, and personalities involved.[98] The proportions Chapman allocated to each expositional step also varied. In evangelistic settings, his weighting of these components leant heavily toward illustration. Indeed, because of his use of "narration" in explaining the Gospels, the entire sermon often felt as though it were a vivid story interspersed lightly with didactic signposts and conclusions.[99] In catechetical settings, Chapman's *semi-inductive arrangement* included these same rhetorical elements (*exordium, narratio, partitio,* and *peroratio*).[100] However, the communicative and logical links between them varied. An opening subject was advanced gradually toward a fuller proposition in a process rich in human interest, excurses, and asides. In such contexts, the

93. Rev. Dick Lucas, Rector Emeritus, in Palmer, "Service of Thanksgiving."

94. Note this pattern in manuscripts 3, 4, 5, 6 and 7. However, in manuscripts 3: "Too Good for Heaven," and 6: "Nothing Recedes Like Success," Chapman examines two parables of Jesus. Consequently, to heighten a sense of suspense and resolution, his homiletic proposition is implied with a question which the parables subsequently solve.

95. Kennedy, *Classical Rhetoric*, 102–03; Kennedy, *Art of Persuasion*, 11, 203.

96. Note this pattern in manuscripts 3, 4, 5, 6, and 7; cf. Kennedy, *Classical Rhetoric*, 102.

97. Note the consistency of this pattern in manuscripts 3, 4, 5, 6, and 7.

98. Note the technique of "narration" in manuscripts 4, 5, 6, and 7 in Appendix 1; cf. Chapel, *Christ-Centered Preaching*, 122–23.

99. See especially manuscripts 4, 5, 6, and 7; cf. Chapel, *Christ-Centered Preaching*, 90–94.

100. See especially manuscripts 1, 2, and 10 in Appendix 1; cf. Kennedy, *Classical Rhetoric*, 102.

weighting of each component was typically more even and the use of humor more sparing.[101] The combined effect was to promote a rhetorical experience and structure suited to the need at hand.

Style, Memory, and Delivery

As a communicator, Chapman appeared to grasp instinctively that to achieve persuasive preaching not only was "teaching" important, but the preacher must also "delight" listeners to retain them and "move" them to impel their wills.[102] Indeed, by both acquisition and innate gift, as Richard Baxter had urged, Chapman seemed to possess the "skill necessary" to "screw the truth into [his hearer's] minds and work Christ into their affections."[103] Chapman's use of humor to achieve this has already been noted as a distinct stylistic trait. However, Chapman's use of clear and vivid language is also notable, as was his ability to move across the register of linguistic styles so as to persuade.

As such, in the mode of "teacher" (using the *plain style*) Chapman's choice of language was typically clear, sober, straightforward, and matter-of-fact. He modelled a reverential attitude to Scripture that elevated the weight of the homiletic event. In the "state," "show," and "explain" steps of exposition he typically employed questions, used clear sentences, and urged listeners to "look with me" so they too might engage the living biblical text.[104] Similarly, Chapman's ability to move seamlessly into the *middle*

---

101. See manuscripts 1, 2, and 10 in Appendix 1; cf. Chapel, *Christ-Centered Preaching*, 90–94.

102. This constitutes Augustine's recasting of Cicero's thesis on style. The "duties" of an orator—to instruct, delight, and move—were tied by Augustine to Cicero's three kinds of style and recast to serve preaching: "teaching" in the plain style, "delighting" in the middle style, and "moving" in the grand style. So Augustine, *De Doctrina Christiana*, 4.27, 33–58.

103. Baxter, *Reformed Pastor*, 6.6, cited in Simeon, *Preaching*, xvii.

104. Indicative of Chapman's "teaching" mode in *catechetical* contexts is this section in manuscript 2. Elucidating the teaching ministry of Paul in Acts 20, he says: "Let me talk first about the content of Paul's ministry as it is described for us here. You will see in verse 20, he said, 'I did not withhold from telling you anything that was profitable.' And verse 24, 'I declared to you the gospel of the grace of God.' . . . He says in verse 25, 'he preached the kingdom.' And in verse 27, he says 'I have not hesitated to proclaim to you the whole will of God.' What was it that he did in three years, in the time at Ephesus? . . . What was it that he did in those three years that when he left, he was able to say to them, 'I have not withheld from telling you anything that was profitable?' . . . Well, what he declared to them was the gospel! The gospel of God's grace. The gospel of the kingdom of God. If you would like me to have put it in the other categories, he told them that Jesus would 'make them wise for salvation as they studied the Scriptures.' They would

style to "delight" listeners was also crucial to his homiletic success. To do this, in the *exordium* and in the "explain," "illustrate," and "apply" steps of exposition, he would typically employ repartee, humorous anecdotes, and illustrations, along with a range of vivid *exempla*, quotes, and asides. Such devices served to command and recall listener attention, reward patience, and renew a sense of rhetorical light and shade. As ex-missionary Jungle Doctor, Paul White, posited of the key to sermon success, one needs to "Hook 'em, hold 'em, humor 'em and hit 'em!"[105] Chapman's ability to delight hearers like this allowed him to constantly do the same.[106]

---

understand God's great plan, the will of God, how in Christ he's reconciling the world to himself. That is what he declared . . . the gospel in its implications."

Indicative of Chapman's "teaching" mode in *evangelistic* contexts is this section in manuscript 3. Elucidating the news of God's redemption in Christ in Romans 3, he says: "The second thing I want to say from this part of the Bible is when a person comes back and seeks for mercy, God declares us right in Christ. And that to me is breath-taking! Let me say it again, God declares us right with him in Christ. Look at verse 23. 'For all have sinned and fall short of the glory of God, and are (what?) . . . 'justified.' Just as if we had never sinned . . . 'We are justified freely by his grace.' How does this come about? 'Through the redemption that comes in Christ Jesus. God presented him as a sacrifice of atonement, through faith in his blood.' In the ancient world . . . If you were in debt beyond paying . . . the last recourse you had was to sell yourself . . . into slavery. And there you stayed . . . unless you were redeemed . . . And on a happy day your owner calls you and says, 'This man has paid the price for your redemption. You are now free. A redemption price has been paid for you.' And God tells us here in this part of the Bible, at 24, you are 'justified freely by his grace. That means just-as-if-ied never sinned.'"

105. White, *Alias Jungle Doctor*, 129.

106. Indicative of Chapman's approach to "delighting" audiences in *catechetical* contexts is the exordium of an address to one thousand English clergy in manuscript 2. As he introduces the theme of "Repentance and Faith Every Sunday" he says: "In the family that I grew up with, it was not a Christian family, although my mother was converted . . . between forty and forty-five, by two of my cousins, who were rip-roaring Christians . . . They evangelized everything that moved, and most things that didn't! (*Laughter.*) They led my mother to Christ . . . before they shot off to Columbia, where they have spent the rest of their life . . . They never came home again, and I'm sure it was a great blessing to both continents (*laughter*). My mother was never too clear on what she had done, although she was fairly clear whenever the pressure was off her. But just to make sure, she made a decision, under every evangelist that ever came to Australia . . . I didn't actually mind that so much until I became an itinerant evangelist. And she used to come with me (*laughter in anticipation*). And I'd say to her in the car, 'If I ask people to come out tonight for counselling dear, you won't come out, will you?' 'No pet, I won't.' I said, 'Why won't you dear?' She said, 'Well, because I'm already Christ's person, aren't I?' I say, 'Yes, that's right. You are, you understand that dear, don't you?' 'Yes.' 'You won't come out!' (*Laughter in anticipation.*) 'No.' And this dear old lady would be seen to be coming in on my arm . . . And then you'd have the dreadful spectacle, of the evangelist saying to the first convert (*through clenched teeth*), 'Go back to your seat!!' (*Uproarious prolonged laughter.*) While she may well have been the bane of every counsellor's life, she was a dream for the evangelist. She kept the figures up all over Sydney

However, it was Chapman's ability to "move" his hearer's by means of an unaffected use of the *grand style* that undoubtedly supplies a key reason for his homiletic success. Typically, in various sections of sermon application and in the *peroratio* Chapman's language became slow, elevated, and earnest. Rhetorically, it was like he was holding out his arms and pleading with his listeners to respond afresh to the love of Christ. To the Christian, he typically sought to impress upon them a renewed sense of wonder at the cross of Christ. To the non-Christian, he sought to depict a sense of their worth and importance to God and how much God had done to win them

---

for many years! When I come to the point of talking about repentance and faith every Sunday, I am not talking about people walking out to the front . . . or standing up. But I *am* talking about a thing which is very serious indeed . . . What I am concerned about is the wedge that's driven between what we think we're doing to the faithful, and what we think we're doing when we're evangelising. And I'm asking, 'Do you think that wedge is there in the Bible? Is the gospel good for the unbeliever, but somehow not good for the believer? Is it something you do to get in by and forget about? Or could it just be that it's something that's good forever?'"

Indicative of Chapman's aptitude to "delight" audiences in *evangelistic* contexts is this section in manuscript 7. Chapman is explaining the importance of Christ's death from Luke 24 and how the Christian can trust that Christ's death was effective. Quoting verse 46 he says: "'The Christ must rise again from the dead.' You see, did it work? That's the question. Did the death of Jesus take? . . . Was his sacrifice a full, perfect, and sufficient sacrifice? Was it big enough for your sin and mine? And do we know? . . . I remember the first time I went overseas. You still had to be vaccinated for smallpox. I went down to the health department and I got on a queue, and it took me quite a long time . . . about half an hour to get up to the front of the queue. And I smiled at the nurse . . . and I said, 'Smallpox?' She said, 'Yellow Fever, you're in the wrong queue.' So, I got in another queue, and I got up to the front again. With less confidence I said, 'Smallpox?' She said, 'Yes, take off your coat, roll up your sleeve, don't muck about.' So, I took off ma' coat, rolled up ma' sleeve. She gave me the little yellow book. She stamped it. She said, 'Come back in three weeks and I'll see if it's taken.' Well, I didn't need the book to be stamped! I didn't need her to tell me. I could feel it had taken! Two days, it was a nice cherry pink. Four days, I'd break out in perspiration, dripping all over, while talking to friends. Their eyeballs'd open like saucers while we were talking! (*Laughter.*) I'd say, 'It's alright . . . smallpox.' They said, 'Have you got it?' (*Laughter.*) I said, 'No the disease must be terrible. I've just got the thing that fixes it!' (*Laughter.*) End of two weeks, it'd risen up like an enormous volcano . . . Did it take? It took! (*Laughter.*) Now, here's the question: Did the death of Jesus take? (*Slow.*) Think it through with me. What does the Bible say the punishment for sin is? . . . Always, the punishment for sin is death. If Jesus takes the punishment our sins deserve, what will you expect? If he does it properly, and he expends everything that death has got, I'm expecting the opposite of death . . . up death . . . resurrection!! So, Paul is able to say, 'If Jesus has not risen from the dead, we of all people are most miserable because there is no forgiveness. We are still in our sins, because his sacrifice did bother all!' But he did. And it did. And it worked! And from the resurrection of Jesus onwards we know that there was sufficient in his death, to deal with the sin of the whole world, because no longer has death got any power over him . . . pssshhtt . . . up death . . . in a great display . . . that his death is big enough for . . . anybody who wants to put their trust in him. The Christ *must* suffer and rise again."

back. Crucially, in such moments the weight and warmth of his tone created a sense of both rhetorical urgency *and* space. Indeed, while the need for repentance was clear, Chapman's Calvinism caused him to resist crowding or overburdening his audience. This produced a sense of both warning *and* wooing in his sermon invitations and appeals. That God had set his love upon his world was abundantly clear. Yet, it was also the responsibility of the listener to open and respond to God's gift of grace.[107]

107. Characteristic of Chapman's approach in seeking to "move" his audience in *catechetical* contexts is a section in manuscript 8. The sermon contrasts the love shown by the "sinful woman" of Luke 7 with the loveless response to Jesus of Simon the Pharisee. Reinforcing the transformative love of Christ for the Christian, he says: "So, I want to ask you at this stage 'Do you think you've been forgiven much? Was that a large thing? Was it a little thing?'... It has never appeared to me to be a small thing. It has only ever appeared to be a large thing, and even now breath-taking in its wonder... that God should set his love upon us, and that he should set his love upon us with a view to our being forgiven and acceptable to him. And that it was at great cost to his Son is a thing to be revelled in and marvelled upon... I am a man who has been forgiven. I need to remind myself of that. And I need to meditate on it. For if I understand this part of the Bible correctly, it is the wellspring from which my love for God is likely to increase. For those who have been forgiven much, love much. 'I tell you,' says Jesus. 'The great love she has shown proves that her many sins have been forgiven. Whoever has been forgiven little shows little love.' I want to ask you if you'll ponder again today on the greatness of forgiveness. On the sheer wonder that God... out of his mercy should take us back. And that at the great cost of the death of the Lord Jesus... Let's pray (*pause*). Our Father, it is a thing of wonder to us, that you should love us and send your Son to die for us. It is a thing of wonder that our many sins have been forgiven. And it is a thing of wonder to me, heavenly Father, how quickly I forget it. Please help us to demonstrate our love to you because of our own forgiveness. We thank you for the way in which this story today shows us in this sister of old, how we ought to act. And our Father, we thank you for preserving the story for us, that we might ponder on it, and love you. Help us to do that, we pray, for Jesus's sake, amen (*audience echo amen*)."

Characteristic of Chapman's approach in seeking to "move" his audience in *evangelistic* settings is this section in manuscript 5. Chapman is moving into the *peroratio* having just expounded one of his best-known sermons on John chapter 3, "A Fresh Start." He says: "I wonder if you'd do an exercise with me. I wonder if you'd say inside your head when I say it out loud, 'Jesus Christ died for me.' 'Jesus Christ died for me.' You've got to be a terrifically important person in God's eyes don't you, for him to do that? Have you ever thought of saying just 'Thank you?'... Just thank you for dying for me. I'll tell you a few things clicked into place that day for me. Do you know what surprised me when I heard this? It surprised me that my sins were so important in God's eyes, that this was the thing that needed to rectify them. I thought I was such a nice sort of a person, really. You know, it came as a big surprise to me. I thought, 'Well I'm not all that bad'... You know the second thing that shocked me. I thought 'If this is the God-given way of dealing with my sin, you can be sure that there is no other way that you can be forgiven, or God wouldn't have picked that one, would he?' And I thought, 'This is the only way. You can't make it by being good, John!' And it took me all the way before I got home from church... before the third thing clicked into place. It was this. Having now heard it, I was totally without excuse in the presence of God. And I remember saying to

Hence, Chapman's ability to slide fluently between the various registers of linguistic style became a key aspect to his effectiveness. It brought a sense of both popular appeal *and* of erudite solemnity to his preaching.[108] Indeed, moving effortlessly from humorous colloquialism to ushering listeners into the heavenly courtroom scene, such rhetorical agility produced a sense of earthiness and of eschatological fervor in his sermons. Added to this was the fact that, like many notable historic preachers, Chapman did not work from a full manuscript but a handwritten summary of his intended address.[109] Hence, while he would typically spend substantial time in rhetorical and spiritual preparation, Chapman's melding of content and form in the heat of the message brought a sense of living authenticity to his preaching that elevated its rhetorical force.[110]

Modes of Persuasion

Notwithstanding the clear presence of such rhetorical artistry, however, the ultimate reason for Chapman's persuasiveness as a preacher lay in the more intangible human and spiritual elements of his work. That is, the efficacy of his preaching could not be divorced from the personal and spiritual sincerity of the man himself. This reality has been long attested in the classical and Christian rhetorical traditions. Of the Aristotelian modes of persuasion (*logos*, *pathos*, and *ethos*) Augustine posited that for the preacher, persuasion first required a sound knowledge of Scripture and

---

myself, 'What would you say, in the presence of God if he said to you now, "Hey listen mate, what are you doing here unforgiven?"' Even I could see it was a stupidity to say, 'Well I, I've lived a fairly decent life.' He'd say, 'What d'ya think I let my Son die for? What are you doing here unforgiven?' (*Pause*.) 'I didn't think it mattered all that much.' He'd say, 'Get Out. You knew it mattered! . . . When you knew that I let my only Son die so that you could be forgiven!' And it is at this point, that we see how much God has taken us seriously. And the Bible is as it were, agog, at the wonder of this. That God should love us and send his only Son to die! So that I could be forgiven! There is no other way." A similarly characteristic sequence appears in the *peroratio* of manuscript 6, "Nothing Recedes Like Success," Luke 12:13–21.

108. On "populist" preaching and the democratic power of winning the crowd, see Old, *Our Time*, 78–81.

109. On the semi-extempore practice of Calvin, Wesley, and Whitefield see Old, *Moderatism*, 110–53; Old, *Reformation*, 91–133.

110. On Chapman's own preparatory sermon regimen, see Chapman, *Setting Hearts on Fire*, 129–38. Note that virtually every one of Chapman's sermon manuscripts across his career displays only a handwritten outline with summary notes. While Chapman preached some of these on numerous occasions, his practice was typically to vary them on each occasion. See Appendix 3.

a determination to elucidate its truth (*logos*).¹¹¹ Augustine also highlighted the importance of *pathos* in preaching. He recognized the power of the emotive features of a sermon—such as the passion, fervor, and feeling a speaker conveys—to influence hearts and minds.¹¹² Ultimately, however, Augustine suggested that the life of the speaker as perceived and known to the listener (*ethos*) carried greater weight than any grandness of eloquence itself.¹¹³ Such an observation has been attested in countless ministries and homiletic works.¹¹⁴ And so it was for Chapman as well.

As such, the power of Chapman's preaching inhered firstly in his faithfulness as a proclaimer of God's word (*logos*).¹¹⁵ Added to this, was the sincerity of the emotive features of his preaching that added depth to its persuasive force (*pathos*). In his younger years, Chapman's preaching exuded a dominant air of "warning."¹¹⁶ However, in later years, Chapman's presentation of Christ grew to offer him with "greater and greater sympathy to a lost and sad world."¹¹⁷ Indeed, as the magnitude of forgiveness and the reality of human resistance to the mercy of God pressed in upon him, this brought a significantly heightened empathy to his preaching work. Consequently, through tears of sorrow or words of benevolent fatherly rebuke, in a string of rhythmic cadences, Chapman would typically exhort listeners to consider why they remained unforgiven when God had sent his Son.¹¹⁸

It was in this sense, then, that like other significant historic ministries, the preeminent power in Chapman's preaching lay in the fusion of personal and spiritual qualities that he imperceptibly conveyed (*ethos*). Chapman's affable larrikin demeanor mixed seamlessly with his enjoyment of life and culture to convey a preacher to whom audiences could easily warm.¹¹⁹ His

---

111. See Augustine, *On Christian Doctrine*, 2.14, 4.6; cf. Kennedy, *Classical Rhetoric*, 82–88.

112. Kennedy, *Classical Rhetoric*, 179.

113. See Augustine, *On Christian Doctrine*, 4.59–63; Kennedy, *Classical Rhetoric*, 170–82; Stott, *Between Two Worlds*, 270, 281.

114. Of Billy Graham, it was remarked that there was "an incontrovertible sincerity" that made him utterly compelling. Similarly, of Charles Simeon, it was said "his whole soul was in his message." Stott, *Between Two Worlds*, 270; Chapel, *Christ-Centered Preaching*, 34–37.

115. See Chapman, *Setting Hearts on Fire*, 13–28. Manuscripts 1 through 10 universally evidence this conviction. See Appendix 1.

116. See Appendix 4, JCCPP/BIO#5, an address by the Rev. Dr. Paul Barnett where he makes this observation. Interview with Simon Manchester, November 18, 2016.

117. Manchester, "Preaching of John Chapman."

118. Typical of the *pathos* in his mature preaching is the *peroratio* (with its rhythmic cadences) in manuscript 9, Appendix 1.

119. Interview with Rico Tice, January 17, 2017.

effervescent persona seemed to reassure them that the God who called them to repentance also "threw in so much of this world to enjoy as well."[120] Similarly, Chapman's unpretentious background combined with his exposure to a variety of cultures to forge a persona who crossed audience barriers with charm and seeming ease.[121] Chiefly, however, it was the unerring spiritual seriousness with which Chapman spoke and conducted his own discipleship that bolstered his persuasive appeal. Listeners seemed to register instinctively that the same Savior Chapman offered them had also powerfully done his work on Chapman as well. Ultimately, then, it was this blend of imperceptible personal and spiritual qualities that came to mark Chapman as a preacher who was simply unique. Indeed, regarding the experience of hearing Chapman preach, a contemporary who heard him often noted:

> We always . . . looked forward to [Chapman's] visits, and we knew that we could ask our most . . . resistant friends to come . . . When he stepped up to speak it was as if he catapulted into the pulpit—he could hardly wait to be preaching . . . It was persuasive, sane and happy preaching—as if he had come with good news (which he had!) . . . He had searched the Scriptures and been searched by the Scriptures, and had worked out the best way to search his listeners with the Scriptures . . . [Chapman] preached like a man who knew "life to the full" . . . He was a natural comedian, but he did not tell jokes . . . his illustrations covered a thousand experiences from travelling to golf to music to shopping to surfing to enjoying every cultural experience he could . . . It was said of George Whitefield that beside him people seemed to be only half alive. In some ways this was true of [Chapman]. He was large, larger than life, and you knew it if he was in the room—or pulpit . . . this animated forcefulness may be what God builds into a real evangelist . . . when [Chapman] was preaching . . . rival ideas or voices were pushed aside. When he took a section of Scripture . . . the authority of Jesus was presented in animated power . . . It was gripping to experience and . . . [marked him] as someone who seemed alight with truth.[122]

---

120. Manchester, "Preaching of John Chapman."

121. On the Australian qualities of a "serious but light touch in dealing with religion," and a "readiness to laugh at oneself," which Chapman embodied and which audiences found so disarming, see Bouma, *Australian Soul*, 32, 45–46.

122. Manchester, "Preaching of John Chapman."

Conclusion

This chapter has sought to distill the essence of Chapman's achievement as a notable Australian homiletician. It has noted firstly his distinctive contribution to the theology of preaching. As such, it has suggested that in distilling a fresh emphasis on the *theocentric* and *missiological* nature of all preaching, Chapman provided needed redress to certain theological and soteriological lacunae that existed in the mid-century evangelical understanding of preaching. The chapter has also analyzed Chapman's praxis as a preacher. It has suggested that Chapman taught and modelled an *expository plain style* of preaching. This approach combined the strengths of postwar evangelical exegesis with the congenial arrangement of the English plain style. It sought to condense the theology of a biblical unit (a text, passage, or theme) under a "lead" idea expounded with the aid of clear rhetorical divisions. The chapter has also suggested that like other expositor-orators, Chapman adhered with relative consistency to the model he espoused. However, the chapter has located the particular power of Chapman's preaching in his ability to employ skillfully the various stylistic registers of language to delight and move his audience, and in the distinctive blend of personal and spiritual qualities that infused his preaching ministry (*pathos* and *ethos*). Like the most compelling of historical preachers, such qualities produced a rhetorical and spiritual experience that favorably disposed the listener while amplifying the sermon's other-worldly force. While not exhibiting the linguistic polish or precision of the likes of Calvin or Stott, Chapman's preaching nevertheless exuded a theological depth *and* simplicity, coupled with a sparkling evangelistic clarity, that made it unreservedly compelling. In Chapman's hands, the sermon became an event. It became a living encounter between God, the preacher, and his audience that was not to be missed.[123] Such factors help to explain why Chapman was propelled to a place of international prominence in his art.

---

123. See Miller, *Way to Biblical Preaching*, 26 on such dynamics in historic preaching.

Part III

Evangelist

5

Public Witness and a Changing Nation

Evangelism in Christian and Post-Christian Australia

> "We must give our whole-hearted attention to the great commission our Lord laid upon us. Men have immortal souls; they have needs which no betterment of their material condition can ever supply ... With all the earnestness and strength that are in me I urge upon you that fact. I urge especially upon my brethren the clergy, study evangelism, preach evangelism, live evangelism."—Anglican Archbishop of Sydney H. W. K. Mowll, 1938[1]

"WHAT A SIGHT!" CRIED the tall American, Billy Graham, as inquirers streamed forward to the crusade podium. "What a sight to see these hundreds coming through the rain. You who are in the Cricket Ground, you come forward too. Come and stand around the fences, and you who are listening to the landline relays, come and stand at the front of the auditorium where you are."[2] As Graham waited incredulously as the large crowd streamed forward, Australia had not seemed to Graham and his team as the likely scene of a crusade that would move a nation. Its population was less than that of New York City and scattered over a land mass the size of the United States (without Alaska). With an expanding economy, a love for sport and the outdoors, and a reputation for independence and bluntness of speech, the nation had proven somewhat ambivalent to foreign evange-

---

1. Howard W. K. Mowll, 1938 Synod Presidential Address, *1939 Sydney Diocesan Yearbook*, 247.
2. Pollock, *Billy Graham Story*, 102.

lists, especially those of the brassy American kind.³ Yet, at this final May 10 meeting of his 1959 Sydney crusade, a crowd of 150,000 was in attendance. A further one million listened by landline or live radio. From its opening week, attendances had ranked favorably alongside Graham's other major crusades in London (1954) and New York (1957). Indeed, over the course of the Australian campaign Graham addressed total audiences of 983,000 in Sydney and 719,000 in Melbourne, of whom 130,000 made "decisions" for Christ. Combined with total audiences of 3.25 million across the wider 1959 Southern Cross Crusade (incorporating Australia and New Zealand) these were said to be the largest crowds ever to have heard the preaching of the gospel, and, to that point, the most successful campaign in Christian history.⁴ Recalling, with a sense of awe, the "solemn audience" that stirred daily "like a giant anthill" at Graham's invitation,⁵ one Sydney clergymen described the spectacle as like "a Pentecost from the very first day."⁶ Another reflected that the response had been "so far beyond anything witnessed in our time that church leaders . . . find it impossible to describe what is taking place."⁷ Australia had not previously experienced anything that could be compared to a nationwide religious awakening. And whether the campaign constituted "revival" in any historic sense was a question that would continue to be debated.⁸ Yet, within the context of this remarkable postwar period of surging evangelical faith, the crusade undoubtedly marked a religious and cultural moment unlike anything the nation had experienced.⁹

Some thirty-five years later, across the other side of the world, a similar invitation was subsequently issued in a vastly different religious context. In "a brave bid to save student sinners," declared Newcastle-upon Tyne's *Courier* newspaper, "Australian evangelist John Chapman will take to the water next week—and preach at that shrine to decadent debauchery, 'The Boat.'" An evangelical mission was "behind the ambitious plan," the *Courier* alleged, which organizers hoped would "bring students into contact

---

3. See Piggin and Linder, *National Soul*, 279–80 for discussion of this ambivalence to "American revivalism" in particular.

4. Pollock, *Billy Graham Story*, 102; *Christian Herald*, May 16, 1959, 1; Piggin, *Billy Graham*, 25–26.

5. This captures the recollections of then Principal of Moore College, Marcus Loane. See Pollock, *Billy Graham Story*, 101.

6. Mitchell, "Sydney Crusade," 283.

7. "Australian Crusade," 5.

8. See Piggin, *Billy Graham*, 23; Piggin, *Spirit*, 158–70; Piggin and Linder, *National Soul*, 279–89 for assessment of the 1959 crusade as constituting "revival." Discussion of this assessment by other historians is noted later in this chapter.

9. Pollock, *Billy Graham Story*, 103; Breward, *Australian Churches*, 167.

with God." Chapman, who was no stranger to preaching before substantial crowds of his own, was in Newcastle in November 1994 at the invitation of the Jesmond Anglican Parish to prepare for a larger mission campaign the following year. Chapman had become a regular visitor to England. English crowds and clergy loved to exploit the "down-under" "upside-downness" of the "Aussie vicar," while Chapman loved to exhort the English to let "Christ turn *their* lives the right way up."[10] On this particular evening, added *The Courier*, Chapman would be "spreading the word from the club's world-famous revolving dance-floor." Chris Back, of Newcastle University's Christian Union, told *The Courier*: "If Jesus was around today, he'd have gone where the people were, like 'The Boat.'" "Back refused to comment," remarked *The Courier* wryly, "on whether the animals would be attending 'two by two' and denied rumors that the club's managers had bought enough hay and shovels to last 'forty days and forty nights.'"[11] Much, of course, was now different about this context in which the Australian evangelist preached. Gone were the historic postwar crowds and the congenial societal reception. Yet, as Chapman opened his Bible and asked students if they were "Right with God," many on the fringes of the revolving dancefloor that evening still found themselves drawn inexorably to Christian faith.[12]

In the generation between these distinctive missionary contexts, the climate in which churches across Western society promoted and defended Christian belief changed significantly. Indeed, following the religious surge of the 1950s, the speed of societal change left many breathless and many churches and denominational leaders flat-footed in finding a vocabulary and an approach with which to respond. By the late 1950s there were signs that the bonds of faith were weakening as moral and religious boundaries began to blur, and as percentage church attendances began to decline, even as overall religious indicators continued to rise.[13] Yet, as the "long 1960s" continued and the centuries-long enlightenment critique of religious certitudes and turn-of-the-century ideas of the intellectual elite began to impinge on the public at large, a tidal surge of protest and change was released.[14] Such realities marked a sudden and disruptive end to the

---

10. *Preaching Christ Newsletter*, no. 1, February–April 1995, 7; *Preaching Christ Newsletter*, February–April 1992, 5; Rev. R. Bewes (Rector, All Soul's Langham Place, London) to J. Kearsley (Administrator, DOE), January 21, 1992. BDM Box 1, SDA.

11. *The Courier*, Newcastle-Upon Tyne, cited in *Preaching Christ Newsletter*, no. 1, February–April, 1995, 7.

12. *Preaching Christ Newsletter*, no. 1, February–April 1995, 7; Appendix 5, *Historic Speaking Engagements*.

13. See Mol, *Religion in Australia*, 5; Breward, *History*, 167.

14. Bebbington, *Evangelicalism*, 232–33.

religious and social contract of the postwar era. In the passage of little over a decade, Christian churches moved from the center of Australian life to its periphery.[15] In such an environment, the challenges confronting evangelicals seeking to reach this culture with an approach that held firmly to traditional doctrine while recognizing the shifting milieu, were felt by clergy and congregations across the world.[16]

The following three chapters examine aspects of the evangelical response to this shifting milieu and the role played by figures like Chapman as a missionary leader within it. As previously noted, a significant aspect of Chapman's legacy was to offer leadership within the post-1960s Australian Christian world, both to re-amplify the theological foundations of the evangelistic task and to stimulate new approaches to mission more suited to reaching a secularizing public. Indeed, into a context in which little sustained reflection on evangelism had previously existed, Chapman's work became an early standard-bearer for a crucicentric and biblicist missiological approach. Such an approach emphasized Reformed theological categories, a stress on the personal responsibility of the Christian in evangelism, and a dialogical approach that gave space to enquirers to engage at length with biblical truth. The following chapters examine each of these emphases with respect to Chapman's work in Australia and overseas. The chapters also explore the oftentimes complex relationship between Sydney evangelicals and other local and international Christian movements. This includes the prominent Billy Graham Evangelistic Association (BGEA) and Lausanne movements (chapters 5 and 6) alongside the influence of certain local Australian theologies that Chapman viewed as counterproductive to forging a proactive culture of evangelism (chapter 7).

In the present chapter a portrait of evangelistic endeavor within Australian Protestantism in the pre-1960s era is first sketched. This supplies an important means by which to assess the degree of continuity and change between two distinct societal eras. Chapman's evangelistic leadership in the post-1960s context is then examined. This includes his involvements *with*, and methodological innovations *toward*, the ubiquitous crusade and pan-evangelical networks of the 1950s to 1980s, as well as his pioneering work in a variety of evangelistic strategies, initiatives, and endeavors. In this way, the study illuminates an influential twentieth-century Australian legacy of missiological advocacy. Moreover, given the relative spiritual vitality experienced by Sydney evangelical churches across this era of rapid

---

15. Mol, *Religion in Australia*, 302–3.

16. See the discussion of the causes of 1960s secularization in chapter 1. See also McLeod, *Religious Crisis*, 1–15.

change the analysis adds further color to the developing scholarly portrait of the complex determinants of religious decline and vitality during the twentieth century.[17]

Public Witness and The Protestant Ascendancy

Australian Civic Protestantism

By the time of Chapman's rise as a leading Australian evangelist, Protestant churches had pursued patterns of public witness that were at least a century old.[18] Following the early colonial period, in which the formative footprint of Australian Evangelicalism was laid by the colonial chaplains in a largely penal context, the influence of convictism faded and "religion distinctly gained ground."[19] From the mid-1830s, a combination of state aid to major religious denominations and a spirit of competition produced an upward surge in the number of church buildings and clergymen. The gold rushes in New South Wales and Victoria in the 1850s also brought to Australia a large wave of immigrants who swamped the ex-convict component of the population. These were accompanied by thousands of free settlers and assisted immigrants from all parts of the British Isles, who imported an attachment to the idea of a "common Christianity."[20] A growing belief across the Australian press of religion's positive social utility was accompanied by the rise of religious and philanthropic organizations. From the 1870s, a more voluntarist religious climate emerged by means of a centralized system of "free, compulsory and secular" education and the withdrawal of state aid to churches and their schools. Yet, during this period, Australian governments of all tempers still saw themselves as committed to the

---

17. See Bruce, "History, Sociology," 199–200; McLeod, "Perspectives," 465; Stanley, *Global Diffusion*, 15, on the need for such analysis to nuance the postwar Christian story and twentieth-century determinants of religious decline and vitality.

18. Breward, *History*, 173.

19. Murray, *Australian Christian Life*, 86–94; Hilliard, "Secularization," 76, cf. chapter 3 on the spiritual temper of the colonial period.

20. Amongst the free settler class (beginning in the 1820s) significant numbers of Congregationalists, Presbyterians, and Baptists arrived in the 1850s, permeating Australian Protestantism and society at large. They were drawn from rural districts of England, Scotland, and Ireland, where religious beliefs were still strongly entrenched, and where, by 1850, evangelical Christianity and religious participation was at its apogee in Britain. The opinion of respectable people was for a Sunday reserved for rest and attendance at public worship. Observance of a strict sexual code was increasingly expected of public figures, and there was a large demand for published sermons. See Hilliard, "Secularization," 76; Jupp, "Introduction," 1–2.

architecture and maintenance of a Christian society. This was demonstrated in various ways: in the introduction from the 1860s of daily prayers into the proceedings of both houses of each colonial legislature; in the support through legislation of a largely Christian social-moral consensus; and by the insertion of religious sensibilities into the preamble of the Constitution for the Commonwealth of Australia (1901).[21]

None of this warrants the conclusion that Australians became fanatically religious or grasped *en masse* the finer theological points upon which the various Christian denominations disagreed. As elsewhere, religious loyalties were determined not by faith alone but by family traditions, communal and social solidarity, conversion through mission work, marriage, school attendance, and other social factors. Each division of Christianity constituted a social network within which it was possible to live safely and comfortably in the sure and certain knowledge of salvation. Baptism, marriage, and burial within a denomination were considered normal behavior and breaking out of these confines could result in social isolation and even ostracism. In most parts of the country, gathering for worship was the most regular form of social interaction. Religious communities created sporting clubs and hobby groups, hosted scout and guide troops, choirs and debating societies, kindergartens and creches, youth fellowships, and missionary auxiliaries. One could live an entire life in the bosom of the church, and the breadth of such initiatives effectively brought together the sacred and secular aspects of life, making them mutually reinforcing.[22] Consequently, the period from 1870 to 1913 marked the high noon of Australian Protestantism, as forty percent of the population attended Christian worship regularly, while the vast majority reflexively named the faith to which they were connected.[23] The unprecedented destruction associated with the Great War of 1914–18 promoted a questioning of conventional religious teaching about God, and was for some years the source of resentment towards the churches for their part in ennobling and sanctioning the violent conflict. The confident assertions of the "new sciences" and of biblical "higher criticism" also posed a threat to traditional religious belief during this period. However, the evidence still suggests that Australia maintained a high degree of religious participation and sympathy well into the mid-twentieth

---

21. Hilliard, "Secularization," 76; Jupp, "Social Role," 30–31.

22. Jupp, "Introduction," 2; Frame, *Losing My Religion*, 62; Davison, "Religion," 219.

23. Fletcher, "Free Society," 97, 99–108; Gladwin, "Public Life," 4–9; Jupp, "Introduction," 2.

century.[24] As Richard Ely enumerates, of the shared "civic Protestantism" that was ascendant in Australia until the 1960s:

> All one can safely say is . . . that a non-denominational, civically-focused Protestantism was, until recent decades, widespread in Australian society; that most or many Australians were literate . . . in its Old Testament oriented vocabulary; that it was nationally-focused, although in the inclusive sense of presupposing that individual Australians were members both of God's Australian people in this continent, and God's Imperial British people on whom the sun never sets; and that, finally, it was civic, in addressing not just a people, but the polity they lived under.[25]

Anglicanism: The Church of the Establishment

Turning to the modes of engagement of Anglican churches, in particular, during this era, it is evident that since Reformation times the destiny and identity of the English nation had been intricately bound up with that of the church. Following the Henrician *Act of Supremacy*, English rulers saw religion as essential to their own legitimacy, and although the secular and sacred were distinguished, they were not divorced.[26] The missionary awakening in Britain at the end of the eighteenth century also came at a time when European interest in the non-European world had markedly increased and, from its outset, had undeniable connections with British imperialism. A common conviction was that Christianity had made Britain great, and that divine providence willed Britain to create more nations on the same pattern. This coalesced with a cultural Protestantism, an enlightenment ethic concerning human progress, and evangelical missionary zeal to forge a widespread belief that the benefits of Western civilization and Christianity ought to be established in the new British colonies. Five pillars of British identity—that it was Christian, Protestant, prosperous, civilized, and free—were considered worthy of universal dissemination. The devotion of British Protestants to this imperial project (while bound up with economic, racial, and political aspirations and fears) also indicates they believed in their role as God's agents for bringing the light of Christian civilization to the ends

---

24. Garton and Stanley, "Great War," 62–63; Frame, *Losing My Religion*, 62–3; Carey, "Historical Outline," 18–19.

25. Ely, "Forgotten Nationalism," 59–67. See also the recent contributions of Chilton, "Christian Australia," 49–85 with Piggin and Linder, *Public Prosperity*, 47–356 on these themes.

26. Chavura, "Secularization Thesis," 65–92; Colley, *Britons*, 1–54.

of the earth.[27] Indeed, as the nation's established church, the Church of England was viewed as a key instrument to implement the government's objectives. Hence, despite the presence of dedicated laymen and a strong sense of missionary vocation among colonial clergy, the history of Australian Anglicanism before the 1840s was largely that of a church which was evangelical in persuasion, under the auspices of state control, and active in a range of religious and civic duties.[28] The increase of cultural and religious plurality in industrial England eventually signaled the death of an "Erastinian" paradigm. The 1829 *Catholic Emancipation Bill* and 1832 *Great Reform Bill* removed all historic restrictions on Catholics and dissenting Christians from possessing full rights as citizens. This signalled the end of Anglican hegemony and the formal identification of Britain as a Protestant state. Such developments in Britain were echoed in NSW via Governor Bourke's 1836 *Church Act*, which sought "religious equality on a just and firm basis" and committed the colony to financially supporting all major denominations equitably.[29] Yet, as John Gascoigne avers, once its "constitutional position had quietened, the Church of England in its *actual* pastoral practice had little alternative but to continue to work on the assumption that it was responsible for the nation as a whole . . . after the 1880s the operative idea of the church which emerged . . . was still essentially that of Hooker." Such assumptions carried over to the Australian context where Anglicanism's establishment status endured, albeit with various local distinctives.[30]

Within this environment, a strong correlation existed between the promotion of Christian society, and the advancement of the social and institutional aims of the church. Indeed, prior to the 1890s, within Anglicanism there had been sparingly little emphasis on direct evangelism. Anglicanism was geared more toward pastoral teaching and moral and social

27. Stanley, *Bible and the Flag*, 57–58, 157–62; Le Couteur, "Anglican High Churchmen," 193–215.

28. Colonial Anglican clergy were active in three interrelated roles that were seen as vehicles toward the shaping of the Christian social, moral, and political order: ecclesiastical (the provision of worship, preaching, and sacraments); civil and governmental (magisterial duties, the inculcation of civic loyalty and public morality, and various chaplaincy works); and social (the provision of social welfare, benevolent and philanthropic societies, and the development of societies' cultural and intellectual institutions). See Gladwin, *Anglican Clergy*, 97–188; Fletcher, "Anglican Ascendancy," 7–30.

29. Stoneman, "Richard Bourke," 341–55.

30. Richard Hooker advanced a theory of church and civil law that gave the rationale *par excellence* for the Elizabethan Settlement and a confessional state. This model became strained after the 1660 *Act of Toleration* yet was invoked by clergy who were nostalgic for a nation united politically and religiously. See Gascoigne, "Church and State," 78; Kaye, "Australian Anglican Identity," 154–76. Note also Hugh Chilton's discussion of such themes in Chilton, "Christian Australia," 55–57.

improvement than to reaching outward with the gospel. The way of Christianizing the nation was seen as through the sanctifying effects of home and parochial activity, the education of the nation's children, and campaigns for temperance, censorship, and sabbatarianism.[31] Such causes sprang not purely from social conservatism, but from a view of British Australia as a godly Commonwealth, with a duty to preserve the habits and injunctions of Scripture lest it lose the favor of God and go the way of fallen empires.[32] Moreover, as the churches began to swell with the ascendant civic Protestantism, Anglicanism's association with legitimacy and monarchy appealed to those predisposed to ties with empire and memories of British prominence and grandeur. The presence of leading citizens and the magistracy in Anglican churches became common. This cemented its establishment ethos and gave an air of vitality that belied the mixed devotional sincerity of a percentage of adherents.[33] During the early twentieth century, the evangelical sea change that took place in the Sydney diocese under the leadership of Archbishop Mowll and T. C. Hammond saw a renewed focus on Reformed doctrine and a desire to stimulate the diocese into visible evangelistic witness.[34] Yet, despite the achievements of this period, the modes of public witness employed still traded softly on imperialist notions. In the postwar era, Australia's relationship with the "mother country" attenuated rapidly. Yet, in the period from 1901, the "crimson thread of kinship" with Britain saw most Australians still viewing themselves as "independent Australian Britons." This influenced the attitudes of clergy at all levels, for whom, motivations for the promotion of Christian Britain lay never far away.[35]

31. Even the archetypical Sydney evangelical, Bishop Barker, pursued the spread of Protestantism largely via the widening of Anglicanism's footprint. This included the multiplying of Anglican schools, the establishment of the Home Mission Society which funded new parishes as centers of Christian formation (1856), and the establishment of numerous benevolent works and societies. Under Barker, clergy carried the weight of church work, while many lay members engaged energetically in the many diverse areas of the church's institutional footprint. Maple, "Barker," 23–6; Judd and Cable, *Sydney Anglicans*, 125–28.

32. Breward, *History*, 80–83; cf. Brown, *Thomas Chalmers*.

33. Murray, *Australian Christian Life*, 92–94; Bouma, *Australian Soul*, 108; Carey, "Historical Outline," 10.

34. McIntosh, *Anglican Evangelicalism*, 267–390. Note the discussion of this period of change in chapter 2.

35. At the outbreak of the Second World War, for example, clerical attitudes may not have evoked the same religious jingoism expressed during the Great War. Yet, Mowll described Nazism as a "spiritual evil" that must be purged. As such, via the Church of England National Emergency Relief Fund (CENEF) Mowll laid out a sweeping agenda to provide help for the spiritual, moral, and social welfare of Australian servicemen in the battle against German aggression. This involved the establishment of hostels

The decade and a half following the Second World War proved a period of both opportunity and threat. It was a climate highly conducive to the expansion of evangelical witness, but it also created some of the conditions that fed into the religious crisis of the 1960s. Postwar churches were buoyant as suburbs expanded around cities, and standards of living and leisure time rose. The mainstream press affirmed Christian faith as part of a moral society, linked to democracy, security, and happy homes. Cold War fears of another protracted conflict were widespread, giving rise to a mood of social conservatism.[36] Undeniably, for Sydney Anglicanism, much of the architecture of its latter-century strength was put in place during this period.[37] Yet, rather than treating such years as halcyon days, Sydney Anglicans, like much of the wider communion, overlooked an opportunity to move beyond their associations with middle-class conservatism, British imperialism, and English cultural hegemony.[38] Instead, the participation of every "Anglican" in parish life alongside a focus on reaching the "inactive Anglicans" in the community became major themes of church thinking and clerical sermonizing. The work of groups like the Church of England Men's Movement, the Mother's Union, the Girl's Friendly Society, and Church of England Boys' Society were each seen as weaponry for the defeat of nominalism. Together with parish sporting and social clubs, these groups catered for Anglicans of all ages and marked a return to the kind of normality and respectability that many imagined had existed before the war.[39] From 1953 to 1954 churches capitalized on economic growth and suburban expansion through major parish building campaigns and membership drives. Using the fundraising

---

for servicemen on leave, mobile canteens to serve others on duty and the provision of equipment for chaplains and a host of voluntary workers. When war commenced, clergy counselled calm and called for courage, enthusiastically supporting the national effort. As the war continued, attention was turned to the kind of society that would be fashioned from its ashes. A pastoral letter from the Anglican bishops in 1941 linked the need for success in the war with the future of Christian civilization and urged able-bodied men and women to support the war effort as best they could. See Frappell, "Imperial Fervour," 76–99; Bridge, "British Commonwealth," 518–36; Loane, "Mowll," 273–74; Frame, "Identity," 111–14.

36. Massam, "Christian Churches," 260.

37. This involved the strengthening of its scholarship and missionary vision via Moore College and CMS, building and financial reform programs, and the multiplication of ministries and clergy numbers. See Judd and Cable, *Sydney Anglicans*, 251–312.

38. After the war, energy was also given to the Australian Anglican Constitution and the World Council of Churches. Positive developments flowed from each of these. Yet, they also marked a trend inward and growing fissures within the national church at a time when the church could, in hindsight, least afford it. Fletcher, "Identity," 332; Frame, *Anglicans*, 243.

39. Frame, *Anglicans*, 242–43. See also Frith, "Role of the Laity," 55–60.

methods of the Wells Organization and concentrating on an "Every Member Canvass," the so-called "Wells Way Scheme" brought the needs of local parishes to all those claiming some affiliation with Anglicanism. A Department of Promotion was established in the Sydney diocese to direct the campaign effort of as many as nine thousand canvassers. They knocked on doors and hosted "loyalty dinners," calling the parish's nominal adherents to become financially and practically involved in the life of the church. The Wells Way canvasses demonstrated the persistence of Protestant belief in the "godly commonwealth" and in the idea that many Australians were nominally Christian but merely in need of a spiritual awakening.[40] In 1957, the "Church Attendance Movement" was launched in the Sydney diocese as a follow-up to the Wells Way scheme. Employing similar methods of visitation and literature distribution, this movement aimed "to increase regular Church attendance, to arouse indifferent Church members into action, to recapture the power of Christian fellowship [and to] bring men and women into touch with God through [the] Church."[41] Other initiatives like the Church of England Television Society sought to exploit the rise of television for mass communication. Producing some of the first live programming on any commercial station in Australia, Sydney Anglican leaders believed their "Anglican contribution [which was] comparable with the 'Lutheran Hour' seen by millions in the United States, would undoubtedly serve a valuable purpose" and could open the possibility of reaching a "vast number of non-Churchgoers . . . as never before."[42] Sydney diocesan leaders also enthusiastically supported the nation's "Bring out a Briton" campaign in the 1950s. This scheme, seen as a subtle rejoinder to the rising number of Catholic and southern European immigrants arriving in the postwar era, was considered advantageous on account of the higher number of "Anglicans" among the scores of British migrants. Support for such programs was indicative of Anglicanism's belated adjustment to the changing nature of Australian society. Indeed, the smaller percentage of postwar migrants deriving from Britain altered the composition of Australian society which had been so conducive to the flourishing of Anglicanism in the past. Nevertheless, the church did little to change its essentially English character to cater for such realities.

---

40. By 1972, the Wells Way programs had raised more than $125m across the various Protestant churches. See Hilliard, "God in the Suburbs," 310; Breward, *History*, 136. On critique of this scheme, see Judd and Cable, *Sydney Anglicans*, 261. Sydney Archbishop Mowll, however, was in strong support of the program. 1956 Presidential Address, 1957 *Sydney Yearbook*.

41. H. W. K. Mowll, 1956 and 1957 Presidential Addresses, 1957 and 1958 *Sydney Yearbook*.

42. H. W. K. Mowll, 1957 Presidential Address, 1958 *Sydney Yearbook*.

While Australian cultural identity was gaining momentum and Australians were developing greater confidence in their own institutions, severing the ties of British kinship was causing sentimental unease. Hence, a creative way of being Anglican *and* Australian was slow to emerge.[43]

During the postwar era, an implicit clericalism also set the tone for Anglican patterns of public witness. Anglican leaders remained confident in their role of societal leadership and received respectful attention in much of the news media as favored public opinion shapers.[44] A committed stable of clerical evangelists also facilitated the work of the Sydney Anglican "Board of Diocesan Missions" (BDM) in the postwar era. Established in 1927, poor funding, short missioner tenure and the disruption of the Depression and war had curtailed the BDM's impact until the late 1940s.[45] Yet, even as its impact began to revive, a technique-led and values-oriented approach tended to dominate its missionary formula. While a clear call to follow Christ was not entirely absent from the BDM's platform, an emphasis on "happy homes," "time for God," and a "folksy" style of evangelism that appealed to latent community piety resounded more loudly still. Weeklong "Parish Teaching Missions" examined a range of themes. These included the basics of "Victorious Christian Living," or sermons entitled "A Happy Thought," "That's my Business," and "May I Come In?" Other BDM missions held screenings of "A Pilgrim's Progress" on three-and-a-quarter inch glass lanternslides. Still others utilized thirty-five milimeter slides and explored themes like "The Gospel in Wildflowers," "The Word from the Windows" (showing pictures of church windows), or "The Gospel in Stones" (testifying to the work of God in creation). Common items like soap, bread, matches, gloves, and petrol slogans were used by other BDM missioners as starting points through which to introduce a Christian message.[46] In keeping with the mood of the home-centered, independent individualism of the Menzies era, several parishes in early 1951 ran the "Better Homes Campaign." Here

---

43. Bridge, "British Commonwealth," 530; Frame, "Differences," 117; 1957 Presidential Address, 1958 *Sydney Yearbook*.

44. As noted, the Cathedral Luncheon Club became a prominent vehicle for public engagement in the 1950s. It examined predominantly current events and received patronage from many attendees who came to absorb the opinions of clergy as leading opinion shapers. So enthusiastically received were the opinions of leading clergy that the program times for the gladiatorial debates between T. C. Hammond and various Catholic spokespersons on radio 2CH were scheduled for maximum audience exposure. See Nelson, "Hammond," 152. On the Cathedral Luncheon Club program see chapter 3.

45. Orpwood, *Sake of the Gospel*, 45–60; "Diocesan Missioner Stipend Ordinance of 1927," *Sydney Yearbook* 1928.

46. David Hewetson to Michael Orpwood, BDM Box 1, SDA; BDM Box 3, SDA.

invitees were questioned, "Does Australia Need Better Homes?" In their promotional material, the visiting diocesan missioner was billed as a "family man whom God has blessed with a Christian wife and three bonny children. He believes the person of Christ received into the heart and home is the secret of a BETTER HOME." Parish bulletins featured news of such missions. They also included advertisements by local businesses that fell within "parish" boundaries and included news of visiting missioners, replete with their theological qualifications, ministry histories, and "family-man" status.[47] Other parish missions, like that of St. Andrew's Lane Cove in 1964, promoted "A Feast of Good Things for 1,400 Families." The mission invited all "Church of England people in the Parish . . . to an awareness of what the Parish Mission can do for you and the whole parish family." It aimed "to create in all 1,400 families an urgent awareness that anything short of total committal to Christ just misses the bus—and that there isn't any other way to experience the joy, fellowship and deep satisfaction of a faith that works." Invitations promised an experience of "Singing, Friendship, Supper, and Films." On the reverse side of the invitation was a commendation of the mission from Archbishop Hugh Gough—signed simply "Hugh Sydney."[48]

It is evident, then, that while there was a strong desire among Sydney Anglicans during this period to reach the community with the news of Christ, their approach also enmeshed strongly with the inherited superstructure of Anglo-Christian identity and was numerically bolstered by the inward tide of nominal adherence. Aside from the wholly pious desire to bring spiritual blessing to the nation, and to ensure the life and liberty of

47. See assorted BDM mission pamphlets, leaflets and invitations, BDM Box 3, SDA; Frame, *Anglicans*, 242–43.

48. Another mission in the Parish of Como was entitled "The Key to a Satisfactory Life," at which enquirers were invited to "gain the knowledge and find the faith that will enable you to put your trust in God. Your life can take on an entirely new meaning and you will find that inner peace 'which passeth all understanding.'" The Parish of St. Swithun's Pymble held a "Time for God" Crusade in July 1963, where the theme "The Keys to the Kingdom" was examined. In April 1964 the parishes of Bexley and Bardwell Park held a mission entitled "The Key to Vital Questions." Operation Friendship was promoted as the key to unlock the door to "Love, Pardon, Joy, Power, Peace, Purpose." Invitees were urged not to "let unfortunate happenings, disappointments, prejudices, old habits, scepticism, guilt or unbelief be a barrier." In April 1963 the Parish of Merrylands ran an "Open Door Crusade." Invitees were asked "Is the Door Open to God?" BDM Box 3, SDA. Note also that in signing his name "Hugh Sydney," Archbishop Gough was adopting the custom of metropolitan bishops who used the city of their See as their surname. Gough's chosen signature gestures in the direction of his formality. It also demonstrates the degree to which, during this era, clergy remained confident in their role of societal leadership and their employment of and enmeshment within the inherited superstructure of Anglo-Christian identity for the purpose of reaching the Australian community of the time.

the nation lay rooted in the Christian faith, little attention was given to a guiding theology of the church's mode of witness. By the religious indicators of the previous decade, Anglicans had every reason to be optimistic about the spread of "the righteousness which exalts a nation." The religious future seemed bright. Indeed, it seemed that "the 1960s would be rather like the previous decade, but better."[49] Harbingers of change were already becoming apparent. Yet, none could have foreseen the speed of transition away from the intellectual and cultural norms that had framed the lives of Anglicans for almost half a millennium toward a society that would increasingly be seen as no longer British, and no longer Christian.

Reviving the Nation

Overlapping such developments in Australia, as elsewhere in the Western Christian world, was the flourishing revivalist movement that both reinforced and challenged the ascendant societal Protestantism.[50] As noted, leading revivalists like Charles Finney and D. L. Moody in the nineteenth century, along with R. A. Torrey, D. G. Barnhouse, and Billy Graham in the twentieth, set the tone for this expansionist movement, under which a cavalcade of others joined the developing industry of soul winning. Several Protestant strands fed into this movement. The dissenting traditions from which the movement had sprung (notably Pietists, Methodists, and Baptists) had begun as explicit or implicit critiques of the alleged mediocrity of the established churches of Western Europe and the United States. Their very mobility was based on the assumption that confessional churches had failed to sustain the purity and vibrancy of early Christianity, thus carrying with them a built-in revival impetus.[51] Similarly, proto-Fundamentalism combined with holiness millenarianism to shape the movement's message. Whether the flavor was classic postmillennial or dispensational-premillennial, the import of such teaching was to stress the turmoil of world events as signs of the end times, in a context of which the urgent need for conversion and a life of holiness was emphasized.[52] Classic revivalist teaching (harboring millenialist convictions that the revival of Christianity was a precondition

---

49. Hilliard, "Crisis," 211; cf. Babbage and Siggins, *Light Beneath the Cross*, 181; Snape, "War, Religion and Revival," 135.

50. Carey, "Historical Outline," 17.

51. McClymond, "Issues," 1–47; Bebbington, *Victorian Religious Revivals*, 1–19; Massam, "Christian Churches," 251–53; Hempton, "Protestant Migrations," 41–45.

52. Francis and Surridge, "End Times," 378–79, 383–85; Bebbington, *Evangelicalism*, 152–53, 191–92.

to Christ's return) thus routinely took its stand against the moral confusions of the age. Temperance legislation, gambling, prostitution, and family planning were stressed as key issues.[53] Moreover, a highly experiential proto-Pentecostal revivalism developed in the early nineteenth century in England and the United States. It was marked by the holding of frontier style meetings, at which the fervor of preaching could result in rapturous dancing, singing, shouting, exorcisms, healings, and vivid dreams. As the century wore on, spontaneity slowly gave way to a practice of more arranged, even choreographed religious revivals. A landmark was the appearance in 1839 of Charles Finney's *Lectures on Revivals of Religion*. In this immensely popular work Finney presented revivalism as a science and suggested that just as there were laws of the physical universe, so there were laws of the spiritual universe. Conversions could be encouraged, he suggested, by the use of techniques like the isolated "anxious seat" for the troubled sinner seeking salvation. Although the book was a major stimulus to the more uncontrived revivalist tradition, it also heralded a new age of revival planning.[54] Under the influence of D. L. Moody (whose ministry became emblematic for much of North American religion in the late nineteenth century) revivalism transitioned from such early patterns toward the use of professionally planned revival-like occasions. Alongside the use of hymnody, testimony, and evocative preaching, such choreographed occasions boasted the more conventional spectacle of "decisions for Christ" and the pervasive use of the "altar call" in response to the conviction of sin.[55]

In Australia, during the late nineteenth and early twentieth century, such expansionary United States style revivalism and British Keswick style holiness revivalism fired simmering expectations of religious awakenings and appeared in several local waves.[56] However, the apogee of the revivalist

---

53. The revivalism of the late nineteenth century was therefore very different from that of the 1740s in Britain and North America. It was a less exacting religion than the undiluted Calvinism of Jonathan Edwards or the Arminian holiness stressed by Wesley. Long doctrinal sermons and catechizing gave way to bright, simple, sentimental preaching and a standardized catalogue of moral vices and spiritual errors. So Piggin, "Revival in Australia," 190–91; Davison, "Religion," 223. On the interconnectedness yet distinctiveness of Evangelicalism, revivalism, and fundamentalism in late nineteenth-century American religion, see Marsden, *Understanding Fundamentalism*, 1–42.

54. McClymond, "Issues," 5; Bebbington, *Evangelicalism*, 8, 115–17; Bebbington, *Victorian Religious Revivals*, 15; Spinks, "Liturgy," 481.

55. Bebbington, *Evangelicalism*, 162–63; Old, *Modern Age*, 501–9; Stanley, *Diffusion*, 66.

56. Three waves of Australian revival-style awakenings are discernible. In 1859–60 the revivals were linked with the missions of William Taylor and Thomas Spurgeon; between 1889–1912, the "Australasian awakening" was associated with the missions of John MacNeil, George Grubb, Reuben Torrey, Charles Alexander, Florence Young, and

movement in Australia was reached with the arrival of the Billy Graham evangelistic machine at the height of the postwar Indian Summer of Australian Protestantism. Graham's style of mass evangelism stood clearly enough in the American revivalist tradition of Finney, Moody, and Torrey while his profile and unprecedented geographical reach surpassed them all.[57] Tall and dressed like a movie star with a million-dollar smile to match, Graham was enticing for the many Westerners enthralled by the flood of postwar American films and cultural products. He golfed with presidents, dined with royals, vacationed with moguls, and schmoozed with anchormen. Graham had carefully studied the style of the revivalist and fundamentalist paladins of the age. While he carefully differentiated his platform from the worst revivalist excesses of the previous generation and some contemporaries, elements of the revivalist cloth from which he was cut still remained.[58] Finely tuning this inherited template and enjoying the benefaction of a collection of American backers, Graham's 1959 campaign machinery was impressive. Alongside the executive leadership of local Anglicans, a team of Billy Graham Evangelistic Association (BGEA) staff maintained the campaign's administration from a central office. Chairmen of a dozen committees built up teams numbered in the tens of thousands: prayer partners, follow-up personnel, choir members, ushers, counsellors, logistics specialists, and many others. Never before had Australian Evangelicalism seen a level of organization or unity on a scale like this.[59] Supplying impetus toward the

---

J. Wilbur Chapman; and that of the 1950s, featuring J. Edwin Orr, Alan Walker, Oral Roberts, and Billy Graham. Piggin, "Revival," 177; Piggin, *Spirit*, 59; Lawton, *Better Time*, 7, 9, 141–44. From the 1870s, advocates of "holiness" teaching promoted the possibility of a "subsequent" experience of sanctification beyond conversion, so as to attain to an elevated state of holiness. Such teaching became synonymous with the English Keswick convention and began to infuse the preaching of Keswick-style revivalists such as George Grubb, who visited Australia in 1891. Bebbington, *Evangelicalism*, 151. See the discussion in chapter 9.

57. Stanley, *Diffusion*, 66; Wacker, *America's Pastor*, 139.

58. Noll, *American Evangelical Christianity*, 50; Wacker, *America's Pastor*, 254; Martin, *Prophet with Honour*, 69. McClymond, "Issues," 18–19 describes Graham as "revivalism at its best" and notes the stain that befell revivalism by the 1920s around abuses of technique, the misappropriation of funds, and sexual scandals—giving rise to the slight on revivalists as religious "hucksters." Indeed, Graham's arrival marked a shift toward the greater infusion of American Evangelicalism within its Australian counterpart, in the words of one historian, moving it "from British sycophant to American lickspittle." This was a dynamic that drew a high degree of criticism at the time. See McLean, "British Colony," 64–79; Chilton, "Christian Australia," 175–80.

59. The scale of the logistical superstructure supporting the campaign was herculean. More than nine thousand counsellors completed seven weeks in training. A roster of three thousand singers served in rotation for the nightly choir, and nearly one thousand made up the usher corps. A "Census Visitation" program was underway

campaign's success was also a national mood that welcomed Graham with the enthusiasm of a visiting celebrity. Indeed, arriving on the crest of the religious surge of the postwar era and coalescing with lingering national security fears and concerns for a society beginning to totter into moral decline, such a confluence of causalities seemed to resonate across the nation at large. Local media outlets gave Graham almost euphoric support. Civic dignitaries rushed to offer enthusiastic patronage.[60] Graham's written endorsements from Presidents Nixon and Eisenhower and his rising fame and statesmanship also combined to give the campaign a quasi-political air. No Australian religious event had ever been treated so favorably. Indeed, the 1959 crusade became not merely a religious affair, but a cultural one; and Billy Graham was the talk of the town.[61]

Graham's message mixed evangelistic imperatives with civic and moral. Addressing the fifty-thousand-strong crowd on the opening night of the Sydney crusade, Graham insisted he had "a simple message" and asked his audience to "listen with the ears of your soul."[62] He spoke of the "mounting confusion" and "despair" of the present age. In a manner calling Australians back to an almost covenantal-like fidelity, he exclaimed: "We find a generation coming along which ignores the Ten Commandments and the Sermon on the Mount. We need to be reminded that the moral law is absolute, and God means what He says."[63] Like his predecessors, Graham spoke of truth and falsehood. Yet his warm Southern tones managed to jettison much of his predecessors' abrasive and artificial air. Taking a note from the revivalist playbook, Graham rarely elaborated the historical and theological implications of the text *du jour*. Instead, he hurried on to a

---

in the weeks preceding the crusade, whereby several thousand attempted to visit every dwelling in Sydney. Fervent daily prayer (linking five thousand homes) was also a feature of the Sydney campaign, supported by organized networks across the globe. "Sydney Preparations," 1. *Billy Graham Center Archives*, Wheaton Illinois (BGCA), Collection (CN) 360, Scrapbook (SB) 467, no. 94, April 1959, sec. 2; Kitchen, "Spiritual Awakening." BGCA, CN 360, SB 466. On the role of Sydney Anglicans in securing and supplying crucial support for the 1959 crusade, see Loane, "Graham Crusade," 2.

60. Herring, Governor of Victoria, for example, described Graham's visit as "an exciting, thrilling prospect for the city" for which he beseeched the "blessing of Almighty God." See *Christian Life*, April 1959, 26. BGCA, CN 360, SB 466; Prior, "Graham's Sydney Campaign." BGCA, CN 360, SB 469.

61. Piggin, "American and British Contributions," 299; Martin, *Prophet with Honor*, 254–55.

62. "Billy Graham in Sydney." BGCA, CN 360, SB 466.

63. Prior, "Graham's Sydney Campaign."

laundry list of national and world crises and declared Christ offered the solution for one as much as the other.[64]

In the tradition of revivalism Graham also concluded each message with an invitation. This displayed a remarkable if not choreographed and deeply ritualized consistency.[65] From its earliest days the revivalist impulse was pervaded by a consciousness of an inevitable and momentous spiritual choice to be made. Such an impulse extended deep into the Protestant psyche and drew from biblical and historical precedent: Paul on the Damascus Road, Augustine in the garden, Martin Luther in his tower. Similarly, John Wesley had a sudden conversion experience at Aldersgate in London, where "an assurance was given me that Christ had taken away my sins ... and saved me from the law of sin and death."[66] Billy Graham, with a religious upbringing, regularly recounted the meeting led by evangelist, Mordecai Ham, at which he himself was converted. Evangelical culture, and Graham in particular, typically described such an experience as a definable event in time. In his more reflective moments, Graham knew the reality of conversion was often more complex.[67] Yet, this did not alter the standard narrative. Revivalism represented an intensification of the Protestant-conversionist impulse and treated such experiences as normal, or even essential, for Christian faith. Furthermore, resisting the idea that dark nights of the soul or seasons of God's silence would be a normal part of the Christian journey, revivalism thus sought an environment that encouraged such an experience as a route to fresh assurance and as an invitation to pursue a personal "Aldersgate" moment.[68] Thus, in every service, Graham aimed for "a verdict."

---

64. Chapman, *Ambition*, 42; Wacker, *America's Pastor*, 55–59. A stress on moral formation also addressed the needs of the hour. For example, during a mid-week Sydney crusade address, Graham tackled the subject of "The Problems of the Home." Referring to Proverbs 31 and Psalm 15 he stressed that a happy home was one where the "Lord God was honored, His word revered, and prayer was made a living reality." The lady at the crusade switchboard was overrun by testimonies from happy wives. Reports also flooded in regarding the way in which this address had been discussed in offices, factories, and clubs across the metropolitan area. See Mitchell, "Sydney Crusade."

65. Long, "Preaching the Good Always," 13.

66. McClymond, "Issues," 10–23.

67. Graham was mindful that conversion was often a longer process of spiritual awakening, and an understanding of grace as a work always in progress was not entirely absent from Graham's matrix. Analysts of his ministry have estimated that 60 percent of those making "decisions" already moved in the churches' orbit. Critics repeated such statistics breathlessly. And to some extent they had a reason for doing so, since the BGEA often allowed the perception of blue-sky conversions. Yet, Graham was candid that as many as 80 percent of crusade "decisions" were "rededications." So McClymond, "Issues," 10–23.

68. Nominalism, they reasoned, sapped Christianity's vitality. And Graham's ability

Signaling the transition from exposition to invitation, Graham slowed his tempo, carefully choosing each word and requiring silence. Even in a vast stadium, the slightest distraction could eclipse the momentous decision at hand. Urging hearers "there is no decision in your whole life that compares to this. You come," his posture sharply etched the scene. Tearless, standing tall and arrow straight, with left elbow in right palm, Graham's entire frame signaled the weight of the decision at hand. And as the giant choir sang, the multitude invariably streamed to the platform.[69]

People frequented the Graham crusades for an array of reasons: the experience of the worship, hearing the "world's greatest living orator" and feeling the force of his invitation to come to Christ.[70] For others, the reasons were not definably religious. They saw it as a spectacle, a media event not to be missed. Others felt drawn in the expectation of a time-out-of-time experience, different from the mundane.[71] Sociologists explained the phenomenon in purely socioeconomic terms. They saw in Graham's principally middle-class base an audience who were drawn to a leader who viewed and accessed the world much as they did.[72] Still others critiqued the legitimacy of the entire approach. "The church did not meet the world at the stadium," decried a critic of Graham's 1957 New York Crusade, but "the church met itself—convinced Christians convinced convinced Christians."[73] Undoubtedly, some validity may be granted to such critique. For, while Sydney churches experienced a burst of campaign enthusiasm, many clergy were also conscious of the percentage of the faithful embedded in statistical responses. Indeed, reinforcing this cautionary note, leading historians have suggested that while the 1959 crusade undoubtedly took "Australia closer to a spiritual awakening than at any time before or since," even so, the crusade stopped short of achieving a widescale "breakthrough" in reaching the "unchurched."[74] Despite such assessments, it is evident that in reaching audi-

---

to prompt audiences to pause and shoulder the responsibilities of the Christian life alongside the textbook conversion constituted a defining contribution. See Johnson et al., "Attendance," 300–309; McClymond, "Issues," 15; Drummond, *Evangelist*, 18–27.

69. "Australian Crusade," 5. BGCA, CN 360, SB 469.
70. Powell, "Why Did Billy Graham Succeed?," 16. BGCA, CN 360, SB 469.
71. Wacker, *America's Pastor*, 255, 261–65.
72. Clelland et al., "Company of the Converted," 47–49.
73. Firebaugh, "City-Wide Crusades," 24–29.
74. Jackson, *Christian God*, 185–86. Such varying assessments reflect the difficulty that historians face in analysing the conflicting micro and macro religious data informing the 1950s to 1960s period. As noted, Stuart Piggin has advanced a case to suggest that the 1959 crusade represented a season of religious "awakening," if not of "revival." Piggin defines revival as "an outpouring of the Holy Spirit on large numbers of people at the same time . . . usually preceded by an extraordinary unity and prayerfulness among

ences of 1.7 million people (alongside a majority of the population via live radio) and registering "decisions" from as many as 2 percent of the population, the 1959 Billy Graham Crusade marked a religious event that was unique in Australian history.[75] Evangelical history offered few reasons to believe that a person of Graham's gifts would arise again anytime soon. By the mid-1960s he had preached to estimated audiences of 32 million people, and a unique set of conditions produced his vast impact.[76] Graham returned in 1968 and 1979 to crusades in Sydney, of which the 1979 crusade still ranked only behind the 1977 crusades in India as the largest 1970s crusade outside North America.[77] Nevertheless, in a rapidly secularizing nation, increasingly thoughtful approaches would be required to break new ground or to achieve what appeared to be ever-diminishing results. However, one does not diminish the unique achievements of the Graham crusade era by observing that when the conditions changed, so did the required approach.

Public Witness in the Era of the Protestant Retreat

Against such a backdrop of swelling civic Protestantism, establishment Anglicanism, and postwar revivalism, the shocking extent of rising 1960s indifference to organized Christianity invited a chorus of reassessment among the various ecclesiastical polities. As noted, the range of Protestant responses to the fracturing religious consensus was diverse. They ranged from the exuberant yet morally conservative charismatic movement to the various strands of liberal Protestantism which promoted a more radical

---

Christians; and . . . always accompanied by the revitalisation of the church, the conversion of large numbers of unbelievers, and the diminution of sinful practices in the community." Piggin suggests that "the 1959 campaign exhibits all these features." See Piggin, "Revivals?," 23; Piggin, *Spirit*, 158–70; Piggin and Linder, *Soul*, 279–89. Hugh Jackson demurs from this assessment. Jackson highlights that many 1959 "inquirers" were "those who had been in the borderlands of church life" and that while many of these "became regular churchgoers . . . there was no breakthrough to the unchurched." Indeed, Jackson highlights data suggesting little increase in overall churchgoing between 1956 and 1960 and cites other polls that point to overall religious decline by 1966. Jackson, *Christian God*, 185–87; cf. Hilliard, "Secularization," 82 for a similarly negative appraisal, and Chilton, "Christian Australia," 180 for a more positive. In reality, the balance probably allows for an acceptance of Piggin's micro-indicators of religious vitality within a broader (and longer) macro-statistical picture of 1960's religious decline.

75. Piggin, *Billy Graham*, 25–26; Pollock, *Graham Story*, 102.

76. By 2005, Graham had preached (live) in ninety-nine countries to an estimated 215 million people and to another (estimated) two billion people through live closed-circuit telecasts. See Drummond, *Evangelist*, 177; Wacker, *America's Pastor*, 21, 291.

77. Note the further assessments of the 1968 and 1979 Australian Billy Graham crusades later in this chapter.

re-evaluation of how Christian doctrine should relate to modern culture. Such responses were each expressions of the disorienting challenge of addressing Christianity's growing marginalization due to the tide of secular modernism.[78] In Sydney diocese, the early 1960s ushered in a range of competing trajectories. Student enrolments at Moore College expanded under the direction of Knox and Robinson.[79] A desire for soul winning also continued to permeate diocesan culture and its structures. Although the spirited university missions of the 1950s had begun to attenuate, the visits of international evangelists like Leighton Ford (1961) alongside a range of local mission initiatives sought to consolidate and extend the effects of the crusade era.[80] Such continuing buoyancy was overlaid by a diocesan political mood that was increasingly vexed. The archiepiscopal term of Englishman Hugh Gough (1959–66) inaugurated an era of rising discord. Gough's autocratic manner and moderate evangelical commitments drew criticism from a coterie of Sydney leaders. Moreover, Gough's establishment of an *Archbishop's Commission* in 1960 (which began a protracted review of diocesan administration and finances) combined with his mismanagement of various tensions concerning the proposed Anglican Constitution to create a drain on diocesan energies at a time when (in hindsight) the church could least afford it.[81] By 1966, the percentage of Australians claiming an allegiance to Anglicanism was declining and a growing sense began to permeate church leadership that the national mood had altered significantly.[82] Yet, as the tone of political discord began to abate under the archiepiscopacy of Marcus Loane (1966–82) and with the successes of 1959 still fresh in leaders' memories, an invitation was issued to Billy Graham to return in 1968 for another crusade under the "shadow of the boomerang."[83]

78. Hutchinson and Wolffe, *Short History*, 246–53; Cox, "Progress Report," 22–23. See also chapter 1.

79. Stanley, *Diffusion*, 12–13; Piggin, *Spirit*, 167. See chapter 2 for analysis of Knox and Robinson's scholarly legacy.

80. *SUEU Handbook*, 24–26. This era saw the rejuvenation of the CMS Summer School in Katoomba, which supplied a steady diet of missionary fervour. The Sydney BDM also continued their various "teaching missions," seeking to consolidate the effects of the crusade era and reach the religiously inactive outside the church. The BDM sponsored the 1961 Leighton Ford Crusade, which saw ninety-seven thousand attend the Showground meetings. Orpwood, *For the Sake*, 78–83; Cameron, *Phenomenal Sydney*, 92, 102.

81. See Cameron, *Phenomenal Sydney*, 78–107; Judd and Cable, *Sydney Anglicans*, 264–301 for analysis of Hugh Gough's archiepiscopacy.

82. See Mol, *Religion in Australia*, 5; Jupp, "Social Status," 42.

83. Many believed Graham's previous visit had imparted a unity to the Australian churches that "gave strength and purpose to all their aims." So Loane, "Objections

Internationally, throughout the 1960s Graham's stocks remained comparatively high. His notoriety and growing crusade ministry had seen the BGEA's work extend beyond Western capitals into Africa, the Middle East, the Caribbean, and South America. It took its first steps behind the Iron Curtain in 1966.[84] The shadow of the "revivalist huckster" still subtly stalked Graham's ministry. Combined with Graham's occasionally naive political partisanship and the breadth of ecclesiastical platforms the BGEA was required to negotiate to achieve consensus for its crusades, the 1960s and 1970s thus witnessed bright days of praise *and* dark days of criticism for Graham.[85] Yet, Graham's star was still ascendant. Alongside his crusade and media profile Graham stepped effortlessly into his role as a leading statesman. Convening the 1966 Berlin World Congress on Evangelism, Graham brought together the largest gathering of evangelicals for its time. This established the movement as a third worldwide ecumenical force alongside Vatican II and the World Council of Churches, and signaled that conservative Evangelicalism could no longer be dismissed as a peculiarity of Anglo-American culture, but was now a vigorous force in all continents. Indeed, having secured "Christendom's number one public figure"[86] to spearhead a much longed-for spiritual advance, the sentiment of Australian delegates to the Berlin Congress was fairly typical of wider hopes for the 1968 Australian campaign. "Our greatest need," opined Berlin delegate Reginald Jarrott, "is a deepening spirit of evangelism, determined boldness. To achieve this, we need revival . . . Whatever strategy is used it will need to be big—very big."[87]

Answered," 9. BGCA, CN 360, SB 307. Moreover, "the 1959 crusade *had* resulted in significant additions to church membership," declared bishop A. J. Dain. Thus, with a desire to see a "spiritual awakening" among the 1960s generation, Dain opined "we are praying for a lasting work of the Holy Spirit [that will see this] happen again." Dain, "Sydney Awaits Billy Graham."

84. On the rise of the crusade ministry outside of the large Western capital cities, see Graham, *Just As I Am*, 325–86.

85. For critique of Graham's "melodramatic" revivalism, see Oram, "Challenge Billy Graham." BGCA, CN 360, SB 308. Indeed, given the ongoing stigma of "fundamentalism" in mainline American circles, the patronage Graham received from Sydney Anglicans as an "establishment" church was a boost to Graham's stocks. Following the 1959 crusade, Graham asked Marcus Loane (now a warm personal friend) to write an appraisal indicating the "infusion of new life into Anglican congregations" that could be traced to the crusade. Indeed, Graham persevered in this request "until it was impossible to say no." This formed the basis of a booklet (*Decade of Decision*) that was circulated before the 1968 crusade along numerous pathways. So M. L. Loane, Interview with Lois Ferm, 1982. BGCA, CN 141, Box 3/28.

86. Martin, *Prophet with Honor*, 341, 519, 608; Stanley, *Diffusion*, 65–70.

87. Jarrott, "Australasia," 236, 238.

Such a spirit of expectation formed the prelude to the 1968 Sydney Crusade (April 20–28). Indeed, played out against a backdrop of momentous events—including the assassination of Martin Luther King Jr. and decisions of President Johnson concerning Vietnam and the future of his administration—the 1968 campaign architecture was also decidedly "big."[88] A vigorous propaganda machine commenced in the months prior, defending Graham's methods and stimulating interest.[89] Crusade planning was again meticulous, occasioning opportunities for wide prayer and lay training. Moreover, on account of a pointed strategy to reach the throng of youth swept up in the so-called "hippie drop-out" generation, the campaign became dubbed affectionately as Sydney's "Youth Crusade."[90] Thus, as Graham challenged his audiences on sin, war, hippies, and the end of the world—with 80 percent of respondents under the age of twenty-five—it was with a flash of "blazers, mini-skirts, jeans, yellow stretch-pants, and brown leather-jackets" that the Sydney Showground came alive each night to the sound of Graham's appeal.[91] In terms of the crusade's success and relative impact, with a total attendance of 418,000 and 22,420 registered "decisions," crusade officials enthused that such an outcome represented another moment of historic proportions. Undoubtedly, there were compelling reasons to view the crusade in such terms. Measured by such indicators as the conversion of future clergy, or the enlivened piety and enthusiasm seen in local ministries as a result, or in the eleven thousand respondents who named the Church of England as the church to which they wished to be referred, so it was held the result of the crusade would only be made "apparent in the decade at hand."[92]

88. Nichols, "Cross Over Sydney." BGCA, CN 360, SB 309.

89. "Most Evangelical City," 1–2. BGCA, CN 360, SB 308.

90. Campaign architecture was again herculean. Two thirds of the Sydney churches (roughly eight hundred) of all denominations actively prepared for the crusade, and crusade committees operated in 115 major country centers. Three thousand homes were coordinated in prayer. Those who undertook "Christian Life and Witness" classes numbered 12,500, of whom six thousand were trained as counsellors. Teams totalling twenty thousand visited the 750,000 homes in the metropolitan area with invitations. Youth teams visited Sydney beaches and "milk bars" with invitations. Evangelistic rallies called "The Big Meet" aimed to give Christian youths an opportunity to "practice" by bringing friends to a "mini-crusade" with "modern style music," an invitation and counselling. Special youth Bible studies sold eleven thousand copies, along with a special audiovisual by Clifford Warne (Church of England TV) which was shown at 120 meetings to an audience of ten thousand. Approximately three hundred ministers also attended the BGEA "School of Evangelism" at the Anglican Chapter House (April 22–26) and were instructed by BGEA staff. "Sydney Crusade Preparation"; "Crusade for the Young."

91. Olsen, "Sydney Crusade Report."

92. Over half the students at Moore College in 1978 traced their conversion or

Indeed, such indicators, it was believed, were merely portents of a "great harvest" that the cities' churches might soon "gather in."[93]

Yet, for the many gains of the 1968 crusade, as the campaign's fuller impact began to register, it also became difficult to avoid the conclusion that while it remained a "fruitful crusade," it had also lacked a measure of the "width and depth" of its counterpart a decade earlier.[94] A detailed appraisal, along with a wide-ranging assessment of contemporary outreach strategies, was conducted by the Sydney Anglican *Commission of Enquiry* between 1968 and 1971. The commission (of which John Chapman played a leading role as secretary and theological consultant) made observations about the 1968 crusade in particular, and about the approach of "mass evangelism" in general, of which the BGEA was considered to be a pace setter. Among its more important findings, the commission observed a number of key dynamics with regard to the 1968 crusade. They included: an apparent diminished prayerful expectancy among the wider churches; a lower cumulative campaign effect on account of the campaign's relative brevity; and an alarmingly high percentage of 1968 "converts" who had ceased active Christian adherence by as early as 1971. In an age "attuned to having the experience of the moment without attention to its consequences," it was suggested that perhaps "too much attention" had been given to "the experience of 'deciding for Christ' without enough attention paid to the nature of that decision." Additionally, it was suggested that by failing to grasp the nature of true repentance, many converts had sought merely to assuage feelings of personal guilt rather than to shoulder the responsibility of genuine spiritual reformation.[95] "Affluence, existentialism and secularism have made the work of evangelism much more difficult in the last decade," the commission advised. While close attention to the "causes of the

---

sense of "calling" to the 1968 crusade. M. Loane Interview with L. Ferm, 1982. BGCA, CN 141, Box 3/28. Cf. *Move in For Action*, 106–10 on such other indicators.

93. Loane, "From the Archbishop," 1–2. BGCA, CN 360, SB 309.

94. Marcus Loane Interview with Lois Ferm, 1982. BGCA, CN 141, Box 3/28.

95. The commission observed regarding 1) prayer: while opportunities for prayer were commensurate with those of 1959, there had also been a "frightening decline" in the "enthusiasm and expectancy" which had marked the various prayer initiatives for 1968. Regarding 2) brevity: while the 1959 crusade had run long enough (one month) to enable cumulative interest, the 1968 crusade (nine days) was considered to have concluded "just as it was getting into the swing." Many people, the report advised, "are so busy they need more than a week's notice to accept an invitation to attend anything." Regarding 3) the perseverance of converts: given diminishing societal understanding of the "things of God," greater attention needed to have been given to "teaching the nature of Christianity" than to merely exhorting audiences to "decision." *Move in For Action*, 106–10.

large drop-out" was urged before other initiatives were undertaken, the commission conceded circumspectly that the role of crusade-style meetings might be a declining one. "The large open-air religious meeting," it advised, might not be "the one which will attract the sophisticated man of the affluent age."[96] Indeed, concerning the general climate for Australian evangelism, others observed wryly that the national mood had changed "almost as drastically as the length of women's skirts."[97]

Added to questions about the efficacy of the crusade approach, were questions about its all-constraining form. For, as the iconic centerpiece of the BGEA's institutional empire, a growing consensus began to emerge that the crusades had become both a stimulant *and* deterrent to effective outreach in local contexts. As a consummately professional religious experience—exuding meticulous planning, enormous advertising, and the inimitable charisma of a unique personality—the crusades had become the all-constraining pattern of most of the mass evangelization initiatives across the Protestant world since the mid-1950s. Indeed, so iconic had the crusades become, that were other pillars of Graham's influence to recede (including publications, radio and television broadcasts, and access to the highest echelons of political power), it remained impossible to imagine Graham's influence as being commensurate without the crusades.[98] Like the imitators of the titanic figures of Whitefield, Spurgeon, and other notables had proven in their own time, the dominance of Graham and the crusade impulse had invited the rapid proliferation of crusade "duplicates" (both of the larger professional *and* home-spun varieties) in Australia and across the world.[99] In Australia, such spectacles—complete with crusade-style hymns, altar calls, and counsellors, and even the jarring presence of Australian preachers projecting softly intoned American accents—proved increasingly "grating."[100] Eventually, with the changing societal mood, the growing estrangement of communities from traditional belief and community structures, and the rise of home-centric activities and newer forms of entertainment,[101] it became painfully apparent that crusade-style endeavors

96. "Surveying Present Outreach" in *Move in For Action*, 106–10, 109.

97. Nichols, "Australia Crusade." BGCA, CN 360, SB 308.

98. *Move in For Action*, 107; Wacker, *America's Pastor*, 61; Ward, "Colonialism," 87.

99. Edwards, *History*, 429–40. See details of such revival-style campaigns in Australia since 1859 earlier in the chapter.

100. John Chapman, "Report on the Parramatta Youth Crusade 1969," n.d., BDM Box 3, SDA.

101. As with early radio, the television became a coveted second-wave consumer item, focusing entertainment more within the home environment and radically transforming Australian family life in the process. See Carter and Griffin-Folet, "Culture and

were no longer drawing comparable crowds. It was also evident that attendances varied little across a given week (indicating the presence of fewer guests) and that clergy and missioners were now frequently and lamentably "preaching to the choir." Thus, a nostalgic loyalty to previously assumed modes of witness had become increasingly untenable.[102] "Evangelism used to be a fairly simple matter," decried a prominent Sydney clergyman in 1970, "parish missions, beach missions, house parties, and Billy Graham! But the more we go into the seventies the more complicated evangelism becomes."[103] Evidently, with the fracturing of religious consensus, the methods which had relied upon such consensus—particularly the crusade as a form of mass evangelism and as a symbol of evangelical success—had begun to wane. This provoked a frantic search for alternatives that could discerningly "follow the cultural energy."[104]

Dialoguing with the Nation: A Re-envisioned Approach

One such Australian alternative to the waning crusade model, which in time began to exert an influence of its own upon the wider evangelical missiological culture, was the development of a dialogical approach. This was not a wholesale replacement of the crusade impulse *per se*, given the involvement of its key exponents (like John Chapman) in future Australian crusade initiatives.[105] Nevertheless, it was a model which sought to resonate with the modern appetite for "dialogue and participation" in emerging religious forms, and offered a more epistemically nuanced approach to the evangelization of cultural moderns.[106] It was also a response to the challenge of energizing continuing mission and lay involvement in light

---

Media," 254.

102. "Move in Summary"; John Chapman, *Evangelical Minister's Assembly*, 1985.

103. Nichols, "Evangelism by Confusion," 5.

104. Hutchinson and Wolffe, *Short History*, 206. Note that the most extensive appraisal of the 1968–69 Australian Crusade meetings (which included three meetings in Brisbane and ten in Melbourne in March 1969, alongside the Sydney meetings) is that of Chilton, "Christian Australia," 182–222. Chilton notes the comparatively high attendances at the 1968–69 meetings relative to crusades of similar length. However, Chilton also concludes of the 1968–69 meetings that ultimately, the "glories of 1959 had not been repeated." Rather, the crusade marked a "transition" point for Australian evangelicals in reconsidering their place within the nation and the new approaches to mission that were required to reach it. Chilton, "Christian Australia," 209–14.

105. John Chapman played a key role in the 1979 Sydney Billy Graham Crusade. This will be examined shortly.

106. "Move in Summary," 12–13; Bruce, "Secularization," 205.

of the all-consuming requirements of the crusade format.[107] Hence, as he developed his own comprehensive missiology, and building on insights of the *Campus Crusade* lay-training material and of various Australian university ministries, in the early 1970s Chapman cultivated a mode of outreach centered on the home environment. As a place of "sympathetic, unjudging fellowship," the home was considered an ideal context for engaging the unchurched and providing a bridge to span the emerging gulf between organized Christianity and secular culture.[108] Highly conscious of the changing milieu, Chapman averred in 1972 that:

> Understanding the world in which we are living is almost as important as understanding the message we have to preach. The message never changes but the sociological factors of life change and these will affect the methods we use in trying to preach the gospel . . . One of the side effects of the affluent society in which we are living is that people's options are greater than ever before. There are many more things to do and more money to enable people to do them. Time is an ever-decreasing commodity. People have little time to spare. This factor must be considered when working out a method of evangelism. For too long we have continued in the security of the old "well tried and reliable" methods without ever having taken an objective look at them . . . Twenty years ago, people were willing to come to a series of meetings. Public meetings were well attended, and even open-air meetings were fairly respectable . . . Those days are gone . . . At the present moment we need to ask: Where do we have meaningful contact with non-Christians? Will they come to the church building? Under what conditions? Many Christians wish to evangelize, but do not know where to begin. *Dialogue evangelism* was begun to show people a way in which their homes could be used [to] meet with non-Christians and talk about the gospel. The message never changes, but we need a renewed confidence in it. The gospel is *very* powerful (Rom 1:16), indeed, it is the power of God and it will bring salvation to those who

---

107. Of the crusade format, Sydney clergyman Rev. David Hewetson recalled of 1959 that many had "blown themselves out on the crusade, we went really full bore . . . everybody was worn out." D. Hewetson to M. Orpwood, BDM Box 1, SDA. See also Frith, "Role of the Laity," 69–85.

108. The model was developed during Chapman's tenure as Director of Christian Education in the Armidale diocese and incorporated insights from various contemporary ministries. Chapman to Orpwood, February 1, 1994, BDM Box 1, SDA; *Move in For Action*, 103; "Dialogue Evangelism" in 1993 *Moore College Missions Resource Book*, 22–50, Appendix 4, JCCPP/MC#2. Cf. Stowers, "Social Status," 59–82 on the early church's changing modes of evangelism in response to changing conditions.

believe. We must also have a renewed confidence in the Holy Spirit who will guide us into new ways when necessary.[109]

In tandem, then, with his escalating preaching ministry, a key model of engagement Chapman advanced in response to the changing context involved the use of the home environment. Such an approach (entitled "dialogue evangelism") involved Christians offering hospitality (usually over supper) to invited guests to discuss the "nature of Christianity." A trained dialogue leader, ideally an "outsider" to the group, led discussion. A brief presentation on the nature of Christianity was used as a basis for discussion. The meetings, being intentionally small (ideally 10–15) supplied a relaxed atmosphere where guests could listen and interact on issues they did not grasp, or with which they disagreed. Such evenings could be stand-alone or integrated into a parish mission.[110] While decidedly simple in format, the model was developed extensively and supplemented with material that supported it theologically *and* sociologically. This allowed it to be scaled and replicated in different contexts. Extensive material was provided to hosts and dialogue leaders on how to ensure meetings were engaging, warm, and conducive to discussion. Sample outlines gave guidance on the elements of a simple presentation of the gospel, as well as detailed apologetic answers for hosts and group members to assist in answering common questions. Such an approach, it was considered, required neither the military-like planning and infrastructure of crusade models nor the specialized knowledge of the cleric-practitioner. The approach began to take hold rapidly.[111]

Following the initial development of this approach, Chapman began training large numbers of Sydney clergy, theological students, and Christian laity in the methodology and its content. By 1970 Chapman's schedule was heavily weighted to the conducting of dialogue-style missions across the region. At the instigation of diocesan leaders, the 1971 Lenten season

---

109. Chapman, "Evangelism Today," 11.

110. Chapman, "What? Why? How?," 3–4.

111. Sociologically, the material reflected extensively on the dynamics of human interaction within the context of a society in which "fewer people have any knowledge of Christianity." Instructions for hosts covered the basics of group dynamics, seating, and discussion arrangements. Informality for clergy was stressed, in order to facilitate the most natural forum for exploration. The content of the recommended gospel presentation mirrored the content of Chapman's tract, "What is a Christian?" By virtue of its clear presentation of a Reformed creation-fall-redemption sequence, this laid the template for later gospel presentations of a similar nature. Commonly asked questions were distilled from a survey of five hundred dialogue meetings and became the basis of another training course provided by the DOE (*Tough Questions*) used to train Christians in biblical apologetics. See the extensive course notes in the *Moore College Missions Resource Book*, 1993, 22–50.

was dedicated to a coordinated mission (entitled *Christ Cares*) following a pattern of dialogue meetings.[112] Four hundred private home meetings were arranged, alongside six town-hall-style rallies at which Archbishop Loane spoke. Ninety clergy and lay leaders took part in the home meetings, which drew a total of 4,500 people.[113] In the enthusiasm surrounding the initiative and in the numbers of unchurched Australians who were being reached by it, the initiative was repeated in 1972 and 1973. Fifty-two parishes enlisted for the 1972 campaign. With training courses drawing several hundred participants and on account of the large numbers of guests attending "whose first contact with Christianity was through the dialogue meetings and [who were] converted," it became the largest dialogue outreach initiative undertaken, and was even more effective than that of 1971.[114] With similar outcomes experienced during the 1973 *Christ Cares* mission, by May 1973 an estimated fifteen thousand nonchurchgoers had been reached by the new and inventive mission approach.[115]

By 1974, reports of dialogue evangelism had spread overseas, and Chapman was invited, as part of his representation of the Oceania delegation at the *Lausanne Congress on World Evangelization*—the largest gathering of world evangelical leaders of its time—to give demonstrations on dialogue evangelism on July 17, 18, 19, and 22. This was a substantial stage, on which Chapman and other leading exponents of evangelistic technique were able to showcase various missiological tools and approaches. Thirty-four demonstrations of evangelistic methods were given over four afternoons at the Lausanne Congress by "well-known exponents of specialized evangelism." Numerous participants expressed the view that "the demonstration groups were among the most valuable aspects of the congress."[116] With rising exposure and enthusiasm, throughout the 1970s dialogue evangelism was introduced to many other parts of Australia and North America as well as numerous locations in the United Kingdom (where it became particularly influential). Rippling outward from Chapman's connection with St. Helen's

---

112. The Sydney Standing Committee set up a subcommittee to promote the program. BDM Prayer Letter, September 1970.

113. "Archbishop Writes," 9; "Dialogue Meeting Draws 4500," 18.

114. BDM Prayer Letter, November 1971; BDM Prayer Letter, October 1972; BDM Prayer Letter, March 1972; BDM Prayer Letter, June 1972.

115. *Southern Cross*, February 1973, 29; "Missioner's Report," May 1973. BDM Box 1, SDA.

116. Others presenting alongside Chapman were Bill Bright (*Campus Crusade*), James Kennedy (*Evangelism Explosion*), George Verwer (*Operation Mobilisation*), and Nigel Goodwin (*Arts Centre Group*, London). Capon, "Lausanne 74," 23–33; "Lausanne 1974 Notice."

Bishopsgate in London, beginning in 1976 the approach was championed among student and businessmen's congregations. Many English theological students and rising evangelical leaders from various countries were also trained in the methodology during regular visits to the United Kingdom.[117] Additionally, by virtue of Chapman's teaching and advocacy at Sydney's *Moore Theological College* and *Sydney Missionary Bible College*, the methodology secured a prominent place in the apologetic diet of Sydney theological college students for some twenty-five years. It enjoyed favored status as a tool for the yearly Moore College missions, which took place within a range of diverse evangelical networks in urban and rural Australia, as well as across wider international evangelical networks like Southern Africa.[118]

In Australia the effects of the radical individualism and social innovation of the 1960s eventually began to moderate. In the Fraser era (1975–83) the percentage of those practicing no religion expanded while only 26 percent of the population regularly attended Christian worship. However, with the influence of a resurgent American conservatism in global affairs, alongside the influence of religious pressure groups, religious immigration, and a growing distaste for 1960s social permissiveness, there arose a newly conservative social mood.[119] This softening national mood facilitated the partial renaissance of larger-scale evangelistic initiatives among Australian evangelical churches. As noted, Chapman played a leading role in such developments. Hence, his schedule began to fill during this era with activities perceived to be most amenable to promoting Christian faith—including large-scale university, regional, and crusade-style guest initiatives. Additionally, with the proliferation of other evangelistic tools, the saturation of Christians conversant in the dialogue model, and with the publication of Chapman's acclaimed *Know and Tell the Gospel*

---

117. Chapman spent four months in 1974 demonstrating the method in America and England and continued to present on methods of evangelism in North America into the 1980s. BDM Prayer Letter, June 1975. In 1976, Chapman lectured at Trinity College, Bristol on evangelism and the dialogue model. Intensive training was also conducted at a St. Helen's Clergy Conference and at the Southampton School of Christian Studies during a three month visit in 1980. Interview with David Jackman, January 16, 2017; DOE Prayer Letter, March 1980. Leading English evangelicals, such as Mark Ashton (Rector of the Round Church Cambridge in the 1990s), suggested Chapman's dialogical approach had become "foundational" to his own approach to evangelism and to that of many other English clergy. Mark Ashton to Michael Orpwood, February 10, 1995, BDM Box 1, SDA. Dialogue evangelism was also taken up in locations such as Toronto, Canada, by church leaders who had attended workshops at Lausanne, requested materials, and begun to implement the model. BDM Newsletter, June 1975.

118. DOE Prayer Letter, February–April 1986; David Cook (SMBC Principal) to John Chapman, January 20, 1986, BDM Box 1, SDA.

119. Bolton, *History*, 247–56; Mol, "Australian Christianity Today," 65–70.

in 1980 (which incorporated and expanded the methodology's insights), the need for its explicit promotion somewhat lessened.[120] Nevertheless, the insights of the dialogue methodology began to find fresh expression in Australia and elsewhere. The 1980s and 1990s saw the embrace of new communication and home entertainment technologies (like video recording equipment) by Australian consumers.[121] As a result, in the mid-1980s Chapman pioneered "Video Evangelism" as an experimental foray into such new media forms. Indeed, echoing the iconic live audience genre of Australia's *Countdown* (1974–87) and the studied irreverence of *The Norman Gunston Show* (1975–76),[122] in 1986 an energetic audience of several hundred attended a live studio recording of a series of presentations by Chapman exploring the Gospel of Luke.[123] The first of its kind in the Australian marketplace, the video series became widely employed in churches and home groups, or as follow-up material for church enquirers. Many also employed the resource in a similar way to an extended dialogue course. In such contexts, leaders would convene a supper meeting at which the video presentations were played and used to facilitate discussion over a stand-alone evening or a period of weeks.[124] Stuart Robinson, a Moore College student in 1986 and later bishop of Australia's Canberra-Goulburn diocese, enthused about Chapman's pioneering approach:

> My first experience of "video evangelism" happened the other week when our neighbors came over to watch Chappo on the small screen. They brought the cake and we supplied the loungeroom, television and coffee. In a relaxed, convenient and non-threatening environment we listened and watched the new "Telling the Gospel's Truth" video series. The messages were exceptionally clear and challenging and led us quite naturally into fruitful discussion . . . John's combination of wit and clear Bible teaching have not been stifled by the camera . . .

---

120. DOE Prayer Letter, November 1981–January 1982. The contours of this work will be examined in chapter 7.

121. Carter and Griffen-Foley, "Culture and Media," 260.

122. The live audience genre prospered in Australia with programs like *Bandstand* (1958–72), *Countdown* (1974–87), and *Hey Hey Its Saturday* (1971–99) holding national audiences. Parodies of Australian life by Gary McDonald (*Norman Gunston*) and Graham Bond (*Aunty Jack*) also shaped the genre's irreverent humor. Carter and Griffen-Foley, "Culture and Media," 257.

123. Chapman to Lane, May 14, 1986. Box 3, Adrian Lane Papers 1973–2005, Mitchell Library NSW.

124. The producer of this resource, "Australian Religious Films," commented as early as 1985 that the videos were the first evangelistic videos that they were aware of, certainly by an Australian evangelist. DOE Prayer Letter, May–July 1985.

> The tapes themselves were well produced ... dialogue evangelism, baptism interviews and backyard barbies will never be the same again when you have a set of "Telling the Gospel's Truth" ready to roll![125]

Such a pioneering initiative added impetus to the indigenization of Australian Christianity as it established firmer roots in its own post-imperial soil and offered the gospel in a form that did much to commend it to Australian culture.[126] Chapman's dialogue model (including its later video expression) also proved to be an important stimulus in the development of notable second-generation evangelistic tools that appeared in the 1990s. Whether directly or implicitly, Chapman's earlier work had, according to Stephen Abbott (Chapman's former student and colleague), pioneered a fresh missiological genre and given permission for a subsequent generation to experiment with new tools and forms.[127] As such, investigative courses like *Christianity Explored*, *The Life of Jesus*, *Introducing God*, and the *Alpha Course* each echoed, in varying degrees, the theological and sociological insights of Chapman's earlier dialogue methodology. This included its narrative-expository approach, the need among cultural moderns for an unhurried exposure to biblical truth, and Chapman's innovative video format. Indeed, leading English and Australian evangelists like Rico Tice and Dominic Steele credited Chapman's earlier work and mentorship as being deeply influential in informing the assumptions that undergirded their own missiological ideals and tools. Moreover, Chapman's influence was also discernible in methods of evangelism employed in English and Australian parish and university contexts. Leading tools, including the British Christian Union's (UCCF) *Uncover* resource or St. Helen's Bishopsgate's *Word One to One* (both of which assume a model of interactive biblical exploration) traced their inspiration to Chapman's earlier missional forms. The more generalist Australian tools, like *Everyday Evangelism* and *Two Ways to Live*, in either their theology or general approach, also echoed Chapman's earlier work.[128]

125. DOE Prayer Letter, November 1986–January 1987.

126. Millikan, "Identity," 30; Frame, *Losing My Religion*, 70–77. Cf. the discussion in chapter 1 on contextualization.

127. Interview with Stephen Abbott, February 14, 2017.

128. Rico Tice (author of *Christianity Explored*) sought Chapman as a mentor in the 1990s. This was an experience that was "foundational" to his ministry. Chapman's theology of evangelism thus became integral to the substructure and training modules of *Christianity Explored*, as did numerous assumptions of the dialogue method. Interview with Rico Tice, January 17, 2017. The leading Australian courses such as *Introducing God* (authored by Dominic Steele) and *Simply Christianity/The Life of*

In terms of the significance of such developments, there is little doubt that, prior to this, biblical and historical antecedents had offered a profusion of examples of the apologetic task being adapted to the changing assumptions of human culture. Indeed, if apologetics is defined as the process of "witness and dialogue [for the purpose of] the intellectual justification of the truth and relevance of the Christian life,"[129] then a dialogical approach cannot be acclaimed as unique *or* novel in missiological history. Like many of its antecedents, Chapman's approach reflected a propositional apologetic, coupled with an Augustinian epistemology. Such an approach employed rational proofs as a component of the apologetic task, while allowing the ultimate cause of spiritual persuasion to reside in biblical revelation, illuminated and made effectual by divine agency.[130]

However, perhaps the key significance of this aspect of Chapman's work lay not in its place at the vanguard of missional approaches to social change or as a supplement to the crusade mentality. Rather, it also formed a key part of a first wave of postwar Australian evangelical scholarship and missional advocacy. For, in the early and mid century the international apologetic landscape had seen concerted industry from Catholic, Neoorthodox, and Evangelical theologian apologists.[131] Yet, as a largely receptor

---

Jesus (authored by John Dickson) also echo many contours of Chapman's work. Both courses employ the sociological insights of a dialogue/course approach. The *Introducing God* material reflects a creation-fall-redemption format (consistent with Chapman's earlier summarization). Dickson's material also reflects Chapman's video format and narrative approach. His apologetic material also echoes, and in some cases explicitly quotes and relies on Chapman's apologetic work. Steele and Dickson studied at Moore College where Chapman's model was prevalent. Steele also sought Chapman's input in the development of his own work. *Sydney Yearbook*, 2015, 166, 233; *Preaching Christ*, September–November 2002. See the approach of such courses as outlined in: Tice, *Christianity Explored*, 9–66; Steele, *Introducing God*, 13–20; Dickson, *Simply Christianity*, 5–9, 34–37. The *Uncover* material produced by the UCCF (the modern CICCU) and the *Word One to One* (a St. Helen's Bishopsgate resource) also assume a process of interactively reading a gospel with enquiring students or friends. See UCCF, "Uncover"; "Word One to One." William Taylor, Rector of St. Helen's confirms the influence of Chapman's approach upon their own. Interview with William Taylor, February 10, 2017. Regarding the Australian tools for personal evangelism, Stephen Abbott (author of *Everyday Evangelism*) credits Chapman as being influential in his contemporary approach. Interview with Stephen Abbott, February 14, 2017. The widely used *Two Ways to Live* resource (author, Phillip Jensen) also follows a creation-fall-redemption narrative and assumes a dialogical approach in personal evangelism. Prior to his ministry on the campus of UNSW, Jensen trained as an evangelist under Chapman, as the dialogue method was being developed in Sydney.

129. Van den Toren, *Christian Apologetics*, 27.

130. Hoover, "Apologetics," 69.

131. Dulles, *History of Apologetics*, 325–65.

culture, Australian Evangelicalism had, prior to the 1960s, produced little in-depth reflection with which to aid its own defense, self-replenishment, or wider contribution. As noted, it relied heavily upon the inherited superstructures of Anglo-Christian identity. Moreover, within an evangelical culture that many believed had become "subjective" and "sentimental," it lacked a consistent conception of the biblical gospel or a coherent theory for its dissemination.[132] Chapman's missiological advocacy must therefore be appreciated in this light. Indeed, given the paucity of careful reflection available in his own context and to the wider evangelical constituency, Chapman's development of such experimental forms began a process that culminated in the publication of his widely acclaimed works *Know and Tell the Gospel* (1980) and *A Fresh Start* (1984). These works distilled and expanded the insights garnered from his extensive domestic and international evangelistic ministry. They also sought to promote these insights to the wider Christian and non-Christian constituencies in a plainspoken and culturally accessible way. As a result, Chapman's missiological contribution by means of these works rose in tandem with other Australian works in the field of biblical studies and theology (like those of Leon Morris, D. B. Knox, and D. W. B. Robinson). Chapman's *Know and Tell the Gospel* came to be regarded as a benchmark resource by a generation of clergy and laity across the Western world. They testified to its worth in helping them not only to gain a rigorously biblical conception of the gospel but also to share the gospel with greater clarity. Chapman's *A Fresh Start* also became one of the best-selling Australian Christian works of its generation. Geared heavily towards the non-Christian, the work memorably distilled a creation/fall/redemption presentation of the gospel while addressing a range of apologetic and discipleship concerns. Pointing to Chapman's disarming and humorous style, many clergy testified to the work's usefulness as a resource for their own ministries, while many non-Christians confessed to being pleasantly surprised by their enjoyment in reading it. On account of its clear and engaging presentation of the gospel the work remained an effective tool in the evangelization of many thousands of people across the globe.[133]

132. Nelson, "Hammond," 151; Judd and Cable, *Sydney Anglicans*, 150–51. See discussion earlier in this chapter and in chapter 4.

133. Notable in this first wave of Australian evangelical advocacy is the work of Morris, *Apostolic Preaching* and Knox and Robinson (see chapter 2 for discussion). Chapman's *Know and Tell the Gospel* had sold forty thousand copies worldwide by the 1990s. Regarding the significance of *Know and Tell the Gospel*, numerous evangelistic works from the subsequent generation are quick to highlight its pioneering influence. See Tice, *Honest Evangelism*, 1; Chan, *Skeptical World*, 11; Chapman's *A Fresh Start* sold upwards of ninety thousand copies and remains in print. Preaching Christ Prayer Letter, August–October 1986; Goodreads, "A Fresh Start."

Notwithstanding such gains, compared with the preceding era of civic Protestantism, a palpable sense lingered that the Christian church had, at least for a time, entered a day of smaller things. Ever greater effort was expended for what appeared to be modest results. Nevertheless, Chapman's pioneering work supplied a needed "unfettering" from the strategies of a previous generation.[134] By virtue of its wide reception and clear presentation of the soteriological themes of Scripture, it became a key influence in the development of an emerging Australian Evangelicalism and an important tool in shaping gospel communication methods across the evangelical world.

Crusade Evangelism 2.0: "Christ's American Son" Returns

In February 1976, the *Anglican Press Service* called a news conference, at which Archbishop Sir Marcus Loane—then Anglican Primate of Australia—was due to make "a major announcement in connection with the spiritual state of the nation."[135] Convinced that the archbishop would issue a "Call to Australia" similar to that issued by the Archbishop of Canterbury, Donald Coggan, who had recently chastised Britain as a nation "drifting towards chaos" and its people for being "like children fighting each other for cream buns," reporters responded with gusto.[136] In contrast, however, Archbishop Loane's "call" was somewhat different. No lover of things American, Loane had summoned the press corps to announce that he had invited the American evangelist, Billy Graham, to revisit Australia, and that a crusade would be held in Sydney from April to May 1979.[137] Loane's decision to invite Graham had been an almost entirely personal and unilateral undertaking. While in the hills of Irian Jaya in 1975, as he walked along jungle trails where two Australian missionaries had recently been martyred, Loane had prayed about the spiritual state of Australia. From Loane's perspective, with a nominal one million believers under his spiritual jurisdiction, his conviction—as he explained months later at St. Andrew's Cathedral to garner the support of church leaders—was that "the city of Sydney and indeed the Commonwealth of Australia stand in need of a proclamation of the gospel on the widest possible scale." Moreover, "in the providence of God" such a crusade, he suggested, "may be the means of a spiritual impact on the city of Sydney . . . not merely in 1979, but for the twenty years that remain in

---

134. Davies, "Dialogue Evangelism," 35.
135. Gill, "Countdown to Crusade." BGCA, CN 360, SB 318.
136. Gill, "Archbishop Describes British."
137. Gill, "Countdown to Crusade."

the twentieth century."[138] Loane subsequently took counsel from close aides and other Protestant leaders about the advisability of such an undertaking. As a result, with a trace of nostalgia, mixed with the weight of evident spiritual need, Loane invited Graham to embark on the first three-week crusade he had conducted since 1963. And the revival juggernaut, now twice refined in Sydney, began to roll.[139]

On his return, at sixty years of age, Graham had now risen to become every bit the global evangelical superstar. Indeed, to many of the evangelical base in the United States, Graham had become "nothing less than the nearest thing to Jesus on this earth. He's sort of like 'Christ's American son,'" suggested one observer. "At the very least, Graham has abided for thirty years as a folk-totem figure, virtually a mythic eminence, in the life of the nation: the icon, the breathing, embodied image of native American rectitude."[140] "Even now, at sixty," opined *Esquire Fortnightly*:

> He has that look of some blond, gallant, crystal-eyed prince out of a Nordic fairy tale—young Hansel grown to a stalwart golden manhood, un-aging, changeless . . . Since his first exuberant emergence in America, back in those days of brave, sunny simplicities after victory in World War Two, he has somehow preserved, through all the abrasions of the years . . . the cold war,

---

138. Nicholls, "Australian Archbishop." BGCA, CN 360, SB 317.

139. Loane described the 1979 crusade as having an "almost romantic start." Attending a missionary conference in West Irian Jaya, Loane went for a walk on his own. He recalled: "I was thinking about the next few years in Sydney before my retirement. Was there anything that could be done to bring the gospel home in a more effective and enduring way in the life of the city . . . I thought 'Well, 1979 would be the 20th anniversary of the great crusade in 1959. I wonder if Billy would consider coming again?' On my return, I wrote a letter and asked if he would consider coming [stipulating] the minimum period for such a crusade should be three weeks . . . when [Graham arrived] he said, 'I wish you'd asked me to come for four weeks.' I could only say 'I wanted to ask for four, but my faith wasn't strong enough!'" Loane convened a meeting of the heads of Protestant churches where he secured unanimous support for a combined invitation. M. Loane interview with L. Ferm, 1982. BGCA, CN 141, Box 3/28. Evidently, the world of the great revivals was a world still manifestly present to Loane. In a farewell address after the crusade, Loane appraised Graham's predecessors as being George Whitefield and D. L. Moody, while intimating Graham's pre-eminence in this venerable succession. Loane recalled travelling as a young man in the same car as a man who "had been converted during Moody's great London Mission in 1875, and his joy was irrepressible." Loane's invitation thus reflected both his esteem for Graham and a consciousness of standing in a revered, if fading, succession. "M. Loane at the Presentation to Billy Graham on 19 May 1979." BGCA, CN 245, Box 25/14.

140. Frady, "Use and Abuse." BGCA, CN 360, SB 816.

racial convulsions, assassinations, Vietnam, Watergate . . . that chaste glamour of Sunday sanctity.[141]

By the late 1970s, the BGEA had proliferated into a megacomplex of agencies and enterprises with a yearly budget of some $40 million; it was a virtual revival behemoth.[142] And yet, arriving in Australia, aside from the predictable chorus of muted critique, Graham—like one who had emerged "straight up out of the grass into the pulpit, sort of God's own divine bumpkin"—conveyed a persona of "ferociously wholesome earnestness" that had many in the press corps enthralled.[143] Stepping out of the service at St. Andrew's Cathedral on the Sunday before the crusade, as "the world's best-known living Christian," Graham was described by one of the press as "deeply tanned" and sporting a suit that was "businessman-black, the shirt an enviable white." Graham, however, spoke self-effacingly of his talents and said: "I have very little. I'm just an ordinary person . . . there are many clergymen in New South Wales that can preach a better sermon than I can. I heard one this morning!" Asked if he would be "sticking to the formula which [had] made him a master evangelist," he replied: "When I was here 20 years ago, someone asked if I was going to speak on an old message. I said: 'Yes, it'll be 2,000 years old.'"[144] Addressing an audience of seven hundred clergy and lay workers at Sydney's Town Hall on April 26 as the crusade began in earnest, Graham was described again by the press as "impeccable really, the initial impression was one of controlled power. To begin with, the voice was soft. But after the jagged 'praise the Lord' phrases Graham suggested he would later thump his message home with all the velvet of Hiroshima."[145]

141. Frady, "Use and Abuse."
142. Frady, "Use and Abuse."
143. Frady, "Use and Abuse."
144. Simper, "E1 Evangelism."
145. "Billy Graham," *Australian*. The bulk of the Australian press were surprisingly positive. The *Australian* editorialized that "Billy Graham has been hailed as a modern Messiah, God's own special agent, a super-showman and a super-salesman. He's been called a charlatan and equated to a real-life Elmer Gantry. He's been courted and feted—and quite possibly misused—by presidents and film stars, by the rich and the famous. His pugnacious belief in Christ, eternal judgment and damnation, has seen him sneered at, scoffed at and ridiculed. But at what he does he's the world champion." The *Sunday Telegraph* ran a four-page souvenir supplement on the crusade, and Graham appeared live across the country on the "Mike Walsh Show" where he memorably prayed for the conversion of Australians. Graham also benefitted from an array of media appearances and interest from major television and radio outlets such as "Four Corners," "60 Minutes," and the "Mike Willessee Show." Nichols, "Graham Crusade Lifts"; W. B. Berryman to Gene L. Jeffries, April 25, 1979. BGCA, CN, 245 Box 29/19.

The "Best Prepared Crusade City"

For all the controlled intensity of the Graham and BGEA aura, however, there lay the reality that the effectiveness of any given campaign was perhaps more *reflective* of local church health than *productive* of it.[146] On this measure, as he arrived in Sydney in April 1979, Graham described Sydney appreciatively as perhaps the "best prepared crusade city he had ever seen."[147] A degree of initial concern had been expressed about the desirability of another BGEA crusade. Yet, with the invitation issued and the press corps notified, local figures swung behind the Anglican primate for what many considered would be the "religious event of the current decade."[148] The crusade machinery—now well-polished in Sydney—invited the energies of nine Protestant denominations onto the Crusade Executive, who busied themselves in three years of intensive preparation. A now familiar rhythm of crusade planning also began to unfold as a flurry of logistics, transport, and communications teams enacted plans. This occurred alongside promotional activity in the local press and widely among churches, minister's fraternals, and men's and women's ministry guilds.[149]

---

146. Stanley, *Global Diffusion*, 71.

147. W. B. Berryman to W. Meloon, May 29, 1979. BGCA, CN 245, Box 29/19; Pollock, *Graham Story*, 161 for a similar appraisal.

148. Gill, "Countdown to Crusade."

149. The crusade was built primarily on a close working relationship between Anglicans and Baptists, while the Salvation Army, the Churches of Christ, the continuing Presbyterian Church, Lutheran, and Brethren, and sections of the Uniting Church provided some support. (Participating churches numbered more than one thousand by the time of the crusade). The Crusade Executive of fifty (under the leadership of Bishop A. J. Dain as Chairman and Barry Berryman as Crusade Director) comprised twenty-six chairpersons of major campaign portfolios, like "Follow-up," "Transport," "Communications" and "Finance." The executive was charged with strategic decision making, while a Council of Reference made representations to the executive on other matters. A budget of $850,000 was accepted and funded by local donors. The challenge of transforming the Randwick Racecourse into a suitable venue was also significant. Government bus services ran shuttles from Central Railway Station to Randwick. The Public Transportation Commission and private bus companies also shuttled people from parish centers or beyond the city. Three thousand ushers were recruited, while a three-thousand-member choir alternated each evening. Half nights of prayer were held in twenty-four regions in the Sydney metropolitan area during April. Five thousand prayer cells formed to pray for the crusade, which averaged ten members. On November 5, 1978, "Operation Andrew" was designed to encourage church people to interest others in the crusade. On April 22, 1979, "Operation Doorstep" sent thirty thousand visitors to visit one million Sydney homes. Special meetings for clergy were held in August 1978 and February 1979. Many pre-crusade meetings were also held, including regional men's and women's meetings, and a day crusade in the Town Hall on May 2, 1979. Simultaneous translation was offered each evening into nine languages,

In the final analysis, the crusade was judged to be a triumph of planning and precision. Yet, with bitterly cold, wet weather in the first ten days keeping many would-be attendees away and worrying crusade organizers, the length of the campaign, together with major contracts secured to televise select crusade meetings, arguably became its salvation. It was the most inclement weather that Graham had experienced, aside from his Wembley and Taipei crusades. Indeed, Graham joked, it was "so wet, that even the greyhounds weren't racing!" Speaking at Sydney's Randwick Racecourse, from a dais above a crusade logo of a black and orange double-boomerang, Graham clipped out his message with the professionalism and elegance for which he was noted. Listening crowds wrapped themselves in coats and woolen caps, and shared flasks of coffee while rain soaked the entire metropolitan area for ten days.[150] As skies cleared, attendances swelled to an aggregate of 491,000 with 22,000 decisions. This ranked among the highest crusade attendance figures in a Western capital in the 1970s period.[151] Numerous metropolitan churches saw parish statistics expand considerably after the crusade. Others spoke of a rising "obedience" among their members alongside a new "optimism and drive" amongst the clergy.[152] A sizeable endowment from a Sydney businessman to televise three of Graham's meetings saw the crusade's media coverage expand dramatically. Consequently, continuing into the third week, sixty-eight television programs carried

---

and follow-up material for ethnic groups was also prepared. A "School of Evangelism and Church Growth" was held May 8–11, 1979 at St. Andrew's Cathedral. BGEA team members spoke, while John Stott also gave three lectures. Berryman, "School of Evangelism"; Nichols, "Graham Crusade Lifts"; Oliver, "Half Nights of Prayer." BGCA, CN 245, Box 29/4; Berryman, "Thousands of Christians." BGCA, CN 245, Box 29/4; "Archbishop Loane Writes."

150. "Young and Old."

151. While the clearing weather signalled a change in attendances, it also signalled a change in tone. Graham himself speculated that at the crusade's midpoint it "took a different course than anticipated, something deeper is happening that is beyond my understanding." Attributing the result to rising spiritual hunger, Graham declared that "Australia has one of the highest standards of living in the world. And yet many people are discovering . . . that a high standard of living is not enough; that education is not enough; that increased leisure time is not enough . . . I have been to Australia before . . . but this time I sense a new atmosphere. I sense that Australia may be on the verge of a spiritual awakening." Graham's assessment bore echoes of his commitment to reviving both church and society. Whether it is to be judged anecdotally, or as reflective of a wider mood, aggregate attendances *were* comparatively high. Regarding the crusade's success, Graham was circumspect. He told a press conference "the success is relative. Whether it's been a success or failure will have to stand the ultimate test of divine judgement." "Only God Can Judge"; Graham, "Australia: Spiritual Superpower"; Nichols, "Graham Crusade Lifts."

152. Nichols, "Graham Crusade Lifts."

crusade news or related content, ensuring that Graham remained news across the nation. Rarely had such a complex communications operation been mounted in Australia, nor had any individual or domestic political leader reached such an audience. This expanded the crusade's impact from an essentially local to a national one. And as the crusade curtain fell, more than four million Australians had heard or seen Graham in what became hailed fittingly as the "Australian Crusade."[153]

Post-Crusade Innovations and Impact

Several features of the 1979 Sydney Crusade are of particular note, however, in both heightening its proportional impact and in placing a subtle yet growing dissonance between Sydney leadership and its generation-long bond with the BGEA. The first lay in the area of counselling and follow-up, where it was considered by senior BGEA figures that the penetration the crusade achieved became one of the "most intensive" in BGEA crusade history.[154] The causes of such a high penetration rate (including a historically high local church co-operation rate, a comparatively high percentage of crusade attendees with no formal church affiliation, and a local follow-up campaign which became a benchmark for the BGEA's ongoing approach)[155] lay in the initial stages of crusade preparation. Members of a synod-appointed committee to help the Sydney diocese prepare for the 1979 crusade had expressed a desire, as early as 1976, to address the causes of the high numbers of people referred from the 1968 Sydney crusade who did not "stick" in terms of continuing on in Christian maturity.[156] Recognizing this to be both a spiritual and sociological issue, the issue became a significant point of critique among local church leaders concerning the value of another crusade.[157] A key objective of this synod committee, therefore, was the desire to motivate the Sydney polity "to make the best of the 1979 opportunity in an increasingly secular age" and to provide "maximum help" to new converts without trying to "over-organize them."[158] John Chapman played a defin-

153. Burney, "They Came to God." Team associates also held satellite crusades in Orange, Tamworth, Canberra, the Gold Coast, Brisbane, and Newcastle, along with 220 additional meetings held in other meeting places. Berryman, "Sydney's Randwick Crusade."

154. Berryman, "Sydney's Randwick Crusade."

155. Berryman, "Sydney's Randwick Crusade."

156. "Archbishop's 1977 Lenten Rallies Leaflet," BGCA, CN 245, Box 29/7.

157. John C. Chapman to W. B. Berryman, June 6, 1978. BGCA, CN 245, Box 25/20.

158. "Archbishop's 1977 Lenten Rallies Leaflet," BGCA, CN 245, Box 29/7; DOE Prayer Letter, August 1978.

ing role in the establishment and operation of this synod committee. He asked the 1976 session of Synod that the Standing Committee be directed to establish a *1979 Crusade Committee* to: "(a) stimulate interest in and prayer for evangelism; (b) make suggestions to parishes as to the best way to prepare for the crusade and to follow it up in a well-planned context of ongoing education and pastoral care; and (c) initiate preparations on a regional basis."[159] In view of Chapman's widely respected and influential missiological contribution, he was also invited to assume the leadership of the major portfolio of "Counselling and Follow-up," alongside taking a leading role in diverse areas of crusade advocacy.[160] Hence, under the rubric of "Getting ready for Billy Graham," during 1977 and 1978 Chapman aligned the work of the Department of Evangelism with that of the crusade preparation committee. He developed regional "schools of evangelism" which offered training in modes of outreach (including "dialogue evangelism") to assist local churches to develop ongoing missiological capacity. Indeed, Chapman reflected, regarding such preparatory initiatives "we took the opportunity to do all we had ever dreamed of doing [in evangelism]" such that "all would have been worthwhile, even if Billy had been unable to come."[161]

In consultation with veteran BGEA figures like Charlie Riggs (who had overseen the Christian Life and Witness and follow-up programs of the BGEA since the 1950s),[162] Chapman and the Sydney Follow-up Committee also conducted an extensive review of BGEA material and its procedures. Seeing limitations in the resources provided by the BGEA, their aim was to provide material whose language was more suited to Australian culture, would encourage greater engagement with the text of Scripture, and would

---

159. Canon J. C. Chapman. Resolution 19/76, 1979 Billy Graham Crusade. 1978 *Sydney Anglican Yearbook.*

160. In light of the vastly changed "climate," Chapman had initially approached the campaign with some reserve. However, he eventually gave strong, yet qualified support and maintained that the strong clerical support the crusade enjoyed was a function of the clergy's high esteem for Loane. Chapman to Orpwood, February 1, 1994, BDM, Box 1, SDA. Archbishop Loane had previously requested Chapman's presence alongside him at the meeting of denominational heads (which issued the invitation to Graham) and a wider meeting of church leaders at St. Andrew's Cathedral in 1976. Loane recognized, in the words of Chapman's colleague, Phillip Jensen, that "if you wanted to achieve anything in evangelism at the time, it benefitted your cause to have John's endorsement." Interview with Phillip Jensen, February 17, 2017. Chapman's advocacy in the Christian Life and Witness classes, the minister's meetings, and the many prayer breakfasts at which he spoke in the lead-up to the crusade was also significant. W. B. Berryman Circular, March 15, 1979. BGCA, CN 245, Box 29/1.

161. Gill, "Countdown to Crusade," 161–62.

162. Navigators, "Remembering."

enhance the post-crusade completion rate of such follow-up materials.[163] To achieve this, the Australian team reduced adult follow-up materials in number (from the previous four booklets to two) and developed a series of lessons dealing with the individual's "commitment, walk and witness" (by means of an examination of John's Gospel).[164]

Central to the revised approach of the 1979 Sydney crusade was a substantially strengthened process for the nurture and integration of crusade respondents. In an innovation initially unique to the Sydney crusade, several thousand "Nurture Group" leaders were selected and trained to continue the process of discipleship and the integration of crusade enquirers into churches across Sydney metropolitan and country areas. An impressively detailed set of procedures was designed to manage the process of communication with all such crusade enquirers until they were established in local fellowships.[165] Such a meticulously detailed process, enthused

---

163. Correspondence between Chapman and the BGEA indicates a need for the revision of existing materials on the grounds that 1) previous material, while positive, had not expressly encouraged engagement with Scripture; 2) language changes were advised "which we think will be more acceptable to Australians . . . because only 15 percent of the population attend church, we consider that little should be taken for granted"; 3) existing BGEA processes involved the completion of numerous follow-up studies followed by a "certificate," which experienced "considerable shortfall after Lesson 1." J. C. Chapman to W. B. Berryman. "Revisions to 'Knowing Christ,'" December 1, 1978. BGCA, CN 245, Box 25/20; Rev. Noble W. Scroggins (Director of Spiritual Counselling and Follow-up, BGEA) to W. B. Berryman, January 12, 1979. BGCA, CN 245, Box 29/19. Previous follow-up procedures had been largely conducted via correspondence with the BGEA. Such lesson material was sent to the BGEA and its affiliates for grading before being sent back to the enquirer. Rapidly rising postage costs (via rising 1970s inflation) and the work entailed in grading such material was placing an almost "intolerable burden" on BGEA resources. Scroggins to Berryman, January 12, 1979; Berryman to Scroggins, January 26, 1979. BGCA, CN 245, Box 29/19.

164. W. B. Berryman to J. C. Chapman, August 31, 1978. BGCA, CN 245, Box 25/20.

165. The revisioned follow-up procedure is captured in material sent to Australian minister's fraternals ahead of the crusade. It states: "To ensure that each crusade enquirer is firmly established in a local church and that he receives continuing Christian growth assistance through the avenue of church-fellowship, personal-counsel and nurture-group Bible study, the follow-up programme has been developed. Prior to the crusade, lay-men and women from participating churches are given small group leadership training to assist them in conducting meaningful and practical Bible studies to help the crusade enquirer. These leaders are equipped to establish 'nurture groups' in their respective churches, university and military service group. Special 'nurture group' study books and 'studies in discipleship' have been developed by the *Sydney Billy Graham Crusade* and this ministry. At each crusade service, Dr Graham presents a gospel sermon to reach the uncommitted. He invites people to come to the platform area in an act of commitment to Jesus Christ. After a brief talk to the enquirers by Dr Graham and a prayer on their behalf, personal counselling begins. Each enquirer will be given a

crusade director Barry Berryman, had received "wide commendation" from Australian clergy, who indicated that "it has been the best we have had thus far."[166] The "depth of penetration and church acceptance of post-Crusade Follow-up" had "undoubtedly had a very considerable effect,"[167] Berryman further observed, and was considered "far greater than we experienced in 1959 and 1968,"[168] and "higher than what is normally achieved overseas."[169] The Crusade Executive were also buoyed by news, enthusiastically relayed from churches where the follow-up and nurture program was under way "that the crusade has by no means finished, for there are still

---

Bible study booklet by the counsellor ("Knowing Christ" if an adult, or "Trusting Jesus" if a child). This study is a series of lessons dealing with the individual's commitment, walk and witness. During the counselling the counsellor will fill out a 'card' registering the enquirer's name, address, church affiliation; keeping a record for themselves and handing the other to a supervisor. The decision card is then collected and sent to the crusade follow-up department for processing. A group of volunteers, known as the Co-labor Corps, process the enquirer's cards following each crusade service. Statistics are recorded before the card is passed on to the committee for church referral. After the crusade, the name of each enquirer is sent to a local church within 24 hours of the decision, along with a report which provides the minister with the enquirer's name, address and recommendations about what would benefit the enquirer, based on the counsellor's report. The minister is asked to get in touch with the person, to encourage him in his Christian walk and invite him to become involved in his church. Counsellors will contact the enquirers they counselled with a phone call, visit, or letter within 48 hours of their initial talk. This is to give interim follow-up encouragement and counsel until they are established in a church. A letter from Dr Graham will be sent to each enquirer several days following the commitment. Bible study nurture groups, under the leadership of the trained group leaders, will be formed in small cell groups in churches and homes. Special programmes have been organised on the university campuses, and in school ISCF and Crusader Union groups." "Summary of Follow-Up for the Billy Graham Crusade," BGCA, CN 245, Box 25/20; "Minister's Information Bulletin No. 9 Dec–Jan 1979," BGCA, CN 245, Box 29/8. This process was supplemented with a telephone survey. Three weeks after the crusade, the Co-Labor Corp phoned each enquirer individually. Where church follow-up was proceeding, no further contact was made. Where this was not occurring, alternative follow-up was arranged via church or parachurch nurture groups. Information was mailed to nurture group leaders by the Co-Labour Corps, including names and addresses of enquirers, whom they were asked to call, inviting them to the scheduled Bible study, and returning to the crusade office names of all who would not be attending. "Follow-Up Procedure," BGCA, CN 245, Box 25/20. The Co-Labour Corps comprised over one thousand people recruited from the eleven thousand strong Christian Life and Witness Classes, along with 4,798 counsellors and 845 supervisors. "Co-Labour Corps," BGCA, CN 245, Box 25/15; "Executive Committee: Minutes 26 April 1979," BGCA, CN 245, Box 29/1.

166. W. B. Berryman to Jack Humphreys, May 31, 1979. BGCA, CN 245, Box 29/19.

167. W. B. Berryman to W. Meloon, May 29, 1979. BGCA, CN 245, Box 29/19.

168. W. B. Berryman to A. P. Margosian, June 5, 1979. BGCA, CN 245, Box 29/19.

169. W. B. Berryman to Rev. Dr. J. Graham Miller, July 1979. BGCA, CN 245, Box 25/20.

people finding Christ . . . and we still seem to be extremely busy with the sale of crusade literature . . . to cope with the additional enquirers that are being gathered in."[170] Veteran BGEA figures like Charlie Riggs and Noble Scroggins (who oversaw the BGEA's work of counselling and follow-up) considered that the material and procedures were of such quality and utility that they formed the basis of the BGEA's ongoing follow-up approach in North American and European crusades into the 1980s.[171]

Revivalism and the Altar Call: A "Reformed Approach"

The frenetic pace that Chapman set in this revisioned follow-up campaign was driven, at least in part, by a growing conviction about the process of conversion that had begun to diverge from the established procedures of crusade-style revivalism. While not discounting the possibility of the spontaneous conversion or the value of a call to "decision" at crusade meetings, in his own thought and praxis Chapman had begun to break the nexus between the appeal and the public response. The BGEA, alert to the breadth of motivations that compelled the typical crusade respondent, still invested the activity of the "altar call" with substantial theological and spiritual freight. Indeed, in intensifying the evangelical-conversionist impulse, and in seeking an environment that encouraged the experience of "decision" as a route to the assurance of salvation or spiritual renewal, the BGEA championed the public act of "decision" as an almost indispensable component of saving faith.[172] However, seeking a praxis more in sympathy

---

170. W. B. Berryman to F. Dienert, June 21, 1979. BGCA, CN 245, Box 29/19.

171. Rev. N. W. Scroggins to W. B. Berryman, April 26, 1979. BGCA, CN 245, Box 29/19. In 1980, Riggs enclosed copies of their ongoing training and follow-up material, observing that the work done by the Sydney team formed the basis of their material going forward. See Charles Riggs to W. B. Berryman, April 11, 1980. BGCA, CN 245, Box 43/17. Evidence of the material's ongoing use in future Graham crusades is found in materials used in campaigns in Baltimore, Alberta, and Southern England. See "Crusade Procedure Books 1981," Billy Graham Baltimore Crusade, June 7–14; Southern Alberta Crusade, August 29–30; "Crusade Procedure Books, 1984," Mission England. Assorted English Cities, May 12–19, 1984. Vol. 1, BGCA, CN 16. News of the crusade and its follow-up also became the subject of interest from representatives of the Wheaton Graduate School of Communication, who requested behind the scenes access to the Sydney crusade, "to see evangelism at its best." J. Gibson (Wheaton College) to S. W. Huston, BGEA, February 11, 1979. BGCA, CN 245, Box 29/19.

172. McClymond, "Issues," 15. In a letter to Australian clergy ahead of the 1979 Crusade, the BGEA defended their practice of the "altar call": "We believe that if people are not willing to couple their faith with action, their faith is too weak to count. Christ demanded action of almost everyone he blessed . . . When persons come reverently at a crusade, they testify they want to receive Christ and desire to live in Him." "Information

with his Reformed influences and alert to the sensitivities of human sociology and culture, Chapman respectfully demurred. In a revealing 1985 exchange, Chapman enunciated how his Reformed soteriology coalesced with the nuanced art of the public appeal. Drawing on his extensive experience of public evangelism, he stated:

> Coming to Christ, I do not believe has to be done publicly to be valid. Once you give assent to that, what you do then is a pragmatic matter. But if you think a person has got to make a public declaration of his coming to Christ, it'll be part of repentance. But to me, they are separate. And therefore, I don't call on people to do things which will embarrass them. Because I can't see any value in embarrassing people. The fact that you stand up so you can be counselled has got little to do with the cost of following Christ . . . My difficulty is that the average Australian male will not . . . walk out to the front no matter what you do. If evangelists tell the truth (and I am one who tries), let me tell you who comes out to appeals. First the counsellors. You can tell them because of the Bibles. Then there are people like my mother, who walk out to help others come out. Then there are the people who are re-dedicating their life to Christ . . . the greater bulk. Then the rest are teenagers. They have no difficulties stepping out anywhere. Does that mean the gospel works better on teenagers than adults? The adults get converted. They just don't tell you. And I want to find a way where I can find them and give them the same help . . . The last thing I want to do on the night a person has come to Christ is scrape the icing off the cake . . . if he's come to Christ, I want him to go home with his head in the clouds! Nothing better has, can, or ever will happen. [So] don't scrape the icing off by telling him that if he won't walk up the front and stand up straight like a soldier, he hasn't come to Christ . . . However, to lead people to the point of taking action, and not tell them precisely what the action is, is to leave them . . . completely up the pole. I normally lead people in a prayer of repentance and use the prayer as a part of the preaching.[173]

Theologically, such a position rested more squarely in evangelical Calvinism than in Arminian and volitional notions of the salvific process.[174]

Bulletin No. 5, August 1978." BGCA, CN 245, Box 29/8.

173. Such comments, articulated some six years later at the Evangelical Minister's Assembly in London, 1985, arguably reflect Chapman's developing earlier convictions. See J. C. Chapman, "Evangelism Today 1," Evangelical Minister's Assembly Address, London, 1985. Proclamation Trust, "PT Resources."

174. As noted earlier, the theological stance of Jakob Arminius, a contemporary

Indeed, emphasizing the primacy of the preached word and the work of the Holy Spirit in conversion, Chapman later articulated his settled belief that:

> The Holy Spirit will take the gospel we have preached and do with it what he will. I will try to persuade people by every legitimate means to respond to the gospel with repentance and faith. But telling us about your response and asking for further help, has nothing to do with repentance and faith. If a person turns to Christ [they are] truly a child of God whether they tell us or not.[175]

Such an approach, energetically championed, would claim an ascendancy all of its own in Reformed circles in Sydney and elsewhere in the later century. Seeking to separate the "act of repentance" from "the overt witness to that act," Chapman's approach was given expression in the widespread practice of "praying the prayer" at evangelistic meetings and in the collecting of "response cards" to connect respondents to investigative courses, in preference to the pervasive singularity of the "altar call." Importantly, however, Chapman stressed a degree of liberty in these matters. Provided an opportunity for response was issued by the evangelist or hosting ministry, the manner in which this response was facilitated could be nuanced and varied.[176] It was in such a spirit that the 1979 crusade and its follow-up campaign proceeded. While tacitly endorsing the BGEA's practice and not discounting the need for "decision," nevertheless the Sydney team judged conversion to be more often a process than an event. It thus placed substantial emphasis on post-crusade nurture and on equipping co-operating churches to continue the ongoing work of witness.

---

of Calvin and Theodore Beza, was that of "conditional predestination." This doctrine suggests that the destiny of individuals is based on God's foreknowledge of the way they will either freely reject or freely accept Christ. Such "volitionalism" was mediated via Wesleyan holiness revivalism to the modern revivalist movement. Conversely, evangelical Calvinism holds that it is God alone who saves by the Holy Spirit's operation by and with the word upon the soul. The decisive difference is that evangelical Calvinist soteriology rests the cause of salvation in God's pre-temporal "election" irrespective of human merit, action or the capacity of the human will. Grider, "Arminianism," 79–81; Reymond, *Systematic Theology*, 472–73; Hoekema, *Saved*, 80–92.

175. Chapman, *Setting Hearts on Fire*, 143.

176. Chapman advised that depending on the context, respondents may fill out a card, call a published phone number, stay behind to speak to a counsellor, fill out a clipboard at a response table, or elect to receive further materials. Chapman, *Setting Hearts on Fire*, 142–50.

The BGEA, Evangelical Expansionism, and Reformed Soteriology: The Narrow Path

Notwithstanding the relative magnanimity accompanying the planning phase of the 1979 Sydney crusade, no small controversy surrounded the question of "participating churches" and the procedures envisaged for the counselling and referral of crusade enquirers. Indeed, in view of the historic denominational breadth of the BGEA platform, a question that exercised the Crusade Executive and gave rise to considerable tension was the question of the involvement of Roman Catholic and Pentecostal Churches. In this regard, the history of Graham's ministry had been an ambitious one— both for his message and his movement. As Graham's star rose, and as the unparalleled scope and diversity of his ministry mushroomed, the BGEA were forced to confront the question of how best to work with those of divergent views in the common cause of evangelism, without surrendering an identifiable evangelical core. Graham's answer, historically, had been to adopt the posture of irenic and ecumenical bridge builder. This was not the vertical ecumenism of mainline Protestantism where distinctions were often collapsed, but the horizontal ecumenism of the missionary, seeking common ground with which to advance his gospel agenda.[177] Graham's ecumenism had hitherto established *certain* limits, in his affirmations that cooperation with "extreme liberal and Unitarian clergy" remained unlikely (given their dismissal of the deity of Christ).[178] However, in his crusade ministry and wider endeavors, Graham had engaged and affirmed virtually every definable Protestant group as viable conversation partners, many of which fell outside the evangelical mainstream.[179] Following the success of his landmark 1950 Boston and 1957 New York Crusades (which rose on the support of mainline Protestant *and* Catholic congregations and clergy), over the next twenty-five years Graham also enjoyed expanding friendships with leading Catholics.[180] As a result, while admitting cautiously that he stumbled over the doctrine of papal infallibility, Graham routinely sought to emphasize his shared conviction with Catholics regarding their "commitment to

---

177. Wacker, *America's Pastor*, 180–83.

178. Martin, *Prophet with Honour*, 218.

179. Graham had famously stated that he intended "to go anywhere, sponsored by anybody, to preach the gospel, if there are no strings attached to my message." "Lost Chord of Evangelism."

180. Graham received warm appraisal in Catholic papers and from Catholic clergy; was compared favourably with Father Theodore Hesburgh, the iconic President of Notre Dame University; and agreed that if asked to preach in St. Peter's Rome he "would gladly and humbly accept it." So Graham, *Just As I Am*, 161, 423, 692; Martin, *Prophet with Honour*, 345; Wacker, *America's Pastor*, 191.

evangelism" and shared "focus on Christ."[181] And yet, for all Graham's munificent overtures and missionary ecumenism, boulders strewn on the path by centuries of theological disagreement did not crumble easily. Most mid-century evangelicals still judged Catholic soteriology to be heavily compromised, while Catholics responded in kind. They chastised Protestants for placing salvation outside the sacraments of the church and placing priority on the individual's quest for salvation through private decision.[182] Indeed, for Graham, the issue ultimately turned from a rift with the conservative channels out of which he had arisen into an unbridgeable chasm, and stoked fears that his soteriological vision had become blurred.[183]

Within the context of the 1979 Sydney crusade, similar concerns threatened to unravel the crusade's coalition of support. The participation of Pentecostal churches was considered to be a more uncomplicated matter.[184] A note of caution had certainly been expressed over the effect that Pentecostal "word of faith" teachings and their convictions on "direct revelation" might have on the integrity of crusade counselling.[185] Yet, given the wide involvement of such churches "at every level of crusade activity" in the North American context and given their (as yet) modest influence on the Australian Protestant landscape, it was resolved to affirm the Assemblies of God, the Foursquare Gospel Church, and the Apostolic Church of Australia as participating churches. An invitation was also extended to representatives of these churches to sit on the Crusade Council of Reference.[186] Regarding the

---

181. Graham, *Just As I Am*, 251, 693.

182. See Noll, *American Evangelical Christianity*, ch. 7.

183. See the concerned editorial: "Graham's Beliefs Still Intact." There was, of course, in the background of the BGEA's approach, the slightly more unseemly question of the "rhetoric of crusade statistics," and the pressure this placed on the inclusion of variegated expressions of Christianity. While the BGEA invested considerable effort in reciting and recording accurate statistics, expansionist evangelical movements had always "counted the house." Indeed, numbers portended more than they documented. The charismatic power of vast crowds made for spectacular headlines. And spectacular headlines safeguarded the success of future campaigns—validating their authenticity, offering a tangible narrative of divine blessing, and firing a subtle pressure towards numerical "inclusion." See Chaves, *American Religion*, 117–25; Wacker, *America's Pastor*, 182.

184. On the taxonomy of "Pentecostalism" and the "Charismatic Movement," see Anderson, "Pentecostal and Charismatic," 89–107. For a fuller discussion of the impact on and relationship of these movements to Australian Evangelicalism, see chapter 9.

185. Revised follow-up and counselling materials had sought a greater emphasis on scriptural content and sought to resist any influences that could diminish this. J. C. Chapman to W. B. Berryman, January 16, 1979. BGCA, CN 245, Box 25/20.

186. Protestant denominational differences pertaining to baptism, gifts of the Spirit, and charismata, as well as other ecclesiological particularities, were considered

participation of Roman Catholics, concerns had been voiced by local clergy in the early stages of crusade planning that aimed to safeguard the crusade's essentially Protestant fabric. Highly aware of the BGEA's practice and contemporary claims to a process of Vatican-II-led Catholic renewal, many clergy nevertheless remained unconvinced.[187] The prospective "involvement of Catholics, Greek Orthodox and Charismatics ... is an important issue and is getting our attention," Chapman advised to crusade chairman, A. J. Dain, and is among the "more serious points of criticism I am encountering ... as I seek to promote the crusade."[188] Indeed, given that previous Sydney crusades had been solely "a Protestant endeavor involving churches of evangelical persuasion," it was considered imperative that only churches able to support the crusade's "stated objectives" should be admitted into partnership.[189] Initially, given that no Catholic churches had either sought or received approval as participating churches and had not been involved previously in any official capacity, the Executive foresaw no mood for any change to this historic policy.[190] However, by August 1978, following an approach made by officers of the Roman Catholic Church (advisedly from within "the biblical renewal movements" of the Archdiocese of Sydney), the Executive were asked to resubmit the issue for examination.[191]

A flurry of meetings between the Crusade Executive and Catholic office-bearers promptly ensued. The first of these, in October 1978 (involving Bishops Dain and Reid and W. B. Berryman) fielded the representations

---

matters appropriately dealt with in the ongoing ministry of the church that the crusade enquirer might subsequently join. "Executive Committee: Minutes 27 July 1978," BGCA, CN 245, Box 29/1.

187. On the effect of charismatic and Vatican-II-led (1963-65) reform movements within Catholicism, see J. Pollard, "Papacy," 29-49, esp 39-40; Piggin, "Roman Catholicism," 955-59; McIntyre, "Vatican Council II," 1135-37.

188. J. C. Chapman to W. B. Berryman, June 6, 1978. BGCA, CN 245, Box 25/20.

189. A. J. Dain to Canon J. C. Chapman, May 2, 1978. BGCA, CN 245, Box 25/20; Report: J. C. Chapman to Executive Committee, May 25, 1978. "Participating Churches," BGCA, CN 245, Box 25/20.

190. "Executive Committee: Minutes 27 July 1978," BGCA, CN 245, Box 29/1.

191. Harbingers of such developments had arisen at a crusade support breakfast, where a Catholic priest had made representations to John Chapman some months before the formal approach. J. C. Chapman to Executive Committee, August 24, 1978. BGCA, CN 245, Box 25/20. Some observers suggested that it was the "substantial influence of the charismatic movement" upon contemporary Catholicism that encouraged the request for involvement. Indeed, some alleged that "within the Roman Catholic Church of Australia, charismatics have introduced Bible study for the first time. Hundreds of parish groups are participating, and some predict a second Reformation." Nichols, "Graham Crusade Lifts."

of Catholic officials regarding the terms of any possible involvement.[192] A diversity of opinion pervaded the executive as the matter was considered. Believing that significant progress had recently been made in the Roman Catholic "communion" regarding the "doctrine of justification by faith alone and the supreme authority of Holy Scripture," Bishop Reid had expressed his view that the committee should be willing to "explore whether there are any areas in which we can discover a common interest in supporting the gospel." Indeed, he suggested, the committee should not "close [their] eyes to the great things God is doing in that communion," nor withdraw their fellowship "from Catholic Christians seeking to live under the authority of the scriptures."[193] Others, however, were far more guarded. In a strongly worded communication to campaign director, Barry Berryman, in December 1978 John Chapman urged the executive to be unequivocally clear that this "area of co-operation is a *very* sensitive one" that involved fundamental judgments about the "authenticity of the Roman Catholic gospel" and the advisability of "referring people back to churches where there may be an absence of adequate bible teaching."[194] Indeed, for other local clergymen, who had already voiced concerns that the selection of crusade counsellors from participating Protestant churches was not sufficiently rigorous (in light of the important role of spiritual formation that such a role entailed), any suggestion of the inclusion of Roman Catholics in this process of spiritual nurture was an even more perplexing prospect.[195]

Eventually, with the Sydney crusade not more than two months away, and with pressure mounting for the impasse to be resolved, negotiations led by Bishop Reid on the morning of March 8, 1979, saw a proposal put to the Crusade Executive that same evening. It proposed the qualified inclusion of Roman Catholics as crusade counsellors and nurture leaders. The terms of the proposal stipulated: first, that any "letter of recommendation from the Catholic Cardinal" regarding prospective Catholic counsellors and nurture group leaders should stipulate their belonging to the "biblical renewal movements which are in the diocese and the people so recruited must be

---

192. "Executive Committee Minutes 26 October 1978," BGCA, CN 245, Box 29/1.

193. J. R. Reid to M. Glinatsis, June 15, 1978. BGCA, CN 245, Box 29/8. This letter, sent to the Pastor of the Greek Baptist Church in Ashfield was in response to earlier concerns raised by Glinatsis (a member of the 1979 Crusade Ethnic Committee) regarding the inclusion of Greek Orthodox representatives on the Crusade Committee. Reid's letter addresses Glinatsis's concerns, citing developments within Catholicism as reasons to proceed with cautious optimism in such matters.

194. J. C. Chapman to W. B. Berryman, December 20, 1978. BGCA, CN 245, Box 25/20.

195. John S. Webb to A. J. Dain, March 13, 1979. BGCA, CN 245, Box 25/16.

genuinely in sympathy with the crusade and its objectives"; second, "that nurture for all enquirers from non-participating congregations ... should be held at a variety of central sites, and that the Roman-Catholic-trained nurture group leaders ... using [crusade] material should be eligible to lead in these small groups"; and third, that "Roman Catholic nuns [be asked] not to wear religious habit if they are engaged in counselling or crusade nurture groups."[196] The motion was debated strongly and at considerable length among members of the executive, with a growing majority appearing to favor what seemed to be a reasoned and measured proposal. However, unpersuaded that recent developments had seen any substantial shift in Catholic soteriology or sacerdotal vision by which to be satisfied that the proposed course was a responsible one, John Chapman opposed the motion strongly. In Chapman's view, post-Vatican II formulations still inferred that Scripture's correct interpretation occurred only alongside the Catholic Church's magisterium and sacred tradition. Moreover, by repromulgating Catholicism's soteriological vision (in which God dealt mediately with the soul via the church and its instrumentalities), post-Vatican II formulations, he believed, continued to render the church, and not the gospel, as the conveyor of saving grace to humanity.[197] Hence, while expressing regret at what appeared to be a hard-nosed and "exclusionary" stance, and notwithstanding the green shoots of potential reform, to refer enquirers to Catholic-led groups or parishes, Chapman held, would dilute the integrity of the post-crusade process and constitute a breach of received wisdom and pastoral duty of care.[198] Following considerable and at times acrimonious debate, the motion was eventually put to the executive. It was resolved forty-eight to two in favor of qualified Catholic involvement, before being announced to the metropolitan church support base. A principled compromise, so it was held, had been reached.[199]

---

196. "Executive Committee: Minutes 8 March 1979," BGCA, CN 245, Box 29/1.

197. On Catholicism's post-Vatican II soteriological vision, which maintained the Church's interpretive role alongside Scripture, as well as its role as the conveyor of sacramental grace, ie. God's imparting of "supernaturally endowed instrumentalities" with the "powers essential to the salvation of the soul being mediated *ex opera operato* through these instrumentalities," see Reymond, *Systematic Theology*, 470–71; Piggin, "Catholicism," 955–59; Tanner *Vatican II*, 29–189. Cf. Chapman to Berryman, December 20, 1978. BGCA, CN 245, Box 25/20.

198. "Executive Committee: Minutes 8 March 1979"; Interview with Phillip Jensen, February 16, 2017.

199. Executive Committee minutes record that Canon John C. Chapman and the Rev. Phillip Jensen were the sole dissenting voices. "Executive Committee: Minutes 8 March 1979"; Interview with Phillip Jensen, February 16, 2017.

However, if the matter was considered to be settled, news of the decision provoked a strength of response that was somewhat unexpected. Trenchant critique from key local Protestant newspapers combined swiftly with rumbles of discontent and threats of the withdrawal of support. Crucially, a series of representations in the weeks after the decision were made to Bishop Dain by senior members of the Baptist Union (the second major denominational pillar of crusade support). They made clear that unless the decision was overturned, they would be left with the regrettable prospect of withdrawing their support for the crusade.[200] Hence, with the prospective loss of key coalition partners, the motion was recommitted at the following meeting of the Crusade Executive on March 29. After lengthy discussion the motion was modified. In its place, a new compromise solution stated that enquirers who expressed a Catholic affiliation would be directed to non-denominational "nurture groups" where they would be encouraged to consider the question of church membership independently.[201] A groundswell conservative response had brought a surprising reinstatement of the historic policy of Roman Catholic exclusion from crusade affairs.

Sydney Anglicans and BGEA Revivalism: Beginning to Walk Apart

There is little doubt that the presence of senior BGEA figures and the breadth of its denominational sympathies, together with the amount of time already invested in negotiations, had placed no small pressure on the outcome of the initial decision taken by the Crusade Executive.[202] Moreover, the need for principled and pragmatic concession making was an unavoidable reality of all expansionary Christian movements.[203] This reality was not lost on senior Sydney figures like Bishops Dain and Reid, who having begun to engage widely with the BGEA's global ministry were disconcerted by what

---

200. These representations were made independently of other Sydney Anglicans, and of Canon John Chapman, who was engaged for a nine-day evangelistic crusade at the Melbourne Showground in the weeks following the March 8 decision. "Executive Committee: Minutes 8 March 1979"; Interview with Phillip Jensen, February 16, 2017.

201. "Executive Committee: Minutes 29 March 1979"; Nichols, "Graham Crusade Lifts."

202. Charlie Riggs, for example, the global figurehead of the BGEA's Christian Life and Witness Classes, having been in Australia for some months, was present at the March 8 meeting. "Executive Committee: Minutes 8 March 1979."

203. McLeod, *Religious Crisis*, 248; Hempton, "Protestant Migrations," 41–48; Bebbington, *Victorian Religious Revivals*, 11–18.

they considered to be a regressive, if not unnecessary, outcome.[204] Yet, such prominent tensions surrounding the 1979 Sydney crusade also portended something more. They were harbingers of a pattern that would increasingly characterize the attitude of senior Sydney leadership, in the later century, to the pervasive expansionism of the BGEA, in favor of an approach considered more doctrinally, culturally, and organizationally discreet. Indeed, with the dizzying postwar expansion and consequent diversity that Evangelicalism experienced (in large measure under the influence of pan-evangelical superstructures like the BGEA, IVF, and other missionary societies), the challenge the movement began to face was one of fragmentation. More diverse in geographical distribution, cultural orientation, and theological emphasis than at any time since its eighteenth-century origins, and seeking to balance the gospel's universal missionary imperative with the doctrinal, cultural, ethical, and ecclesiological particularities of its application, expansive Evangelicalism began to exhibit signs of fatigue under the strain of its own now sizeable frame. The result was that a "new phase of realignment and redefinition" began to emerge within global Evangelicalism, the particularities of which were reflected in specific contexts like Sydney.[205]

Chapman's ruminations in the wake of the 1983 *Amsterdam International Congress for Itinerant Evangelists* are particularly telling in this regard. The Amsterdam Congress—itself a reaction to the overbearing demands of Lausanne-driven "social concern" perceived by some to be subtly assailing world efforts in evangelization—devoted itself exclusively to the "training and encouragement" of those who "carry the Gospel from place to place."[206] Funded by the largesse of the BGEA and dwarfing even the 1974 Lausanne Congress, Amsterdam drew four thousand practitioners from 133 nations. Seventy percent of these attended from Majority World countries. Plenary sessions by leaders from every continent were supplemented with workshops on other areas of the evangelist's tool kit. One hundred and seven workshops covered subjects as varied as family life and apologetics, and were accompanied by how-to-do-it films, interviews, testimonies, group

---

204. Interview with Phillip Jensen, February 16, 2017. Bishop John Reid would soon assume the chairmanship of the *Lausanne Theology Work Group* (from 1981) and served as Vice-Chairman of the *Lausanne Committee for World Evangelisation* (an offshoot of the BGEA) into the 1990s. Bishop A. J. Dain, a British-born Sydney Anglican assistant bishop and close confidant of Billy Graham, served as Chairman of the *1974 Lausanne Congress on World Evangelisation*. So Hutchinson, "Dain, Arthur John."

205. On similar evangelical realignments experienced in the 1830s, 1910s, and 1950s, see Stanley, *Global Diffusion*, 11, 235–39.

206. Foster, "Amsterdam '83," 7. BGCA, CN 253, Box 21/8. A full examination of the Lausanne Congress and the issue of evangelical "social concern" follows in chapter 6.

discussions, and "lots of music"—participants were heard singing "even between sessions, and in the dining hall."[207] Few could discount the "spirit of koinonia, inspiration and motivation" that was imparted via the congress, enthused Billy Graham, "our vision was lifted, and our sickles sharpened as we learned from one another how to more effectively proclaim the gospel of Christ to our generation."[208]

Undoubtedly, Australian leaders like Chapman heartily agreed with Graham's assessment. As convener and keynote presenter for the Oceania regional workshop on "Message Preparation and Delivery," Chapman was enthusiastically engaged in the congress's vision and its many proceedings.[209] Exhilarated at being part of such a historic forum, and aghast at the financial largesse of the BGEA, Chapman wrote to his Australian support base following the congress:

> Who but Billy Graham could have pulled off such a coup? Is there anyone else in whom so many have sufficient confidence to attend such a gathering? Is there anyone else who so freely uses their resources to encourage the spread of the gospel? . . . The opening ceremony was a thrill . . . Billy Graham spoke on this occasion on the topic of the "The Evangelist and a Torn World." It was vintage Billy Graham, with his passion to see the lost saved and a clear call to make preaching a top priority while not neglecting the other needs of people. I was inspired by it.[210]

Nevertheless, while emphasizing his overall response to be "thoroughly positive" and not wishing to "detract from what I am certain will be a highly significant event," other concerns in relation to the Amsterdam platform provided reason to be more circumspect. For example, the linking in congress promotional and audiovisual material of numerous countervailing theological traditions—in the succession of "great evangelists down the ages"—posed perplexing questions, Chapman suggested, about the theological breadth of the modern BGEA movement.[211] This, together with an apparent insufficient use of Scripture among congress plenary speakers who championed the "preaching of the Bible," yet appeared to leave

207. Foster, "Amsterdam '83"; Wirt, "Amsterdam '83," 9.

208. Graham, "Foreword," 2. BGCA, CN 253, Box 21/8.

209. See J. C. Chapman, "Message Preparation and Delivery (Oceania)," July 14, ICIE 1983. BGCA, CN 245, T216.

210. J. C. Chapman: *Report on The International Congress for Itinerant Evangelists*, Amsterdam, August 1983. BDM Box 1, SDA.

211. For example, "Cyprian, Savonarola and the seventeenth-century Jesuits who 'evangelised' China," were linked together with "Wesley, Whitefield, Moody and even Billy himself." Chapman, *Report on the ICIE*, Amsterdam, August 1983.

it largely unopened in their own expositions, only amplified Chapman's concerns.[212] Furthermore, for a congress with the goal of exploring new initiatives in world evangelization, the promotion of prefabricated crusade templates as the ostensibly cure-all panacea (however historically successful such templates had been) provided further cause for apprehension.[213] In response to such concerns, Chapman informed his supporters of the need to be investing in the development of Australian evangelists and in missiological patterns that were more "appropriate to culture and tastes." This, he suggested, ought to contrast the now ingrained pattern of "looking overseas" and to the BGEA, whose "roll all before it" approach had begun to bear the hallmarks of cultural obtuseness and insensitivity.[214]

The effect of such concerns—alongside a growing self-confidence in the Sydney evangelical polity and a strengthening of its ties with other conservative movements—was to create a subtle breach in the generation-long association between Sydney and the BGEA. Indeed, while immense goodwill remained between these two movements and shared objectives endured, conflicting beliefs regarding the methods required to achieve such objectives saw these historic allies begin to now walk at a distance, more as "family" but no longer as "brothers" in the work of global mission.

Making good on his post-Amsterdam ruminations, in 1984 Chapman formalized a process of developing Australian evangelists and preachers. Between 1984 and 2009, as many as eighty-nine student-practitioners were selected and trained by Chapman and his successors at the Department of Evangelism. Many of these would go on to be leading figures in Australian (and to some extent world) Evangelicalism.[215] This combined with the intensification of local church planting initiatives, a focus on strengthening the landscape of Australian parochial ministries, and the expansion of evangelical Australian publishing ministries and parachurch bodies (initiatives in

212. Chapman, *Report on the ICIE*; Foster, "Amsterdam '83," 47–48.

213. Alongside other resources, the BGEA gave copies of *The Billy Graham Crusade Handbook* to all Majority World participants and sponsored a plethora of crusade-oriented workshops such as "Setting up City-Wide Crusades for Large Cities," "Setting up Small Town and Rural Area Crusades," "Conducting Single-Church Evangelistic Crusades," together with numerous workshops on "Giving the Invitation," and "Crusade Follow-Up." *Decision*, ICIE November 1983, 10.

214. Chapman, *Report on the ICIE*.

215. They served in future roles as Anglican bishops and deans, theological college principals and scholars, leading church planters and evangelists in both Anglican and independent evangelical church networks, directors of national student ministries, as well as missionaries, school principals and leading local and international clergy. See Appendix 2. Names have been drawn from historic Department of Evangelism/Preaching Christ Newsletters. BDM Box 2, SDA.

which Chapman also played a leading role) to mark a period of transition in which the once largely receptor culture of Australian Evangelicalism began to emerge from infancy toward a self-assured adolescence.[216]

Ultimately, the juggernaut of BGEA-led evangelism showed no signs of abating during this period. It pursued further (and larger) conferences for evangelists in 1986 and 2000 and expanded its crusade ministry into unexpected areas of Asia and Eastern Europe. Together with the parallel Lausanne movement, the BGEA's breadth of vision brooked few rivals in either contemporary or historic Christian settings.[217] In perhaps its most ambitious endeavor of all, following Amsterdam II (which saw eight thousand evangelists convene in Amsterdam in 1986) the BGEA began gauging support for a global "mission originating from one city and [being] beamed by satellite to hundreds of cities at the same time." Having trialed the model during 1986, in a letter to gauge the level of Australian support, Graham enthused to Chapman that because the "technology exists to do the same thing worldwide," the BGEA had begun "prayerfully thinking about holding this project in 1989." With "millions of Christians" making "this their major prayer concern," Graham alleged, "I believe God would bless it beyond our expectations," and "I would like to know your thoughts."[218] Tellingly, however, Chapman's enthusiasm at the prospect of such an enterprise was subdued. He replied:

> Dr. Graham, Thank you very much for your letter and for the note about *Mission World '89*. I've taken a wide sample of people within the Diocese of Sydney and especially of the Board of the Department of Evangelism. Although we think the vision

---

216. During the 1990s, the theme of "mission and the local church" reached a crescendo in Sydney. This was driven in part by a continuing response to perceived BGEA overreach and by the influence of the Knox-Robinson ecclesiology and its view on mission and the church (see ch. 7). Chapman and his successors at the DOE offered impetus to the intensification of local ministry, resourcing the DOE in the 1990s with parish "consultants" to aid parishes in refining their mission agenda. David Mansfield (Chapman's successor) in tandem with leading figures like Phillip Jensen, in the mid-1990s sponsored the exploration of church-planting initiatives, which took shape in concrete initiatives like the establishment of the College of Church Planters and Fellowship of Independent Evangelical Churches, and prefigured a wave of church planting in and from Sydney in the late 1990s. This was in concert with the rise of the Church Growth Movement, which emphasized church-centric models. The rise of publishing ministries and training bodies (like Matthias Media and The Ministry Training Strategy) is also significant. *Preaching Christ Newsletters*, February–April 1996, March–May 2003, September–November 2004.

217. Olsen, "Amsterdam 2000."

218. Rev. Dr. Billy Graham to Rev. Canon John Chapman, March 1987, BDM Box 1, SDA.

of trying to evangelize the world is a great one, we don't really think that this is the way we want to go about it. Our fears lie in two directions: 1) That we think it's not possible to do something which will be culturally acceptable to everybody at the same time; and 2) We think that we will have great difficulty in motivating the Christians for this sort of venture. We therefore believe this is not the best way forward. I know this will be a disappointment to hear us express it in this way, but this is our honest opinion.[219]

In unison with Chapman, and on Chapman's advice, Archbishop Robinson also replied:

Dear Dr. Graham, this is to acknowledge your March letter in which you seek my thoughts about the possibility of a satellite ministry in 1989. While I appreciate the vision . . . I have to say that it is not a proposal I feel able to commend so far as the city of Sydney is concerned. We give constant thought to the responsibility for evangelization in our own area, and indeed will be engaged in a consultation this very week to discover the best means by which we can fulfill our task in relation to this Diocese . . . We have a number of proposals and activities planned in this connection. However, there are aspects of a large international exercise by the means you have suggested which do not appeal to me at all, and I think I should say that frankly in response to your enquiry . . . I cannot say there would be no effect, but I certainly do not think it is necessarily the most effective way of conducting evangelistic ministry in Sydney in 1989.[220]

Almost certainly, a mood of rising confidence during the 1980s also played a role in the more independent note struck by Chapman and Robinson regarding such a prospective venture. The fruits of national reform under the Frazer and Hawke administrations combined with the impact of new technologies and the liberalization of Australian money markets to foster an expansionary mood. The land, once considered prohibitively remote, was becoming a magnet for travelers and foreign capital, accelerating the rise of a new breed of Australian entrepreneur and global citizenry, and the emergence of a nation come of age.[221] In this context, Australian Evangeli-

219. Rev. Canon John Chapman to Rev. Dr. Billy Graham, May 1, 1987 (dictated April 15), BDM Box 1, SDA.

220. Most Rev. D. W. B. Robinson to Rev. Dr. Billy Graham, April 8, 1987, BDM Box 1, SDA; Rev. Canon John C. Chapman to the Most Rev. D. W. B. Robinson, March 31, 1987, BDM Box 1, SDA.

221. MacIntyre, *Concise History*, 236–47; Walter, "Growth Resumed," 162–86.

calism was beginning to find its own voice, just as the nation had begun to as well. Yet, in contrast to the variegated theological tones that aggregated under the banner of BGEA-led expansivity, the strong antipodean evangelical voice that emerged in this period was distinctly conservative in its tone. While not abandoning the ambition of world evangelization, a sense that newer (or perhaps the revival of older) alliances were emerging as the vehicle to achieve this, had already begun to firm. Paralleling similar developments in its dealings with the contemporary Lausanne movement (also an offshoot of the BGEA) Sydney's breaking step with the BGEA marked the twilight of the long crusade era and of "big Evangelicalism" in Australia, in favor of an evangelical vision considered to be more doctrinally, culturally, and organizationally discreet and consistent, yet equally ambitious.[222]

Conclusion

This chapter has located the missiological contribution of John Chapman within a period of defining social and religious change that transformed Western society and brought widespread challenges to Christian churches as they sought to maintain an effective witness in this new milieu. The chapter demonstrates the degree to which the modes of Australian Protestant public witness (*including* those of Anglican evangelicals) prior to this sea change were enmeshed with the inherited superstructures of Anglo-Christian culture and identity. This created a context in which Australian churches were largely ill-equipped to converse with their culture once the bulwarks conducive to the flourishing of Christian identity began to fall away. The chapter demonstrates the vital, yet nuanced role Chapman played as a missiological leader in this context. Chapman's approach was Augustinian in epistemology; Reformed and biblically conservative in theology; and pragmatic in its desired ends. Alert to the changing realities of culture, he successfully differentiated evangelical modes of witness from the models of the previous era. This involved, *inter alia*, the pioneering of an interactive and contextualized model of evangelism (*dialogue evangelism*) and the publication of a range of influential works (*Know and Tell the Gospel* and *A Fresh Start*) that distilled the many theological and practical evangelistic insights discerned throughout his career. This body of work

222. The BGEA's pursuit of a global crusade-style initiative came to fruition in March 1995, with Dr. Graham's preaching by satellite to an audience of more than one billion people in 185 countries from a stadium in San Juan, Puerto Rico. It received enthusiastic support from certain Sydney parishes. However, no formal crusade partnerships were entered into with Australian cities after the 1979 Sydney crusade. See "Billy Graham Activates."

became a standard bearer for conservative evangelical missional advocacy and reflection among evangelical clergy and laity across many parts of the world. It also gave rise to a subsequent generation of evangelistic resources in Australia and overseas that drew upon his earlier pioneering contribution. The positions Chapman adopted in his roles of public gospel advocacy were also highly pragmatic. Indeed, having previously differentiated evangelical modes of witness from the institutional and revivalist modes of the past, inasmuch as such modes could still serve the advance of the gospel, he actively promoted them. Chapman played a leading role in the success of the 1979 Sydney Graham Crusade. He also pursued a strategy of successful larger-scale crusades across Sydney regions in the 1980s (albeit utilizing his own modified approach to the public appeal). Ultimately, Chapman came to perceive a degree of dissonance between the objectives of expansive evangelical movements (like the BGEA) and the ability of Australian evangelicals to maintain a consistently Reformed and contextualized approach to mission. In response, Chapman became a leading advocate for the development of Australian evangelists and patterns of mission, as well as the pursuit of alliances considered more amenable to such an agenda. Chapman believed such a pragmatic, yet muscular conservatism, to be an authentic expression of apostolic faith (1 Cor 9:22).

6

The Gospel and Social Reform

Lausanne and the Challenge of Missiological Priority

"If the gospel is to be preached to all men, it must be done while they are living . . . To us who are responsible for preaching the gospel it means [the evangelization of the World] in this generation."—John Raleigh Mott, New York 1900[1]

IN THE NORTHERN SUMMER of 1974, 115 Australians gathered with over 2,400 evangelical leaders, 3,600 participants, and 410 press reporters from 150 nations in the Palais de Bailleau in Lausanne, Switzerland, for what became the most widely representative gathering of evangelicals of its time.[2] According to *Time Magazine*, the hotly anticipated congress "served notice" of the rising contemporary "vigor of conservative, resolutely biblical, fervently mission-minded Christianity" across the world.[3] Similarly, in the mind of its convener, Billy Graham, the congress stood resolutely in the tradition of the great missionary conferences at New York (1900) and Edinburgh (1910) whose vision of world evangelization he hoped to recapture.[4] Indeed, convinced that "never before have the opportunities been so great nor the means at our command to proclaim the gospel so manifold,"[5]

---

1. Bebbington, *Evangelicalism*, 192.
2. The Lausanne Congress for World Evangelisation took place between July 16–25, 1974. Chester, *Awakening*, 70n4; Chilton, "Christian Australia," 300–301.
3. "Challenge from Evangelicals," 48.
4. Graham, "Why Lausanne?," 22–36, esp. 25–26.
5. "Church Leaders." BGCA, CN 46, Box 1/1.

Graham's vision for the 1974 congress was "to unite all evangelicals in the task of total evangelization of the world" and finish the job.[6] The Australian delegation to the congress comprised fifty-three clergy and thirty-eight laymen, alongside a number of observers, media representatives, and spouses. A collection of Sydney Anglicans formed part of the Australian delegation. They included well-known figures like Bishop John Reid, Canon D. B. Knox, Canon Ken Short, Canon John Chapman, the Very Rev. Lance Shilton, and the Rev. David Claydon.[7] Emerging leaders from the "Australian Jesus Movement" (like John Hirt and Peter Campbell from the "House of the New World," John Smith from the "God's Squad" Motorcycle Club, and the movement's leading theologian, Dr. Athol Gill) were also invited to the congress as observers. This group of self-described radicals had fast become the Australian face of a new countercultural Evangelicalism. In their ministries they had pursued a range of initiatives in their quest to subvert the idols of Western culture, including the renunciation of wealth, showing solidarity with the underprivileged and the promotion of allegedly "fresh biblical answers" to social evils.[8] As the congress began, a mood of optimism pervaded. Yet, it was also apparent that the diversity of such a gathering posed significant risks. Indeed, as one observer suggested, the challenge of combining "paternalistic North Americans, radical central Americans, [and] revivalistic East Africans" with "a mixture of Europeans, Australians [and] the rest of the world" presented a scenario of "potential chaos."[9] Sharp congress tensions did ultimately arise. However, what surprised most observers was not the presence of such tensions, but the direction from which they came. Raising their voices with various co-sympathizers from across the world, it was the diverse members of the Australian delegation (not least the figure of John Chapman) who supplied some of the more incendiary dynamics of the ten-day event. Moreover, the issue around which tensions primarily arose was the historically delicate question of the relationship between evangelism and social concern.

The following chapter examines this defining twentieth-century question (of the relationship between evangelism and social concern) through the lens of the 1974 Lausanne Congress and its context. This was a question that occupied the energies of many across the evangelical landscape,

6. Billy Graham to John Stott, April 3, 1972, JWRS Pre-Congress Correspondence. International Congress on World Evangelisation (ICOWE). BGCA, CN 590, Folder 4:1.

7. Chilton, "Christian Australia," 301; Olsen, "Congress Participants." BGCA, CN 46, Box 32/8.

8. "After the Congress with Jack Dain." Interview with B. Kaye, n.d., BGCA, CN 46, Box 32/2; Chilton, "Christian Australia," 320–25.

9. Knox, "Lausanne and After."

revealing the conflicting theological and missiological trajectories the movement sought to bestride.[10] However, it also became a defining issue within the Australian evangelical constituency. Indeed, as a leading Australian evangelical, Chapman himself regarded the issue to be central. "Without a doubt," wrote David Mansfield (Chapman's colleague and successor at the Department of Evangelism), Chapman "was never more rigorous in his theological vigilance than when it came to the definition, integrity and clarity of the gospel and the primacy of evangelism." To be sure, Mansfield contended, while Chapman "recognized the importance of Christian social responsibility, he [nevertheless] countered any attempt to make it integral to mission or part of the essence of evangelism or the gospel."[11] Indeed, along with other leading conservatives, Chapman's advocacy for the priority of evangelism ultimately came to such prominence it became a virtual conservative shibboleth. It drew passionate discussion from many who were invested in a more social vision of the gospel and who felt compelled to voice their disagreement with his widely articulated views.[12] This chapter therefore seeks to examine the role of figures like Chapman in the ongoing debate. A degree of context will first be supplied to situate the congress and its key developments. After this, the events of the congress and its key outcomes will be examined. In turn, this chapter illuminates unique trends and pressure points that arose within Australian and world Evangelicalism during this period. It also reveals something of the prolonged struggle the movement faced to balance the quest for "world evangelization" with the highly visible responsibility of caring for a world in need.

The Great Reversal?

It is well known that from its earliest days the Christian movement was at the vanguard of social activism and bold calls for the reformation and providential ordering of society. In the opening centuries of the Christian era, the "wholeness" of the Christian missionary witness (including the Christian's moral excellences, their deeds of mercy, and reputation as carers for the sick) combined with the intellectual defense of the Christian

10. Stanley, "Lausanne 1974," 533–51; Chapman, "International Relations," 355–68.

11. Mansfield, *Chappo Collection*, 194. This work by Mansfield (Chapman's longtime friend and colleague of forty-three years) provides a compendium of professional and biographical reflections regarding Chapman's legacy by colleagues and friends from across the world.

12. Jensen, *Anglicanism*, 120. Chapman revealed to his biographer that "in other denominations our Department is heavily criticised because of my stand on this issue." Chapman to Orpwood, February 1, 1995, BDM Box 1, SDA.

faith to affirm the plausibility of Christian teaching in a culture inimical to the message.[13] Similarly, in the evangelization of Europe and Britain in the medieval period, the Christian qualities of self-discipline, orderliness, patience, and service to others mixed seamlessly with Christian teachings in the evangelization of unreached people groups.[14] In the eighteenth century, the Evangelical Revival in Britain and North America also proved a great stimulus to philanthropy and evangelism in the founding of missionary societies and the giving by many Christians of generous service in societal life.[15] Moreover, across the late eighteenth and nineteenth century the sick and disadvantaged received attention from an "empire of philanthropy" that arose via the development of charitable societies that were a fruit of the evangelical impulse.[16]

In colonial Australia, alongside their ecclesiastical responsibilities, many Anglican clergy were active in a range of social and governmental activities that were seen as vehicles for the shaping of the Christian social and political order. The establishment of a panoply of benevolent and philanthropic societies also mirrored their earlier development in Britain.[17] In the early twentieth century, leading Sydney Anglican clergymen like Canon F. B. Boyce led the struggle for old age pensions and slum clearance. Boyce's objectives were shared by another social reformer, the Rev. R. B. S Hammond of St. Barnabas's Broadway. Alongside a vigorous preaching ministry in the inner city, Hammond (and the teams he administered) made thousands of visits to the poor and sick. They were also active in finding housing for homeless families, sourcing seed loans to get men started in self-employment, and serving more than a quarter of a million meals in a single year.[18] Indeed, building on the work of such predecessors, Sydney Anglicans built

---

13. McClymond, "Mission and Evangelism," 341–54 suggests that "missionary propaganda" and "dogmatic completeness" were not the sole catalysts for the conversion of the Greco-Roman world. It was the "wholeness" of the church's "missionary witness" that the Greco-Roman world found compelling. Cf. Walls, *Missionary Movement*, chs. 1–4; Stark, *Rise*, 84–87. See also Holland, *Dominion*, chs. 8–11; and Judge and Scholer, *Social Distinctives* on the rising Christian influence in the cultures of antiquity.

14. McClymond, "Mission and Evangelism," 346.

15. On the philanthropy of Wesley, Whitefield, and Lord Shaftesbury, see Bebbington, *Evangelicalism*, 71–74, 120–21.

16. Of the charitable organizations that arose in Britain by the later nineteenth century, it is estimated that three-quarters were evangelical in character and control. Fletcher, "Anglican Ascendancy," 9; Frame, *Anglicans*, 49; Piggin, *Spirit*, vi.

17. Gladwin, *Anglican Clergy*, 97–188; Dickey, *No Charity There*, chs. 1–3.

18. Fletcher, "Anglican Ascendancy," 12–14; Gladwin, *Anglican Clergy*, 97–188; Judd, "Robert Brodribb Hammond," 148–50; Withycombe, "Francis Bertie Boyce," 46. See also Lake, *Faith in Action*, 11–109.

up over one hundred years a diocesan welfare network, described in 1979 by the Archbishop of Canterbury, Donald Coggan, as "the largest welfare work conducted by any diocese in the Anglican Communion."[19] However, by the time of the 1974 Lausanne Congress, rising concerns over the conflation of two interrelated activities (namely evangelism and social concern), which had previously seemed harmonized in the evangelical inheritance, began to circulate in Sydney and elsewhere. Indeed, some evangelical leaders like John Stott began to argue that by the mid-twentieth century a "great reversal" had taken place that amounted to the repudiation of Evangelicalism's historic legacy of social concern.[20]

The roots of this apparent reversal lay in the profound social and economic changes that occurred during the mid-nineteenth century, alongside the growing fissures that emerged within Protestantism in relation to the fundamentalist and liberal-modernist divide. During the nineteenth century the twin processes of industrialization and urbanization strongly impacted the larger economies of Western society (chiefly the imperial powers of Western Europe and the United States). These processes began to produce significant structural inequalities between the prosperous capitalist classes and the new urban poor of these nations, as well as the exploited populations of the Western colonies on whom their prosperity depended. Such developments aroused both movements of protest and new forms of understanding society and the economy. The socialist and Marxist critique of the structural inequalities produced by capitalism arose as a related phenomenon, with Marxism being a later nineteenth-century phenomenon on that continuum. Resonating with such critique, Christian socialists regarded the masses of the urban poor as both the victims of capitalist developments and the core of new movements for change. They saw in the Old Testament prophetic denunciation of injustice and in the teachings of Jesus the threads of a contrasting social order to the unrestrained competition and individualism of the capitalist model. In response, they urged churches to identify more closely with the industrial working class and to guide the community toward improving the conditions of these citizens as quickly as possible. Such a socially and economically oriented application of Christian principles (which became commonly known as the "Social Gospel") was given particular expression at the turn of the twentieth century in contexts such as Germany, the United States, and Britain.[21]

19. Cited in Nichols, "Australian Archbishop," 58.

20. Moberg, *Great Reversal*, 28–66.

21. Forrester, "Wealth and Poverty," 514–33; Douglas, "Christian Socialism," 1029. In Germany, the leading liberal theologian, Adolf Von Harnack, considered the question of "the gospel and the poor" to be *the* social question to be addressed. In America,

While such Christian responses to inequality were to be commended, the connection of leading advocates of this enhanced social vision to the liberal wings of the churches also created a sense of unease. Indeed, many of the early century clerical advocates of such a social vision had also previously promoted an accommodationist stance in relation to the "new sciences" and the conclusions of "higher criticism." Such figures typically demurred from a historically orthodox conception of Christianity. Coupled with a broadening postmillennial tradition and an optimism in the potential of human progress, such figures implied that humanity could, via its own efforts, bring in God's kingdom of justice and peace on earth.[22] Conservative leaders naturally responded to such developments with reserve. They perceived in such assertions a reductionist Christology (that focused solely on Christ's example of mercy at the expense of his atoning work), a false eschatology and a misplaced humanistic optimism. Moreover, a perception lingered among some early-century evangelicals that the promotion of social reform was merely a more palatable pathway for some than preaching sin and salvation, and they were quick to cite historic examples where socially constructive Christian work had become secularized.[23]

In the interwar era, an intermediate (neo-orthodox) response emanated from the American theologian-ethicist Reinhold Neibuhr and Swiss theologian Karl Barth, who highlighted the need to work for justice in light of God's coming kingdom.[24] Among American evangelicals, Harold J. Ockenga and Carl F. Henry emerged after the Second World War as mediating figures in this debate. Ockenga (president of the new Fuller Seminary) sponsored a range of scholarship that encouraged a more socially enlightened ministry, while Henry (editor of the influential evangelical publication *Christianity Today*) famously claimed fundamentalism had lost its social conscience, and urged evangelicals to work out the social implications of the gospel.[25] In Britain, with the dawn of the television era (which brought the

---

the work of Walter Rauschenbusch (*Christianity and the Social Crisis*, 1907) inspired a new generation of Christians with an eagerness for social involvement. In Britain, R. H. Tawney and W. Temple issued calls for social and economic justice rooted in Christian faith. This was coupled in British Nonconformist channels with a view of Christian social engagement generated primarily as a response to the challenges of mission in urban contexts and in situations of economic deprivation. In Australia, Christian socialism enjoyed support from prominent figures at St. John's Morpeth and from several clergy and prominent lay academics in Sydney. Mansfield, "Social Gospel," 411–33; Bebbington, *Evangelicalism*, 211–13.

22. Magnuson, "Social Gospel," 1027–29; Bebbington, *Evangelicalism*, 216.
23. Sugden, "Social Gospel," 799–800; McClymond, "Issues," 349.
24. Sturch, "Reinhold Neibuhr," 628–29; Bloesch, "Karl Barth," 184–85.
25. Marsden, *Reforming Fundamentalism*, 4; Henry, *Uneasy Conscience*, 17, 26, 30.

scale of human suffering unmistakably into the lounge rooms of the world), and with the rise of 1960s protest culture, a desire to reexamine the broader social dimensions of the gospel began to intensify.[26] Moreover, with the rising postwar confidence of British evangelicals and the emergence of numerous evangelical charitable works (like the TEAR Fund and Shaftesbury Project) alongside the impact of leading publications urging for change, there was, on both sides of the Atlantic, a strengthening of the application of evangelical thought to issues of social concern and a determination to renew their engagement in the public square.[27]

Despite such developments, the specter of a more liberally oriented "social gospel" had not entirely departed from world Christian networks, and its reamplification via the World Council of Churches (WCC) framed the immediate prelude to the Lausanne Congress in 1974. As a formal successor to the great missionary conferences in the early century, the WCC represented a drive toward church unity and the unity of the churches in mission. It was able to draw on the large financial resources of member denominations and their mission agencies, as well as the interest of Western governments in encouraging a range of developmental programs in the Majority World. Thus engaged, from the 1950s, the WCC moved toward a more expansive understanding of the *missio Dei* that included far more than evangelism in the Christian mandate.[28] Emerging ecumenical missiology reflected a serious attempt to overcome the many apparent dualisms of previous missionary views.[29] Hence, a defining characteristic of the WCC's approach became a considered openness towards the world. God, it was held, was not primarily interested in the church or in saved individuals but in the "totality of human experience." Indeed, while reconciling man to God had been the goal of "traditional" mission, the concern of "new mission" (as articulated at the WCC's Uppsala Assembly, 1968) was rather the desire to cultivate *true* man and to foster the *humanization* of society.[30] Also challenged was the conviction that God related to the world through the church. Rather, in the WCC's formulations, the world was moved from

---

26. Chester, *Awakening*, 22.

27. Stanley, *Global Diffusion*, 153–55; cf. the later discussion in this chapter regarding developments in the Global South.

28. Bosch, *Witness to the World*, 18; Hunt, "Lausanne Movement," 81–84.

29. Such dualisms included: the eternal and temporal, soul and body, religion and culture, evangelization and social involvement, salvation and liberation, religious and secular, church and world. Bosch, *Witness to the World*, 35.

30. As Uppsala formulated it, this would find expression in a range of reforms in the areas of race relations, industrial relations, rural development, business and professional ethics, intellectual honesty, and integrity. Bosch, *Witness to the World*, 35–37.

the periphery of the missionary portrait to its epicenter. Consequently, it alleged, to be a "missionary" meant to be God's co-worker *in* the world, and the task of the church in mission became that of "entering into partnership with God in history" (Uppsala Assembly, 1968). Ecumenical missiology thus made a quantum shift away from a conception of *God speaking to the world via the church* to one of *God speaking to the church through what he was doing in the world*. Within such a conception, the *missio Dei* was framed in terms of the totality of spiritual and secular movements which the church was charged to discern, support, and facilitate.[31] Climactically, with the call from ecumenical leaders in the early 1970s for a "moratorium" on "traditional missions," the attitude of many evangelical leaders hardened. They charged that ecumenical missiology promoted a "secularized gospel," that it advanced a form of syncretism which conflated the spiritual and secular, and finally, that it betrayed the urgent needs of the world's two billion people who had not yet heard of Christ.[32] While a round of dialogue was attempted after Uppsala (1968), the settled direction of the WCC was maintained. This served to freshly polarize the ecumenical and evangelical divide, and renewed suspicions in the minds of evangelicals of any advocacy in relation to social concern.[33]

The Rise of the Lausanne Movement

It is in light of such contrasting missiological trajectories that the 1974 Lausanne Congress and its immediate antecedents and successors must be viewed. After the 1966 Berlin Congress, in November 1971, Graham and the BGEA convened a small international group of advisors to consider if a sequel to the Berlin Congress might be desirable. In light of the radical turn taken by ecumenism in the wake of the Uppsala Assembly, conservative evangelicals felt that a restatement of a more orthodox yet properly comprehensive view of Christian mission was pressing.[34] Indeed, believing that "radical theology" had created a "vacuum in the world church,"[35] a consensus of opinion emerged among this advisory group that a congress examining the theme of "the whole gospel, for the whole world by the whole

31. Bosch, *Transforming Mission*, 326–27.
32. McGavran, "Will Uppsala Betray?"; Glasser, "Salvation Today," 33.
33. Stott, "Biblical Basis," 65; Chester, *Awakening*, 28.
34. John Stott to Jack Dain, June 15, 1973. LCWE, BGCA 46, Box 35/35; Hunt, "Lausanne Movement," 82.
35. Meeting of the Consultative Conference, LCWE, Florida, March 23–24, 1972. BGCA, CN 46, Box 30/27.

church" would be desirable.[36] In time, the precise meaning of such a phrase would become *the* defining issue of the congress. However, at this early stage, in light of the growth of Christianity in the developing world, the advisory group considered it imperative that "representatives of the younger churches" be invited to share on the congress planning committee from the outset.[37] Additionally, it was believed that if the congress was to attract broad international support then it should enlist the cooperation of a wide cross section of world evangelical leaders by inviting them to serve as congress convenors. Consequently, thirty-one members of the planning committee (including eleven from the Global South) joined with 150 "convenors" (selected from eight strategic regions) to garner support for what they hoped would become a defining moment in the history of Christian mission.[38] Undoubtedly, the congress did prove to be such a moment. However, in a postcolonial world as evangelicals from the Global South became increasingly willing to criticize their brethren from Evangelicalism's heartlands in the West, the congress also served to illuminate the rising complexity of the evangelical landscape. Indeed, no longer content simply to be the recipients of the overtures of their Western counterparts, a chorus of voices on the congress planning committee (notably the leading Latin Americans) proved to be the most controversial voices of all.[39]

Signs of the explosivity that was to follow at Lausanne began to surface during the congress's preparatory stages and became more apparent in a series of plenary addresses that were judged to be considerably at odds with each other. Prior to the congress, the planning committee decided that if Lausanne was to be a properly prepared study conference with meaningful outcomes, then a series of plenary papers would be circulated before the conference. They suggested that the gathering should also produce a unified "covenant," a comprehensive restatement of evangelical beliefs.[40] Accordingly, as the congress began, the opening charge of Billy Graham aroused cheers from the faithful for a staunchly "prioritist" position on evangelism.[41]

---

36. Minutes, "World Evangelisation Strategy Consultation," December 2, 1971, BGCA 46, Box 1/1.

37. Dain to Troutman, February 17, 1972, BGCA CN 46, Box 30/1.

38. "Regional Summary Reports," in Douglas, *Let the Earth Hear*, 1318–37; Stanley, "Lausanne 1974," 540.

39. Stanley, "Lausanne 1974," 536–37, 540–42.

40. Capon, "Lausanne 74," 23–33, 25.

41. David Hesselgrave identifies the positions taken by evangelicals in regard to social concern on a spectrum: "Revisionist holism" emphasizes ministry to society *and* individuals and rejects as unbiblical any dichotomies between the physical and spiritual. "Restrained holism" emphasizes the necessity of social responsibility while

Addressing the most diverse gathering of evangelicals ever assembled to "pray and plan for world evangelization," Graham spoke of a modern missionary movement that had lost its way. The corrosive effects of liberal ecumenism, he charged, had diverted many from the "conversion of souls" towards "the materialistic salvation of the *community*." Thus, as the world plunged foreseeably to the brink of "Armageddon," Graham expressed his desire to recapture the prioritist fervor of a previous day.[42] As chair of the covenant drafting committee, the contribution of John Stott was also highly anticipated. Stott's address was the "usual helping of patient, lucid exposition" as he unpacked a series of definitions on mission, evangelism, salvation, and conversion to tease out a biblical basis for contemporary mission.[43] Stott had notably shifted since Berlin (1966) from a more "prioritist" position to one that argued for a sturdier link between Christ's "Great Commission" to missionary witness (Matt 28:19–20) and his "Great Commandment" to neighborly love (Luke 10:37). Indeed, in the years immediately preceding Lausanne, Stott had become acutely conscious that ecumenical-evangelical relations had hardened significantly. Stott himself had begun to resonate closely with the non-Western critique of Western Christianity.[44] Indeed, coming to see himself as something of a broker between evangelicals and the ecumenical movement, at the WCC meetings in Uppsala (1968) and Nairobi (1975) Stott would urge upon ecumenical leaders a greater attention to Christ's commission to preach the gospel. Conversely, at Lausanne (1974) he highlighted the elements of truth in the ecumenical critique of Evangelicalism and sought a note of "repentance" from evangelicals, coupled with a compassionate and intellectual reengagement with the world.[45]

Stott's critique, delivered early in the congress proceedings, was enthusiastically received by many Western and non-Western leaders, especially those with connections to the WCC.[46] However, as the congress progressed,

---

upholding the priority of evangelism. "Traditional prioritism" gives strict priority to evangelism and holds social action to be a secondary task of the church. Hesselgrave (like other conservatives) favors prioritism, while not mitigating the possibility of restrained holism. See Hesselgrave, *Paradigms in Conflict*, 118–38.

42. Graham spoke of the nineteenth century as the great era of missionary expansion, energized by their commitment to the "authority of Scripture." The New York (1900) and Edinburgh (1910) conferences stood in such a tradition, he alleged. It was thus Graham's hope that Lausanne would take evangelicals "back to the vision" of that era. Graham, "Why Lausanne?," 25.

43. Capon, "Lausanne 74," 25; Stott, "Biblical Basis," 65–78.

44. Stott, "Biblical Basis," 67, 65; Chapman, *Godly Ambition*, 122.

45. Stott, "Biblical Basis," 65–66, 78; On the progression in Stott's social conviction, see Chapman, *Godly Ambition*, 118–19.

46. Michael Green (Principal of St. John's College, Nottingham) also argued the

it also became apparent that Stott's entreaty was merely a harbinger of a wave of further criticism that would follow from a group of outspoken leaders of the Global South. Indeed, the stinging diatribe of Dr. René Padilla on the topic of "Evangelism and the World" soon "set the congress alight" and was adjudged as "a collective broadside" against a "truncated" form of Christianity with which he had "little sympathy."[47] In his address, Padilla (the associate General Secretary of IFES for Latin America and a member of the covenant drafting committee) insisted that the gospel had cosmic as well as personal dimensions. He took aim at what he considered to be Americanized forms of "culture Christianity." These, he alleged, had reduced the gospel to a form of cheap grace, a marketed product designed to guarantee the "consumer" the eschatological equivalent of the Western values of "happiness" and "success." Padilla also criticized the strategists of the Church Growth Movement (led by Fuller Theological Seminary's Donald McGavran and Ralph Winter) for treating the task of mission as merely a formulaic equation. Dividing the world into geographical and cultural enclaves, such strategists, Padilla alleged, believed that they could "produce the greatest number of Christians at the least possible cost." For Padilla, the path to enhanced effectiveness lay not in "research-driven action" but in lasting evangelical "repentance."[48] Similarly, the address of Samuel Escobar (the Peruvian-born director of IVF Canada and member of the covenant

---

case for greater evangelical social responsibility. Such contributions were all the more significant, given their provenance not from the lips of Majority World "rebels" but from recognizably centrist figures in the Western evangelical tradition. Green, "Methods and Strategy," 159–80; Capon, "Lausanne 74," 25; Chapman, *Godly Ambition*, 140.

47. Capon, "Lausanne 74," 23–33.

48. Padilla, "Evangelism and the World," 116–33; cf. McGavran, "Dimensions," 94–107, 108–15; Winter, "Highest Priority," 213–58. Latin American Evangelicalism had encountered the influence of Marxist ideology to a greater extent than any other continent. Accordingly, emerging Latin American leaders such as Padilla placed a high priority on a thoughtful response to the Marxist analysis of structural injustice in society. They were also sensitive to the perceived dangers of an American style "militant conservatism" that advocated "prefabricated patterns of action and witness," and in dividing the world along Cold War fault lines, was blinding them to the positive processes of social transformation taking place in non-Western contexts. Latin evangelicals viewed such conservatism to be sub-biblical and neo-imperialist. Instead, they promoted an emphasis that was penetrating in its social criticism and concern. Fuelling the force of the Latin American critique was also the fact that the influence of the American missionary presence on the global landscape had become overwhelming. Consequently, with the growth of Christianity in the Majority World and the clash of religious, cultural, and political ideologies that this generated with Western leaders, such dynamics introduced a primary source of instability to the congress. Walls, "American Dimension," 1–28. On the contours of the "Liberation Theology" that lay behind the Latin American critique, see Rowland, "Liberation Theology," 551–62.

drafting committee) also proved challenging to northern ears. Drawing on the "Nazareth Manifesto" (Luke 4:18–19), Escobar insisted that it could *not* be spiritualized in a world where millions were brokenhearted, blind, and bruised.[49] Following this, Orlanda Costas (a missiologist at the Latin American Biblical Seminary) rendered the message of Padilla and Escobar still more explicit by arguing that the Great Commission had an inescapably structural dimension. Indeed, he charged, to evangelize "in-depth" meant bringing the gospel to bear not merely on individuals but upon the socioeconomic structures of the present age.[50] Consequently, speaking within a context of rising anti-American sentiment and displaying an indebtedness to left-wing political and theological discourse, the diatribes of the Latin Americans called not just for new methods but for a theology of gospel and society that emphasized questions of justice in the here and now, as well as the promise of justice in the eschatological future. This was the only remedy for the illness of American pragmatism that was, in their view, infecting world Evangelicalism.[51]

The Challenge of "Radical Discipleship"

Within a congress of such size and representative breadth, the disagreements were seen as both a mark of its maturity and as a distraction.[52] Jack Dain, the Sydney bishop and congress executive chairman, noted that while the level of disagreement had left some "shaken," he was also heartened that significant "agreement" remained on the essentials and that the congress had been "sufficiently mature" to "agree to disagree."[53] Similarly, others saw the congress policy of "comprehension" as key to its development of a more "representative" final covenant. As such, they believed it represented a "major breakthrough for evangelicals on questions of social ethics" such that "obscurantism will never be respectable

---

49. Indeed, Escobar explicitly linked the injustices of the contemporary world with political and financial corruption and the failure of Western Christians to be engaged in social realignments for change. Accordingly, he charged, while the church continued to wait for Christ's eschatological kingdom, it *must* do more than merely "proclaim." Rather, it must "demonstrate" a new way of dealing with "power, inequality, and privilege" as "evidence" it expected the promise of a "new creation" to appear. Escobar, "Man's Search,"303–26.

50. Costas, "Depth in Evangelism," 682; Carl Henry, *Christianity Today*, September 13, 1974, 66.

51. Chapman, "International Relations," 359–60; Escobar, "Man's Search," 304.

52. Chapman, "International Relations," 361–62.

53. "Evangelicals Learn." BGCA, CN 46, Box 1/16.

again."[54] Others, like the conservative American figures of Billy Graham, Donald McGavran, and Harold Lindsell, celebrated the opportunity for dialogue the congress afforded. Yet they came to see its focus on social issues as ultimately a distraction to the pressing task of world evangelization—which they would later redouble their efforts to pursue.[55] Finally, however, as the congress careered towards its conclusion in the signing of the Lausanne Covenant, it was the outspoken voices in the Australian delegation (represented by the Reverends John Chapman, Paul Barnett, and D. B. Knox) who voiced the most strident defense of a "prioritist" position. This was against the claims of the self-styled "Theology and Radical Discipleship" group whose fringe meeting of eight hundred participants provided a tense conclusion to congress proceedings.[56]

The Lausanne Covenant itself had originated in a fifteen-paragraph statement, drafted on the basis of the precirculated papers in March 1974. It was revised twice, before the third draft (now known as the Covenant) was circulated to delegates in the closing days of the congress. Several hundred revisions were submitted during this process, of which the largest contributors—the "Theology and Radical Discipleship Group"—felt that even in its revised form the Covenant did not express their concerns strongly enough. They therefore invited others to join them in pressing for the inclusion of a more radical statement regarding Christian social concern.[57] Among the leaders of this unofficial group were the Latin American evangelical leaders (Padilla and Escobar), Jim Punton of Britain's Frontier Youth Trust, David Claydon of Scripture Union in Australia, Dr. Athol Gill (the leading theologian of the "Australian Jesus Movement"), and other Americans like the Menonnite John Howard Yoder.[58] Before the

54. Kaye, "Freedom and Maturity." BGCA, CN 46, Box 1/16.

55. "Billy Graham Challenges," 3; McGavran, *Understanding Church Growth*, 257–58; *Christianity Today*, August 30, 1974, 27.

56. Stanley, "Lausanne 1974," 545.

57. Capon, "Lausanne 74," 26; Stanley, "Lausanne 1974," 545.

58. Stanley, "Lausanne 1974," 546. The Australian members of this fringe delegation comprised the youthful leaders of the "Australian Jesus Movement" (John Hirt and Peter Campbell from the "House of the New World," John Smith from the "God's Squad" Motorcycle Club, and Baptist scholar Dr. Athol Gill). Invited to the congress as "observers," the group met *ad hoc* under the Palais clock tower after each plenary paper and seminar for discussion. The group brandished information to delegates on their countercultural initiatives in Australia and began to "agitate." Finding ready allies among the Latin Americans, the group petitioned Jack Dain for permission to hold a special meeting to showcase more about "theology and radical discipleship." "After the Congress with Jack Dain," Interview with B. Kaye, BGCA 46, Box 32/2; Chilton, "Christian Australia," 320–28.

final version of the Covenant appeared, the group widely circulated an alternative statement of its own, entitled "A Response to Lausanne." This statement affirmed the cosmic scope of redemption and repudiated any attempt to "drive a wedge between evangelism and social action" as being patently "demonic."[59] Consequently, on the Sunday evening of day six of the congress, in a session incorporating vigorous contributions from both the platform and the floor, a crowd of eight hundred listened for several hours to impassioned pleas for greater penitence for past evangelical failures and a stronger commitment to social concern.[60]

Nevertheless, convinced of the priority of evangelism in the church's mission and not unaware of the prospect of disagreement at Lausanne, the contribution of the conservative Australians (in the later words of John Stott) was akin to an "evangelical watchdog" barking "loud and long."[61] Indeed, speaking in June 1974 in an interview prior to the congress, John Chapman affirmed his hope that the congress would rekindle a widespread desire to evangelize amongst the global evangelical constituency. Yet, having reflected on the congress papers, he had become more circumspect in light of their clear accent upon social concern. "It's easy for us to band together to gather milk for India, and we do it very successfully," he charged lightheartedly, "but it's very hard to band together to evangelize, because it brings out the very essence of the Gospel."[62] Similarly, Chapman observed that the gospel undoubtedly brought moral and social transformation and that first-century evangelism had occurred in the context of widespread permissiveness and social dislocation in urban centers like Athens, Ephesus, and Rome. Such realities marked out the early Christians as being radically distinct from their own communities, a fact that was just as crucial in first-century witness as in the contemporary world. Nevertheless, he added, the "remediation" of these social conditions at any "systemic level" did not seem "to be the major concern of the Pauline epistles."[63] The Rev. Paul Barnett (now Rector of a large Anglican Church in Adelaide and a key protagonist in the unscheduled meeting) also resonated with a "prioritist" position as he considered the Lausanne documents. Barnett noted the pressing needs of four-fifths of the world's population who had no opportunity to know Christ unless the church mobilized itself for evangelism as its highest

59. "A Response to Lausanne," 2, BGCA, CN 46, Box 32/2.

60. Capon, "Lausanne 74," 29.

61. This is a phrase Stott used to describe conservative responses to any signs "of a diminished commitment to evangelism," responses for which he remained "grateful." Stott, *Contemporary Christian*, 352.

62. "Chat with Chapman," 8-9.

63. "Chat with Chapman," 8-9.

priority. Indeed, referencing the contributions of many of the conservative North American leaders approvingly as he surveyed the Lausanne documents, Barnett exhorted the church to be vehicles of God's salvific plan for the nations and emphasized the pursuit of cross-centric and cross-cultural evangelism as the means through which to do this.[64] D. B. Knox likewise voiced a degree of apprehension about the pre-congress papers. Speaking ahead of the congress, Knox stated that a conference the size of Lausanne represented a "significant event in the Christian world." If it was to be fruitful, it was crucially "important that it should be based on a clear and accurate Biblical-theological foundation."[65] Indeed, advancing a strongly "prioritist" position, Knox suggested that there were "three points that must be absolutely Biblical" if Christian missionary activity was to be fruitful. The first was the "message," the second was the church's apprehension of its eschatological "context," and the third was its missionary "objective." Emphasizing the gospel to be a *message* of reconciliation with God ahead of God's eschatological judgment, Knox stressed that the preaching of this gospel took place in a present eschatological *context* under the authority of Christ, the exalted Son of Man (Matt 26:64, cf. Dan 7:13,14). Therefore, he charged, the preaching of this gospel "will not lack power so long as it is a true word from Him. It will cast down strongholds and turn the world up-side-down . . . We ourselves are weak, but the power of Christ through the Word of God is irresistible." Consequently, regarding the *objective* of Christian mission, recalling Christ's commission on which the authority of all missionary activity rested and the love of Christ that compelled the Christian (2 Cor 5:14–15), Knox stridently asserted that:

> God will accomplish his purposes . . . He has His people throughout the world and we are sent by the call and commission of Christ to bring them the gospel that they may call upon His name and be saved . . . Thus, in our ministry of evangelism there should be confidence, devotion, assiduity, and endurance, for we are God's messengers, sent to call His elect from the four winds, to gather them together to Christ. But not a note of this is evident in the Lausanne documents.[66]

---

64. See Barnett and Court, *Message of Lausanne*, 4–5. BGCA, CN 46, Box 32/2. This publication contains four sermons preached at Holy Trinity Adelaide in 1974 in which Barnett and Court distill a set of congregational priorities from the Lausanne material. While the sermon series was given retrospectively (August 1974), there is little doubt it also reflected Barnett's pre-congress missiological judgments, as will be seen below.

65. D. B. Knox, "World Mission," unpublished, June 1974, 1. BGCA, CN 46, Box 32/2.

66. D. B. Knox, "World Mission," 5; cf. Knox, "Message of the Gospel," 25–46.

Such were the convictions informing the responses of the conservative Australian leaders as the Sunday evening meeting began to unfold. The objective of the unprogrammed session (in the words of its chairman) was "to get down to some tin-tacks on the question of radical discipleship" and to address the question of "coming to grips with the social structures of our society and how we as Christians should relate to them."[67] On the night before delegates were asked to endorse the contents of the Lausanne Covenant, it was considered imperative they be given an opportunity to wrestle with Scripture and to remove any vestiges of "prejudice" that might preclude them from embracing a biblically rigorous social vision. Athol Gill opened the meeting with an exposition of the group's biblical convictions and spoke of mission in highly incarnational terms.[68] After this, René Padilla echoed the appeals of his earlier paper concerning the ethical, racial, and political dimensions of the gospel. He contended that Christian discipleship *must* go beyond "right doctrine, good concepts and orthodox-creeds." Indeed, Padilla insisted, the demand for a new ethical orientation was an "essential" component of the gospel message. Consequently, authentic Christian mission required the church to proclaim and to embody "the arrival of God's new order" which Christ came to convey.[69] Following this, Samuel Escobar

67. International Congress on World Evangelisation (ICOWE), "Unprogrammed Session on Radical Discipleship," July 21, 1974. BGCA, CN 53, Series II, Subseries D, Tapes 180–84. The session was chaired by the Australian David Claydon.

68. Gill identified Mark 10:38 ("Can you drink the cup I drink?") as the hinge on which the disciple should expect to identify with Christ in his ministry (including his message, deeds, and subsequent rejection). Having been called into Christ's "new community," Gill suggested, the disciple was then "sent out to preach the gospel of the Kingdom and continue Christ's ministry." This, Gill posited, involved "doing the sort of things Christ did . . . associating with tax collectors, sinners, the underprivileged." Further, the message they were to preach was that "it is not because of race or colour [but] simply because the grace of God has come to us that we belong to a new community . . . And the gospel we are to preach [is good news] to the poor, deliverance to the captives, sight to the blind, in words and action, even as [Christ] did." Such a foundation, he suggested, was the "starting point not only for evangelism, but for social and political action." ICOWE, "Discipleship."

69. Padilla charged that a key failing of the Western church was that it had "intellectualised the gospel." Rather, Christ's lordship and ethical teaching demanded a "total commitment to Christ in practical life . . . God wants us to be an expression of our doctrine, an incarnation of the gospel." Padilla took aim at the view which prioritized "the preaching of the gospel" over the demand for ethical transformation. Instead, Padilla countered, to "proclaim the gospel" was to proclaim the "arrival of God's new order." It was to proclaim a message intended to "deliver man *from* the evil world, in order to release man *into* the world as a new man in Christ . . . Christ came not just to save my soul, but to form a new society." Padilla cited the example of his own Latin American context that was moving toward "totalitarianism." He suggested that for the evangelistic witness of the Latin American church to be effective it required the "manifestation of

also suggested (somewhat surprisingly) that Protestant missions since the Reformation era had never truly "touched the structures of society" but had bequeathed a largely syncretistic legacy of "pagan and Christian elements." Thus, he urged, if the church was to be faithful to its mission mandate, then wherever it advanced it *must* be willing to "challenge society at every level" and to authentically "incarnate the gospel's demands."[70]

It was, therefore, in response to such forceful assertions that the conservative Australian figures (notably Chapman and Barnett) rose expeditiously to their feet to take the floor. They appreciated the exhortation to ethical living; nevertheless, having heard in the presentations of the Latin American leaders what appeared to be a dilution of the biblical gospel, they felt compelled to seek clarity publicly. "How much of the Christian ethic does a man have to know before he can respond to the gospel?" Chapman argued incredulously in response to their entreaties for a strongly "incarnated" Christian witness. "I remain concerned," he charged, "if I have heard you correctly as saying that ethics are an essential part of the apostolic gospel."[71] Similarly, Barnett rose promptly to suggest that what was occurring was the conflation of the church's *ethical response* to the biblical gospel with the *gospel itself*. Rather, he countered, the "apostolic evangel" consisted in:

> Propositions about God the Creator, Christ, and the end, and the need . . . for a man to re-orientate his entire life with respect to those propositions . . . I believe there is a [continual] distinction made in the New Testament between the apostolic evangel and Christian ethics. Paul says, "We preach not ourselves but Christ as Lord." And I don't believe that we are to preach ourselves or to preach *the church* as the gospel, but *only Christ*. Consequently,

---

a kingdom here and now." It required the church to demonstrate it had *authentically become* God's "new man in Christ." Consequently, Padilla urged his congress auditors towards "a serious commitment to *be the church* in the fullness of that word." ICOWE, "Discipleship."

70. Such a critique was in keeping with the Latin American analysis of Western missionary practices which it viewed as both "imperialistic" and "captive" to Western culture. The panacea, Escobar suggested, lay in the ministry of Christ who both proclaimed *and* incarnated the kingdom. If the church could not do this, he charged, it would continue to produce "pagans or semi-Christians . . . instead of really evangelizing." The American theologian and ethicist John H. Yoder also presented on the session platform. He cited material from his 1972 work *The Politics of Jesus* to sketch a more political vision of "radical discipleship." However, it was the presentations of the Latin Americans that was of greatest concern to conservative ears. ICOWE, "Discipleship"; see Pierard, "*Pax Americana*," 155–79; cf. "Books of the Century" on the significance of Yoder's 1972 work.

71. ICOWE, "Discipleship."

I believe that Dr. Padilla's emphasis [may represent] a polarization from "cheap grace" toward "no grace."[72]

As the evening session continued, Chapman again took to the floor to suggest that the panel's criticizing of delegates in pursuing patterns of discipleship that were radically flawed was unnecessarily pejorative and inaccurate. Congress delegates, Chapman suggested, *did* share a deep and holistic love for Christ, their communities, and countrymen. Moreover, quoting John 18:36 ("My kingdom is *not* of this world"), Chapman urged the panel to give more careful consideration to the New Testament's reluctance to prescribe systemic solutions to questions of societal reform. Instead, he averred, the radically eschatological and spiritual nature of Christ's kingdom (as a realized, yet ultimately future reality) ought to caution Christian movements from pursuing a primarily this-worldly agenda and brandishing their activism as a means to disparage the dedication of others.[73] In response, Os Guinness, the English evangelist and social critic offered a stinging counter-assertion from the floor. He suggested that the Australians (and other conservatives) were merely "theorizing," were holding "their bibles and playing church," and defining "evangelization" in a purely "culturally determined" way. This needed to be rather "earthed," he suggested, by hearing what the Spirit of God was saying through the "prophetic voices" of the Latin Americans. In reply, Barnett retorted that the Australian entreaties were not at all merely culturally "conditioned." Rather, they had been posed out of a strong concern that a satisfactorily "biblical hermeneutic" was not being applied to issues of crucial importance.[74] Indeed, there was a substantive dissonance, Barnett suggested, in what was being presented as the essence of the gospel. Moreover, he advised, progress would not be achieved, until, using sound theological and hermeneutical principles, study and dialogue, a degree of unanimity could be reached on the gospel's essential biblical character.[75]

The fissiparous nature of this unscheduled meeting on "radical discipleship," rather than unifying the congress, appeared to seriously polarize it. It served to illuminate just how wide a chasm had opened across the global evangelical constituency on this seminal issue. Following the initial barbs of the Australians, supporting commentary was supplied from the

---

72. An audible sense of shock permeated the audience following Barnett's charge to Padilla, which carried an inference that Padilla was stretching the bounds of orthodoxy. ICOWE, "Discipleship."

73. Meeting participants, Alan Nichols and David Claydon, recall Chapman as being the chief advocate for a conservative position. Interview with A. Nichols, January 16, 2013, cited in Chilton, "Christian Australia," 326; ICOWE, "Discipleship."

74. ICOWE, "Discipleship."

75. ICOWE, "Discipleship."

floor in a manner consistent with the emerging polarities. Progressive voices continued to argue that we "do away with this pseudo doctrine of souls and talk about wholeness and humanness," to the sound of enthusiastic applause. Conservatives, however, continued to decry this "most dangerous of tendencies . . . in terms of redeeming society, as opposed to redeeming man."[76] As chairman of the drafting committee, John Stott held a series of cordial meetings with the group's leaders. Although Stott privately regretted the undermining of evangelical unity their unilateral actions represented, he nevertheless borrowed some key phrases from their "Response" to the draft covenant to include in the final version.[77] Moreover, on account of the strength of the conservative response, Stott also took some of the wind out of the radicals' sails by preemptively announcing that he would happily sign their "Response" in addition to the covenant itself. This had the effect of framing their more radical submission merely as an addendum, and not as a rival to the Lausanne Covenant.[78]

Following two long nights of editorial work, Stott skillfully amended the covenant's text in ways that were calculated to bridge the gap between the emerging radical and conservative voices. The section on Christian social responsibility was promoted from paragraph seven to paragraph five and was significantly strengthened in phrasing.[79] On day nine of the congress, Stott presented the final text of the Lausanne Covenant to all participants. This was not for official "adoption," but with the invitation that those who wished should sign it. Two thirds of the delegates did so.

Undoubtedly, Stott's performance in this presentation established him as one of the leading statesmen of world Evangelicalism at the time. More than any other, Stott had taken the concerns of evangelicals from the Majority World and interpreted them sympathetically to conservatives who remained uneasy that the emerging radicalism was simply a reembodiment of the older social gospel. This, they believed, had led inexorably to the bankruptcy of the WCC.[80] Positively, conservatives like Billy Graham declared that the congress had succeeded in framing a mandate for world evangelization that held evangelism to be preeminent in the mission of the church.[81]

76. ICOWE "Discipleship."

77. Capon, "Lausanne 74," 29; Dudley-Smith, *Global Ministry*, 213–14; Chilton, "Christian Australia," 327.

78. Stanley, "Lausanne 1974," 546; Capon, "Lausanne 74," 29.

79. Compare the third draft, issued to congress participants during the congress itself (in BGCA, CN 46, Box 27/4), with the "Lausanne Covenant" in its final form in Douglas, *Let the Earth Hear*, 3–9; Stanley, "Lausanne 1974," 547.

80. Stanley, "Lausanne 1974," 547; Capon, "Lausanne 74," 29.

81. Bruce Kaye, "Lausanne Congress Ends with a Bang and a Covenant,"

Similarly, by signing the Covenant, thousands of delegates had also affirmed (via the heavily contested Clause 5) that while "reconciliation with man is not reconciliation with God, nor is social action evangelism, nor is political liberation salvation, nevertheless we affirm that evangelism and sociopolitical involvement are both part of our Christian duty."[82] Even so, many in the departure hall of the Lausanne airport still sensed that global Evangelicalism remained not only "dappled," but heavily "divided" in its understanding of how such a mission should be pursued. Indeed, the subsequent history of the movement would only make such divisions clearer, as it negotiated a winding path between divergent interpretations of what the "true" message of the congress was. The Lausanne Covenant remained a contested text, yielding a diversity of interpretations. And reconciling the diversity of its global constituency became an unenviable and difficult task.[83]

Post-Lausanne Developments

After the congress, Graham and the BGEA oversaw the establishment of the Lausanne Committee on World Evangelization (LCWE).[84] Its objective was to continue the work begun in Switzerland by disseminating information on global mission and arranging further gatherings. The "theological work group" of the LCWE chaired by Stott sponsored four comparatively small consultations between 1977 and 1982. These consultations dealt with topics arising from the congress and produced reports that were published as Lausanne Occasional Papers. The fourth of these was the 1982 Grand Rapids Consultation on the Relationship Between Evangelism and Social Responsibility.[85] While the issues it surveyed were undeniably complex,[86] the consultation ultimately agreed on and promoted a threefold relationship between evangelism and social responsibility. First, Christian social activity was articulated as a *consequence* of evangelism, since it was the evangelized who engaged in it and one of the aims of a changed life was to serve others.

---

unpublished, BGCA, CN 46, Box 32/2; see Lausanne Covenant: Clause 6, "The Church and Evangelism," in Douglas, *Let the Earth Hear*, 4.

82. See Lausanne Covenant: Clause 5, "Christian Social Responsibility," in Douglas, *Let the Earth Hear*, 3–4.

83. Chapman, "International Relations," 357; Stanley, *Global Diffusion*, 177.

84. Note the discussion of the BGEA and its expanding network of global missiological influence in chapter 5.

85. Stott, "Twenty Years," 50–55.

86. Eight major papers were circulated prior to the 1982 Consultation which explored the question kaleidoscopically from the perspectives of church history, historical theology, sociology, and biblical studies. BGCA, CN 46, Box 3/10.

Second, it was a *bridge* to evangelism, since it expressed God's love and so overcame prejudice and opened closed doors. Third, it was a *partner* to evangelism, such that while evangelism remained primary ("like the two blades of a pair of scissors or the two wings of a bird") the church was to witness to Christ in both word and deed.[87] In 1989, the second Lausanne Congress convened 3,600 leaders from 170 countries in Manila. Fifty percent larger than the 1974 congress and drawing half of its delegates from the Global South, the congress also marked the first significant involvement of evangelicals associated with the charismatic movement. Moreover, reflecting the influence of the Church Growth Movement and seeing the reemergence of "strategic thought" as a tool for evangelization, the congress was dominated by "strategic" definitions of "unreached people groups" living in the "10/40 window" and by the goal of evangelizing the entire world by the year 2000.[88] On the question of Christian social responsibility, prior to the congress Majority World leaders like René Padilla had expressed a degree of concern that a "holistic" paradigm had not been sufficiently embraced by evangelicals following 1974. Consequently, alongside other leading progressive figures, Padilla advocated strongly across a variety of forums (largely connected to the WCC) for the renewed embrace of missiological "holism." His advocacy shaped the ideals of a new wave of Majority World leaders who came to prominence at Manila.[89] The result was that the Manila Manifesto strongly reaffirmed the "primacy" of evangelism. However, echoing the divisions of 1974 it also reaffirmed that the proclamation of the gospel *demanded* "the prophetic denunciation of all that is incompatible with it" and that all "true mission" was unalterably "incarnational."[90] Such developments were viewed with fresh alarm by leading conservatives. They charged that a new wave of radicalism was again seeking to turn "social action into evangelism" and perceived in the Manila statement the conflation of missiological categories that were, in their mind, distinct.[91]

Despite the presence of such continuing acrimony, following the 1974 Congress the world landscape altered significantly in a way that rendered its concerns, to a certain degree, time bound. From the 1970s, the rhetoric that had characterized an era of anti-American sentiment (catalyzed by the

---

87. See "Evangelism and Social Responsibility: An Evangelical Commitment. Report from CRESR 82," June 1982. BGCA, CN 46, Box 3/13, also published as Lausanne Occasional Paper 21. Lausanne Movement, "Lausanne Occasional Paper."

88. The "10/40 window" is the area of North Africa, the Middle East, and Asia between ten and forty degrees north latitude. Coote, "Lausanne II," 10–17.

89. Coote, "Lausanne II," 12; Padilla, "Politics of the Kingdom," 180–98.

90. "Manila Manifesto," in Hedlund, *Great Debate*, 419–32.

91. Coote, "Lausanne II," 13; Stott, "Twenty Years," 52.

dynamics of the Cold War, Vietnam, and the OPEC crisis) was steadily declining.[92] Added to this was the fact that the unifying figures of Stott and Graham had begun to recede from the Lausanne stage by the later century. Stott was no longer the bestriding figure at Manila that he had been at Lausanne in 1974. Having lost substantial credibility among American and Australian evangelicals for his published, albeit tentative, views on divine judgment and the nature of hell, his addresses, and theologically unifying presence no longer set the Lausanne agenda.[93] Moreover, there are indications that Graham himself had also lost interest in Lausanne. Graham had not resiled from his determination to pursue world evangelization. He had merely resolved that the objective was better served by diverting resources to those who, in his words, were "actually doing the work"; and he began increasingly referring to Lausanne as "something of a diversion" from this goal.[94] Additionally, reflecting the majority conservative North American response to the tensions of Lausanne 1974—a strategy of avoidance and even reinterpretation of its outcomes rather than engagement—as early as 1983 Graham sponsored another congress (this time in Amsterdam) which gathered four thousand evangelistic practitioners from 133 countries.[95] Three years later, he brought more than twice that number to a similar gathering that dwarfed any of the Lausanne events.[96]

92. Indeed, the first Lausanne Congress occurred at a time when a heightened degree of American criticism may have opened the platform to the many non-American voices who felt at liberty to reflect the wider sentiment being espoused. From the 1970s, such rhetoric steadily declined. Similarly, the 1980s collapse of many African countries and the crumbling of the Eastern Bloc by 1989 also led many churches in these societies to be more amenable to overseas sources of funding. This rendered the hubris of the "independence generation" to be somewhat "dented." The US culture wars of the 1990s also increasingly isolated the concerns of American evangelicals from those of the rest of the world and rendered as further irrelevant the politics of American evangelism in the international realm. Further, a combination of theological, sociological, and economic analyses of unevangelized humanity would bring an array of fresh concerns to light. These included the tide of environmentalism and a kaleidoscopic variety of ways for evangelicals to parse "missiological" and "social concern." That the world was in need of the gospel was affirmed. Yet, it was also a world of rising complexity, making totemic "statements" on issues of social concern and acerbic geo-political partisan critique appear glib and even naive. See Hunt, "Lausanne Movement," 84; Chapman, "International Relations," 359–60; Shenk, "2004 Forum," 31.

93. See Edwards and Stott, *Evangelical Essentials*, 312–20 for Stott's published views on such questions; Dudley-Smith, *Global Ministry*, 351–55.

94. "Graham Announces," 16; Graham, *Just as I Am*, 574.

95. "From Amsterdam," 3–5. BGCA, CN 253, Box 21/8. Cf. chapter 5. On the conservative reinterpretation of the 1974 congress by leading North Americans, see Harold Lindsell, *Christianity Today*, August 16, 1974; Wagner, "Lausanne," 7–9.

96. "Amsterdam Conference."

There is little doubt that through this period Lausanne continued to be a valuable "instrument of spiritual motivation"—providing a forum for the development of new theological fellowships and missional tools. Yet, unable to reconcile the growing diversity within Lausanne's constituency, and seeking to offer leadership to a movement that lacked a controlling center, Graham's decision was merely reflective of similar decisions made by others in relation to the Lausanne movement. Such leaders came to believe they could fruitfully advance their mission objectives without anxiety about who controlled the center. For there *was* no organizing or theological center—no evangelical Vatican. Rather, consistent with its historic fabric, and retaining a curious mix of theological certitudes *and* religious pluralism, world Evangelicalism continued to be a movement characterized more by individualism and activism than by consensus and reflection. Indeed, Evangelicalism's propensity to elevate the individual conscience in theological judgments had, by this time, become a subtle corrective to the euphoric claims of comprehensivity with which Lausanne had begun.[97]

Post-Lausanne Australian Developments

In the Australian context, the development of Lausanne's contentious legacy on evangelism and social responsibility was no less delicate, providing stimulus *and* enlarging tensions within the progressive and conservative wings of Australian Evangelicalism. The themes of Lausanne were the subject of substantial discussion in the years after the congress as a range of conferences, organizations, and individuals responded to Lausanne's entreaty for a fresh engagement with the nation and world. Within the progressive wing of the movement many continued to laud Lausanne as a tipping point toward a "socially informed missiology" and regarded it favorably as a mandate for the transformation of Australian society and contemporary churches away from "affluence, militarism, and unjust social and economic structures."[98]

---

97. Beyerhaus, "Evangelism and Theology," 8; Chapman, "International Relations," 357; Hesselgrave, *Paradigms in Conflict*, 135–38.

98. See Tizon, *Transformation after Lausanne*, 1–8. Tokens of a progressive social vision are evident in the closing report by the Lausanne "Australian Strategy Group." Following the congress, this group co-opted the help of the Evangelical Alliance to take "immediate action" to explore "the meaning and content of the gospel" in relation to issues of national ethics, youth culture, ethnic minorities, and problems in industry and commerce (see below). "Australian Strategy Group Report," in Douglas, *Let the Earth Hear*, 1340–41. Similarly buoyant that Australian Evangelicalism was "coming of age," Gerald Davis, editor of the Anglican newspaper *Church Scene* also believed that Lausanne had inaugurated a new "generous evangelicalism" more adept at "isolating essentials from peripherals." Davis, "Movement," 12. Athol Gill restated his belief that the

Anxious about the potential for acrimony as the concerns of Lausanne were discussed, the Australian Evangelical Alliance (AEA) promoted a range of forums through which a new consensus might possibly be secured. Less than a month after the congress, the AEA's national council meeting saw Lausanne's "Australian Strategy Group Report" being carefully studied.[99] This was followed up in February 1976 when the alliance gathered fifty-four evangelical leaders for a consultation at Whitley College in Melbourne.[100] Presided over by Sydney Bishop John Reid, the consultation explored topics advised by the Australian Strategy Group. The majority of conference papers largely affirmed Lausanne's "holistic" vision, while differing over the degree of penitent "breast beating" that was felt appropriate for past failures and in the strategies championed to make real-world progress in areas of social concern.[101] In the Sydney diocese, in an effort to ensure Lausanne's "holistic" vision penetrated to the diocese's "grass roots," Bishop A. J. Dain (the congress executive chairman) circulated copies of the Lausanne materials among Sydney parishes and clergy, and to delegates of the 1974 synod.[102] Other leading advocates of Lausanne's social vision (like Bishop Reid and the dean, Lance Shilton) sponsored the publication, in 1981, of a set of

---

congress had opened the eyes of many to the shape of true discipleship and had given rise to an exciting future for the radical cause. Melbourne's Truth and Liberation staff workers (led by John Smith) were the most serious students of the Lausanne material. The *Free Slave* newspaper (from John Hirt's "House of the New World") also published the Australian "radical discipleship" group's "Response to Lausanne," along with John Stott's endorsement of it. Cutler, "Radicals," 12; "Response to Lausanne," 4–5. Bishop Gerald Muston (largely a theological conservative) also cautioned the danger of "separating proclamation from life" and urged the Melbourne Anglican Synod "to be radical in any area where God is leading us into new approaches." G. Muston, "Lausanne and World Trends in Evangelism," *An Address to the Melbourne Anglican Diocesan Synod on 30 Sept 1974*. BGCA, CN 46, Box 32/2; See Chilton, "Christian Australia," 321–25 for further analysis.

99. "Lausanne Call for Action," 3. The "Australian Strategy Group" was an outworking of Lausanne's strategy of "involvement." Strategy groups across eight geographies crystallized plans (derived during the congress) for the evangelization of their geographies. The Australian Evangelical Alliance (AEA) had been formed in June 1972. It was affiliated with the World Evangelical Fellowship (formed in 1951) which looked back over a century to the formation in 1846 of the British Evangelical Alliance. The final "Australian Strategy Group Report" requested that the Australian Evangelical Alliance act as an "initiating group" for further discussion of the lessons learnt at Lausanne. See Chilton, "Christian Australia," 331–33; "Introduction," vii, and "Regional Summary Reports," in Douglas, *Let the Earth Hear*, 1318–61.

100. "Fanning the Fires," 21.

101. Proceedings of the Lausanne Australia Consultation, February 1976. BGCA, CN 46, Box 20/2.

102. Rt. Rev. A. J. Dain to Dr. Leighton Ford, October 1, 1974. BGCA, CN 46, Box 1/20.

studies on the biblical basis for social involvement. In publicly commending this volume, Reid declared the Lausanne vision to be symbolic of a new evangelical consciousness and urged the church body to engage in a range of societal initiatives.[103]

Within the conservative wing of the Australian movement, however, not all were in support of Lausanne's broadening vision. Indeed, joining with other local and international conservatives, leading Sydney figures like Loane and Knox continued to demur from it.[104] Similarly, following the publication of the 1982 Lausanne Occasional Paper on "Evangelism and Social Responsibility," and in light of what he considered to be a continuing confusion within the evangelical constituency on this key question, Chapman himself reflected on the issue in a series of communications. In the months prior, Chapman had spent a considerable amount of time in international engagements. During this period, he had begun to perceive a loss of confidence in Scripture, alongside a decline in missiological urgency and a swathe of distractions to evangelism across the many church networks with which he had interacted. Consequently, wishing to highlight and address these concerns, Chapman wrote in a regular prayer letter distributed to his supporters across the world:

103. See Mears, *Christian and Social Concern*, 2–3, 53–63. See also the preparatory studies for the 1981 *National Evangelical Anglican Congress* published as Wallace and Mears, *Living Gospel*, ch. 2. Bishop Reid served as Chairman of the Lausanne Theology Working Group from 1981 and was Vice-Chairman of the LCWE at Manila in 1989. Interserve, "Remembering John Reid." Lance Shilton (Dean of St. Andrew's Cathedral 1973–88) shared Lausanne's holistic social vision and a sensitivity to Majority World challenges. Shilton, "Aftermath of Lausanne," 5. BGCA, CN 46, Box 32/2.

104. In 1976, as he announced news of the forthcoming Graham Crusade (1979) and urged parish rectors to lend their support, Archbishop Loane acknowledged the vexed nature of contemporary dialogue. Addressing the synod, Loane acknowledged the vigor of the evangelical legacy in social concern, and that, paying "heed to the words of the Lausanne Covenant" we affirm that "evangelism and sociopolitical involvement are both part of our Christian duty." However, Loane was also quick to draw the synod's attention to the primacy of proclamation. Marcus Loane Presidential Address, 1977 *Sydney Diocesan Yearbook*, 221. Similarly, in 1976, in a criticism directed specifically at the radicalism emerging from Lausanne, Knox cautioned against the popularization of the gospel by aligning it with a "radical" agenda. Instead, he suggested, if the gospel was "to be the salt of society" then Christians needed to "avoid the temptation" to "minimize its supernaturalism," to follow "fads" and constantly seek to be "in the swim." One such "modern fad," he continued, was to elevate "a consequence of the gospel, namely social concern" to "*be part* of the gospel itself." Such an approach, he advised, "detract[ed] from the uniqueness of the gospel, which is the news about Jesus Emmanuel, the coming judgement and the salvation that can be found in him." See D. B. Knox, "The Gospel and Society," *The Protestant Faith* radio broadcast, April 4, 1976, repr. In Payne and Beilharz, *D. Broughton Knox Vol. III*, 155–57. Note the conservative position editorialized in the *Victorian Baptist Witness*, February 5, 1975, 2.

> The work of evangelism is always under threat ... Even among those believing the Bible [to be] the Word of God, evangelism [does] not seem to be in its rightful place ... Amongst evangelical Christians there [is] still a great deal of confusion over the relationship between evangelism and social concern for people. In its extreme form it results in people saying they are doing evangelism when they are [merely] meeting people's needs physically, socially and emotionally ... it still represents a problem for us to know the relationship between the idea of "doing good to all men" (Gal 6:10) and that "God commands all men everywhere to repent" (Acts 17:30). Notwithstanding every good work done by the Lausanne Continuation Committee I myself am still convinced that "gospelling" is the more important of these activities. The need to be saved does not take its place on a list of other needs people have. People's need to be reconciled to God is of paramount importance. Social welfare work is, in one sense, easier to do than evangelism. You see the results of your work, the recipients are usually grateful and the world at large approves of the work. Evangelism ... has none of these benefits. My fear is that when we think that evangelism and social welfare work are equally important then in time the easier will take more of our time and money. Assuming this life is all there is, then relieving the lot of our fellow man is the most important. Assuming eternity is true, then evangelism is of the highest importance. This can be seen in the priority of the Lord Jesus, and it must be so with us (see Luke 4:42–44; Luke 5:15–16; Mark 1:32–39). I do not think people's needs are unimportant, but the priority of the way Jesus met the needs of the man in Luke 5:17–26 should be ours as well.[105]

Chapman courted substantial controversy as a result of such remarks, particularly in their inference of a certain faintheartedness or misplaced priority on the part of other evangelicals. Consequently, in subsequent communications he sought to affirm the value of the recent Lausanne material in clarifying the "balance" between these two activities.[106] He also clarified his desire not to diminish the work of Christians engaged directly in roles of societal service. Nevertheless, he advised, he remained uneasy about "making socio-political involvement part of discipleship" or binding the conscience of Christians on matters about which Scripture was not explicit. In substantiating

---

105. DOE Prayer Letter, no. 1, February–April 1983, 2.

106. Chapman commended, in particular, the Lausanne Occasional Paper that had been published as a result of the 1982 Grand Rapids Consultation on Evangelism and Social Responsibility. DOE Prayer Letter, no. 2, May–July 1983.

such comments, Chapman re-emphasized "the lack of New Testament teaching or even a model" upon which to base a template for social action. He also highlighted the ministries of Christ and the apostles who eschewed "human need" and sociopolitical involvement in order to prioritize matters of "godliness and the spread of the gospel" (Matt 22:21; 26:1; Mark 1:32–39; Luke 4:42–44; 5:17–26; Acts 6:2–4).[107] In light of these realities Chapman restated what seemed to be "crystal clear from Scripture," namely: "that evangelism is to have *top priority* in our thinking, doing and giving. People's needs are important and meeting them with love and concern is an obligation on all Christians." Nevertheless, he stated, "there is a need which only the gospel can heal, the need to be forgiven and reconciled to God . . . In Jesus' ministry it had priority. It should be so for us."[108]

Chapman's "prioritism" came to prominence again in August 1983 when he delivered a plenary response to the more progressive presentation of the English apologist, Os Guinness, at the National Evangelical Anglican Conference (NEAC), the third Australia-wide conference of evangelicals held at Sydney's Macquarie University, on "Evangelism and Social Responsibility."[109] After this, continuing his "prioritist" advocacy across an array of theological colleges, student, clerical, and conference settings, Chapman was widely critiqued by clergy of other tempers in subsequent years. Indeed, Chapman later reflected that it became difficult to maintain such a position while not being "misunderstood as someone who is disinterested in the physical or social plight of the underprivileged."[110] Such accusations

107. DOE Prayer Letter, August–October 1983.

108. Chapman was aware of the arguments which suggested: a) that the New Testament's "silence" on issues of sociopolitical action was merely because first-century Christians lacked the resources through which to take action; and b) that people "cannot hear the gospel until their other needs are met." He replied, once again, by highlighting the paucity of Christ's sociopolitical instruction as a significant reason to be cautious in such matters. He also highlighted that the pressing physical needs that were present in first-century Israel did not stop Christ from consistently prioritizing the proclamation of the gospel (Luke 4:42–44; 5:17–26). DOE Prayer Letter, May–July 1983, 2; DOE Prayer Letter, August–October 1983.

109. DOE Prayer Letter, no. 3, August–October 1983, 4.

110. Chapman to Orpwood, February 2, 1995, BDM Box 1. Jensen, *Anglicanism*, 120–21 notes the contentious nature of the "Sydney position" on Christian social concern (defined in significant ways by Chapman's advocacy). Indeed, David Mansfield notes the combative nature of discussions among Australian evangelicals on such matters in the early 1990s. Mansfield notes the strong critique levelled against those "who didn't hold to a view that the gospel, by definition, included social concern" and suggests that Chapman was "singled out for special attention" in such criticism. Mansfield, *Chappo Collection*, 298, 303. Typical of Chapman's more private advocacy was his correspondence with David Claydon (Federal Secretary of CMS Australia) in which he sought to clarify the substance of a CMS article where aid work was promoted

became especially acute for Chapman given his propensity (on account of his formative influences) to "lean toward socialism" in his political convictions, a position that was uncommon among the "majority" of his "Anglican peers." Indeed, raised and still drawn to the proletarian vision of the "fair go" and of "kindness in another's trouble, and courage in your own,"[111] such accusations of indifference became especially difficult to bear.[112]

Notwithstanding the strength of such critique, the paradox of such seemingly belligerent Sydney conservatism was the reality of the diocese's highly developed programs of social concern. Indeed, while leading figures like Chapman and others continued to promote the proclamation of the gospel as the church's foremost priority, there was little evidence in the diocese's theological or sociopolitical discourse of a world-denying pessimism that repudiated the value of a range of this-worldly concerns.[113] On the contrary, during the 1970s to 1990s a variety of diocesan committees made submissions to Australian Federal and State Governments on an array of social and political issues. As a member of the Standing Committee (1975–93) Chapman gave eager assent to such initiatives. The Social Issues Committee of the Standing Committee also sought, over several decades, to develop and promote a wide range of Christian ethical and public social policy. It sought to develop Christian thought on issues like the environment, families, adoption law reform, disability policy, religious freedom, sexuality, labor law reform, climate, poverty, aged policy, abortion, and matters of bioethics.[114] Moreover, the work of the diocese's expanding social welfare agencies like Anglicare, the Anglican Retirement Village network, the Archbishop's Overseas Appeal

---

as "mission." See Appendix 4, JCCPP/LEAD#3, "Is Development a Missionary Task?" *Checkpoint Magazine* (Spring 1997) 6–8. Typical of his public advocacy was his 2002 Sydney synod studies on Mark's Gospel in which he reiterated the themes of his long-standing "prioritism." See Appendix 3, JCCPPB24W29, "A Matter of Priority"; cf. Chester, "Social Involvement (Part I)"; Chester and Payne, "Social Involvement (Part II)"; Raiter, "Social Involvement (Part III)," for the shape of ongoing Sydney dialogue on such matters.

111. McMullin, *Light on the Hill*, 56; Clark, *History of Australia Vol. 6*, 118.

112. Chapman to Orpwood, February 2, 1995, BDM Box 1, SDA.

113. Such an accusation had been levelled at Sydney Anglicans in a study of the diocese from 1885 to 1914 by Bill Lawton. Lawton portrayed a world-denying isolationism in the diocese. By inferring that a similar genealogy of ideas characterized the modern diocese his study suggested that their social vision was equally antiquarian. Lawton, *Better Time*, 89.

114. Judd and Cable, *Sydney Anglicans*, 277; Anglican Diocese of Sydney, "Social Issues Committee." The representations of Marcus Loane on questions of poverty and social equity are also widely held to have influenced the Federal Government's appointment of a Commission of Enquiry resulting in the landmark 1975 Henderson Commission's report on *Poverty in Australia*. Blanch, *Strength to Strength*, 271.

Fund (Anglican Aid) and HammondCare (an independent welfare agency with historic links to the diocese) was also significant. With an operating budget of $361.5 million in 2018, the scale of Sydney's Anglicare, for example, may be appreciated by noting that in 2018 the high-profile Salvation Army's national budget was $445 million. When aggregated, such combined relief and aid agencies thus mark the diocese's social relief program as one of the most significant non-government care and development programs across the Sydney region, if not the nation.[115]

Such a tangibly applied program of social concern thus demonstrates that the position of leading Sydney figures like Chapman constituted an authentically "prioritist" conviction.[116] Indeed, for Chapman the ultimate resolution to the tension between the responsibilities of evangelism and social concern was an eschatological one. In this vein, Chapman did not develop a comprehensive political or social theology among his published works. His purpose was rather the mobilization of Christians to evangelistic activism. However, he did give extensive insight into the eschatological framework that informed his position. In so doing, he was persuaded that an "inaugurated" eschatological framework provided the strongest synthesis of the biblical material. Such a position contended that the Christian lives in an epoch in which Christ's life, death, and resurrection *both* affirms the worth of human life and culture while pointing inexorably to a coming age that transcends it. Indeed, such a conviction contended that while aspects of the coming age *may be glimpsed* in the present creation, nevertheless the resurrection of the body and the complete redemption of the created order *all await* the final consummation of God's purposes. Hence, while resisting a pervasive pessimism toward the created order, such a view nevertheless held that the balance of the church's contemporary energies should be directed

---

115. Such agencies are funded in part, via donations from individual, parish, and diocesan means. However, during the Menzies administration the philanthropic work of the Australian churches began to receive additional state aid. This transformed them from being providers of volunteers into major employers with national budgets. In 2018, for example, Sydney's "Anglicare" (a merger of the diocese's former aged care and social relief arms) had income of $361.5 million and assets valued at $1803.1 million. See Anglicare, "2018 Annual Review," 36–39. In 2017, the Archbishop of Sydney's Anglican Aid also administered $4.7 million from individual donations (accepting no government funding) in the provision of Christian aid to vulnerable communities throughout the world. Anglican Aid, "Annual Report 2016–17." On HammondCare, see Hilliard, "Pluralism," 148. On the Salvation Army, see Salvation Army, "2018 Annual Report"; Horsburgh, "Government and Social Welfare," 41–46. For insightful recent analysis of the development of Sydney diocese's socially oriented programs, see Frith, "Role of the Laity," 103–12.

116. See the definitions of missiological "prioritism" and "holism" in Hesselgrave, *Paradigms in Conflict*, 118–38.

toward the proclamation of God's coming eschatological reign and to the work of Christ as the means of participating in it.[117]

Such was Chapman's considered view. Chapman acknowledged the beauty *and* brokenness of the present creation and believed Christians did less than justice to Scripture if they ignored either of these realities. Such an eschatological conviction, he suggested, ought to inspire the enjoyment of the present world (1 Tim 6:17), a concern for the upholding of civil society (1 Tim 2:1–8), and a commitment (where possible) of "doing good to all people" (Gal 6:10) via the remediation of poverty and worldly oppression.[118] Yet, Chapman was also highly conscious of the challenges of evangelism in a secularizing age and of the ease with which society's transcendent needs (in the preaching of the gospel) may be rapidly overshadowed by efforts to serve society's imminent needs (in the provision of social care).[119] Hence, into this environment Chapman and other conservatives sought in their advocacy to "lean harder into the breeze" to ensure the church was not found to be in neglect of its foremost priority.[120] Such an approach bore the inherent risk that, anxious to guard the purity of their doctrinal commitments, they appeared indifferent toward the welfare of the community they sought to serve and were seen to be engaged in needless combative conservatism. Others charged that such a position was, in fact, already evidence of their growing marginalization and proof of their desire to seek a less demanding position on the edges of society than to pursue a centrist position requiring

---

117. Such a view broadly coheres with an amillennial eschatology. This is in contrast to premillennialism (which carries the expectation of a supernatural inbreaking of God's rule in history followed by a literal millennium reign of Christ) as well as postmillennialism (which emphasizes the present aspects of God's kingdom that will reach fruition in the future and the belief that Christ's millennium reign will come through Christian preaching and activism). Instead, amillennialism suggests that a continuous development of good and evil will characterize the present world until Christ's return. It holds that the kingdom of God is now present in the world (as the victorious Christ rules his church) prior to its final glorious consummation at the *parousia*. Amillennialism eschews an overly pessimistic view of the present world, yet it is less optimistic than postmillennialism regarding the possibility of pervasive societal reform. See Brower, "Eschatology," 459–64; Clouse, "Views of the Millennium," 714–18; DOE Prayer Letter, July 1983, 2. The propagation of this view in Sydney owes much to the eschatological reflections of D. W. B. Robinson in the 1950s. Shiner, *Reading*, 60.

118. Chapman, *Fresh Start*, 215–18; Chapman, *Know and Tell*, 66, 213; Chapman, *Foot in Two Worlds*, 19–38.

119. See Chapman, *Know and Tell*, 109–19 on challenges to evangelism, including the gospel's divisiveness and foolishness (Mark 10:34–36; 1 Cor 1:18–2:5), worldly opposition (John 15:18–25), and the Christian impulse to be "ashamed" (Rom 1:18).

120. Interview with Alan Stewart, December 7, 2016; Interview with Rico Tice, January 17, 2017.

thoughtful civic engagement.[121] However, it is perhaps more apt to suggest that, drawing more deeply from the "biblicist" and "conversionist" quadrants of their heritage than the "activist" strand, Chapman and other leading conservatives sought merely to elevate the importance of the former activity (conversion) without diminishing the worth of the latter (activist concern).[122] Somewhat instructively, the rise of the "church growth" school of missiology would later reveal salient parallels between a strongly prioritist position and some of the core findings of the school's research concerning the benefits of religious recruitment. Indeed, a key finding of a complement of studies in Europe and the United States has been to suggest that, other things being equal, churches that have exhibited a greater intentionality in promoting evangelistic initiative and who have been committed to a "vivid otherworldliness" have seen greater spiritual and numerical buoyancy than those pursuing the priorities of institutional maintenance, social justice, or the quest for influence in public life.[123] Within the context of a national church that experienced falling participation rates in the later century, compared to the Sydney diocese which saw modest expansion during the same period, such insights are not wholly immaterial.[124]

Revisioning Lausanne: New Alignments

Over time the Lausanne movement received diminishing patronage from Sydney conservatives. While support continued into the 1990s, conservative interest (in a manner almost emblematic of the movement) began to wilt. Indeed, reflecting on the 2004 Lausanne Forum for World Evangelization in Thailand, leading Sydney missiologist Michael Raiter confessed that although he was thankful for the gains in contemporary world mission that had been made and were reported at the 2004 forum, he remained concerned for the movement's direction. In his estimation it had begun to shadow the course of other similar historic movements. "A holistic understanding of mission [had

---

121. Jensen, *Apology*, 111; Piggin, "Concrete," 190; Fletcher, "Diocese of Sydney," 111–32; Bouma, *Australian Soul*, 130.

122. See Bebbington, *Evangelicalism*, 2, 4–17 on the "Bebbington quadrilateral."

123. Cox, "Progress Report," 21. In a study of American religion between 1776–2005, Finke and Stark, *Churching of America*, 2–4, claim that American churches who "rejected traditional doctrines and ceased to make serious demands on their followers" typically "ceased to prosper," while evangelistically expansive churches "committed to vivid otherworldliness" more commonly experienced growth; cf. Olson, *American Church*, ch. 2.

124. Anglican Church of Australia, *Report of the Viability and Structures Taskforce*, 31.

become] unquestioned," Raiter submitted, "and there [were] even open attacks on those who [wanted] to critique this or argue for the primacy of proclamation." "Strikingly," he contended, "every '-ing' was mentioned except the one for which we'd been called to come together: Proclaiming! . . . When asked, where is the gospel of the forgiveness of sins, the reply comes that it is implied . . . at a conference on world evangelization it needs to be more than implied; it needs to be loudly heralded."[125] Such an "implied gospel of forgiveness," Raiter opined, "should cause us grave concern. One generation heralds a message. The next implies it. By the third it has been forgotten."[126] Tellingly, by the time of the 2010 Cape Town Congress it seemed that Raiter's warning had been prescient. Indeed, at the 2010 congress many believed that Lausanne's constituency had become so diffuse that the "prioritist" fervor championed by the likes of Graham and Chapman some thirty-six years earlier remained merely a fading hope.[127]

In the new century, fresh coalitions of conservatives would begin to emerge under the shadow of Lausanne's more conservative historic American, British, and Australian constituencies. Schooled in the lessons of Lausanne's perceived missteps, such coalitions aligned behind a freshly conservative theological agenda and more modest missiological goals.[128] More loosely aligned "coalitions" (such as The Gospel Coalition and Together for the Gospel) formed across North America at this juncture, inviting partnership with conservatives across the evangelical world. Reformed statements of belief and a vision for ministry committed these churches and their leaders to continual doctrinal and missiological renewal.[129] More circumspect in their aims, more emphatically Reformed in their orientation, and less prescriptive concerning the nexus between the gospel and its sociocultural application, such coalitions garnered the support and involvement of conservative networks across the English-speaking world. This included a strong complement of conservative leaders within Sydney and across Australia.[130] At the denominational level,

---

125. Raiter, "Years On," 4.

126. Raiter, "Social Involvement (Part III)."

127. Hunt, "Lausanne Movement," 84; Stott, *Contemporary Christian*, 352; cf. Billy Graham, "Why Lausanne?," 25–26.

128. Warner, "Evangelical Bases," 334.

129. Gospel Coalition, "Foundation Documents."

130. The foremost of these, "The Gospel Coalition," represented a leading international network of evangelical practitioners, with growing representation across the English, Spanish, and French-speaking worlds. With links to the conservative networks within which Lausanne first flourished (such as Chicago's Wheaton College and Trinity Evangelical Divinity School) this coalition represented a more modest

the formation of the GAFCON Fellowship (The Global Anglican Future Conference) was also driven, at least in part, by the desire for global theological and missiological renewal left unfulfilled by the fading hopes of conservatives in the Lausanne movement. Indeed, while the GAFCON movement itself was essentially a response to theological compromise within the Anglican Communion, for the leading Sydney and English figures who played a role in its architecture, the movement represented a new vehicle toward the goal of world evangelization via the "proclamation" of the "biblical gospel." Concerned to bring the gospel "to areas of the world where it had been obscured [and to the world's] unreached people," GAFCON's foundational missiological objectives thus arguably represented a reflowering (within a denominational scaffold) of the earlier conservative and "prioritist" hopes for the Lausanne movement.[131]

Such coalitions are evidence that for conservative evangelicals the desire for missiological cooperation and theological enrichment remained strong. Yet, with an even stronger commitment to the foundational markers of evangelical identity (such as its commitment to biblical authority and to the atoning work of Christ on the cross) such desires were necessarily tempered when the movement's more foundational commitments were seen to be compromised. From a conservative frame of reference, this would appear to be a defining lesson from the Lausanne experiment. A desire to see Christ's commission realized—which became hampered by theological

---

reflowering of similar historic missiological ambitions. Note also the Australian arm of this conservative network which includes numerous representatives from within Sydney Anglicanism. See Gospel Coalition, "Foundation Documents." Another coalition, "Together for the Gospel," emerged from similar conservative North American channels and focused more on Reformed "theological renewal." While seeking to "reaffirm and reiterate the central doctrine of the Christian faith and to encourage local churches around the world to do the same," this network remained far more North American-centric in its outlook. See TG4, "About Us."

131. The GAFCON movement was formalized in 2008 via the "Jerusalem Declaration," following the meeting of 291 bishops and 1148 lay and clerical leaders who met in Jerusalem to consider how to "take a stand against the collapse of biblical witness in parts of the Anglican Communion." Reflecting the inexorable "drift south" within the power base of global Evangelicalism, conservative African leaders assumed a place of central prominence within the leadership and organizational architecture of the GAFCON movement. Importantly, however, the General Secretary of GAFCON from 2008 (widely considered to have provided critical impetus toward GAFCON's formation and a close friend of Chapman's) was Sydney Archbishop Dr. P. F. Jensen (2001–2012). GAFCON, "History"; cf. Hutchison and Wolffe, Short History, 219. British impetus for the movement arose out of the "Reform" movement of the 1990s. A response to the open Evangelicalism of figures like Anthony Thiselton and Tom Wright, "Reform" was committed to a Calvinist soteriology and to a renewed conservatism on the many issues of progressive "drift" arising in the wake of Lausanne. Warner, "Evangelical Bases," 334.

discord, overblown claims of comprehensivity and acrimony between constituent members—was eventually subordinated to a pattern of resistance, reform, and renewal. More specifically, conservative *resistance* to perceived compromise saw calls for *reform* to safeguard the movement's integrity, which led to a *renewal* of earlier missiological objectives in the formation of newer quasi-institutional instruments of global mission and the renewal of historic missionary aims.[132] It is thus possible to argue that the debate surrounding the relationship between evangelism and Christian social responsibility (refracted through the 1974 Lausanne Congress and its offshoots) provides a window into the intrinsic strengths of historic Evangelicalism in balancing wide cultural and ecclesiastical tradition on the fulcrum of deeply held foundational commitments. The Lausanne movement also serves as a flashpoint that illustrates the process by which Evangelicalism has balanced the provisional instruments of its missiological aims with its higher and non-provisional theological ideals. Undoubtedly, the force of conservative advocacy during this process occasioned missteps, just as the promotion of a progressive agenda elicited missteps as well. Yet, as Leon Morris notes, while the vigor with which such commitments were held and the evangelical habit "of mounting their horses and riding off in all directions" was at times ungainly, it nevertheless remained "central" to the movement's "vitality" and "strength."[133] Furthermore, as Brian Stanley observes, in at least partial explanation of the force of conservative advocacy on this question:

> If the global diffusion of evangelicalism proves eventually to have transmuted into the global disintegration of evangelicalism, it will not be because of the philosophical and hermeneutical boldness of a few post-conservative evangelical theologians in the North. It will rather be because in the explosive popular Christianity of the southern hemisphere the balance will have been tipped away from a Bible-centered gospel that, while being properly holistic, still holds to the soteriological centrality and ethical normativity of the cross, towards a form of religious materialism that subordinates the cross [of Christ] to a crude theology of divine blessing [and to] the daily realities of endemic poverty, hunger, pandemic disease and structural injustice.[134]

---

132. See this pattern of evangelical engagement and reform outlined in Atherstone and Maiden, "Anglican Evangelicalism," 1–47.

133. Morris, "Lausanne '74," 1–11; cf. Turnbull, *Anglican and Evangelical?*, 165.

134. Stanley, *Global Diffusion*, 247.

Conclusion

It is to such realities—in seeking to safeguard the centrality of the cross in evangelical witness—that figures like Chapman addressed themselves in their preaching and advocacy along the winding course of the Lausanne experiment. Indeed, as has been demonstrated, Chapman's advocacy not only supplied one of the more incendiary dynamics of the 1974 congress, but the persistence and extent with which it was offered (while at times decidedly polemical) almost certainly played a cumulative role in the consolidation of conservative opinion across world evangelical networks and in the renewal of prioritist missiological instruments across the Reformed evangelical world.

7

Evangelism and the Church

Christian Witness and the Challenge of Ecclesiology

"I find evangelism hard. The problem with being an evangelist is that people assume that you find evangelism effortless; but I don't find it easy, and never have . . . I know there's a painline that needs to be crossed if I tell someone the gospel; but I want to stay the comfortable side of [it]."—Rico Tice, English author and evangelist[1]

IN THE BASEMENT OF old Sydney Church House lay the insalubrious offices of the Sydney Board of Diocesan Missions.[2] In October 1968, the waggish director of the Board of Diocesan Missions, the Rev. Geoff Fletcher, was meeting with his newly appointed assistant missioner, the Rev. John Chapman. Chapman had recently joined Fletcher in his pursuit to proclaim Christ across the length of the Sydney region. Unused to the drab mustiness of his new office environment, Chapman began to make light of their simple and incommodious surroundings: "This place certainly tells you what the diocese thinks of evangelism, doesn't it Geoff?" Chapman quipped, confident of Fletcher's wholehearted agreement. "No Chappo," Fletcher roared with wry indignation, "it tells you that the whole of the diocesan structure is built on our foundation!"[3]

---

1. Tice, *Honest Evangelism*, 11, 15.
2. Sydney "Church House" (in Cathedral Square) was replaced in the 1970s by the modern St. Andrew's House complex.
3. Interview with Phillip Jensen, February 16, 2017.

Whether consciously or not, Fletcher's roguish reply gestures towards a subtle tension that has come to permeate the historiography of the evangelistic legacy of Sydney Anglicanism. Within this body of commentary even leading critics of Sydney's legacy have tended to depict its commitment to evangelism as an indomitable reality of its corporate life. Portraying the diocese as a "monolithic" entity standing "alone" among world Anglicans in its brand of "ultra-conservative fundamentalism," such critics have suggested the diocese's shared "imperative to evangelize the lost" has constituted an unwavering foundation upon which its bold missionary agenda has been forged.[4] Others have suggested that Sydney's almost "casual confidence" in the face of opposition to its expansive agenda has been a posture that has often driven its detractors "to distraction."[5] Similarly, even those who offer a more sympathetic perspective on the diocese (written largely from an insider's vantage point) have tended to highlight the diocese's "passion for evangelism" as a defining reason for its historic strength and as central to the dexterity with which it navigated the tide of overwhelming twentieth-century cultural change.[6] While there is undoubtedly some truth in all of these observations, the present study has demonstrated a more nuanced picture of Sydney's evangelistic legacy. It has demonstrated the diocese's enmeshment with the inherited superstructures of Anglo-Christian identity and the struggle it faced (led, in large part, through the agency of figures like Chapman) to open fresh avenues of missional vitality once traditional bulwarks conducive to the flourishing of Christian identity began to fall away.

However, in addition to having examined external threats to the diocese's evangelistic vitality, the following chapter seeks to examine subtle *internal* missional challenges that arose from within *and* as a result of the unique theological and ecclesiological ecosystem of Sydney Anglicanism. Indeed, one of the more intriguing products of this environment was the stimulating scholarship on the doctrine of the church advanced by leading Sydney theologians D. B. Knox and D. W. B. Robinson. The "Knox-Robinson doctrine of church" was widely regarded as a needed "corrective" to certain overblown views of denominationalism in circulation during the mid-century. However, several of the innovations that characterized their position also came to be regarded as a significant *disincentive* to the work of evangelism in local churches.[7] Indeed, Chapman himself came to regard

---

4. This represents the impression and critique of Porter, *Anglicanism*, 2, 12, 17 regarding Sydney's missional legacy.

5. Jensen, *Apology*, 1–3.

6. Ballantine-Jones, *Political Factor*, 28–29; Jensen, *Apology*, 117.

7. Shiner, *Reading*, 62–65; Jensen, *Apology*, 75–76.

their formulations as having had a deleterious impact on the desire, among local Christians, to be engaged in a lifestyle of evangelism, and thus sought to provide redress to these disincentives to evangelism which their work had espoused (albeit inadvertently).[8] Chapman's contributions on such questions also resulted in a lively ongoing dialogue on the place of evangelism in the church that continued across the closing decades of the twentieth century. This chapter examines these stimulating developments. Beginning with an assessment of the contours of Knox and Robinson's ecclesiological thought and praxis, the chapter then assesses Chapman's response and its ongoing impact. In so doing, the discussion provides a further lens through which to appreciate Chapman's unique missiological contribution to Australian Evangelicalism and to the Sydney diocese.

The Knox-Robinson Doctrine of Church

Historical and Theological Context

Regarding the origins of the "Knox-Robinson view of church," it is evident that while the view itself began to make its presence felt within Sydney and Australian evangelical circles in the 1970s and 1980s, the impetus for the view derived from their reflections within the atmosphere of the postwar biblical theology movement, and in light of the significant ecumenical and denominational developments taking place at the time.[9]

---

8. J. C. Chapman, BDM Prayer Letter, March 1975, 1; Chapman, *Know and Tell*, 5–6, 9–12, 46.

9. The origins of the "Knox-Robinson view of church" are a somewhat contested feature of recent historiography. In his study of Robinson's work Rory Shiner provides extensive analysis of how the theology and nomenclature of the Knox-Robinson view developed. He notes that the nomenclature of the "Knox-Robinson doctrine" first began to appear in print in the 1980s. Judd and Cable's diocesan history (1987) discussed Knox and Robinson's views but did not introduce the compound term "Knox-Robinson." In 1987, Graham Cole presented a paper at Moore College's School of Theology in which he outlined a view called "the Robinson-Knox Corrective." In the essay that responded to Cole, Robert Doyle spoke of the "Knox-Robinson view" of church. This provided the first instance in print of the now "canonical nomenclature" which shows Knox's name as taking priority. However, alongside Chase Kuhn's extended study of Knox and Robinson's work, Shiner demonstrates that Cole's compound ("Robinson-Knox") is the most accurate representation of the view's substance. Shiner (with Kuhn) speculates that Knox's seniority and charisma may have resulted in Knox's name taking precedence when describing their thought. However, Shiner demonstrates that in the development of ideas that shaped the view, Robinson's linguistic work supplied the preliminary foundation upon which both scholars built. See Shiner, *Reading*, 62–68; Kuhn, "Ecclesiology," 247; Judd and Cable, *Sydney Anglicans*, 285–291; Cole, "Doctrine of Church," 3–17; Doyle, "Response," 19–25.

Within this mid-century environment, the concept of "the Church" had not previously been high on the doctrinal agenda in evangelical circles. Themes of justification, atonement, and the authority of Scripture were far more central. The concept of "the Church" had certainly featured in the Protestant psyche as a reaction to the authoritarian claims of Roman Catholicism. Moreover, for Anglicans, their historic liturgy and expanding international footprint had also affirmed their participation in the church "universal" and promoted a sense of solidarity with Christians in other times and places. However, many mid-century evangelicals' conception of "church" was still framed more in terms of what it was *not* than what it *was*. Such a paucity of overt ecclesiological reflection, however, was soon challenged by the rise of international ecumenism and the formation of the national Anglican Church of Australia.[10]

The ecumenical movement was a movement that gained critical momentum in the decades following the Edinburgh International Missionary Conference (1910). An ecumenical vision for the unity and missionary renewal of the church had begun to build for more than a century. By the early twentieth century a coalition of missionary leaders and parachurch bodies had begun to bring together Christians of various traditions in the belief that historic Christian factionalism and denominationalism had curtailed the church's missionary effectiveness. At the same time, there was a growing recognition that such early ecumenism required greater coordination to be effective and that the churches themselves (not just the parachurch bodies) needed to be brought more fully into the heart of concerns for Christian unity.[11] Following these early ecumenical impulses, the priorities of the movement were articulated at the first gathering of the World Council of Churches in Amsterdam (1948). These priorities testified that the movement aspired to achieve something beyond merely a superficial denominational harmony, or even simply common cause in missionary endeavor.[12]

---

10. Shiner, *Reading*, 64–65, 88–89; Judd and Cable, *Sydney Anglicans*, 289; Jensen, *Apology*, 76; Cole, "Doctrine of Church," 3–4.

11. As early as 1810 William Carey had proposed a decennial gathering of churches to discuss missionary partnerships. By the early 1900s various parachurch and mission bodies (such as the YMCA, the Student Christian Movement, the World Missionary Council, the World Council of Christian Education, the Faith and Order Movement, and the World Alliance for Friendship through Churches) had begun to claim that denominational divisions were hampering missionary effectiveness. Prayer for reconciliation and unity was also expressed through gatherings associated with the World Day of Prayer. See Latourette, "Ecumenical Bearings," 355; Fitzgerald, *Ecumenical Movement*, 104–6.

12. The priorities of the Ecumenical Movement as articulated at the first gathering of the WCC in Amsterdam (1948) were fourfold: 1) *Common Service* in promoting

However, by the time of the WCC's 1961 New Delhi congress it had become increasingly apparent that the nature of the unity the council was seeking was in fact far more than merely a spiritual unity—it was also deeply institutional. Indeed, the definitive statement produced for the 1961 WCC congress enthusiastically stated that the "unity" which was both "God's will and gift to his Church" was "being made visible" in the contemporary church as all who were "baptized into Christ" were being "brought by the Holy Spirit into one fully committed [global] fellowship" which exhibited a common mission, communion, orders of ministry, and organization.[13]

Yet, while the desire for such shared fellowship and witness was certainly admirable, with considerable variety in doctrine and practice still evident across the denominations engaged with the WCC, the question of how a true spiritual (and institutional) unity *could* be achieved without genuine agreement on foundational matters became pressing.[14] Similarly, within the Australian environment, the establishment of the new *Constitution of the Anglican Church of Australia* (1962) gave rise to concerns regarding the variety of doctrine and practice that existed across the Australian church and the degree of unity that could be achieved across such disparate expressions of Anglicanism. On account of such concerns the road toward a national constitutional agreement had already been vexed. However, with episcopal leaders persuaded that the national church must face the world as a national entity, a constitutional draft was ratified in 1955 and instated in 1962. Following its enactment, the Australian dioceses became part of the "autocephalous Anglican Church of Australia." The agreed constitution contained a number of compromises that sought to safeguard a degree of diocesan autonomy in matters of doctrine, order, and financial obligation to the national body. However, the degree of coercive authority that any new national structure would hold continued to raise fears of compromise, particularly among evangelicals, if the national church should seek to impose standardized doctrine on all the dioceses irrespective of their theological

---

justice and working cooperatively to provide interchurch aid to victims of war, poverty, and oppression; 2) *Common Fellowship* in a common apostolic faith, a mutual recognition of members and ministers, and working towards the removal of barriers to sharing the Eucharist; 3) *Common Witness* in cooperative mission and evangelism; and 4) *Common Renewal* in the transformation that comes through receiving the gifts that others contribute to the body of Christ. Subsequent WCC meetings were held in Evanston (1954), New Delhi (1961), Uppsala (1968), Nairobi (1975), Vancouver (1983), Canberra (1991), Harare (1998), Porto Alegre (2006), and Busan (2013). Kinnamon and Cope, *Ecumenical Movement*, 2–4.

13. "Report on the Section on Unity," Third Assembly of the WCC, New Delhi 1961, in Kinnamon and Cope, *Ecumenical Movement*, 88–89.

14. Kuhn, "Ecclesiology," 46.

and ecclesiological commitments. Comprehensivity, it was believed, could amount to compromise. And in conceding too much to any national Anglican ecclesiological structure, many evangelicals feared that the new constitution *could* amount to the demise of evangelical theology among Australian Anglicans as a by-product of coercivity.[15]

The Nature and Location of the Church: The Knox-Robinson Corrective

Such was the context into which Robinson and Knox began to offer their reflections on the nature, unity, and locality of the Christian church. Robinson had been stimulated in his reflections in this area through his engagement with leading scholars (like C. F. D. Moule, F. J. A. Hort, and Karl Barth) during his studies at Cambridge (1940s) and his early lecturing at Moore College (1950s). Such scholars had helped him to wrestle with the "confusion" that can often arise when speaking of "what has generally come to be called the church, meaning . . . 'the whole congregation of Christian people dispersed throughout the world' and what the New Testament means by the word *ekklēsia*."[16] Indeed, he reflected, given the "confusion" surrounding the application of the New Testament's use of *ekklēsia* to bodies like the WCC and the "Church of England in Australia," beginning in 1959 (with his first article on such themes) Robinson felt compelled to "go public" with his views.[17] Similarly, during the 1950s Knox had also been somewhat critical of the proposals surrounding the new Anglican Constitution.[18] However, in contrast to Robinson, Knox's initial scholarship in this area had been largely reflective of "traditional evangelical categories."[19] It was not until later that Knox began to reflect what would become the

---

15. On the loose federal structure that existed between the Australian dioceses prior to 1962 and the vexed process of constitutional negotiation, see Davis, *Australian Anglicans*, 138–50; Knox, "Undefined Comprehensiveness," 2; Judd and Cable, *Sydney Anglicans*, 255–56; Judd, "Defenders of Their Faith," 448–53; Frame, *Anglicans*, 72–86; Frame, "Anglicans," 122–28; Kaye, "Identity," 154–76.

16. Robinson, "Church Revisited," 259–71.

17. Robinson, "Church Revisited," 263, 267. Robinson's key outputs on this topic were offered in 1959 ("The Church in the New Testament"), 1960 ("Origin's Conception of 'Church' in the *Contra Celsum*"), 1962 ("The Biblical Doctrine of the Church"), 1962 ("Church"), 1962 ("The 'Authority' of the Church"), 1965 ("The Church of God: Its Forms and Unity"), and 1990 ("The Diocese of Sydney and Its Purpose") in Bolt and Thompson, *Donald Robinson, Vol. 1*, 205–317.

18. Knox, "Four Fatal Flaws," 8.

19. In his initial 1950 paper Knox offered a relatively conventional claim that "church" meant "called out." Shiner, *Reading*, 67; Knox, "People of God," 9–17.

crucial linguistic contention regarding the use of *ekklēsia* in the Knox-Robinson view.[20] In terms of the essence of the doctrine that came to bear their name, however, neither Knox *nor* Robinson ever distilled a summary of their view. Their work did, however, share sufficient commonality that it is possible to speak of a distinct theological construct that emerged displaying certain "recognizable features." Accordingly, while resisting the language of institutionalism used to describe "church" in common discourse, the essence of the Knox-Robinson ecclesiology was to suggest that "church" was in fact the *function* of the people of God when they gathered. It was the actual meeting of believers, an intermittent activity of congregation rather than its continuous aggregation. As Robinson lucidly explained:

> "Church" in the NT . . . renders Gk. *ekklēsia*, which mostly designates a local congregation of Christians and never a building. Although we often speak of these congregations collectively as the NT church . . . no NT writer uses *ekklēsia* in this collective way . . . In Acts, James, 3 John, Revelation and the earlier Pauline letters, "church" is always a particular congregation . . . [In] Colossians and Ephesians Paul generalizes his use of "church" to indicate, not an ecumenical church, but the spiritual and heavenly significance of each . . . local "body" . . . there is only one church, one gathering of all under the headship of Christ. But on earth it is pluriform, seen wherever two of three gather in his name . . . Like the believer, the church is both local *and* "in heaven" . . . "Church" is not a synonym for "people of God"; it is rather an *activity* of the "people of God" . . . assembled with Christ in the midst (Matt. 18.20; Heb. 2:12).[21]

Within such a statement (written in 1962) the essential elements of their ecclesiology began to emerge. Indeed, for Knox and Robinson, "church" was to be regarded more as a verb than a noun. It was an "activity, a meeting,

20. Regarding the development of the view that came to bear their name, Knox's crucial contributions were offered in 1964 as Knox, "Church and the Denominations," 44–53; in 1973, "De-Mythologizing the Church," in 1986, "Biblical Concept of Fellowship," and in 1989, "Church, the Churches," 23–31, 57–84, 85–98. By 1964 (when Knox's first published work exhibiting the traits of the later "doctrine" appeared) Robinson had already published at least five articles propounding the view that he had developed during the 1950s. Given such an observable chronology in the development of their ideas it is evident that as both scholars developed their work as part of a wider theological conversation, the line of influence in their thought appears to have gone from Robinson to Knox, rather than the other way around. As Shiner notes, however, Knox *was* teaching and broadcasting on the topic across the 1960s to 1980s. Hence, his views *were* being disseminated beyond merely his academic outputs. This gives some weight to the possibility of "mutual influence" during this period. Shiner, *Reading*, 68, 96–97.

21. Robinson, "Church of God," 221–229, 222–23.

rather than a continuous society or organization." Certainly, in its "ultimate heavenly aspect" the "church" could be described as a "continuous" reality. Drawing on the language of Hebrews 12:22–24 and Ephesians 2:6, Robinson suggested that the Christian had come to participate (spiritually) in the heavenly *ekklēsia* gathered around Christ's throne. The local congregation was simply an *intermittent* expression of this *continuous* heavenly reality.[22] Indeed, regarding the church's continuous nature Robinson suggested that "believers may regard themselves as *continuously* partaking of the life of the church *above* inasmuch as they are already risen with Christ, are part of his body, and have their minds set on things above where He is exalted (Col. 3:1–4)." However, he concluded, "believers cannot think of themselves as in the same way *continuously* partaking of the life of the earthly church." For, "although an earthly church is an expression of the heavenly church . . . it has this character only in so far as, and only as often as, there is an actual meeting. There is no greater source of confusion in our speaking about the church today," he alleged, "than the practice of using *church* to mean the organized structures built up to ensure the continuance of formalized Christianity, and to show a certain face to the world."[23]

From such a stimulating, yet provocative, viewpoint several corollaries followed. The first was that the unity of the church was not to be found in the institutional arrangements of the earthly church, but in the gospel. In fact, Robinson averred, little was known of the organization of the New Testament churches in general. Rather, their "unity lay in the gospel, acceptance of the OT Scriptures and acknowledgement of Jesus as 'Lord and Christ.'" Indeed, he suggested, "differences of church government" and "forms of ministry" among the New Testament churches were probably "greater than we realize." Nor did any "NT church, nor all the churches together" exercise "authority" over the rest. This "authority belong[ed] only to the apostolic gospel as contained in the whole of the Scriptures."[24] Consequently, he alleged, any contemporary quest that sought to achieve an organizational unity *outside* the unity found in the gospel was surely misplaced. Moreover, on such a reading, the historic denominations were to be regarded more as a federation of churches. They could not assume for themselves the status of "church" accorded to the assemblies of the New Testament. Rather, Knox suggested, the denominations were more accurately to be seen as "service

---

22. Robinson, "Church of God," 230–253, 234–236.

23. Robinson, "Church of God," 236, emphasis original. See also Knox, "De-Mythologizing," 26–30.

24. Robinson, "Church of God," 229.

structures to assist congregations which are real churches."[25] Such structures were useful in the promotion of fellowship, providing a forum for doctrinal enrichment, dispute resolution, and a stable repository for congregational assets.[26] Indeed, Robinson reflected, "however imperfectly they may have functioned," the denominations *had* played a role in keeping "local churches on the rails" and fine-tuning a service structure that aided the life of the churches. Nevertheless, they were not in themselves to be regarded as "church" in the strictest New Testament sense.[27]

The second corollary of this view was that the local Christian gathering could *not* be said to *have a mission*. In fact, according to Robinson, evangelism was not strictly speaking a purpose for which the church existed. For, he reasoned, if the "church" existed *only when it gathered* (giving it a focus inward and upward but not outward) then mission was not to be regarded as a legitimate activity of the "church." Indeed, fearing that to speak of the church's "corporate witness" could "sanction" the language of "institutionalism" that had given rise to such recent confusions, Robinson stressed that the responsibility for evangelism rested with the scattered people of God and not the gathered church. "The church," he stated, "has no such task or role. Christians do . . . [but] I cannot think of anything in the New Testament which suggests that the church . . . or even Christians as a visibly organized body, have a function of witness or service *vis-à-vis* the world."[28] Rather, Robinson maintained, "the purpose of the *ekklēsia* [is] that God's children . . . scattered in the world might strengthen one another's hands in the sharing of ministries to their mutual edification . . . but the church [itself] has no such *face* to the world and is therefore not a direct agent in evangelism."[29] Naturally, Robinson placed a high premium on the power of the "evangel" as the instrument that established the church by calling

25. Knox, "De-Mythologizing," 23–34, 31.

26. Knox, "Christian Unity," 33–34; Robinson, "Authority of the Church," 298–311.

27. Robinson, "Church Revisited," 270. This provides some insight into the enigmatic relationship between Knox and Robinson's highly congregationalist views of church versus their conservative approach to the denomination. Driven to protect the heritage they saw to be resident in their diocese and to fine-tune a "service structure" that safeguarded the health of the local churches, Knox *and* Robinson's ecclesiology drove them not to withdraw but to be heavily involved in denominational affairs to achieve this (Knox as Principal of Moore College and Robinson as bishop). Indeed, for both scholars, denominationalism was not to be despised. Yet, Robinson in particular, had a complex understanding of ecclesiological tradition. This meant his application of ecclesiology to contemporary practice was a complex affair, as his 1980s episcopacy showed. Shiner, *Reading*, 97.

28. Robinson, "Church of God," 242.

29. Robinson, "Doctrine of the Church," 109.

humanity into fellowship with Christ. As such, the church was ultimately the end point of evangelism, even if it was neither its means or its agent.[30] Robinson also stressed that while the church had no direct evangelistic responsibility, it *did* partner in the work of evangelism in three ways: "(a) to pray the Lord of the harvest to send out laborers, (b) to . . . attest to the authority of the Spirit in the call of a missionary, and (c) to join in fellowship, through prayer and . . . financial aid with such as God sends forth."[31] Despite such concessions, however, Robinson's strenuous attempts to conceptually compartmentalize these activities ("assembling" and "evangelizing") were considered to have become a significant *disincentive* to the proclamation of the gospel both *from* and *within* the local church. Indeed, while seeking to remediate the effects of ecclesiastical authoritarianism on the one front, such a view was considered to be doing harm on another. If left conceptually isolated, some suggested, it might "limit Christian self-understanding" and "promote ghetto-ism . . . and a remnant mentality."[32]

A third corollary of Robinson's views on the nature of church[33] was related to evangelistic gifting and its expression among and by the people of God. Indeed, on account of Robinson's strenuous congregationalism, he was compelled (almost as a step of logic) to comment on *where* and *by whom* the work of evangelism was therefore conducted if it was not strictly a function of the local church. In answer to this, Robinson advanced a view that both *elevated* the nature of the gospel as being a "proclamation" of an "authoritative" quality, while also *limiting* the identity of the "evangelist" as being that of a "qualified office bearer" who was "sent" to proclaim it. He wrote:

> "Evangel" (εὐαγγέλιον) and "evangelize" (εὐαγγελίζωμαι) occur frequently in the . . . vocabulary of the NT. "Evangelist" (εὐαγγελιστής) also occurs, but . . . only three times. There is no term in this word-group exactly equivalent to our word "evangelism." Nevertheless, if we are not to [use] "evangelism" to mean anything we like, we are bound to define it in connection with the biblical terms from which it is derived. And here, "evangel" means a proclamation or announcement. Whatever may be the derivation of the word "gospel" in English, the Greek noun . . .

---

30. Robinson, "Doctrine of the Church," 112–13. Cf. Emil Brunner's well-known maxim in the early twentieth-century that "the church exists by mission, just as a fire exists by burning," in *Word and the World*, 108.

31. Robinson, "Authority of the Church," 305.

32. Cole, "Doctrine of the Church," 3–17, 5; Edwards, "Romance," 39.

33. While Knox's scholarship contributed to the broader architecture of the so-called "Knox-Robinson view," it was largely Robinson who developed the implications of their work in relation to evangelism, as evidenced by this analysis.

does not simply mean "good news" . . . it means *a proclamation of an authoritative character conveyed by a properly qualified person*. It is something to be "preached." It calls for acceptance or acknowledgement, and for that wholehearted adjustment of the mind that the NT calls μετάνοια or "repentance."[34]

In addition, the implication of such a particularized definition of the gospel was also the need to specify whose responsibility it was to be an emissary of such an "authoritative proclamation." In answer to this, Robinson stressed that as the author of the *evangel* it was ultimately God himself who gave utterance to the gospel. Such utterance had been conveyed in the Scriptures by the work of various emissaries whom God authorized and sent (including the prophets, various messianic forerunners, and the New Testament apostles who bore a unique witness to Christ). However, in addition to such emissaries, in the New Testament "certain others were seen to possess the gift of evangelism." Such "evangelists," Robinson alleged, were "associates of the apostles and shared their ministry" in the bearing of God's word and in the founding of congregations (Eph 4:11; Acts 8:14–15). Like the apostles, such figures functioned alongside the churches and were "sent" by them. Moreover, while not "exercis[ing] the gift of evangelism," many in the churches became "partners" with such emissaries by the offering of "material help" and encouragement (Phil 1:3–11; 4:2, 3, 18). However, the church's task, he argued, was primarily to recognize "the sovereignty of God in bestowing his gifts of evangelism and directing their use."[35] From such a pattern, Robinson urged, it was clear that the work of "evangelism generally proceed[ed] independently of the church." He wrote:

> What emerges is that evangelism in the proper NT sense is not a . . . responsibility resting directly on all Christians. [Such a view] does not stand up to a careful exegetical examination and is at . . . variance with the NT teaching concerning the diversity of gifts. Every Christian must of course bear witness to the God he serves, by his good works (which will include what he says) and by his direct confession when this may be called for. But this is not evangelism. [Every] Christian should be encouraged by the examples of the NT to have fellowship in the furtherance of the gospel with those whom God *has* called to be evangelists. Above all, the heart of the [Christian and] of each church should alike be constantly turned to God . . . asking that the owner of

---

34. Robinson, "Doctrine of the Church," 103. Emphasis not original.
35. Robinson, "Doctrine of the Church," 106–12.

the harvest will send his laborers into the harvest, and that the gospel will be proclaimed in all the world.[36]

A final related corollary of Robinson (and Knox's) view of the particularized nature of evangelism was its implications for the contours of the Christian meeting. Indeed, according to Knox the "main task" of the Christian minister was almost singularly that of a "teacher of God's word" (2 Tim 2:2), a task that lacked an overtly evangelistic function. Similarly, as noted, Robinson regarded the *ekklēsia* as largely a context for the edification of believers and one which lacked an inherently evangelistic function, given that the work of evangelism occurred extraneously to it.[37] It followed that if the speaking activity of such a specialized cast of evangelistic emissary was of a different order from that which normally occurred in the *ekklēsia*, and if the *ekklēsia* was not the place where the gospel was preached to "those outside," then one ought logically to concede a diminished expectancy not only of the evangelistic potential of the church meeting but of the preaching activity of the Christian pastor.[38] Certainly, Robinson's compartmentalization of the activities of "gathering" and "evangelizing" was not intended to stifle evangelism *per se*. Indeed, in some respects, Robinson felt that in his day evangelism had not become *too radical* but *not radical enough*. That is, he judged that if the Christian meeting was being relied upon to carry the weight of contemporary missionary endeavor, then this was evidence that the Christian community had lost the kind of "frontier with the genuine non-Christian" world that "St Paul had when he spoke at Athens."[39] Despite such qualifications, it is evident that what was largely *heard* by many clergy and parishes as a result of Robinson's and Knox's "introverted" ecclesiology

---

36. Robinson, "Doctrine of the Church," 113; cf. Robinson, "Theology of Evangelism," 99–102.

37. Payne, "On Training," 25; Robinson, "Evangelism," 99–102.

38. Robinson, "Doctrine of the Church," 106. Related to such concerns was Robinson's view on the role of the bishop. Robinson equated the work of the modern bishop with the biblical figure of Timothy. He described Timothy as "Paul's colleague in missionary and apostolic evangelisation" charged with conveying and proclaiming the apostolic testimony. Robinson also saw in Timothy an early example of the monarchical episcopate. Robinson therefore viewed the modern bishop as an ecclesiastical defender of the faith and as one of a limited cast of evangelistic emissaries operating extraneously to the local church. Robinson gave little consideration to Timothy's pastoral work (2 Tim 4:1–5) wherein the two activities of teaching and evangelism were integrated components of his ministry. For discussion of Timothy's dual work of congregational teaching and evangelism and the possible relation of his ministry to later structures, see Knight, *Pastoral Epistles*, 28–31, 451–58; Cf. Robinson, "Bishop as Evangelist," 85–98.

39. Robinson, "Doctrine of the Church," 106.

was that of an essentially cautionary note regarding the pursuit of a strongly missionally oriented church life and culture.[40]

Evangelism and the Church: A Rejoinder

For the director of the Sydney Department of Evangelism, who had sought across a twenty-five-year directorship to promote a widespread missional culture among evangelicals, such an "introverted" doctrine on the church and evangelism was undoubtedly troubling. Indeed, between 1969 and 1993 Chapman had striven relentlessly in a range of contexts to promote a grassroots confidence in the gospel among his evangelical constituency, and a passion to see it widely shared and proclaimed.[41] Without question, Chap-

---

40. Edwards, "Romance," 39; Interview with Dr. Peter Jensen, December 2, 2016. Note: Sydney clergy were primarily exposed to Knox and Robinson's views in the context of their training within the environment of Sydney's Moore College.

41. One of the clearest written evidences of this was the "Director's Addresses" in the quarterly Department of Evangelism newsletters. Without exception, these widely distributed newsletters contained reflections by Chapman in which he took up a passage or verse from Scripture through which to examine an aspect of the gospel and the Christian motivation to see it shared and proclaimed. These newsletters also contained reports on the ministry activity of Chapman and his associates to give readers confidence by observing the "gospel in action" in churches across the world (cf. chapter 5 for details of Chapman's efforts to mobilize churches evangelistically through initiatives such as "dialogue evangelism" and "investigative courses"). The passages and titles of these "Director's Addresses" (beginning in 1969) are illustrative of Chapman's relentless missiological focus: June 1969, Eph 1:9–10, "God's World Plan"; Sept. 1969, 2 Thess 1:5–10, "Evangelism: Does it Really Work?"; Dec. 1969, Matt 1:21, "He Will Save His People from Their Sins"; Mar. 1970, 1 Tim 2:5–6, "One God: One Way"; June 1970, Matt 9:35–38, "A Heart Filled with Pity"; Sept. 1970, Col 2:13–15, "God's Forgiveness and the Cross"; Feb. 1971, John 3:16, "God's Love and Our Love"; May 1971, 1 Thess 1:5, 2:3–13, "True Ministry"; Aug. 1971, 1 Thess 2:13, "True Conversion"; Nov. 1971, 1 Thess 1:10, "True Anticipation"; June 1972, Rom 1:16, "Not Ashamed"; Oct. 1972, Ps 14:1, "Man Cannot Live by Bread Alone"; Dec. 1972, Gal 4:4, "When the Time Had Fully Come, God Sent his Son"; June 1973, Col 4:2–3, "Prayer for the Spread of the Gospel"; Sept. 1973, Luke 24:44–47, "Three Imperatives of the Gospel"; Dec. 1973, 2 Cor 4:3–6, "Paul: In Defence of Evangelism"; Mar. 1974, 2 Cor 5:17—6:1, "Paul: The Grandeur and Permanence of the New Covenant Ministry"; June 1974, 2 Thess 2:13–14, "The Gospel is Integral to God's Plan and Purpose"; Oct. 1974, Rom 1:1–6, "The Nature of the Gospel"; Dec. 1974, Mark 9:43–48, "Hell is No Joking Matter"; Mar. 1975, 2 Thess 3:1, "The Work of Evangelism"; Sept. 1975, Heb 2:14–15, "The Work of Christ and Eternity"; June 1975, Acts 14:26–27, "All That God Has Done"; Dec. 1975, Matt 2:1–17, "A Gospel for All"; Feb. 1976, Matt 24:30–31, "Sign of the Son of Man"; Apr. 1976, Eph 6:18–20, "Boldness in Preaching and Praying"; Aug 1976, Heb 10:35, "Don't Throw it Away"; Nov. 1976, Mark 10:45, "The Servant Savior"; Mar. 1977, Matt 28:18–20, "Disciples Must Be Made"; May 1977, Phil 4:18–19, "Partnership in the Gospel"; Aug. 1977, 1 Thess 1:9–10, "Repentance and Faith"; Nov. 1977, 1 John 2:1–2, "A Friend at Court";

man had found many aspects of Knox and Robinson's scholarship stimulating and had sought to maintain a warm, collegial relationship with both figures. However, he also confessed to investing significant energy in trying to redress the disincentives he believed they provided to the emphasis he sought to promote.[42] Out of respect for their piety and scholarship, in his work *Know and Tell the Gospel* (1980) Chapman refrained from identifying Knox and Robinson as a target of his rebuttal. Nevertheless, a central theme of this work was to remove the barriers to evangelism that arose as

---

May 1978, Matt 20:25–27, "Service in the Gospel"; Aug. 1978, Rev 14:6–8, "An Eternal Gospel"; Nov. 1978, Rev 3:15–20, "Hot or Cold"; Feb. 1979, 1 Cor 9:22–23, "A Slave of All"; May 1979, Titus 3:4–7, "The Goodness and Loving Kindness of God"; Aug. 1979, Col 1:3–6, "We Always Thank God . . . For the Gospel"; Nov. 1979, 1 Thess 1:5, 2:2, 3:2, "Whose Gospel?"; June–Mar. 1980, Rev 4:11, "Worthy Art Thou O God and Worthy Is the Lamb"; May–July 1980, "Two Quotes on Personal Witnessing"; Aug–Oct. 1980, John 4:34–37, "The Harvest is Now"; Nov. 1980–Jan. 1981, John 11:33–38, "The Angry Jesus"; Feb–Apr. 1981, 2 Tim 4:1–5, "The Teaching Office of the Christian Leader"; Aug–Oct. 1981, 1 Cor 3:5–9, "Co-workers with God"; Nov. 1981–Jan. 1982, Rom 8:31–35, "Three Great Questions"; Feb–Apr. 1982, Heb 10:23–24, "Let Us Encourage One Another"; May–Jul. 1982, Rom 5:1, 5, "The Holy Spirit and Evangelism"; Aug–Oct. 1982, Acts 21:27–35, "A Man Obsessed with the Gospel"; Nov. 1982–Jan. 1983, Matt 19:26, "With God All Things are Possible"; Feb–Apr. 1983, Luke 11:27–28, "Sentimentality and Reality"; May–Jul 1983, Ezek. 2:9–3:3, "Good News or Bad News?"; Aug–Oct 1983, Luke 4:42–44, "The Priority of Need"; Nov. 1983–Jan. 1984, Ezek 36:22–23, "God's Glory: Our Prime Motivation"; Feb–Apr. 1984, Acts 3:13–15, "What We Did: What God Did"; May–July 1984, Luke 4:1–4, "Temptation and the Gospel"; Aug–Oct. 1984, Matt 16:26, "How Valuable is the Person Next Door?"; Nov. 1984–Jan. 1985, Ps 34:6, "God Hears and Saves"; Feb–Apr. 1985, Matt 24:4–6, "The Sign of the End of the Age"; May–July 1985, Mark 8:34–35, "Suffering for the Gospel"; Aug–Oct. 1985, Rom 15:19b–20, 23–24a, "Fully Proclaiming the Gospel"; Nov. 1985–Jan. 1986, Luke 11:23, "To Do Nothing Is Not to Be Neutral"; Feb–Apr. 1986, John 4:34–36, "The Reaper and the Reward"; May–July 1986, Acts 11:14, "All Done By Words"; Aug–Oct. 1986, Isa 6:11–12, "For How Long?"; Nov. 1986–Jan. 1987, Acts 1:8, "Power for Witnessing"; Feb–Apr. 1987, Heb 2:2–3, "Such a Great Salvation"; Aug–Oct. 1987, Ezek 37:3, "Can These Bones Live?"; Nov. 1987–Jan. 1988, 1 Cor 2:2, "Top Priority"; Feb–Apr. 1988, Matt 16:23, "What is Essential?"; May–July 1988, Eph 1:3–14, "Evangelism is Speaking!!"; Nov. 1988–Jan. 1989, 1 Thess 1:4–6, "What Sort of Power?"; Feb–Apr. 1989, Ps 108:3, "Did You Know that Evangelism is Praise?"; May–July 1989, Rev 5:12, "The Gospel Goes on Forever"; Aug–Oct. 1989, 1 Cor 9:16, "The Gospel Must Be Preached"; Nov. 1989–Jan. 1990, Matt 28:18–20, "Is There Any Condition to the Promise?"; Feb–Apr. 1990, 1 Pet 2:9, "Why Are the Citizens of Heaven Left on Earth?"; May–July 1990, Luke 15:20, "The God Who Welcomes Sinners"; Aug–Oct. 1990, Matt 26:38, "Christ in Gethsemane"; Nov. 1990–Jan. 1991, Gal 3:8, "God the Evangelist"; Feb–Apr. 1991, Rev 21:3, 4, 27, "The Conclusion of History"; May–July 1991, "I Thank God"; Aug–Oct. 1991, "Twenty Twenty Vision"; Nov. 1991–Jan. 1992, 2 Chron 7:21, "What Appears to Be Permanent Can Often Be Temporary"; Feb–Apr. 1992, John 5:24, "Crossed Over from Death to Life"; May–July 1992, 1 Cor 15, "Death Has Been Swallowed Up in Victory"; Aug–Oct. 1992, 1 Cor 2:2, "Power Through Weakness."

42. John Chapman, BDM Prayer Letter, March 1975, 1; Edwards, "Romance," 39.

a consequence of their ecclesiology. Indeed, in giving a rationale for this work, Chapman described a variety of views which, he alleged, in both his own missional development *and* among the Christian constituency had resulted in a "go-slow campaign" on the work of evangelism.[43] The impact of such views, he contended, were significant. He wrote:

> The New Testament pulsates with the wonder of the spread of the gospel . . . We should reflect this same spirit . . . We should be those who long . . . to see the word of the Lord spread rapidly. However, a strange fashion has crept into our thinking of late which I believe has not helped us. People have drawn our attention . . . to the fact that one of the gifts which the Holy Spirit gives is that of the evangelist (Eph 4:11). However, the conclusion which many have drawn from this fact seems strange. They reason that since all men do not have this gift then only those who have this gift are obligated to be engaged in evangelism. It has had a *devastating result*. Suddenly everyone has decided they don't have the gift and are . . . absolved from engaging in the spread of the gospel!![44]

Hence, through the body of this popular work Chapman sought, among an array of objectives, to redress the obstacles to evangelism that had arisen as a result of Knox and Robinson's influential views. Beginning with the breadth of the Bible's exhortation to "make disciples," he argued:

---

43. In introducing *Know and Tell the Gospel*, 9–14, Chapman described the views of certain advocates who (1) believed they "had discovered a 'theological' reason . . . not to bother about evangelism," (2) multiplied uncertainty about the specific work of the "evangelist" and the work of "witnessing," and (3) contended that the work of the pastor/teacher was *not* that of evangelism and that the church meeting was an *inappropriate* place for evangelism. From this, it is evident that he was primarily interacting with the views of Robinson and Knox. Chapman himself perceived that Robinson's more "specialized" views on ministry had arisen, in part, as a by-product of the widespread reassessment of ministry roles that emerged as a result of the mid-century ecumenical movement. Indeed, in a 1978 interview in *Church Scene* magazine, noting the pervasive clericalism of the previous era which had received a degree of redress by the rediscovery of a "more biblical vision of the ministry of all believers," Chapman suggested that what followed this "in our part of the world" could be described as a "panic situation . . . if everybody has a ministry [then] what is the ministry of the minister? Some clergy got defensive; some questioned the idea and others [wondered] whether they were going to be displaced and become redundant." See Davis, "Lay Leader," 9. On the widespread reassessment of ministry roles that developed as a by-product of the Faith and Order Movement (a subset of the WCC) and the impact this had upon discussions within the ACA on questions relating to ordination and ministry, see Collins, *Diakonia Studies*, 165–70; *Ordination: Its Meaning*.

44. BDM Prayer Letter, March 1975, 1. These comments, while earlier than his 1980 work, reveal the emerging issue.

> In regard to the Great Commission, it ... seems likely that Jesus had more than just the eleven disciples in mind when he said ... "[Go] and make disciples of all nations" (Matthew 28:18–19). In Matthew's Gospel, the eleven are called disciples not because they are an exclusive group, but because they are prototype disciples ... Their commission is our commission. This would seem to be borne out by the promise of the Lord Jesus: "Lo I am with you always even to the close of the age" (Matthew 28:20). Since none of the eleven lived to the close of the age, we might presume that the promise, and also the command, is for all "disciples" to the end of the age.[45]

Additionally, Chapman cited various parallel exhortations in Luke's and John's Gospels. He noted that in Luke, Christ's commission was given to "the eleven and those with them" (Luke 24:33). From this he concluded that "according to Luke, the group who are 'witnesses' and who will presumably preach to the nations is larger than the eleven." Likewise, in John's Gospel, Chapman suggested that the picture was "even stronger in seeing that all believers will continue the work of Jesus in making God known." Quoting John 14:9–12, Chapman suggested that according to John:

> Anyone who believes will do the "works" that Jesus has been doing, only more so. In this passage, and in John's Gospel generally, this refers to Jesus' "work" of revealing the Father through what he has been saying and doing. The ongoing work of all believers will not be greater than what Jesus did in the sense that we will do even more amazing miracles, [but rather that] the full impact of the Father's love and his salvation will be seen even more starkly. After the cross, the revelation of the Father [made known through the testimony of believers] is even greater.[46]

In the same way, Chapman argued, "when we come to the book of Acts we see the expectation of the Gospels borne out." For "it was not just the apostles who spread the word. In fact, when the believers were scattered throughout Judea and Samaria by persecution in Acts 8, *they* went about preaching the word, while the *apostles* were left back in Jerusalem." Consequently, he argued, the New Testament did not envisage that it would be solely the job of the apostles to make disciples.[47]

Furthermore, regarding the correlation of the New Testament "evangelist" with the continuing work *of* evangelism, Chapman was equally

---

45. Chapman, *Know and Tell*, 43.
46. Chapman, *Know and Tell*, 43–44.
47. Chapman, *Know and Tell*, 44. Emphasis not original.

emphatic. Indeed, while he conceded the difficulty that scholars faced in isolating the identity of such figures, even so, such uncertainties *did not* discount the need for a widespread Christian witness. Regarding the ministry of "the evangelist," he wrote:

> In Ephesians 4:11, Paul tells us the ascended Christ gave gifts to his Church. Among these are the "evangelists." Knowing what their role was presents us no small difficulty. This arises because we hardly know anything about them. There are only three references to them in the NT. We know they are (or were) the gift of the victorious Christ to the Church (Ephesians 4:11). We know that Philip was one (Acts 21:8), and that Timothy is told to do the work of an evangelist (2 Tim 4:5)! . . . These three references do not give us a really clear picture of the role of the evangelist. He may have been an itinerant preacher [or] someone gifted in leading people to Christ. He may have been a NT extension of the OT prophet; or a person recognized [in] congregations whose job it was to go around proclaiming the gospel. We just aren't sure. However, even if we *were* more sure, would that mean . . . we could just leave evangelism to him (or her) while the rest of us played a supporting role? I remember well when this idea first came to us in the late 1960s . . . in Sydney. It was welcomed with open arms. Everyone immediately discovered they didn't have to bother unless they were "evangelists." They were equally certain . . . none of them was! It was the only time in . . . our country when we were left with no "evangelists." What a foolishness it all was. That there were people in the NT who were known as "evangelists" by no means excludes all Christians from having a role to play in . . . evangelism, any more than the existence of gifted . . . "teachers" in the NT means that all Christians don't have a role in teaching . . . and exhorting one another in the Lord. We are all to "speak the truth in love" to one another. We might say the same thing about the special gift of "faith" . . . in 1 Corinthians 12—it does not mean that "faith" is the special possession of only a few, but [merely] that some are particularly strong in this area.[48]

---

48. In the same way, in response to the assertion that the Bible provided a paucity of explicit "commands" that the Christian should "evangelize," Chapman suggested that the same could be said of the paucity of unambiguous "commands" that the Christian should "read the Bible and go to church regularly." Yet, he charged, "very few would argue against the idea . . . A simple direct command is not the only way the Bible instructs . . . The Christian standard is not to limit obedience down to what is barely commanded, and feel satisfied that we have fulfilled our obligation . . . there is ample encouragement . . . for Christians to be rolling up their sleeves to get involved in the

Regarding the evangelistic contours of the Christian *ekklēsia* Chapman was equally eager to safeguard the missiological potential of the local church gathering and the preaching office of the Christian minister-overseer. In this connection, highlighting Paul's emphatic exhortation to Timothy (the overseer of the church in Ephesus) that he should "do the work of an evangelist [and] discharge all the duties of [his] ministry" (2 Timothy 4:1–5), Chapman enquired:

> Why did Paul need to urge [Timothy] to do the work of an evangelist? . . . He is to do the work of an evangelist *because* he is a teacher of God's word. As a teacher he must be able to teach the *evangel—the word*—and so it is proper to urge him to do so. For too long we have driven a wedge between teaching as a function and preaching the gospel or evangelizing. Paul describes the way the Christians were converted in Colossae in these terms . . . they *heard, understood* and *learned* the gospel [Col. 1:5–7]. Epaphras taught it to them. He was the teacher/evangelist. The gospel cannot be *caught* unless it is *taught*. Timothy is urged to do the same. He is urged to "do the work of an evangelist, discharge all the duties of your ministry" (2 Tim. 4:5), because that was part of "preaching the word" (2 Tim. 4:1–2). [Christian] ministers, because of their teaching office, need to "do the work of an evangelist" as well as take responsibility to teach the congregation . . . [For] a pulpit ministry which teaches the necessity of evangelism but never does it, or which stresses the urgency of the call of the gospel but never practices it, in the end cannot be sustained. [Rather] evangelistic preaching will, like the New Testament be varied . . . and like a diamond which flashes light in every direction, the gospel in its many facets [will never be] monotonous.[49]

Regarding the teaching office of the pastor, Chapman suggested that if Paul could summarize his own pastoral ministry as being *simultaneously* a work of preaching "the whole will of God" (Acts 20:27) alongside the sustained work of preaching "repentance and faith in our Lord Jesus Christ" (Acts 20:21) then this provided strong evidence of Paul's desired shape for the Christian pastorate. Indeed, Chapman concluded, in the mind of the apostle there *was* no essential distinction between the objectives of an evangelistically oriented and regular preaching ministry. Rather, "whether a sermon was specifically evangelistic" or contained a diet of "teaching on the Christian life," if Paul sought to elicit the twin responses of "repentance and faith" as

---

work of the gospel." Chapman, *Know and Tell*, 45–46.

49. Chapman, *Know and Tell*, 96–99. Emphasis not original.

he discharged his own pulpit ministry, then so too must the contemporary Christian pastorate. Consequently, Chapman contended, the regular preaching ministry was to be a work of "evangelism every Sunday."[50]

Ultimately, as Chapman sought to address the particular implications of Knox and Robinson's views, he highlighted the importance of "love" as the driving motivation for all Christian activity and speech. Such an attitude was to be expressed in the sacrificial actions of Christians who sought "the good of the other" and demonstrated authentic discipleship to the world (1 John 3:16). It extended to the running of the church meeting so as to "build up" the believer *and* to ensure that the meeting was "intelligible and constructive, so that visitors may be drawn in and brought to acknowledge God" (1 Cor 14:23–25). It extended to the exercise *and* restriction of one's "liberty" so that no obstacle might be placed in another person's way (1 Cor 9:1–22). Whatever the context, Chapman argued, the essential shape of the Christian life was to be the pursuit of a lifestyle and patterns of speech that made it easy for people to hear and receive the good news of Jesus Christ.[51]

Evangelism and the Church: A Continuing Debate

As Knox and Robinson's scholarship began to be absorbed and responded to by Chapman and other leading figures, aspects of their work faced increasing scrutiny. The implication of their views for the church and evangelism was not the sole line of critique. Their work had undoubtedly brought clarity to matters of church polity and fresh perspectives to issues of denominationalism and its relationship to the local church. Yet, as scholars began to grapple with the particular nuances of their work, Knox and Robinson's somewhat incomplete explanation of the relationship *between* the heavenly (universal and continuous) and local (intermittent and discontinuous) nature of the church received particular attention.[52] Various contemporaries highlighted a range of language beyond the New Testament's use of *ekklēsia* (like "temple," "body," and "bride of Christ" imagery) which suggested an

---

50. Chapman, "Preaching that Converts," 168; Cf. the discussion of Chapman's preaching theology in chapter 4.

51. Of such a lifestyle Chapman wrote, it is a: "'sacrificial-flexible-identification' with all people . . . that they may come to salvation. It is simply love, and it is evangelistic in its thrust . . . That attitude which 'seeks and saves the lost' is to be the attitude of all Christians." Chapman, *Know and Tell*, 48–50. Alongside the wide distribution of *Know and Tell the Gospel*, its contents formed part of Chapman's lecturing material in Sydney seminaries, thus impacting a generation of students.

52. See Kuhn, "Ecclesiology," 128–35, 194–202, 212–16, 228–32, 252 for careful analysis of this shortcoming.

ongoing corporate reality to the earthly church *beyond* merely the "intermittent nature of the local gathering."[53] Others echoed the essence of Chapman's critique concerning the propensity of their scholarship to diminish the ministry of all believers in the work of evangelism, to devalue the missional potential of the church gathering, and to encourage congregations to become "inward-looking and preoccupied with their own worship and order."[54] However, by the late 1990s, aspects of Robinson's work were given renewed voice by the contentions of well-known Sydney evangelist and clergyman John Dickson. This was the result of Dickson's published scholarship alongside his participation in a debate through the pages of the diocesan magazine *Southern Cross*, around the question "Is every Christian an evangelist?" In a series of exchanges on this question Dickson sought to establish the "no" case, while David Mansfield (Chapman's successor at the Anglican Department of Evangelism) put forward the "yes" case.[55]

The echoes of Chapman's and Robinson's earlier contrasting positions in this 1990s debate are striking. Mansfield's opening remarks highlighted the "privileged responsibility" of every Christian to be involved in the work of evangelism, as opposed to being a work conferred only upon a select few. While he conceded that the Bible did not speak of a generalized "gift" of evangelism, nevertheless, it did say much regarding a way of life that urgently sought to win the lost.[56] Mansfield continued by highlighting the way

---

53. See especially Cole, "Church of God," 3–11; O'Brien, "Eschatological Entity," 88–119.

54. Note, in this vein, the critique of Foulkes, "Church and Evangelism," 26–33. Additionally, in a 1991 interchange (in the pages of *Southern Cross* magazine) between Robinson (then Archbishop of Sydney) and Bruce Harris (Professor of History at Macquarie University) a similar critique was aired. In a thrice-delivered paper Robinson laid out his customary caveats concerning the church and evangelism, which Harris sought to respectfully refute. Supporting his article with detailed textual analysis, Harris suggested that according to the New Testament, "communicating the faith was not regarded as the preserve of the very zealous or the officially designated evangelist. Christianity was supremely a lay movement, spread by informal missionaries. The clergy saw it as their responsibility too: bishops and presbyters . . . saw the propagation of the gospel as their prime concern." Robinson, "Gospel and Church"; Harris, "Gospel and Church."

55. Interview with David Mansfield, November 29, 2016. The request by the magazine's editor for a more public dialogue followed a comment made by Dickson (then an evangelist for the Northern Region of Sydney diocese) in the October 1997 issue of *Southern Cross* in which Dickson claimed that "he didn't believe we were all evangelists." *Southern Cross*, February 1998, 17.

56. Mansfield wrote: "I have never been taught that we are all evangelists . . . But I *have* been thankfully taught that we all have a *responsibility* to evangelize . . . Christian maturity means to become more and more like the Lord Jesus . . . Jesus came to seek and save the lost. If this is what God is like, then this is what we are to be like . . . Paul

in which the gift of the evangelist in Ephesians 4:11 occurred within a list of gifts bestowed for the preparation of God's people for works of service. From this he concluded that one of the functions of the evangelistic "specialist" was to equip others to be effective within their own evangelistic context and that such giftings (the evangelistic "specialist" and the "generalist") should work together within the local church for effective mission.[57]

Dickson replied that such a view represented a "one-tier" approach to God's mission that had become a "potential hindrance" to the gospel cause. Instead, Dickson advanced what he described as a "two-tier" approach. This stressed that while all Christians undoubtedly have a role to play in Christian "outreach," this did not necessarily involve every Christian in the ministry of "evangelism." Rather, Dickson advised, while "all Christians should engage in God's mission, they do so at *two significantly different levels*. Some will do evangelism and be called "proclaimers," while most will do non-evangelistic outreach and be called "partners."[58] In support of this view, Dickson drew attention to the apparent absence of explicit biblical exhortations that Christians "evangelize." He also reexamined a range of biblical texts (Phil 1:5; 2:16; Eph 6:14; 1 Cor 10:31–11:1; 1 Pet 2:9; Acts 8:4) that were traditionally used to urge Christians toward a "one-tier" approach. From this he concluded "evangelism" was chiefly a more technical activity of the specialist declaring the rule of the risen Christ. Somewhat provocatively, Dickson added that a one-tier approach was a view that was largely absent from church history.[59] Indeed, noting the range of activities by which Christians may participate in God's mission (like godly living, generosity, and cultivating the apt reply) such activities, he charged, were part of the ever-widening sphere of "outreach" for the committed Christian. By stressing the required evangelistic activity of the many, while leaving undeveloped the clearer gifts of the few, we create needless anxiety, Dickson advised. Instead, by differentiating the roles of all believers from the work of "evangelists," we will "free up a great mass of

---

says 'for I am not seeking my own good but the good of many so that they may be saved. Follow my example as I follow the example of Christ' (1 Cor 10:33–11:1). Christ, Paul, us. The one who came 'not to be served but to serve' (Mark 10:45) is followed by the one who made himself 'everyone's slave to win as many as possible' (1 Cor 9:19) . . . He is to be followed by us . . . just as . . . Jesus . . . called us the light of the world (Matt 5:14) whose light is to shine before others that they may see our good works and glorify our Father in Heaven." So Mansfield, "Are We All Evangelists?," 17.

57. Mansfield, "Are We All Evangelists?," 17.

58. Dickson, "Players," 21–23.

59. Indeed, surveying a range of historic ecclesial periods in which a "one tier" approach was said to be unknown, Dickson supposed that such a view had only arisen in the last forty years in the Sydney diocese! Dickson, "Players," 23.

currently guilty and anxious Christians, enabling them to play their part in God's mission with renewed vigor and optimism; and we will spur on the many evangelists in our congregations who have been kept hidden under the huge blanket of a one-tier view of outreach." While the Bible obliged all Christians to be engaged in a range of "outreach" activities, Dickson concluded, "evangelism is not one of them." Consequently, "few Christians will operate in the first tier of God's mission."[60]

In the following edition of the *Southern Cross* magazine Mansfield replied to Dickson, offering further reflection and critique. He highlighted certain key omissions in Dickson's treatment of the biblical texts (Phil 1:14; Eph 6:17) which suggested that a pervasive evangelistic witness beyond merely the "specialists" *was* characteristic of New Testament ministry.[61] He also critiqued Dickson's claim that a so-called "one-tier" approach was "suffocating" the "gifted" evangelists and suggested that such an approach would, in fact, encourage them. Primarily, however, Mansfield suggested that Dickson's view failed to give appropriate regard to the overall "panorama" of the Bible and its implications for Christian missional resolve. For at the heart of the Bible's account, Mansfield argued, lay the "consuming passion of a relentlessly loving creator" and a "message of forgiveness to be communicated to . . . the world." In light of this, he charged, how "could the person who was once dead, but is now alive long for anything less than to bring that . . . message to [others]? The very nature of the Gospel implies that those who enjoy its benefits will want to pass them around."[62]

Dickson eventually pursued his synthesis at both an academic and popular level. This ensured that the long-running discussion received renewed attention well into the opening decade of the new century. Consequently, via a historical and philological examination of Greek, Jewish, and Christian

---

60. Dickson, "Players," 23. The resonance of Robinson's thought in Dickson's work is strikingly evident. As noted, Robinson had *elevated* the gospel to be a "proclamation" of a specific and authoritative nature and *limited* the identity of the "evangelist" to be that of a "qualified office bearer" "sent" to proclaim it. Robinson also contended that while many in the New Testament churches "did not exercise the gift of evangelism" they became "partners" with such missionary emissaries by the offering of "material help" and "encouragement." The responsibility of the church member was primarily to bear "witness" through "conversation" and "deeds" that reflected Christ—a pattern that Dickson echoed. Robinson, "Doctrine of the Church," 106–12.

61. For example, on the view advanced by various New Testament scholars (notably E. E. Ellis in 1978) that suggested Paul's reference to "the brothers" in Philippians 1:14 was in fact a quasi-technical term for Paul's "co-workers" and could not be used to justify a widespread (but rather a restricted) evangelistic witness, see Fee, *Paul's Letter*, 113–16; cf. Ellis, "Paul," 3–22. This was a view that Dickson himself reprised in his later academic work.

62. Mansfield, "Privilege and Responsibility," 17–18.

sources, Dickson amplified his claim that Christian "mission" encompassed a wide range of outreach-related activities, while "evangelism" referred almost exclusively to the "foundational proclamation" of the gospel by specialist New Testament emissaries.[63] This scholarship was later published in popular form (*Promoting the Gospel*, 2005) in which Dickson reiterated his distinction between the work of gospel "promotion" (by the church body) and that of gospel "proclamation" (by the evangelistic specialist), and emphasized "evangelism" to be properly only the preserve of the few.[64]

Naturally, reactions to Dickson's provocative views among the evangelical community were varied. Like the reception of Robinson's earlier work, some applauded Dickson for releasing Christians from the "guilt" they carried in not possessing the passion of the "door-knockers and street preachers,"[65] and for unburdening them from doing that which they felt ill-equipped to do (evangelism) while urging them to participate in that which they did (varied service).[66] Others celebrated Dickson's achievement in addressing an important scholarly lacuna and in underscoring "the range of activities" that were needed to establish an "effective" Christian witness in the modern world.[67]

However, not all were convinced of Dickson's position. Against this backdrop, further editions of Chapman's *Know and Tell the Gospel* were published that were intended to reinforce the "traditional evangelical view" of evangelism. Chapman was familiar with the substance of Dickson's position and aware that such editions would be seen as something of "a response" to Dickson's views.[68] Hence, alongside his customary exhortations in support

63. Dickson, *Mission-Commitment*, 133–52, 311. In a supporting academic article during this period, Dickson surveyed the use of the εὐαγγελ word group within Greek, Jewish, and Christian literature. He concluded that this word group was used to connote "a message or an act of proclamation" of previously unknown news by "the εὐαγγελος" (the official messenger). Thus, he advised, a "broad-ranging" use of this word group to describe speech employed in "missionary *and* congregational" settings could not be supported. Dickson, "Gospel as News," 212–30.

64. Dickson, *Promoting the Gospel*. Dickson's scholarship did arise in the context of a wider academic debate on the role of the New Testament congregations in the Pauline mission. For an excellent summary of this debate as well as critical engagement with Dickson's views (including the contention that the Pauline congregations *were* engaged in "spreading the word of the Lord," 1 Thess 1), see Ware, *Mission*, 1–22.

65. Michael Frost, "Testimonials," in Dickson, *Promoting the Gospel*, 221.

66. Interview with Alan Stewart, December 7, 2016.

67. I. H. Marshall, "Testimonials," in Dickson, *Promoting the Gospel*, 221; Ware, *Mission*, 5.

68. Appendix 4, JCCPP/PUB#1, Correspondence from Matthias Media to Chapman, August 29, 1998. This correspondence between Tony Payne (editorial director of Matthias Media) and Chapman contains a draft chapter 4 ("Who Should Do the

of a widespread missional culture, these editions emphasized "love" as the key motivator in Christian evangelism as opposed to a "command-driven" approach that looked for specific "biblical imperatives" to evangelize instead.[69] Chapman's revised work was supplemented by contributions from a range of local evangelical leaders. Responding to Dickson's scholarship, they emphasized the inadequacy of a mission strategy that promoted exemplary living without a corresponding need for broadscale evangelistic "speech" and criticized the premise of a command-driven approach.[70] In time, the voices of a new generation of influential English and Australian evangelists such as Rico Tice and Sam Chan (who had each been mentored by Chapman) weighed in on this long-running debate. While their engagement with Dickson's scholarship (and by implication that of Robinson's) was more implicit than overt, their contributions did evidence an innate familiarity with the questions that such scholarship had raised.[71] Consequently, while Tice and Chan acknowledged the varying shades of evangelistic gifting and confidence that existed across the Christian community, they nevertheless contended that evangelism was an activity of verbal witness that was the privilege and responsibility of all Christians. Reminiscent of Chapman's earlier emphasis, Chan (*Evangelism in a Skeptical World*, 2018) defined evangelism as the communication of the *euangelion*—the good news about Jesus Christ as Lord—to believers *and* nonbelievers in a range of linguistic modes and contexts in the hope that God would use such means to elicit repentance and obedience to Jesus as Lord. Chan suggested that the act of "communicating the gospel" (conveyed by the New Testament verb *euangelizo*) incorporated a broad range of speech activities. Consequently, "evangelism" could be conceived in a "broad" sense as the process of establishing *and* maturing believers in the gospel (Col 1:28). However, in a "narrower" sense, he added, evangelism related specifically to communicating the gospel to nonbelievers

---

Work of Evangelism?") of Chapman's revised *Know and Tell the Gospel* (2005). It reveals Chapman's familiarity with the arguments advanced by Dickson and their collective desire to put forward a considered "response."

69. Chapman, *Know and Tell* (2005), 48–50. A "deontic" command-driven approach motivates Christian behavior on the basis of duty and obligation. Cameron, *Joined Up Life*, 20. Such an approach was considered central to Dickson's view. Appendix 4, JCCPP/PUB#1. Matthias Media to Chapman.

70. See the series of interchanges in the *Briefing*: Perkins, "Danger of Living"; Payne, "Ethics of Everyday Evangelism"; Windsor, "Speech and Salvation."

71. International evangelicals had become aware of the contours of this more localized debate and the questions it posed regarding evangelistic responsibility. However, the debate had not gained the same profile nor exerted the same influence in popular English and American evangelical circles as it had in Australia. Interview with Rico Tice, January 17, 2017.

and urging them to follow Christ.[72] In the same way, while highly aware of the more technical aspects of evangelism, Tice (*Honest Evangelism*, 2015) primarily emphasized the motivational and methodological elements of evangelism. "God is the great evangelist, the great seeker and finder of people," he wrote, "and he's called his followers to the same pursuit and . . . emotion."[73] Indeed, Tice conceded, in a world of increasing opposition to the gospel message, few Christians would find the work of evangelism to be easy. Yet, conscious of the growing spiritual hunger of a secular world and drawing motivation from a concern for Christ's glory and the certainty of the coming age, Tice issued an impassioned plea for Christians to "cross the painline." "Evangelism is not about saying everything, or saying it eloquently," he stated, but "if you've explained [Christ] to someone, however hard you found it and however haltingly you said it . . . you've preached Christ as he asks you to. The rest is up to God."[74]

Evangelism and the Church: Interrelated Theological and Social Concerns

What then is to be made of this seemingly prolix and idiosyncratic debate that occupied leading evangelicals over the course of half a century?[75] It would be easy to categorize such a dialogue on the church and evangelism as the interests of a belligerent evangelical minority and to relegate such questions to the periphery of historic Christian experience and concern.[76] However, there is little doubt that a concern for the church's advancement has been one of the defining hallmarks not only of historic Evangelicalism but of historic Christian orthodoxy. Leading commentators have suggested that a concern for Christian mission connotes one of the primary

---

72. Chan, *Skeptical World*, 13–38; cf. the resonance of Chapman's earlier work in *Know and Tell*, 16–28, 35–57, 71–84.

73. Tice, *Honest Evangelism*, 11; cf. Tice, *Christianity Explored*, 9–66 on Tice's detailed evangelistic content and method.

74. Tice's confidence to "cross the pain-line" was a confidence he credits to Chapman. Interview with Rico Tice, January 17, 2017. Tice's *Honest Evangelism* was considered by some to be the *Know and Tell the Gospel* for a new century. Chan's work was also received enthusiastically in evangelical Australian and American leadership circles. Tice, *Honest Evangelism*, 1, 25–40; Chan, *Skeptical World*, 1–2.

75. Robinson's initial scholarship on "the church" and its related doctrines was published in 1959.

76. Note the sentiment of commentators such as Porter, *Anglicanism*, 72–73 in this regard.

markers of Christian health[77] and has represented the essence of "original, apostolic, New Testament Christianity" across the length of the Christian era.[78] Others have observed, in this connection, that within Christianity's "philosophical structure is the idea of universality—that the message it proclaims . . . should be shared with all peoples" such that across its "history are myriad examples of Christians being sent or else informally crossing geographic or cultural barriers and founding new groups of believers wherever they go."[79] Moreover, as the reformer John Calvin observed in an earlier period of the importance of Christian missional fervor: "nothing could be more inconsistent concerning the nature of faith than that deadness which would lead a man to disregard his brethren and keep the light of knowledge . . . choked up in his own breast. The greater the eminence which any man has received from his calling, so much the more diligently ought he to labor to enlighten others."[80]

A concern for the church's missional advancement is therefore historically uncontroversial. The contours of this particular debate, however, ought rather to be seen as the product of a set of dynamics that converged within the Australian environment (in particular) in the mid-century. The mid-century ecumenical movement and development of a constitution for the Anglican Church of Australia undoubtedly created the conditions necessary for fresh reflection on the nature of the church.[81] Added to this within the Australian (and particularly Sydney) evangelical environment was the brand of stimulating postwar scholarship exemplified by Knox and Robinson. Given the provocative and heuristic approach they pursued, it is unsurprising their work had the propensity to generate such debate.[82] Overlaid onto these dynamics was the reality of a historically robust local missiological culture. Indeed, as previously noted, Sydney Anglicanism *was* undoubtedly characterized by such a culture. However, it was also a culture which itself was emerging from an implicit dependence on the bulwarks of historic Anglo-Christian identity and seeking to confront the rising challenges of a secular world.[83] That questions relating to the breadth of Christian evangelistic responsibility came to be so contentious in this environment would

77. McGrath, *Evangelicalism*, 55–56.
78. Stott, *Evangelical Truth*, 16.
79. Robert, *Christian Mission*, 1.
80. Calvin, *Commentary on Isaiah*, 2:3, 94.
81. See Kärkkäinen, *Introduction to Ecclesiology*, 7–20 for discussion of the relative paucity of historic ecclesiological reflection and its late-century resurgence.
82. Note the discussion of their scholarly method in chapter 2.
83. See the extensive discussion of these dynamics in chapter 5 and Chapman's role in redressing them.

not only seem to confirm the strength of its missiological fervor. It would also seem to demonstrate this culture's emergence into a period in which questions that were once implicit (like "How should the church be advanced in 'Christian Australia'?") had now become more complex and overt (like "What *did* the Bible say about Christian witness and how should this be conducted in a rapidly changing world?").

The result of this confluence of factors was that as Knox and Robinson began to apply their heuristic scholarship to the changing mid-century world, what began as an enquiry into the nature of the church soon became refracted into a set of wider interrelated concerns. These included the nature, purpose, and mission of the church; the identity of those charged with the missional advancement of the church and the breadth of the Holy Spirit's administration of such gifts; the appropriate location and purpose for the use of such gifts; and the nature of the wider church's involvement in such missional activity. Knox and Robinson answered the first three of these propositions in a more restrictive sense, while answering the fourth more expansively. That is, while not wishing to discourage evangelism *per se*, their strong congregationalism and more circumscribed view of "the church's mission" nevertheless led them to express a restricted view of evangelistic gifting as an activity occurring outside "the church" by "specialist" emissaries, a restricted view of the use and purpose of such gifts *within* the local church, and a correspondingly expansive view of the *non-verbal* partnership needed across the church body for effective mission to occur.

Chapman's response might be characterized differently. Indeed, given the convictions that underlay his strenuous evangelistic activism, Chapman answered all four propositions expansively. That is, given his expansive view of the church's mission, he expressed an expansive view of evangelistic gifting as an activity occurring *within and beyond* the local church by specialists *and* generalists, and a corresponding belief that for effective evangelism to occur, widespread proclamation and non-verbal gospel partnership *alongside* the ethical witness of Christians was required. Such a view Chapman believed to be no more than "original, apostolic, New Testament Christianity." It was a view that he championed both in relation to the scholarship of Knox and Robinson and as a matter of ongoing concern.[84] Chapman was mindful of the challenges of personal evangelistic practice and the wisdom required for its effective regular execution. In this vein he urged that in effective evangelism the doctrines of creation and redemption needed to operate in a delicate unison. Such an approach was

---

84. Stott, *Evangelical Truth*, 16. Cf. Chapman's long-standing advocacy for this view in this and earlier chapters.

careful to honor a person's humanity and to treat them with respect and compassion. A robust theology of divine sovereignty was also key. This fostered a prayerfulness in the evangelistic exchange that looked for the apposite moment to speak.[85] Yet, Chapman was adamant that a widespread culture of evangelism not only reflected the New Testament pattern but was urgently needed in the modern world. "In a time like our own," he stated, "when the number of people who turn to Christ seem so few . . . we might long that God would raise up clever, eloquent and persuasive evangelists!" Yet, "what we must not do is lose our nerve on the gospel," he charged, for "it is the way God will demonstrate the Spirit's power!"[86] In order to address the missional challenges of the modern era, it was as vital as ever that evangelism was regarded as a way of life. "It is the privilege [and] the responsibility of every Christian," he argued, "to be engaged in evangelism, according to each one's gifts and opportunities . . . every situation is one" in which both "by the way we live" and "by speaking," the Christian may witness to the fact that "Jesus is Lord."[87] Most importantly, however, within the array of activities the church could pursue to fulfill its mission mandate, he urged that it must *not* lose sight of the fact that the power of the gospel lay ultimately in its *verbal* proclamation. Of this reality, he wrote:

> The work of Christ is applied to us *through the gospel*. Paul reminds the Ephesians that it was when they heard the gospel and believed it that they were included in Christ (1:13). There may be many things which cause a person to want to listen to the gospel. It may be the kindness of a Christian friend, or the winsomeness of a life lived before them, but in the end *it is the gospel which saves them*. There is no way I can live my life so that a person will understand Christ has died and risen again for them. They may perceive they are sinful, but they cannot perceive the remedy unless they are told. Pre-evangelism is important, but it is not evangelism. Bridge-building is for "crossing the gap." It is not an end in itself. It was when the Ephesians heard the gospel

---

85. Cf. Chapman, *Know and Tell*, 123–206 on evangelistic practice. Regarding Chapman's own nuanced practice of such convictions, Rico Tice recounts the occasion when Chapman spent an entire day playing golf with Tice's father. As a senior executive in the tobacco industry, Tice's father expected a clergyman to berate him for this and was apprehensive about the experience. However, Chapman spent the day asking Tice's father about his life and work and appeared highly informed in conversation. He elicited laughter from Tice's father in a way that was unexpected. Consequently, Tice was able to give Chapman's books to his father who, in reading them, came to faith in his seventies. Interview with Rico Tice, January 17, 2017.

86. *Preaching Christ Newsletter*, August–October 1992.

87. Chapman, *Know and Tell*, 93–94.

that they [possessed] "redemption through his blood" . . . the forgiveness of sins by putting their trust in Christ. We are called to live for the praise of his glory. Part of that will be through speaking the gospel . . . *Evangelism is speaking.*[88]

Conclusion

This chapter has explored one of the more intriguing by-products of Sydney Anglicanism's robust missiological and theological tradition, alongside Chapman's place at the vanguard of a stimulating debate that emerged as a result. Arising out of the complexities of the mid-century ecumenical movement and the response of leading figures (D. B. Knox and D. W. B. Robinson) to this movement, the question of the nature and mission of the church received increasing focus. In responding to the perceived excesses of this movement, one of the inadvertent results of Knox and Robinson's scholarship was the promotion of an essentially limited view of the church's mission and the work of evangelism in the local church. Consistent with the portrait that has emerged in previous chapters, the chapter demonstrates Chapman's advocacy for a widespread missional culture among evangelical churches. In the face of such a scholarly challenge to this agenda Chapman sought to reestablish "the church" as a legitimate context for evangelism and to promote a view of the church's mission in which both leaders *and* members played an active role.

88. *Preaching Christ Newsletter*, May–July 1988.

Part IV

Pugilist and Pioneer

8

Semper Reformanda[1]

The Gospel, The Church, and a Changing World

> "The gospel and its growth is what animates Sydney Anglicans . . . we are evangelicals first and Anglicans second. The gospel is our passion, our song, our motive force. The gospel explains us."—Tony Payne[2]

ON THE MORNING OF March 13, 1934, Howard W. K. Mowll was enthroned as the third Archbishop of Sydney in a service at St. Andrew's Anglican Cathedral.[3] On the day of consecration, the cathedral was crowded to capacity. Two thousand people filled every portion of the building while another thousand joined the many well-wishers outside in the square. Governor Sir Philip Game and Lord Mayor Parker were present. They were flanked by a complement of military and academic figures, together with a host of provincial bishops and Sydney clergy in one of the largest and most representative congregations to have assembled in the historic edifice.[4] Conducted according to the rites of the 1662 *Book of Common*

---

1. The complete phrase *ecclesia reformata, semper reformanda, secundum verbum dei* ("The reformed church, always reforming, under the word of God") is frequently cited as a slogan that captures the essence of the reforming impulse in every generation. See Atherstone, "Semper Reformanda," 31.

2. Payne, "Magic Potion."

3. Archbishop Mowll was the third Archbishop of Sydney and the sixth Diocesan of the See of Sydney. The title of Archbishop of Sydney was first bestowed upon Archbishop William Saumarez Smith (1890–1909).

4. "Archbishop Mowll Enthroned," 13.

Prayer, the enthronement was dignified and measured. At 10:35 a.m. Mowll knocked three times on the cathedral's great west door where he was admitted by Bishop S. J. Kirby and led in procession to the cathedral chancel to be handed his pastoral staff. Following a shortened form of morning service that included choral liturgy, hymns, and ordered prayers, Mowll took up his text of 2 Corinthians 4:5. Seizing upon the diocesan and imperial heritage that was collectively theirs to maintain, Mowll stressed that by the workings of the "principles of Christianity" throughout the British Empire's civil and ecclesiastical interests, they had each become stewards of a trust that was instrumental to the flourishing of all humanity. Urging that their conduct, in their many civil and ecclesiastical vocations, should not proclaim themselves but Jesus Christ their Lord, Mowll invited the congregation to stand silently as they each rededicated themselves to the service of Christ. That same evening, Mowll arrived to a capacity public reception at Sydney's Town Hall. Welcomed with sustained applause by a sea of societal, political, and clerical leaders, a distinguished twenty-five-year archiepiscopacy had begun.[5]

Some sixty-seven years later, a very different consecration and welcome to the See of Sydney would unfold. On the evening of Friday June 29, 2001, the Rev. Dr. Peter Jensen was consecrated as the eighth Archbishop of Sydney in the same cathedral. With Governor Bashir and Prime Minister Howard present amidst a capacity crowd, the occasion was similarly ebullient. Conducted according to the rites of the 1978 *Australian Prayer Book*, the service exuded respect for the weight of ecclesiastical office being assumed. However, it also bespoke a simplicity symbolic of a process of wider ecclesiastical change that had taken place in the intervening years. The robed archbishop was led to the cathedral chancel. This was followed by a ceremony punctuated with choral items, prayers, hymns, and modern songs.[6] However, instead of the episcopal cope, miter, and staff, a Bible was symbolically placed in Jensen's hands. Then, by the laying on of hands Jensen was instated into his episcopal ministry of shepherding Christ's flock by the preaching of God's word.[7] Perhaps even more indicative of the wider changes that had transpired, however, was the official welcome for Jensen in August 2001. Four thousand cheering well-wishers attended the occasion at Sydney's State Sports Centre. Performances from musician Colin Buchanan and a 250-strong choir were interwoven with an impromptu "rap" performance by Jensen himself. Assuming a "Blues Brothers" persona in dark

---

5. "Archbishop Mowll Enthroned," 13; Loane, *Archbishop Mowll*, 132–33.
6. Burke, "New House of God," 7.
7. Cleary, "Sunday Nights."

sunglasses and a suit, Jensen joined Buchanan in a "rap" performance of Isaiah 53:6.[8] Of greatest significance on this occasion, however, was Jensen's impassioned address. "I do not believe I have been brought to this position [to] acquiesce silently in the passing away of Anglican Christianity in this region," Jensen stated. "Church-going Anglicans in Sydney . . . are becoming invisible . . . We are poised to become exotic . . . How will our neighbors hear the gospel from us?" An assumed imperialism was absent from this episcopal address. Nor was there any presumption about the Christian fabric of society at large. Rather, Jensen advised, if Sydney Anglicans wished to have a "deep impact" upon their society, then, in a bid to win many thousands of Sydneysiders to Christ, perseverance in the proclamation of the gospel and a commitment to change at all levels of diocesan and parish life constituted the pressing and overwhelming need.[9]

The era between these two archiepiscopal inaugurations was an era that witnessed a revolution not only in the fabric of Western society but in the worship styles and practices of churches throughout the Western world.[10] Until the mid-twentieth century the liturgical rites of the Anglican Communion had rested on a tradition of carefully crafted formularies that stretched back to Reformation times.[11] Indeed, while the framers of the 1662 *Book of Common Prayer* had acknowledged the desire for flexibility to accommodate changing stylistic needs, by the mid-twentieth century the majority of Anglican churches had strayed little from the 1662 language and forms. This resulted in the use of forms of Anglican expression that had stood more or less unaltered within Britain and her colonies for over three hundred years.[12] The period after the Second World War marked the subsequent withdrawal of British oversight from its colonies and a movement within receptor cultures towards indigenous patterns of leadership and expression. Such factors combined with a rapidly changing culture and the impact of statistical decline in mainline churches to fuel a widespread movement for ministry and liturgical reform.[13]

Within the Anglican Church of Australia, Sydney Anglicans were considered pace setters in this process of change. Over time, the adoption of new clerical attire, service forms, and music became commonplace

8. *Southern Cross*, September 2001, 1.

9. Archbishop Dr. Peter Jensen, Address, "Deep Impact Rally," cited in *Sydney Diocesan Yearbook*, 2002, 376.

10. Spinks, "Liturgy," 471.

11. Old, *Reformation*, 149–52; Avis, "Prayer Book Use," 128–130.

12. Spinks, "Liturgy," 471.

13. O'Farrell, "General History," 66; Ward, "Colonialism," 86; Milikan, "Australian Identity," 30; Chapman, "International Relations," 355.

in Sydney churches and the outward expression of conservative faith in corporate worship took on a very different form from that of a previous generation. Reflecting back on this somewhat turbulent period, in 2007 Archbishop Jensen observed that the decline of formality in worship had been an inescapable cost of the "need to be missionaries" to their culture. While missteps in this process were regrettable, he contended, they were nevertheless signs of life—akin to the messiness of the "teenager's bedroom"—from which there could be no going back.[14] Indeed, given the uniformity that had previously typified Anglican worship, such changes in Sydney and elsewhere might rightly be regarded as the "remaking of Anglicanism" for the modern world.[15] Once again, John Chapman played an active and important role in this remaking.

The following chapter thus traces key features of this movement to contextualize worship and ministry practices within Australian (particularly Sydney) Anglicanism and the role played by Chapman and other leading figures in this process. It is important at the outset not to claim too much for Chapman in terms of the role that he *or any single individual* played in this process of reform. Indeed, as a complex ecclesiastical entity the Sydney diocese itself has been described in Churchillian terms as a "riddle wrapped in a mystery inside an enigma."[16] It consists of approximately 270 autonomous parishes. The government of the diocese is divided between the archbishop who shares his power with a democratic and independently minded synod.[17] Meeting annually, the synod is modelled on the Westminster parliamentary system. Renowned as a chamber of vigorous debate, success in attaining policy or legislative objectives within this forum has often required the presence of active caucusing, wide procedural knowledge, and the deployment of speakers proficient in debate. Indeed, on account of the somewhat diffuse and independent nature of the diocese's episcopal, parish,

---

14. Archbishop P. F. Jensen, Presidential Address, 2008 *Sydney Yearbook*.
15. Null and Yates, "Manifesto," 186–201; Lewis, "Introduction," 1–8.
16. Ballantine-Jones, *Political Factor*, 31.
17. The Synod consists of a host of clerical and lay members (rectors, parish representatives, and others appointed by the archbishop) who in turn elect the representatives of approximately fifty committees that manage the diocese's wider financial and administrative interests. These fifty bodies comprise a total membership of well over six hundred people and often consist of volunteers who exercise significant leadership in professional life. These bodies include the Standing Committee of the Synod, the Property Trust, regional councils, church schools, university colleges, disciplinary tribunals, and ministry organizations such as Moore College, Anglicare, and Youthworks. This is supplemented by the work of committees that manage the diocese's financial and administrative arrangements. For extensive analysis, see Ballantine-Jones, *Political Factor*, 21–40.

and administrative arrangements, the attainment of desired policy goals and objectives in this context has consistently resisted an expressly *coercive* or *centralized approach*. Rather, it has necessitated the ability to *woo, persuade, and inspire*.[18] Given the constraints of such an environment, the contribution of any single political or reforming figure must not be unduly stressed. At the same time, Chapman *was* a figure who wielded a significant public profile. While he never held an episcopal office, throughout his formal ministry in the diocese Chapman exercised a significant extra-parochial leadership presence that spanned three archiepiscopates. He occupied the high-profile directorship of the diocese's Department of Evangelism (1969–93) and operated as a key figure within important diocesan and extra-diocesan political and decision-making forums.[19] The contours of Chapman's public ministry (as outlined in previous chapters) placed him in regular and extended contact with the clergy of the diocese *and* numerous other national and international Anglican and evangelical denominational groups. This led to the cultivation of long-standing collegial friendships with Christian leaders of many persuasions. Indeed, in the context of Chapman's wide preaching sojourns (in which he preached as many as 7,500 sermons across five continents) and in his receipt of hospitality from these colleagues, Chapman developed an extensive web of relationships with leaders across the evangelical world. These leaders not only benefited from Chapman's preaching in the context of their own ministries but regularly sought his counsel on a range of theological, missiological, and pastoral concerns.[20] In an era before

18. In his study of the Sydney diocese (1966–2013) Ballantine-Jones details three factors that precipitate the need for a *persuasive* political approach in this environment, namely: 1) the operational independence of virtually all of the diocese's entities (parishes and major organizations) is such that it is difficult for bishops and administrative leaders to initiate major programs without their co-operation; 2) the distribution of power between the Synod and the Archbishop means that when they disagree over policy matters, an essential stalemate occurs (given that neither can exercise sufficient authority to overcome the independence of the diocese's constituent entities); and 3) the public-service-like culture of "the center" (with its committee-run structures) creates inefficiencies that often work against the achievement of the objectives being sought. Sydney Archbishops themselves, he notes, exercise influence over central committees and organizations as well as regulations relating to worship and statutory services. They exercise influence in the appointment of parish incumbents and retain the right of veto over the Synod's legislative decisions. Yet even their influence remains *primarily* spiritual and persuasive—a reality that has frustrated the programs of numerous archiepiscopacies. Ballantine-Jones, *Political Factor*, 22–23, 38–39.

19. Chapman was a member of the Moore College Council (1969–1992), Sydney Diocesan Standing Committee (1975–1993), the Australian General Synod (1973–1993), and was a Canon of the St. Andrew's Cathedral Chapter (1975–2012).

20. One might even say that, while his ministry did not share the same function of formal oversight, Chapman exercised something of an informal "missiological-bishopric"

the internet and social media, the extent of Chapman's presence across this array of forums thus forged an influential platform from which he was able to effect widely clerical conviction and resolve. In addition to these informal lines of influence, within the various political contexts in which Chapman engaged he was also widely regarded as a figure of substantial influence. A cultivated ability to debate and carry opinion shaped his reputation in such arenas. Indeed, it was precisely Chapman's ability to *woo, persuade, and inspire* that marked his contribution as being particularly effectual in the very fora wherein a capacity for persuasion was required.[21]

Consequently, while an exhaustive account of Chapman's legacy as a reforming figure is not possible, this chapter charts key aspects of Chapman's work in promoting widespread and often contentious ministry reforms. This includes changes in relation to liturgy, service forms and attire, alongside various interventions in areas such as lay presidency of Holy Communion and women's ordination. In so doing the chapter assesses the principles by which Chapman and other leading figures sought to reshape Anglicanism according to the missiological needs of a changing world.

Politician and Provocateur

Politics in the Blood

Chapman was undoubtedly a man with politics in his blood. As noted, Chapman was raised in an intelligent working-class Sydney home that extolled the virtues of "Australian Labor" to the back teeth.[22] Marching his sons to hear politicians campaigning from the back of trucks or allowing the wireless parliamentary broadcast to reverberate throughout the home, Chapman's father Albury had instilled in him an innate fascination with political exchange.[23] Such a fondness for the rhetoric of public disputation left its mark on Chapman's homelife and his emerging career. Quick-witted family banter often evolved rapidly into vigorous discussion of important concerns. Indeed, born and raised at a time when political ideologies were profoundly reshaping the course of nations, such looming

---

to extensive networks of clergy in Australia and abroad. See, in particular, Appendix 5, *Historic Speaking Engagements* for insight into the breadth and extent of such clerical connections.

21. Interview with Rev. Dr. Paul Barnett, December 2, 2016.
22. Interview with David Mansfield, November 29, 2016.
23. Jensen and Freney, "Majoring on the Majors."

realities were a common focus in family debate.[24] Chapman also saw the process of dialectical exchange as something of a tool in the formation of theological and personal judgments. Discussions between Chapman and his many ministry colleagues were often characterized by energetic theological dialogue and debate. Chapman held his convictions strongly. However, if it could be shown convincingly from Scripture that another position had greater merit, Chapman was readily willing to change his point of view.[25] Indeed, in preparing for his own speaking and ministry engagements, Chapman frequently sought the opinion of a wide network of colleagues. Pushing, prodding, and wrestling in an animated contest of minds, Chapman would press relentlessly (sometimes exhaustively) on the details of a policy or theological matter until he had understood to his satisfaction the nuance of the issue at hand.[26] Such a schooling in the dialectical art of opinion-shaping undoubtedly forged in Chapman a robustness and mental intensity, and a cultivated instinct for the rhetorical and logical elements required to build a case.

Chapman's fascination with the political process was to be an absorption that continued throughout his life. In addition to a strikingly disciplined daily devotional life, one of Chapman's other personal habits was his pattern of seeking to digest what was occurring across a variety of secular and ecclesiastical political forums. Indeed, not unlike his father before him, Chapman took an almost recreational interest in the dynamics of the political state of play. This is illustrated in an extended series of letters written by Chapman to colleagues ministering in the United States in the 1980s. In an era before the rapid dissemination of news via internet media, Chapman wrote regularly (often from across the globe) to convey theological and pastoral exhortations alongside reflections on the state of domestic and international political and ecclesiastical life. This included commentary on an array of policy and procedural developments in Australian state and federal parliaments, alongside various state and federal electoral contests, and the fortunes of their leading figures. Additionally, Chapman reflected on the progress of numerous national and international ecclesiastical forums with which he was engaged. This included developments in the Sydney and Australian Anglican synods alongside the challenges facing evangelicals in Europe, North America, and Asia with whom he interacted. Such reflections reveal a figure with wide

---

24. Interview with David Mansfield, November 29, 2016; Bongiorno, "Search for a Solution," 64–65; Darian-Smith, "World War 2," 88–90.

25. See the recollections of Steve Abbott and Phillip Jensen in Mansfield, *Chappo Collection*, 164–65.

26. See the recollections of Dr. Peter O'Brien in Mansfield, *Chappo Collection*, 192.

ministry influence and an appreciation for the elements needed to champion change in an array of political contexts.[27]

Party Whip and Anchorman

Alongside Chapman's cultivated appreciation for the art of political theatre, he also discovered a personal aptitude as a leader in the process of change. Indeed, while he eschewed the language of "strategic planning" that came to dominate 1980s and 1990s corporate (and increasingly ecclesial) organizational culture, Chapman's approach to leadership nevertheless exuded the attributes of a "sharp, shrewd, strategic practitioner."[28] Such attributes were sharpened considerably by his early ministry forays in the diocese of Armidale. Following the success of his early activities in this rural diocese—a diocese that exuded a socially oriented formal Anglicanism—Chapman became "fixed with a vision" to see evangelical conviction flourish widely in this diocese. Initially convinced that such an objective would require a long-term commitment, Chapman began to promote widely the needs of this diocese and to actively solicit evangelical clergy to minister alongside him there.[29] Rapidly gaining the confidence of Bishop Moyes, Chapman was granted increasing influence. This resulted in a stream of Moore College trained clergy commencing ministry across the diocese in the 1960s.[30] Indeed, foreshadowing the role Chapman would later play across numerous other forums, the peripatetic nature of

---

27. This extended series of letters (1985–1989) was written primarily to Chapman's younger colleague, Adrian Lane, who at that time was studying at Gordon-Conwell Seminary in the United States. Chapman sent duplicate copies of numerous letters to another colleague, Ray Smith, who was serving as Director of Education at Trinity Episcopal School for Ministry in Pittsburgh. Only the letters to Lane survive. The detailed content of Chapman's political remarks related to issues concerning enterprise bargaining, trade, and budgetary reform by Australian State and National Governments; details of the Fitzgerald Inquiry into Police corruption; the results of numerous electoral contests in South Australia, Tasmania, New South Wales, and Queensland, as well as the political fortunes of leading figures like John Howard, Andrew Peacock, Bob Hawke, and Joh Bjelke-Petersen. Alongside his remarks on the progress of evangelical faith in the various world ecclesiastical forums with which he was engaged, Chapman's comments on the workings of various national church forums included the passage of legislation concerning the ordination of women, the reform of statutory services, and rulings of the Anglican Appellate Tribunal and Doctrine Commission. Box 3, Adrian Lane Papers 1973–2005, Mitchell Library NSW.

28. Mansfield, *Chappo Collection*, 167.

29. Chapman to Orpwood, January 15, 1995. BDM Box 1, SDA. See also the analysis in chapter 2.

30. Jensen and Freney, "Majoring on the Majors."

his Armidale ministry and his growing influence on its diocesan council confirmed his role as the unofficial organizing secretary of the evangelical group. Maintaining a fast-paced schedule of preaching across this expansive diocese, in the course of his travels Chapman offered direction and encouragement to a growing number of evangelical clergy.

Chapman's political leadership was also crucial. He gathered the evangelical clergy in his residence ahead of the annual synod. While such meetings were called ostensibly for the purpose of "prayer," a large percentage of the time was spent discussing how evangelical interests might be established more firmly via synodical proceedings and how to secure evangelical preferment on to diocesan committees. There was little doubt in the minds of the clergy present about who held them together nor about the strategic value of the task at hand.[31] Indeed, it is significant that on account of Chapman's influence, by the time of Bishop Moyes's retirement in 1964 the evangelical presence in the diocese had risen to such an extent that Clive Kerle (the evangelical Bishop Coadjutor of Sydney) was elected to replace him. While no single figure may be credited for this outcome, those who regarded this as a retrograde step for the diocese were in no doubt about who was primarily responsible. This ultimately resulted in the resignation of numerous High Churchmen from the diocese—a dynamic that only solidified its increasing shift toward Evangelicalism.[32]

Chapman's political dexterity was also demonstrated in the critical role he played in two Sydney archiepiscopal election synods. This was seen firstly in the successful election, in 1982, of Archbishop Robinson. In 1993, Chapman again played a defining role in the campaign to elect Paul Barnett, who ultimately lost to Archbishop Goodhew. Both occasions provide insights into Chapman's capacity as a political animal and the criteria that shaped his judgments in the quest for change.[33]

In the case of the 1982 election, upon the retirement of Archbishop Loane (1966–82) the diocese was poised between the stability of the past and the uncertainty of the future. It was clear to many at this juncture that the Bishop of South Sydney, John Reid, was the heir apparent to Archbishop Loane. An establishment figure with a strong media profile, Reid

---

31. John Wheeler to Michael Orpwood, BDM Box 1, *Sydney Diocesan Archives*; Orpwood, *For the Sake*, 38.

32. Given that the voting margin which led to Kerle's election was somewhat modest, this also instilled in Chapman an awareness of the importance of the political process in securing important ecclesiastical change even via the narrowest of margins. For analysis see Orpwood, *For the Sake*, 38–42; Jensen and Freney, "Majoring on the Majors."

33. Mansfield, *Chappo Collection*, 171.

(somewhat paradoxically) enjoyed the support of many of the ecclesiastically conservative, yet theologically progressive voices within the synod. This was a reality that sat uncomfortably with many of the synod's theologically conservative (primarily clerical) members. Consequently, while Reid was considered the figure best placed to lead the diocese through a time of change, his own theological inclusivity led many to doubt that Reid could be trusted to lead it.[34] In contrast, as a respected scholar and biblical theologian, Robinson (then Bishop of Parramatta) was known as a traditionalist who was unlikely to support radical change. Such a combination ultimately sowed the seeds of significant tension during Robinson's episcopacy.[35] However, many members of the clergy were drawn to Robinson's predictability and his firm adherence to the principles of Reformed thought.[36] Hence, placing their desire for "change" behind the more foundational desire for stable doctrinal leadership, many conservative members of the synod, led by Chapman, campaigned strongly for Robinson. Indeed, like a "general" marshalling his troops, Chapman carefully organized the process both on and off the synod floor. He ordered the speakers, positioning himself last so as to strongly anchor the bid. The result was an electoral victory that went against the tide of expectation and saw the elevation of Robinson, the enigmatic scholar-bishop, to the Sydney archiepiscopal see.[37]

During the 1993 archiepiscopal election Chapman again exerted significant influence, and, in his choice of preferred candidate, manifested his convictions concerning the pursuit of change. Like the nation at large, which was in the thrall of a political contest between incumbency and change, in 1993 the Sydney synod faced a choice between an unknown future or the security of men already serving on the episcopal bench. According to the secular press, the choice before them was between a "radical conservative with a huge and devoted following" in the younger Phillip Jensen,

---

34. Ballantine-Jones, *Political Factor*, 169. Note the discussion in chapters 5 and 6 regarding Reid's theological inclusivity.

35. The tensions surrounding Robinson's archiepiscopacy will be examined shortly.

36. Shiner notes that key to grasping the mix of factors that informed Robinson's approach to change was to recognize his belief that to be Anglican was to be an inheritor of "Reformed Catholicism." That is, to be *Reformed* was to be part of the Church of the Elizabethan Settlement, moderately Calvinistic, and Protestant in relation to Rome. However, to be Anglican was also to be a Reformed *Catholic*. It was to be a member of a *reformed* rather than *ex-nihilo* liturgical tradition, to be in continuity with an ancient communion, and to be in fellowship with all creed-affirming Christians. Such a conviction, combined with Robinson's biblical empiricism, Shiner notes, often made for "strange bedfellows." Shiner, *Reading*, 29.

37. Mansfield, *Chappo Collection*, 171. Ballantine-Jones, *Political Factor*, 172 records the vote as 243–223 in the laity and 149–76 in the clergy.

or that of a coterie of "establishment figures" in the incumbent Sydney Bishops Reid, Barnett, and Goodhew.[38] By 1993, Jensen (one of Chapman's earliest protégés) had established an international reputation as a preacher, evangelical churchman, and advocate for sweeping ecclesiastical change.[39] However, together with a group of younger Sydney rectors who believed the pace of reform under Archbishop Robinson had now rendered the diocese captive to institutionalism and blunted its missional effectiveness, in 1992 Jensen launched the Reformed Evangelical Protestant Association (REPA) as a grassroots vehicle for change. The widespread support the association received soon shook many in the diocesan establishment to the core.[40] Such a backdrop unmistakably informed the election narratives of the leading candidates. Consequently, much of the pre-election publicity and the debate on the synod floor focused on the appropriateness of radical change (typical of the supporters of Jensen) or an approach to change that was slower and more evolutionary (typical of support for the incumbent bishops).[41] Chapman himself was sympathetic to much of Jensen's agenda and had already emerged as one of the chief architects and agitators for change over the preceding decades. However, before Jensen's election bid had even been launched Chapman had already thrown his support behind the Bishop of North Sydney, Paul Barnett, as the man best placed to lead the diocese. Somewhat scandalized by the highly negative characterization of Jensen by various establishment voices during the election campaign, Chapman had verged on lending Jensen his support.[42] However, Chapman's

38. Williams and Robinson, "War in the Cloisters," 39.

39. Within evangelical church networks in Britain, for example, Jensen's advocacy for ecclesiastical change (which he articulated emphatically at the 1986 Evangelical Minister's Assembly) was said to have "revolutionized" many English clergy "overnight" and earned him an "almost cult status among ministers in training." Phillip Jensen, "Changing the Church," Talk 3, *Evangelical Minister's Assembly*, London, 1986. Proclamation Trust, "Question Time"; Green, "Preaching," 18.

40. To encourage what they regarded as more missiologically oriented churches, REPA leaders championed the need for "a thousand changes in the same direction . . . based in theology and evangelism rather than liturgy and structuralism." Dozens of think tanks were held across the diocese and a newsletter was published. REPA members flooded the business paper of the 1992 Synod with notices of motions in areas they believed required change. By early 1993 REPA leaders announced that two-thirds of all Sydney Anglicans attended churches under the oversight of rectors associated with REPA. Such actions were regarded by establishment figures as highly destabilizing and divisive. Ballantine-Jones, *Political Factor*, 190–94.

41. Ballantine-Jones, *Political Factor*, 198.

42. Chapman to Lane, September 2, 1989; Chapman to Lane, March 27, 1993. Box 3, Adrian Lane Papers 1973–2005. Note that Chapman's own contribution as a leading agitator for change will be assessed later in the current chapter.

continued support for Barnett was reflective of the esteem in which he held Barnett as a colleague, scholar, and leader. It was also reflective of Chapman's recognition (even his innate disposition) that in an ecclesiastical environment of such size and complexity, the path toward effective reform was one of moderation. It required the securing of archiepiscopal leadership in whom sufficient numbers across a variety of outlooks had sufficient confidence to command the consensus needed for change. In his leadership of Barnett's campaign, Chapman thus garnered the support of a range of respected synodical voices.[43] After the first evening of voting, the names of Reid, Goodhew, Jensen, and Barnett subsequently progressed to the second ballot. However, after the second evening, with Jensen's bid falling short primarily in the house of the laity and Reid again falling short with the Sydney clergy, only the names of Barnett and Goodhew progressed to the final list. The result on the final evening was to be a victory for Goodhew—an irenic figure with a sound episcopal and pastoral track record that championed strategies for church growth. Various commentators have suggested that such an outcome reflected the fracturing of the more radical element within the synod's evangelical base. Indeed, they suggest, had there been swifter coordination in transferring Jensen's support to Barnett (a figure with whose agenda Jensen's supporters perhaps shared a greater affinity), the result may have secured victory for Barnett. Nevertheless, with the weight of expectation for "change" following Goodhew into office and a wave of cultural flashpoints (such as debates around the ordination of women) consuming the interests of the Sydney and national synods during the 1990s, Goodhew's episcopacy was not to be the period of calm and incremental reform that had been hoped for. Indeed, in pursuing the path of moderation, it is arguable that proponents like Chapman had helped to secure an outcome which, by frustrating the path of radical change, in fact inflamed it. Even so, the passage of the 1993 election is illustrative of Chapman's political instincts and leadership, as well as the sheer difficulty of securing policy and strategic outcomes within such a complex ecclesiastical forum.[44]

---

43. These included Chris Bellenger (Professor of Veterinary Surgery), Edwin Judge (Professor of History, Macquarie University), John Mason (Rector of Mosman), and Boak Jobbins (Anglican Dean of Sydney). Ballantine-Jones, *Political Factor*, 200.

44. For analysis of the 1993 election, the passage of voting in both houses (clerical and lay) for Reid, Jensen, Barnett, and Goodhew, as well as the resultant tensions during Goodhew's episcopacy, see Ballantine-Jones, *Political Factor*, 193–243.

Ecclesiastical Promoter and Provocateur

As a leading figure in a tradition that was episcopally led and synodically governed Chapman was undoubtedly a believer in evangelical Anglicanism as a vehicle for gospel mission. Indeed, in an address to the bishops of the province of NSW in 1989, as he reflected on the approaching "Decade of Evangelism,"[45] Chapman outlined the benefits of Anglican polity and establishment privilege as a vehicle for gospel promotion. Recounting the contents of this address, he later wrote:

> Last Monday I addressed the Bishops of the Province on the Decade of Evangelism. It was great fun. The general thrust went like this. The key to ongoing evangelism is an informed, articulate and motivated laity. The key to that is an informed, articulate, motivated clergy who can teach this to their people. And the key to this is complex. There are at least three factors which create clergy like this. The first . . . is the Bishop as leader of the Diocese. He should set a lead in gospelling on every occasion he [can]. I urged them to buy-up every opportunity they could get before the cameras but to make sure they preached the gospel whatever else they say . . . I urged them to evangelize at confirmations and ordinations and to conduct the Ordination Service so the non-Christian relatives of the Ordinands were [engaged]. The second area that affects clergy and their evangelism is the theological college where they were trained, which should equip them to be informed about the gospel [and] motivate them to see [preaching it] as the most important work of their ministry. The third area which leads to the informed . . . motivated clergyman is his peers in the ordained ministry. Every time anyone gets up and [preaches the gospel] he challenges and informs his peers to do the same. I explained to the Bishops that the clergyman who takes initiative in leading his people in this form of evangelism is typified by being a lateral thinker. They often think of new ways outside of the "system." They regularly challenge the institution because they see it getting in the way of the gospel. They can often be [tiresome] to their Bishop. However, I tried to point out that men and women of vision were so rare that they needed to be cultivated and not crushed. With many similar and gentle words I exhorted them.

---

45. The "Decade of Evangelism" was an initiative of the Lambeth Bishops and called on the Anglican Communion to renew efforts in evangelism as the new millennium approached. 6/90 "Decade of Evangelism," 1993 *Sydney Yearbook*, 343.

I'm sure you will be surprised that on the last point they only "heard" that they were the key to everything.[46]

Notwithstanding such a confident (albeit roguish) assessment of evangelical Anglicanism as an effective vehicle for gospel mission, the waggish irreverence of Chapman's own social background also combined with his preference for low-church evangelical expression to fuel a distaste for the vestiges of all ecclesiastical pomp and display. Chapman frequently caricatured heavily liturgical or cathedral-like worship as akin to "religious theatre" in which "players" in "fancy costume" and "funny hats" engaged in religious activity so "complicated and technical" that it bespoke a scene from a bygone world. In modern Australia, he feared, such activity had a largely repellant effect on the average un-churched person.[47] Indeed, such a mischievous disdain for ecclesial pageantry endured to the concluding days of Chapman's life. Only days before his death, Chapman's long-time colleague, Archbishop Jensen, conducted a pastoral visit to Chapman's hospital bedside. Sitting upright as Jensen entered the room, Chapman gestured with his hands in a cross shape on his chest and cried impishly, "Ox's Blockses" (a mid-century Protestant pun on the mysticism of the Catholic Mass), before sinking back into his bed.[48] Chapman's deference to ecclesiastical leadership was therefore infused with a characteristic Australian wariness of the "straighteners," "God's police," and the "guardians of purity," alongside an evangelical Anglican wariness of the influence of Anglo-Catholicism and heavily liturgical expression. The result of this blend of establishment and non-establishment impulses would see Chapman work to preserve the strengths of Anglicanism in his career, while also campaigning to reform those elements of the tradition he believed to be hampering its missional effectiveness.[49] Indeed, echoing the apostolic imperative to remove all impediments to the gospel's reception (both cultural *and* theological, 1 Cor 9:22), Chapman sought eagerly in his ministry to fine-tune Anglicanism to meet the missiological needs of a changing world.[50]

---

46. Chapman to Lane, November 11, 1989. Box 3, Adrian Lane Papers, Mitchell Library NSW.

47. Chapman to Lane, August 25, 1989. Box 3, Adrian Lane Papers, Mitchell Library NSW.

48. Interview with Peter Jensen, December 2, 2016. This saying derives from *hocus pocus*, which was itself a parody of the Latin *hoc est corpus meum* ("this is my body") spoken by the priest at the Catholic Mass. Guiley, *Witches and Witchcraft*, 161.

49. Bouma, *Australian Soul*, 45–47; Interview with Dr. Bruce Ballantine-Jones, February 13, 2017.

50. Whiteman, "Contextualization," 3.

Reforming Anglicanism

From its very inception Anglicanism has been a reforming tradition. The liturgical reforms of Thomas Cranmer had sought a genuine reformation of the ministry of the word of God by opening the whole of Scripture to the English people, while the 1563 *Act of Uniformity* sought to consolidate a diversity of belief and practice. Retaining the historic creeds, together with a corporate life shaped by the sacraments and Thirty-Nine Articles of Religion, Cranmer's reforms became a touchstone of theological orthodoxy and unity in Anglican faith and expression.[51] However, while Cranmer and the later framers of the 1662 *Book of Common Prayer* acknowledged the desire for flexibility to accommodate changing stylistic needs, by the mid-twentieth century the majority of Anglican churches had strayed little from the 1662 language and forms.[52] Harbingers of the process of twentieth-century liturgical and ministry reform appeared in the early part of the century. Within the Anglican Communion a round of liturgical revision took place in 1928 with new prayer books in England, South Africa, and the United States. This was driven, in large part, by the strength of early century Anglo-Catholicism and ritualism.[53] Anglo-Catholic emphases continued to influence the Church of England during the 1930s and postwar era.[54] One of the firstfruits of this Anglo-Catholic liturgical movement was the liturgy of the Church of South India (1950). The revised liturgy of this church was the first to break with the Cranmerian mold.[55] As

---

51. Old, *Reformation*, 149–52; Avis, "Prayer Book Use," 128–130.

52. The 1662 *Book of Common Prayer* substantially ratified Cranmer's reforms. Avis, "Prayer Book Use," 132.

53. The push for Prayer Book revision began, following a 1904 ruling by the Royal Commission on Ecclesiastical Discipline, which suggested greater freedoms should be offered to laws around public worship. With High Churchmen assuming a majority position of episcopal leadership in England by the early century, the controversial 1928 English Revised Prayer Book promoted a reversion to pre-Reformation practices including prayers for the dead, reservation of the sacrament, and vestments. The British Parliament, imbued with an ancient fear of Rome, rejected the book twice, stalling the advance of early century revisionism. Jupp, "Anglican Catholic Church," 118–19; Morris, "Oxford Movement," 406–27.

54. During the 1930s, such influences derived primarily from the work of Henry de Candole (1895–1971) and Gabriel Herbert (1886–1963). In the postwar era, the work of Gregory Dix (*The Shape of the Liturgy*, 1945) also contended that the Cranmerian reforms had failed to express the richness and beauty of the early church's sacramental legacy. His recommendations established themselves as a pattern within many later century eucharistic liturgies. Spinks, "Liturgy," 477.

55. It introduced a separate service of the word and placed the confession and absolution at the beginning of the service, while its eucharistic prayer was closer in structure to those of the fourth and fifth centuries. Spinks, "Liturgy," 477.

various provinces, spurred on by South India, appointed commissions to undertake liturgical revision, it was feared that what held the Communion together—namely books of common prayer grown from the Cranmerian root—would fly apart as provinces acted independently. As such, the Church of England appointed a Liturgical Commission in 1954 to prepare a liturgical guide for the 1958 Lambeth Conference. Further pan-Anglican liturgical guides were issued in 1965 and 1969.[56]

In Australia, Anglo-Catholic influence also swelled in the early twentieth century as Anglo-Catholic and High Churchmen became dominant over much of the national church between 1914 and 1939.[57] Within the Sydney diocese, Anglo-Catholic influence swelled under the influence of Bishops Saumarez Smith (1889–1909) and Wright (1909–33). These leaders promoted a broad spectrum of theological sympathy and did little to stem the growth of ritualist practices in a number of significant Sydney parishes.[58] Tensions came to a head during the infamous "Red Book Case" of the 1940s. The Red Book Case was so called on account of the actions of Bishop Wylde of Bathurst, who published an unauthorized prayer book (bound in red) which contained a number of prayers and rubrics that pointed to a Roman Catholic conception of the Lord's Supper. This provoked a legal response supported by Sydney leaders Archbishop Mowll and T. C. Hammond. The case dominated the greater part of the 1940s for Australian Anglicans. In light of the divergent theological and liturgical visions that now buffeted the national church, the case was instrumental in exposing the need for prayer book revision. This, in turn, was reliant upon the establishment of a new constitution for the Anglican Church of Australia.[59]

The instatement of an independent Australian Anglican constitution on January 1, 1962, opened the way for Australian liturgical revision. With the constitution in full effect, revision of the *Book of Common Prayer* began

---

56. Spinks, "Liturgy," 477; Avis, "Prayer Book Use," 133–34.

57. Jupp, "Anglican Catholic Church," 118; Frame, *Anglicans*, 76.

58. The most notable example of this was the growth of ritualism at St. James King Street and Christ Church St. Laurence, both Anglican churches in inner-city Sydney. Judd and Cable, *Sydney Anglicans*, 123–207; McIntosh, *Anglican Evangelicalism*, 57.

59. The details of the Red Book Case involved twenty-three laymen from Bathurst diocese (aided by Mowll and Hammond) filing a complaint in the Equity Court of NSW against Bishop Wylde. The case appealed to the *BCP* to suggest that the bishop had committed heresy. Wylde rejected the laymen's complaints and refused to withdraw his prayer book. The laymen persisted, appealing to a new charge under the *NSW Church of England Property Trust Act* (1917–1923) of misappropriation of properties endowed for Church of England purposes. The charge was upheld in 1948. On appeal, it was limited to a group of only twenty churches wherein the trusts had been proved. Teale, "Red Book Case," 74–89.

in earnest. A liturgical commission was appointed by the 1962 General Synod to explore a range of draft liturgies. This included new orders of service and vernacular versions of the old. After validating these trial forms, the 1977 General Synod authorized the publication of *An Australian Prayer Book* 1978 (AAPB). This was actively promoted by the primate, Archbishop Loane. Alongside Donald Robinson, Loane played a defining role in its development.[60] Representing a remarkable agreement between churchmen of different persuasions, the 1978 *Australian Prayer Book* was widely employed and, for a time, helped to create something close to a sense of national identity for Australian Anglicans. Despite assurances that the AAPB was offered for "use with" and not as a "replacement of" the *Book of Common Prayer* as the standard of doctrine and worship in the Australian Church, use of the 1662 prayer book attenuated rapidly from this point, or was relegated to early services and nostalgic special events.[61]

The Need for More Pervasive Ministry Reforms

The 1968 Commission of Enquiry

Notwithstanding the achievements of this period of reform and consensus building, many Sydney leaders (alongside their international counterparts) were conscious that liturgical reform alone was not sufficient to meet the challenges that pervasive secularization was bringing to light. Alongside the renewed standard of liturgical orthodoxy that had been secured as a result of such reforms, many had also hoped it would lift Anglican worship from its oftentimes "lifeless" expression and allow the churches to present a fresh and modern public face.[62] Gradually, however, a more endemic challenge was becoming apparent. Indeed, even as the process of liturgical review continued and fresh service forms were drafted in the 1960s, widespread decline in churchgoing accelerated, matched by a corresponding decline in occasional service use. A decade after Australians had ceased regular attendance at Sunday worship and were freed to be more candid about their religious misgivings, many had also begun to discard the church's rites of passage and liturgical observances.[63] Hence, by the 1970s it was apparent

60. Frame, *Anglicans*, 127–28; Hilliard, "Church of England in Australia," 138; Judd and Cable, *Sydney Anglicans*, 292–93.

61. Preface, *Australian Prayer Book 1978*, 7; Frame, *Anglicans*, 129; Kaye, "Identity," 174. See also the edition of *St Mark's Review* 222 (November 2012) dedicated to the *Book of Common Prayer* on its 250th anniversary.

62. Barnett and Jensen, *Quest for Power*, 77; Frame, *Anglicans*, 130.

63. Frame, *Anglicans*, 130; Jupp, "Social Role," 38; Hilliard, "Secularization," 75.

that even fresh expressions of the historic liturgies were affecting little change in curbing the alienation of the "man-in-the-street." While clerical leaders could continue to "follow hunches" in diagnosing the situation, it was evident that a more "thorough review" of the church's worship and ministry patterns was "long overdue."[64]

Such stirrings for a process of sweeping review were given voice under the episcopal term of Marcus Loane (1966–82). Despite his cautious and consensus-oriented manner, alongside the liturgical reforms that Loane had sponsored, he also sponsored a plethora of enquiries to investigate the application of theology to pressing contemporary concerns. With such a resolutely conservative figure presiding over diocesan affairs, this brought a degree of comfort to many synodical figures that the exploration of change appeared to be a reasonable and appropriate pursuit.[65] Standing at the apex of these many reviews was the 1968 *Commission of Enquiry*. Following a series of notable synodical addresses by Loane in the late 1960s that sounded a bold missionary call to arms, the 1968 Commission was charged with the task of investigating the "whole problem of modern communication of the gospel" within the "prevailing intellectual outlook."[66] Chapman himself played a defining role as secretary and theological consultant for this commission, which spent three years in deliberation. The commission conducted a sociological assessment of Australian society. It also undertook an assessment of contemporary church practices and forms, alongside a reanalysis of New Testament missiological principles.[67] The resultant report, entitled *Move in For Action* (1971) was made publicly available with the aim of stimulating the Sydney diocese and "the whole of the Australian church to assess accurately its present outreach." Among its recommendations, the report concluded that for too long the "church has been

---

64. "Foreword," *Move in For Action*, 7; cf. Breward, *Australian Churches*, 169, 172 on similar concerns.

65. The process of change began in Sydney during the term of Archbishop Gough (1958–1966). Gough's progressive sympathies and conservative churchmanship galvanized evangelical advocacy for change and inaugurated a series of financial and managerial reforms that facilitated change in later years. Illustrative of the degree of reform under Loane, however, is that between 1964 and 1987 there were seventy-four reviews undertaken by the sitting archbishop. Ballantine-Jones, *Political Factor*, 158–60; Cameron, *Phenomenal Sydney*, 78–84. Similar realizations of the need for change were being felt by English Evangelicals. The 1967 Keele Congress demonstrated an appetite for reform. Key leaders such as John Stott and James Packer also attempted to put distance between their movement and fundamentalism. Stott championed a case for "relevance" in public worship and warned of the perils of failing to adjust "to the contemporary scene." Dudley-Smith, *Global Ministry*, 206–26; Chapman, *Ambition*, 59–60.

66. See 1968 *Sydney Yearbook*, 354; 1969 *Sydney Yearbook*, 220; *Move in For Action*, 7.

67. *Move in For Action*, 11–33, 34–48, 49–98, 99–126.

answering questions that no-one has been asking" and suggested that while "the gospel of Christ has been *faithfully* preached for generations, yet in our times it does not appear to have been *effectively* preached." Indeed, whether tied up in questions of "orthodoxy" or "corporate" identity or hindered by a pervasive insularity within local church life, the church's essential work of "witness," the report alleged, had become lost in a "haze" of other objectives. Consequently, conceding the need for continued cultural sensitivity so as to communicate "relevantly" and an openness to new ministry structures and activities so as to operate "creatively," the report urged the need for a pervasive missionary outlook at the core of church life. This was to be the result of a "vital spiritual life" that permeated the congregation rather than being merely a "panacea" to stem decline.[68] In a parallel yet supplementary process, another report entitled *Looking into the Parish* (1972) was developed. This applied the assessments of the 1968 Commission to the life of the Sydney diocese. The resultant report proposed a raft of extensive changes to the polity and culture of Sydney parishes and to the diocesan structures that existed to support them.[69] Many of these sat uncomfortably with aspects of traditional Anglican polity and practice. The report was therefore considered excessively radical and few of its recommendations were implemented at the time. Nevertheless, these dual reports of the 1968 *Commission of Enquiry* effectively inaugurated the theme of "change" as an ongoing diocesan preoccupation. This generated numerous enquiries in subsequent years that built on their earlier themes and resulted in significant long-term structural and ministry reforms.[70]

Continuing Reform Initiatives

During the decades that followed these enquiries, a plethora of official and unofficial initiatives pursued changes in Sydney diocesan life. The role of a coterie of key clerical leaders was notable in this process. The stimulating

---

68. *Move in For Action*, 7, 8, 9, 127, 133; cf. "Move in For Action," 12.

69. *Looking into the Parish*, 2.

70. John Chapman was not involved in the production of the *Looking into the Parish* report of 1972 (known as the "Reid Commission"). He restricted his involvement to the concerns of missiological culture addressed in *Move in For Action* (1971). The report, however, combined numerous recommendations on a system of "shared eldership" in Anglican parishes as well as a series of recommendations on clerical effectiveness and licensing that constituted a direct challenge to the long-held tradition of clerical tenure (*Looking into the Parish*, 2–7). Together with other suggestions for diocesan restructuring, many believed the report had gone too far. Judd and Cable, *Sydney Anglicans*, 289–92; Ballantine-Jones, *Political Factor*, 41–42, 54, 161.

theological leadership of D. B. Knox and D. W. B. Robinson continued to challenge prevailing assumptions and call for fresh thought. This was supplemented by the influence, within the diocese's many political forums, of a number of figures who significantly shaped the generation of clergy who rose to prominence in the 1990s. This included A. J. Dain, P. R. Watson, R. H. Goodhew, D. T. Foord, J. R. Reid, and P. W. Barnett. Working in sympathy with such figures, Chapman was also highly prominent as an agent for change.[71] Across his many formal representative roles and the networks of clergy with whom he interacted, Chapman campaigned strongly for issues that he judged to be of central importance to maintaining the evangelical temper of the diocese and to promoting the cause of mission. He lobbied strongly within such forums, in particular, for the independence of Sydney parishes and their incumbents, alongside the evangelical integrity of the diocese's training college.[72] As a member of the standing committee, Chapman also played a leading role as chairman or secretary in the passage of a range of synodical initiatives. Movers and seconders of such initiatives (often members of the standing committee who had taken charge of an initiative's development) were responsible for persuading the synod of an initiative's merits as well as dealing with the concerns expressed by synod members to allow passage of the legislation to proceed.[73] In this vein, between 1970 and 1990 Chapman provided leadership to the synod regarding the establishment of the College of Preachers (1970) and the development of expository preaching. He was engaged with the Commission on Mass Media (1971) which advised the synod on the use of emerging media technologies for the purposes of parish evangelism. He lobbied strongly for enquiries to be made in the synod's response to the charismatic movement (1971) and questions concerning lay administration of the Lord's Supper (1977). He provided leadership in the synod's engagement with the 1979 Billy Graham Crusade (1976–79) and the 1990s "Decade on Evangelism" initiative (1990). He also provided leadership in the synod's handling of the major report on "The Meaning and Value of Ordination"—a report produced to answer questions pertaining to women's ordination and lay administration of the Lord's

---

71. In cataloguing the contributions of key clerical figures, many other contributions are of course overlooked. Those highlighted here were judged to be the preeminent figures for "change" in their generation (1970–1980s) who, by virtue of their office, or native ability to command influence, rose to prominence. Interview with Dr. Bruce Ballantine-Jones, February 13, 2017.

72. Interview with Rev. Dr. Peter Jensen, December 2, 2016.

73. See *Conduct of the Business of Synod Ordinance 2000*, 8–15. Sydney Diocesan Services, "Recognised Churches."

Supper (1981) that arose in the 1980s.[74] Chapman's secretarial leadership of the 1986 "Report on Cross-Cultural Ministries" also identified the urgent need to more effectively reach the multitude of cultures in urban Australia. Indeed, recognizing the decline in historic Anglican constituencies across the Sydney region, the report highlighted the need to transcend racial barriers and to extend the gospel's blessings to the people of all nations. The report called for a renewed cultural "sensitivity" in Anglican worship conventions and for a coordinated approach to be taken to the many green shoots of diocesan cross-cultural initiative. Seeking to safeguard what was "precious" in the Anglican heritage while fostering a "dynamic Anglican" culture more representative of the "richness" of modern Australia, many of the report's recommendations became influential in establishing new patterns of diocesan cross-cultural ministry. This included the development of a growing number of multiethnic congregations and a range of strategies to reach the expanding number of ethnic minorities within the city. Indeed, on account of the simplified service formats that emerged in such congregations, such

---

74. Note Chapman's synodical involvement, chairmanship or secretarial leadership in the following forums: *Move in for Action* (Secretary); Resolution 10/1970 "College of Preachers," 1972 *Sydney Yearbook*, 350–51 (Committee member); Resolution 4/1971 "College of Preachers," 1973 *Sydney Yearbook*, 309 (Committee member); Resolution 4/72, "Charismatic Movement," 1973 *Yearbook*, 291 (Committee member); "Both Sides" (Committee member); Resolution 39/1968 "Commission on Evangelism," 1972 *Yearbook*, 352–52 (Committee member); Resolution 9/71 "Commission on Evangelism, 1972 *Yearbook*, 286–87; Resolution 26/71 "Study of Charismatic Movement," 1972 *Yearbook*, 290–91; Resolution 9/1971 "Suggested Diocesan Congress on Evangelism," 1973 *Yearbook*, 309; "Interim Report of Commission on Mass Media to the Synod of the Diocese," October 1971, *Supplement to Southern Cross* (Committee member); Canon J. C. Chapman, 4.10.77, Resolution 9/77 "Licensing Lay Persons for Ministry of Word and Sacrament," 1978 *Yearbook*, 242; Canon J. C. Chapman, Resolution 19/76, "1979 Billy Graham Crusade," 1977 *Yearbook*; Canon J. C. Chapman, 6.10.77, Resolution 21/77 "Billy Graham Crusade," 1978 *Yearbook*, 245; Canon J. C. Chapman, "A Report on the Anglican Involvement in the 1979 Sydney Billy Graham Crusade," August 9, 1979, 1980 *Yearbook*, 380; Canon J. C. Chapman, 6.10.81, Resolution 3/81, "Meaning, Value and Theology of Ordination," 1982 *Yearbook*, 251; Canon J. C. Chapman (Secretary), "Report of the Standing Committee Re Cross-Cultural Ministries," 1987 *Yearbook*, 287; Canon J. C. Chapman, 11.10.88, "Consultants on Parish Evangelism," 1989 *Yearbook*, 260; Canon J. C. Chapman (Secretary), Resolution 11/88 "A Report from the Committee Re Church Growth," 1990 *Yearbook*, 373–84; Resolution 7/90 "Church Growth," 1991 *Yearbook*, 238; "Decade of Evangelism: Means for More Effective Evangelism," 1990 *Yearbook*, 257; Canon J. C. Chapman (Secretary), Resolution 6/90, "Report from the Committee Re Decade of Evangelism," 1992 *Yearbook*, 342–43; J. C. Chapman, *Submission to the Most Rev DWB Robinson on Training Men for the Ministry*, September 6, 1982, BDM Box 1, SDA. This submission (alongside others to Bishops E. Cameron and R. Goodhew) detail Chapman's advocacy for a commission to revise the system of training for Sydney Anglican ordinands.

developments came to play an important role in the simplification of worship patterns across the diocese.[75]

In 1988 Chapman also lobbied the synod to establish a committee on church growth. This was intended to provide a comprehensive response to the challenges presented by the Kaldor Report (*Going to Church in Australia*) and the findings of a "Joint Churches Census" concerning the crisis of churchgoing in Australia.[76] Chapman became secretary of the committee that formed as a result. The committee conducted a wide-ranging review of current church practices, while offering strategies for the pursuit of "qualitative" and "numerical" church growth.[77] The subsequent report noted areas of diminishing growth across sectors of the Sydney churches alongside pockets of positive ministry activity.[78] Notwithstanding such tokens of progress, it was noted with a sense of alarm that Anglicanism was "facing a critical phase of its life" wherein resistance to change would precipitate a "major decline in our already marginal impact on society."[79] Consequently, appealing to the Anglican formularies which conceded the need for changing worship patterns, the report stressed the need for wide-reaching reforms at the personal, congregational, and denominational level. Church members were urged toward a "personal" readiness to jettison "inflexible" commitments "to secondary issues"; toward a "congregational" readiness to examine the weaknesses of present ministries and to encourage "leaders of creativity, vision and ingenuity"; and to a "denominational" readiness to redress patterns of "over-regulation" in aspects of public worship especially around traditional "forms of service, dress codes and furnishings."[80] The report was

75. By 2012, sixty-one language-specific congregations existed across the diocese, 2012 *Sydney Yearbook*, 153.

76. J. C. Chapman, 10.10.88, "Resolution 11/88: Committee Re Church Growth," 1989 *Sydney Yearbook*, 257; Chapman, "Forum on Church Growth," 13. Dr. Peter Kaldor (founding director of the National Church Life Survey, NCLS) was commissioned by the Uniting Church to research church life in Australia. The results of this research, alongside a corresponding statistical analysis (the "Joint Churches Census") were published in 1987. The ongoing NCLS, which flowed out of this initial research, was incorporated in 1991 as a joint venture between church mission agencies. It gave rise to the five-yearly survey which today incorporates more than twenty Australian denominations. Kaldor, *Who Goes Where?*; NCLS, "NCLS Research."

77. "Report: Synod Resolution 11/88 Re Church Growth," 1990 *Sydney Yearbook*, 373–84, 376–77.

78. Positive progress was occurring chiefly among ethnic and special interest groups, the middle-class, student ministries, and churches that had begun to engage contemporary worship styles. "Report: Resolution 11/88," 374–75.

79. "Report: Resolution 11/88," 375.

80. "Report: Resolution 11/88," 378, nos. 26–27, 43–45. The report made reference to the preface of the 1978 *Australian Prayer Book*, 9–13 which (quoting Anglican

commended for consideration among deaneries, parish councils, and across the leadership structures of numerous diocesan ministries.[81] Commenting on the foreseeable effects of such recommendations, Chapman himself suggested that should the diocese rise to the challenge that had been issued to it, in any given church "we may soon have services as different as chalk and cheese... yuppies meeting on Wednesday nights; traditional Anglicans on Sunday mornings, a family service later in the morning and an evening service more 'charismatic' in its music style."[82]

In addition to such formalized legislative and committee-based initiatives, the growing popularity of guest-style Sunday and occasional services alongside the burgeoning regional and university missions of the 1970s to 1990s played a role in the reform of public worship styles.[83] Chapman played a leading role as both preacher and organizer of such initiatives. Indeed, throughout this era Chapman preached across a strikingly wide array of guest contexts including student and parish missions, cathedrals, stadiums, parks, civic halls, schools, luncheons, and lecture theatres. In preparation for such initiatives Chapman and his staff forwarded information advising the various hosting ministries on the desired shape of such meetings, to ensure they were suitable for the non-churched visitor to attend. This included the desire to strike a balance between a formal and informal meeting atmosphere, alongside recommendations on the appropriate use of congregational singing, dramas, musical items, and audio-visual presentations. It also included the consideration of elements of the meeting that could foreseeably alienate visitors, like excessive notices, in-house jokes, and heavily liturgical expression. The entire focus of the meeting, Chapman advised, was to be geared such that no element of the meeting detracted from the proclamation of the gospel given in the address.[84] Chapman averred that the regional crusade-style meetings of the 1980s and 1990s were also designed to be "snappy." Such meetings (held across the breadth of the Sydney region and attended by thousands of Christians and visitors during this period) typically involved a musical item, testimony or book review, followed by the Bible reading and the

---

Article 34, and chapter 2, §4 of the 1962 *Australian Anglican Constitution*) notes the expectation, by the framers of Anglican liturgy, of the development of culturally appropriate worship forms in every place.

81. Bishop J. R. Reid, 8.10.90, "Resolution 7/90 Church Growth," 1991 *Sydney Yearbook*, 238.

82. Chapman, "Forum on Church Growth," 13.

83. See the discussion of such missions and the growth of Australian tertiary ministries in chapter 3.

84. "Preparing for an Evangelistic Event," BDM Box 3, SDA.

address. Given the ever-increasing unfamiliarity of audiences with the format of Christian worship services and with the Bible itself, such events were run to as high a standard as possible and aimed to do nothing that might distract from the hearing of the gospel. Indeed, Chapman opined, by lasting little more than an hour such minimalist gatherings were designed to have visitors "at home having coffee by 9.30 pm."[85] Their entire objective was to establish a mode of "public evangelism that was able to fit happily into the contemporary Australian scene."[86] Together with the insights of Chapman's widely modelled "dialogue evangelism" methodology (that emphasized an environment of relaxed informality) alongside his practice of non-liturgical attire, plain speech, and a larrikin demeanor, such initiatives played a significant role in shaping Christian meeting styles during this period. Indeed, alongside the influence in Sydney churches of United States-style "seeker-sensitive" and charismatic "soft-rock" approaches,[87] the influence of 1990s church planting methodologies,[88] and a raft of initiatives growing out of the "Decade of Evangelism,"[89] such developments began to amplify the now two-decade-long groundswell for change. As such, the note of "change" that had been first struck in the 1970s, which foresaw that the emerging society would "not tolerate traditionalism nor retreat from the revolutionary future," was beginning to intensify.[90] Prior to the 1970s, the archetypal Sydney evangelical clergyman had unselfconsciously worn clerical attire, attended "reformation rallies," resisted crosses and candles, and enthusiastically observed the weekly rhythm of the *Book of Common Prayer*.[91] However, by the early new century, the conventions of most Sydney Anglican churches had altered dramatically. Traditional hymns were replaced with contemporary songs.[92] Communion tables were often relocated, and the church nave was used as a stage. Many pulpits were cut down to the size of reading desks. Church pews were replaced with

85. Chapman, "Regional Evangelism," 11.

86. Chapman, "Regional Evangelism," 11; "About the GOZpel!," 12–14.

87. Stanley, *Gospel Diffusion*, 24; McIntosh, *Evaluating*, 12–20; Ballantine-Jones, *Political Factor*, 51; Webster and Jones, "New Music," 169–70.

88. "8/94 Planting and Developing New Churches: Report from a Synod Working Party," 1995 *Sydney Yearbook*, 383–91.

89. Bishop R. H. Goodhew, "6/90 Decade of Evangelism," 1991 *Sydney Yearbook*, 238, 347; Canon J. C. Chapman, 28.7.1992, "6/90 Decade of Evangelism," 1993 *Sydney Yearbook*, 342–43.

90. *Move in For Action*, 28.

91. Judd and Cable, *Sydney Anglicans*, 307, 295–96.

92. This was reflective of the shifts in youth and pop culture in the post-1960s era. Webster and Jones, "New Music," 169.

movable seats. Authorized forms of services were replaced by extempore forms. In most parishes, any vesture beyond the clerical collar had also been unceremoniously discarded.[93] While fresh attempts were made in the 1990s to revive the diocese's liturgical tradition, formal liturgical services had nonetheless become the exception rather than the rule. Such developments ushered in a style of Anglican worship that was almost unrecognizable from the patterns of a previous era.[94]

Anglicanism and the Passage of Change

Ecclesiastical Inflexibility and Anxiety about the Pace of Reform

Given the foregoing assessment, there is little doubt that the magnitude of change in public worship culture experienced during this era was substantial. However, the fact that such changes *did* eventuate should not mask the fact that the path to attaining them was difficult and highly contentious. Indeed, during the archiepiscopacies of Robinson and Goodhew, the struggle for "change" produced a context in which the Sydney diocese was said to resemble a "powder keg."[95] Two dynamics in particular could be said to have produced this situation. The first was the ecclesiastical meticulousness of Archbishop Robinson and the impact this had upon his leadership. The second was the shape of Anglicanism and, in particular, Australian Anglicanism itself. In this vein, Archbishop Robinson had been elected in 1982 on the back of support from a young and theologically conservative constituency in the synod. Known for his traditionalism yet admired for his integrity and scholarship, Robinson had drawn support as a steadfastly conservative figure in a time of theological unease.[96] However, as the complexities of Robinson's ecclesiology and his views on Anglican polity began to manifest themselves in his leadership of diocesan affairs, this produced a volatile dynamic between Robinson and members of his own support base. For, while they represented the more theologically conservative members of the synod, they were also the more eager to see change. The result was that during Robinson's term, a concern

---

93. 2007 *Sydney Yearbook*, 370.

94. Anglican Church of Australia, "Sunday Services"; Ballantine-Jones, *Political Factor*, 43.

95. Ballantine-Jones, *Political* Factor, 45, 187.

96. Judd and Cable, *Sydney Anglicans*, 286–87; Ballantine-Jones, *Political Factor*, 169, 172.

for the "lawful" application of church authority came to be expressed *and* regarded in an increasingly stifling way.[97]

Also contributing to the highly politicized nature of reform in Australian Anglicanism was the way in which its national synodical arrangement had been conceived. Established originally by the imprimatur of the state under English civil law, Anglicanism's *via media* had undoubtedly created a legal and theological compact that produced an ongoing struggle for the soul of the English church. By 1605, the Church of England had established its own statements of faith, forms of worship, and body of canon law, declaring its submission to the apostolic witness and the authority of Holy Scripture. The Thirty-Nine Articles, the *Book of Common Prayer*, and the three historic creeds (Apostles', Nicene, and Athanasian) had also become definitive of Anglican belief and custom. Across its history, Anglicanism had undoubtedly become home to a range of theological traditions under this essentially erastian arrangement. Nevertheless, it was these formularies that formed the basis of any legal appeal to reform.[98] Consequently, when the Australian Anglican constitution was ratified in 1962, synodical decisions at all levels were linked back to these formularies. However, as distinct from other provinces, an essentially "bottom-up" (versus "top-down") structure was woven into the Australian constitution. This meant that decision-making power in the Australian church was not vested in the General Synod but in the diocesan synods themselves. Hence, within Australian Anglicanism, if a canon of its General Synod was to affect matters of doctrine, order or financial obligation, the canon applied in a diocese *only*

---

97. As examined in chapter seven, Robinson's ecclesiology elevated the local church to be the primary unit in ecclesiastical life and viewed the denomination as a "service structure" tasked with serving the local church. Paradoxically, however, such a view did not drive Robinson to be disinterested in denominational affairs. Rather, driven to protect the heritage he saw to be resident in his diocese and to fine-tune a service structure that best aided the life of the local churches, Robinson's ecclesiology drove him to be heavily involved in denominational affairs. Moreover, in Robinson's mind, to be Anglican was to be an inheritor of "Reformed Catholicism." On such a view, Anglicanism and its liturgical inheritance was not to be parted with nor discarded lightly. Robinson's views on the diocesan "bishop" as the "chief pastor and ruler of a diocese" also undoubtedly infused his handling of diocesan affairs. Indeed, Robinson contended that in a time of doctrinal and constitutional "change and uncertainty such as we Anglicans are going through at present," like a "latter-day Timothy," the "final line of defence in many instances may be simply that 'the bishop' is faithful to his charge." Conscious of this, Robinson invested heavy significance in the "lawful" authority that an archbishop exercised over his diocese and clergy. Robinson, "Bishop as Evangelist," 85; Shiner, *Reading*, 29; Robinson, "Church of God," 230–52.

98. "Erastianism" refers to an ecclesiastical system wherein the state possesses authority in matters pertaining to the church. Frame, "Anglican History," 120–28, 124; MacCulloch, *Reformation*, 30; Lindberg, *European Reformations*, 321–29.

if the diocese adopted it. This rendered the General Synod's contribution to national unity to be more a persuasive and permissive influence than a coercive one. It also presented a challenge to national cohesion in the face of the diversity of the Australian dioceses—establishing a context wherein each diocese was mindful of their *independence from* the national body while being *dependent upon* it for the realization of key reforms.[99]

Such a combination of factors undoubtedly created a recipe for heightened tension. In this regard, Robinson's handling of several pastorally charged issues (like the ordination of women to the priesthood and the remarriage of divorced persons) was seen by many to be framed more in terms of a desire to uphold the faith and order of Anglicanism than by any principled recourse to Scripture. To many clergy who had been raised on Robinson's scholarship, such an appeal *primarily* to ecclesiastical order became somewhat perplexing.[100] Such actions were matched by Robinson's curtailing of the passage of two other 1985 bills (on lay administration of the Lord's Supper and the ordination of women as deacons) which had passed the synod.[101] Robinson's conservatism regarding the reform of clerical vesture and the modernization of Sunday services, alongside his conservatism in the area of church architecture and furnishings, also intensified the mood of clerical frustration. Indeed, in 1991, Robinson courted outrage by publicly chastising clergy who had "released themselves" from the obligation to use only authorized prayer book forms. He charged that such actions ignored the principle of consensus on which the AAPB was produced, as well as "the terms of a minister's license" and the evident "law of

---

99. Kaye, "Anglican Identity," 154–76.

100. On the ordination of women to the priesthood Robinson was opposed to the proposition as a "non-negotiable matter." However, Robinson nowhere published a scriptural rationale for his opposition. Instead, in 1987 he reasoned that to ordain women as priests without securing "canonical authority" would place Anglicans "at variance with the faith and order we receive from the apostolic church." On the question of remarriage Robinson was similarly obstructive. Indeed, against the advice of three Synod committees who had each issued calls for principled reform in this area, Robinson cited his responsibility to administer the ecclesiastical law and refused to consider their proposals. Indeed, in 1985 Robinson refused to grant assent to the related ordinance (which had passed the Synod) that sought to legislate the reforms proposed by these committees. This was only the second time a Sydney Archbishop had declined to give assent on a matter of principle. Yet, believing the Synod was not at liberty to act *without* a canon of General Synod, under Robinson the issue lapsed. This left clergy with the prospect of needing to act without an approved framework and denied Anglican rites to those wishing to remarry even on legitimate scriptural grounds. Judd and Cable, *Sydney Anglicans*, 305; Ballantine-Jones, *Political Factor*, 172–82.

101. Judd and Cable, *Sydney Anglicans*, 305; Cameron, *Phenomenal Sydney*, 162.

the Church."[102] For figures like Chapman—who had supported Robinson's election and continued to hold him in high regard—such tendencies were increasingly concerning.[103] Indeed, while Chapman took "no joy" in being at odds with his archbishop,[104] he began to share privately the concerns of a growing number that Robinson's leadership was approaching a point of crisis.[105] In private correspondence he wrote:

> At standing committee the archbishop told us he is contemplating withholding his assent to no less than five ordinances... He is consulting the world about them! How I wish he'd consulted the Bible. It will be the all-time record—five!!! I have written to him about [the ordinance relating to] relief from wearing the surplice and told him that it will provoke anarchy and call in a spate of non-statutory services where men [simply] don't wear them. I took the opportunity to point out that men of initiative will not be ordained when there is no chance of any reform taking place... I have never known a time when morale is so low ... It is so unhappy and so many are complaining that it can't go on much longer I hope. Autocratic leadership is so ugly and so unlike the Bible. I hate it because it reminds me so much about those early days in Armidale when old Bishop Moyes not only had unlimited power but took twice as much more than he should have. It was the worst face of Episcopacy. Pray that we will know what to do and when to oppose him. I don't want to be ungodly but he seems to me to be systematically dismantling the show. The last thing we need is princely bishops strutting around... However, the gospel is as good as ever.[106]

In 1985, the proposed ordinance giving relief to the wearing of a surplice one service per Sunday passed the synod unanimously. However, following this, Robinson addressed the synod. He described the ordinance as "a most radical departure from tradition" and cast doubt on whether he would assent to it. Reflecting on Robinson's response, Chapman again expressed his concern that if "such a simple reform could not be made,

---

102. 1992 *Yearbook*, 265–69; cf. Robinson, "Liturgical Patterns," 331.
103. Chapman to Lane, October 19, 1985. Box 3, Adrian Lane Papers.
104. Chapman to Lane, October 1, 1988. Box 3, Adrian Lane Papers.
105. Chapman to Lane, November 5, 1985. Box 3, Adrian Lane Papers.
106. The ordinances for which Robinson had advised he may withhold assent were: "Relief to the Wearing of Surplice," "Ordinance to Ordain Women as Deacons," "Bishop to the Defence Forces," "A Service for Ordaining Deacons," and "Ordinance to Allow for Remarriage of Divorced Persons." So Chapman to Lane, October 1, 1988, Box 3, Adrian Lane Papers.

then NOTHING can be changed."[107] Such comments were undoubtedly indicative of a growing collective frustration during this period as even the most elementary kind of change became seemingly subject to the stifling effects of ecclesiastical process.

With the election of Archbishop Goodhew at the height of this era, a weight of expectation for change thus followed Goodhew into office. As a widely respected consensus builder with a firm but gracious manner, Goodhew had declared that *his approach* to achieving the desired changes would not be by force, but by the inexorable power of positive consensus and the gradual reform of Anglican polity.[108] As Bishop of Wollongong, Goodhew had supported a range of growth and evangelistic initiatives. He had also been sympathetic toward a more radical change agenda via his support for moves toward lay administration of the Lord's Supper.[109] However, in assuming office, like his predecessors Goodhew was faced with the unenviable task of promoting consensus *and* change among members of a diocese geared to proceed according to different speeds and agendas. Indeed, while numerous gains in missional strategy were achieved during Goodhew's term,[110] attaining the hoped-for consensus assumed an order of complexity that was almost insuperable. New social trends in the areas of gender and sexual ethics remained a source of contention in the synod and across the secular press.[111] Goodhew's inelegant management of a Sydney parish's efforts to divest itself of its newly installed rector also precipitated a firestorm of disapproval.[112] Moreover, while making tentative steps toward the production of more contextualized liturgies, Goodhew's caution in this area exasperated many

107. Chapman to Lane, October 19, 1985. Box 3, Adrian Lane Papers.

108. Goodhew sought to "stir [the] imagination" of his synod and invited them to embark with him on "major experiments" across the city to see "the kingdom of God growing." Yet, the path to achieving this, he advised, lay not in the abandonment of the past, but in reigniting the fires of corporate spiritual growth and becoming "dynamically Anglican." 1994 *Sydney Yearbook*, 305–8, 315–17, 321–22; Ballantine-Jones, *Political Factor*, 193.

109. Goodhew, "Evangelism Explosion"; Bishop R. H. Goodhew, "Resolution 18/85. Lay Presidency at the Holy Communion," 1986 *Sydney Yearbook*, 244.

110. The pursuit of church planting as a missional strategy gained momentum during Goodhew's term. In 2000 the Sydney Synod passed the "Recognised Churches Ordinance." This resulted in a wave of extra-parochial fellowships being established across Sydney and the national church. Despite the potential for friction with other dioceses that such actions raised, Goodhew played a permissive role. DOE Newsletter, August–October 1998; Sydney Diocesan Services, "Recognised Churches."

111. Baird, "Brothers Huddle"; *Southern Cross*, December 1994, 5; *Southern Cross*, April 2000, 8.

112. 1995 *Sydney Yearbook*, 310–16. For analysis of the 1993 events in the Parish of Pymble, see Cameron, *Phenomenal Sydney*, 188–89.

(including Chapman) who were pressing for more rapid change to worship culture within Sydney churches.[113] Their critique was driven by the belief (as articulated by Chapman) that on account of the diminishing percentage of Australians attending Anglican worship there was now little room (even in the relatively robust Sydney context) for pretending Anglicans remained a "large, powerful" religious constituency.[114] Rather, Chapman averred, only a realistic acceptance of Anglicanism's diminished status would precipitate the kind of reforming energy that might reverse such trends and rescue the diocese from the world of ecclesiastical tedium in which it often engaged.[115] Consequently, during Goodhew's term Chapman privately, and forcefully voiced such concerns to the archbishop. This was a painful development in their long association, which was later restored.[116] Yet, such sentiments reflected a continuing conviction, especially among the ranks of younger clergy, that excessive caution did little to imbue the diocese with a culture necessary to respond to the challenges of a secularizing world.[117]

During Archbishop Jensen's episcopacy (2001–13) the revolution in culture and practice that had long been championed by such prominent change agents as Chapman received a high degree of official support. Elected with the goodwill of this largely younger clerical constituency, in 2002 Jensen launched what became known as the "Diocesan Mission." One of the most ambitious projects the diocese had ever undertaken, this mission aspired to sweeping changes at all levels of diocesan life and to a realignment of its resources to reach 10 percent of the city's population. The mission culminated in a year-long evangelistic initiative entitled "Connect 09." Marking fifty years since the 1959 Graham Crusade, the initiative pooled the dioceses' energies towards an ambitious "make-Jesus-known" campaign.

---

113. In the face of calls for speedier liturgical reform, Goodhew acknowledged the need to be culturally "relevant" while considering the "long-term consequences of our practices." "I am of the opinion," he charged, "that ordered worship that has a degree of commonality is a distinctive feature of Anglicanism." Goodhew thus issued a "challenge" to the Sydney Liturgical Commission "to engage in a long-term process of producing contemporary material that will contribute to the ongoing work of liturgical revision." This resulted in the publication of the *Sunday Services* resource in 2001—the first authorized liturgical resource for Sydney congregations since the 1978 *Australian Prayer Book*. The "Sunday Services" resource was also motivated after the rejection of the 1995 General Synod's *A Prayer Book for Australia* (APBA), which many in Sydney felt sanctioned the reintroduction of Catholic symbolism. Cameron, *Phenomenal Sydney*, 218; 1993 *Sydney Yearbook*, 306–7; 1996 *Sydney Yearbook*, 303.

114. Chapman to Lane, 16 October 1987. Box 3, Adrian Lane Papers.

115. Chapman to Lane, 19 October 1985. Box 3, Adrian Lane Papers.

116. Interview with Harry Goodhew, November 4, 2016.

117. Ballantine-Jones, *Political Factor*, 221–30.

Resources were developed by a steering committee alongside the encouragement of a range of initiatives in parishes and the staging of city-wide mission events.[118] In net terms, during the period of the diocesan mission, a 127 percent increase in parish giving across the diocese translated into a modest 7.2 percent increase in Sydney parish attendances. Sydney leaders (and especially those having advocated for widespread systemic change) had undoubtedly desired a far deeper impact than was realized from either the diocesan mission or its Connect 09 focal point. Such a reality, however, was perhaps as much indicative of the magnitude of the external threats and obstacles to Christian belief in a relentlessly secular culture as it was reflective of any lingering deficiencies in the church's attempts to reach that culture.[119] Indeed, with one in five Australians living in the Sydney region—an estimated 60 percent of whom had little or no contact with organized Christianity—the task before the diocese had moved beyond merely the need for religious revival.[120] Rather, in an increasingly post-Christian society the entire re-evangelization of the society had become the overwhelming task at hand. The complexity of this task and the somewhat modest progress made toward achieving it (even in the Jensen era when the balance between episcopal "authority" and "change" was perhaps in strongest alignment) was a sobering realization for many.[121] Indeed, the modest success that even the vast energy of the Jensen era met with posed a subtle corrective to the assumptions of a generation of clergy—including Chapman—who had often inferred that the impediments to missionally driven growth were all substantially *internal* and were of the diocese's own making. Rather, for all the sound and fury exerted in their protracted quest for "change," by the early new century it had become increasingly evident that the path toward religious renewal was no linear or straightforward affair.

Principles and Legacies of Reform

Principles of Reform

For all the strenuous advocacy of this era, however, was there a consistent vision that guided the choices of Chapman and others as they championed the need for change? For indeed, one of the frustrations of leaders across the

---

118. Ballantine-Jones, *Political Factor*, 245–70.

119. McLeod, *Religious Crisis*, 14, 208; Brown, "Religious Crisis," 473–79; Bruce, "Secularization," 10.

120. Percy, "Connection."

121. Ballantine-Jones, *Political Factor*, 267–78.

national church during this era concerning the stance of Sydney Anglicans on various policy matters was the simultaneously restrictive *and* radical positions that were seemingly taken.[122] Was there a coherent policy framework that may be said to explain the various positions adopted? Such a question may be assessed with reference to two key policy issues of this era, namely: the ordination of women and the lay administration of the Lord's Supper.

The Ordination of Women

The question of the ordination of women to the priesthood was undoubtedly one of the most contentious policy issues to confront the diocese and wider denomination during this period. While the issue itself invited wide-ranging theological dialogue, the need to attain assent at both local *and* national synodical levels for any reform to Anglican practice was a dynamic that fueled an extended confrontation across the national church. In this vein, following a wave of ordination ceremonies for women in various dioceses across the world, the issue came to a head in the Australian church in 1977 when the General Synod Doctrine Commission concluded that it saw no objection to women being ordained to any of the three orders of Anglican ministry.[123] Seeking to apply this ruling, in 1981 the General Synod passed a canon allowing each diocese to ordain women to all three orders of ministry. However, the Sydney diocese effectively vetoed this canon and continually opposed it on theological grounds throughout the 1980s.[124] Sydney's opposition led ultimately to the 1992 case (known as *Scandrett v Dowling*) that came before the NSW Supreme Court. In this

---

122. See for example the critique of Porter, *Melbourne Anglicans*, 80–111; Porter, "Debates and Issues," 141–48.

123. Such a position was motivated by a range of opinions, including: 1) prevailing feminist ideology that opposed all gender distinctions; 2) a belief that the prohibition of women's ordination was a denial of the rights of women as equal members of Christ's church; and 3) a positive view of the work done by women in churches and on the mission field which reinforced the belief that there should be no impediment to their also being permitted to serve in the ordained ministry. For detailed analysis of such views, see Beck, *Two Views on Women*; Grenz and Muir Kjesbo, *Women in the Church*.

124. Known as the "headship principle," the opposition of Sydney leaders to the ordination of women to the priesthood derived from an exegesis of passages like 1 Corinthians 11:2–16, 1 Timothy 2–3, and Ephesians 5:22–33. Such a position stated that while men and women enjoy an equality of status as beings created in the image of God, this did not correlate to a sameness of role in the family or in the church. Indeed, grounded in an equality in the persons of the Godhead which is nevertheless expressed by a difference in role and function, proponents of this view suggest that such a reality supplies a template for equality *and* difference in gender roles in the church. Thiselton, *First Epistle*, 799–806; Knight, *Pastoral Epistles*, 138–42.

highly publicized case (carrying echoes of the "Red Book Case") leading Sydney figures sought an injunction against the actions of Bishop Owen Dowling of Canberra-Goulburn who, in frustration, had announced his intention to ordain a number of women to the priesthood in 1991. Appealing to the constitution of the Anglican Church of Australia (ACA), the Sydney plaintiffs sought a determination that Dowling had no authority to proceed. However, in July 1992 the full bench of the NSW Court of Appeal found *against* the Sydney plaintiffs. In a ruling that had far-reaching implications for the cohesion of the national church, the court ruled that the constitution of the ACA was not a legally enforceable instrument except in matters pertaining to church property. This left each local synod at increasing liberty to organize its own affairs, and the ordination of women followed as a matter of course across the national church.[125]

However, notwithstanding the commitment of figures like Chapman to what became the majority position of the Sydney synod on the ordination of women to the priesthood, Chapman himself was also sensitive to the quest for change. Chapman was present at the General Synod sessions in 1985, 1987, and 1989 in which the initial requests for reform were made and had supported a conservative position on all three occasions. However, Chapman also lamented the injury done to Anglican unity and the loss in transferability of ordination rites across the Australian dioceses as a result of the eventual outcome. He also lamented the injury done to the many Anglican women who had genuinely sought change in this area only to see it consistently denied.[126] Moreover, despite his innate conservatism on such questions, as a member of the Sydney standing committee Chapman had also been one of the instigators of what he regarded to be a measured and scripturally sanctioned reform. In 1985 he moved in the standing committee that a bill authorizing the ordination of women as deacons *should* be promoted to the General Synod[127] and expressed frustration when Archbishop Robinson curtailed the passage of this reform.[128] Indeed, for Chapman, the holding of a "conservative" position on the question of female ordination

---

125. For extended analysis see Cameron, *Phenomenal Sydney*, 151–70; Ballantine-Jones, *Political Factor*, 75–84.

126. Chapman articulated and outlined each of these positions in a series of private correspondences with Adrian Lane during the 1980s. See Chapman to Lane, September 7, 1985; Chapman to Lane, September 7, 1987; Chapman to Lane, November 28, 1988; Chapman to Lane, August 25, 1989; Chapman to Lane, October 7, 1989. Box 3, Adrian Lane Papers.

127. W. Gotley to J. Chapman, February 16, 1994, BDM Box 1, SDA (Gotley was Diocesan Secretary from 1973–1994).

128. Chapman to Lane, October 19, 1985, Box 3, Adrian Lane Papers.

to the *priesthood* and a "progressive" position on female ordination to the *diaconate* was an unconflicted matter of biblical principle. He reasoned that since deacons would not serve as parish incumbents (church overseers) such a reform did not threaten what he regarded to be the legitimate principle of the servant leadership of Christian men in the home and in the church as the household of God (1 Tim 3:15).[129] As such, in unison with other Sydney figures, Chapman tailored his advocacy for the reform of ecclesiastical practice in each case by the application of biblically driven principles.

Lay Administration of the Lord's Supper

Similarly, with the equally incendiary issue of Lay Administration of the Lord's Supper, Chapman's advocacy for the reform of ecclesiastical practice assumed an ostensibly "radical" rather than "conservative" position. In the Anglican Communion only bishops and priests had customarily been permitted to preside at services of Holy Communion. Significant conjecture surrounds the origins of this precedent.[130] However, by the mid-twentieth century, the rise of a gifted and theologically qualified laity began to see a surge in the participation of lay people in aspects of Anglican worship previously reserved for the clergy alone. Indeed, regarding services of the Lord's Supper, while a strict adherence to the rubrics of the *Book of Common Prayer* demanded they all be read *only* by an ordained clergyman, by this time it had become commonplace that only "The Prayer of Consecration" now retained the original priestly hedge. This created a context in which lay persons came to participate in almost every aspect of Anglican worship *except* that which had now become an ostensibly "priestly" rite.[131] Even more concerning for evangelicals was the fact that for many of their Anglican peers the celebration

---

129. On such arguments, see Thiselton, *First Epistle*, 799–806; Knight, *Pastoral Epistles*, 138–42.

130. The Reformers rejected much of the mystical understanding of the Lord's Supper that developed via the Catholic tradition and played down the significance of the role of the priest. Following this, however, significant restrictions came to surround the ministries of the church which, while well intentioned, ultimately came to undermine the understanding of the sacrament they sought to protect. Within the context of a newly reformed English Church the *Book of Common Prayer* (1662) prohibited the taking part by *any* lay person in public worship and specified that only those episcopally ordained could administer the sacrament. This was not reflective of an innate suitability on the part of the priest for this task. Rather, in a day of widespread theological illiteracy the restriction was issued to guard the gospel from error by leaving *all* ministry in clerical hands. Thompson, "Theological Considerations," 21–35; Woodhouse, "Stay the Same," 12.

131. Woodhouse, "Stay the Same," 10.

of Communion had come to be seen as in fact "central to the life of the church" and "presidency at the eucharist" as *the* "focal point of the ministry of word, sacrament and pastoral care to which a man is . . . ordained."[132] Such was the strength of feeling about this now essentially "priestly" rite that many Anglican leaders declared themselves "scandalized" by calls for reform and suggested that any change to this restriction was "more radical than any changes in belief and practice over the previous 400 years."[133] As a result of such developments, many evangelicals felt strongly that the prohibition of the "non-priest" from administering the Lord's Supper had begun to obscure the very gospel they sought to uphold.[134]

Such concerns gave rise in the Sydney diocese to a protracted campaign for the removal of this priestly restriction that lasted some forty years. Though no single figure could be said to have led the prosecution of this issue, John Chapman supplied critical impetus (both formally and informally), particularly in the campaign's early years. In the initial mid-1970s stages of this campaign, the actions of Sydney diocesan figures were primarily in response to the actions of the General Synod which itself had taken steps to account for the irregularities caused by the rise of lay ministries across the nation.[135] This culminated in the request by the 1976 Sydney synod for a study of "The Meaning, Value and Theology of Ordination."[136] In 1977, Chapman led the synod in requesting the committee responsible for this study to "investigate the issue of licensing lay persons for the ministry of Word and Sacrament and to report to the next session of Synod."[137] Such actions led ultimately to a report produced by the synod in 1981 that offered

---

132. Anglican Church of Australia, "Theology of Ordination," 43.

133. Porter, "Debates and Issues," 145; Woodhouse, "Stay the Same," 7–9.

134. Woodhouse, "Stay the Same," 8.

135. In this vein, the question of lay involvement in the Lord's Supper had first emerged across the Australian church *outside* the Sydney diocese in various missionary contexts and under pressures associated with inadequate clergy numbers. In an effort to account for such irregularities and the involvement of lay persons in public ministries, at the 1971 General Synod urgent consideration was requested to be given to "whether laymen might rightly be given a commission of local and temporary effect to preside at the Eucharist." This resulted in the passing of the 1973 General Synod *Lay Assistants at the Holy Communion Canon* which authorized lay persons to "assist the priest in the ministration of the Holy Communion" while giving Australian dioceses the right to limit the ministries of the laity under the canon. For background see Bolt, "Timeline," 36–67; Frith, "Role of the Laity," 37–50.

136. Bolt, "Timeline," 36, 64.

137. J. C. Chapman, 4.10.77, "9/77. Licensing Lay Persons for Ministry of Word and Sacrament," 1978 *Yearbook*, 242.

tentative support for the removal of the priestly restriction.[138] Despite such affirmations, the position of the Australian General Synod simultaneously hardened. A report produced by the General Synod Doctrine Commission in 1981 stated emphatically that while no *identifiable* doctrinal obstacle could be raised against the practice, in its judgment lay presidency would nevertheless "be inimical to the good order of the church."[139]

In the early 1980s the campaign continued at the national and synodical levels. At the 1981 National Evangelical Anglican Conference (NEAC) Chapman presented a paper in which he vigorously argued the case for reform. Examining the (albeit limited) biblical teaching on the Lord's Supper, he described it as a "visible preaching of the Gospel" in which the believer was reminded of Christ's atonement, coming judgment, and the promise of God's acceptance when combined with a life of active faith.[140] He also critically appraised a range of historic precedents suggesting the "Bishop" (understood as the overseer of a congregation) to have been the figure most likely to "preside" at communion. However, in light of the Bible's *complete silence* on the question of eucharistic "presidency," Chapman consequently issued an impassioned charge to his colleagues across the national church. He said:

> At the present time we have arrived, in most dioceses in Australia, where duly authorized persons can perform everything at our . . . services *except* say the prayer of consecration . . . It is possible . . . to have the prayers read by a lay person, others to read Bible readings, others to say the prayer for the church, a lay-reader to preach and distribute the bread and wine. In fact, he may do it all *except* say the prayer of consecration. Consequently it is now an urgent matter to authorize lay persons to conduct the Lord's Supper for the following reasons: . . . a) If the present "new" situation is allowed to become our practice, we will have endorsed a doctrine about the Lord's Supper and ordained minister (by default). This will make the prayer of consecration almost a magic act. There is *no* doctrinal reason why an authorized preacher of God's word should not be authorized to take a service of the Lord's Supper, b) To refuse to do this will drive a wedge between the ministry of the Word

---

138. The report concluded there was insufficient evidence to know who regularly administered baptism in the New Testament and even less evidence concerning the administration of the Lord's Supper. *Report: Meaning, Value and Theology*, 8.

139. *1981 Report of the General Synod Commission on Doctrine*, 28, 43–45.

140. Chapman, "Lay Presidency," 103–9. In his analysis, Chapman discussed the major biblical passages on the Supper: 1 Cor 10:14–17; 11:17–33; Luke 22:17–23; Mark 14:23–25, Matt 26:26–29, Acts 2:38–41; John 6.

and sacrament, as well as the sacrament of baptism which can be administered by a lay person and that of the Lord's Supper which may not . . . c) In many dioceses in Australia there are isolated groups of Christians who because of their numbers cannot afford a minister . . . These people have the Lord's Supper when the Rector [can] come . . . This is a highly unsatisfactory situation . . . It (i) challenges the validity of the ministry of the local leaders, (ii) gives the people a false view of the ministry of the ordained minister, (iii) gives the ordained minister a false view of his ministry, and (iv) gives a false view of the sacrament of the Holy Communion, d) There are some situations where deaconesses exercise the ministry of chaplains in girls' schools . . . hospitals, jails and other institutions. It is absurd to have to bring in an ordained minister to conduct the Holy Communion in such situations. It cannot but undermine the ministry of the deaconess . . . and e) These difficulties are felt more acutely in some dioceses than others. Some have "solved" the problem by "reserving the elements" and having lay-readers take the service without the prayer of consecration. This is so unsatisfactory to me as an evangelical that it provides yet another reason why it is [now urgent] to take action for change.[141]

In tandem with such protestations, the Sydney synod continued to pursue avenues for how the findings of its 1981 report (*The Meaning, Value and Theology of Ordination*) might be implemented. This precipitated a series of maneuvers that culminated in the Sydney synod (1985) and its standing committee (1986) passing resolutions affirming their belief that there existed "no doctrinal objections to lay presidency in the context contemplated by the Synod" and that the practice did "not contravene any "principle of worship" of the *Book of Common Prayer*."[142] Despite the clarity of the synod's position, however, a lengthy process ensued which, alongside a rapidly changing Anglican landscape, combined to forestall the practice of even "diaconal administration" until 2008. A series of resolutions and counter-resolutions by the Sydney and national synods in the early 1990s led ultimately to a 1998 ruling by the General Synod Appellate Tribunal (when invited to arbitrate) which stated that it *was* consistent with the 1961 constitution for lay people to administer Communion provided that a canon of the General Synod authorizing the practice was in place.[143]

141. Chapman, "Lay Presidency," 106–7.

142. "Report of Standing Committee," 1987 *Sydney Yearbook*, 258–59, cited in Bolt, "Timeline," 41, 65.

143. For extensive analysis, including the referral of Sydney's course to the Appellate

Notwithstanding the Appellate Tribunal's significant affirmation, however, in August 1998 the Archbishop of Canterbury announced that Resolution 1.10 of the Lambeth Conference had passed by a significant majority. This resolution, which upheld biblical teaching on questions of marriage and sexual ethics, was to mark a watershed moment for the Anglican Communion.[144] The deliberate breach of this resolution in 2002 by the actions of the Bishop of New Westminster (Canada) and the Diocese of New Hampshire in 2003 (USA) set in motion forces which severely tested the ties that bound the communion together.[145] Such watershed realignments directly impacted the campaign for lay administration. Indeed, in what appeared to be a long-coveted victory in which it ratified its previous affirmations, the 1999 Sydney synod voted to allow lay administration for a trial period of five years.[146] However, reflecting the heavy encroachment of such wider developments, in November 1999 Archbishop Goodhew indicated that he would not assent to the synod's decision. He indicated that the 1998 Appellate Tribunal's opinion that a diocese should not act unilaterally without a canon of General Synod weighed heavily upon him. He also explained that since Lambeth 1998 he had added his voice to wider calls for bishops to avoid all unilateral action on questions of sexual ethics. Consequently, he felt that "to act unilaterally" on an issue that was also seen as being contrary to the will of the global communion would undermine not only his, but also the diocese's credibility in such ongoing debates. It would also add impetus to the dynamics rending the communion apart.[147] Goodhew's caution, coupled with such wider considerations, gave rise to an acceptance among members of the synod that to find "a constitutionally legal way to proceed" that neither compromised the instruments of Anglican unity *nor* Sydney's standing in the wider communion at this juncture,

---

Tribunal see Bolt, "Timeline," 44.

144. Skidmore, "Lambeth Struggles"; Bolt, "Timeline," 53.

145. In 2002 the Bishop of New Westminster authorized a service for the blessing of same-sex couples. The election in 2003 of an openly homosexual man as Bishop of New Hampshire (USA) caused further strain. The Report of a Primatial Committee set up to examine the implications of these developments (the Windsor Report) concluded strongly that both the Episcopal Church of the United States of America (ECUSA) and the Diocese of New Westminster had deviated from "the standard of Anglican teaching" and had departed "from genuine, apostolic faith." ECUSA, however, responded by questioning the existence of any universal jurisdiction within Anglicanism. This placed significant strain on the instruments of Anglican unity and led directly to a more permanent state of impaired global communion. Frame, *Anglicans*, 188–202.

146. The 1999 Sydney Synod passed the legislation by a 346 to 194 majority. Bolt, "Timeline," 55.

147. 2000 *Sydney Yearbook*, 402.

presented the best (indeed the only) path to reform.[148] Crucially, having sought a range of constitutionally sanctioned paths forward, in 2007 the synod received a standing committee report advising that in light of the 1998 Appellate Tribunal ruling, a legitimate legal pathway toward lay presidency *may* already exist. Drawing attention to a 1985 General Synod Canon (*Ordination Service for Deacons*) which negotiated a range of changes in a deacon's responsibilities, the report suggested that the administration of Holy Communion was *already* an activity *implicit* in a deacon's responsibilities as recognized by the General Synod.[149] In light of this, the 2007 Standing Committee Report concluded that "for diaconal administration . . . at least, there *is* a way forward by simply licensing deacons to administer the sacraments in accordance with their ordination responsibilities."[150] Persuaded by this rationale, the 2008 Sydney Synod passed a resolution that sanctioned the practice of diaconal administration, while reaffirming its support for lay administration. After that time, although lay administration remained unauthorized and legislation for both practices remained outstanding at the national level, tacit permission was granted in Sydney for diaconal administration to occur.[151]

Legacies of Reform

What then is to be made of the long-running nature of this and other issues that were fought or which transpired during this highly contentious era of reform? It is undoubtedly the case that the scale and extent of the reforms that were sought and enacted during this era can be correlated closely with the scale and extent of the cultural change that was taking place. Indeed, in an era which numerous religious historians have described as a moment of religious and cultural "rupture" as profound as the Reformation or Enlightenment eras, the magnitude of the changes negotiated by Chapman and other leading figures was little short of a revolution.[152] As a result of their advocacy a flood of change in church attire, architecture, fellowship

---

148. Bolt, "Timeline," 57.

149. In the 1985 Canon, the bishop declared: "receive this sign of your authority to proclaim God's word and assist in the administration of the sacraments." Sydney figures argued that this implicitly included the administration of Communion in a deacon's responsibilities. Davies, "Authorisation," 68–69.

150. "26/03 Lay and Diaconal Administration of Holy Communion Legal Impediments," 2008 *Yearbook*, 528–43.

151. Ballantine-Jones, *Political Factor*, 117, 145; Bolt, "Timeline," 63.

152. McLeod, *Religious Crisis*; McLeod, "Crisis of Christianity," 327–40; Brown, "Religious Crisis," 468–79.

practices, liturgy, and worship rendered the experience of contemporary Sydney Anglicans almost unrecognizable from that of their forebears who stood in an equally Reformed-conservative tradition.[153] What then constituted the key vision that shaped the choices made by such figures as they championed the case for change? It is arguable that the initiatives they championed may be explained by seeing their choices as operating between the balance of two poles—namely a desire to advance and defend the gospel *and* an equal desire to uphold the scriptural integrity of Anglicanism. When viewed through this lens, the seemingly countervailing positions adopted (both conservative *and* radical) become more easily understood.

Such a paradigm can be seen, for example, in the reforms to liturgical and ministry practice. What motivated the quest to so radically alter the forms of clothing, speech, and services that had characterized Anglican worship for generations? Viewing with a sense of alarm the sharp decline in church attendances across Western societies, leading evangelicals like Chapman evidently sought to promote a range of reforms and new ministries they believed might best advance the gospel and aid the church's mission in a changing context. Undoubtedly, this strategy brought with it a variety of challenges and (in the opinion of some) the potential for significant losses to the richness of Anglican worship.[154] Not unaware of such pitfalls, Chapman and other change leaders continued to urge, however, that built into Anglicanism's formularies was the expectation of *ongoing* reform. Consequently, while the process of change *would* continue to be unsettling, he suggested, the growth of the gospel "demanded" that contemporary Anglicans continue to strive in their ministries to present the "unchanging gospel in new and appropriate ways."[155] Notwithstanding such a commitment to bold mission-driven reform, the equal commitment of Chapman and others to the process of *legally sanctioned* change is also noteworthy. Indeed, seeing in Anglicanism's liturgical inheritance a highpoint of Anglican doctrine to which the church had submitted itself, evangelicals like Chapman were also mindful that this supplied a rule of faith against which *all change* was to be measured and a safeguard against the threat of deleterious doctrinal innovation. Consequently, the often painstaking process of reform pursued by such figures is

---

153. Spinks, "Liturgy," 471; Whiteman, "Contextualization," 3; Atherstone, "Semper Reformanda," 35–37.

154. Some suggested that while the abandoning of traditional liturgies was to be applauded as a striving for relevance, others believed the style of worship that replaced such liturgies was doctrinally thin, lacking balance or the unifying rhythm of prayer book worship. See D. Peterson, 1993 *Sydney Yearbook*, 307; Horsburgh, "High Politics."

155. See J. C. Chapman, "Committee Re Church Growth," *Sydney Diocesan Yearbook* 1991, 378, nos. 26–27, 43–45.

evidence of their recognition of the scriptural integrity of such formularies and their desire not to compromise but to uphold them.

The same dynamic can be seen in the handling of such issues as the ordination of women and lay administration of the Lord's Supper. For, as noted, the simultaneously conservative *and* radical positions taken by Chapman and others on such questions can be explained by seeing their advocacy as charting a balance between these poles. That is, seeking to reform all practice according to scriptural principles (as they saw it) such figures adopted a conservative stance on the question of female ordination to the priesthood (mixed with a supportive stance on female deaconesses) and defended this in the Sydney and national synods. Similarly, those elements of Anglicanism that were seen as vestiges of the church's only partially reformed past (such as the "presidency" of the "priest" at the Supper) were viewed as impediments to a more consistently Reformed future and were opposed. Either way, whether a radical or conservative position was adopted, the exhaustive legal pursuit of these issues by Chapman and others via the Sydney and national synods is evidence of their commitment to upholding the scriptural fidelity of Anglicanism. Often this involved the expenditure of vast political capital and the straining and even the loss of goodwill. Yet, amidst a changing secular and ecclesial environment, such measures were seen not only as an inescapable cost of the gospel's preservation but as a legitimate avenue for attaining reform objectives that were both consensual *and* constitutional. Convinced of this, leading Sydney figures invested substantial energy in campaigns to both placate and persuade their co-religionists.[156]

In the final analysis, however, all of this is evidence that the modern transformation in liturgical and ministry expression in Sydney and across the Anglican Communion constituted the inescapable remaking of Anglicanism for the contemporary world. For, the speed of twentieth-century cultural change and the fissures emerging across the Anglican Communion left many asking questions of foundational importance about the nature of Anglicanism. Such questions gave rise to even deeper questions about the nature of authentic faith and the application of Scripture in the contemporary world.[157] Indeed, drawing parallels with the Reformation era—in which the Reformers were thrust back upon Scripture and the interpretive traditions of the early church to answer such questions in their own time—leading contemporary commentators suggested that a process of similar magnitude was occurring (and would continue) in the contemporary

---

156. MacCulloch, *Reformation*, 30; Frame, "History," 122–28; Kaye, "Anglican Identity," 154–76; Bolt, "Timeline," 43.

157. "Preface," in Null and Yates, "Manifesto," 11.

world.[158] In this sense, drawing on the continually reforming vision of worship emerging from the Anglican formularies, an effectively "remade Anglicanism," they posited, would continue to exhibit a continuity with key aspects of its historic DNA.[159] Moreover, Anglicanism's historically "porous" nature and its appropriation of the strengths of other traditions would also likely see it continue to creatively assimilate new influences.[160] However, they posited, perhaps the *greatest constant* that would define an effectively remade Anglicanism in such a rapidly shifting milieu, would be the reality of ongoing missionally driven change. Such change and constancy, flexibility, and rigidity, they suggested, has marked the commitment of the church in each age, as it has sought to promote timeless truths via timely means and to mold all ecclesiastical practice in the service of Christ.[161] Furthermore, as the foregoing analysis has shown, such a commitment arguably defines the central agenda of the generation of evangelical Anglican leaders of which Chapman was a crucial member.

Conclusion

This chapter has examined the legacy of Chapman as a key figure in a generation of clerical leaders tasked with navigating the church's response to one of the most significant cultural and religious revolutions since the Reformation and Enlightenment eras. In this environment Chapman gave leadership and expression to a movement which championed a wave of missionally driven change that rendered the experience of contemporary Sydney Anglicans almost unrecognizable from that of their forebears. At the same time, as an enthusiastic advocate of evangelical Anglicanism as a vehicle for effective gospel mission, Chapman sought to promote a kind of change that vigorously safeguarded the formularies of Anglicanism, inasmuch as they were seen to uphold the authority of Scripture to which the church had submitted. Such an offensive *and* defensive reform agenda issued in the investment (by Chapman and other change leaders) in extended political campaigns by which they sought to placate *and* persuade their Anglican co-religionists of the benefits of change or the maintenance of present ministry practice. Amidst a rapidly changing context such (often contentious) measures were seen as an inescapable cost of the gospel's progress *and* preservation.

158. "Preface," in Null and Yates, "Manifesto," 12; Avis, "Prayer Book Use," 135.

159. Null and Yates, "Manifesto," 186–201; Atherstone, "Semper Reformanda," 33–37.

160. McGrath, "Anglicanism," 314.

161. Whiteman, "Contextualization," 3.

Moreover, given the scale of the changes that ultimately accrued, this marks Chapman as a key figure in the development of a contextualized, twentieth-century Australian evangelical ministry culture.

9

The Spirit, the Word, and the Christian Life

Charismatic Renewal and Spirit-Filled Christianity

> "Jesus, in his earthly ministry, showed again and again that it was his will and practice to heal those who were sick . . . Jesus healed, he always healed, he never failed to heal, and he healed them all. Healing is what God wants done in the world and it is our responsibility to see it is carried out."—Canon Jim Glennon[1]

IN THE SMALL RURAL town of Moree in north-western New South Wales the arrival of an international religious figure was a significant event. In 1959 as Pentecostal evangelists began to proliferate in waves of transnational influence, a leading Pentecostal evangelist campaigned in Moree as part of a whistle-stop tour. The message of such evangelists was uncomplicated. The call to "surrender to Christ" alongside an invitation to experience the "full life" of New Testament Christianity was usually exhorted. Evidenced by the restoration of the charismatic gifts of tongues-speaking, prophecy, and miracles, God's end-time power, it was said, would be seen in the bodies and lives of those who truly believed in Him. "Divine healing" was therefore a significant element in their repertoire.[2] Conscious that his youth

---

1. Glennon, *Healing*, 28–29, 92. Jim Glennon was the founding leader of the healing ministry at St. Andrew's Cathedral in Sydney from 1960 to 1988.

2. Leading international healing revivalists such as A. S. Worley, O. Roberts, A. C. Valdez, and T. Hicks toured Australia between 1952 and 1959. Hutchinson,

fellowship would likely attend the meetings regardless of his own misgivings, the young Anglican curate, John Chapman, chaperoned the Moree Anglican youth fellowship to the revival tent in the middle of town. The emphasis on this particular evening was typical Pentecostal fare. Revival-style choruses were punctuated with an address that built to a poignant and emotive crescendo. However, as the meeting swelled to its conclusion with the invitation to surrender to Christ and receive healing, one of the better-known town personalities went forward to have his eyes healed. Wearing thick "coke-bottle-like" glasses, the man's eyesight had been a relentlessly frustrating experience. Seeking to reverse this situation, the evangelist laid hands on the man and prayed for the full restoration of his sight. Rubbing his eyes and looking around him after the prayer, the man exclaimed excitedly, "I can see!" Then, in an effort to demonstrate confidence that his healing had been received, the man promptly threw his glasses on the ground and forcefully stomped on them. However, upon leaving the stage the man promptly walked headlong and unceremoniously into a tent pole! Perhaps unsurprisingly, the event added a note of caution to the audience's heightening curiosity at the movement's energetic advance.[3]

In 1972, Chapman, now an emerging evangelical leader, attended another meeting, this time concerned with the *evaluation* of Pentecostal experience. Convened by the rector of the Sydney Parish of Darlinghurst, Bernard Gook, the meeting was called to discuss the rising tide of charismatic renewal which had begun to touch the mainline denominations since the early 1960s.[4] Over one hundred clergy attended the lengthy and at times emotionally charged meeting. The expanding healing ministry at St. Andrew's Cathedral and the influence of figures like Michael Harper of England's Fountain Trust had amplified such influences in the diocese.[5] As a result, some twenty-five rectors had become heavily influenced by charismatic thought and expression. Indeed, rallying under the leadership of Gook, these clergy spoke of a dryness that had consumed their ministries. Yet, they alleged, having experienced the "baptism of the Holy Spirit," evidenced in an experience of new joy and the reception of tongues-speaking, they spoke of ministries now transformed with a fervency they had not previously known. Moreover, they suggested, if the church was to renew its corporate power

---

"Pentecostals," 517–23; Chant, "Australian Pentecostal Movement," 97–122.

3. Interview with Phillip Jensen, February 16, 2017. This event was relayed to Jensen by Chapman.

4. Hutchinson, "Australia," 26–29.

5. Hutchinson, "Australia," 26–29; Interview with Rev. Dr. Peter Jensen, December 2, 2016.

for witness, then such an experience was to be believed and received by all.[6] Many clergy responded to such representations with considerable reserve. For, within the mainline churches the movement had emerged with such speed that it seemed to be "everywhere before it was anywhere" and its theological propositions were not yet well known.[7] Still others responded with a sense of incredulity at the realities being proposed. They jested that if they experienced a joy in their ministry now, then perhaps they had already experienced the blessing without knowing it.

Leading the conservative reply on this particular evening was the figure of John Chapman. Rising to his feet, Chapman led a tightly argued theological cross-examination that sought to clarify what was being claimed. Increasingly frustrated at the lengthy rebuttal, Gook replied that ultimately if one allowed rationalism to obstruct the reception of divine blessing, then such blessing would never be received. Yet, conscious of the impact of a spirituality which, if inaccurate, posed a burden to Christian conscience and a distorted view of divine grace, Chapman sought to add a note of carefully argued biblical reasoning to one of the most divisive issues of the era.[8]

The following chapter examines the rise and impact of Pentecostal and charismatic thought and expression in Australian Evangelicalism and the response of leading figures like Chapman in the historic denominations to this phenomenon.[9] Such an examination provides important insights into modern Evangelicalism. For, alongside its distinctive spiritual qualities,

---

6. Glennon, *Healing*, 92; Williams, "Baptism in the Holy Spirit," 359–60.

7. Hutchinson, "Pentecostals," 517.

8. Interview with Phillip Jensen, February 16, 2017; Barnett and Jensen, *Quest for Power*, 2.

9. The term "Pentecostalism" describes a cluster of related Christian restorationist movements with roots in Methodism and the nineteenth-century holiness and healing movements. "Pentecostalism" has exhibited three related but distinct stages. "Classic Pentecostalism" began among evangelicals in the early twentieth century. It espoused a post-conversion experience of "baptism in the Spirit," *glossolalia*, and divine healing. "Second-wave Pentecostalism" (or the "charismatic movement") impacted the historic denominations from the 1960s espousing a post-conversion experience of "renewal" and the exercise of *charismata* (spiritual gifts). "Third-wave Pentecostalism" emerged in the 1980s as charismatic renewal weakened in the historic churches. It grew rapidly in the Global South giving rise to hundreds of independent networks emphasizing the Spirit's empowerment in the Christian life. Pursuing the modernization of worship practices, third-wave Pentecostalism aided the renewal of classic Pentecostalism (via the rise of denominationally affiliated "new-style Pentecostal churches") across many parts of the world. "Pentecostalism" is used in this chapter to describe these related movements as a phenomenological whole, while the language of "classic Pentecostalism," "charismatic movement" and "third-wave Pentecostalism" denotes the distinctive movements. See Piggin and Linder, *National Soul*, 382–87; Anderson, "Pentecostal and Charismatic," 89–106; Anderson, *Ends of the Earth*, 1–10.

"Pentecostalism" was also an experiential response to the challenges of stifling traditionalism and rationalism in mainline churches. In this regard, it was highly successful in achieving a vibrant and contextualized public ministry culture. Indeed, by the end of the century Pentecostalism had established a pervasive global presence. It boasted some six hundred million adherents and had strongly influenced the mainline churches with its distinctive forms of ministry and worship. However, a strong reaction to aspects of charismatic expression (second-wave Pentecostalism) developed in mainline churches during the 1960s to 1980s. The strength of this mainline reaction moderated by the end of the century. However, by the 1990s many charismatic Christians had already departed the mainline churches to join separatist networks and denominations. Moreover, sufficient doctrinal and cultural distinctives had become embedded within Pentecostalism such that the compartmentalization between it and the mainline churches largely remained.[10] The following chapter thus details the growth of Pentecostalism and its impact on Australian Evangelicalism. By then detailing the theological and pastoral concerns that energized the local conservative reply, the chapter seeks to throw new light on one of the most dynamic yet divisive influences to impact Evangelicalism in the modern era. Once again, it will be seen that John Chapman played an important role in the conservative Australian response.

Origins of Pentecostalism

At the most foundational level, historic disparities over Pentecostal theology and expression may be reduced to a question of eschatology. That is, between the inauguration of the kingdom of God in the events of biblical history and its consummation in the return of Christ, the question over which disagreement has ranged concerns the shape of God's rule and the working of his Spirit in the world, church, and Christian life.[11] In answer to this question, Christian sympathies have ranged across a continuum between cessationist and continuationist thought. Cessationists have emphasized that the extraordinary working of God's Spirit in the events of biblical revelation and the endowment of "charismata" to the early church served as aids to establish the church in its infancy and accredit its teaching. However, in light of their chiefly authenticating and foundational role, such manifestations, cessationists allege, did not continue beyond the close

---

10. Maddox, "Mega-Churches," 325–29; Anderson, *Ends of the Earth*, 4; Satyavrata, "Globalization," 218–20; Piggin and Linder, *National Soul*, 385–86.

11. Brower, "Eschatology," 459–64.

of the apostolic era.[12] Continuationists on the other hand have stressed the availability (even necessity) of contemporary encounters of God's empowerment. They have maintained that the New Testament manifestations of the Spirit (like tongues-speaking, prophecy, healing, and visions) ought to mark Christian experience today, no less than in the first century. Hence, following the occurrence in the late nineteenth and early twentieth century of numerous revivals in parts of the world which manifested the reemergence of such charismata, early Pentecostals saw signs of the end of the age and the elevation of the church to its former level of "power" in preparation for Christ's return.[13]

While Pentecostal impulses have undoubtedly appeared at numerous historical junctures, the seeds of the modern movement were sown via the contours of Methodist enthusiasm.[14] Methodist historians have naturally emphasized the scientific and enlightenment interests of their founder and the social and spiritual benefits the movement produced. Nevertheless, while Wesley's co-religionists were far more circumspect about the place of extraordinary spiritual manifestations, Wesley appeared to encourage them. Narratives of dreams, faith healings, and exorcisms published in the *Arminian Magazine* provided the movement with material for inspiration and became a key contributor to Methodist spirituality. This played a role in establishing a climate of plausibility for later Pentecostal supernaturalism

---

12. Ruthven, "Cessationism," 84–86; Twelftree, "Signs and Wonders," 775.

13. Warrington, "Gifts of Healing," 232–34; Michaels, "Gifts of the Spirit," 215–18; Burgess, "Antecedents of Pentecostalism," 30–33.

14. For analysis of the antecedents of Pentecostalism, see Anderson, *Introduction to Pentecostalism*, 19–26. Regarding attitudes of the Christian mainstream to "continuationist" spirituality, the Reformation era was especially influential. Various reformers employed "cessationism" as a weapon to undercut Catholic claims to evolving doctrine and the authority of the pope. The supernatural interventions cited in medieval literature in support of Catholic dogma were said to be no more than the "lying wonders" of the false prophets Christ warned would proliferate in the last days. In contrast, the reformers stressed that their faith needed no external supports to prove its authenticity. Rather, Scripture was to be the anchor for all Christian belief. However, it was also the more nuanced position of reformers like John Calvin, in his work on providence, that combined with new intellectual challenges to revive the category of the miraculous in Protestant thought. By the late seventeenth century, the impact of Enlightenment ideals began to soften the hard line of some Protestants to the cessation of miracles. Indeed, for many (especially English) Protestants, once the battle with Catholicism had lessened and the nonconformists were tamed by toleration, a growing challenge was holding back the "flood of irreligion." In fact, if the seventeenth century saw a willingness to defend supernatural occurrences, this was because they were seen as a bulwark against the tide of skepticism many felt was sweeping England. As such, the recording of providences and miracles was seen by some as an antidote to the rising "atheism of the age." Walsham, "Miracles," 273–306.

to bloom.[15] Heavily influenced by German Pietism (which stressed the importance of a personal experience of God), Wesley's conversion experience (1738) also became central to his emerging spirituality. Indeed, a central emphasis of early Methodism was Wesley's doctrine of a "second blessing" — a crisis experience *subsequent to conversion* that he called "sanctification" or "Christian perfection." Such a state, he alleged, was a second stage in Christian development in which a believer was said to experience "a total death to sin and an entire renewal in the love and image of God." Crucially, although progress in holiness was said to precede and follow the attainment of this state, the experience itself was held to be instantaneous. It was received, Wesley insisted, by faith. In so emphasizing such a state of grace attainable after conversion, Wesley began to lay the groundwork for an experiential theology that became foundational to Pentecostal spirituality. This opened the door for other aspects of spirituality to be made "subsequent" to and distinct from regeneration.[16] Building on Wesley's ideals, mid-nineteenth century holiness teaching began to promote sanctification as a "second blessing" of grace available after conversion. Penitents received pardon from sin at conversion. However, in the "subsequent" experience of sanctification the dominance of the sinful nature was said to be broken through faith in the work of Christ. This notion of a "second blessing" of sanctification was promoted on both sides of the Atlantic. In the decades after 1875 it became central to the Keswick Convention in the United Kingdom and the growing North American revivalist movement. Travelling such pathways and bringing the believer into fresh "consecration," deeper "apprehension of the fullness of the Spirit" and ongoing "victory" over sin, second blessing theology became foundational to holiness spirituality and was considered a necessary step in the possession of the "higher" Christian life.[17]

While Pentecostalism's origins thus reach deep into the history of ecstatic Christianity, the birth of its twentieth century emphases can be traced to the holiness wing of American Methodism at the dawn of the century. As the holiness movement expanded a stress on the outward evidences of sanctification began to emerge. This came to particular expression in the belief, popularized by Charles Parham of the Topeka Bible School in Kansas, of a "third blessing" of the Holy Spirit. Following the ecstatic experiences of Parham's students (1901), which were accompanied by tongues-speaking,

15. Rack, "Early Methodist Healing," 137–52; Gladwin, "Mission and Colonialism," 282–304.

16. Anderson, *Introduction to Pentecostalism*, 25–26. Note the critique of Wesleyan Perfectionism in Hoekema, *Saved by Grace*, 202–24.

17. Anderson, *Introduction to Pentecostalism*, 25–28; Synan, "Second Work of Grace," 430; Gladwin, "Missions," 293.

Parham began to promote the idea that a "third blessing" or "baptism of the Holy Ghost" was the final work of grace to be sought by every Christian. Parham's "third-blessing" theology impacted other holiness leaders like William Seymour who became instrumental in the famed Azusa Street Revival in Los Angeles. The Azusa Street Revival (1906–09) was marked by experiences like ecstatic singing, dancing, prophecy, and tongues-speaking. With thousands flocking to the Azusa Street revival hall, news of the revival and the associated "baptism" spread quickly along holiness pathways. It also broke new ground within the established denominations. From the soil of such influences, overtaking the earlier holiness emphasis on "perfection" sprang the use, among classic Pentecostals, of "Spirit-Baptism" as the central metaphor for describing an experience of renewal and "power" for witness. It was a search for the "power" of Pentecost, evidenced in "glossolalia" and the "charismata" of the early church. Moreover, from this first wave of development, second-wave Pentecostalism (or "charismatic renewal") had a major impact upon the mainline denominations in the 1960s to 1970s, while a third wave is associated with the ministry of American John Wimber in the 1980s and the demand, in particular, for "signs and wonders."[18]

Australian Pentecostalism

Within Australian churches, conditions for the emergence of Pentecostalism also coalesced in the late nineteenth century, infused by a host of international influences and a number of local particularities. Instances of

---

18. The antecedents of twentieth-century Pentecostalism are numerous. Alongside its roots in Methodism, historians trace the influences as far back as Jonathan Edwards (1703–58) and later William Carey (1761–1834). The spirituality of Edwards privileged the need for a personal experience of conversion, growth in moral perfection, and heightened religious affections. The expectation (especially among nineteenth-century premillennials) of an outpouring of the Spirit to restore miraculous power to the church's mission before the end of the age, gave impetus to the nineteenth-century revivalist, healing, and missionary movements. This saw the development among radical evangelicals (on both sides of the Atlantic and in some British colonies) of intense religious activity, faith missions, and an increased expectation for the restoration of the biblical charismata. The restoration of tongues-speaking was seen as necessary for the effective preaching of the gospel to the nations, setting the scene for this doctrine to become the hallmark of early Pentecostalism. Charles Parham's linking of tongues with spirit baptism was the new idea that caught fire in the early twentieth century. This web of historic expectation demonstrates that instead of a sudden new start in 1901, there was a growth of ideas that have their origins much earlier. For a fuller examination of these influences including that of Edward Irving in England (1792–1834) and the late nineteenth-century influence of A. B. Simpson and F. Sanford in America, see Hocken, "Charismatic Movement," 477–519; Anderson, *Ends of the Earth*, 11–26.

tongues-speaking were reported in Victoria as early as 1870 and among Methodist prayer groups in the 1890s.[19] "Higher life" holiness teaching was also transplanted to Australia in 1891 by the formation of the Geelong Convention. This was a sister ministry to the Keswick Convention, which produced a litany of Australian emulators. Such conventions became conduits for the rise of revivalist practices that were elemental in creating a climate of expectation for the spiritually extraordinary to occur.[20] However, the best claimant to the title of "founder" of Australian Pentecostalism is said to be Jeannie Lancaster. Lancaster was influenced by northern hemisphere literature that spoke of "back to Pentecost" experiences. She subsequently obtained her own Pentecost experience in 1908. Gathering a number of people around her, Lancaster bought an old temperance hall in 1909 which she transformed into the Good News Hall, Australia's first Pentecostal congregation. The "Good News Hall" publication eventually circulated to more than three thousand people across Australia and was a key element in the spread of early Pentecostal expression.[21]

The influence of Alexander Dowie is also significant. Dowie's extraordinary itinerant ministry in South Australia, Sydney, and Melbourne in the 1870s fueled a particular interest in divine healing within early Australian Pentecostalism.[22] Indeed, on account of Dowie's influence, first-wave Australian Pentecostalism appeared to be less a "tongues" movement than a storefront healing mission. Personal experience remained secondary to the dominant emphases of prophetic utterance, missions support, and the evidence of God's presence through miraculous healing. A series of east-coast campaigns during the 1920s, headlined by leading international and local Pentecostal figures, also supplied the Australian movement with early impetus and organization.[23] Such early-century "enthusiasm" invited a growing following among the Protestant fringe and saw the movement swell from eighteen congregations in 1924 to eighty in 1939. Despite such growth, as a largely separatist movement with as few as three thousand members, prewar

19. Hutchinson, "Australia," 26–29.

20. These included the Belgrave Heights and Katoomba Conventions. It was through such channels that key figures such as R. A. Torrey, G. Grubb, and C. Alexander were introduced to Australia. Chant, "Origins," 117; Piggin, *Spirit*, 56–61.

21. Lancaster became a founding figure in the "Apostolic Faith Mission" (1926). Hutchinson, "Pentecostals," 518.

22. Following several influential Australian healing and preaching tours, in 1896 Dowie migrated to the United States where he established the Zion City Christian Church outside Chicago. Hutchinson, "Australia," 26; Chant, "Origins," 106–10.

23. Aimee Semple McPherson, Smith Wigglesworth, F. B. Van Eyk, and A.C. Valdez were some of the more significant names conducting Australian "healing" campaigns in the early twentieth century. So Hutchinson, "Pentecostals," 518.

Pentecostals made only a modest impact on overall Census figures and on the nation's conception of the Christian faith.[24]

Within this first phase of Australian Pentecostalism, perfectionist[25] and healing ideals exerted a degree of influence on pockets of Australian denominationalism. In Sydney, a strain of holiness perfectionism made inroads among several of Sydney's evangelical university groups and parachurch organizations in the 1930s.[26] After the war, a strain of holiness perfectionism was also propagated in Sydney by the ministry of Geoffrey Bingham (1919–2009) at Miller's Point Anglican Parish.[27] Bingham was influenced by the spirituality of the East African Revival. This emphasized the language of "repentance" and the daily "infilling of the Spirit."[28] Bingham was also influenced by L. E. Maxwell's work, *Born Crucified*, which emphasized a soteriological schema that eschewed a merely "legal and lifeless imputation of righteousness."[29] Rather, seeking a more dynamic expression of the believer's union with Christ, Bingham urged that the path to "higher living" lay in a deeper consecration and in the need to daily "reckon" oneself dead to sin "by faith."[30] Holding revival-like meetings (1953–57), Bingham saw hundreds flocking to his services, while numerous clergy followed Bingham in forging a closer unity between Keswick and Reformed spirituality.[31]

Important in the rise of healing ministries in the Anglican Communion and Sydney diocese was also the ministry of Englishman, James

24. Hutchinson, "Pentecostals," 518; Anderson, "Pentecostal and Charismatic," 101.

25. "Perfectionism" is a doctrine stating a Christian is able to attain a sinless state. Thomas, "Perfectionism," 363–65.

26. The groups affected included the Sydney University Evangelical Union and Crusader Union. Projecting a spiritually elitist and cultlike approach, such ideals were refuted by T. C. Hammond, who allegedly "brought a sledgehammer down on the perfectionists" by reasserting an Augustinian soteriology. This emphasized the Christian's legal justification ("imputed righteousness") alongside the progressive sanctification of the believer. Piggin, *Spirit*, 105–20; Loane, *Warriors*, 89–90.

27. Bleby, *Quiet Revival*, 139.

28. Also emphasized was the primacy of visions and dreams, prophecy, speaking in tongues, prayers, hymns, singing, and dancing. Ward and Wild-Wood, *East African Revival*, 1–12.

29. Bleby, *Quiet Revival*, 134, 143.

30. The memory of 1930's perfectionism aroused opposition to Bingham's teaching among those who feared a return to such elitist doctrines. Bingham's teaching was closer to a "sanctification by faith" position than Wesleyan perfectionism. Yet, in emphasizing "higher life" spirituality in contrast to Augustinian soteriology, Bingham's teaching introduced a note of conditionality in relation to the Christian's daily soteriological experience. Bleby, *Quiet Revival*, 141–45; Loane, *Warriors*, 89–90.

31. Egan, "Healing Ministries," 48–52; Piggin, *Spirit*, 148–56; Piggin and Linder, *National Soul*, 275–76.

Moore Hickson. A layman, Hickson's thaumaturgic ability initially met with cool reserve from the Anglican establishment. However, after a successful global healing tour between 1919 and 1924 Hickson emerged as a "religious superstar." This was a reality that melted the reserve of many in the episcopacy.[32] Indeed, following a successful Australian tour in 1923, the entire Australian Anglican episcopate signed a letter about his ministry. They testified to "the wonder of divine healing" which was "incapable of explanation on any merely physical or mental basis."[33] After 1945, the topic of healing gained new salience on account of the ministry of American Episcopalian, Agnes Sanford (1897–1982). Sanford's interest in healing stemmed from her own deliverance from depression by the laying on of hands.[34] After a powerful spiritual encounter in the early 1950s, Sanford's ministry acquired a marked charismatic quality. Becoming influential in American mainline and Episcopalian circles and in the "The Order of St. Luke" (an international healing fraternity), Sanford and her husband widely disseminated an awareness of spiritual gifts and "the power of the Spirit" to effect healing of "physical, mental and social ills."[35] In 1960, Sanford's book, *The Healing Light*, impacted Sydney clergyman James Glennon. Sanford visited Australia to conduct a mission at St. Andrew's Cathedral in 1961. With Glennon receiving "spirit baptism" during this mission, Sanford's ideals thus became formative in his establishment of what would become one of the largest healing ministries in the Anglican world.[36]

Following such early-century developments, second-wave Pentecostalism (also known as the charismatic movement) made its presence felt in Australian mainline churches from the mid-1950s. A host of interconnected influences gave rise to this second wave.[37] However, the tipping point

---

32. Mews, "Revival," 300–301, 306, 314.

33. Supported by Sydney's Archbishop Wright, Hickson held meetings at St. Andrew's Cathedral, addressing six thousand in six days. The mission was considered "the most striking experience since the War." Egan, "Healing Ministries," 33–34; Mews, "Revival," 304, 329.

34. Egan, "Healing Ministries," 26–27.

35. Stanley, *Global Diffusion*, 183; Egan, "Healing Ministries," 27; Hocken, "Charismatic Movement," 478.

36. Mews, "Revival," 309; Glennon, *Healing*, 99; Egan, "Healing Ministries," 32–40, 66–67; Hutchinson, "Australia," 28.

37. In this vein, the postwar internationalization of Australian and world culture brought with it a proliferation of smaller charismatic offshoots that energized the local movement. Enhanced global communication and transport networks also supplied a profusion of personalities and publications that exposed the Christian mainstream to the movement's claims. The ministry of David Du Plessis did more than any other to bridge the divide between the charismatic movement and the historic churches. Du

that brought the movement to public consciousness and ensured news of its development reverberated around the world was a series of encounters in Californian Episcopalianism. Between 1959 and 1961 a number of Californian churches (the Parish of the Holy Spirit in Monterey Park and St. Mark's Van Nuys) entered into charismatic "renewal." News stories of such outbreaks published in *Newsweek* and *Time* magazines subsequently made these developments a topic of national interest. News quickly rippled across to Britain where it came to the attention of notable Anglicans like John Stott and Philip Hughes. Hughes, a well-credentialled scholar and editor of *The Churchman* magazine, subsequently published a favorable editorial on the movement.[38] Such an upbeat assessment had a major impact on various Anglican clergy such as Michael Harper and John Collins, who became pioneers of renewal in Britain.[39] The appearance of other key journals and publications promoting the movement was also important in broadcasting charismatic ideals across Britain and much of the English-speaking world. The result was that by the early 1960s people in virtually every major Protestant and Catholic tradition were reportedly receiving the "Baptism of the Holy Spirit." While differences in belief and behavior existed between such diverse groups, they were united in the belief that they had received the renewing outpouring of God's Holy Spirit.[40]

Plessis (nicknamed "Mr Pentecost") travelled the world from 1951 and brought many from the historic churches into charismatic experience. The return of missionaries from places like Africa, China, South America, and Pakistan also created a bank of charismatic experience and awareness which entered the consciousness of mainstream clergy and congregations. The theatrical campaigns of healing revivalists like Oral Roberts, T. L. Osborn, and A.C. Valdez Jr also played an important role in firing a hunger for fresh outpourings of the Spirit, while popularizing the message of divine healing and building growing local bases of support. The prevalence of high-profile figures who became influenced by charismatic renewal is also significant. Baptist evangelist John Ridley had a newfound spiritual experience in the early 1950s, while in the 1960s, Methodist evangelist Alan Walker returned from South America and spoke publicly of the "thrilling story of Methodist-Pentecostal progress in South America." Hutchinson, "Australia," 28; Hocken, "Charismatic," 487.

38. Indeed, travelling to the United States to investigate such claims, Hughes's article enthusiastically suggested the movement was "transforming lives" and "revitalising congregations." Stanley, *Global Diffusion*, 187–90.

39. Harper established the *Fountain Trust* as a service agency for charismatic renewal. John Collins was vicar of Holy Trinity Brompton (1980–1985). Collin's curates David Watson (1933–1984) and David MacInnes (1932–) were to become the best-known figures in the British renewal movement. Dudley-Smith, *Global Ministry*, 37; Bebbington, *Evangelicalism*, 230.

40. Cartledge, "Charismatic Theology," 177–90.

Charismatic Renewal and Sydney Anglicanism

The response of leading Sydney Anglicans to this fast-moving tide of charismatic renewal was one of caution and concern. This was coupled with a desire to reframe, within a broader biblical-theological context, the questions the movement was posing to their wider constituency. From the mid-1960s, the movement quickly gained momentum within the diocese as numerous rectors embraced the movement and experienced the deepening power and intensity of spirit baptism and its associated manifestations. Charismatic sympathies developed rapidly in the parishes of Picton, Malabar, Clovelly, Darlinghurst, Normanhurst, Northbridge, Baulkham Hills, Avalon, Manly, Longueville, St. Paul's Wahroonga, St. Claire, Waverley, and Surry Hills. Among the more concerning developments at Surry Hills was the fact that alongside the exploration of prophecy and healing, under the rector, Peter Hobson, the parish also attained a reputation for exorcisms.[41]

The growing healing ministry of St. Andrew's Cathedral, under the leadership of Jim Glennon, also supplied a significant rallying point for charismatic renewal. This ministry lay, somewhat paradoxically, at the center of the diocese geographically, while at its outer margins theologically. However, with Glennon's book[42] selling over two hundred thousand copies and remaining in print for some twenty-five years, combined with the size of the healing service which grew to become one of the largest weeknight healing services in the Anglican world, Glennon's influence among the ever-widening circles of charismatic enthusiasm was considerable. This meant that for those drawn to the movement's claims of spiritual immediacy and refreshment, the healing ministry became a key rallying point for the spread of charismatic enthusiasm across the city.[43]

---

41. "Australia's Top Exorcist"; Egan, "Healing Ministries," 77–78; Interview with Peter Jensen, December 2, 2016.

42. Glennon, *Healing*.

43. Although the local movement lacked a significant leader to prosecute its claims, Glennon was its most widely recognized advocate. At its highpoint the mid-week healing service at the cathedral drew as many as seven hundred people from churches across the city. At the opening of the ministry's Healing Centre in 1985 messages were sent from Anglican dignitaries across the world. In his address, Archbishop Robinson, an esteemed figure and New Testament scholar himself, quipped that in his travels it was often "nice to be recognized" alongside the likes of Jim Glennon. Judd and Cable, *Sydney Anglicans*, 294; Egan, "Healing Ministries," 171. For statistics on the scale of other world healing ministries, see Anderson, *Pentecostalism*, 1–8.

A Reformed Theological Framework

Such developments raised sufficient concern in the diocese that over the course of the 1970s and 1980s a chorus of leading figures offered a series of reflections intended to both affirm *and* offer correction to the movement.[44] A key shaper of this response was the Reformed emphasis that had been in the ascendancy at Moore College in the postwar era. Three elements of this emphasis are noteworthy. First, a key feature of Augustinian Christianity upon which the Reformers, especially Calvin, had placed fresh if not unprecedented emphasis was the question of divine omnipotence. This preoccupation with the supreme majesty of God was a side-effect of Protestantism's fierce determination to eliminate all intermediaries between God and the believer. It was also a function of the Reformation tenet of justification by faith, which highlighted that human beings could take no steps of their own to achieve salvation but were dependent upon divine grace alone.[45] Combining these two impulses, leading Reformers like Calvin envisaged a universe ruled over by a God who foreknew all events and dynamically intervened to bring them about. The corollary to this was that while Calvin *had* strongly refuted the miraculous claims of medieval Catholicism, he was also reluctant to rule out *a priori* the possibility that miracles might still be manifested. This would have been to bind the hands of God and impose limits on a deity who was, by definition, omnipotent. Moreover, by framing the question of miracles within the broader biblical category of providence, Calvin was also able to place the question of supernaturalism onto a far larger canvas. In this, Calvin emphasized that God was able to operate both mediately and immediately. He could employ the intricate network of instruments and forces established at creation, while being equally able to transcend them. According to Calvin, therefore, the activity of God was to be detected in the mundane and trivial occurrences of life, no less than in the earth-shattering.[46]

Second, the Trinitarianism and Christology of the Reformers also had implications for their conception of the Holy Spirit. Commenting on the Pentecost event, Calvin reflected that the purpose of the Father's sending

---

44. While leading figures expressed some sympathy with the movement, they felt that if the spiritual pattern being advocated was inaccurate then it posed an unwelcome burden to the believer and a distorted view of authentic spiritual life. See Woodhouse, "Signs and Wonders," 7–8; Barnett and Jensen, *Quest for Power*, 1–2.

45. Such views were heavily contested by subsequent figures like Arminius and Beza. Grider, "Arminianism," 79–81.

46. Walsham, "Miracles," 284–85; See Calvin, *Institutes*, 1:16.13.

the Spirit was "to make the whole church partakers of Christ's life."[47] Indeed, Calvin taught that the entire efficacy of Pentecost is "contained in Christ." For, by the outpouring of his Spirit, Christ had marked the beginning of his eschatological reign and the renewal of the world.[48] In order to communicate the benefits of this life and reign, Calvin suggested, Christ "had to become ours and dwell with us." This was done by the "secret energy of the Spirit, by which we come to enjoy Christ and all his benefits," offered "through the gospel."[49] This binding of pneumatology with Christology (the fusion of the spirit of Christ, with the person, work, and Word of Christ) marks one of Calvin's enduring contributions. Consequently, for Calvin, the significance of the work of the Holy Spirit was not just a matter of spiritual renewal and the bestowal of charismata. Rather, it lay *primarily* in the fact that in the preaching of the gospel Christ conveyed his personal rule and presence. And by the agency of his Word and Spirit the believer "possesses heaven along with him" and has received the assurance of a kingdom whose blessings were inaugurated yet still predominantly in the future. Thus, for Calvin, authentic spirituality was intimately tied to the Christian's reception *of* and perseverance *in* the biblical gospel.[50]

A third Reformed emphasis which underlay the Sydney Anglican response was in soteriology. Reformed soteriology held that the elements of Christian conversion formed an inseparable unity. At the moment of faith, it taught, the believer is justified, sanctified, adopted, and sealed with the Spirit, by whose power they experience the process of progressive sanctification. Such a non-elitist and egalitarian schema, the Reformers held, was foundational in laying bare all soteriological error. Indeed, while gradations in maturity were certainly evident in Christian experience, nevertheless, leaving no room for the undermining of assurance by claims to "subsequent" or "higher" blessing, Reformed soteriology consistently sought to safeguard the blessings of salvation as the possession of every believer.[51]

Given the presence of such Reformed thought in the Sydney diocese in the postwar era, it is unsurprising that much of the response of its leadership to the charismatic movement bore the hallmarks of this approach. Two of the significant early responses arose via the work of leading clergymen Paul

---

47. Doyle, *Eschatology*, 197; Calvin, *Commentary on Acts*, 2:32, 109.

48. Calvin, *Commentary on Acts*, 2:38, 118.

49. Calvin, *Institutes*, 3.1.1.

50. See especially Calvin, *Commentary on John*, chs. 14–17, esp. 16. On Calvin's inaugurated eschatology, see Doyle, *Eschatology*, 192–96. See also Bruce, "Eschatology," 362–65; Goldsworthy, *Goldsworthy Trilogy*, 119–20; Reymond, *Systematic Theology*, 983–84; Hoekema, *Bible and the Future*, 20–21.

51. Hoekema, *Saved by Grace*, 153; Reymond, *Systematic Theology*, 711–90.

Barnett and Peter Jensen, alongside a response commissioned by the synod. In their 1973 publication *The Quest for Power: Neo Pentecostals and the New Testament*, Barnett and Jensen took issue with the charismatic doctrine of "subsequence." The charismatic, they suggested, agreed that the Holy Spirit was given at conversion "for sanctification and growth in grace," but was subsequently urged to "seek the *fullness of the Spirit* . . . to be a *powerful Christian.*" Such fullness was allegedly obtained by spirit-baptism and was a "gift" to be sought by "every Christian *subsequent to conversion.*" Barnett and Jensen highlighted what they saw as the troubling corollaries of such teaching. They noted the bifurcation of Christian life and experience it produced, in proposing a strata of Christian who may be saved but who will not be "supernaturally endowed" for service.[52] Moreover, in proposing certain needed spiritual preconditions for such an experience to be received (such as a deeper consecration and an ardent faith) such teaching had the propensity to undermine biblical soteriology and assurance by suggesting the possession of such blessing was attainable only via ongoing spiritual "achievement."[53] Thus, while not discounting the depth of charismatic experience nor even the place of such phenomena in the Christian life, Barnett and Jensen located their disagreement with the movement in the *interpretation* and *priority* given to such phenomena and urged a rediscovery of the "power" of the gospel as Christ's instrument to nourish his church.[54]

Alongside the early scholarly work of Barnett and Jensen, at the 1971 Sydney synod John Reid and John Chapman led the synod in requesting a committee be appointed to study the charismatic movement from a scholarly and pastoral standpoint. The committee was asked to give attention

---

52. Barnett and Jensen, *Quest for Power*, 1–4. Emphasis not original.

53. This contrasts with Reformed doctrine which holds that the various elements of conversion (such as regeneration, justification, sanctification, and the sealing of the Spirit) even if viewed as functionally distinct, form a unity, akin to the moment of "turning on the light switch and flooding a room with light." In contrast, when the elements of conversion are chronologically separated (as in Charismatic doctrine) and conditions are attached to their attainment (such as a deeper repentance or a truer faith to receive the "baptism") these conditions effectively become "works" which, only if sufficient, may illicit divine blessing and renewal. Hoekema, *Grace*, 153; Reymond, *Systematic Theology*, 711; Barnett and Jensen, *Quest for Power*, 70, 76.

54. In their analysis, Barnett and Jensen in *Quest for Power* reaffirmed the place of Scripture for the light needed to establish Christian maturity (7–15), examined biblical teaching on the work of the Holy Spirit (15–27, 42–54), critiqued the structure of Charismatic hermeneutics (29–41) and examined the cross-centric nature of New Testament ministry (57–66). They concluded that, on closer inspection, the passages cited by charismatics in support of their schema were either distinct events in salvation history (not to be sought as normative Christian experience) or were synonyms for conversion (86).

via the disciplines of theology, medicine, and the social sciences to questions of tongues-speaking, prophecy, healing, and spiritual gifts, and their place in the worship and witness of the church. The committee that was formed (on which Chapman played a leading role) included figures across a spectrum of charismatic sympathy and deliberated over a period of two years.[55] Recognizing the growing crisis in the contemporary church was not a divide "between Catholics and Protestants but between *traditional* and *experiential* forms of Church life," the committee were at pains to highlight that the Reformed and charismatic approaches to Scripture and experience constituted the central fault line along which much of their disagreement ran. The dividing issue was whether Scripture was to be understood via the lens of experience, or Christian experience in light of Scripture.

The charismatic, the report suggested, was "experience-centered in [their] approach to the bible" and "restorationist" in hermeneutical intent. This meant that the lens of experience shaped their reading of Scripture (on questions of spirit baptism, tongues, and prophecy). Conscious of this underlying disagreement, the report examined the nature of the New Testament charismata from numerous angles. Presenting arguments from both sides of the spectrum, the report urged a greater caution in the rush to equate contemporary spiritual manifestations with the charismata of the early church. Furthermore, while it lent no authority to the view that such charismata had ceased, the report advised that a more careful reading of the New Testament may recognize that the miraculous gifts were largely initiatory gifts and belonged "more to church founding and revival situations" than to being normative gifts "for the entire Church age."[56] Crucially, on the question of whether Scripture authorizes contemporary Christians to "exercise a Spirit-given ability to heal, apart from medical means," the report echoed the work of Calvin by framing its discussion of this issue against the larger backdrop of the sovereign power and providence of God. Citing the charismatic appeal to texts like 1 Corinthians 12 and James 5:15 (as precedents for the expectation of healing today) the report cautioned against the making of ironclad promises for healing. The report certainly recognized the freedom of God to effect contemporary healing. However, within the framework of a providentially ordered world, the "natural" processes of bodily healing and the use of medical aids were

---

55. The twelve committee members were Revs. A. M. Blanch, J. C. Chapman, D. H. Crawford, G. H. Feltham, D. T. Foord, R. E. Lamb, A. J. Glennon, D. B. Knox, J. R. Reid (Chairman), Dr. B. B. Hamilton, R. B. Hobart, and D. Treloar. *Both Sides*, 3–4.

56. *Both Sides*, 6, 8–29. On Reformed and charismatic hermeneutics, see Fee and Stuart, *Read the Bible*, 119–27. On the relationship between Scripture and experience, see Packer, *Concise Theology*, 8; Jensen, *Revelation of God*, 95–144.

also to be considered providential "means" by which God answered prayer for healing. To see God's hand only in the supernatural, the report advised, constituted a deficient view. Rather, "whatever the agency," all healing was to be seen as divinely ordained.[57]

The St. Andrew's Cathedral Healing Ministry

Other similar reflections were offered in the Sydney context in the 1970s and 1980s by a host of domestic and international figures like D. W. B Robinson, D. B. Knox, Dick Lucas, Phillip Jensen, Robert Forsyth, and John Woodhouse. In their desire to provide a Reformed counterpoint to the claims of charismatic renewal, such figures sought, in various fora, to reframe the discussion by presenting "charismatic" Christianity as being simply no more or less than "biblical Christianity."[58]

---

57. *Both Sides*, 51–57. Of greatest concern to the committee were the charismatic claims that surrounded the "prayer of faith" in James 5:14–15. The report cautioned that the "prayer of faith" was not a special kind of prayer that mandated divine favour. Rather, it advised, "James teaches us the uncertainty of life, both in its continuity and in all its circumstances, and tells us that we ought to say 'if the Lord will' in regard to all these things (James 4:13–16) . . . Far from being a denial of faith [such a prayer] is a mark of quiet trust in the loving heavenly Father who *can* do what we ask but who *may not* because His glory and our well-being and spiritual maturity are better advanced by His not doing it." Furthermore, the report advised, "the pastoral reasons for rejecting the [charismatic] definition of the 'prayer of faith' are that it places on a sick person an additional burden. Should healing not occur, they feel their faithfulness is the cause" (51–53). The report also advised the need for scrutiny of claims to instantaneous healing, strongly suggesting that the relief of symptoms were not the same as receiving "cure." Indeed, numerous studies had shown that "cure" rates from "healings" were in most cases equal only to the "spontaneous recovery rate" for certain ailments. Other studies had sought to establish documented instances of cure by the intervention of a "faith healer," yet in twenty years of research no instance had been found (56–57).

58. Robinson and Knox sought to reframe the discussion by reaffirming the Holy Spirit as being the possession of every Christian. Moreover, reflecting the high Trinitarianism and Christology of the Reformers they argued that to speak of a non-charismatic Christianity was a misnomer. Indeed, they advised, all gifts were by definition "charismatic" inasmuch as all Christians were recipients of God's gifting by means of the spirit of Christ. At the height of his own engagement with the renewal movement in Britain, Dick Lucas gave a series of addresses at the CMS Summer School and College of Preachers in which he expounded John's Gospel and 1 Corinthians to suggest that the "greater works" (John 14) and "mature Christianity" (1 Cor 2–3) spoken of in such texts were not to be equated with the presence of charismata but were bound up with the preaching of the cross of Christ. Similarly, a Reformed Trinitarianism pervaded the major Sydney university ministries of Phillip Jensen and Robert Forsyth. It also shaped the response of local leaders to the third-wave Pentecostalism of figures like John Wimber (1980s). Indeed, in response to renewed calls for eye-catching phenomena to characterize the Christian life, such leaders continued to reframe the

In addition to such responses, another significant aspect of the response of Sydney figures (and in particular the response of Chapman) to the tide of charismatic renewal was the response taken to the influential St. Andrew's Cathedral healing ministry. The ministry's founder, Jim Glennon, was one of a coterie of Sydney clergy who had embraced the charismatic movement as it made inroads into the mainline churches in the 1960s. Energized by his own experience of charismatic renewal in 1961, Glennon became a proponent of charismatic doctrine and experience. He conducted healing missions in the early 1960s and residential healing retreats. Glennon was an important contributor to the 1973 Diocesan Report on the charismatic movement where he strongly advocated for "second blessing" theology and a view of divine healing, which held that it was a contemporary gift *and* command for the church today. Such convictions found expression in Glennon's teaching at the St. Andrew's healing service and in his published work *Your Healing is Within You* (1978). In such teaching contexts Glennon drew heavily on the allegedly "irrevocable promise" of healing in James 5:14–15. Here, on condition of the Christian's fervent belief that they had been healed "regardless of what their sight might suggest," the Christian, it was said, was able to come into the full blessing of God for bodily healing. Indeed, Glennon even suggested that if healing was *not* "received" immediately, then just as the kingdom of God grows like a "mustard seed," so, much contemporary healing also had a "progressive character." It grew in unison with a believer's faith. Such was the teaching Glennon conveyed to his mid-week congregation of as many as seven hundred from churches across the city. Coupled with his regular spot on radio 2CBA FM and the wide dissemination of his sermon transcripts and monthly newspaper, Glennon's teaching thus began to significantly influence the convictions of Christians across a swathe of local churches.[59]

---

discussion by suggesting the "signs and wonders that mattered for true faith" were "God's historic acts of redemption" seen in the cross of Christ. See Robinson, "Gifts of the Spirit," 172–83; Robinson, "Charismatic Christianity," 191–201; Knox, "Holy Spirit," 109–14; *Preaching Christ Newsletter*, no. 3, 1982, 2–3; Jensen, "True Spirituality"; Forsyth "Holy Spirit"; Woodhouse, "Signs and Wonders," 7–15, 39; Barnett, "Miraculous and Ministry," 73–100.

59. Glennon taught that while the will of God was for all Christians to experience healing, certain conditions were also needed for healing to be "received." These included the degree of a believer's repentance, faith, and forgiveness of others. Glennon thus taught that "only a minority of people are healed at once." Glennon also promoted the idea that many illnesses were emotionally caused. Hence, in a more disputed technique, he emphasized the possibility of healing for conscious and unconscious memories. At the ministries' height, seven thousand sermon transcripts were distributed weekly, the ministries' newspaper was distributed internationally and Christians from across the world frequented the services to hear Glennon teach and to receive divine

Consequently, the response of diocesan leaders to this ministry was one of caution and containment. Undoubtedly, the life of the cathedral had been energized by the healing service.[60] Nevertheless, there was sufficient concern among the cathedral's leadership and its chapter regarding the content of Glennon's teaching that over the course of Glennon's ministry numerous requests for clarification, retraction, and reform of his public communications were made.

Chief among those assuming responsibility for this process of reproof and containment was John Chapman.[61] Chapman himself was intimately familiar with the substructure of charismatic belief and some of its more troubling pastoral implications. In his youth, Chapman had been heavily affected by the strain of holiness enthusiasm that emanated from Miller's Point Anglican Church during the 1950s under Geoffrey Bingham. A Keswick-oriented teaching from Romans 6 suggesting the believer could know "continuous victory over sin" by exercising faith in the fact they had "died to sin" previously had a "devastating effect" on his Christian life, Chapman recalled. The result was that in his youth Chapman had "rocketed into sin faster than ever, because [he] was not resisting, fleeing or fighting as [he] should have been." Such an experience was not only spiritually harmful but also alerted Chapman to the "subsequent" nature of charismatic spirituality. Such "second blessing" theology, he suggested (whether expressed as an expectation of deeper holiness, heightened spiritual power or divine healing) was a misappropriation of biblical faith and inadvertently diminished the work of Christ.[62] Chapman was also acutely conscious of the injury caused to vulnerable Christians when promises of healing could not be sustained. Having counselled several people whose faith had been heavily bruised by unfounded claims of healing, Chapman had witnessed the damage that such teaching could produce. Led to believe their "lack of faith" was the cause of their regression in health, such people subsequently

---

healing. Somewhat paradoxically, however, Glennon himself remained blind in one eye throughout his life. Egan, "Healing Ministries," 68–101; *Both Sides*, 4, 11, 29–44; Glennon, *Healing*, 26–34, 74–80; Interview with Dr. Peter Jensen, December 2, 2016.

60. Indeed, as an evangelical pietist, Archbishop Loane had sought to encourage all endeavours toward a Christian's growing relationship with Christ. While he discouraged the presence of Charismatic distinctives in Christian worship, Loane had also shown a degree of sympathy for a ministry he perceived to be promoting a desirable spiritual end. Egan, "Healing Ministries," 83–85.

61. Interview with Canon Chris Allan, March 7, 2017. Chris Allan, a conservative evangelical Sydney clergyman assumed the role of leader of the healing ministry from 2008. Egan, "Healing Ministries," 83–85, 231–32; 2015 *Sydney Yearbook*, 141.

62. Chapman, *Foot in Two Worlds*, 59, 69.

THE SPIRIT, THE WORD, AND THE CHRISTIAN LIFE   345

voiced profound existential questions about the faithfulness of God and the Christian's worthiness before him.⁶³

Such significant repercussions energized the role Chapman played in the 1973 Synod Report on the charismatic movement and saw him offer leadership on aspects of charismatic renewal in the 1970s and 1980s. He spoke widely in conference and church contexts, emphasizing the Reformed themes of the possession of the Holy Spirit by every believer, alongside the Spirit's key work of regeneration, illumination, and sanctification. He also offered critique on the charismatic doctrine of revelation "by the direct agency of the Spirit" and was quick to challenge any teaching that diminished the primacy of Scripture or the centrality of the cross as the lifeblood of the church.⁶⁴ Such strong views undoubtedly played a role in the position Chapman adopted as a member of the cathedral chapter, and as its lead spokesperson to the healing ministry. Given the profile of the healing ministry and the role it played as a conduit for charismatic excess, Chapman thus conferred regularly with Glennon to address a range of significant concerns. These included matters of complaint about Glennon's disparagement of medical practice and the promotion of a form of perfectionism that championed "the power of faith" as a necessary precondition for the reception of divine favor.⁶⁵

One of the more contentious moments in Chapman's involvement with the healing ministry came with the search for Glennon's replacement.

63. Chapman to Lane, March 14, 1988, Box 3, Adrian Lane Papers 1973–2005. Instructively, Chapman himself was not a cessationist. As articulated in the 1973 Synod Report, and expressed throughout his ministry, he held that God was able to act both mediately and immediately through supernatural as well as natural means. Consequently, in the last weeks of his life as he struggled with an illness from which he finally succumbed, Chapman invited the director of the cathedral healing ministry, Canon Chris Allan, to his hospital bedside to pray for healing. Interview with Canon Chris Allan, March 7, 2017.

64. Chapman delivered major addresses at the 1972 Katoomba Convention on "The Holy Spirit," the 1986 Katoomba Convention on "Biblical Holiness," and a late 1980s CMS Summer School on John 13–17. He also offered a host of teaching in Australian and overseas contexts on these same themes. See Appendix 3, JCCPPHW57, JCCPPHW102, JCCPPB10W12, JCCPPB12W1, JCCPPB12W6, JCCPPB16W22, JCCPPB20W14, JCCPPB23W27–30. Chapman also frequently addressed evangelical distinctives in relation to charismatic renewal to a wide support base in his quarterly newsletters. See: "All Done by Words" (Acts 11:14). DOE Prayer Letter, no. 2 (May–July 1986); "Power for Witnessing" (Acts 1:8), DOE Prayer Letter, no. 4 (November 1986–January 1987); "Can These Bones Live?" (Ezekiel 37:3), *Preaching Christ Newsletter*, August–October 1987.

65. Glennon's association with figures like Norman Vincent Peale (the New York pastor and author whom most Reformed leaders regarded as being heretical) also presented cause for concern. Interview with Chris Allan, March 7, 2017.

Glennon's retirement was a watershed in the life of the ministry. Having grown organically under his leadership for twenty-five years, a degree of uncertainty surrounded the ministry when it came to electing a successor. Following negotiations between Dean Shilton, the cathedral chapter, and the healing ministry leadership committee, it was agreed the healing ministry would submit a candidate to the dean who would recommend the name to the chapter for endorsement by the archbishop. The first name formally considered for the position was the Rev. John Squires. Squires was a product of the healing ministry and a natural successor to Glennon. He had received the ministry's support as a Moore College student and maintained active links thereafter. Consequently, much enthusiasm greeted his nomination to the chapter in January 1985.[66] However, two factors combined to preclude Squires's appointment. Leading the work of the chapter subcommittee (charged with their own assessment before a recommendation was made to the archbishop) was John Chapman. Following an examination of Squires's theology and an extensive interview between Squires and the chapter subcommittee, concerns were raised about Squires's convictions, particularly regarding his views on "unqualified promises of healing." While Squires sought an audience with Dean Shilton and engaged in lengthy discussions with both Chapman and Bishop Reid, significant unease still surrounded Squires's nomination. Nevertheless, the healing ministry committee sought Squires's appointment "at any price."[67] At the same time, during the course of negotiations with the healing ministry, Squires began to make what came to be regarded as "onerous financial demands" as a condition of his employment. This strained the goodwill of the selection committee, who began doubting the wisdom of their choice. With the committee unwilling to meet his conditions, Squires withdrew his acceptance of the appointment. Such developments, however, were largely obscured from the public eye. Instead, a view long perpetuated in healing ministry circles was that Chapman and the chapter's undue concerns had been damaging to Squires and precipitated the collapse of negotiations. Yet, Squires's own role in this breakdown was overlooked.[68] Such developments placed further strain on the relationship between the chapter and healing ministry and saw the extension of Glennon's tenure until 1987.

In 1987, with the support of Chapman and the cathedral chapter the more moderate figure of Jim Holbeck (Dean of Armidale Diocese) was

---

66. Egan, "Healing Ministries," 102–6.

67. Chapman to Lane, September 16, 1985, Box 3, Adrian Lane Papers; Chapman to Lane, November 5, 1985, Adrian Lane Papers.

68. Egan, "Healing Ministries," 106; Interview with Chris Allan, March 7, 2017.

appointed to succeed Glennon (1988–2005). A self-described conservative with an "openness to the working of the Spirit," Holbeck judiciously avoided adopting a charismatic label. Indeed, as a relative "outsider" to the diocese, Holbeck sought to accommodate more fully the wishes of the dean and cathedral chapter regarding charismatic worship practices (like tongues and prophecy) and pursued a largely orthodox teaching ministry. This improved Holbeck's standing with diocesan leaders and forged a bridge between the overtly charismatic ethos of his predecessor and that of the diocesan mainstream. Notwithstanding such positive developments, the healing ministry experienced a set of rising challenges in the wake of Glennon's departure. The acquisition of a residential facility for the healing ministry in innercity Newtown placed a growing administrative burden on Holbeck and his fledgling team. Moreover, during the 1990s, increasingly mindful of their differing convictions and uncertain of their ability to maintain a presence within the older denominations any longer, large numbers of charismatic Christians left the mainline churches to join a host of proliferating independent churches like the Christian City Church, Christian Life Centre, and Vineyard church movements.[69] Consequently, while the healing ministry retained a degree of vitality in this period and remained one of the larger cathedral ministries, such developments undoubtedly had a diminishing effect on the size and sustainability of the ministry. Moreover, lacking the mercurial charisma of its founder and many original supporters, it also began to assume a more conservative evangelical character. Divine healing was promoted within a framework of Bible teaching that emphasized providence, spiritual growth, and sanctification, while leaving room for spontaneous "manifestations of the Spirit."[70]

A Reformed Spirituality in Print

In time, the shape of Chapman's advocacy for Reformed spirituality was distilled in print. In a series of popular works in his later career, Chapman sought to amplify his earlier protestations. These works reiterated the centrality of Scripture, the cross of Christ, and the "now-but-not-yet" nature of biblical eschatology as the key facets of a pastorally and spiritually responsible view of the Christian life. Revealing something of his earlier struggle with charismatic spirituality, he wrote:

---

69. Egan, "Healing Ministries," 183–88, 196–97; Hutchinson, "Australia," 28–29; Piggin and Linder, *National Soul*, 385–87.

70. Egan, "Healing Ministries," 184–85, 188–89.

> On several occasions during my Christian life, I have been offered quick fix methods of obtaining holiness without the hard work of self-discipline. Some told me that I would obtain it by a method of absolute surrender. Others suggested that I might need to be baptized with the Holy Spirit, after which the Christian life would grow ever easier. Still others told of continuous victory over all my sins, and how I could have that if I asked for it. They all turned out to be waterless springs, promising me things . . . they were simply unable to deliver. They offered me heaven (which was irresistible) and the assurance that it would happen now (which was impossible).[71]

Consequently, in these widely distributed works Chapman examined and sought to reframe the underlying spirituality of charismatic-style belief. Echoing the motifs of J. C. Ryle's classic work on holiness a century earlier, in *A Sinner's Guide to Holiness* (2005) and *A Foot in Two Worlds* (2009), Chapman sought to confute the various expressions of "higher-life" teaching by offering a description of what Ryle had called "real practical holiness."[72] Conscious that holiness enthusiasm and charismatic claims to "subsequent" blessing had moderated by the latter-century, nevertheless, the promise of "quick fix" or "two-tier" spirituality, he believed, remained ever present. Accordingly, in these works Chapman examined the challenges of a range of two-tier spiritualities (including perfectionist, second blessing, healing, and prosperity related teaching) and sought to outline an approach to help Christians live with and not seek to "relieve the tension caused by [their] membership of . . . this world *and* the world to come."[73] While he did not deny the possibility of refreshing spiritual experiences and cautioned Christians against assuming that "God will never do anything out of the ordinary," the biblical expectation for normal Christian experience, he charged, was the embrace of a gradual growth in Christlikeness. This occurred "positively by bringing forth the fruit of the Spirit, and negatively by putting to death the desires of the flesh."[74]

Similarly, in his work *Making the Most of the Rest of Your Life* (2007), Chapman examined the human predicament of a fractured world as seen in the presence of evil, suffering, frailty, and death. Contrasting the exuberant

---

71. Chapman, *Sinner's Guide*, 46, 75–78.

72. Ryle wrote: "Real practical holiness does not receive the attention it deserves . . . I am increasingly convinced that the zealous efforts of some well-meaning persons to promote a higher standard of spiritual life are often not 'according to knowledge.'" Ryle, *Holiness*, xiii–xv.

73. Chapman, *Foot in Two Worlds*, 57–71; Chapman, *Sinner's Guide*, 58–64.

74. Chapman, *Foot in Two Worlds*, 60–71; Chapman, *Sinner's Guide*, 38–49.

claims of charismatic-style belief which suggested that victory over many such realities *was* attainable in the present age, Chapman sought instead to convey an inaugurated eschatological framework.[75] To do this he examined the ministry of Christ in the Gospel of Mark and noted how Christ's ministry functioned as *both* a testimony to Christ's majesty *and* a window into the new creation he came to bring about. As such, Chapman suggested, Christ's earthly ministry had opened a window onto a world in which suffering, evil, disaster, and death would ultimately be overcome by Christ's transformative power. Consequently, while the Christian continued to experience the inexorable effects of life in a world that was passing away, so certain was their participation in the new creation Christ had inaugurated that they could experience the contemporary world in an attitude of confident hope, for "the best was yet to come."[76]

Additionally, in his works *Making the Most of the Cross* (2011) and *Making the Most of the Bible* (2012), Chapman sought to position the realities of the gospel and the witness of Scripture as containing both the grounds and the shape of the authentic spiritual life. Indeed, echoing Calvin's earlier contention that it was "through the gospel" that the Holy Spirit enabled the Christian to enjoy the benefits of Christ's resurrection life and reign, Chapman sought to bind closely the categories of Christology and pneumatology. He spoke of the Scriptures as being Christ's gift to the church by the aid of the Holy Spirit, through whose agency the gospel had been preached, believed, and established across the world (John 14–17).[77] Moreover, it was as Christians received Christ's invitation, held out in the gospel, that they were united to Christ by faith and "the beneficial effects" of Christ's death and resurrection became theirs as well. This included their reception of justification and peace with God and their being raised with Christ to a state of new spiritual life (Rom 6). Such a reality occurred definitively at the moment of faith, while also being a "lifelong" process to be "completed only when Christ returns." Consequently, Chapman concluded, in imitation of the character of Christ—as outlined in Scripture—the Christian was to "live a life dominated not by sin . . . but by God-honoring behavior appropriate for the resurrection life."[78]

---

75. Inaugurated eschatology views the events of Christ's life, death, and resurrection as having inaugurated yet not fully consummated Christ's messianic rule and his restoration of the created order. Doyle, *Eschatology*, 196; Bruce, "Eschatology," 365.

76. Chapman, *Most of the Rest*, 19–28, 29–45.

77. Chapman, *Most of the Bible*, 31–34; cf. Calvin, *Institutes*, 3.1.1.

78. Chapman, *Most of the Cross*, 93–98.

Conclusion

What then is to be made of the rise of Pentecostal and charismatic expression and theology in twentieth-century Christianity? The scale and influence of these now global faith movements has invited a host of pastoral and scholarly explanations.[79] At the pastoral level, those who found their experience of Christian worship rejuvenated by charismatic renewal were in no doubt they were the beneficiaries of a decisive move of the Spirit, which was opening the hardened arteries of evangelical faith and restoring Christian confidence in the capacity of God to transform lives in ways no less dramatic than in biblical times. Others, however, viewed the phenomenon through a more academic and cultural lens. They judged these movements to be a reaction to the strictures of a defensive and overly propositional Protestantism that left too little room for the freedom of the Spirit. Eventually, they suggested, as Western societies began to espouse the "Modernist" values of experience over dogma, self-expression over decorum, and fluidity over structure, Christian communities worldwide moved with them. The result, as evidenced in the renewal movement, was merely a readjustment of the evangelical tradition to the altered mood of the "Modernist" era.[80]

Given the growing structural compartmentalization between mainline and charismatic churches and the ongoing theological disagreements between them, one of the distinctive (albeit unexpected) outcomes of the later century was the convergence of Christian worship culture. Indeed, so successfully did the charismatic movement appropriate *and* propagate the

---

79. Hutchinson, "Australia," 28–29; cf. Anderson, *Ends of the Earth*, 1–4, 248–50, and Miller et al., *Spirit and Power* on the growth of Pentecostalism as a transnational movement.

80. Stanley, *Global Diffusion*, 209–11. "Cultural Modernism" represents a movement with origins at the start of the twentieth century among theorists, artists, and *litterateurs*. Rejecting all metaphysical certitudes, this movement gave rise in twentieth-century culture to the values of self-expression, anti-authoritarianism, experience over dogma, and spontaneity over structure. This is distinct from "theological Modernism," a movement which sought to remodel Christianity along Enlightenment and Romantic lines. So Bebbington, "Modernism," 1–8. In this vein, David Bebbington has argued persuasively that just as the confidence of Evangelicalism was born out of the combination of Reformed theology and enlightenment epistemology, and holiness revivalism was fuelled by the Romantic fondness for "the affections" and "the growth of the soul," so the charismatic movement became an especially effective conduit for the application of "Modernist" values. Bebbington even likens the charismatic movement to the "evangelical equivalent" of the "youth counter-culture of the swinging 60s" (which itself was an outgrowth of the "Modernism" that first impinged upon mass-culture in the 1960s). As such, he suggests, the movement's successful appropriation and even "Christianisation" of the modernist values of self-expression and experientialism is a major reason for its highly attractional and contextualized appeal. Bebbington, "Romanticism," 9–15.

expressivity of modernist culture (alongside its organic structures and empowering spiritual appeal), that by the close of the century many of the distinctive features of charismatic worship came to pervade both charismatic *and* mainline churches. As such, by the 1990s churches worldwide began singing songs of charismatic origin and promoting the language of "gifts" and "spirit empowerment," all without attaching an overtly "charismatic" label to such activity. At the same time, within the newer charismatic churches, worship patterns altered. Indeed, while questions of spirit-baptism and tongues still functioned as an entry point into charismatic involvement, a growing realization among charismatic leaders of the complexities of their own origins and theology, together with a rising mainstream mindset, combined to see many historic Pentecostal distinctives disappear from charismatic gatherings.[81] Some have seen in this emerging *rapprochement* signs of an ecumenical flowing together of "the streams of faith . . . into a mighty movement of the Spirit."[82] Still others suggest that such developments are illustrative of the work of the Spirit in both spheres and of their need for one another. They suggest that the historic churches needed the challenge of the newer churches to face their own limitations and the dangers of complacency, inflexibility, and rationalistic anti-supernaturalism. Conversely, they suggest, the newer churches also needed the long experience of mainline struggle for renewal in patterns of worship, doctrine, and governance to bolster their authenticity and to provide an antidote to the dangers of anti-intellectualism, theological naivete, and the idealization of numerical success.[83] Whichever way the movement is ultimately construed, there is little doubt that it provided a potent growth dynamic and embedded lasting changes within worship practices across the world. Indeed, on current estimates the number of Pentecostal Christians is projected to surpass one billion before 2050, warranting its identification as one of the most successful spiritual and social movements of the past century.[84]

Regarding the response of conservative evangelical leaders to the rise of this renewal movement (including the influential response of Chapman) what then may be said? Some have characterized the conservative Sydney

---

81. Hocken, "Charismatic Movement," 501; Maddox, "Mega-Churches," 325–29; Stanley, *Global Diffusion*, 182, 195–97.

82. Hocken, "Charismatic Movement," 518; Miller and Yamamori, *Global Pentecostalism*, 211–15.

83. Stanley, *Global Diffusion*, 209; Anderson, "Pentecostal and Charismatic," 89; Anderson, *Ends of the Earth*, 249–50, 254–55.

84. Jenkins, *Next Christendom*, 7–9, 245–49; Stanley, *Global Diffusion*, 195–97, 209–10. This estimate includes Christians within classic Pentecostal as well as charismatic-style denominational networks and gatherings.

response to the fast-moving tide of charismatic renewal as typical of a movement that privileged the importance of doctrine over those that emphasized a "freedom in the Spirit" and resisted definition by such traditional doctrinal strictures.[85] Indeed, they suggest, holding to a belligerent form of Calvinism, Sydney evangelical leaders alternated between a strict form of "cessationism" and "aggressive counterattacks based on stereotyped accounts of charismatic extremes." This in turn sparked "a Reformed separatism" which showed itself to be indifferent to the movement's spiritual aims and the strength of its piety and missional vitality.[86] There is little doubt that the tendency of renewal leaders to threaten key aspects of Reformed theology *did* motivate a spirited response among conservative Sydney leaders. Yet, as the preceding discussion has highlighted, while they did not entirely avoid the specter of invective and disagreed with their charismatic brethren on the means of attaining desired spiritual ends, Sydney figures like Chapman shared a greater sympathy with the movement's claims than is commonly alleged, and were united with them in the desire for a revival of faith across Australian churches. Indeed, as has been noted, while they demurred from the theology of second baptism and the necessity of glossolalia, Sydney leaders often accepted in principle the validity of charismatic experience and the availability of the charismata. Moreover, by uniting the categories of word and Spirit, and amplifying themes of God's providence and Trinitarian gifting of his church, they sought to reclaim the language of "spirit-filled Christianity" as being no more or less than "biblical Christianity."[87]

Conservative leaders like Chapman also sought to hold in tension the positions of cessationism and continuationism by promoting an "inaugurated eschatology." This view stressed the freedom of God to advance his kingdom via the outpouring of his Spirit in times of revival and the intermittent appearance of the miraculous. However, it also stressed that while Christ's endowment of his church secured a fullness of spiritual life and the promise of the kingdom's final consummation, the full possession of this kingdom was still a future reality. Such a conviction, it was held, was the only reasonable synthesis of the "now-but-not-yet" nature of biblical revelation.[88]

Fundamentally, however, in both his public protestations and his writings, Chapman sought to promote a theology that provided a reliable core of expectation regarding the shape of authentic spiritual life. In

85. Satyavrata, "Globalization," 221; Hocken, "Charismatic Movement," 483.

86. Hutchinson and Wolffe, *Short History*, 201; cf. Stanley, *Global Diffusion*, 182.

87. Chapman, *Sinner's Guide*, 38–49. Cf. *Both Sides*, 33–46; Robinson, "Charismatic Christianity," 191–201; Chapman, *Foot in Two Worlds*, 60–71.

88. Chapman, *Foot in Two Worlds*, 60–71; Chapman, *Rest of Your Life*, 19–28, 30–45. Cf. Bruce, "Eschatology," 362–65.

unison with classic Reformed thought, such a spirituality refused to rule out *a priori* the place of the extraordinary in the Christian life, but it also privileged a doctrine of the Spirit that elevated his revelatory work. That is, by enabling the Christian to discern the glory of Christ and to taste his gifts of life and truth, the preeminent work of the Holy Spirit was to draw the believer to Christ, who drew near to them spiritually by his word. Such a spirituality was also one that was profoundly "tied to the cross." Indeed, true spirituality, it alleged, was to align oneself with the preeminent reality to which the Holy Spirit himself pointed—the "message of the cross, God's secret wisdom."[89] It was undoubtedly to such a reality that Chapman pointed in 1988. Indeed, at the height of the controversies of the 1980s he sought to publicly contrast the "power" claims of charismatic renewal with Calvinist spirituality. Examining 1 Thessalonians 1:4-6, for example, he noted that while Paul had performed miracles elsewhere and likely in Thessalonica, the miracle he consistently chose to dwell upon was the miracle of divine illumination in the gospel. He wrote:

> If anything marks the latter half of this decade it is the great debate as to whether there are modern day miracles. . . . Closely akin to that is the desire, which I share, to see the power of the Holy Spirit manifest in our midst more and more. When Paul wrote to the Thessalonians . . . the Thessalonians [had received] the word of God, and with joy. That joy was God-given. . . . A miracle had taken place. Paul, a human, had visited them. He had preached the gospel to them and through it they heard God addressing them. We have grown accustomed to God doing this and are often neglectful of the wonder of this miracle . . . The Bible makes it clear that all of us are "dead in our sins." We are unresponsive to God's voice and cannot understand His ways unless he . . . opens our eyes and brings us to the new birth, changing us by the powerful work of his Spirit. This miracle has taken place in the life of every believer. Our churches are full of them! Whatever the answer to the present debate we should not lose sight of the many clear indications that God is at work in our midst . . . The ultimate test of the power of the gospel is that it changes lives. Right understanding of the gospel in the mind and heart . . . is always a miracle.[90]

---

89. Chapman, *Most of the Cross*, 93-98. Cf. Packer, *Keep in Step*, 65-66; Carson, *Christian Ministry*, 62-66, 26-41.

90. "What Sort of Miracles and What Sort of Power?" *Preaching Christ Newsletter*, November 1988-January 1989.

Preeminently, then, echoing Calvin's earlier emphases, Chapman's overriding theological and pastoral concern was to suggest that the significance of the Spirit's work lay not just in the presence of charismata. Rather, it lay *primarily* in the fact that in the preaching of the gospel Christ conveyed his personal rule and presence. Consequently, Chapman urged, authentic spirituality was intimately tied to the Christian's reception *of* and perseverance *in* Christ and the biblical gospel.[91]

---

91. Calvin, *Commentary on John*, 16.16.

10

Conclusion: The Shaping of Anglican Evangelicalism

A Gospel-Centered, Practical Hermeneutic

> "It seems that just once in a while someone is raised up by God of whom his contemporaries say with complete sincerity, 'We shall never see his like again.' And that is what those of us who knew him found ourselves saying . . . He was unique, but his influence will continue to be felt."—John Eddison[1]

THE STIMULATING CAREER OF John Charles Chapman arose during a century marked by unprecedented changes to the social, economic, and religious fabric of Western society. This gave rise to a host of threats and opportunities for the promotion of Christian faith. It was an era in which an early-century optimism was shattered by the onset of two global military conflicts and an economic contraction that reshaped the geopolitical and cultural landscape. As has been noted, by the end of the "long 1960s" Protestant churches across the denominational spectrum no longer enjoyed the fruits of their historic ascendancy. They were confronted in the 1960s by a wave of social and religious change that many now assess as epochal, and by the rise of a culture that saw the keys to progress in a secular humanism free from the encumbrance of religion. Such realities saw a statistical decline across mainline denominations and marked a sudden end to the social and religious contract that had regulated Western society, as the bulwarks condu-

---

1. Eddison, "Introduction," ix.

cive to the flourishing of Christian identity began to fall away.[2] At the same time, the century also marked a time of great opportunity for evangelical faith. In the Global South, the seeds sown during the nineteenth century by countless missionaries and Bible translators began to bear fruit in parts of Africa, Asia, Latin America, and Australasia. As a result, the mid- and late twentieth century witnessed church growth in large parts of the Majority World on a scale unprecedented in any period of history.[3] In Western societies new catalysts for the expansion of evangelical faith also coalesced. A confident evangelical scholarship emerged after 1945. This gave rise to new approaches in preaching, apologetics, biblical studies, the philosophy of religion, and to a confident response to the liberal theological ideals that had pervaded the earlier part of the century. Such realities combined with new developments in communications and transport to see the rise of pan-evangelical alliances like the BGEA and Lausanne movements. Drawing evangelicals together across the globe, such alliances imbued the movement with a vitality not seen, some suggest, since its eighteenth-century origins. As a result, the second half of the twentieth century saw evangelical churches across the West experience growth and even renewal amidst wider secularizing trends. For Anglicans specifically, evangelicals formed a larger portion of their constituency than ever before.[4]

It was into an environment of such conflicting religious and social trajectories that John Charles Chapman—the inimitable preacher, evangelist, and statesman—emerged. The breadth of Chapman's ministry interests and impact are striking. Chapman stood at the vanguard of the growing evangelical movement in Australia for a generation, while playing a significant role in the development of the movement in prominent pockets of the English-speaking world. A figure with access (in his early life) to only a modest formal education and limited socioeconomic opportunity, Chapman nevertheless emerged to offer defining contributions to homiletics, missiology, and public Christian advocacy that were highly regarded by a host of evangelical leaders across the world. In this vein, as perhaps Australia's "most-capped" preacher (preaching more often, in more places, and to larger combined audiences that any other Australian before him), Chapman's extensive speaking and writing ministry across five continents was judged by many evangelicals across this array of contexts to have brought (either directly or derivatively) a new clarity and energy to their

---

2. McLeod, "Introduction," 1, 6–9; Stanley, *Bible and the Flag*, 1–10.

3. McLeod, *Religious Crisis*, 1–15; Hilliard, "Radical," 99–102; Barrett et al., *World Christian Encyclopaedia*, 22; Stanley, *Twentieth Century*, 1–10.

4. Noll, *Between Faith and Criticism*, 102; Noble, *Tyndale House Fellowship*, 48–57; Hilliard, "Pluralism," 133; O'Brien, "Transatlantic Community," 811–32.

CONCLUSION: THE SHAPING OF ANGLICAN EVANGELICALISM   357

ministries. Indeed, the regularity with which Christian leaders across these diverse contexts affectionately recall Chapman's many sayings and aphorisms bears witness to the extent to which his contribution came to shape the popular consciousness of a movement.[5]

The present study has examined Chapman's important contribution chiefly along three distinct yet interrelated lines: as a preacher, as an evangelist, and as a vigorous advocate for the central tenets of Reformed evangelical faith. As a preacher, Chapman came to prominence on the crest of a wave that saw the reemergence of an expository model of preaching across swathes of the evangelical world. This was a model that originally flourished during the apostolic, patristic, and Reformation eras.[6] However, due to the dominance of the "textual sermon" and various developments during the English Reformation, such insights did not carry over into English preaching at that time. This gave rise to the pervasive use of the "textual" or Protestant plain style as the conventional preaching pattern in England and her colonies until the twentieth century.[7] The tradition of expository preaching developed in English-speaking contexts in the mid-twentieth century as a result of the revival of conservative biblical scholarship in the prewar and postwar eras. Under the influence of leading figures like John Stott, the insights of a pattern of rigorous textual study were combined during this era with various rhetorical features of the older plain style. Catalyzed by Stott's approach, after the 1960s Chapman subsequently became one of the leading Australian preachers to exemplify, popularize, and refine this model for use in congregational and evangelistic settings. Chapman's renown as a preacher was forged by the exposure of many thousands of listeners to his preaching in an array of contexts and rose in prominence by virtue of its positive reception. Chapman's preaching combined a unique mixture of clarity, brevity, and levity—in the words of a contemporary "it brought forth the word of God with such force and freshness and fun" that unbelief seemed wanting and Christians were filled with renewed thanks for the wonder of

---

5. Throughout the interview phase for this research numerous subjects vividly recalled phrases of Chapman's or opinions he held by their use of the phrase "As Chappo used to say." Hugh Palmer (Rector of All Souls, Langham Place) used this very phrase in highlighting an aspect of Chapman's legacy in an address at Chapman's English memorial service in 2013. Palmer, "Service of Thanksgiving."

6. As noted in chapter 3, "expository preaching" sought to handle the text of Scripture such that its essential meaning in the mind of the biblical writer and, as it related to the wider themes of Scripture, were made clear to the hearer.

7. As also noted, this model had affinities with the classical tradition. It sought a rhetorically cohesive examination of a biblical "text" by expounding the propositions drawn from the text utilizing "divisions," "proofs," and tools of "arrangement."

God's salvation.[8] Chapman preached an estimated 7,500 sermons across five continents to audiences of three quarters of a million people. Few Australian preachers may lay claim to such a legacy. This also ensured that his homiletic theory and praxis became an influential model in the formation of Australian and international practitioners, as he sought to distill a model of exegesis that served the gospel message *and* his listeners well. The extent of Chapman's preaching, and the esteem in which it was held, doubtless secured his place at the vanguard of the evangelical movement. Such a reality is evidence of the recognition, increasingly given by historians, to the power of sermons and preaching to galvanize Christian movements. In this light, it is perhaps unsurprising that, mirroring the network of preachers who had energized previous periods of evangelical advance, the figures that came to lead the alliance of twentieth-century Evangelicalism (of which Chapman was a key part) were also a network of notable preachers.[9]

Chapman's contribution as an evangelist was no less significant. As noted above, in the generation in which Chapman's ministry took shape, the climate in which churches across the West promoted and defended Christian belief altered dramatically. Consequently, the challenges of trying to reach this culture, with an approach that held firmly to Protestant doctrine while being sensitive to the rapidly changing milieu, were felt by clergy and congregations across the world.[10] Regarding the Sydney Anglican approach to such challenges, the present study has contended that while there *was* a strong desire among members of this ecclesiastical fellowship to reach the community with the good news of the gospel, the methods it had historically promoted and employed were also enmeshed with the inherited superstructures of Anglo-Christian identity. Indeed, aside from the pious desire to ensure that the life and liberty of the nation remained rooted in the Christian faith, little attention was given to a guiding theology of the church's mode of witness or to how it might fulfill its missionary mandate should the tide of nominal adherence ever recede.[11]

It was in such a context that Chapman's missional contribution must chiefly be understood, as he sought to address these lacunae by various pragmatic and theological means. As it became clearer that the well-trodden missional pathways (like revivalism and the residual patterns of civic Protestantism) were diminishing in their effect, Chapman emerged as a key figure

---

8. Manchester, "Preaching of John Chapman."

9. Tennant, "Sermons," 114–32; O'Brien, "Transatlantic Community," 811–15; Gladwin, "Editorial," ix.

10. Mol, *Religion*, 302–3; McLeod, "Crisis of Christianity," 337–39.

11. Note the extensive discussion of these realities in chapter 5.

in the development of new missional tools. In the 1970s he pioneered an approach to mission (entitled dialogue evangelism) that sought to resonate with the modern appetite for "dialogue and participation" in emerging religious forms, and which offered an epistemically and culturally nuanced approach to the evangelization of cultural moderns.[12] So effective was this approach that it gained credence across swathes of the evangelical world and inspired numerous second-generation offspring in the production of a range of later video- and course-based missional tools.[13] Added to this was Chapman's development of a first generation of postwar theologically oriented mission resources. For, as this study has also demonstrated, as a movement shaped (to this point) primarily by influences from overseas, Australian Evangelicalism had produced little in-depth reflection with which to aid its own defense or self-replenishment. It lacked a rigorous conception of the gospel or a coherent theory for its dissemination. In this context Chapman's theologically oriented and popular evangelistic works (*Know and Tell the Gospel* and *A Fresh Start*) alongside his insightful public missional advocacy (presented in seminars, regional and national conventions, churches, and other civic forums), were said to have supplied motivation as well as a framework and vocabulary for a generation of Christians to re-engage their culture with the claims of Christ.[14] Ever alert to changing realities, however, the positions Chapman adopted as a public gospel advocate were also highly pragmatic. Indeed, having previously differentiated evangelical modes of witness from the institutional and revivalist modes of the past, inasmuch as such older modes could still effectively serve the advance of the gospel, he actively promoted them. Consequently, Chapman played a lead role in the planning and promotion of the 1979 Sydney Billy Graham Crusade (which boasted one of the highest crusade attendances in a Western city in the 1970s period) and pursued a strategy of successful medium-size crusades across Sydney regions in the 1980s. Ultimately, however, as Australian Evangelicalism began to strengthen and find its own voice under the leadership of figures like Chapman, a degree of dissonance was perceived between the objectives of pan-evangelical movements like the BGEA and the ability of Australian evangelicals to promote patterns of mission that were appropriate for the Australian context. Consequently, while immense goodwill remained between these historic allies, throughout the 1980s Chapman promoted and invested heavily in the development of Australian evangelists and the

---

12. "Move in for Action," 12–13; Bruce, "Secularization," 205.
13. Note the extensive discussion of these developments in chapter 5.
14. Note the extensive discussion of these developments in chapter 5.

establishment of missional alliances and activities considered more amenable to the promotion of Reformed evangelical faith.

Alongside Chapman's significant contributions in homiletics and missional advocacy, however, perhaps the defining reality that energized and united the other aspects of his ministry was his gospel-centered pragmatism. While his writings and patterns of advocacy exuded a freshness and originality like that of other pioneering figures, evidently, much of his contribution was offered in reply to a range of contextual concerns.[15] In the case of Chapman's written work, for example, many of his publications were developed to address a range of contemporary questions. This meant that Chapman's writings were rarely abstract but rather applied. They were rarely impersonal, but rather pastoral and practical. Reflecting the interests of the era, they inferred on the basis of Scripture, logic, and experience a response to the homiletic, missional, and discipleship concerns at hand.[16]

In addition to this, however, the positions that Chapman adopted on an array of other contemporary matters might also be described as polemical. Indeed, as the present study has shown, the range of committees, synodical bodies, networks, and congresses with which Chapman was engaged and through which he sought the promotion of Christian truth was remarkable. It was for this reason that contemporaries such as Dick Lucas affectionately described him as like the "ecclesiastical weatherman." Indeed, Lucas opined, by virtue of Chapman's peripatetic ministry and extensive international network "he could always give you the temperature of things." And by virtue of his "uncommon commonsense" he could "often see three or four steps ahead!"[17] Consequently, as Chapman sought across this wide array of fora to secure the promotion *and* preservation of gospel truth, he adopted a range of positions that appeared radical *or* conservative, flexible *or* inflexible, depending on the degree to which the gospel, in his estimation, would be advanced by them. The foundational question asked in each instance appeared to be, "What will advance *or* safeguard the gospel?" Such an approach is evident in his posture toward the pan-Evangelicalism of the BGEA and Lausanne movements. In relation to such movements Chapman was as eager as any other leader to promote the cause of local and global

---

15. For stimulating overviews of the innately polemical nature of biblical, apologetic, and historic Christian thought, see Craig, *Reasonable Faith*; Frame, *Apologetics*.

16. Note the extensive discussion in preceding chapters regarding the environment into which Chapman's works in preaching (*Setting Hearts on Fire*), evangelism (*Know and Tell the Gospel, A Fresh Start*) and Christian discipleship (*A Foot in Two Worlds, Sinner's Guide to Holiness, Making the Most of: the Cross, the Bible, the Rest of Your Life*) were developed and published.

17. Interview with Dick Lucas, January 21, 2017.

CONCLUSION: THE SHAPING OF ANGLICAN EVANGELICALISM 361

mission, enthusiastically cooperating with and promoting these movements where it was perceived that gospel objectives could be achieved. However, when it was perceived that the priorities or methods of such movements were at odds with gospel imperatives or if the message of the cross was in danger of being obscured, Chapman's support notably waned. In this vein, Chapman's withdrawal of support from the BGEA and Lausanne movements ultimately resulted, in both cases, in the formation of more discreet conservative missional alliances with other parts of the evangelical world. This was on the grounds of the BGEA's broadening theological commitments and acontextual, prefabricated approach to mission, and Lausanne's eclipsing of a cross-centered message in favor of social reform.[18]

Chapman's response to the challenge of Sydney Anglican ecclesiology reflected something of this same approach. Indeed, in the face of a challenge to the development of a widespread missional culture among evangelicals that was mounted (albeit inadvertently) via the scholarly reflections of Robinson and Knox, Chapman sought to reestablish "the church" as a legitimate context for evangelism and a view of the church's mission in which leaders *and* members played an active role.[19] Similarly, in his extensive political involvements at both diocesan and national levels, Chapman played an energetic role in the reform of church structures to promote a contextualized missional culture, while also promoting a series of measures (in the areas of lay presidency and ordination practice) aimed at the conservation of biblical authority as he understood it. Such measures (within the same political forum) might be described as being radical *and* conservative at the same time.[20] Finally, in his dealings with the charismatic renewal movement Chapman sought, in both his written work and public advocacy, to promote a reliable core of expectation for the shape of authentic spiritual life. In this regard, he vigorously refuted what he deemed to be an essentially two-tier spirituality. Furthermore, while he gave no credence to the view that the biblical *charismata* had ceased, by binding categories of Christology and pneumatology together he stressed that authentic spirituality was intimately tied to one's reception *of* and perseverance *in* the gospel of Christ.[21] Thus, while they were unarguably polemical, even "pugilistic" at times, by the

---

18. This study has noted a strong link between Chapman's waning support for BGEA-led pan-Evangelicalism and the rise of more discreet local and conservative mission initiatives, as well as the formation of newer and more discreet alliances in the shadow of the waning Lausanne movement (like GAFCON and other gospel coalitions). See chapters 5 and 6.

19. Note the extensive discussion of these dynamics in chapter 7.

20. Note the extensive discussion of these developments in chapter 8.

21. Note the extensive discussion of these contentions and developments in chapter 9.

employment of such measures Chapman sought to prioritize the centrality of the gospel in Christian life, mission, and thought.

Many evangelicals contend that a strong historical and biblical precedent exists for such an approach.[22] Indeed, they have contended that it represents a "gospel-centered hermeneutic." That is, recognizing Scripture's focus to be on "Christ's soteriological priority" and the gospel as being the "interpretative norm" for the Bible and the Christian life,[23] such a recognition, they allege, produces a "gospel-centered ministry." Such a ministry in turn produces "a series of balances" that are neither wholly radical *nor* conservative, separatist *nor* accommodationist, and nor do they operate rigidly within any inherited ecclesial pattern.[24] Rather, in seeking to renew constantly the church's life and witness "'in line with the truth of the gospel' (Gal 2:14)," the resultant ministry culture displays a flexibility which issues in actions and attitudes that appear radical *or* conservative, separatist *or* accommodationist, to the degree that the gospel of Christ is advanced by them. Such an approach, they contend, represents the essence of the apostolic and reformation spirit (1 Cor 9:19–23).[25] Reflecting on this dynamic (which he terms the "theological and practical centrality of the gospel"), evangelical commentator Tony Payne suggests that such a paradigm explains much in relation to an ecclesiastical entity like late-century Sydney Anglicanism. Indeed, citing the radical and conservative tendencies the movement displayed during this period, Payne suggests it was the productive fusion of its commitment to missional endeavor *and* to biblical fidelity that produced the diocese's ostensibly "gospel-centered" (and numerically fruitful) approach.[26] Furthermore, describing the figure of Chapman as the "emblematic Sydney Anglican" for whom "the gospel was the central preoccupation of his life," Payne suggests that more than any figure in the movement's recent history, it was Chapman who preeminently exemplified and embodied such an approach.[27]

Without question, then, the twentieth century was an era of immense challenge for the promotion of Christian faith. In its examination of the

---

22. Carson and Keller, "Gospel-Centered Ministry," 20–21; Köstenberger and O'Brien, *Salvation*, 161–201; O'Brien, *Consumed By Passion*, 83–86; Null and Yates, "Manifesto," 183–204.

23. Goldsworthy, *Gospel-Centred Hermeneutics*, 59, 63.

24. Carson and Keller, "Gospel-Centered Ministry," 18–19.

25. Carson and Keller, "Gospel-Centered Ministry," 20–21; Köstenberger and O'Brien, *Salvation*, 161–201; O'Brien, *Consumed By Passion*, 83–107; Null and Yates, "Manifesto," 183–204.

26. Payne, "Magic Potion."

27. Payne, "Magic Potion"; cf. Ballantine-Jones, *Political Factor*, 54–56.

CONCLUSION: THE SHAPING OF ANGLICAN EVANGELICALISM

post-1960s era, an earlier religious historiography showed a proclivity for dwelling only on the negative side of this ledger. It suggested that the tide of secularization continued inexorably to erode the edifice of religious adherence and its place in Western societal life.[28] More recent historiography has begun to challenge the adequacy of this view. It has noted the expansion of other world religions, the massive growth of Christianity in the Global South and increasingly animated contemporary discussion about the place of religion in Western cultures. Increasingly, however, the surprising element in the twentieth-century historiographical story line has been the presence of resurgent, even buoyant, religious (specifically evangelical Christian) faith.[29] This study has sought to cast fresh light on this emerging narrative. More specifically, it has sought to examine a peculiarly Australian strand within this story.[30] For, as noted, during the later twentieth century, as Australian Evangelicalism emerged from infancy to a self-assured adolescence, a new chorus of voices with a distinctly antipodean accent came to play a lively role in the global network of evangelical faith. They offered new evangelistic and missiological insights, the energy of a youthful church and national culture, and a dash of straight-talking gospel zealotry. John Chapman was a central figure in this story. He worked at the vanguard of a movement that sought a revival of confidence in Evangelicalism's message, and a careful and constantly reforming vision of Evangelicalism's method. Alongside the significant theological and ecclesiological contributions of figures like D. B. Knox, D. W. B. Robinson, and Marcus Loane, Chapman became a key figure within the generation of postwar leaders whose work coalesced to give the Australian evangelical movement its contemporary rhythm, shape, and dynamism. It was not a story of linear triumph, nor were missteps entirely absent. However, in explaining the unique qualities that energized the Australian movement which Chapman strongly shaped, perhaps the most important element was its possession of a heightened confidence in the efficacy, urgency, and universality of the gospel of Christ. As Chapman stated in 1972 and repeated across his career, "we need to recapture Paul's confidence in the power and effectiveness of the gospel. The gospel is not weak. It is a word of power of which we need not be ashamed."[31] Indeed, he later declared, because Christ is a risen Sav-

---

28. Bruce, *God is Dead*, 30; Bruce, "Secularization," 191–93; Warner, *Secularization*, 2. Berger, "Desecularization," 1–19.

29. Davie, "Thinking Broadly," 220; Stanley, *Global Diffusion*, 14–15.

30. Note the scholarly invitation to examine the religious contours of the "new Britains" like Australia in chapter 1.

31. J. C. Chapman, Director's commentary on Romans 1:16. BDM Department of Evangelism, Prayer Letter, no. 2, 1972.

ior to whom "all authority belongs," the gospel is a message which in both its bold call to repentance and its comforting words of grace, is of universal significance and saving efficacy for all.[32] Future studies may seek a fuller examination of the qualities and personalities that shaped this distinctive Australian story and the ecclesiastical realignments that emerged as a result. They may also seek a fuller appraisal of the missteps and tensions that arose. However, it is clear that such studies would be incomplete without careful reflection on the inimitable personality, tireless energy, and reforming gospel vision of the figure termed affectionately "Chappo"—John Charles Chapman—"Sydney's one special evangelist."[33]

32. Chapman, "Director's Commentary."
33. Manchester, "Preaching of John Chapman."

Appendices[1]

CHAPMAN'S PERSONAL PAPERS HAVE been accessed with permission for this research through the generosity of the Rev. David Mansfield (Chapman's colleague, friend, and estate executor). Among these papers include previously unpublished and unknown theological works by Chapman, biographical material, handwritten sermon notes (dating to the mid-1970s) as well as study notes (dating to the beginning of Chapman's formal ministry in Armidale Diocese in 1960). These sources have been itemized and coded. Each source is coded with a general prefix, followed by a suffix itemizing it according to the area of ministry to which it relates.

General Prefix Code:

JCCPP = John Charles Chapman Personal Papers

Sermon Papers
Suffix Code:
B#W# = Book Number, Work Number
HW# = Handwritten Work #

---

1. Access to appendices 1–5 is available through the Digital Repository and Archive of Moore College (the Ark). http://johnchapman.moore.edu.au

Biographical/Ministry Sources
Suffix Code:
/MC# = Moore College Files
/SMBC# = SMBC Files
/PROC# = Proclamation Files
/PUB# = Publisher Files
/LEAD# = Leadership Files
/BIO# = Biographical Files
/CAL = Calendar File

APPENDIX I

Historical Sermon Manuscripts

THE FOLLOWING SERMONS WERE preached over a ten-year period at a range of domestic and international clerical, parish, and theological college contexts. The sermons are *thematic*, *catechetical*, and *evangelistic* in genre and expound some of Chapman's most favored narrative and epistolary texts and themes. The sermons have been transcribed from audio recordings. The title, text (if preached on a Bible passage), manuscript location (if known), and location the sermon was given are noted in the introductory rubric. The arrangement and genre of each sermon is also noted. Editorial rubrics have been inserted into the transcript to mark the flow of the sermon's "arrangement" and to indicate the live audience response.

Sermon Manuscript #1

Sermon Title: Evangelism Every Sunday

Location: Evangelical Minister's Assembly 1991, London England

https://www.proctrust.org.uk/resources/

Rhetorical Arrangement and Genre: semi-inductive, thematic/catechetical

Sermon Transcription

Exordium

Thank you, Dick, very much indeed.

Er, brothers and sisters, would you like to pray with me that I would do it properly? Our heavenly Father, we thank you for your word. I pray that I will teach it properly. Speak to us out of it today and give us wills that want to do your will, we pray, for Jesus's sake, amen.

Now, in your folder you will find an outline, which, unlike Peter Jensen who says it doesn't do anything for you, this will do something for you. It will tell you what I've said, while you've been asleep! (*Crowd laughter.*) Our Lord says that, touching his return, you must pray that your flight be not in the winter. If you are to pray that your flight be not in the winter, let me tell you the next thing you ought to pray . . . that you don't have to speak after lunch (*crowd laughter*). That's the second thing you ought to pray you don't have to do. When you see yourself nodding off, stand straight up, because when you go to sleep when you're standing up, you'll fall over and wake up, and it saves an enormous amount of time. Have you got the . . . this is called, filling in time, while you get the blue sheet out. Do you have the blue sheet out? You won't have Buckley's if you haven't got it. Do you know what Buckley's is? No, you don't, that's another thing you don't know (*crowd laughter*). In Melbourne there is a firm called Nunn and Buckley's (*audience member interjects*). Beg your pardon? (*Listens and interacts.*) So you say (*crowd laughter*). In Melbourne, there is a firm called Buckley's and Nunn. So, to have your chance and Buckley's, it's to have no chance at all. Do you have that out now? Can I start? Please nod? Are you out there? (*Crowd laughter.*) Thank you very much indeed. (1 min 44)

Propositio: Evangelism Every Sunday (Stated as Subject to Be Completed Inductively)

Right, what am I going to talk about? I'm going to talk about evangelism every Sunday. And I want to talk about evangelistic preaching, every time you do it. So, let me start off by telling you what I'm not talking about. Have you got that . . . what I am not talking about.

Confirmatio (Proof) in Negative #1

In 1957, I was ordained, and I went to work in northern New South Wales, with a clergyman there whom I had known when I was a layman. Whether there was any correlation between these two facts, I am not able to tell ... but six months after we worked together, he had a very severe heart attack, and was taken off for another four months. During that four months, the ministers in that town asked if they could use our building for a Billy Graham landline. It was difficult for me to know what the Archdeacon would say to that question. He was not an evangelical. He had never been exposed to evangelicals. He had not trained in an evangelical college. In fact, it was unlikely that he'd even known that the word existed. And he was thoroughly Anglican in an exclusive sort of way. And it was always very difficult for me to work out if he would be happy about something like this, or not. And since I knew that I would have to face him when he came back, and since if I was responsible for the first heart attack, I certainly didn't want to be responsible for a relapse (*laughter*).

I spent a little bit of time thinking about and praying about what the answer ought to be. And it came to me that it ought to be yes, whatever the cost (*murmur*). Yes, thank you, that is a joke, you may smile (*sustained laughter*). I said to the ministers, yes you may use our building. Then of course I had the difficulty of telling him when he came back, that I had committed us to the Billy Graham landline. And so, I waited for a good opportunity. And I told him. He said, "I'm very glad to hear that, John." He said, "I saw him in a newsreel in the movies, and he's such a nice man" (*audience laughter*). I was glad too (*laughter*). He said, "Have they sent us up some sort of manual, to tell us how to get ready?" Well, those of course, of you, who know the Billy Graham Crusade know that there is always a manual! (*Audience laughter.*) So, I said "Yes, as a matter of fact they have." So, I pulled it out, and we opened it up on the first page, and it said, "the first thing to do to prepare for this crusade is prayer." He said, "Quite right. Tell the ministers we'll all pray in our chapel, every morning at 7 o'clock." Well, can I say, this was no big deal for us, because we said Morning Prayer every morning at 7 o'clock. But I think the rest of the ministers had not really thought that they ... this was quite on their agenda. They lasted two days at this 7 o'clock ritual every morning. However, the Archdeacon lent on them, and put this notice out in their churches. And many of the Christians climbed out of the woodwork and joined us at 7 o'clock. And by virtue of the fact that he was running it every morning, he became the patriarch of all the Christians in our village.

Next thing we had to do was train counsellors. We didn't know what a counsellor was. Then nobody knew. So, the Archdeacon simply announced to the praying group, that we all had to get trained as counsellors, and that we were to meet in his sitting room. On the next Wednesday night, we would be trained. I said to him, "How are we going to be trained?" He said, "I don't know, read on!" (*Sustained laughter.*) So, we read on, and discovered that Charlie Riggs was going to send us records. And so, come the next Wednesday night, there we all were, in the sitting room, with the gramophone, and on went the record. And the voice said (*projecting American accent*): "Welcome to the Billy Graham Organization training talk for counsellors. We will be learning many memory verses, during the time we are together. Right then, Romans 3:23 (*with thick accent*): 'ALL have sinned, and come short of the glory of GOD,' Romans 3:23 (*sustained crowd laughter*). Say that verse together with me." So, all around the sitting room, we all said (*thick accent*): "ALL have sinned and come short of the glory of GOD!" (*Laughter.*)

Those of you who know Charlie Riggs that . . . em . . . indeed, the Billy Graham Organization, that although you may be in the counsellor training course it's primarily designed for evangelism. You might be at a course to learn how to put people in their seats, but you will be evangelized. The one thing you can be certain about is no matter what they're teaching you to do, you will be evangelized. So, by the time we got to the end of that first night, we got to Revelation 3:20. And so he told us, (*projecting American accent*): "Behold, I stand at the door and KNOCK! Any man hear my voice and open the door, I'll come into him, and sup with him, and he with me. Revelation 3:20." But then came the crunch. He said, "Every night, Dr. Graham will use this verse, at the end of his Crusade. And you will be helping people, who've opened the heart's door to the Lord Jesus. I don't need to point out to you" . . . does it sound familiar? (*Chapman asks crowd*) . . . (*heavy accent*) "I don't need to point out to you, it is impossible to help somebody who has not done this themself. Now, I wonder, if there's somebody with you listening to my voice right now, who's never asked the Lord Jesus into their life. And I'll pray a prayer for that person right now. All heads bowed, and eyes closed." So, the whole fifteen of us . . . round the sitting room . . . and Charlie Rigg's voice said: "Dear LORD Jesus." And a voice next to me said (*crowd goes quieter*), "Dear Lord Jesus." Well at that stage, fourteen people in the room went (*Chapman gestures . . . sustained laughter*) all to focus on the old man sitting next to me.

Can I say there's nothing like having a converted clergyman is there!! It's an enormous help for the work!! (*Laughter.*) And what happened from that day onwards, every one of the Archdeacon's sermons, no matter where it began, it ended with Revelation 3:20! (*Sustained laughter.*) Even the ones on baptismal regeneration!! (*Sustained laughter*.) Let me tell you, you've got to do an enormous amount of theological footwork, to get from baptismal regeneration to Revelation 3:20 (*sustained laughter*). Okay, that is NOT what I am talking about! (*Sustained laughter*) . . . I am NOT talking about those sermons which, it doesn't matter where they begin, they irrevocably end up at Revelation 3:20, or John 3:16, or both. (8 min 34 sec)

Confirmatio (Proof) in Negative #2

Let me tell you about the other thing I'm NOT talking about. This is a very funny way to start a talk, isn't it? I'm not talking about that. I'm also not talking about the fact . . . I once saw outside a church building at the time when the Prime Minister and the Government of Australia had changed the national anthem from yours to ours . . . and from God Save the Queen, to Advance Australia . . . something or other, which none of us know now so none of us can sing it. I mean in the past we could sing yours quite well, but now we can't sing any (*audience laughter*). Outside of the church, was put this sign: "Advance" . . . it it it advertised the sermon . . . "Advance Australia Where?" And I thought it was such a clever title. And I thought I would hear a sermon on national apostasy, or the gospel for the nation. It was so clever. So, I went along, and the first five minutes was taken up with a terrible tirade . . . against the Australian government for changing a prayer, to a secular statement. And I was assured that we would never sing that in this church, and that we would always pray the prayer which we had sung many times in the past. And here were five reasons why you can be sure, why Jesus rose from the dead (*sustained laughter . . . long pause*). If you fail to see the connection, I join with you! Now let me say that is NOT what I am talking about. I'm not talking about the sermon which jumps illogically onto the gospel as if it is a postscript, at the end, in case there is somebody hiding behind the pillar. (10 min 25 sec)

Narratio

Well then, what is it that I AM talking about? Can I say, that with my friends, and since I'm not the minister at a church anywhere, I'm more like a layman in the church where I go than I am like a clergyman. I am lucky to be able to choose the Sunday my non-Christian friends will come with me. If they will come on any Sunday, I am lucky to be able to pull that off. Sorry, I'm not to use that word am I . . . fortunate. Are you able to choose the Sunday you can get your friends to come? I'm going to tell you that most of the people who sit in your pews are lucky to get anyone to come with them on any given day. They cannot . . . they are unable to pick the day if they're like mine. So, I'm saying, I want it to happen whenever I bring my friends to church. And I want to have the confidence so that any time I ask them, I won't have to say to them, "Well, it's a great pity, if you'd only come last week, or if you could come with me next week."

Can I say that it's interesting to me, as an itinerant evangelist, that where I turn up at places where evangelism keeps being done regularly from the pulpit . . . my job as an evangelist, seems to bear more fruit, than when that does not take place. Now, you'd think it'd be the reverse, wouldn't you? That is, where there is a regular ministry from the pulpit of gospelling, when the itinerant arrives, we see more fruit as it were, than where there is not a regular one. And that is a constant mystery to me, because I would have expected the opposite to happen. (12 min 33)

Partitio

Inductive Proposition #1: Christ is the Key Who Shows from Both the Old and New Testaments How We Might Be Saved

(*Tone moderates.*) Okay then, what is the message of the Bible? Will you go with me then please to 2 Timothy chapter 3, fifteen and sixteen? Now, what a relief, I can see Dick's finally relaxed . . . we've got to the Bible (*laughter*). He thought we were never going to touch it the whole afternoon. Alright, 2 Timothy 3:15 . . . you will remember this great passage. You will have preached on it on Scripture Union Sundays regularly, won't you? If you didn't in your church, you did in somebody else's, and don't worry, somebody else did it in yours. "How, from infancy, you have known the Holy Scriptures, which are able to make you wise for salvation through faith in Jesus Christ. All Scripture is God-breathed, and is useful for teaching, correcting, rebuking, and training in righteousness, so that the man of God may be thoroughly equipped for every good work." Now, he's saying to this man . . . God, is saying through the apostle to Timothy "that the Scriptures which he was trained in from infancy, those Holy Scriptures . . . which can only be the Old Testament . . . those Old Testament Scriptures which from infancy he was trained in, are able to make him wise for salvation through Jesus Christ. That is, Jesus is the key which shows us both from the Old and the New . . . how we can be saved. These Scriptures are Christ-directed, and when we teach them, it is to teach Christ, the only way of salvation. If a Jew or Muslim is happy with our treatment of any part of the Scriptures, it cannot be Christian. Let me say it again. If a Jew or a Muslim is happy with our treatment of any part of the Bible, it cannot be Christian. (14 min)

Inductive Proposition #2: The Entire Old Testament Scriptures Spoke of Christ (Which the Pharisees Failed to Recognize)

Narratio

I wonder if you'd be kind enough to go to John chapter 5. Same idea is taught again, this time by our Lord. John chapter 5, verse 36. I don't need to tell you do I, that this is in the aftermath of the man who'd been lame for thirty-eight years, and not only did Jesus repeatedly break the Sabbath, but he repeatedly called God his Father, in such a way as to claim equality with God. And you remember in John's Gospel, the fat is in the fire, from that moment onwards. And the opposition of the Pharisees to the Lord Jesus in John's Gospel starts here and begins to increase and increase and increase and increase, until in the end they want to kill Lazarus, to get rid of the evidence.

"I have testimony weightier than that of John's," says the Lord Jesus. "For the very works that the Father has given me to finish, and which I am doing, testify that the Father has sent me. And the Father who sent me, has himself testified concerning me. You have never heard his voice nor seen his form. Nor does his word dwell in you, for you do not believe the one he sent. You diligently search the Scriptures, because you think that by them you possess eternal life. These are the Scriptures that testify about me. Yet you refuse to come to me to have life. I do not accept praise from men, but I know you. I know that you do not have the love of God in your hearts. I have come in my Father's name, and you do not accept me. But if somebody else comes in his own name, you will accept him. How can you believe if you accept praise from one another, yet make no effort to obtain the praise that comes from only God (*tone heightens*). But do not think that I will accuse you before the Father. Your accuser is Moses, on whom your hopes are set. If you believed Moses, you would believe me because he wrote about me. But since you did not believe what he wrote, how are you going to believe what I say?"

Okay, got the message there? The Pharisees are here castigated by the Lord Jesus because God's word did not dwell in them, and that although they had diligently searched the Scriptures, they had failed to recognize that they were talking about HIM. And Moses would accuse them because it was about Jesus that he was writing. Now, why am I making such a big meal out of this? It is because often I hear the Old Testament dealt with as if it is not about the Lord Jesus. But he thinks it is about him!! And the apostle Paul thinks it is about him. Indeed, the Old Testament Scriptures will make you wise to salvation, through faith in Jesus Christ. (17 min 50 sec)

Inductive Proposition #3: Everything Written in the Law, the Prophets, and Psalms about Christ Had to Be Fulfilled

Well, lest you might the more be thoroughly convinced, go to Luke . . . ah . . . please, and Luke 24. Luke 24 is this marvelous two passages . . . the two appearances of the Lord Jesus. You remember there were the two walking on the way to Emmaus. At verse 25, I don't need to fill you in on this, do I? Jesus comes alongside them, they don't recognize him, "What is the problem, why are you so down at mouth?" They say, "are you the only person in Jerusalem who doesn't know what's been happening?" "No, no," he says, "fill me in." And then they use those words about how they had hoped that he would have been, or the one who would have fulfilled all their hopes. Verse 25 he said to them, "How foolish you are, and slow of heart (*slows pace*) to believe all that the prophets had spoken." He said, "trouble with you lot is, if you'd had your quiet times properly and put your mind to it, you wouldn't have been in the state you're in now." I don't know if you've noticed that the women are not commended for their devotion, which is misplaced? "What are you seeking the living, where the dead are for?" (*Pause.*) Doesn't sound to me like a pat on the back for devotion (*castigating tone*). "If you'd had your wits about you and read your Bible, you wouldn't have wasted time by being here this morning. What are you seeking the living amongst the dead? He is not here, he's risen." Now the two on the way to Emmaus, "What are you talking about? You don't understand anything . . . in the Bible? How foolish you are, and slow of heart to believe all that the prophets have spoken. Did not the Christ have to suffer these things and then enter into his glory?" And beginning with Moses and all the prophets, he explained to them what was said in ALL the Scriptures (*pace slows*) concerning himself (*lengthy pause*). When he appears to them in the upper room, verse 44, "This is what I told you while I was still with you, everything must be fulfilled that was written about me in the Law of Moses, and the Prophets, and the Psalms." And he opened their minds, so they could understand the Scriptures (*pause*). Got it? "Everything must be fulfilled that is written about me, in the Law of Moses, and the Prophets and the Psalms." The whole sweep of the Old Testament, everything must be fulfilled. (20 min 35 sec)

Cumulative Proposition: Overarching All of Scripture is Christ —By Whom God Has Reconciled the World to Himself

Now, overarching everything in the Bible is Jesus and salvation (*pause*). If I were to say to you, "What is the book about? Not, a book of the Bible. But what is the whole revelation about? That is, from Genesis right through to Revelation. If you were to summarize it for me, can you do that? What is the book about . . . what is the revelation about? Well, I've suggested, it could be summarized under this idea, "God was in Christ, reconciling the world to himself." That'd be a possible summary, wouldn't it? You could describe it under a kingdom model. You could describe it under a covenant model. For it seems to me that the Bible does both of those, and many others! But let me just pick the one, "God was in Christ, reconciling the world to himself." If I am right in saying, that is a reasonable summary of what the revelation is about, then when it comes to preaching, it seems to me that preaching must be done within the context in which it comes.

Sub-Proposition #1: Set Scripture within its Immediate Context

Now, I'm teaching my grandmothers how to suck eggs now, aren't I? Because you know that I know that you know that everything has gotta be preached within its context. A great friend of mine said to me his favorite verse in the Bible comes from Isaiah 5, "Woe unto them, who rise up early in the morning" (*laughter*). That's not a bad verse. I might pick it for my verse for the year, next year (*laughter*). In its context, it is to follow after strong drink! Now, I don't need to tell you about putting it into its immediate context. You will know all about that. But a verse if it's rightly to be understood, there are three contexts in which it's got to be placed.

There is its immediate context. It means something, where it comes, with the bit that comes before and the bit that comes after it. The most elementary form of exegesis knows that. So, if you don't know that, you might as well blow your brains out as a preacher! Or, better still, learn how to do it, but don't open your mouth again 'til you've learned how to do it (*laughter*). Alright. It must be set within its context. It means something where it comes, with the bit that comes before and the bit after.

Sub-Propositions #2 and #3: Set Scripture within its Context in the Biblical Book and within the Bible's Revelation as a Whole

But it means something, within the context of the book! Now, I don't need to teach you that either, do I? . . . that you do not transport Johannine ideas into Paul. Or, if you want to do it simply, the way in which John sees you are to respond to the gospel, is to believe on the Lord Jesus Christ. The way Luke calls you to respond is to repent and believe the gospel, for the forgiveness of your sins. I assume they're talking about the same response. It's not that there is a Johannine way that you can get in, and there is a Lukan way that is different. And some can come by the John door, and some by the Luke door. And some by no door at all. See what I mean? There is its immediate context in which it's to be set. But it also means something within the context of the book. Now what I want to ask you brothers and sisters is, "Does it also have to take its place in the context of the revelation as a whole? That is, if I'm right in saying the revelation as a whole, is to direct me towards Christ and the way of salvation, is it too much to ask, that when the little piece is dealt with, that you've got to be able to fit it into the big mosaic? What is it telling me about how God reconciles the world to himself in Christ? (*Heightened tone.*) And I want to say to you, "until that is done, I don't think it is set in its context (*pause*). And when it is set into its wide context, then it must be evangelistic. Because you will show me how this piece, wherever it comes from, fits into the overall of what the whole revelation is doing." (25 min 20 sec)

IMPLICIT PROPOSITION: If we demonstrate how the section of Scripture we are dealing with is situated within the overall revelation God has made (about God reconciling the world to himself in Christ) then if a non-Christian walks in any Sunday they should be hearing the gospel.

Now I don't want you to jump up there too quickly. I don't want you to jump up until you've set it in its immediate context, and in the context of the book. But I don't want you to leave it there, and never show me how it fits in to what God is doing Christ, for the salvation of people. Let me ask you this question, "Do you think it's too much to ask if a pagan man comes for a look see, one night, it's too much to expect he'll know what we're on about?" And I'm saying, it's not too much to ask, surely!! Since I can't pick the night when my friends say yes, and I've to take a punt, I can't ring up the Rector and say, "He's coming tonight! Can you whip onto John 3:16, or round the twist somewhere?" No, it is when it is done like this, that it doesn't matter what night he says yes, I'm happy to bring him. Do you think it could be brothers and sisters, that this could be one of the reasons why our people lack confidence to bring people, all the time? Because for them, many times, they can't see how it does fit into the overall. They themselves don't know . . . how the bit I'm dealing with right now fits into the overall, so they can't even explain it on the way home. We are so anxious, I want to suggest you . . . I'm sorry, let me rephrase that, could it be possible that some preachers somewhere, are so anxious to deal with the text faithfully, but it sounds as if it isn't in the whole? Or that it has validity, outside of the whole? And I want to suggest to you, it doesn't. It cannot stand except in the context, and the book cannot stand except in the whole. What is it, do you think, I am doing when I arrive on the scene as an evangelist? (*Pause.*) Why I pick bits that allow me to jump up into the whole. I pick those summary parts, like the one I've given you from 2 Corinthians 5, or 1 Corinthians 15, or John 3:16, (*voice heightens*) which somehow seem to telescope the whole up into one little verse . . . it's so distilled. And that's what enables me to say the whole quickly . . . because the bit I choose to preach on, enables me to do it. (28 min 12 sec)

Confirmatio: Worked Example #1 of an Exegetical Process to Achieve Implicit Proposition

Now, let me give you two quick illustrations, and then there'll be time for you to ask me a question, if I'm going to stick my neck out in the way that I have. The first illustration I give you is from 1 Samuel 17, and I'm not going to read the fifty-eight verses. You will be relieved to know. On the basis that I will not need to do that, for it is the slaying of Goliath by David. Is there anyone here, who has never read that story? (*Laughter.*) Right, that's not a bad . . . ah . . . move about is there. It is a well-known story. Let me try and set it for you in its immediate context. We know that Saul has been rejected by God as ruler, protector of his people, because he has already told Samuel that Saul is rejected. We know that David has been anointed by God, to be king over his people, and Samuel has already done this. He's done it privately and is a bit edgy about doing it (*pause*). Whether the rest of the family know or not, they probably do. But it is not widely known. God's people are oppressed, by his and their enemies. And they are powerless to deal with the situation. That is abundantly clear when we read the story. And God's anointed one comes in apparent weakness, and, almost from obscurity, and brings salvation to God's people. Have I understood it properly in its context? Now, what is the context of 1 and 2 Samuel, and 1 and 2 Kings? To try and put in within the framework of its book, God has promised that David's kingdom will be established forever. Yet there seems no way that this is going to happen as king after king fails. And even in great high moments, like Josiah and Hezekiah, when your spirits are buoyed up for a bit, they don't last the distance. And even though David's victory is very great here, it is not permanent. So, does that not lead you to the question, "How then will God's promise prevail?" And it is only in Jesus, and only in Jesus do we see the permanent salvation for God's people, and he through his death and resurrection, achieves it.

Can I say that to identify David with us and our struggles, in my judgment, is to fail to set this in any one of its three contexts, let alone to even miss it in one or two. If the writer thought that he was talking about our struggle against sin (which I'm all for, I mean, struggling against sin) . . . if the writer thought that that's what he was on about, I'll walk from here to Redding on a cold winter's night on ma hands! Without any pants on! (*Laughter.*) See what I'm saying. But can I say, to set it in the first context, and even to set it in the second, and not to set it in the context of the whole, is not to do justice to what is taking place in the wide sweep of the revelation. And to set it in its whole . . . is to tell me the gospel, is it not? Can I say, you'll find it exciting. We will find it exciting. And unbelievers will find it exciting. And I believe that when I start to do that, our people will have more confidence than ever, to bring their friends. Because they will say "it doesn't matter what night you bring them, it doesn't matter what he's on about, he will set it in the context of the gospel." (32 min 45 sec)

Confirmatio: Worked Example #2 of an Exegetical Process to Achieve Implicit Proposition

Let me try and do one more for you, and then I'll stop, and you may ask me some questions. If you'll go to Judges 3, I'll show you another illustration (*murmurs as he flicks Bible*). Where abouts do the Judges come? In the church that I go to, my minister announces the Bible reading, and begins to read it. I look it up. And he is still reading. He finishes. And I find it (*laughter*). I've neither heard it, nor read it. I have a continuing nightmare. It is that I am reading the lesson in St. Andrew's Cathedral. It is from Obadiah. The boy with the wand has picked me up from my stall and has led me with unerring accuracy to the lectern. It's not all that far in St. Andrew's Cathedral, but you still need a guide, to make sure you don't get lost on the way! (*Laughter.*) I get to the lectern, and to my great horror, I discover that the table of contents has been pulled out of the Bible (*laughter*). The Magnificat long since finished, and I am still going through the slow turn, looking for Obadiah (*laughter*). By the way, have you found Judges 3? (*Laughter.*)

Alright, let's have a look at Judges 3. "The Israelites did evil in the eyes of the Lord. They forgot the Lord their God, and they served the Baals, and the Ashtaroths. The anger of the LORD burned against Israel, so that he sold them into the hands of Cushan (*omits Rishathaim king of Aram Naharaim*), to whom the Israelites were subject for eight years (*laughter at Chapman's omission*)." You thought I was going to make a go at it, didn't ya (*laughter*)? "But when they cried out to the LORD, he raised up for them a deliverer, Othniel son of Kenaz, Caleb's younger brother, who saved them. The Spirit of the LORD came upon him, so that he became Israel's judge and went to war. And the LORD gave that King of Aram into the hands of Othniel, who overpowered him. So, the land had peace for forty years, until Othniel died."

Now, I don't need to tell you about what this book is about, because mercifully, the author tells us. It's always a great relief in the Bible when the author tells you what he's on about, isn't it? I'm always hoping my commentators will tell me what the book is about, when the author doesn't. And I'm doubly irritated when my commentator seems to miss what the author has said, and says he couldn't possibly have meant this, but tells you another. Have a look at Judges 2, ten and onwards. "After that whole generation had been gathered to their fathers, another generation grew up, who knew neither the LORD, nor what he had done for Israel. Then the Israelites did evil in the eyes of the LORD and served the Baals. They forsook the LORD, the God of their fathers, who had brought them up out of Egypt. They followed and worshipped various gods of the peoples around about them. They provoked the LORD to anger, because they forsook him and served the Baals and the Ashtaroths. And in his anger against Israel, the LORD handed them over to raiders who plundered them. He sold them to their enemies all about, whom they were no longer able to resist. And whenever Israel went out to fight, the hand of the LORD was against them, to defeat them, just as he had sworn to them. They were in great distress. Then the LORD raised up judges who saved them out of the hands of these raiders. Yet they would not listen to their judges but prostituted themselves to other gods and worshipped them. Unlike their fathers, they quickly turned from the way in which their fathers had walked, the ways of obedience to the LORD's command. And whenever the LORD raised up a judge for them, he was with the judge, and saved them out of the hand of their enemies as long as the judge lived, for the LORD had compassion on them, as they groaned under those who oppressed them and afflicted them. But when the judge died, the people returned to ways even more corrupt than those of their fathers . . . etcetera, etcetera, etcetera.

So, we know what the book is about! It is about the never-ending cycle of rebellion, punishment, repentance, deliverance. Rebellion, punishment, repentance, deliverance (*pause*). But when you finally get to the end of this book, there is that terrible despair. There is now no judge, and they have been in this awful, calamitous situation. And the writer finishes, "In those days, Israel had no king. Everyone did as he saw fit." And you say to them, then how did God's people ever survive? And now, this permanent solution is in Christ, who rescues God's people from a permanent judgment. And to deal with the little cameo of Othniel, and not to get me to Jesus, is not to do what the writer of that book wants you to do. Now, he may not have known of the final victory that God would give. But he knew that if God's people were going to survive, they certainly hadn't done it by the time he got to end of his story! That thing is abundantly clear from reading the whole book. It's that sort of thing I'm asking for I think brothers and sisters.

OVERALL PROPOSITION: Whenever a verse or a verse is set in its biblical theology, then the gospel will be set out clearly.

Not to do this, is to fail to set it in its context, and I think is to leave our people *awash* to know what the Old Testament is about. If they don't know what that is about, they won't know much of what the New Testament is about. But when they understand all of them to be pointing to Christ, the way of salvation, it'll give them great confidence in their reading, and great confidence in bringing their friends. And I say, "any believer listening to any sermon, should not be in the dark about our basic message." I'm not talking about how long it will take. It may not take very long to point people to Jesus, the one who is the fulfiller of it all. But I want to plead with you not to fail to do this.

Peroratio

Can I say so far as outreach is concerned, I do not, I believe, I agree with Peter Jensen, that the pulpit ministry itself is not sufficient to meet the needs of our moment, but evangelism MUST BEGIN THERE! It must begin there. People must know that you and I are concerned about the spread of the gospel, and that we regularly proclaim HIM! HIM, no matter where it is that I begin. To have no plan for outreach to the Parish, will be absolutely certain, brothers and sisters, you'll achieve your aim. To aim at nothing, you will certainly hit it! But can I say that any plan for the Parish which does not have PREACHING as its first priority, I think will never convince our people that it really matters at all. (41 min 5 sec) Mike . . . Mike . . . Mike Neville asked me to say something about both of these books. And I will. There is a book by Mark Strom, which is a biblical theology, called "Days are Coming." You no doubt will have read a biblical theology. If you haven't read one, that's not a bad one. That's the sort of thing I'm talking about. Haddon Robinson has a book called "Expository Preaching." You may have a copy already under "Biblical Preaching." If you've got one under "Biblical Preaching," don't buy "Expository Preaching" because it is identical. They've just changed the title. I think I might change the title of "A Fresh Start." You know . . . something like "Still Fresh" (*laughter*). Mind you, it's been out for so long, I can't work out why it hasn't gone off (*laughter*). This book is a great help on putting sermons together after you've understood what the text is about. Okay, if you're looking for that sort of a book, you'll find it helpful. It's time for questions. (42 min 10 sec)

Sermon Manuscript #2

Sermon Title: Repentance and Faith Every Sunday

Location: Evangelical Minister's Assembly 1991, London England

https://www.proctrust.org.uk/resources/

Rhetorical Arrangement and Genre: semi-inductive, thematic/catechetical

Sermon Transcription

Exordium

In your folder, there is a blue sheet. It is called "Repentance and Faith Every Sunday." "Repentance and Faith Every Sunday." It will help to keep you awake if you've got that sheet there. And it says what I wish I was going to say, if I remember to say what I wanted to say correctly. Okay, so if I say what is not on the notes, what I meant to say is on the notes. Is that alright? Not what is on the tape, which is going to be very hard for those who get the tape. Have you ever thought, in about a thousand years' time, they'll find places, rooms full of tapes. Some eager beaver will dig them up. And by great scientific effort they will play them. And people will do PhD's on whether the tapes have been spliced, or whether they are one person, speaking the whole way through (*laughter*). But the one which will occupy the greater bulk of their thinking time was why we thought they were so valuable to record. That is meant to be a joke. You might just smile (*chuckles and laughter . . . pause*).

In the family that I grew up with, it was not a Christian family, although my mother was converted in her forty . . . forty plus years. Between forty and forty-five, by two of my cousins, who were rip-roaring Christians. It's difficult to know how quite to describe them. They evangelized everything that moved, and most things that didn't! (*Laughter.*) They led my mother to Christ and a few other Australians, before they shot off to Columbia, where they have spent the rest of their life. And they are seventy-two and seventy-four respectively. They never came home again, and I'm sure it was a great blessing to both continents (*laughter*). My mother was never too clear on what she had done, although she was fairly clear whenever the pressure was off her. But just to make sure, she made a decision, under every evangelist that ever came to Australia. And when we cleaned up her house after the aftermath of her death, there was, going back, for about the last thirty-five years, a set of counselling material, from every major and minor crusade that had ever been invented (*chuckles*). I didn't actually mind that so much until I became an itinerant evangelist. And she used to come with me (*laughter in anticipation*). And I'd say to her in the car, "If I ask people to come out tonight for counselling dear, you won't come out, will you?" "No pet, I won't." I said, "Why won't you dear?" She said, "Well, because I'm already Christ's person, aren't I?" I say, "Yes, that's right. You are, you understand that dear, don't you?" "Yes." "You won't come out!" (*Laughter in anticipation.*) "No." And this dear old lady would be seen to be coming in on my arm and ushered into her pew. And then you'd have the dreadful spectacle, of the evangelist saying to the first convert (*through clenched teeth*), "Go back to your seat!!" (*Uproarious prolonged laughter.*) While she may have been the bane of every counsellor's life, she was a dream for the evangelist. She kept the figures up enormously, all over Sydney for many years!

Propositio: Repentance and Faith Every Sunday
(Stated as Subject To Be Completed Inductively)

When I come to the point of talking about repentance and faith every Sunday, I am not talking about people walking out to the front, putting up their hand, sitting down, or standing up. But I *am* talking about a thing which to me is very serious indeed. And you will have noted from what I said on Monday, if you can remember back that far, for a lot of water has gone under the bridge since then, a lot of very good water I might say too, and jolly glad I am to have been associated with this conference. I mean can you imagine; you get asked to speak, and you can listen to everybody else as well. I just think it has been brilliant, don't you? Yes, thank you for asking me Dick. Would you like me to get onto the text? I'm sure you would. Quite right.

Now, what I am concerned about is the wedge that's driven between what we think we're doing to the faithful, and what we think we're doing when we're evangelizing. And I'm asking, "Do you think that wedge is there in the Bible? Is the gospel good for the unbeliever, but somehow not good for the believer? Is it something you do to get in by and forget about? Or could it just be that it's something that's good forever? And if you leave it, it's bad news indeed."

Now, I spoke briefly, er, on the last occasion, about setting everything in its biblical theology. And what I want to talk today . . . is about how we're coming to end every sermon. Where are we heading in preaching?

Partitio

Inductive Proposition #1:
What/Who is the Evangelist?

INDUCTIVE SUB-PROPOSITION #1.1: The Bible Teacher Is an Evangelist and Evangelizes as He Teaches

First thing I want to say is "What is the evangelist?" Well, not too many references in the Bible for the evangelist are there? We're told . . . we know why Philip is one. He does it. Philip's an evangelist. We're told that the gifts of the ascended Christ . . . one of those is the evangelist. And Timothy is told to do the work of one. Not too much to build a doctrine on, is it? However, let me tell you, it doesn't stop almost everybody who writes their book on evangelism. They all seem to be able to juggle it all together, and they know exactly who it is. Who is that evangelist? Is it somebody like Billy Graham? Or is it like the boy, who every time I go down to Kiama, which is in the South . . . the south coast of New South Wales, first year I go, and here he is, a little insignificant wart about this high. And he wheels up a friend to me at the end of the sermon, and he says, "Mr. Chapman, this is my friend, Bill Blogs. He doesn't love Jesus. And there's no doubt about the implication of what I'm supposed to do." Next year I come back, they're all two inches higher. There is Bill Blogs and two more. And so, the two of them wheeled up another two. And the next year, they're all another two inches higher, and he's at the head of it all. And by the time I come down for the fifth year, he's got three pews full of them. Now whatever gift that is . . . an outbreak of it, wouldn't do any church any harm at all would it! (*Laughter.*) And I wonder, is he the evangelist? And who will know?

Is Timothy told to do the work of the evangelist in 2 Timothy 4:5, because he's multi-gifted, or because he's a teacher of the Bible and therefore can do it! And I am inclined to think, the latter. For anyone who can teach the Bible, surely, *must* be able to teach the evangel. Which I note that Dick has pointed out to me, in Acts 8, Philip teaches the Ethiopian eunuch the Bible. The man says, "How can I understand what I'm reading, unless somebody explains it to me?" And in verse 35, "Philip began with that very passage of the Scriptures and told him the good news about Jesus." So, he had his biblical theology sorted out completely, no doubt that's why he was told to do the job. No good asking somebody to do it who can't do it. So, he is there called upon to do it. In Colossians 1:7, contrary to what everybody says about the gospel being caught not taught, Epaphras taught the Colossians, the gospel. (*Slow pace.*) They learned it from him. That is how they went about evangelizing. (8 min 43 sec)

INDUCTIVE SUB-PROPOSITION #1.2: As Paul Taught the Whole Counsel of God in His Regular Teaching Ministry He Declared the Gospel

Um, I want to talk about exposition and evangelism. And I wonder if you'd go to Acts 20, because here we've got Luke's account of Paul's farewell address to the elders at Miletus, the Ephesian elders at Miletus. And I want to look at this, because of the things which it says. There is no doubt in my mind, that the exhortation in 28 and 29, "Keep watch over yourselves, and over the whole flock of which the Holy Spirit has made you overseers. Be shepherds of the church of God, which he bought with his own blood" . . . there's no doubt in my mind, that that exhortation comes because Paul has rehearsed before them, the ministry which he exercised, as the model for the ministry that he wants them to exercise. That is what I'm saying about this. What is this discourse about? It is so we can know how, as overseers of the flock, to exercise a ministry . . . a true, apostolic ministry, and that is why the apostle goes and tells them precisely what he did when he was with them, so they will have a pattern for their ministry. I want to ask you to have a look at it. Perhaps I ought to read it. I'll pick it up at seventeen.

"From Miletus, Paul sent to Ephesus for the elders of the church. When they arrived, he said to them: 'You know how I lived the whole time I was with you, from the first day I came into the province of Asia. I served the Lord with great humility and with tears, although I was severely tested by the plots of the Jews. You know that I have not hesitated to preach anything that would be helpful to you, but have taught you publicly, and from house to house. I have declared to both Jews and Greeks that they must turn to God in repentance and have faith in our Lord Jesus. And now, compelled by the Spirit, I am going to Jerusalem, not knowing what will happen to me there. I only know that in every city, the Holy Spirit warns me that prison and hardships are facing me. However, I consider my life worth nothing to me, if only I may finish the race and complete the task the Lord Jesus has given me, the task of testifying to the gospel of the grace of God. Now I know that none of you among whom I've gone about preaching the gospel will ever see me again. Therefore, I declare to you today, that I am innocent of the blood of you all, for I have not hesitated to proclaim to you the whole will of God.'" (11 min 37 sec)

Let me talk first about the content of Paul's ministry as it is described for us here. You will see in verse 20, he said, "I did not withhold from telling you anything that was profitable." Verse 24, "I declared to you the gospel of the grace of God," I think it should read, shouldn't it? The gospel of the grace of God. He says in verse 25, "he preached the kingdom." And in verse 27, he says, "I have not hesitated to proclaim to you the whole will of God."

What was it that he did in three years, in the time at Ephesus, which at the end of that time he was able to say, "I have declared to you the whole counsel of God?" What was it that he did in those three years, that when he left, he was able to say to them, "I have not withheld from telling you anything that was profitable?" That is, he was able to leave them with confidence, that all they needed to go on in the Christian life, anything that was profitable, indeed the whole counsel of God had been declared to them. Well, what he declared to them was the gospel!! The gospel of God's grace. The gospel of the kingdom of God. If you would have liked me to have put it in the other categories, he told them that Jesus would "make them wise for salvation as they studied the Scriptures." They would understand God's great plan, the will of God, how in Christ he's reconciling the world to himself. That is what he declared to them, the gospel in its implications. (13 min 38 sec)

IMPLICIT PROPOSITION: What Paul did in his ministry, he also expected other ministers/elders to do, to evangelize.

Can I say to you, will you note, that the gospel of the grace of God can be rightly described as "preaching the kingdom." They are not opposed to each other. They describe the same gospel, which in 1 Corinthians 15 can be described as "the death of Jesus, for the forgiveness of our sins, and his resurrection, according to the Scriptures." It's all the same gospel. It isn't that sometimes, he preached the kingdom of God, and sometimes he preached the grace of God in its truth, and sometimes he preached the death and resurrection of Jesus for the forgiveness of sins. But they are all of a piece!! And they were never in opposition to each other. That is, he preached the grace of God . . . that free . . . unmerited . . . forgiveness of God whereby a sinful man can be said by God to be right with him, because of the death of Jesus. And that I can stand in the presence of the holy God as if I'd never sinned, and that because of the death and resurrection of Jesus, that is the position I may occupy! And it is free! God takes the initiative. When I am dead because of my trespasses and sins, he raises me to life in Christ. When I am blind, and cannot see the truth about Christ, he graciously opens my eyes, and I see the glory of God in the face of Jesus. When I am *unable* to come to my own aid, he comes to my aid, at the right time, Christ died for the ungodly. When I could not recognize Jesus was King, he brought me to new birth, and by his Spirit enabled me to recognize Jesus as King. (16 min)

Now, if we only had one of those, we might think we were pushing them a wee bit far, wouldn't it? But when all of the illustrations of how I am before God all converge to that one point, there is no doubt that if God does not take the initiative, and save me, I cannot save myself.

See, it's no good saying to a corpse, "Up, Up, Up!" I mean you can say it if you like, so long as you don't think anything's going to happen. They are totally unresponsive. The definition of being lost is that you cannot find the way. I remember once taking my Sunday school class hiking in the Royal National Park, down in Audley, outside of Sydney. And as we passed the same tree for the fourth time, and I had recognized it for the fourth time (mind you, we might have passed it more times than four, I only recognized it for the fourth time), I remember little Graham Noble said to me, "Hey Mister Chapman, wouldn't it be great fun if we got lost!" (*Laughter.*) It didn't seem to me at that moment to be all that much fun, to be perfectly honest. But the definition of being lost is that you cannot find the way. Blind, that you cannot see. Dead, that you are lifeless and need to be brought to life. Helpless means you cannot help yourself. And all of them come to that one great moment, if God does not deal with the situation that I am in, I am finished! I cannot cry out for help. Not until God gives me the wherewithal, that I might do it. (*Slow.*) The gospel . . . of the grace of God.

But the gospel of the grace of God can be equally described as the gospel of the kingdom. And no doubt Paul and Luke have put this in so that you and I are not in any doubt at all that the gospel Jesus preached is identical with the gospel Paul preached! Why do you think he bothered to put in in? Why did Paul bother to say it to them? Was somebody already suggesting he had a different gospel to the gospel of Jesus? Well, Luke who wrote his gospel of Jesus, is the one who wrote this down, so that you and I are not in the faintest shadow of a doubt, they understood their gospel to be identical. But it's possible, isn't it, to talk about the grace of God as if that does not put you under the kingly rule of Jesus. It's possible to talk about a free pardon, and free forgiveness, without realizing, that . . . if you want to put it this way, the obligations that come with that are that I am under the kingly rule of Christ. And it's equally possible to talk about the kingdom of God and the need for me to put myself under the kingly rule of Christ as if that good work subsumes all the others. And therefore, it is nothing more than a new doctrine of works by a different name. But not so with him. The gospel of the grace of God was the gospel of the kingdom. And he rightly understood that the kingly rule of Christ was established unmistakably through his death and resurrection for the forgiveness of our sins. Now, brothers and sisters, that's the first thing I want to say. When you're banging away at the gospel, can all of those three ideas be seen quite clearly in the presentation that's coming through, so that if I listen to you, I could say to you, "That is the gospel of the grace of God." The man sitting next to me could say "That is the gospel of the kingdom." And yet a third would say, "Isn't it great to hear the preaching of the death and resurrection for the forgiveness of sins." And all three talking about the same sermon. I want to suggest to you, that is what Paul expected the elders from Ephesus to do. For, it was three ways of describing the very gospel which he proclaimed. It's important that I should get that clear, don't you think? (20 min 27 sec)

Inductive Proposition #2: What is the Nature of the Teaching Ministry? (Stated as an Implicit Subject)

INDUCTIVE SUB-PROPOSITION #2.1: In Paul's Mind There Was No Distinction between Pastoring, Preaching, and Evangelism

Second thing I want to say is that in the apostle's mind, there was no distinction between pastoring, and preaching, and evangelism. What he did publicly, he did privately. See that in verse 20? "You know that I did not hesitate to preach to you anything that would be helpful but have taught you publicly and from house to house." What he did privately, is what he did publicly. I take it pastoring is that, isn't it? That's the only thing you've been taught to do, isn't it? I mean, you might have some counselling skills on the side, well bully for you. Might as well use them, and not let them go to waste. But if you want to be a counsellor, don't become the pastor. Let me say it again, "Pastoring and teaching the Bible are one in the same thing. It's just that you do one, one to one and bring the mind of God from the Scriptures to bear on the particular issue, where publicly you do it for everybody." At least in the apostle's mind, what he thought he was doing publicly, is what he thought he thought he was doing privately. That's not a bad model to do, do you think?

Confirmatio: Excursus. If you Dismiss or Upstage your Apostle, You Dismiss Christ

Are we got any Jews here? All gentiles . . . stick with your apostle then! Let me tell you, you only got one apostle, the gentiles haven't they? If you're a

Jew, you've got twelve! That's how important they are! . . . Or slow learners (*laughter*). I don't know which it is. But if you're a gentile, you've got one apostle . . . stick with your apostle. No wonder the gentile churches are in the bog they're in! They've said goodbye to their only apostle. I was talking to a man at the General Synod in Australia. I was putting forward a point of view. He said, "That's novel." I said, (*heightened tone*) "It's not novel, what are you talking about? That's the apostle Paul!" "Well," he said, "Who's he?" (*Laughter.*) "He's your apostle, he's your apostle! I said, aren't you a gentile? Well, he's your apostle!" Well, he said, "He's a man like us." I said, "He's not." I said, "Did Christ commission you on the Damascus Road? Did he? You've seen the risen Christ on the Damascus Road? BULL!! You haven't seen him anywhere!!" And I said, "He did not anoint you to be an apostle to the gentiles. Say goodbye to him . . . you've said goodbye to Christ! For that is the one who is commissioned by Christ to be the apostle to the gentiles" (*pause*). Dear brothers and sisters, don't upstage your apostle! What he was doing publicly, he was doing privately. (23 min 15 sec)

INDUCTIVE SUB-PROPOSITION #2.2: Paul's Aim in Every Sermon Was To Preach Repentance and Faith

Look at the next thing will you, verse 21, verse 21, "I have declared to both Jews and Greeks that they must turn to God in repentance and have faith in the Lord Jesus Christ." Now, this is very interesting to me, and it's where I want to spend some time. First of all, what he did publicly, he did privately. But what he did to Greeks, he was also doing to Jews. That is, he was aiming to bring everybody who heard him to the position, whether they were Greeks or Jews, publicly or privately, to that position where they showed repentance towards God and faith in the Lord Jesus. Now, I want to point that out to you. There is no doubt about where his preaching was aimed. Young and old. Private, public. Jew and Greek. Same end. Although, I want to suggest to you that the way, the place he began, and the way the sermons were put together seemed to me to be different if you read Acts 13—the sermon in the Synagogue in Antioch in Pisidia, and Acts 17—to the Greeks at the Areopagus. But in the Apostle's mind, that's where he was irrevocably leading: (*pause*) repentance towards God and faith in the Lord Jesus. And I want to suggest to you that all preaching should be focusing in that direction. ALL PREACHING! Or do you think every sermon the apostle preached while he was at Ephesus was evangelistic? Well, yes. And . . . no. Yes, I think it was, according to the ones I was talking about on Monday. Because he had his biblical theology properly . . . in spite of the fact that he had been deprived of studying at Moore College (*laughter*). But nonetheless . . . yes that is meant to be a joke (*laughter*). You know that English people laugh three times at every joke, don't you? Once, when they hear it out of politeness. Secondly, after it's explained to them. And then, thirdly, when they get it! (*Sustained laughter.*) But Australians only ever laugh twice (*sustained laughter*). Well done. (25 min 40 sec)

INDUCTIVE SUB-PROPOSITION #2.3: The Thessalonians, Who Turned to God from Idols, Demonstrated Repentance and Faith

Let's have a look then at the response that was sought, and I'm asking you to think with me now . . . please think about last Sunday's sermon, the one you've just preached. Or, better still, forget it (*laughter*). Think about next Sunday's . . . the one you're about to preach . . . that's even better. Think about that one. Where is it heading? What response are you looking for? I wonder if you'd like to keep your finger in the place. I want to come back there. And go over to 1 Thessalonians 1, where it seems to me that we have a brilliant illustration of repentance and faith.

Do you remember the Thessalonians are described as the model church on a couple of occasions, and I don't need to point that out to you, in this sort of company. But they were a model church in the way they responded, so that Paul is able to use them as an example of a good, clear-cut response to the preaching of his gospel. Have a look at 1 Thessalonians 1:9. "For they themself report what kind of reception you gave us. They tell us how you" . . . What was the first thing they did? Look at it? Tell me . . . "Turned to God from idols, to serve the true and living God." Is that not repentance towards God? When I turn my back on the idols, whatever they are, and turn my face towards the living God and say, "You will have your God's place over me!" And though I list all the sins that I think I've ever committed, and I feel sorry in my heart of hearts, and say "I will not do it ever again," I suggest to you that I have never repented until I look the living God . . . as it were . . . face to face and say, "I serve you with lips, and life forever." And that is what I'm called upon to do. And publicly and privately, and Jew and Gentile, he was moving to that position, where they turned their back on the idols.

Now, no doubt in the Thessalonian world that was a relatively simple thing to identify. In the Western world, it may not be so easily able to be identified. Friend of mine was at a conference recently where an overseas guest was trying to get the Australians to grapple with what they thought were the great idols of Australians. And they to a man said, "It is materialism that marks the whole Australian thinking." To which a Canadian fell on the floor in shrieks of laughter. He said, "It's not materialism. It's hedonism." He said, "It's not money you want, it's money to go on holidays! Don't you understand that?" Well, that's right smack on the ball for us. It is not without good cause that our country is called "The Land of the Long Weekend."

We'll have a Bank Holiday for any Monday you can name. And we've got a string of them. But give us another one, we'll have it. It is why the present Labor Party's idea of becoming a Republic is doomed to failure! We'll lose the Queen's Birthday holidays (*laughter*), and all the holidays that come with every successive royal visit. No Australian will vote for fewer holidays! (*Chuckles.*)

Let me say to you brothers and sisters, if you want to identify the idols of the, of the Western World right now, ask this question, "What do you want for your children, that you couldn't get for yourself? Does that focus towards the gospel? Or is it focusing somewhere else?" And you'll be very close to the raw. And I want to say to you right now, "Do you want other things for your children that you haven't had for yourself? And does that focus up into the gospel, or somewhere else?"

There are two very godly ex-missionaries, retired missionaries in our country. They're Brits. They live in Canberra. It's a long way from home. I said to them, "Why ever did you come into retirement here?" He said, "We want our kids to go back into South-East Asia as missionaries. And England is a long way from South-East Asia." Does it not grieve you to discover Christian parents who are dissuading their children from going to the mission field? It is an appalling scandal. And it shows that our repentance has never touched at the point of the idols. And my job and your job is to try and expose them in the Western world at the present moment, and say, "What is that thing, that gets in the way of wholehearted obedience to the living God?" They turned their back on the idols. They may have had to say, "We were wrong." They had to say at least that we were wrong. They must have had to say, "We were willful! We knew it was wrong but stuck to it." Whatever it was they needed to do, that's what they did. They turned their back on their idols. They turned their front to the true and living God and said, "I'm your slave forever."

Notice the second part of the response. They showed repentance towards God and they put their faith in the Lord Jesus. In verse 10, "They waited for his Son from heaven, whom he raised from the dead." They were in no doubt about who the judge was! It was the one he had raised from the dead . . . Jesus, who rescues from the coming wrath. And it wouldn't be a bad idea to sit down one day with a pencil and piece of paper, do it on a wet Sunday afternoon, which will be any one . . . On a wet Sunday afternoon with a scrap of paper and note down the things the apostle must have taught in his gospel for them to be able to make this response. "They turned to God from idols, to serve a true and living God, and to wait for his Son from heaven, whom he raised from the dead, Jesus who delivers from the coming wrath." Wouldn't be a bad idea to check the last evangelistic sermon against what you've got on the list. See how you fared, according to your apostle. They waited for his Son.

IMPLICIT PROPOSITION: Every sermon should lead to repentance and faith in Christ.

Now, did he do this because all his sermons were evangelistic? Yes and no. He taught them everything that was profitable. He didn't withhold from telling them the whole counsel of God. But what was profitable was heading towards repentance and faith. So, I want to suggest to you . . . humph . . . it's very pretentious for a little idea . . . towards the theology of application. When I come to the application, what is it that I think I'm doing? I certainly don't need to elucidate what Jim said yesterday. It was like music to my ears. But is it not when I come to the end of a sermon, that I am calling on you, or you when you preach to me, are calling . . . there'll be a component of repentance and faith irrespective of what part of God's word it is. Is that not so? Well, I want to suggest to you, that that's what Paul was doing. That . . . moving on . . . wherever he was in the Bible . . . whatever it was he was teaching them . . . that was the response he was looking for . . . repentance towards God and faith in the Lord Jesus.

Confirmatio: Worked Example #1 of a Parable that Demonstrates the Need to Repent of Prayerlessness—Part of a Life of Repentance and Faith

Let me see if I can give you an example of this. I wonder if you'd like to turn to Luke 18. I have chosen this parable, because it is the easiest one I can think of. I keep constantly telling new preachers, "Choose the easiest part of the Bible, which is impossible to muck up." Get the stories, which of themselves, you have to really work overtime to ruin. And there's a good chance you'll pull it off. Spend the first ten years on the bits that you understand so clearly, you cannot confuse anybody. And then, you'll be so well practiced that you won't be game to go anywhere else. Luke 18. I picked this parable for two reasons. Both the aim is clearly stated, and the application is clearly stated. So, I ought to be able to get the inside part right, if I've got the aim right, and I've got the conclusion right. "Jesus told his disciples a parable" . . . here comes the aim . . . "to show them that they should always pray and not give up."

Okay, so the aim is crystal clear, isn't it? What should I do with regards to prayer? I should stay with it. What should I do with regard to prayer? I should be persistent. What should I do with regard to prayer? I should stay with it and be persistent, and NOT give up. And here is a parable to encourage me to do it. Does that appear to you to be what is here? Does that appear to you to be ambiguous? Well, that's good? Are you awake? Good, I think that's what it means.

"In a certain town, there was a judge, who never feared God, nor cared about men. And there was a widow in that town who kept coming to him with the plea, 'Grant me justice against my adversary.' For some time, he refused. But finally, he said to himself, 'Even though I don't fear God or care about men, yet because this widow keeps bothering me, I will see that she gets justice, so that she won't eventually wear me out with her coming.'" Conclusion . . . "The Lord said, 'Listen to what the unjust judge says. And will not God bring about justice to his chosen ones, who cry out to him day and night? Will he keep putting them off? I tell you, he will see that they get justice quickly.'"

If you've preached this sermon to me, what is it you want me to do with regard to repentance? Why, surely, you want me to repent of the idea that I may live a normal Christian life and be prayerless, don't you? Do you not want me to repent of the fact that I don't stay at prayer? That I get worn out by it? And I give up! And you want me to see that for what it is, don't you? Sin! And deal with it. You want me to get back to prayer, and to stay at it, persistently. And not give up. Well then, if I'm right in saying that . . . what is the faith component? Why, you want me to trust that God is a God, who hears and answers prayer, and will vindicate me, and not forget about me. So, whatever I might have been doing in the past, if I'd repented in the past, you want and will still keep doing, that is, I haven't given up in prayer, you want to say to me, "Stay with it brother! Stay with it. Whatever temptation you're under, don't give up! You are not forgotten. God will vindicate the elect, who cry to him. It isn't because he's tired, or forgetful, or has gone on a journey. That's another god that gets mocked like that. But not the true and living God. He will vindicate you. Hang in. Don't let your confidence in this great and gracious God waver." (39 min)

Now let me ask you brothers and sisters, is that repentance and faith that you are calling upon me to exercise with regard to prayer, not but a tiny portion, of a whole life which is lived by repentance and faith? Is that not so? Is it not because when I came to Christ, I turned my back on the idols and I turned my face to the living God, and I said, "It is to you that I serve. Lip and life forever," that you say to me, "Don't go back on your persistent prayer. Stay with it. Remember what it was when you committed your life to Christ. Remember what it was when you showed repentance towards God. Don't back away from it now." You see, in this tiny little area of the whole area of obedience, you are saying, "Live it out now Chappo. Live it out like you set your hand to the plow at the beginning. And don't look back." And you say, "do you remember what it was like, right at the very beginning, when with the whole of your life, you put your trust in the living Christ who is going to be the judge of all men, and who saves you from the wrath to come? And how you put your whole trust and confidence in . . . don't back away from trusting now!" You see, the little bit, is like the whole! And that is why, there is only a half a hair's breadth between saying it to God's people and saying to somebody in the congregation, "You would be a foolish person, to put your trust in a God who hears and answers prayer, if you've not turned your whole life towards him, and thrown your whole confidence!"

So, every sermon at that point becomes evangelistic, because you are recalling me always to the gospel. Christianity is the only place you make progress by going backwards. But then, pretty everything is on its head in Christianity, isn't it? Thing about Christianity is, if you get asked a question, work out what you think the answer is, don't speak. Say the opposite, and nine times out of ten you're right! Isn't that so? Can you think of anywhere else where the greatest are the least? Did you work that out? That's got to come by inspiration, doesn't it? Nobody's ever dreamt that up. Even the people who believe it can't pull it off (*chuckles*). And here in this one, we make progress by constantly going back to the gospel. See, it's Dick I learnt this from, and a hundred others too . . . the gospel is not a junction, that takes you off somewhere else. The gospel is a terminus! When you've arrived at the gospel, you've arrived at all there is for living the Christian life. All you've gotta do is spend a lifetime of working it out. It's not half so hard to understand as it is to pull it off. That's about Christianity, is that it's harder to do, than it is to understand, isn't it? And when people discover how hard it is, they think it's because they haven't understood it properly. So, they keep hoping that there'll be a secret teaching somewhere that will make it easier. So, they say "could we have the deeper life teaching?" I said, "I understand that to be John 3:16." The deeper life convention is an evangelistic crusade!! There's no deeper life than the gospel. Can I say to you brothers and sisters, if you're tired of hearing the gospel, you're sick nigh unto death, or you're unconverted, or you've not understood it. But if I tell you the gospel today, does it not come home with a freshness it always had? Do you not with me say, "Dear Chappo, don't forget that you turned your back on the idols. Do it again now. Do it again. Do it again on any other issue you want to name. Remember will you, that you've got a wedding ring on your finger, don't behave like a single . . . don't behave like a single man again. You are committed and you must live that out today.

Peroratio

OVERALL SERMON PROPOSITION: Ministers must preach in such a way that helps people to see repentance and faith in God in every area.

And it's in this area I want to say to you that what Paul thought he did, which equipped them forever, was repentance towards God, that was a response, and faith in the Lord Jesus. And it's in that sense, that I want to ask you, "Do you think that the time you spend in application can be easily identified?" I hear lots of sermons. I hear a sermon, apart from my own, which of course are always the exception, but I hear many sermons in my own Parish church . . . often I get to the end, and a lot of time has been spent in exegesis. A lot of things I am told should have been left in the study, and some, should have been put in the WPB. But invariably, in the last two minutes, I am exhorted to pray God that we'll do it. And nine times out of ten, it's a complete mystery to me what God is supposed to do. For no time has been spent, showing me how I'm to repent, and put my faith in a God who will deal with me. And I want to ask you if you'll think on that one, even as I ask you to preach everything within its biblical frame, so it will be evangelistic. So, the response you call for from the faithful is only a hair's breadth away from the total response you will call for an unbeliever. And I want to say now what I said at the beginning, "Do you think that our preaching could cause the fact, could cause it, that our people have lost confidence in the fact that if they bring their friends, they'll hear a word for them?" I think our division between teaching the faithful, and evangelizing the unconverted . . . I'm asking you to ask whether the apostle would have recognized it? I think he wouldn't have. I think there was a universality in the message which did for all hearers on the day. And I think if you'd like people to have confidence to start bringing their unconverted friends, if we start doing this, they'll start saying to themselves, "I should have brought my brother tonight you know. I should have brought my mother. That's exactly what he, she, they need to hear." And I don't believe we can afford to wait till they bring them, because it's like the hen and the egg. It's gotta break the cycle somewhere. And it'll only be done as we put them into its biblical context and apply it with repentance and faith. Well, if you think that's what the Bible's saying, do it. And if you think it isn't it, forget it. And if you'd like to correct me, there's time for questions . . . (47 min 15 sec)

Sermon Manuscript #3

Sermon Title: How Can God Declare Me Right When I'm Wrong?

Text: Romans 3:21–25

Location: Giving the Talk—A Training Video on Biblical Preaching Featuring John Chapman. Club 5 Conference, early 1990s

Manuscript Location: JCCPPB10W18

Rhetorical Arrangement and Genre: inductive-deductive, evangelistic

Sermon Transcription

Exordium

Let me put a scenario to you. Here is a situation.

In a particular high school, a state high school, there is a principal who is a Christian. And this person has made a good witness in the school. He has openly witnessed to the staff that he is Christian. And he has declared himself to the student body that he is so. And he's known as a person who acts fairly and rightly. You can trust him to do that. In the school, there is a girl called Jane, and she also is a Christian. And although she is not the brightest person in the school, she certainly is a fine leader. And the staff, have awarded her fairest and best and most improved scholar. And there is a medal to be had at speech day. On the day before speech day, she comes to the headmaster and tells him that at the exam she has cheated. She wished she hadn't done it. But this has weighed heavily on her. And she doesn't want to be awarded the prize under false pretenses. And she feels that she ought to tell him. She hasn't told anyone else, but she doesn't feel right about it, and she wants to get it off her conscience.

And he is now confronted with a decision. Does he tell the staff? Does he go on as if nothing's happened? Does he overlook this because she's come now and confessed it? Do they not award the medal for that year? What will it do, if he doesn't act rightly now? And how does his longing to do the right thing interact with what is the best thing for her and the school and the staff? Well thank goodness I'm not the headmaster and don't have to make the decision. That'd be a hard one, wouldn't it? (2 min 30 sec)

Propositio: God Declares Us Right When We Are Wrong (Implicit Question: How?)

Narratio

It's while I've been thinking about it that I thought to myself, the situation I find myself is not unlike that. That God is actually a God who acts fairly. And I haven't done the right thing by God. And even though he tells me I'm forgiven; do you ever feel as if you're not? I wake up sometimes and I think of the sort of things I've done, and I keep on doing. And I wonder "Am I really acceptable to God? How does he do that? Does he go through some mental fiction? How can he say, "I'm right," when I'm not right? How can he be right and say that I'm right when I'm not right? And how can I feel as if I am right when I'm not right? And how does it all intersect with each other? Now, I think the Bible speaks directly into this. And if you'd like to open your Bible now at Romans chapter 3 at verse 21, I'm going to read it to you, because I think the answers to these questions are locked up in this passage.

How can God be right and say that I'm right when in fact I'm wrong? That's the question I'm addressing my mind to. Have a look at Romans 3:21: "But now a righteousness from God apart from law, has been made known, to which the Law and the Prophets testify. This righteousness from God comes through faith in Jesus Christ to all who believe. There is no difference, for all have sinned and fall short of the glory of God and are justified freely by his grace through the redemption that comes by Christ Jesus. God presented him as a sacrifice of atonement, through faith in his blood. He did this to demonstrate his justice, because in his forbearance he has left the sins committed beforehand unpunished. He did it to demonstrate his justice at the present time, so as to be just and the one who justifies those who have faith in Jesus Christ." (5 min)

Partitio

Proposition #1: I am Not Right with God

STATE AND SHOW

The first thing I want to draw our attention to in solving the question . . . in solving the problem "How can God be right and say that wrong people are right, how can God be right when he says I am right when I am wrong," well we need to establish that I am in fact not right with God. That's the first thing I want to draw to your attention. I am not right with God. Indeed, none of us are. And where did I find that? In verse 23. Let me read it to you: "For all have sinned and fall short of the glory of God."

If we'd had time to read the three chapters that come before this, the argument up to this point is proving that everybody is sinful. The Jews are sinful because God gave them a special revelation of himself, but instead of saying "Yes" to God, and responding to God by way of this revelation, they said "No" to the God of revelation and they said "Yes" to themself as God. They said, "In spite of the fact that God has spoken (they wouldn't have ever put it like this) . . . in spite of the fact that God has spoken, we know better." Now of course to have said it so starkly would have shaken them. So, they find ways around it. But they turned their back on the God who had revealed himself to them by words in Law. They said "No" to God as God, and they said "Yes" to themself as God.

The writer of this letter also argues that the rest of people in the world have done this too. The Jews did it by saying "No" to the special revelation that God had given them. But those who weren't Jews (and I'm not a Jew, so that's me) the rest of the people in the world said "No" to the God who'd shown himself in the creation. God had revealed himself, and they'd said "No" to that revelation. And instead of worshipping the God who made the world, they said "No" to that God as God, and they said "Yes" to themselves as God.

That's the very nature of sin. When he says here "All have sinned" that's what we're talking about. We're not talking about some small thing like nicking a ruler from a shop one day, or peaches from the back fence. We're really talking about a whole lifestyle that says to God "No" and to me "Yes." "No" to God as God, and "Yes" to myself as God.

And that is so very very destructive. It is so very destructive. (8 min 4 sec)

Explain

Think with me for a moment. If I'm pretending to be God, and Mike Neville is pretending to be God, when we meet together, which one of us is going to be God? See that puts me into collision course with him straightaway, doesn't it? I'm against him. You see this with little children. They solve the problems by the physical method, don't they? They just pick the nearest available toy and bash each other over the head with it. When you become an adult of course, that is socially unacceptable, isn't it? You've got to work out another way to do it. I think it's called manipulation, isn't it? I think you recover from the physical method quicker than you do? And see, if I can do it with some suave sophistication, and get you to do what I want you to do, and make you see that I am God, so much the easier for me, and so much the hurt on you. And Bosnia, and Rwanda, and Northern Ireland, and Ethiopia are all about who is going to be in charge. Who is going to be God? We believe that until you get God in the right place in your thinking, you don't have the where-with-all to start being cooperative with each other. Sin is so utterly destructive. And that is why it is so serious in God's eyes. No good pretending that six million people through the gas chamber is a small thing! Or ethnic cleansing. I mean it's appalling to think about it isn't it, until suddenly I realize that I'm born of the same stuff. Given the same set of circumstances I'd behave like that. Aren't you angry when you see people killing other people because they belong to a different ethnic group? Does that not really appall you? And do you think God is made of lesser stuff than you? Is he not appalled?

Illustrate

Several years ago, I was working in a church in England, and in that church a man said to me one day, "Would you like to have lunch with me?" Well the answer to that is always "Yes," isn't it? (*Murmurs of laughter.*) He said, "At the House of Lords." Well I thought, "Well he's probably a cleaner." But he turned out to be a proper one. And we made arrangements. And I fronted up to the palace of Westminster. And when you walk through the archway at the front there are two guards in livery who've got those big spear things with the axe on the end of it. When you get closer to it, it looks a wee bit sharper than it does on tele (*laughter*). And as I approached (*makes sound indicating action of closing spears together*) they barred the way. He said, "Do you have business in the palace of Westminster? I said, "I'm the guest of Lord Ashborne." He said, "Your name is?" I said, "I'm John Chapman."

They clicked to attention. He said, "You're expected Mr. Chapman. If you walk through the arch and go down to the left, there's a waiting room. His Lordship will meet you there. And I hope you enjoy lunch." And I did! (*Laughter.*)

During the course of lunch, he said to me, "Would you like to look into the chamber. We're not sitting at the present moment, but I can show you around." I said, "Of course." And there he took me in. And there were the red leather seats. And a wool bale on which the Lord Chancellor sits. And when you're standing at the back looking to the front, on the right-hand side, six stairs above the floor level is the throne on which the monarch sits when she comes to address the Lords. It's designed so that when she is seated, she is head and shoulders above the tallest peers standing. There is no doubt who they think is important there. It's designed like that. I said to me friend, "Hey wouldn't it be alright if I sit up there on that chair, and you take my photograph! (*Laughter.*) It'll be an absolute smash back in Australia!" Well, it was dreadful, the blood rushed straight out of... I thought he was going to have a stroke. I said, "It's a joke. It's a joke." I'm telling you; it was no joke. It was no joke. (12 min)

Apply

Ladies and gentlemen, what if you were to come up for air one day and discover you are not sitting on the throne of the Queen of England, but on the great God who is King of the universe. And you are on his seat. What you doing there, for goodness sake? Wouldn't you be wise to get off that quickly, and make an apology? Say "Oops, I should never have got here. I shouldn't be telling you how to run the world. I'm not God. What am I doing in God's place?"

And the whole shove here. It is very very destructive. Wouldn't you get off that quickly and admit the situation and stop pretending that what you've done is small. We should beg God to have mercy on us. We find ourselves in that situation. I want to ask you right up front, "Do you remember doing that?" Do you remember the day when you came before God and said, "I need mercy! Will you have mercy on me? Or I'm done." You remember that day? Well, if you can't remember it, it's odds on you haven't done it! And today's the day to do it. I wouldn't push your luck any further. I remember the day when I've done it. And a happy day it was too.

And the question comes to mind, "If I do do it, will God have me back again?"

*Proposition #2: God Declares Us Right in Christ
When We Ask for Mercy*

STATE AND SHOW: REDEMPTION

And the second thing I want to say from this part of the Bible is when a person comes back and seeks for mercy, God declares us right in Christ. And that to me is breathtaking. Let me say it again, God declares us right with him in Christ. Look at verse 24 will you.

See what it says. I'll backtrack to 23: For all have sinned and fall short of the glory of God, and are (what?) . . . justified. Just as if we had never sinned. Just as if we had never sinned. We are justified freely by his grace. How does this come about? Through the redemption that comes in Christ Jesus. God presented him as a sacrifice of atonement, through faith in his blood.

EXPLAIN

In the ancient world, there was no such thing as bankruptcy. If you were in debt beyond paying, what happened was the last recourse you had was to sell yourself and your spouse, and your children into slavery. And there you stayed. You were owned by another. They had total power of you, and total control. And there you stayed . . . unless you were redeemed. Try and imagine yourself in that situation. You've got a brother who's as poor as a church mouse. And he gets a job, at night as well. And day and night he works and slaves away. He deprives his own family, and on a happy day your owner calls you and says, "This man has paid the price for your redemption. You are now free. Go. Take your wife. Take your little ones. A redemption price has been paid for you. And God tells us here in this part of the Bible, see at 24, you are "justified freely by his grace. That means just-as-if-ied never sinned, freely by his grace through the redemption . . . the paying of the price by the Lord Jesus to set us free. Free from what?

Well, free from slavery? What slavery? Well, slavery that's fear of judgment. You don't have to be frightened about judgment anymore. You've been set free from that slavery. We've been set free from the terrible slavery of trying to make ourselves good enough for God. Did you know that slavery? Of endlessly trying to make yourself good enough. You say, "Have I notched up enough brownie points yet? Am I good enough yet?" Or that awful slavery of remembering things in the past when done and feeling unclean and unworthy in the presence of God. You know that sort of slavery? I'm talking about what I know about. That awful slavery to Satan who can accuse us in the presence of God because our track record is very bad indeed.

And Jesus has paid for release from that. It's good, isn't it? God says, you will be treated as if you had never sinned, because Jesus has done something, in his death that enables us to be set free.

Illustrate: Redemption

In the ancient world (whether he's talking about the Jewish sacrifices or pagan ones, we can't be clear here). But in the ancient world, what happened in religions where there were sacrifices, well you felt yourself to be sinful because you knew you were sinful. You fronted up with your animal that was sacrificed. You laid your hands on the animal. You confessed your sins. It was a symbolic way of transferring your sins onto the animal. And when you witnessed its killing you said, "What is taking place now on the animal is what I deserve. But because there is a substitute, I am able to be forgiven." That was what the symbolism was about.

Apply and Restate: Sacrifice of Atonement

And God tells us in this part of the Bible, Jesus was like the sacrifice. Where do I find that? Have a look in verse 25. "God presented Him" Jesus "as a sacrifice of atonement."

Show and Explain

What's he talking about? Well, he's talking about the great day when Jesus died on the cross. Remember that? Picture in your mind's eye Jesus on the cross. Remember the thief on either side. Jesus in the middle. Above his head "King of the Jews." Others walked around the bottom. "He saved others . . . himself," are you with me? Got that in your mind's eye fixed?

Listen to this terrible cry, "My God, My God. Why have you forsaken me?" What is going on?

Here is the Son of God asking why his Father has left him bereft. What is taking place? The Bible says that in this terrible moment Jesus is taking the punishment my sins deserve. Yours. Everybody in Australia. Bosnia. Six million in the gas chambers. It's mind-boggling, isn't it? I don't pretend to have a handle on that. The Bible says, "He who was without sin was made sin, that we could be right with God."

Illustrate

One year my Aunty Milly gave me a magnifying glass for Christmas. Her knowledge of juvenile delinquency was very bad indeed. She thought I was going to have loads of fun making little things big. I did have quite a bit of fun doing that. When I got it out in the sunlight, I discovered you could have loads of fun doing other things. Loads more fun (*laughter*). That you could converge the rays of the sun down to a sharp point. And the energy and heat generated there, you could burn little pieces of paper. You could burn a big piece of paper. I burned my name into the front fence. It did not please my father at all. And when I burned down the fowl house (*laughter*) my father said, "Enough is enough." And he confiscated it and gave me what I deserved.

Try and imagine an enormous moral magnifying glass through which you are able to converge the punishment due for sin. For all time, for all people in history. And you were able to converge it down and down and down and down until in one moment of time, on one person, the whole power and force of it all were to come. And hear the terrified cry, "My God, My God, why have you forsaken me?"

Apply

It is a big, big deal that's taking place here. See what is being said? When Jesus died, my sin, the punishment for my sin was laid on him. Not in a symbolic way like on the animal, but in reality. And yours, and the sin of the whole world, so that you and I could be set free. And God says, "I will treat you just-as-if-you-have-never sinned because of that which Jesus has done on your behalf. If you trust me, put your trust in what he has done, and take your trust away from yourself, and that awful agony of trying to make ourselves good enough for God." He says, "I declare you in Christ to be right with me."

Now, I want to say to you brothers and sisters if you've done that, if you've put your trust in the death of Jesus, know that God accepts you. You may feel unacceptable and that feeling is an accurate one. But because of what Jesus has done you can be thoroughly acceptable to God. Ponder on that today. That is an incredible thing, isn't it? That God should do that to us, and for us? For you, for me.

Proposition #3: God is Right in Declaring Us Right When We're Wrong

Show and Explain

Well, the last thing I want to say is that God is right when he acts like this. That God is right when he declares us right, who are in Christ Jesus. It's not some mental fiction that God has gone through. He doesn't say, "Let's pretend it didn't happen." He says, "No, I always act rightly." Look at verse 26: "He did it to demonstrate his justice at the present time, so as to be just, and the one who justifies those who have faith in Jesus." God doesn't say about our sins, "Let's skip it." You look at the cross and it says, "They matter." God never says, "My love will nullify your sin." He doesn't say that. You look at the cross and you say, "God punishes sin." But when you look at the cross, what do you discover but that God's love and his holiness and his righteousness and his justice have all kissed together in the death of Christ. The cross of Christ says, "I love you." The cross of Christ says, "I hate sin." The cross of Christ says, "I can forgive you." The cross of Christ says, "I act rightly when I forgive you. Because in the death of Jesus, everything is done that satisfies love, and holiness, and justice." Pretty clever, isn't it? God found a way to say that we are right even when we're wrong, and still act rightly.

Peroratio/Application

Well, there you go. That's what I want to say. How do you reckon we ought to react to this? Let me ask you to think about that. Should this not fill us with wonder and awe? That God has acted on our behalf like this? Is it not the source of our love for God? Why do we love God? Why, because he's loved us and sent his Son for us. And since this is something we latch onto by faith, should we not ask God to strengthen our faith? Hey, it's just possible you haven't ever done this, isn't it? As you listen to me, somebody in the room right now you say, "Well, no I'm still on the throne." Get off it quickly. Where's your apology, quickly. Thank Jesus for dying for you. Do it quickly. Ask him to forgive you, and God to accept you. And because now you know don't push your luck any further. Why don't we just take a moment where we can just stop and think. And you might like to pray something to God that's really right for you now. Then I'll pray for us all in a moment. Want to do that? (27 min)

Sermon Manuscript #4

Sermon Title: Too Good for Heaven

Text: Luke 18:9–14

Location: St. Helen's Bishopsgate, London England, December 16, 1986

http://www.st-helens.org.uk/resources/media-library/src/talk/2155/title/too-good-for-heaven

Manuscript Location: JCCPPHW80

Rhetorical Arrangement and Genre: inductive-deductive, evangelistic

Sermon Transcription

Exordium

(Chapman, immediately following reading, leads in prayer):
Let us pray. Our heavenly Father, we thank you for your word. And as we come to that word now, we pray that you'll speak to us, in our hearts and in our minds, and that hearing your voice, we will be quick to hear and quick to obey. We ask this for Jesus's sake, amen.

Our Father, who art in heaven, hallowed be thy name.
Thy kingdom come, thy will be done on earth as it is in heaven.
Give us this day our daily bread,
And forgive us our trespasses as we forgive those who trespass against us.
And lead us not into temptation but deliver us from evil.
For thine is the kingdom, the power and the glory, for ever and ever. Amen. (*pause*)

Well, it's a funny thing about Christianity, but if you think out what you think it ought to be, and then reverse it, you generally get it right. Now,

I'll say that again, because you can't believe that I've said it. Right... you say, "he's left out a negative somewhere." So, I'll say it again. "With Christianity, if you think out the way you think it ought to be, then you reverse it, you normally always get it right." Now here's a funny thing.

When I first started to go to church, I never listened to sermons. I thought they were a terrible pain in the neck. I hope that was because I didn't listen to them. I don't think they were, but I didn't ever listen to them, so I didn't understand anything about Christianity. But what I thought was it went like this—that God kept a book on you, not unlike a cash book, only on one column they wrote the good things, and on the other column they wrote the bad things. And when you snuffed it in the end, they drew a line along the bottom, and whichever column was in front, you went in or out or up or down, depending on what it was like. Now, I don't think I'm Robinson Crusoe in this matter, to be perfectly honest, because I think people think that's the way it goes. 'Course the wretched part about that is it always breeds a terrible amount of uncertainty, doesn't it? You never get a monthly statement on where you're standing (*prolonged laughter*) you see. You never know where it is. You're not sure which column's in front.

In your best moments, you feel that that column might be in front. In your worst you know only too well that that column is miles in front. And so, after a while, you can't live with that, so you invent the other stupidity which is "If you do enough good things, they'll cancel out the bad things." So you know, you go on holidays and help old ladies across the bus stop and all things like that in the valiant effort to hope, that all those good deeds will somehow cross out the bad ones (which of course is utter nonsense). If you go and rob the bank and give the money away to the poor, you haven't stopped being a bank robber, have you? Well, just in case you're acquiescing in that nonsense, don't do it anymore (*laughter*). (3 min)

Propositio: Goodness Will Not Make Us Right with God

But let me say that that idea, that idea could not be further away from the truth! (*Emphatic tone.*) That's what I always believed. If you were good enough, in the end you'll make it. Well, let me say, that the better you are, the better you are, the less chance you've got. Now just in case the press are here, let me get this clearly said now, "I am for goodness. I like people to be good, especially if they are my neighbors (*laughter*). It just isn't the way you get right with God." (4 min)

Narratio

Now let's have a look at the story before us, because here are two men at church, just like we are. And, they're both at prayer, just like we've been. One of them goes out of the building, and he could not be further away from God if he'd just killed his grandmother. And the other man, who hardly hopes against hope, that God will take him back on again, walks away friends with God. Now, from every outward appearance, you and I couldn't tell the difference. Can't tell the difference here, can you? I can't. One of the nice things about coming as a visitor is you know that I don't know if you're a visitor. I mean you all look like regulars to me. I don't know how you tell a regular from a non-regular? All got two eyes, two ears. Some of them have got no hair. But then I normally don't speak about that (*laughter given Chapman's own baldness*). See, if we'd have been there on this day, we'd have seen two men at church. Both at their prayers. And only God who looks on the heart can tell the difference. That's a bit spooky that, isn't it? Bit unnerving? (*Pause.*) You can't hide from God! And they don't hide from God either. He looks straight down into the heart and says "bpwut . . . bpwut (*Chapman makes sound effect*) you are miles away from me. You continue like that you can never be right with me."

To this man, he walks away friends with God. You know what, it'll be like that today. There'll be not a single person who walks out of the building today in neither of those categories. You'll be in one or the other. You'll walk out of the building an enemy of God, or you'll walk out of the building friends with God, and there's no neutral ground, at that point. (5 min)

Partitio

Implied Proposition #1: The First Man's Confidence was Misplaced—It Was in Himself

Narratio: Mixes Show, Explain, Illustrate
Steps of Exposition

Let's see if we can work out where the divide is. Where's the big divide? Let's have a look at the first man. It's a funny sort of a prayer. It's addressed to God, but it is really speaking about himself. "Oh God." (That's all God gets a look in there . . . okay, all finished with God now.) "Oh God." (That's out of the road. Now he gets on with himself.) "I thank you, that I am not like other men." First mistake! He'll never get it right from now onwards. He doesn't. I can't use that word here, can I? You don't know what it means. If I was in

Australia, I'd say he's got "Yours and Buckley's of ever getting it right." That means he's got no chance whatever of getting it right.

You know what, he looks in the wrong place to start with. He said, "Oh God, I know plenty of people who are worse than I am." Ladies and gentlemen, you have to be wicked beyond all belief not to find somebody worse than you, because they're all in our living room every night on the news now. Isn't that so? You can't make it on the news in our country unless you're bad. And there they are, one bad person coming up after another. You say, "Well I haven't done that. I haven't done that." Unless you have, in which case, you're terribly wicked. And there's good news for you.

But you see this man looks in the wrong place, doesn't he? He ought to be looking to Jesus. If he'd looked at his God, that he'd addressed, instead of looking at himself, he'd have known that he'd not loved that God with his heart, mind, soul, and strength. He'd have known that he hadn't loved his neighbor as himself. But he didn't. He looked around, and he said, "God, you must be really proud of me." (*Pause*.) A man said to me one day, "If you've got to be better than I have to get to heaven, you've got to be very good, don't you?" And you do. You have to be perfect. And any of you who are perfect, snooze on. I've got nothing to say to you. He looked in the wrong place. "Oh God," he said, "I thank you that I'm not wicked like other men. I'm not an adulterer. I'm honest in business. I'm not an extortioner. I'm not like that tax collector over there. I fast twice a week. I give tithes of all that I get." And that was true.

We sometimes think the Pharisees were sort of religious ratbags. They weren't that. They were as straight as a die. Let me tell you in the English scene where you would find them. I'm not saying you're one if you're there. I'm just saying you are one if you are (*laughter*). Right. Where would you find one? He'd be on the P. C. C for sure. He'd be at church Sundy morning and Sundy night, and at the prayer meeting on Wednesday. He said, "I fast twice a week." He only had to do it once. He was an over and above in religious observance. Church on Sunday. Church on Sunday. Prayer meeting on Wednesday evening. For sure, he'd have a Sunday school class. Couldn't miss out on the P. C. C because he was a big giver. "I give tithes of all that I possess." He didn't have to do that. That was over and above. He'd have been as straight as a die (*pace slows*). And I don't doubt that people said to their kids, "I hope when you grow up, you're like Mr. Blogs. Honest, straight, good citizen." Couldn't do anything worse than to be like this man here. "Oh God, I thank you, I thank you that I'm not . . ." And he went home a total stranger to God. You know what? He is light-years away from everything that God stands for. And you know what? "Everybody who exalts himself will be humiliated" is what Jesus says. You know what will happen to this man? (*Heightened voice.*) He'll stand in the presence of the risen Christ on the day of judgment. (That's what we sang about: "Lo, he comes with clouds descending.") This man will stand in the presence of the risen Christ, and he will see the scars where the nails went through his hands. And he'll hear himself saying, "Oh God, I thank you that you did not need to die for me. I thank you that I am better than other men." And Jesus will say, "You are mistaken! It was for you that I died." You see, the death of Jesus puts the cross straight through the man who thinks he can make himself good enough for God. For would he needed to have died for you, if you could make it by any other way? What does the Bible say? "God loved the world in such a way, that he gave his only begotten Son." Has that sunk in for you? That God sent his Son into the world to die for you, so you could be forgiven. "God loved the world in such a way, that he gave his only begotten Son, that whoever believes in him should not perish, but have eternal life." It didn't sink in for years and years to me, that God had loved me and sent his Son to die for me. And I'm going to say the verse again, so I can be specially reminded today. "God loved John Chapman in such a way, that he gave his only begotten Son, that if John Chapman believes in him, he will not perish but have eternal life." And I'll say it yet once more. And I'll leave a blank. You say your name in the blank, as I want you to know it was for you. (*Slow pace.*) "God loved (*pause for their name*) in such a way that he gave his only begotten Son, that if (*pause for their name*) believes in him (*pause for their name*) will not perish, but have eternal life." There'd have been no need for Christ to have come. There'd have been no need for Christ to die if we could have made it on our own. No one is good enough. And the day of judgment, and the death of Jesus keeps saying, "it's time for you to turn back, and repent." You see, had he looked at his God, had he looked at the Lord Jesus, he'd have said, "I have not lived properly before you." (13 mins)

Implied Proposition #2: This Man's Confidence Was Well Placed, in God

Narratio: Mixes Show, Explain, Illustrate Steps of Exposition

Well, let's look at the other man. I think he's probably in church for the first time, this other man. He's ill-at-ease in church. He doesn't know the right form. He stands well at the back. You always do that when you don't know the form don't you, unless you're Anglicans, and you do it all your life (*laughter*). He stood at the back. He doesn't even lift his eyes to heaven. He looks into his own heart, and he sees it for what it is. And he says (*slow and with heavy tone*), "Oh God, have mercy on me, sinner that I am. Oh God, have mercy on me, sinner that I am." I don't know what came to his mind at that moment. The tax-collectors were notoriously bad people. They were extortioners. And they did it under the protection of the government. They were dishonest. Whether he had that in mind. Whether it was something he'd done against other people, I don't know. But in the presence of the Holy God, he didn't fool around and pretend. He knew what he was like. He didn't look at the bloke up the front. He didn't need to look past his own heart. It rightly accused him in the presence of God, like yours does (*slow pause*). Your conscience tells you you need to be forgiven. The death of Jesus tells you, you need to be forgiven. God in his great love sent his Son because I need to be forgiven. And it ill-behooves me in the presence of the Holy God to tell him he doesn't know his business. This man didn't. He came right out in the open. And he said, "Oh God, when I think about what I've done, when I think about what I've thought of, and when I think about what you've done for me, I am finished, unless you are a merciful God." And praise be to that merciful God, he is! He's able to say, "Because of the death of my Son, there is a full and free, total pardon, to anyone who humbles himself."

That poor wretched creature walked home (these are the words of Jesus), I wouldn't have made it up this way, would you? I would have had the good bloke go to heaven and the rat get it in the neck (*laughter murmurs*). I'm sorry, is it possible to put that in English? (*Laughter murmurs.*) It must be by inspiration, mustn't it? Do you know anyone who's ever made up anything like this? It's straight from God himself. He said, "That man went home in the right with God." He didn't pretend. He said, "The death of Jesus is for me. It was necessary, so that I could be forgiven. And I want to plug-in on that. Oh God," he said, "have mercy on me, sinner that I am."

Jesus says, "I tell you, he was right with God when he went home." Will you be? Will you be right with God when you walk out the building? (*Pause.*) Where's your trust pinned? I'll ask you a quick question. And wherever you place your answer here will demonstrate exactly where your trust is pinned, in the presence of God. Supposing you were to die tonight, and God said to you, "Why should I let you into heaven? Why should I let you into heaven?" Whatever answer you give to that will show exactly where your trust is pinned. If you begin by saying "Because I . . ." well that's where your trust is pinned. If on the other hand you say, "Because Christ died for me . . ." that's where your trust is pinned. Let me ask you the question again. If you were to die tonight and God said to you, "Where is the focus of your trust? Is it in yourself? Or is it in something that Christ has done for you?" (*Long pause.*) (18 min)

Today would be a good day to swing the focus of your trust in the right direction, wouldn't it? There'll be people in the building who answered with a good and honest heart, "My trust is in the fact that Christ has died for me." And there'll be people in the building today who've honestly got their focus in another direction.

Peroratio

Have a look at the prayer will you on the back of the sheet.

The prayer on the back of the sheet is designed for people whose trust is in the wrong place, to swing it in a right direction. See what it says. "Heavenly Father, I've not been trusting in the death of the Lord Jesus as the only way to friendship with you. Please forgive me and take over the running of my life."

It is not possible in a gathering as large as this that there are not many people here today who've walked in the building with their trust in their own goodness. You're proud of your achievements. You might be proud of your abilities. You might be proud of your religious knowledge. But you never stand in the presence of the Holy God and say, "Oh God, have mercy on me." And I'm saying, "Today would be a great day for you to pray the prayer."

You may be the sort of person who can hardly hope that God would actually do it. And I'm saying, "The death of Jesus says, put your trust in this direction, where-ever it's been."

Prayer

And I'm going to pray this prayer. I'm going to pray it sentence by sentence and then I'll stop. If it's appropriate for you (and there will be many people for whom it will be appropriate), if it's appropriate for you, echo it to God inside your own mind and make it yours. And if it's not appropriate, we'll just wait for a moment.

Let me just read that, and you can think about it while I'm reading it.

"Heavenly Father, I've not been trusting in the death of the Lord Jesus as the only way to friendship with you. Please forgive me and take over the running of my life."

Is it appropriate for you?

I'll pray it now then, sentence by sentence and stop.

"Heavenly Father." (*Pause.*)

"I've not been trusting in the death of the Lord Jesus." (*Pause.*)

"As the only way to friendship with you." (*Pause.*)
"Please forgive me." (*Pause.*)
"Please take over the running of my life." (*Pause and slow.*)
"Amen."

Narratio: The Choreography of Conversion and Follow-Up

I want to take another moment of your time. I want to say a quick word to people who might have prayed the prayer today. You prayed the prayer and meant it, be sure your prayer's been heard and answered. What a great day it is for you, to start in a new life, with your faith in the right direction. "New" is the operative word. You can't be newer than two minutes, can you? New people need help. Let me make a quick suggestion to you. The only way we can tell the difference between the new ones and the old ones is by them telling. You're the only one who'll know. If you prayed the prayer and you've come with a friend today, tell your friend, ask him or her for help. They're the best ones to give it to you. If you've come today and you don't have a friend, and you'd like help, write your name and your phone number on the sheet, fold it up. Drop it in the box on the way out. Somebody on the staff will contact you and make a time when they can talk to you. It would be to your advantage to get help.

Several years ago, I was shaking hands with people at the door, in a church in Sydney. (I have a quick look around before I say this, I think I'm safe.) A lady came out of church, and she was sufficiently elderly for it not to be an impertinence to ask her her age. So, I gave her a little cuddle and I said, "How old are you darling?" She said, "I'm eighty-nine, or three months." I thought "the poor old thing's lost her marbles for sure!" (*Laughter.*) I said, "What are ya' on about?" (*Laughter.*) "Well," she said, "I'm eighty-nine years old, I'm three months a Christian." I said, "Well, by golly, you just squeaked in by the skin o' your teeth didn't you!" (*Sustained laughter.*) Now, those of you who've got three-months-old babies know that they need constant help. It's no good you saying, "look we haven't had a decent night's sleep since you came into this house. We're going to pop you out in the garage for a couple of weeks, so we can catch up." It's not on, is it? Get the idea? New Christians need the same sort of help. Tell your friend. Write your name. Thanks very much indeed. (24 min 10 sec)

Sermon Manuscript #5

Sermon Title: A Fresh Start

Text: John 3:1–16

Location: St. Helen's Bishopsgate, London England, November 21, 1993

http://www.st-helens.org.uk/resources/media-library/src/talk/4139/title/8-a-fresh-start

Manuscript Location: JCCPPHW87

Rhetorical Arrangement and Genre: inductive-deductive, evangelistic

Sermon Transcription

Exordium

In a moment I'm going to pray, and before I pray, I'm going to tell you what I'm going to say when I pray, so you'll know whether you want to join with me or not. In the church I go to there is a known mechanism for saying I agree with this prayer. There doesn't seem to be any sort of mechanism where you can pull out in midstream. And so, I thought I'd tell you what I'm going to say, so you can work out if you want to do it with me or not.

The first thing I'm going to pray is that I preach well. You'd like me to do that wouldn't you? (*Laughter.*) There's nothing like good preaching. Let me say there's nothing like the opposite. It's the absolute pits! And if I were in your position, even if didn't normally pray, I'd pray that prayer (*prolonged laughter*). For a couple of reasons: first of all, because within twenty minutes or half an hour, you'll know the answer to it. Often you have to wait a long time for an answer to prayer. But that one, I'd do for the sheer exercise (*laughter*).

The second thing I'm going to pray is that God will speak to you, to me. Wouldn't that be a marvelous thing? You came tonight, and here is a man speaking, but in fact you hear the voice of the living God. That is the normal way God speaks as his word is taught. So, I'm going to ask you to pray that God will speak to you. And because God doesn't do that unless we intend to be obedient to him, I'm going to pray that as we hear the voice of God, we'll do the right thing by him. Would you like to join with me in that prayer?

Our heavenly Father, please help me to teach the Bible properly. Please speak to us tonight out of your word. And please give us the where-with-all to do what is right by you. And we ask this for Jesus's sake, amen.

Propositio: It is Essential to Have a Fresh Start with God (Experience the New Birth) to See the Kingdom of God

Well, you've seen the topic for tonight. It's called a fresh start. I don't know if you know that saying, where people say to each other, "If only I had my life to live over again." Mind you, you probably wouldn't have done that if you're under thirty. And many of you are, I think. When you get to my age, it's difficult to tell really. Everybody seems to be young, suddenly. You know if I had my (of course, if you're under thirty, you think you'll get your act together sometime. It's when you get to my age and you become nostalgic, and you say, "If only I had my . . . yes, that'd be nice"). Do you . . . somebody said to me once, "If I had my life to live over again, I'd do exactly what I've already done." Doesn't that appear to you to be a singular lack of imagination? (*Laughter.*) I mean if I had my life to live over again, I'd have done all the things I've done. I'd have a go at something else. I'd like to go hang gliding. I'd love to go bungee jumping (*murmurs of laughter*) . . . all sorts of possibilities. Can I say to you that with regard to Christianity it is not a desirable thing to start again? It's an absolute essential thing . . . to start again. Nobody gets into Christianity, or nobody enters the kingdom of God, unless they do make a fresh start (*emphatic tone*), is what was said to us tonight, in the Bible reading. Did you notice that? And it is spoken by the Lord Jesus himself. I don't need to point out to you that Christianity is basically about the Lord Jesus. It's not basically about us and being good. It's basically about the Lord Jesus and being in relationship with the living God through him. (4 min)

Narratio

(*Tone heightens.*) And in the Bible reading we had tonight, we had an encounter of a man Nicodemus, who comes to Jesus by night. This man is from a group of people known as the Pharisees. They were a lay movement. They weren't clergymen. They were a lay movement. And they were a lay movement of serious people. They said to one another, "Whether our clergy lead us in the right direction or not, we will be true to the living God of Israel." And they played the game for keeps. They were serious in religion as they understood it. And that is why it comes as an enormous shock to this man when Jesus . . . let me read it to you, "Jesus said, I tell you the truth, no one can see the kingdom of God, unless he is born again. No one can see the kingdom of God unless he is born again." And later he goes to describe it as being "Born of the Spirit" or "Being born from above."

Implied Proposition #1: Even the Pharisee (Religious Leader) Needed to Make a Fresh Start with God

Narratio: Mixes Show, Explain, and Illustrate Steps of Exposition

And that is the first thing I want to draw to your attention tonight, I need to make a fresh start in this direction, and you also, if you are to be right with God, need to be born again, or make this fresh start (*pause*). Now, it's interesting to me, that it is to such a man as this man that Jesus says it. See, if anyone had said to me in my non-Christian days, "For you to become a Christian, you'll need to born again," I wouldn't have doubted that for a single moment. I said I'm sure I would need to. Because I certainly wasn't heading in the right direction. And even I knew that. But it isn't to a man like me who was careless about the things of God. It is to a man who was meticulous! (*Emphatic.*)

If this man had lived here today, he'd have been here this morning at church. He'd be here again tonight. And it wouldn't surprise me if he'd stayed for a second dose at 8.30, or 8 o'clock (is it Hugh?), 8 o'clock. He'd have been in a small group and probably ran a Bible study group in his own home. He was honest in business. You could trust him.

About six months ago I did the foolish thing of all foolish things, you know when you fill the car up with petrol, where does your wallet never go? Of course, on top of the car. You need three hands at that moment, don't you? You know, one for the pump, one to unscrew with, and one to hold your wallet. And so, I threw mine on top of the car, filled it with petrol. Just at that moment, my brother passed his hand out and said, "fill it up on me mate." Well, that's the last I'd seen of that wallet. Whether it was stolen before it fell on the ground, or whether it was stolen after it fell on the ground, there was 400 bucks in it! Do you know before I could get the cards cancelled, someone had taken out 570 bucks worth from the Video Easy shop? I tell you it's easy, very easy. I wish a Pharisee had found it. I'd be a grand up! He'd have no more dreamt of keeping it, than he would of flying to the moon! For he knew that God watched his actions and he knew that to steal was against the law of God. And he was sure that the way you got right with God, was by keeping the rules. He'd have been a faithful husband. He'd have been probably a church leader. And he is rightly shaken when Jesus says to him, "I tell you the truth, no one can see the kingdom of God unless he is born again." And then later on Jesus says, "Do not be surprised that I tell you, you must be born again." And I have concluded that if he (*emphatic*) is neither good enough nor can make him good enough for God, then ladies and gentlemen, you and I all fall into the same category.

Why is it possible, why is it like that? Why is it that I need to be born again? Do you know what the Bible says? "All of us at one stage or another have turned our back on God." Sometimes we do that deliberately, and with all our faculties functioning. In my case it was not like that. I just drifted into nothingness, like most Australians. I didn't worry God, and I didn't want God to worry me. And the only time I ever worried God was round about exam times. And that was that I might pass. The Bible says when we do that, we die in the spirit realm. It's catastrophic! It's not just that we become unhealthy, but that we die! We lose our capacity to get back to God. And nothing except a new beginning enables us to do it. However good I am, however bad I am, if I'm ever to get right with God, I need to be born again. That's the first thing I want to say. (9 min 30 sec)

Implied Proposition #2: The New Birth is Something God Does for Us and In Us

Narratio: Mixes Show, Explain, and Illustrate Steps of Exposition

Second thing I want to say is this: What is this new birth that I'm talking about? What is it?

Well, let me talk about what it's not. Get that out of the way to start with.

It's not "turning over a new leaf." It's not like that. It's not like going back on the diet again for the ump-teenth-millionth time. Those of you who are old dieters from ways back. It's not like giving up smoking again for the how many ump-teenth time. It's not like making a New Year's resolution, which you've got a fair idea is not going to last all that long, given our track record. It is not in fact something I do. It is something which God does. It's a radical change. It's a radical change which God does. And it's a radical change which God does through his Spirit.

Let me read the Bible to you again . . . listen:

"Flesh gives birth to flesh. It is the Spirit that gives birth to spirit. The wind blows wherever it wishes, you hear the sound it makes, but you don't know where it's come from or where it is going to. It is the same with everyone who is born of the Spirit."

That it is not something I can do for myself. It is something which God does for me.

In fact, it's not unlike an operation, surgery under anesthetic. That has only ever happened to me once. But it was like this. I was lying in the hospital bed, and an anesthetist came, and plunged something into my arm. I don't know what that was. But in the next quarter of an hour a whole wonderful euphoric feeling swept over me. The hospital was good, lovely. The nurses were lovely (*murmurs of laughter*). The thought of the operation, it was quite good now, up till now I'd been quite apprehensive, but even I was quite looking forward to that (*murmurs*). And then a man came with trolley and he said, "Can you get onto this sport?" I said, "Sure." (*Feigning anesthetic affected voice, laughter.*) I couldn't move a muscle! How he got me on to this day I've no idea. I saw the ceiling drift by, and doors flapped open. And my surgeon was there, and he spoke to me as through a million years and he said, "How d'you feel old man?" I said, "Dr Hughes, I feel absolutely marvelous!" (*Feigning anesthetic affected voice- laughter.*) And suddenly (*claps twice*), he said, "It's all over, old man. Wake up."

Hadn't taken a split second. Do you know within an hour I knew he'd done the operation? Within two hours, I wished he hadn't! (*Laughter.*) A friend of mine visited me at the end of that day, he said, "How d'you feel Chappo?" I said, "I feel appalling!!" He said, "That's surgery isn't it. End of the first day you think you're going to die. End of the second day, you're frightened you won't!" (*Laughter*) Now to this day I still have the scar. I promise I'm not going to show it to any of you (*laughter*). And do you know what ensued in the years that came along? All the benefits of that successful surgery were mine.

Apply

Let me tell you what it's like in the new birth. It is something which God does in us and through us by his Word. And I'll tell you the marks, so you'll know if it's happened to you. This is what it was like with me when God brought me to new birth by his Spirit. What is it? It is a thing which the spirit of God does within us, and he changes our outlook on life. And you'll be able to work out whether this has happened to you or not.

Confirmatio: Evidence of the New Birth (Narrated as a String of Reflections and Personal Testimony)

Before I was born again, I never worried about God. I was never thankful to God. And I never wanted to please God. I didn't give a moment's thought to the things of God, really. Not honestly. I just drifted along. But after the new birth had happened, I was so thankful to God for what he had done for me that I set out to try and please him.

The second thing I noticed about the new birth was, before God did this great work by his Spirit within me, when I went to the Bible, it really was all gobbledygook. I couldn't work out why people made such a big thing about it. And I found it relatively boring. After God had done this new thing, when I came to read the Bible, the living God addressed me through it. And it became an exciting encounter. To hear the voice . . . I don't mean I heard a voice out there. I knew in the very depths of my being that this was God, the living God, speaking to me. And, no great shakes to me. I didn't do anything about it. It was a work which God did on me. And you will know if you've got the marks of the new birth about you.

Before I was born again by the spirit of God prayer was a sort of a . . . zero zero zero (is that what you ring when you're in danger here, or do you ring nine nine nine? Which one? Nine nine nine). That's all my prayers were. "Oh God let me pass tomorrow, and I'll become a missionary" (*laughter*). You know that sort of stupidity. It wasn't prayer. It had nothing to do with me being in a true friendship with the living God. And when I was brought to new birth by the spirit of God working within me, prayer became a true meeting with God. I wanted to talk with him. I wanted to respond to him. I wanted to share my life with him.

One of the other marks I noticed, which was such a surprise to me, even now can hardly get used to it, I strangely became interested in other people. And I can tell you, that is a miracle! I was concerned for their welfare. I never worried about people before that. I just manipulated them to get my own way—when I was a child, crudely, and when I became an adult, with a greater degree of sophistication.

The other thing which amazed me too was, I began to hate evil in the world, and most especially when I encountered it within my own life. It was so ugly. When the spirit of God opened my eyes to see life like God saw it, that's the sort of thing that happens in the new birth. And I want to ask you ladies and gentlemen, have you had that experience? Do you know what that is, for the spirit of God to come on you and change your outlook on life? I need it. And it is a radical thing, which God does. (16 min)

Implied Proposition #3: God Has Sent his Son to Bring about the Fresh Start Humanity Need

Narratio: Mixes Show, Explain, Illustrate, Apply Steps of Exposition

Third thing I want to say is that "What is it that God himself has done, which enables the new birth to happen to people like us?" And for this I want to go to verse 16. Let me read it to you again: "God loved the world so much that he gave his only Son, that whoever believes in him may not perish but have eternal life." What is it that God has done, so the new birth can be affected within us, so that we can make a radical new start? (*Pause.*) God has loved us and sent his Son into the world to die in our place.

I've already told you before that going to church and listening to sermons was a thing which I thought was totally for the birds. I didn't listen. I always thought the person up the front was telling you to be good. And I didn't want to be all that good, so I didn't bother listening. And you know, one day out of sheer boredom I came up as it were for air and listened. And do you know I got the surprise of my life. He wasn't telling me to be good. In fact, he didn't speak about me at all. He told me that God had loved me, and sent his Son to die, in my place, to take the punishment that my sins deserve, so that I could be forgiven. Do you know it shocked me to the very foundation! I'm a fairly slow learner. It takes ages for the penny to drop with me. But the penny dropped that day (*pause*). God loved me! Before I was even born God had taken action so that I could be forgiven. Jesus himself had died in my place. God loved me. I didn't love God! But God loved me and gave his only Son to die in my place! I must have heard that thousands of times and never taken it in. They must have been saying that in that church every week, and I'd never listened! And here we are in church tonight friends, and I don't want it to go on. It's possible for me. It's possible for you!

I wonder if you'd do an exercise with me. I wonder if you'd say inside your head when I say it out loud, "Jesus Christ died for me." "Jesus Christ died for me." You've got to be a terrifically important person in God's eyes don't you, for him to do that? Have you ever thought of saying just "Thank you?" Plain ordinary common decency would do that, wouldn't it? Just thank you for dying for me.

Apply (Presented as a Series of Reflections from the Perspective of Personal Testimony on the Rationale for Faith)

I'll tell you a few things clicked into place that day for me. Do you know what surprised me when I heard this? It surprised me that my sins were so important in God's eyes, that this was the thing that needed to rectify them. I thought I was such a nice sort of a person, really. You know, it came as a big surprise to me. I thought, "Well I'm not all that bad." You may feel like that. You may feel, "Well I, it never occurred . . .'"

You know the second thing that shocked me. I thought, "If this is the God-given way of dealing with my sin, you can be sure that there is no other way that you can be forgiven, or God wouldn't have picked that one, would he?" And I thought, "This is the only way. You can't make it by being good, John!" And it took me all the way before I got home from church to my home before the third thing clicked into place. It was this. Having now heard it, I was totally without excuse in the presence of God. And I remember saying to myself, "What would you say, in the presence of God if he said to you now, 'Hey listen mate, what are you doing here unforgiven?'" Even I could see it was stupidity to say, "Well I, I've lived a fairly decent life." He'd say, "Well you must think I'm mad, do you! What d'ya think I let me Son die for? What are you doing here unforgiven?" (*Pause.*) "I didn't think it mattered all that much." He'd say, "Get Out. You knew it mattered! When you knew that I let my only Son die so that you could be forgiven!" And here it is at this point, that we see how much God has taken us seriously.

And the Bible is as it were . . . agog . . . at the wonder of this. That God should love us and send his only Son to die! So that I could be forgiven! So that you could be forgiven! For there is no way that the spirit of God is going to come and take up residence with somebody who is unforgiven. But know that God has made provision for your forgiveness and for mine. And there is no other way.

Implied Proposition #4: Faith in Jesus is the Key to the Fresh Start

Narratio: Mixes Show, Explain, Illustrate
Steps of Exposition

And finally, what is it that God wants us to do? I'll read the verse to you again. "God loved the world so much that he gave his only Son, so that everybody who believes in him." See, that is what he wants. He wants us to trust him! Trust me! Trust me! People who trust him will not perish but will have eternal life. God says, "Trust me about the death of my Son. Trust me that in the death of Jesus you can be totally forgiven! Trust me and I will send to you the Spirit, and make you into a new person, and give you a fresh start! Trust me!"

I only have one brother. He is older than me by five years. And he lives in Canberra. I often spend Christmas with the Chapmans in Canberra. Christmas in the Chapman household in Canberra is designed to send the most stable people round the twist (*laughter*). Let me tell you the sort of rituals that take place in Canberra on Christmas Day. No pressies are opened until after lunch. Can you believe that? I'm the sort of person who sneaks down late at night and rattles boxes. My own first, and everybody else's. If I can't work out what's in them, I've been known to open mine and do them up again (*laughter*). And sometimes not do them up again at all. The idea of waiting until after lunch seems unnecessary in the extreme. That meal is eaten with great haste, let me tell you. The next ritual that comes is that the youngest child is given all his presents first. Not in a great heap, where you go to them and rip them apart, but one by one. And you know, and we're all cooing and saying, "Oh isn't that lovely, I . . ." "Hurry!" (*Laughter.*) Do you know one Christmas we stopped for tea in the middle, and I'd not even so much as touched a present! I don't need to tell you where I come in the pecking order of the youngest to the oldest (*pause*).

Ladies and gentlemen, let me tell you that I've never once left one of my presents under the Christmas tree. However long I've waited, it's never occurred to me to leave my gifts there. Can you imagine, I drive to Canberra. And I'm driving up the driveway at 3 McPherson Street O'Connor where my brother lives. It's September, and he says, "It's really good to see you mate. I'm so glad you've come. For goodness' sake, take your present from under the Christmas tree! All the pine needles keep falling over the carpet . . . I'm sick of tidying it up. And yours is the only present still there. What is the matter with you?" I say, "It looks like a new set of golf clubs." He said, "You idiot, of course it's golf clubs. How can you gift wrap golf clubs and make them look like anything but golf clubs? You need a set of clubs, don't you? What's the matter with you? Take it for goodness' sake!" I mean, do forgive me, it is so idiotic, isn't it?

Well, you won't mind me saying to you that God says, "Have I not given my Son? The best I have? For you, so that you might have eternal life? Trust me! Why don't you pick it up for goodness' sake!" he says (*perplexed and pleading tone*). "Take it. Take it." And for my part, it is the greatest of all mysteries as to why if you haven't, you don't. Know tonight, it is not God's fault, only ours if this great gift of eternal life and the new beginning with God's Spirit is not ours. (27 min)

Peroratio: Combines a Sequence of State, Explain and Apply Instructions on Conversion

There you go. I've said what I want to say. But it would be remiss of me now not to say, as you listen to me there are people here, and you know in your heart of hearts that this new work has been done. And as I'm going along, you're saying, "Yes. Yes, that's me. That's happened to me." It's so good. And others of you'll be here, and you say, "That's not happened to me." You say, "I know that I need to be forgiven. I know that Jesus died for me. I need to make a new start, and tonight's the night! I'll put my trust in what God says about the death of Jesus. And I'll ask him to send his Spirit to make me into a new person." Is that you? In a gathering this size, there are bound to be many of you like that.

And I'm going to pray a prayer. Let me tell you what I'll say in the prayer. See if it's yours, if it's appropriate for you. Then I'll ask you to echo it in your heart to God. If it's not yours, not appropriate for some reason or other, well, we don't want you to do what's inappropriate before God.

This is what I'll say in my prayer. I'll say: "Heavenly Father, I need to be born again. Please send your Spirit into my life and change it."

Then I'll say: "Lord Jesus, thank you for dying for me. Please forgive me. Please take over the running of my life."

It's a lot of things, isn't it? Can I just run that past you again, so you've got time to think?

Heavenly Father, I need to be born again. Please send your Spirit to change me. Lord Jesus, thank you for dying for me. Please forgive me. Please take over the running of my life.

I'll pray it sentence by sentence and stop.

If it's appropriate for you, echo it to God inside your own head and it'll be yours. Okay? Let's pray.

Heavenly Father, I need to be born again. (*Pause.*)
Please send your Spirit into my life to change me. (*Pause.*)
Lord Jesus, thank you for dying for me. (*Pause.*)
Please forgive me. (*Pause.*)
Please take over the running of my life. Amen. (*Long pause.*)

Narratio: The Choreography of Conversion and Follow-Up

Ladies and gentlemen, may I take just five more minutes of your time? I want to say a word to people who prayed the prayer tonight. If you prayed the prayer tonight and you meant it of course, you prayed the prayer tonight, and you meant it, I just want you to stop and reflect for a moment about what's happened to you. God will have heard your prayer and answered it. It's a great night for you. You may not feel all that different, but it is a great night. Just think with me for a moment, you came unforgiven, and you're walking out tonight forgiven. That's a pretty good night, isn't it? You came tonight, and you weren't right with God, and you're walking home right with God. It's a pretty good night! You came, and you weren't ready to meet your maker. And whether it's sooner or later, you're going home ready. Sounds like a great night to me. The more I talk about it the better it's getting isn't it! (*Laughter.*) It's a great night. Welcome to God's people! You know you've started out a new life with Christ. And new is the operative word. And new people need help. Let me give you some advice about getting help, may I? If you've come with a friend, why don't you tell your friend, and they'll be able to give you the sort of advice you need to go on in the Christian life.

The "Discovering Christianity" group. Wouldn't that be ideal for you? Pop in and say, "Well I don't know that much about it. I made a Fresh Start. I'll go and find out what's really happened." And I'd go along to the desk down there, the welcome desk, or the student desk. Somebody will enroll you. Don't want to go there. Want to talk to me. Want to talk to Hugh. Come and tell us. We'll talk to you about getting into the discovering Christianity. And if you're a person, you say, "Well I'm not up to that yet, I'm ways back down the road from there." I'm saying, "Have you looked properly? Have you looked properly?" From our perspective, we can't bear the idea that people will miss out on what we've got. And we want to say, "Do have a look for yourself." (34 min 10 sec)

Sermon Manuscript #6

Sermon Title: Nothing Recedes Like Success

Text: Luke 12:13–21

Location: St. Helen's Bishopsgate, London England, December 9, 1986

http://st-helens.org.uk/resources/media-library/src/talk/2154/title/nothing-recedes-like-success

Manuscript Location: JCCPPHW8

Rhetorical Arrangement and Genre: inductive-deductive, evangelistic

Sermon Transcription

Exordium

(*Chapman begins with prayer.*)

Let us pray. Our heavenly Father we pray today that I will teach the Bible accurately and truly. Please help me to do that. Please speak to us out of your word and give us wills longing to obey you, for Jesus Christ's sake. Amen.

(*Chapman leads congregation together in the Lord's Prayer.*)

Our Father which art in heaven, hallowed be thy name. Thy kingdom come. Thy will be done on earth as it is in heaven. Give us this day our daily bread and forgive us our trespasses as we forgive them that trespass against us. And lead us not into temptation but deliver us from evil. For thine is the kingdom and the power and the glory, forever and ever. Amen. (*Pause.*)

Thank you for the welcome. It's always good to be back, home. And especially since the Australians have managed to keep on batting for a little bit longer, so I don't have to have the ignominy of having to face you with another terrible defeat. (*Pause.*)

Implied Proposition: It is Possible to Be Successful, Yet for God to Judge You as Having Lived Foolishly—How/Why?

(*Tone heightens.*) I wonder if you'd like to do a small exercise with me. Put your mind at the present moment will you . . . do you think you're a successful person? Do you think you're a successful person? I'm not saying have you been in the past. Or do you think it's just round the corner. But right now, at this moment of time, would you consider yourself to be successful?

Now I suppose if we were honest, we'd have people ranging from every possible answer, wouldn't we? There'd be some people in the building today are fairly certain they're successful. Other people have been put down so regularly that they've lost all confidence in themselves, and would say, "No, I don't think I am successful." And there are bound to be lots in the middle. What would constitute success so far as you're concerned?

There comes before us in this part of the Bible today a man who from every point of view would be considered to be successful. And yet God's judgment on him is that he is a dismal failure. A dismal failure. God says to him, "What a fool you are. What a fool you are." (4 min)

Narratio

Let me see if I can put ma' finger on the dividing things that constitute success in this, or failure. What is it that makes the difference? It's an interesting story really. Let me see if I can put it in . . . I'd like to be able to put it in its English context. I don't know the English context. So, if I say the Australian context . . . be better, won't it?

Here is a man who is very successful and has retired himself at forty-five. They own a lovely house at Mosman overlooking the harbor. When he looks out from his front verandah, he sees the Opera House over the left, and the Bridge over on the right. And it really is quite lovely. And they've bought a block of flats on the Gold Coast, up in Surfers Paradise, just down from Brisbane where it's summer all the year round. And he's going to retire there. They'll live off the rent of the other flats, and they've taken the bottom one, that looks . . . walks straight out of the French windows onto the beach, and it's just so lovely. And they're selling up at Mosman. And they're having a few friends in to say goodbye to them.

And his lady wife, she's in the kitchen busying herself. And he's on the front verandah. He's got a long cool glass of . . . um . . . orange juice . . . do you think? (*Laughter.*) You thought I was going to say Fosters, didn't you? We don't drink it, we export it! (*Long laughter.*) And he says to himself, "You are a lucky bloke! To be able to retire so early! You've got plenty laid up for you for years and years and years! Take life easy. Eat, drink."

There's a searing pain in his chest. And he was dead before they got him to intensive care.

What will happen to all this man's goods? Did you notice it as it was being read? "The land of a certain rich man brought forth plentifully." He said, "I've got nowhere to store my grain and my goods? This is what I'll do. I'll tear down the barn and build a bigger one. And there I'll say to my soul, "soul you've got ample goods laid up for many years. Take life easy. Eat, drink, be merry!" And God said to him, "What a fool you are! Tonight, your soul is required of you. And who will get all the good things for which you've worked?"

Punchline by Jesus: "So it is with everyone who is not rich towards God."

Partitio #1: This Man's First Mistake Was to Live as Though God is Not There

Narratio: Mixes State, Show, Illustrate Expository Steps

Let me tell you what I think his two fatal mistakes were. I think they're fairly common mistakes. That's why I'm glad you're here today, so we can put our mind to what constitutes success in life. I've never met anybody who wants to fail in life. Everybody wants to be successful. What are his two fatal mistakes? His first mistake is he lived as if God wasn't there.

We know almost nothing about this man. We don't know whether he was good or whether he was bad. We don't know whether he was lazy, or whether he was industrious. We don't know whether he was a good wife . . . or a philanderer (*corrects himself*) . . . a good husband, or a philanderer. Dear oh dear . . . What day is it? Who am I? (*Laughter.*) Let's see if I can get that right. We don't know if he was a faithful husband, or otherwise. We don't know if he was a good father, or whether he beat his children. All we know about him is, he was not rich towards God.

I don't doubt for a single moment if you'd stopped him in the street and said, "Do you believe in God?" He'd have said, "Yes." But he lived as if God didn't exist. He's totally self-centered.

"I'll say to my soul, soul you've got ample goods laid up for many years. Take life easy."

Everything is directed in onto himself. Perhaps thinking about God was on the back burner? He really meant to bring it down towards the front one day. But religion was for the wife and the children. Yet, he lived as if God wasn't there. And God said to him, "What a fool you are!"

Why? Why is it, the Psalmist says, "The foolish body has said in his heart there's no God?" Why, because there is a God, that's why! Because God has shown himself (*pause*).

Illustrate

Eighteen months ago, I was staying with friends . . . Rockhampton . . . that's ways ways up in Queensland. I'd been up there to give a series of talks for the week. They had two little boys. They still have, or they're a bit older now. Simon: eighteen months. Andrew: three. Early on in the week they were talking about the fact that they were going to a wedding on the Saturday, and they didn't have anybody to babysit. So, I didn't do anything for then. I mean it was fairly pointed. Though but I thought . . . well, I ought to tell you I'm a bachelor, for those who don't know . . . it's a fairly massive operation to babysit when you've had no practice of your own. So, I gave that some thought . . . couple of days thought, and then I made an offer. I said, "Be helpful if I sat the boys?" Well, that was snapped up with scandalous rapidity! (*Laughter.*)

They took off about 12 o'clock. And ah . . . they came back at 6 o'clock at night.

Well, there were all sorts of things about the afternoon that I found fun. The sleeping part I could handle quite well, while they were asleep. That was good fun. The eating bit. That was good fun too. The bath was terrific fun! It was all the bits in between I found hard to handle. And there seemed to be such a long time in between all of those things.

About 5 o'clock, Andrew said to me, "Shall we play hide and seek?" I said, "Yes, I'd love to do that mate." Now I'm an old hand at games from ways back, and I know you must get the rules clear before you start. Have you ever noticed that? If you ask for a ruling in the middle of a game, it always goes against you, doesn't it? (*Laughter.*) So, I said, "How do you play this game mate?" He said, "Easy! You hide your face and begin to count. I run away and hide behind the laundry door, and you come and look for me (*laughter*)." I said, "Have I got that right? I hide my face and count and you go and hide behind the laundry door, and I come and look for you. Is that correct?" He said, "Yes." Well, I must say I'd never played by those rules before. It's dead easy that game. You don't even have to move your position. I just cried out with a loud voice, "I wonder if Andrew is hiding under his bed?" Whoops of delight from behind the laundry door! (*Laughter.*) "I wonder if Andrew is by the fridge?" Uncontrollable laughter from behind the laundry door! "I wonder if Andrew is behind the laundry door?" And he shot out as if he was spring-loaded. I said, "How do we play now mate?" He said, "I go and hide under the bed, you count, you come and look for me." Now, you and I know he hasn't got the gist of that game yet has he? (*Laughter.*) And I tell you that even though he knows I'm not supposed to know where he is, there's a good six months lag between when he goes and hides, and you yell out, "Are you ready?" And he says, "Yes." You still know where he is.

Apply: Christ is God's Revelation
—Therefore God Can Be Known

Have you stopped to consider why people speak? They speak to draw attention to the fact that they're there. But we speak to enter into relationship with each other. If you don't want to be friends with me, just don't answer me for five or ten minutes. I'll give up. If on the other hand you want to become friends with me, you must speak to me! (*Emphatic.*)

Do you know the incredible thing that the Bible says? God . . . spoke! He drew attention to the fact that he was there. So that we could enter into friendship with him! And so that we could be in absolutely no doubt whatever, he sent his Son Jesus into the world. You can't ask for much better than that can you? He turned up on the scene!

A man said to me last week, "I've been searching for God for a long time!" I said, "I find that very difficult to understand. If you'd been searching for him, you should have found him. He's not hiding! He's been talking all the time. He's been drawing attention to the fact that he is there. He sent his Son Jesus into the world. What do you make of Jesus?"

If we had time to go through this book . . . we'd find the most extraordinary person! A person of great power! Healing the sick. Stilling the waves. I just want to point out to you, because the Bible gets fairly bad press these days, that the man who wrote this gospel we've read said, "I never saw Jesus. I never heard him. But I was anxious for us to have accurate information. So, I wrote nothing down in my book . . . nothing! . . . except that which I could verify from eyewitnesses. And when I got it verified from people who were there, and heard it and saw it, I then put it into an orderly account, so you could be sure. Certain, about the things you believe."

We've got accurate information about Jesus. Is it possible . . . is it possible that he was anybody except the Son of God? He certainly believed he was. He says it repeatedly, both directly and indirectly. What do you make of the person of Jesus? Of this person of great power? Who stills the wind and the waves? Who brings people to life again from the dead? Who is able to heal sick people by changing his mind? All the things that you and I would long to do but can't. He is God in our midst.

Restate

This man lived as if God was not there. And God said to him, "What a fool you are. What a fool you are! To have pushed me aside and lived as if I'm not here. You were meant to live with me right at the very center of your being!"

Would you say with regard to living in friendship with God, that you are successful, or a failure?

That's his first big mistake. He lives as if God isn't there. He ought to know better than that. God has sent his Son into the world. And this man of great power and great love showed us precisely what God was like. Not only to do the most incredible things. But he finally dies, so that my sins can be forgiven. And he died on the cross for you. So that your sins can be forgiven.

Everything that was due to us for living a life of pushing God out, Jesus took upon himself, so that I could be forgiven and come back and start again, friends with God. Can you beat that? God sent his only Son into the world to die, so that we could be forgiven. (16 min)

Illustrate and Apply

I have a friend in Queensland I visited eighteen months ago in Brisbane. On the fridge door was a photograph of a little baby fixed on with a magnet. His children are adult but not yet married. I said, "Whose is the photograph, Graham?" "Oh Chappo," he said. "It's a terrible tragedy in our congregation. Young couple, training to be missionaries . . . their only child. They lived in a little flat. Sunshine only on the driveway and then for a little time in the morning. The mother popped the baby in the basinet in the sun, just for a few minutes on the drive. Didn't tell the father, who jumped into the car and backed out over it and killed it.

Why do I tell you a story like that? It rightly shocks us all! Ladies and gentlemen, is it not a fact, we are not shocked any longer by the fact that God's Son died for us. We've somehow taken it in stride. That God loved us (*emphatic*). And gave his Son to die for us. You think he expects us to treat him seriously? He's treated us seriously! He only had one Son! He loved the world in such a way that he gave that only Son (*pleading emphatic tone*) so that you and I can be forgiven! And God's judgment on this man is right! He says, "What a fool you are to have ignored me like this! What a fool you are!" There's his first mistake. (17 min 30 sec)

Partitio #2: This Man Lives as If There is No Judgment Day

Narratio: Mixes State, Show, Explain, Illustrate Steps of Exposition

What do you think his second mistake is? Well, his first mistake is he lived as if God wasn't there. His second mistake is, he lives as if there is no judgment day. See, he says "Soul, you've got ample goods laid up for many years. Take life easy. Eat, drink, be merry." He did have terrific preparations made for a long time. He just didn't have a long time! He was fresh out of time. He plunged into eternity. We're all so terrified about death in the Western world, that we'll never get round to thinking about judgment because it's what happens after death. If you can't think about death, you certainly won't about judgment.

The Western world's terrified about death, aren't we? So terrified we won't even say the word. We've got all sorts of new synonyms for it: passed on, gone over, fallen asleep, say anything, but no one will say: "He's dead." It's almost immoral when I say it, isn't it? (*Pause.*) You given any thought to your death? Do you ever speak about it? If you want to bring a dinner conversion to a crashing, grinding halt (*laughter*) just lean over to your hostess and whisper quite confidentially, "Have you given any thought to your death lately?" (*Laughter.*) You'll even be scrubbed off their Christmas card list. The trouble with this man is, he pretends that life will go on indefinitely.

Here's a little part from the Sydney Morning Herald of the 21st of the 10th '84.

"A sixteen-year-old schoolboy on a work experience program was killed yesterday in an explosion in Muswellbrook in the Hunter Valley. The police said that 'Peter Simon Richards of Muswellbrook was struck on the head by a piece of metal after a small explosion in a refrigerator repair shop.'" Well I wonder if he was ready to meet God? I certainly wasn't at the age of sixteen. I hadn't given it a moment's thought. And . . . I'm fairly certain that he won't have given it a moment's thought either. But at the end of the day, he was in the presence of God, who either declared his life to be marvelously successful or a dismal failure (*pause*).

I had a letter this morning from my sister-in-law in Canberra. Last paragraph, "I've just been to a funeral. I played golf with this friend on Thursday. She died in half an hour on Friday mornin, bracket—heart attack. This life is so temporary, isn't it?" I spent last week in a home of people in South Hampton where the boy in that household was preparing for exams. And his parents were urging him to keep at it. It was a very important event that would take place, and he ought to prepare himself for it. (20 min 30 sec)

Apply: The Rightness of God's Justice

You made any preparations for your finals? It'd be worth a thought, wouldn't it? You know they're coming. I don't have to go through the exercise about forty-five and fifty-five, and sixty-five, do I? Well, I might? If you're over forty-five you're well past halfway. If you're up to sixty you've lived more than two thirds. If you're past seventy, you're knocking on the door (*knocks on wooden lectern*). Let me say if you're older than that, you're knocking very hard! (*Emphatic.*) And it'll fly open any minute!

"What a fool you are," he said. Be sure that judgment day is a reality. You're far too important to God for that not to take place. Some people acquiesce in the idea it's not going to happen. The only way for judgment to be averted is for God to suddenly become careless about everything. He loves the world so much, you are so important, I am so important, and the world is so important, we will give an account for how we've lived before each other, how we've lived before him, and how we've treated his world. And the only way for that to happen is for nothing to ever matter again! And the thought of that is too horrific to face! (*Emphatic.*) To think that nothing matters. There's no justice ever! But there is.

Peroratio

It's so important to God that you and I will face him. Do you know what the touchstone is? Is Jesus your Lord? Have you been forgiven? Is Jesus your Lord? That means, "Do you live as if God is really there? That his Son Jesus who he has declared to be Lord over the world is Lord over you? If today's the day for you, would your life be successful by God's standards?" That's worth a thought, isn't it? If it happened today, and God said to you, "Whatever are you doing here, unforgiven?" Whatever would you say?

"I didn't really think it mattered all that much."

He'll say, "Come off it! Whatever do you think I let my Son die for if it didn't matter? You knew it mattered. What are you doing here unforgiven?"

"I lived a fairly decent life."

"What do you think I let my Son die for if you could make it by that way?"

You see, in the light of the fact that God has sent his Son to die for us both the urgency and the importance of it take on new meaning. Of course it matters that I should be right with God. Of course it matters that I should live now in friendship with God. Would he have done that if it didn't matter? Here is a man who everybody would have thought to be successful. But God who looks on the heart has declared him to be a failure. (24 min)

Well, you'll walk out of the building either one or the other. And your attitude to Jesus is the big divide. If he is Lord, is he truly your Lord? If he has died for you, have you availed yourself of that forgiveness? Don't you consider yourself to be lucky, still to have time to change?

This lady (*holding up letter from sister-in-law*) has no more time.

This boy (*holding up Herald clipping on 16-year-old*) has no more time.

This man (*in reference to the Rich Fool in the parable*) had no more time.

You . . . have got time (*slow and pleads*).

On the back of the hymn sheet, there is a prayer that I'm going to pray in a moment. It is a prayer for people who say, "It's time for me. It's time for me to take action. I am not successful in the spiritual life." See what I say in the prayer?

Heavenly Father, I've lived as if you were not there, and as if there was no judgment. Today I wish to acknowledge Jesus as my Lord. Lord Jesus, thank you for dying for me. Please forgive me and take over the running of my life.

That would be a thoroughly appropriate prayer for people who wanted to make a new beginning. It won't be appropriate for everybody. But it might just be appropriate for you. And I'm going to pray it. And you'll best be able to judge how appropriate it is for you. And I'm going to invite you to pray it inside your own head as I go along if it's appropriate for you, so that when you walk out of the building today, you will know that you are not a failure in this part of life. (26 min)

Let's pray.

Heavenly Father, I've lived as if you were not there, and as if there was no judgment. (*Pause.*)

Today I wish to acknowledge Jesus as my Lord. (*Pause.*)

Lord Jesus, thank you for dying for me. (*Pause.*)

Please forgive me and take over the running of my life. Amen.

May I take just a moment of your time? If you prayed that prayer and it is a new beginning for you, you'd be wise to tell the friend you came with today. You will need help. You've started out a new life with Christ. But if you did that be sure your prayer's been heard and answered, and it's a great day for you . . . a great great day. I'd get some further help if I were you. And the only way we know if you've prayed it is if you tell somebody. You're bound to have come with a friend. And they'll be glad to know, and glad to advise you of the sort of help you need.

Thanks so much. I'm looking forward to seeing you next week. (27 min 36 sec)

Sermon Manuscript #7

Sermon Title: You Can't Keep a Good Man Down

Text: Luke 24:36–49

Location: Christ Church Anglican, St. Ives, September 20, 1992

http://audio.christchurch.com.au/speaker3.htm#15

Manuscript Location: JCCPPHW75

Rhetorical Arrangement and Genre: inductive-deductive, evangelistic

Sermon Transcription

Exordium

(*Chapman opens sermon in prayer.*)

Our heavenly Father, we pray that as I speak tonight and teach the Bible, that you'll help me to do that carefully and accurately. We pray heavenly Father that you will speak to us in the very depths of our being so that we'll hear your voice. And our Father, we pray that we'll humble ourselves before you and not be proud, be glad to hear what you've got to say, and in our hearts be quick to obey you. And we ask this for Jesus's sake. Amen. (*Pause.*)

Several years ago, I wrote a little booklet called "What is a Christian?" And it was published in a sort of a booklet form . . . not a booklet form . . . it was on a page like this so it could be easily turned over. And um, a boy came into my office one day, about . . . he looked to me to be about fourteen or fifteen, and he had a copy of it that was not unlike this one. It looked as if somebody had screwed it up. And then . . . ah . . . he told me in fact that had happened (*laughter murmurs*). And he'd pulled it out of the garbage bin, and he'd straightened it out (*Chapman reenacts as he tells*). That's what it looked like, just like that one.

And . . . ah . . . he said . . . ah . . . "Do you buy these here?"

I said, "You do."

He said, "How much are they?"

I said, "They're ten cents each."

"Strike," he said, "they're expensive, aren't they?" (*Laughter.*)

I said, "No, they're dirt cheap." I said, "Costs all that, nearly that much to produce them. What do you want them for anyway?"

"Well," he said, "I've got a day off from school and I'm standing outside Parliament House in Macquarie Street witnessing. I'm giving these to people as they come and go in and out of Parliament House. I've made a sign, and I'm just giving those to people."

I said, "That looks a pretty scungy one!"

"Well," he said, "The guy screwed it up and threw it in the bin. So, I pulled it out. If they're worth ten cents each, I'm glad I did." (*Laughter.*)

I said, "Put it back in the bin and leave it there (*condescending fatherly tone*) And if you're doing that, here's a hundred on the house. By the way, what have you written on the sign."

"Well," he said, "I've written on the sign: Jesus Christ rose from the dead. You can't keep a good man down." (*Laughter.*)

Propositio: Because Jesus is Good He Can Die and Take the Punishment for Sin. Because He has Risen, He Demonstrates His Death Was Effective

Now I must say it's not my kettle of fish. But from a point of view of correctness, theological correctness, you couldn't get a better statement of the truth. It is because Jesus is good, through and through, that he can die and take the punishment that our sins deserve. And it's because he's done that, that you can't keep him down. He's risen again from the dead.

And it's that that I want to look at tonight with you. (2 min 30 sec)

Narratio

Please get this color . . . whatever it is . . . out . . . that sheet . . . keep that in front of you. I want to refer to that as we go along. Now, in Luke's Gospel, it's interesting really because let me rehearse the facts to you, as they occur in this gospel.

Can I remind you that Luke says he wrote nothing in his gospel except that which he could verify from eyewitnesses? I know there's an enormous amount of nonsense going on at the present moment about the fact that you cannot trust the Bible.

It's prejudicial! It's not built on fact.

This man says, "He wrote nothing in his book" . . . we don't even . . . he may himself have been an eyewitness . . . we don't know whether he was or whether he wasn't. But he says, "I checked everything from eyewitnesses. And I wrote nothing down except that which could be verified. And then I shook it into an orderly account." Writing to his patron Theophilus he said, "So that you Theophilus might have full knowledge about the things which I'm calling on you to believe."

Now I'm glad about that, because what we're called on to believe is very difficult indeed.

So let me rehearse the facts to you. (*Quick-paced recounting of facts.*)

First of all, Jesus is dead, certified dead and buried. Three days, women come to the tomb, three days later. They're going to embalm the body. When they get there, the stone is rolled away and the body is missing, and the angels are there who say to the women, "What are you doing here, in misguided devotion? Why are you seeking the living among the dead? He told you he would rise again from the dead. Why didn't you believe him?" See? That misguided devotion gets no thanks from God. "What are you seeking the living among the dead for? He is not here."

Then, the two walking on the way to Emmaus . . . talking with each other. Jesus joins them and they don't recognize him. They're full of their own worries. And they're full of the fact that Jesus has gone, and they don't think they'll ever see him again.

And Jesus says, "You look a bit down in the mouth." He said, "You don't look all that happy, what's on?"

And they said, "Are you a stranger in Jerusalem, you don't know what's been happening?"

He said, "Like what?"

And how you have the strangeness of them describing to Jesus, what happened to Jesus. All a bit odd really, isn't it? Then they describe Jesus and their great hopes that he would be the King of Israel. And now they say he's been put to death by the chief priests and rulers. And now women go to the grave at the morning and they find the tomb empty. And they met shining ones . . . angels . . . who said, "Why are you seeking the living among the dead?"

And Jesus says, "What's the trouble with you lot? Don't you remember what's in the Bible?"

Nobody is being thanked, for not knowing the truth and the facts.

"What's up with you lot?" he said. "You don't read the Bible anymore, or don't believe it? Which?" He said, "Oh foolish" . . . that's another Chapman paraphrase . . . "OH foolish you are, and slow of heart not to believe all that the prophets had spoken. Did not the Christ have to suffer these things and enter his glory?" And then all the way through the Old Testament . . . okay . . . for seven miles . . . eleven k's . . . it's quite a long walk really. It's a decent fun-run, isn't it? Well, there's no fun-run about it. They just had a long-extended Bible study as they ambled along the eleven k's. Good job they had a long way to go, because he opened up all the Old Testament to them as they went along, beginning with Moses . . . the first five books of the Bible . . . then the Psalms . . . and all the Prophets . . . he showed them that the Christ must suffer and rise again from the dead . . . and before you could say . . . this is a very strange thing, isn't it? Here you've got Jesus, author of the Bible, teaching them the Bible. Pretty good . . . to be able to have the author explaining it to them! That's what's happening as they're going along.

They get to Emmaus, and they say, "It's late, why don't you pop in and have dinner with us." And he says, "Well why not" . . . sort of. And they do go in. And then at grace, in the breaking of the bread, they recognize that it is Jesus . . . I have always thought, probably by the scars in his hands. And then he disappeared from them. He seems to be able to materialize and de-materialize at will. It doesn't seem to be a problem to him, in his resurrection body.

(*Pace quickens.*) They are terrifically excited. They hotfoot it back . . . all the way back to Jerusalem . . . they've already walked the eleven k's . . . now they do a walk and run. As they can catch their breath. And they rush back, and this is just about where we pick it up in our Bible reading . . . they rush to the upper room . . . and I've always thought this must have been an enormous letdown! Because having done the eleven k's out and the eleven k's back in a hurry, they rush up the back stairs all breathless (*mimics heavy breathing noise*). And before they can get their breath somebody says, "Guess what, Jesus is alive. He's appeared to Peter!" (*Laughter.*) Don't you think that must have been a terrible let down? They'd run all the way back to let them in on the news, and Jesus has got the drop on them again. And that's where our Bible reading picks up.

Show

(*Reads passage.*) "While they are still talking about this . . ." (*Psshew.*) "Jesus himself stood among them. Peace be with you. They were startled and frightened thinking they were seeing a ghost. He said to them, 'Why are you troubled? Why do doubts arise in your mind? Look at my hands and my feet. It is I myself. Touch me! See. A ghost doesn't have flesh and bones.'"

Explain

See, he wants them to be really assured! (*Emphatic.*) He is alive! He has a body. He is not a ghost. You can touch him. You can feel him. And then, to reiterate this, he says, "Have you got anything to eat?" Think he was a bit peckish? 'Course he wasn't. He wants them to know, that he is alive, never to die again. And his resurrection body is real.

"Have you got anything to eat? They gave him a piece of broiled fish, and he took it and ate it in their presence."

These are the facts. This Jesus, the Son of God who was crucified, dead, and buried, is now alive again from the dead, never to die again. Now what does this mean?

Confirmatio: Evidence for the Resurrection is Very Good

By the way, the evidence is very good! You go to John's Gospel, the other gospel, on one occasion when Jesus came back to them, Thomas wasn't there. When he comes back, they say "Thomas, Jesus is alive!"

He says, "Pull the other leg, it whistles!" (*Laughter.*) Well, it's a lose paraphrase.

He said, "I'll believe it when I can shove 'ma finger in the hole where the nail went through, and 'ma fist up his side!" You wouldn't say anything stupid like that if you thought you'd ever get a chance to do it, would you?

When I was growing up as a boy, my father, he'd say, "Listen mate, listen, if that ever comes to pass, I'll walk from here to Bathurst, on a cold winter's night on ma hands, without any pants on!" (*Laughter.*) Now what does that mean? It means it's never going to happen.

That's what Thomas is saying. "It's never going to happen! I'll believe it" ... you'll never been to a hospital have you, to see your friend after surgery and asked if you could poke your finger in the wound! (*Laughter.*) I mean, it's revolting! Absolutely revolting! "I'll believe it, I'll believe it," Thomas says, "when I can poke ma finger in the hole where the nail went through" ... see ... he's saying ... "that'll never happen!"

I'm on his side. I am not easily convinced. You want good evidence for this, don't you? We've got good evidence. We've got the man who's not easily convinced. I walk out the building, and a voice booms out from heaven

"John Chapman," I'll be looking around to see who's playing games with me, wouldn't you? Thomas is that sort of a man. Very down to earth.

A week later, Jesus stood in the midst, and he said, "Oh, I'm glad Tom that you're here. I missed you last time. Here is my hand. Shove your finger in it mate. (*Laughter.*) Poke it in, poke it in. But don't doubt any longer!"

Thomas said, "You are my Lord and my God."

He said, "Thank you, you're dead right (*laughter*). And it's a great pity you didn't believe the others when they told you. What you think they are?"

See, he gets no thanks, for not believing when the evidence was good. Now the evidence is very good. What does it mean?

Partitio #1 and #2: Jesus Has Conquered Death and Is Able to Carry Others through Death as Well

Narratio: Mixes State, Show, Explain, Illustrate Expository Steps

Well three things immediately.

First, Jesus has conquered death and is alive now. He is here. He is privy to what's going on. He knows you. He knows all about you. He knows me. He knows all about me. He is not an idea in my mind! He is real, and is alive, and can be related to in the here and now. He can come to us by his Spirit and be with us. He is alive. He is not dead. That's the first thing.

The second thing is, having gone through death, to life after death, he is able to take people through it with him! I mean wouldn't you like to put your hands in the hands of the person who's already been! You know what it's like in a whole brand-new situation, you've had absolutely no experience in it. What are you looking for? You say to the person, "Have you ever done this?"

I don't know if you know that story, in *Point Man*, about the man, the photographer, who's sent by the editor of his paper to photograph this great bushfire in the States. And he rings him, and he says, "I can't get close enough to it. I really need a plane."

He said, "Well, get one, I'll organize one for you."

He tells him where the aerodrome is, the local aerodrome.

And he says, "You be there, and I'll organize it."

So, he gets in the car and hotfoots it around and there's a plane already warmed up. He jumps in the back and he says, "Let's go." And off the plane takes. He said, "Now I wonder if you can get as close to the fire as you could? And do a low sweep over it."

He said, "A low sweep over the fire? What am I doin' that for?"
He said, "I'm supposed to be photographing it!"
He said, "What do you mean photographing it?"
He said, "Well, that's what I've got in the plane for."

The fella says, "You mean you're not the instructor!!" (*Uproarious laughter.*)

Apply

I want to go with the person who's already done it before! I normally say to my surgeon, "Have you done this operation before? I don't want him practicing on me!"

See . . . I want to put ma hand . . . a person at a meeting said to me one night, "Well the trouble is, no one's ever come back to tell us, have they?" I nearly fell off the chair. I said, "Yes, somebody has come back from the other side, in an unmistakable way!" Not in some mumbo-jumbo where you don't know if it's the truth and you don't know whether you're being caught. Somebody has actually been through death and come back from the dead and says, "I am resurrection and life. If you trust me, even though you die, you will live in life after death with me."

When Jesus was on the cross, and the dying thief looks up to him and says, "Jesus, remember me when you become King." And Jesus says to him, "Today, you and I will be together in Paradise." Is there any truth to that, or is it mumbo-jumbo? Is it like whistling to keep your spirits up in the dark? Well, I'm going to put ma hand in the one whose been through and come back, and says, "Trust me." He can take us through death to life after.

Confirmatio: The Need for an Expert in Death

Australians are terrified about death. You ever think about your death? It's almost immoral when I talk about your death, isn't it? You want to bring a dinner conversation to a crashing grinding halt, whisper intimately to your hostess, "Have you given any thought to your death lately?" (*Laughter.*) See how that goes down. You'll be sure you won't be invited back again, even be struck off the Chrissy card list. Why are we so frightened about death?

See I can't get people to think about life after death. They're so terrified . . . why is everybody pretending they're younger than themselves, unless they're under twenty-one and then they're pretending they're older. What's good about being young? It enables us to forget about the end.

But I spoke recently about death at a church. And the clergyman stood up at the end in conclusion and said, "I've had three funerals this week. An elderly lady, eighty-three, I buried. A young man, twenty-seven. A boy, fifteen. And he concluded this: "People our age died today, all over Australia."

And we think it will never be us. I'll let you in on a secret, it will be! It will be! And I'm going to trust the one who knows the way. And I'm not going to trust to a flip of the coin that it'll be alright. Jesus is alive! He can be related to in the here and now.

Jesus has gone through death and can take us.

Partitio #3: Death is Not the End

STATE

And notice the third thing I want to draw your attention to, "Death is not the end."

Be under no illusion. Death is not the end! We have had somebody come back to tell us to get ready.

Now, this gospel opens with a great promise. Do you remember at the birth of Jesus the angels, they say to the shepherds, "There is good news of great joy to all people. To you is born this day in the city of David a Savior, who is Christ, the Lord." And this gospel finishes with a sort of rounding-off conclusion. And this is the concluding part of the gospel, where Jesus, as it were sums up, in a very pithy way everything he's on about with the three great imperatives.

SHOW

I wonder if you'd have a look at forty-four. He said to them, "This is what I told you while I was still with you: Everything must be fulfilled that is written about me in the Law of Moses, and the Prophets and the Psalms." And here are the three great imperatives. "He opened their minds so they could understand the Scriptures. He told them, 'The Christ will suffer. The Christ will rise from the dead on the third day. And repentance and forgiveness of sins will be preached in his name to all the nations.'"

Explain

See the three great imperatives that sum up the whole of Christianity? If you want to say, what is, what are we really on about, this is a great little summary here by Jesus. And this is how the gospel comes to an end. If this is the only book of the Bible you'd ever read, this is the last thing that's left ringing in your ears. The Christ must suffer. The Christ must rise from the dead. And repentance and forgiveness of sins must be preached. And he showed it to them from the Bible. He opened the Scriptures and he showed them that God's King must suffer.

Well, it'd be interesting to know which part of the Bible he went to, to show them that. I'd put my money on Isaiah 53. You 'member where the servant of God comes, and is wounded for our transgressions? And Isaiah says, "All we like sheep have gone astray. We've turned every man to his own way. And God has laid on Jesus, the sin of us all."

Sub-Partitio #3.1: The Christ Must Suffer

The Christ must suffer. Why is that so? Who's going to make good your sins? Who's going to make good for mine? What is God supposed to do about our sin? Say (*clicks fingers*), "Why don't we just skip it eh? Why don't we just skip it?" You know what happens if God says, "Let's just skip it?" Well, if he skips mine, he skips yours. That's quite a lot of sins by the time we all lump 'em together. (*Casual resigned tone.*) And if he skips ours, he skips everybody at Lindfield, and Pymble, and Sydney, and Melbourne and . . . we're getting quite a collection of sins now, aren't we? They don't really matter. Let's skip 'em. And if you do all of Australia, well you might as well go to China, you might as well go to Russia . . . might as well get to Germany . . . might as well do six million through the gas chamber . . . they don't matter. You say, "Wait on, that ma . . . wait on. Mine don't matter, but that does!"

See, it's stupid. Once God says, "Let's (*clicks fingers*) skip it," nothing ever matters again. But he doesn't say that does he? He said, "No, they matter. If you treat people like that, it matters to me. It mightn't matter to you, but it matters to me. If you treat yourself like that, it mightn't matter to you, but it matters to me. I love the world! I love everything in it! You treat the creation like that, it mightn't matter to you, but it matters to me."

And I'm glad, aren't you? I want justice to be done. When rotten things happen, I've said "Geez, that's not right, is it? That oughtn't be allowed to happen. People oughtn't be allowed to get . . . I want . . . I want justice to happen." Well, you'll be glad to know if you're like that, God's like it.

A man said to me once, "Why doesn't God . . ." it was in the height of the Vietnam War . . . he said, "Why doesn't God stop the war in Vietnam?" I said, "I suppose so you can become a Christian. I'm not sure of all the reasons. But that must be one of them."

He said, "You've got to be joking!"

I said, "I never joke about important things."

He said, "What's the war in Vietnam got to do with me becoming a Christian?"

I said, "You want God to stop evil, do you? You want him to stop people doing the wrong thing in Vietnam?"

"Yes!" he said.

I said, "In New Guinea? You want . . . how far down do you want him to come? You want him to get to Sydney?" I said, "Before you ask God to clean up the garbage, you want to make sure you're not in it." You see . . . you want God to clean up your life. And when you're asking for justice, you're asking . . . you're saying, "Oh God, please call on the judgment day! Come in judgment." That's what we're really saying! "Stop wickedness." How will you go yourself then?

See . . . we can see it better when we're not involved. But it's not on!

And God in his great wisdom finds a way that we can never say again, "You're not just."

We can never say again, "You don't care about justice."

We can never say again, "Our sins don't matter."

And the solution is the death of his Son.

God says "Watch and see how big it is. We'll show you."

"My God, My God, why have you forsaken me?" (*Implying the words of Jesus on the cross.*)

When the perfect one, took the punishment which my sins deserved, and when I look at him dying on the cross, I can never say again, "It didn't matter." It did matter. I can never say again, "You don't love me." He does love me. I can never say again, "Justice will never be done," because he said, "It is done." The full punishment for sin is taken . . . on Jesus.

Clever really, isn't it? When you think it through? In fact, I can't think of any other way it can work.

He opened their minds to understand, that the Christ must suffer. Ladies and gentlemen, can I ask you, "Do you understand that? Has your mind been opened, to understand that Christ must suffer, if you are ever to be forgiven?"

You cannot be forgiven, except you put your trust in the death of Jesus. And I want to ask you, "Have you done that? Have you done that?"

That's the first great imperative. The Christ must suffer.

Sub-Partitio #3.2: The Christ Must Rise from the Dead

State and Explain

Look at the second one: "The Christ must rise again from the dead."

You see, did it work? That's the question. Did the death of Jesus take?

I mean you can't imagine me saying, "I love you all so much, watch this."

I pull out a revolver and blow ma' brains out.

You say, "What are you talking about? How does your dying do anything for me?" Well, my dying doesn't do anything for you. It wouldn't do a single thing, except distress you . . . at least I hope it would. What is this about Jesus dying and rising again from the dead?

Well, did it work? Was his sacrifice a full, perfect, and sufficient sacrifice? Was it big enough for your sin and mine? And do we know? Can we be sure? How can we be sure?

Illustrate: Was Jesus's Death Effective?

I remember the first time I went overseas. You still had to be vaccinated for smallpox. I went down to the health department in the Blackstump, and I got on a queue, and it took me quite a long time . . . about half an hour to get up to the front of the queue. And I smiled at the nurse that was there, and I said, "Smallpox?" She said, "Yellow Fever, you're in the wrong queue." So, I got in another queue, and I got up to the front again with less confidence. I said, "Smallpox?" She said, "Yes, take off your coat, roll up your sleeve, don't muck about." So, I took off ma' coat, rolled up ma' sleeve. She gave me the little yellow book. She stamped it. She said, "Come back in three weeks and I'll see if it's taken."

Well, I didn't need the book to be stamped! I didn't need her to tell me. I could feel it had taken! Two days, it was a nice cherry pink. Four days, I'd break out in perspiration, dripping all over, while talking to friends. Their eye-balls'd open like saucers while we were talking! (*Laughter.*) I'd say, "It's alright . . . smallpox." They said, "Have you got it?" (*Laughter.*) I said, "No the disease must be terrible. I've just got the thing that fixes it!" (*Laughter.*)

End of two weeks, it'd risen up like an enormous volcano. I made a cotton wool pad to go round it. I was going to a wedding. I could hardly bare for ma' shirt to scrape on it. And I remember putting ma' jacket on. Ma' whole arm was hanging limp. And I got to a friend and I said, "Don't touch ma' arm." And he only heard, "Touch ma' arm." He said, "What do you want me to touch it for" (*makes sound of friend hitting arm . . . laughter*).

Apply

Did it take? It took! (*Laughter.*)

Now, here's the question: Did the death of Jesus take? (S*low.*)

Think it through with me. Stay with me.

What does the Bible say the punishment for sin is? "The wages of sin is death." Always, the punishment for sin is death. If Jesus takes the punishment our sins deserve, what will you expect? If he does it properly, and he expends everything that death has got, I'm expecting the opposite of death . . . up death . . . resurrection!!

So Paul is able to say, "If Jesus has not risen from the dead, we of all people are most miserable because there is no forgiveness. We are still in our sins, because his sacrifice did bother all!!

But he did. And it did. And it worked!

And from the resurrection of Jesus onwards we know, that there was sufficient in his death, to deal with the whole sin of the whole world, because no longer has death got any power over him . . . pssshhtt . . . up death . . . in a great display . . . that his death is big enough for you and me . . . and you and you and you and you . . . and anybody who wants to put their trust in him.

The Christ must suffer. He must rise again from the dead. (26 min 30 sec)

Sub-Partitio #3.3: Repentance and Forgiveness of Sins Must be Preached

State and Explain

A listen to the third great imperative. If you've been asleep now, wake up! The important bit is right now. Repentance and forgiveness of sins must be preached . . . and I want to do it now.

What is repentance? Who's gonna run your life? That's what repentance is about.

Will Jesus as God's King run it, or will you fight him?

Let me give you a warning on the side . . . if you fight him, you will not win. You will not win! Go to a gospel, and read about his enormous power, and see if you think you'll be able to beat him. It's a terrible foolishness. You will not win!

Please . . . forget about the idea that you'll do it when you're older! You won't want to when you get older if don't want to do it now! Do you think you'll turn into a different person? You don't! You just can't do things as fast as you used to. You're exactly the same person at sixty as you were at sixteen! . . . Apart from the fact that when you bend down to do up your shoelaces . . . you think of what else you can do while you're still down there (*laughter*), so you don't have to waste time! But you're not going to grow into a different person! You'll still be you! If you're convinced that Jesus is God's King, but you say, "Oh, I'll do that later" . . . you won't!! You won't!!

Illustrate

When I first started to play tennis . . . my father is an old conman from ways back. He said to me, "Mate, I tell you what" . . . we had one of those toilets down the back . . . a little brick building. And he said to me, "Mate, if you were to mow the lawn every day and roll it, you'd get a terrific surface there to practice from." What a con! (*Laughter.*) So, I mowed the lawn there every day and rolled it, and used to belt a ball up against the side of the wall. You know, the first day I tried, I missed the wall, more times than I hit it. Had to go down the back of the yard and pick up the ball. And then I used to do it, and I'd practice until I could do a hundred forehands and not miss it at all. And then a hundred backhands and not miss it. And if I missed it, I'd go back to one, and start again. Then I drew a circle. Three feet across . . . a yard. And I belted a hundred forehands into it and a hundred backhands, and I'd kept going until I could do it without missing. And I reduced the circle . . . till it got to about that wide . . . and if you practice like that, you get quite good in the end.

Apply

Do you know, every time you say "No" to Jesus, you get better at saying "No." I want to give a word of warning to those of you who've said "No" many times in the past. And tonight, you might be saying something like "Oh . . . Jeez . . . the same old jazz! They're on about Jesus and repentance and forgiveness." I'm saying, "You're doing a hundred in the forehand and a hundred in the backhand with great ease." You've become very good at it, haven't you? And after a while you won't need to think about it. You just go straight into your, "Well, I'll do that later" mode. You won't have to give it a moment's thought.

Do take great care. If you think you're neutral . . . you're not. Because tonight, you'll have to say "Yes" or "No." And if you're saying "No" for many times, your chances of doing it later on are rapidly diminishing!! In fact, if it's easy to say "No" you're fairly good at it, aren't you? You mightn't get too many more chances. That's the way it'll go. Oh, you'll hear it many times again. You'll just be soooo locked . . . into that mode, that your chances of changing become almost zero.

Peroratio

I want to ask you to change tonight. I want to ask you to repent.

I want to say, "Come to terms with the reality Jesus is God's King. He's died and risen again for you." And he says, "Don't fight me" (*pleading*). "Don't fight me. I only want to do you good. That's all I want. But if you fight me, you will be overthrown in the end." That's the reality of it.

Repentance must be preached.

And the best part is . . . that when you come back in repentance, what will Christ do?

Total forgiveness. Repentance and the forgiveness of sins must be preached.

Well, it's time to come back and start again. For most people, it is not the want of evidence that gets in the way. You know that Jesus is King in God's world. You know that he's died and risen again for you. Mostly, it's our pride. (32 min)

I was listening to a sermon on tape, which a friend of mine had sent me from England. In it he said as a boy, he used to play a game with his friends called "spot the bike." And he said, "I became so proficient at it that after a while, I could tell what bike it was by the sound of the exhaust." He said, "one day in the car, we were going on holidays, and my young brother said to me there was a car in the freeway a long way ahead of us. He said, 'It's Honda.' I said, 'It's Yamaha.' He said, 'It's Honda.' 'Yamaha' . . . 'Honda' . . . 'Yamaha.'" But he said, "My Dad, sped up." And he said, "As we got close enough, I could see on the back of the seat H O N D A." I said, "It's a Yamaha . . . and he's changed the seat!" (*Laughter.*)

You see, pride in the end, gets in the way of even admitting the facts.

And I want to say, "If it's pride that's stopping you, you have nothing to be proud of."

It's foolishness. It's foolishness in the light of the facts. It's time, to repent. It's time, to be forgiven. From God's point of view, he's done everything. And he says, "Listen to me while there is still time. Come back and let me forgive you."

Now . . . I guess in a gathering like we've got tonight and people over at the hall, there are many people who have never repented properly and never come back to Christ for forgiveness. And I want you to do it now . . .

now. Many people have done it during the course of this week, and over the course of this year. If I thought it wouldn't embarrass them, I'd ask the people who've come to Christ this year to wave their hands around. But I won't. It'll embarrass them. But they're here alright. And all over Sydney this year people have been turning to Christ.

And I'm saying, "You heard God speak to you tonight? Is it your time? Don't say no anymore. You'll get too good at it."

Prayer

I'm going to pray a prayer for people who know they're not Christ's. They say "No, I've never repented, but I'll do it now." And this prayer is for you.

Listen while I tell you what I'll pray so you can think about it. I'll say:
"Lord Jesus, I believe you are King in God's world.
I'm sorry I've been fighting against you.
I want you to take over the running of my life." (That's repentance.)
Then I'll say, "Lord Jesus, thank you for dying for me. Please forgive me."
That a good prayer for you? It will be for many people here tonight.
Let me run it past you again, so you can think.
Lord Jesus, I believe you are King in God's world.
I'm sorry to have been fighting against you.
Please come and take over the running of my life.
Lord Jesus, thank you for dying for me. Please forgive me.

I'll pray it bit by bit. And I'll stop. If it's a good one for you, echo it to God inside your head. Okay, the rest of you stay in prayer . . . will you? Let's bow our heads for prayer.

We just have a moment of quietness, where you can give it thought.
Jesus says, "Today, if you hear my voice, do not harden your heart."
Lord Jesus, I believe you are King in God's world. (*Pause.*)
I'm sorry I've been fighting you. (*Pause.*)
Please come and take over the running of my life. (*Pause.*)
Lord Jesus, thank you for dying for me. (*Pause.*)
Please forgive me. (*Pause.*) Amen. (*Long pause.*)

Narratio: Choreography of Conversion and Follow-up

Ladies and gentlemen, we want to get the best help we can to you. I want to say a quick word to people who might have prayed the prayer tonight. I don't know who you are of course. So, if you think I'm gazing at you, it's because I'm short-sighted. If you prayed the prayer tonight and you meant it, you can be sure that God's heard your prayer and answered it. What a good night it is for you. You came tonight and you weren't forgiven, and you're going home forgiven. Pretty good night. You came tonight and you weren't on the side of the Lord Jesus, and you're going home on his side . . . it's a pretty good night. You started out on a new life with Christ . . . new people need help . . . you are going to need help, and the only way we can get help to you . . . is by asking. I normally used to say to people, "Why don't you tell me on the way out? I'll put you in touch with somebody who can help you." Do you know how many people ever told me? None . . . none. So, I realized that wasn't a very good method. People prayed the prayer alright.

So, the method we've decided is to ask people to fill in a card. Now, you were given a card when you came in. You will have had a peek at that already. If you were here last week, or through the week, you might have filled it in four or five times. I want you to help people who've never seen it before. Take it out and pretend it's your first time. Say, "Oh isn't that interesting, look at that card." It says, "Confidential." Okay?

I'm going to ask everybody if they'd be kind enough to write something on this in a moment. Okay? Now, what is this card for? It's for people who say, "I've taken a step tonight, and I'd like more help." What do you need to do? You need to put a tick where it says "Prayed." And put your name and a contact number. And help is on the way to you. You can join the twenty or so other people who've already asked for help by that way.

Now you might be the sort of person who says, "No, I'm not able to pray that prayer yet Chappo. But I'd be glad to talk, I've made a big step by being here tonight. But I'd be glad to get to a Christianity Explained course, or I'd talk this through with somebody. Is there someone willing to do that?" Of course. Put a tick in the "More." That's what you want, you want more information. Put a name and a contact number, and we're on the way to you with help.

And because we don't want you to feel discriminated against if you didn't pray the prayer and you don't want any more, there's a box there for you, "Enjoyed." And if you didn't enjoy it, write "Not" in front of it. It'll make you feel better . . . or you know . . . so so.

Now, it's pretty clear if you start to write . . . people will see who's writing . . . people next to you will be having a peek. And so, I want to say, like in exams, keep your eyes on your own page. And if we all write a comment, no one will know who's writing what. You want to help other people who want to write but will feel embarrassed? Write a comment.

I'm going to write a comment (*mimics*). "I thought . . ." (*laughter*). Okay. If you're asking for help, we really do need to have name . . . contact number. If you're writing a comment, doesn't matter if you put your name on it or if you don't. If you've written Mr. Keating's name, please do not write it again (*laughter*). And Ken Moser, we've followed up twenty-five times this week already. Okay. Done that. Pop it back in the envelope. Please put your pencil back, and don't nick it, and you'll find a box at the door to put it in, and help is on the way to you.

Oh, there's one more thing I want to say. If you're in the under twenty age bracket, under eighteen, and you'd like somebody about your age to contact you, you might like to stick "under." And of course, if you're my age, you'd put "under forty." Oh . . . forty plus. You know.

So if that'd be a big thing for you, if you'd write a comment along the bottom saying minus eighteen years. Alright? Minus thirty years. Plus forty . . . JCC. Okay. And pop 'em on the way. Only remains for me to say ladies and gentlemen thank you very much for having me as your guest tonight. (41 min 48 sec)

Sermon Manuscript #8

Sermon Title: Forgiven Much, Loved Much

Text: Luke 7:36–50

Location: Moore Theological College Sydney, Chapel Service, October 4, 1994 https://myrrh.library.moore.edu.au/

Manuscript Location: JCCPPHW86

Rhetorical Arrangement and Genre: inductive-deductive, catechetical

Sermon Transcription

Exordium

My introduction to Christianity, or to church at least, was at a little Sunday school at St Paul's at Oatley.

Many things that happened in that Sunday school were a total mystery to me. I had more money in my hand than I'd ever seen. And my brother held it over a brass bowl and shook my hand until it fell in (*murmur*). And then a man gave it to God. How he got it to God, it was a mystery to me. I was told the following Sunday was going to be the feast of St. Thomas (*murmurs and laughter*). The only feasting that was done in our household was at birthdays and at Christmas. And I rather perked up at the idea that St. Thomas was having his birthday and that I was going to be part of it. I realized then that much of what was said in that church did not mean as it sounded. For there was not so much as a broken biscuit to be had at the feast of St. Thomas, let me tell you (*laughter around room*). However, in that little Sunday school, a man who seemed like a giant to me and was wearing a dark suit, looked very solemn and said to us week by week, "Hear O Israel, the LORD your God is one Lord. And you will love the LORD your God with all your heart, and mind and soul and strength."

And even though I didn't grasp much of what he was talking about, there was a great solemnity about it. And I look now at that poor little child, who was desperately trying to psyche up within him that which when God looked into me, would recognize that at least I was making an effort, if not now, but at any other time, to love him.

Propositio: Stated as Implicit Question—How Does Love for God Increase?

Some people seem to love God in a way that makes me long to love him in the way they do. Some people seem to be semi-snakey with God. Some of you have heard me tell this story. No matter. I was at a mission at Oxford earlier in the year, and every night an undergraduate got up and told us how he'd come to Christ. On the last night of this mission, a guy in a wheelchair was lifted up. He maneuvered himself to a little mike. He told us his name. He said, "I've been in the wheelchair since I was eight. It was the result of a family car accident. However, that's of little importance." He said, "I'm a fourth-year classicist. That is of little importance also." He said, "ah, my Godfather wrote a book called *The Enigma of Suffering*. And he gave me a copy of it to read." He said, "I found the book long, involved, and complicated. But because he'd given it to me, I pressed on to the end." He said, "By the time I'd finished reading it, I'd come to the conclusion that God was real and that he was basically good. So, I said to my Godfather, 'Would you like to further direct my reading?'" "He gave me a book," said the young man, "the name of which I have now forgotten. In that book I discovered that I was a great sinner in desperate need of forgiveness." He said, "I also discovered in that book that in the death of Jesus, there was sufficient for my complete forgiveness. And I've availed myself of that forgiveness. And that is important. And the last thing I want to say is that God has been so good to me during my lifetime that I want to spend the rest of my life in serving him. And I think that is important too." And with that he wheeled himself to the edge of the stage, and the ushers lifted him down. I said to the President of the OICCU, "Do you think I ought to say anything, or just make the appeal now?" (*Laughter.*) He said, "I'd just sit still and let it slowly simmer down."

Now, brothers, sisters, is that not a great miracle? That with the possibility of bitterness on the right hand and the left, God allows him the ability to soar above it, and his whole horizon is filled with loving God and wanting to serve him. Well, the part of the Bible you'll be glad to know I'm finally going to get to, is in Luke chapter 7, verse 36. For it is about loving God, and why we love God (*pause*).

Narratio

(*Reading Bible.*) A Pharisee invited Jesus to have dinner with him. Jesus went to his house and sat down to eat. There was a woman in the town who had lived a sinful life. She'd heard that Jesus was eating in the Pharisee's house. So, she brought an alabaster jar full of perfume, stood behind Jesus by his feet crying, wetting his feet with her tears. Then she dried his feet with her hair, kissed them, and poured perfume on them. When the Pharisee who had invited Jesus saw this, he said to himself, "If this man really were a prophet he would know who this woman was who is touching him, and he would know what kind of a sinful life she lives." Jesus spoke up and said, "Simon, I've got something to tell you." "Yes teacher," he said, "tell me." "There were two men who owed money to a moneylender," Jesus began. "One owed him five hundred dollars, the other fifty. Neither one could pay him back. So, he cancelled the debts of both. Which one, then, will love him more?" "I suppose," answered Simon, "that it would be the one who was forgiven more." "Your answer is correct," Jesus said. Then he turned to the woman and said to Simon, "Do you see this woman? I came into your house and you gave me no water for my feet. But she has washed my feet with her tears and dried them with her hair. You did not welcome me with a kiss, but she has not stopped pouring kisses on my feet since I came. You provided no oil for my head, but she has covered my feet with perfume. I tell you then, the great love she has shown proves that her many sins have been forgiven. Whoever has been forgiven little, however, shows only a little love." Then Jesus said to the woman, "Your sins are forgiven." The others sitting at the table began to say to themselves, "Who is this, who even forgives sin?" But Jesus said to the woman, "your faith has saved you, go in peace."

Partitio #1: Examination of Narrative Figure #1
—*The Sinful Woman*

Narratio: Mixes State, Show, Explain, Illustrate,
Apply Steps of Exposition

One of the nice things about the Bible stories is they are so uncluttered. Here are three players in this story.

If you're old like me, and watch Inspector Morse it is a complete fizzer, because after about a quarter of an hour I've dosed off. And I come back again and there are twenty-five more characters walking around who I've never seen. And you think, "Will I ever get to the bottom of this, and is it worth taping it and watching it five more times" (*murmur*) to get it all in. On the other hand, in Columbo, all I've gotta do is stay awake for the first three minutes (*murmurs*) and I know who's done it. And when I come up for air along the way, it's just a matter of how long he's bumbled on towards the end. I'm a Columbo man.

The Bible stories seem to me like that. They're totally uncluttered. Three characters. Simon, the Pharisee. The woman who has lived a sinful life. Jesus, who cares equally for both of them. Let's look at the woman. She is notorious. Now she's probably a prostitute. And the situation has got the possibility of disaster for the ministry of the Lord Jesus. For there she is, crying, fondling his feet, wiping them with her hair. And everybody knows who she is. If that hasn't got the possibility of bringing a good ministry to a crashing halt . . . But he is completely in control. And what is she doing? She is making a desperate bid to say, "Thank you." And the thank you is all about the word of forgiveness which she's heard. Where she's heard the word of forgiveness we're not told. But she's heard the word of forgiveness. She may have been in the house of Levi and heard the gracious words of Jesus that "the doctor comes for the sick" and that "he has come to bring repentance and forgiveness." She could have been there. She might have heard the story of the lost things. She might have heard the story of the lost coin and the lost sheep, and the lost boy . . . with the reiterating theme "there is more joy in heaven over one sinner who repents." She may have heard the story of the two men in the temple at prayer. And she may have identified so thoroughly with the man who beat on his chest and said, "Oh God, have mercy on me sinner that I am," and heard the gracious words of the Lord Jesus, "I tell you . . . that man went home in the right with God." Wherever it was that she'd heard the word of forgiveness of sins she had laid hold of it. And she knew what it was to be forgiven. And she must have heard the gracious words of forgiveness from the Lord Jesus himself because he is the object of her thanksgiving. She hears that he is in the house. My own view for what it's worth is that she may have thought she'd get in, anoint his feet with the ointment, and get back out again, without that much difficulty. But in the situation, she is overcome by emotion and breaks down. And tears are flowing freely. And she lets her hair down now and wipes them. And the wheel has fallen off the bike. And everybody sees her. She is right at the center of everything. And it is embarrassing beyond belief.

I don't know when you've ever been in those situations where you think your emotions will be all completely under control, only to discover that you're not able to control them, and the very worst thing you could've imagined has now materialized. I agreed to preach in a weak moment at my mother's funeral. She said it would be a great way to make sure the gospel got to our relatives. And I thought that would be a piece of cake. But when I actually got into the situation it was much more difficult than I thought it was going to be. In fact, it was for me, very close to being a disaster.

And I think about her now. She comes along with a very precious thing. Some of these were passed on as heirlooms. They may have been for her dowry. Whatever it is, it is very costly. She breaks it open. My parents owned a dinner service, which had never been used. It was a wedding present to them, and they brought it out on high days and let us look at it (*murmurs of laughter*) and put it away again. I inherited it when my mother died, and I have broken several of the pieces in its use. But since all of my stuff is willed to this college, I kept thinking, "What will you lot do with a dinner service?" (*Strong laughter.*) So, I've gone and continued to use it (*uproarious laughter*).

Will you notice what the Lord Jesus says to her? She is commended for this action. There is not a word to condemn her. Although in Simon's mind there certainly is. Jesus said, "I tell you, the great love she has shown proves that her many sins have been forgiven." And that is why she loves so much. To reinforce it, he says to her, "Your sins are forgiven." And so that she will know why this is so, he says, "It is your faith (I take it in the words she had heard of her forgiveness through Jesus), it is your faith which has saved you. Go in peace. Be sure that you are forgiven," is what he is saying.

Partitio #2: Examination of Narrative Figure #2
—Simon the Pharisee

Narratio: Mixes State, Show, Explain

Simon the Pharisee is the second player. He in my judgment is curious to know whether Jesus is a prophet. For, in verse 39, he concludes, "If this man really were a prophet, he would know the sort of woman she is and what is happening."

Well, as ever, you pass judgment on Jesus, you actually discover the judgment is on you. For not only is he a prophet, but he is one of great perception. For he knows what the man is thinking. And the parable is crystal clear.

Two men owe money to a money lender, and neither can pay. And one is an excessive sum. The other is a large sum. And both are cancelled. My difficulty with this is that I cannot imagine a moneylender doing it. However, there it is . . . done. "Which . . . will . . . love . . . most?" (*Asked slowly.*) Well, you don't have to a be a genius to work that out.

So, I want to ask you as this stage, "Do you think you've been forgiven much? Was that a large thing? Was it a little thing?"

Proposition: Loving God Derives from Our Understanding of Forgiveness

For loving God is caught up with my understanding of my forgiveness, at least in part. And the reason why she is able to love much is because she knows that she is acceptable to God (no thanks to what she has done). And ... as I think about it today (certainly no thanks for what I have done) that I should be allowed to be in the presence of God a totally forgiven man ... for everything. It has never appeared to me to be a small thing. It has only ever appeared to me to be a large thing, and even now breathtaking in its wonder, that God should set his love upon us, and that he should set his love upon us with a view to our being forgiven and being acceptable to him. And that that at the great cost to his Son is a thing to be reveled in and marveled upon.

Peroratio

As I conclude, let me draw your attention to how it is Jesus loves both of them.

The woman who he knows thoroughly, and who is delighted at her acts of devotion because of her forgiveness. And of Simon who is severely rebuked, because of the hardness of his heart. And because he is so unlike God in forgiving and in recognizing forgiveness.

Both of them are treated with great care. And both of them are dealt with in the way the situation calls for. For love is both rebuking as well as encouraging. For me, it is very difficult to do the first one, and especially with my friends. It is relatively easy to encourage them than it is to rebuke them. And my own lack of love for my friends is often demonstrated in my total inability to do it when the time is called for. Jesus who cares for both of them deals with both of them as the situation calls for.

I am a man who has been forgiven. I need to remind myself about that. And I need to meditate on it. For if I understand this part of the Bible correctly, it is the wellspring from which my love for God is likely to increase. For those who have been forgiven much, love much. "I tell you," says Jesus. "The great love she has shown proves that her many sins have been forgiven. Whoever has been forgiven little shows little love."

I want to ask you if you'll ponder today again on the greatness of forgiveness. On the sheer wonder that God . . . out of his mercy should take us back. And that at the great cost of the death of the Lord Jesus . . . But today, the great love she has shown proves that her many sins have been forgiven.

Let's pray (*pause*).

Our Father, it is a thing of wonder to us, that you should love us and send your Son to die for us. It is a thing of wonder that our many sins have been forgiven. And it is a thing of wonder to me, heavenly Father, how quickly I forget it. Please help us to demonstrate our love to you because of our own forgiveness. We thank you for the way in which this story today shows us in this sister of old, how we ought to act. And our Father, we thank you for preserving the story for us, that we might ponder on it, and love you. Help us to do that, we pray, for Jesus's sake. Amen (*audience echo amen*). (20 min 46 sec)

Sermon Manuscript #9

Sermon Title: He Must Increase

Text: John 3:22–36

Location: Moore Theological College, Chapel Service, October 22, 1991

https://myrrh.library.moore.edu.au/

Manuscript Location: JCCPPB17W2

Rhetorical Arrangement and Genre: inductive-deductive, catechetical

Sermon Transcription

Exordium

Heavenly Father, I pray that the words I say will be right and true according to your word. Please help me to teach it correctly. Please speak to us from your word now and give us wills longing to hear your voice and to do your will. For Christ's sake, amen.

Well, it occurred to me as I thought about this sermon that the end of the year is near. That might be a rejoicing for you. It certainly is a good year to come to an end from my point of view. Nearly every year is like that. For many of you who listen to me now, ordination is near at hand. Some of you will be leaving and going to full-time work. How am I supposed to think about that? How are you s'posed to think about that more to the point? Most depressing reading at the Synod. They have got to stop taking statistics. You'd think we would have learned that, wouldn't you? We now discover that of the 272 parishes a third of them are under one hundred and in decline. I don't know if it's occurred to you that you might be the Rector of one of those within two or three years. How you s'posed to think about that?

Propositio (Stated as Implied Question): What is the Joy of Christian Ministry and How/Where Is It Found?

Narratio: Mixes State, Show, Explain, Illustrate Expository Steps

Now there are many stories you could tell about good ministers who are frustrated off their brain and worn out. And in some senses the prospect of entering into ministry might daunt you. I don't want to speak about that. I want to speak about the exact opposite. I want to talk tonight about the joy of ministry in God's service, and where to look for that joy. Because it's just possible to miss it if you look in the wrong place. That's what I want to do. I want to focus our mind in John chapter 3. I'm going to read from verse 22. I want to look at the ministry of John the Baptist, note a few things about that and ask what we may learn from it as we come to these Scriptures tonight. John chapter 3, verses 22:

"After this Jesus and his disciples went into the land of Judea, where he remained with them and baptized. John was baptizing near Salem because there was much water there and people came and were baptized. For John had not yet been put in prison. Now a discussion arose between John's disciples and a Jew over purifying. And they came to John and said to him 'Rabbi, he who was with you beyond the Jordan, to whom you bore witness, here he is baptizing, and all are going to him.' John answered, 'No one can receive anything except it is given him from heaven. You yourself bear me witness that I said I am not the Christ. But I have been sent before him. He who has the bride is the bridegroom. The friend of the bridegroom who stands and hears him rejoices greatly at the bridegroom's voice. Therefore, this joy of mine is now complete. He must increase, and I MUST (*emphatically*) decrease.'"

Jesus and John are baptizing simultaneously, so this incident has taken place before anything that Mark tells us in his gospel. You remember Mark begins his gospel by telling us that Jesus's ministry began after John had been arrested. But this incident began before that. There is a dispute between some of the disciples of John the Baptist and a Jew, over what is simply said here as "purification rights." I don't know what they were. It may well have been that some dispute had arisen as to whether you'd been baptized with John's baptism, and to whether you had to engage in any more purification rights. I don't know what the issue was. It's simply told us that there was a dispute. But the bottom line was that whatever the discussion . . . however the discussion sparked off, it ended by their resentment with the fact that Jesus's ministry was becoming much more popular than John's. And in verse

26 there's the bottom line. "Rabbi, he who was with you beyond the Jordan, to whom you bore witness, well . . . he is baptizing, and *everyone* is going to him." So, I do think there is a slight note of resentment there, don't you? (*Laughter.*) Did you pick that up? It appears to me to be like that.

I remember growing up as a child, and saying to my father, "Everybody says" (*in rapid succession imitating father's voice*). "Who says it John, in fact, who?" You can be absolutely certain there was no winning from that moment onwards. The word of defeat was already sounded. Who in fact? The fact that they had not gone over to him showed that at least somebody was not there. Well, "he, beyond the Jordan, of whom you bore witness . . . he is baptizing, and everyone is going to him." Then comes these marvelous words of John the Baptist, which demonstrate how he thinks about his ministry. And there are three things I want to draw to your attention. What he believes is the origin of his ministry. The joy of that ministry. And the goal of that ministry.

Partitio

Inductive Proposition #1: The Origin of John's Ministry is from God

Show and Explain

First the origin of his ministry in verse 27. "John answered, 'No one can receive anything except it is given him from heaven, from God.'" To wish to have another's ministry seems to me to denigrate one's own ministry. To wish to be like someone else is a clear demonstration that you think your own ministry is ineffective, or defective at least. To wish to have another's ministry is to forget the sovereign God who gives that ministry.

Now, we didn't need to do this in the good ol' days, because everybody believed they'd been called by God to ministry. But now that nobody believes, having read "Decision making and the will of God," that we've arrived at it by our own cleverness and or indeed wisdom that's come from above, but not all that much, because we didn't need all that much (*murmur*) . . . But even if you hold that view (which you may believe that I don't all that much) (*laughter*), even if you do hold that view, you must believe that your ministry has come from above. See when Paul speaks to the elders in Acts 20, he says "Take heed to yourself and over the whole church to which the Holy Spirit has made you a guardian." It's his. He is jealous for the church. And those for whom he calls into ministry, or who find their way by an alternative route into ministry, need to take great care at this point. This comes from above (*slowly*). To wish to have another's ministry is to forget that. But in *his* case, to wish to have Messiah's ministry, is the worst arrogance of all. It is to wish to stand where God himself stands. It is to put us straight back into the garden all over again. At this point he is crystal clear. "I am *not* the Christ. I am his witness." Both the Lord Jesus and John have their roles from heaven. And he will not let them forget it for a moment.

Apply

When this principle is understood, all rivalry is at an end, is it not? Now think with me, the great Australian trait of cutting down the tall poppies, where does that come from? That's gotta be a form of rivalry, hasn't it? We don't want others to appear to be better than us. We don't want *anybody* to appear to be better than us. That cannot carry over into Christian living (*pause*). There can be no form of rivalry. No competition. In John's disciple's minds they saw Jesus and John to be competitors. In John's mind, they were on the same side, serving the same God, they were on the same team. Humility before each other is helped if we meditate here . . . a man can receive only that which is given from heaven. That is the first thing I want to draw to our attention about John the Baptist's ministry. He recognizes it to be God-given and he is able to rejoice in the nature of it. It comes from God and therefore it is a thing to be reveled in.

Inductive Proposition #2: The Joy of John's Ministry is That He Heralds the Messiah

Show, Explain

Now, the second thing I want to draw to your attention comes in verse 29 and it is the joy of his ministry. He says, "He who has the bride is the bridegroom. The friend of the bridegroom who stands and hears him rejoices greatly at the bridegroom's voice. Therefore, this joy of mine is now complete." Now, I must say in Australia, the best man at weddings seems to have very little to do. I suppose to make sure that the groom gets to the right church and preferably is sober. I s'pose he's also . . . it's his role to organize the buck's party on the night before. In the land we're talking about, his role was to see to the arrangements of the wedding . . . to bring the bride and to stay with her until the groom arrived. And his joy was to see them united and the whole wedding function go properly. And here John the Baptist is saying, "I've done all the preparations, it's all ready, here is the bride and I'm prepared now I hear his voice, I'm in the last stages of the ministry which has been given to me. It's not possible that those who heard him on this occasion could have missed the allusion to the several times where Israel is betrothed by God to himself. Let me read you the passage from Hosea, "I will betroth you to me forever" (this is chapter 2, verse 19). "I will betroth you to me forever. I will betroth you to me in justice and righteousness, in love and compassion I will betroth you to me in faithfulness and you will acknowledge the Lord." And what is the role of John the Baptist here, as the friend of the bridegroom? Why has he not called out faithful Israel to be ready to meet Messiah? And will he not present them to him, the bride whom he's got to the right place at the right time and made all the preparations for this marriage to take place.

Confirmatio and Restate

I don't need to draw to your attention how this idea keeps running on in the New Testament. Although it appears to me that the apostle in the Corinthian correspondence sees himself much more like the edgy father, who has contracted his daughter in marriage, and is going to make sure she's a virgin by the time she gets there. And he says to them, "Have I not betrothed you? Have I got your guarantee that you're faithful to this vow that I have made on your behalf?" No, I think the Baptist is saying something else at this moment. The disciples are disappointed, but John . . . his joy has reached completion (*emphatic*) in the coming of the Messiah. There's a totally different mindset between them. They are disappointed. They want him to be disappointed. He, on the other hand has reached the apex of ministry. His joy is completed. Calvin has an interesting quote. He says, "We are not called to subdue or dominate the church. But he makes use of us to unite him with us."

Illustrate and Apply

I s'pose all of you have been at one stage or other to the Katoomba Youth Convention. And some of you may in fact have also been those who are organizers at it. You might have been in the carpark. You might have been those who put out chairs. You might have been those who registered people. To pull off a show like that you've got to have an army of behind-the-scenes workers. And if you've been in the inner circle of those who've been lucky enough to wait behind when it's all gone, and you pick up the lolly papers and all the other things, it's not possible (if you've been in those groups, and I've been with them often) you know what it's like when you're exhausted, you sit down at the end of it all, and you don't whinge and gripe about it, because the whole thing has gone so well! You haven't been up on the platform. Somebody else has been up on the platform. In fact, the people on the platform (let me tell you, having been in both positions) never tidy up afterwards (*humorous murmur*). They never do. They get in the car and drive straight home. Somebody else is left to pick up the pieces. What is the joy of the organizers? That the whole thing ran smoothly. That people were edified from the front. That people delivered the goods. And in this John is saying (only that's a bad analogy) my joy is now complete.

Dear brothers and sisters, ponder on it. Here is somebody of the old order, which is just on the brink of passing away. He has never seen the glorified Christ like you and I have. He has not seen him lifted up to draw all men to himself. Nor did he witness his resurrection in the way that you and I have. And in spite of the fact that he was filled with the Holy Spirit from his mother's womb, he knew none of the glorious ministry of the Spirit bringing the glorified Christ to us. Did he know any of that going into the presence of God with great boldness, that the writer to the Hebrews speaks about? I doubt it. Well, if he can say, "My joy is complete" and he be in that order, how much more for me, for my joy to reach completion? In doing that which is the will of God, and that ministry which is given to me?

Inductive Proposition #3: The Goal of John's Ministry is That Christ's Glory Would Increase

SHOW, EXPLAIN, AND APPLY

And it is, as if to reinforce this, he brings me to the third point I want to make . . . the goal of his ministry in verse 30.

"Therefore," he says, "this joy of mine is complete. He MUST increase. I MUST decrease." It is very emphatic. It is the plan of God. Not should, not might, but he MUST, and I must is the very order of things. With these words an old order comes to an end. God did indeed speak in times past through the prophets. But NOW . . . NOW . . . he speaks through a Son, and this Son has come. With this he sees that old order passing away. It will never . . . never be the same again. He MUST increase, and I MUST decrease. For this one who has come is none other than the one who was from the beginning, who was with God and who was God. Much and all as we might be flattered to gather disciples around us, it is only Jesus who can save them. Much and all as we might be flattered by those who keep endlessly telling us how wonderful our ministry is, it is only the Lord Jesus by his Spirit who will bring them to new birth. These are the last recorded words of John the Baptist in this gospel. John the evangelist will not let us forget for a moment that the whole horizon is to be flooded with the Lord Jesus. He MUST increase, and I MUST decrease.

Now, I know that John's ministry is not an exact parallel to ours. Although the greatest of all the prophets, the least in the kingdom is greater than he. What you and I know in reality, he may have had an inkling of, or he may not have dreamt of in his wildest dreams. Would he have known how Christ would enter into his glory through death and resurrection? I repeat again, that great ministry of the Spirit, who was constantly applying the work of the glorified Christ to our lives? If he did, it was just a tiny flicker on the horizon. Did he know that bold access into the presence of God through the work of Jesus? I don't think so. If the ministerial attitudes were valid for him, can I say MUCH MORE for me. NOT LESS . . . MORE (*emphatic tone*). Where is the origin of my ministry? Why, it comes in the gift which God has given me. And the origin of yours? No man can do anything unless he receives it from above. Can I ask if you're happy with the gifts you've got, and if you can rejoice in them? You think they're good gifts? Be careful. Know who the giver is. With regard to joy, can I ask you, do you understand the joy of pointing people to Christ? Of seeing Christ formed in them? And being part of that church which in the end will be his bride. And with regard to the goal of ministry, is it that you want Christ to flood their horizons, and indeed you can say with a good heart, "He, in everything must increase, and I must decrease."

Let us pray. Heavenly Father, for this great one we thank you. But our Father, we thank you for the great ministry which you have wrought in us by the Lord Jesus and through his spirit, that we can cry to you "Abba Father" and come into your presence with great boldness. We thank you our Father that every good gift comes from above, and that ministry gifts come from above, and we pray that you'll help us to be happy to exercise in whatever ministry it is you have for us. And our Father we pray that our joy, like his, might be complete, to see the Lord Jesus, united with his people. And Father we pray that that deep humility which was his will be ours. But with a good and honest heart we'll be able to say, "He MUST increase, and I MUST decrease." And we ask this for Jesus's sake, amen. (21 min 33 sec)

Sermon Manuscript #10

Sermon Title: What Is at the Heart of Ministry?

Text: 2 Timothy 4:1–5

Location: Moore Theological College, Chapel Service, August 18, 1995

https://myrrh.library.moore.edu.au/

Manuscript Location: JCCPPB18W12

Rhetorical Arrangement and Genre: semi-inductive, catechetical

Sermon Transcription

Exordium

(*Chapman prays*) Our heavenly Father, we pray that we will hear your voice address us as we come to your word, and that hearing it we'll be quick to listen, quick to hear, quick to obey. Help us to do that we pray Father, for Jesus's sake. Amen (*pause*).

When I worked in the diocese of Armidale, towards the end of my time there, it fell my lot to represent the diocese on the selection panel for ministers for parishes . . . uh . . . on the presentation board. And, er, during that time I heard people from parishes say what they were looking for in their ministers. They varied widely. I remember on one occasion, the bishop in exasperation says, "Perhaps we ought to get you a public relations officer," to which the gentleman said, "It wouldn't do a scrap of harm, bishop, trust me" (*laughter*).

Propositio: Stated as Implied Question—What Is Ministry About?

It's interesting really, because your expectation of what is required in ministry, and the expectation of the people, the expectation of your peers, the expectation of your family, and the expectation of the diocesan officers, or the denominational officers may never ever coincide. They may at some places intersect. And I want to try and explore with you today, "What is it that ministry is basically about?" Or, what's more "Does God tell us what ministry is about?" That'd be nice to know, wouldn't it? Then you could decide whether you want to be obedient, popular, or just a complete fizz (*laughter*). All of those are possibilities, aren't they? But if we knew what God had in mind for ministry, we'd be able to fix our minds on that. Do we know that? I take it that's what the Pastorals are for, don't you? They seem to me to be addressed more to church leaders. And they seem to be manuals for church leaders. And they're given to us so that we can know what God is saying to the leaders. And if you're one of them, well and good. But if you're not, it's nice to know what you're on about when you're picking. It's nice to know what to look for when the time comes.

So, I'm going to read from 2 Timothy 4, five verses, make a couple of comments (*long pause*). "In the presence of God and of Christ Jesus, who will judge the living and the dead, and in view of his appearing and his kingdom, I give you this charge: Preach the word; be prepared in season and out of season; correct, rebuke and encourage—with great and careful instruction. For the time will come when men will not put up with sound doctrine. Instead, to suit their own desires, they will gather around them a great number of teachers to say what their itching ears want to hear. They will turn their ears away from the truth and turn aside to myths. But you, keep your head in all situations. Endure hardship, do the work of an evangelist, discharge all the duties of your ministry."

Partitio #1: A Very Solemn Charge Regarding Ministry
—It is Conducted Before the Risen Christ

SHOW AND EXPLAIN

The two things which I draw to your attention are the very solemn charge, and the very clear exhortation.

First, look at the solemn nature of this charge. We know that this is the last will and testament of the apostle. The last letter we've got from him. Verse 6, "I'm already being poured out like a drink offering. The time has come for my departure. I've fought the good fight. I've finished the course. I've run the race. It is your job now, not mine any longer. I've been faithful to the ministry given to me. And I charge you to be faithful to the ministry given to you."

In the passage that comes just before this, you remember it comes to that great climax about Timothy, from infancy, having known the Scriptures, which are able to make him wise to salvation through faith in Christ. And then the passage, "All Scripture is God-breathed and is useful for teaching, rebuking and training in righteousness, so that the man of God may be thoroughly equipped for every good work." I take it the term "the man of God" is used for this church leader. Um, it certainly is that way in 1 Timothy 6:11. "But you, man of God." So, I take it what he is saying is, that in the God-breathed Scripture, is everything that is necessary for the teacher, the man of God, *he* will be thoroughly equipped for every good work. I won't go to the stake for that, but by consequence, it must be that it will contain everything necessary for us. But it is to this man, who is the church leader, to whom this is addressed. And everything in those Scriptures, for every good work for him is there.

Now wouldn't you think that he would have immediately gone and said, "Consequently, preach the word, be in season and out of season." But no, he doesn't. He interrupts it with this solemn warning: "In the presence of God, and of Christ Jesus who will judge the living and the dead, in view of his appearing and his kingdom, I give you this charge" (*emphatic*). Well, I don't think you can lay it on much thicker than that, can you? This is the heavy roller being rolled backwards and forwards, isn't it? "In the presence of God."

Illustrate

It's interesting, I've been working on this passage and meditating on it, and it's taken me back to my early Christian roots. Soon after I was converted, I used to go to church at a little Congregational church in Como, where the pastors of that church were students, from the Sydney Missionary Bible College. I always thought they were great giants of biblical knowledge. And now I teach them . . . (*leaves pause . . . laughter*). Say no more . . . say no more. I don't remember a sermon where I wasn't reminded that everything I did in my life was done before the watching Father. I don't remember a day that went by that I didn't remind myself in my prayers, that everything was seen by God. And it did me well to remember that as I set forth on the day. I don't know why I abandoned that early piety that I had. And I think I ought to try and get back to it again. I was reminded that faithfulness will be rewarded by God. And specially if he was the only one who saw it. And that if he did see it in secret, he would reward me openly. And not to forget it. I think it's probably possible that in an endeavor to avoid false and showy piety, we might abandon our piety altogether, do you think? Well, I'm getting back to where I've come from. Everything is done in the presence of God.

Apply

He says, "In the presence of God, and in the presence of the Lord Jesus Christ, who is the judge." And that is emphasized, "Who will judge the living and the dead, who by his appearing, and by the kingdom." Those are the three ways he emphasizes again, again, and again that Jesus will judge us. He says, "in the presence of God, who knows and sees everything, and in the presence of Jesus the judge . . . do not forget he will come . . . do not forget that nothing in that day will prevent his absolute rule to be seen . . . and you, man of God, understand that to be so." It's a very important office, the office of ministry, isn't it? It seems, by God, to be taken very seriously here, do you think? It doesn't seem to matter much what the congregation thinks . . . or the denominational officers . . . or even our peers . . . or even you yourself. But what the Lord Jesus thinks, who has purchased the church with his own blood, he will judge us. Don't forget it. Believe it. It is a serious business. It's the sort of thing which clears your head, and focuses your mind, does it not? "In the presence of God, and of Christ Jesus who will judge the living and the dead, and in view of his appearing and his kingdom, I give you this charge." I suppose it's the idea that grace ought not to be thought of in such a way as to make us careless. But indeed, it ought to have the exact opposite effect, shouldn't it? It's only the sinful heart that will allow grace in us to become the means of our carelessness.

You remember 2 Corinthians 5? "For we must all appear before the judgment seat of Christ, that each one may receive what is due him for the things done in the body, whether good or bad." And then he says, "since then we know what it is to fear the Lord, we try to persuade men." Earlier on in this Epistle, God has said to this man of God that there is a workman who ought to be ashamed, and a workman who does not have God's approval. And there is envisaged a workman who does not need to be ashamed, and who has God's approval. And you remember what the dividing line is? By rightly handling the word of God. Well, there is a very solemn, very, very solemn warning indeed. There is the charge.

APPENDIX 1: HISTORICAL SERMON MANUSCRIPTS

Partitio #2: A Very Clear Exhortation Regarding Ministry
—Teach the Word

SHOW AND EXPLAIN

Now what is the exhortation? What is it that I am to do then? "In the presence of God and of Christ Jesus who will judge the living and the dead, in view of his appearing and his kingdom, here is the charge: Preach the word. Be prepared in season and out of season; correct rebuke, encourage with great patience and careful instruction" (*long pause*). "Keep your head. Endure hardship. Do the work of the evangelist. Discharge all the duties of your office." Herald out that word. What word? The God-breathed-out Scriptures. That is what we're on about. Preach the word. Settle it in your mind. Be decisive. What is it that ministry is basically about? So that we won't be easily side-tracked from it. Brian Telfer was telling me that earlier in the year, he was speaking to a conference of pastors, where they'd abandoned the teaching of the Bible. And they told him quite openly, "It didn't get anywhere." Churches were emptying. They'd abandoned it. They were going into counselling. And when he urged them to get back to teaching the Bible, they became very agro with him. It's a bad business that, isn't it?

What is it that I'm here training for? What is it that I'm going to do? Year in and year out, preach the word! Be prepared in and out of season. What does that mean? Ready all the time? Whether you feel like it. Whether you don't feel like it. Whether it seems like a good opportunity. Whether it doesn't seem like a good opportunity. Whether people are going to listen. Whether they're not going to listen. Preach the word! Be prepared in and out of season.

Do the hard part as well as the easy part. Correct, rebuke, and encourage. The hard part? Don't pull back from that. Brothers and sisters, if we settle it in our mind that we'll only be positive, you'll never correct or rebuke anybody, will you? And then, encourage them. He tells us the manner in which this is to happen and the method. The manner is with great patience . . . over, and over, and over again. If you get bored by the truth, you'll be bored out of your brain. Because you've got to keep going over, and over, and over again. Don't pull back from telling people the truth, because they know it. It's believing it that's hard.

Illustrate

I remember counselling a great friend of mine, soon after his baby had died, and amongst other things I said, "Don't forget, God has got everything in his hands." He said, "I know that Chappo." I said, "I know you know it mate, I'm calling on you to believe it!" That's what's hard. And that's why I need to be exhorted again and again and again. The truth of God's word. Don't make the fatal mistake of saying, "They know it, I've told them." But the fact you've told them doesn't mean they know it to start with. But even if they *do* know it, it needs to be said again and again and again. Why? Because we're quick to forget. Correct, rebuke, and encourage.

Apply

Okay, how will you do that? How do you get that balance? I think the only way you can do that is by systematically teaching through the Bible, isn't it? We're not very good at encouraging, are we? The great Australian knockers. Not much good at it.

I was in a church, the middle of last year, and I was pretty impressed with the staff there. They affirmed each other publicly. They encouraged each other privately. And they spoke with warm affection about the other members when they weren't present. That's pretty impressive, isn't it? I found it impressive. Found it pretty novel too (*pause*).

There it is. Correct, rebuke, encourage. The manner: with great patience. Over and over again. The method: careful instruction.

And then he tells you why. Doesn't this strike terror into the heart of a prospective minister? It ought to. "For the time will come when men will no longer put up with sound doctrine, instead to suit their own desires, they will gather around them a great number of teachers to say what their itching ears want to hear. They will turn their ears from the truth and turn aside to myths."

And settle it in your heart, it's going to be like that. I was converted in 1947, and I can hardly remember a year that went by that some new form of Christian aberration hasn't been on the scene, and we've seen our friends run after it, one after the other. I remember being at a church in the evening where the pastor of that church had told me in the morning, that having preached his heart out somebody said to him, "Do you ever preach when you're filled with the Spirit?" I said, "What you say to him?" He said, "I didn't know what to say." I said, "I always do. Would never occur to me to do it any otherwise." Isn't that a hateful thing to say? But let me say that

I can't remember a year. And whatever the aberration is today, it'll change tomorrow, but it'll be there. And when they walk away, and after you've taught with all patience and perseverance and you've stuck at it for as long as you can, and they walk away, *then* . . . what will you do? Don't lose your head (*slowly*). You've still got your best asset . . . God. It's the congregation that've gone, not him. So, don't lose your head. Don't panic as if he's disappeared off the scene. Okay? Endure hardship. Is that on your agenda? No triumphalist nonsense here, is there? Hard work. Can I say at this stage, please don't assess your gifts by how easy or hard it is to do things. It's got nothing to do with your gifts. It might have to do with working harder. Endure hardship. Do the work of the evangelist. Start all over again. Just plant a new church. That's what he's saying, isn't it? What are your options . . . if they all walk away? (*Heightened tone.*) Start all over again. Get back to the gospel. There isn't anything else. Discharge all the duties of your ministry. How will you find all the duties of your ministry? By reading the Pastorals! You read those regularly so your picture of what you're aiming at is clear. It'd be a good ordination charge this, wouldn't it? Preach the word . . . when you feel like it . . . when you don't. Don't lose your head when the wheel falls off the bike. Endure hardship. Do the work of an evangelist. Discharge all the duties of your ministry.

Peroratio

One of the nice things I think about time and days and months, and years and anniversaries, is that every day is not like the day before. Aren't you glad when some days come to an end? You say, "Well, thank goodness that's over. I'll give it my best shot tomorrow." I'm a bit like that with golf now (*laughter*). I don't know if you've got any anniversary . . . do you remember the day you decided to come to college? This'd be a good thing to read on that anniversary, wouldn't it? I read it on the anniversary of my ordination. There are certain other things I read on my birthday. They roll round, year after year, and just in case you forget, at least you do it once a year. And today wouldn't be a bad day to sit down with this text and let it say to you, "How you been goin'? How you goin' on this?" Let's pray.

    Our heavenly Father, we thank you for the clear and solemn warning and this very clear exhortation. And we pray for our ministers, that they will preach the word, in and out of season, that they will discharge all the duties of their office. And we pray as we prepare to do it, that we'll be faithful too. For Jesus's sake, amen. (22 min 30 sec)

APPENDIX 2

Department of Evangelism Catechists

The following table provides a list of the catechists/student preachers who trained at the DOE, beginning in 1984. Many of these would go on to be leading figures within Australian (and to some extent world) evangelicalism. They have served or continue to serve in roles as Anglican bishops and deans, theological college principals and scholars, leading church planters and evangelists (in both Anglican and independent evangelical church networks), directors of national student ministries, as well as missionaries, school principals, and leading local and international clergy. Names have been distilled from the historic Sydney Department of Evangelism newsletters in which they featured.

Year	Name	Year	Name
1984	David Short	2001	Danny Ruelander
1985	Ian Powell	2001	Rhett Harris
1986	Stuart Robinson	2002	Andrew Lubbock
1987	Alan Stewart	2002	Con Campbell
1987	Rick Lewers	2002	Connan O'Shea
1988	Gordon Cheng	2002	Nigel Fortescue
1988	Ed Vaughan	2003	Michele Underwood
1989	David McDonald	2003	Susan Shiner
1989	Graham Bannister	2003	Geoff Lin
1990	Ray Galea	2003	Jason Ramsay
1990	Matthew Pickering	2003	Wendy Potts

APPENDIX 2: DEPARTMENT OF EVANGELISM CATECHISTS

1991	Nick Foord	2004	Jay Behan
1991	Rob Smith	2004	Emma Fookes
1991	Phil Wheeler	2004	Andrew Lim
1992	Zac Veron	2004	Susan Ravenhall
1992	Bill Salier	2004	Mike Wirth
1992	Andrew Heard	2005	Mike Heptonstall
1993	Lyn Yapp	2005	Glenn Hohnberg
1993	Shaun Potts	2005	Zoe Holloway
1993	Peter Smith	2005	Jen Shadwick
1994	Graham Stanton	2005	Baden Stace
1994	Richard Chin	2006	Martin Shadwick
1994	Mark Leech	2006	Robyn Bain
1994	Richard Shumack	2006	Miriam Chan
1995	Kanishka Raffel	2006	Mike Paget
1995	Sue Willis	2006	Tony Wright
1995	Martin Foord	2007	David Skirving
1996	Steve Calder	2007	Thora Marsh
1996	Greg Peisley	2007	Naomi Chong
1996	Darren Hindle	2007	Steve Chong
1997	Andrew Katay	2007	Luther Symons
1997	Adam Lamb	2007	David Ould
1997	Dominic Steele	2008	Lisa Thompson
1998	Dominic Steele	2008	Joshua Kuswadi
1998	Ruth Muffet	2008	Chris Deacon
1998	Scott Warner	2008	Claire Boyd
1999	Orlando Saer	2008	Sonja Graml
1999	Paul Rees	2009	Jenny Ihn
1999	Marcus Reeves	2009	Nathan Sandon
1999	Rebecca Fulton	2009	Tho Luu
2000	Darren Box	2009	Claire Boyd
2000	Simon France	2009	Alex Koch
2000	Kirsten Hales	2009	Mike Doyle
2001	Tim Bowden	2009	Tim Bradford
2001	Carl Matthei		

Bibliography

Primary Sources

Interviews

Interview with Adrian Lane, March 27, 2017.
Interview with Alan Stewart, December 7, 2016.
Interview with Andrew Cornes, November 24, 2016.
Interview with Bruce Ballantine-Jones, February 13, 2017.
Interview with Chris Allan, March 7, 2017.
Interview with David Jackman, January 16, 2017.
Interview with David Mansfield, November 29, 2016.
Interview with David McDonald, December 6, 2016.
Interview with David Seccombe, February 16, 2017.
Interview with David Short by email correspondence, February 17, 2017.
Interview with Dick Lucas, January 20, 2017.
Interview with Donald Howard, February 17, 2017.
Interview with Grant Retief, August 29, 2017.
Interview with Harry Goodhew, November 14, 2016.
Interview with Ian Powell, March 12, 2017.
Interview with Paul Barnett, December 2, 2016.
Interview with Peter Jensen, December 2, 2016.
Interview with Phillip Jensen, February 16, 2017.
Interview with Ray Smith, February 21, 2017.
Interview with Richard Bewes, January 19, 2017.
Interview with Rico Tice, January 17, 2017.
Interview with Simon Manchester, November 18, 2016.
Interview with Stephen Abbott, February 14, 2017.
Interview with Tony Payne, November 29, 2016.
Interview with William Taylor, February 10, 2017.

Manuscripts and Archival Collections

Armidale Diocesan Registry

Billy Graham Center Archives, Wheaton Illinois

Collection 16. International Crusade Procedure Books.
Collection 16. Volumes 1–2. Billy Graham Crusade, Sydney. April–May, 1979.
Collection 46. Box 1. Folder 1–22. 1974 Lausanne International Congress on World Evangelization.
Collection 46. Box 3. Folder 3–13. 1974 Lausanne ICOWE Continuation Committee.
Collection 46. Box 7. Folder 4–12. 1974 ICOWE Continuation Committee.
Collection 46. Box 32. Folder 1–8. 1974 ICOWE Continuation Committee.
Collection 46. Box 286. Folder 9, 17. 1974 ICOWE Continuation Committee.
Collection 141. Box 2, 3, 13. Oral History Program.
Collection 245. Accession 82–59. Billy Graham Sydney Crusade 1959.
Collection 245. Box 13. ICOWE Correspondence.
Collection 245. Box 16. Billy Graham Sydney Crusade 1979 Correspondence.
Collection 245. Box 19. Billy Graham Sydney Crusade 1968 Correspondence.
Collection 245. Box 25. Folders 5–24. Billy Graham Sydney Crusade 1979 Planning.
Collection 245. Box 26. Folders 6–18. Billy Graham Sydney Crusade 1979 Planning.
Collection 245. Box 29. Folders 1–22. Executive Correspondence.
Collection 245. Box 41. Folder 8. W. B. Berryman Director Correspondence 1976–1979.
Collection 245. Box 42. Folder 4. Billy Graham Sydney Crusade 1979 Follow-Up Program.
Collection 245. Box 43. Folder 5–14. Billy Graham Sydney Crusade 1979 Executive Correspondence.
Collection 245. Box 44. Folder 5–10. Billy Graham Sydney Crusade 1979 Executive Correspondence.
Collection 253. Box 21. Amsterdam International Conference for Itinerant Evangelists 1983. Media.
Collection 253. Box 39. Amsterdam ICIE 1983. Correspondence.
Collection 253. Box 40. Amsterdam ICIE 1983. Program Committee.
Collection 360. Scrapbook 308–11. Billy Graham Sydney Crusade 1968. Media.
Collection 360. Scrapbook 466–69. Billy Graham Sydney Crusade 1959. Media.
Collection 360. Scrapbook 816–17. Billy Graham Sydney Crusade 1979. Media.
Collection 590. John Stott Personal Papers.

John Charles Chapman Estate

Personal Papers 1960–2012.

Sydney Diocesan Archives

Box 1, Board of Diocesan Mission. Board Planning and Correspondence.
Box 2, Board of Diocesan Mission. Newsletters 1969–2010.

Box 3, Board of Diocesan Mission. Missioner News and Media 1955-1963.
Box 4, Board of Diocesan Mission. Billy Graham Sydney Crusade 1979. Planning and Media.
St Andrew's Cathedral, Chapter Minutes.

Mitchell Library Sydney

Adrian Lane Papers 1973-2005.
Box 1. Sydney University Evangelical Union. Volume 1.
Box 3. John Chapman to Adrian Lane Correspondence.
Box 12. Lausanne Australia. Melbourne Department of Evangelism.
Box 15. Sydney University Evangelical Union. Volume 2.
Box 16. St Barnabas Broadway 1976-79.
Box 17. Sydney Department of Evangelism 1972-1985.

Dictionaries, Yearbooks, and Encyclopedias

Alexander, T. Desmond, and Brian S. Rosner, eds. *New Dictionary of Biblical Theology*. Downers Grove: IVP, 2020.
Atkinson, David J., and David H. Field, eds. *New Dictionary of Christian Ethics and Pastoral Theology*. Downers Grove: IVP, 1995.
Barrett, David B., et al., eds. *World Christian Encyclopedia*. New York: Oxford University Press, 2001.
Burgess, Stanley M., ed. *Encyclopedia of Pentecostal and Charismatic Christianity*. New York: Routledge, 2006.
———. *New International Dictionary of Pentecostal and Charismatic Movements*. Grand Rapids: Zondervan, 2002.
Dickey, Brian, ed. *Australian Dictionary of Evangelical Biography*. Sydney: Evangelical History Association, 1994.
Elwell, Walter A., ed. *Evangelical Dictionary of Theology*. Grand Rapids: Baker, 1984.
Freedman, David Noel, et al., eds. *Anchor Bible Dictionary*. New York: Doubleday, 1992.
Guiley, Rosemary Ellen. *The Encyclopedia of Witches and Witchcraft*. New York: Facts on File, 1989.
Jupp, James, ed. *The Encyclopedia of Religion in Australia*. Cambridge: Cambridge University Press, 2009.
Kittel, Gerhard, and Gerhard Friedrich, eds. *Theological Dictionary of the New Testament Volume 3*. Translated by Geoffrey W. Bromiley. Grand Rapids: Eerdmans, 1964-76.
Langmore, Diane, ed. *Australian Dictionary of Biography*. 12 Vols. National Centre of Biography, Australian National University, 1966-2012.
Southern Cross Magazine, 1969-2012. Sydney: Anglican Information Office, 1969-2012.
Yearbooks of the Anglican Diocese of Sydney, 1939-2015. Sydney: Anglican Information Office, 1939-2015.

Reports and Edited Volumes

Agenda for a Biblical Church. Volume 2, Debates and Issues from the National Evangelical Anglican Congress. Sydney: Anglican Information Office, 1981.
An Australian Prayer Book 1978. Sydney Square: Anglican Information Office.
Bellamy, John, and Peter Kaldor. *National Church Life Survey.* Adelaide: Open Book, 2002.
Bolt, Peter G., et al. *The Lord's Supper in Human Hands. Who Should Administer?* Camperdown: Australian Church Record, 2008.
Both Sides to the Question: Report to Synod of the Church of England Diocese of Sydney of the Committee to Study the Neo-Pentecostal Movement. Sydney: Anglican Information Office, 1972.
Castle, Keith, et. al. *The National Church Life Survey Commissioned Report No. 1, the NCLS and Sydney Anglicans—Initial Analysis.* NCLS, 1992.
Douglas, J. D., ed. *Let the Earth Hear His Voice: International Congress on World Evangelization, Lausanne, Switzerland. Official Reference Volume.* Minneapolis: World Wide Publications, 1975.
Henry, Carl F. H., and W. Stanley Mooneyham, eds. *One Race, One Gospel, One Task: World Congress on Evangelism, Berlin 1966, Official Reference Volume.* Minneapolis: World Wide Publications, 1967.
Kaldor, Peter. *Who Goes Where? Who Doesn't Care? Going to Church in Australia.* Homebush: Lancer, 1987.
Kaldor, Peter, et al. *Taking Stock: A Profile of Australian Church Attenders.* Adelaide: Open Book, 1999.
Kinnamon, Michael, and Brian E. Cope, eds. *The Ecumenical Movement: An Anthology of Key Texts and Voices.* Geneva: World Council of Churches, 1997.
Looking into the Parish. Report of the Parish Ministry and Organization Commission. Sydney: Anglican Information Office, 1972.
Mol, Hans. *Religion in Australia: A Sociological Investigation.* Sydney: Thomas Nelson, 1971.
Move in For Action: Report of the Commission on Evangelism of the Church of England, Diocese of Sydney. Sydney: Anzea Publishers, 1971.
"Move in For Action: Report Summary." *Southern Cross*, October 1971, 12–13.
Ordination: Its Meaning, Value and Theology. A Report to the Sydney Diocesan Synod. Sydney: Anglican Information Office, 1981.
"The Report of the Evangelistic Mission Held by Sydney University Evangelical Union 29th June—7th July, 1977: 'Go Back—You're Going The Wrong Way.'"
"Towards a Theology of Ordination." *A Report of the General Synod Commission on Doctrine, Anglican Church of Australia.* Sydney: Church of England in Australia Trust, 1981.

Literary Primary Sources

"Aftermath of Lausanne: Evangelism in a Changing World." *New Life*, August 29, 1974, 5.
"Amsterdam '83: A Pictorial Report." *Decision*, ICIE, November 1983, 2.

"Amsterdam Conference Draws 8,000 Evangelists." *World Evangelization*, December 1, 1986.
"Archbishop Loane Writes." *Southern Cross*, May 1979, 8–9.
"Archbishop Mowll Enthroned. Impressive Ceremony at St. Andrew's." *Sydney Morning Herald*, March 14, 1934, 13.
"Archbishop Writes." *Southern Cross*, April 1971, 9.
"Australian Crusade." *The Southern Presbyterian Journal* 18, no. 2 (May 13, 1959) 5.
"Australia's Top Exorcist." *Sunday Telegraph*, August 17, 1975.
Barnett, Paul. "2 Corinthians 4–5." *Southern Cross*, September 1985, 14–15.
Barnett, Paul, and John Court. *The Message of Lausanne*. Adelaide: Trinity, 1974.
Berryman, Barry. "School of Evangelism." *BGEA News Release*, November 15, 1978.
———. "Sydney's Randwick Crusade Closes with 85,000 Attendance." *BGEA News Release*, May 30, 1979.
———. "Thousands of Christians Already Praying for Graham Crusade." *BGEA News Release*, November 1, 1978.
"Billy Graham." *The Australian*, May 20, 1979.
"Billy Graham Challenges Lausanne Movement." *World Evangelization*, December 1986, 3.
"Billy Graham in Sydney." *Australian Women's Weekly*, April 29, 1959.
"Billy Graham in 'The Most Evangelical City in the World.'" *Crusade Facts*, March 1968, 1–2.
Blake, Phillip. "The Letter to Jude: 4 Studies." *Southern Cross*, July 1985, 14.
Bonwick, James. *Australia's First Preacher: The Rev. Richard Johnson, First Chaplain of New South Wales*. London: Sampson Low, Marston & Co., 1898.
"Books of the Century." *Christianity Today*, April 24, 2000.
Bruce, F. F. "The Tyndale Fellowship for Biblical Research." *Evangelical Quarterly* 19 (1947) 52–61.
Burney, John. "They Came to God in Thousands." *The Daily Telegraph*, May 19, 1979.
Capon, John. "Lausanne 74: Let the Earth Hear Whose Voice?" *Crusade*, September 1974, 23–33.
"A Challenge from Evangelicals." *Time Magazine*, August 5, 1974, 48.
Chaseling, B. "Overland to London." *Sydney Morning Herald*, July 20, 1957.
"A Chat with Chapman." *Southern Cross*, June 1974, 8–9.
"Church Leaders from 6 Continents Meet in Los Angeles to Plan World Congress." *BGEA News Release*, August 25, 1972.
Cole, Graham. "Songs from the Heart: Studies in Psalms 1, 19, 77, 150." *Southern Cross*, April 1985, 14–15.
"A Crusade for the Young." *Woman's Day*, April 11, 1968.
Cutler, Genevieve. "Radicals Meet the Establishment." *See*, July 1976, 12.
Dain, A. J. "Sydney Awaits Billy Graham." *The Life of Faith*, April 18, 1968.
Davis, Gerald. "A Lay Leader at Communion." *Church Scene*, December 14, 1978, 9.
———. "Movement Really Comes of Age." *The Australian*, August 3, 1974, 12.
Dawson, Peter. "The Duties and Responsibilities of a Servant of God: Studies in 2 Timothy." *Southern Cross*, March 1985, 13, 23.
"Dialogue Meeting Draws 4500." *Southern Cross*, May 1971, 18.
Edwards, W. J., Dr. "Why Go to Church?" *Sydney Morning Herald*, July 7, 1956.
"Evangelicals Learn to 'Agree to Disagree.'" *CWN Series*, August 9, 1974, 13.
"Faith of our Fathers." *Sydney Morning Herald*, October 29, 1960.

"Fanning the Fires Lit at Lausanne." *The Australian Evangelical* (March–April, 1976), 21.

Firebaugh, Glenn. "How Effective Are City-Wide Crusades?" *Christianity Today*, March 27, 1981, 24–29.

Foster, Dave. "Amsterdam '83: A Pictorial Report." *International Conference for Itinerant Evangelists*, 7.

Frady, Marshall. "The Use and Abuse of Billy Graham." *Esquire Fortnightly*, April 1979.

"From Amsterdam: To Every People by Every Means." *Decision*, ICIE, November 1983, 3–5.

Gill, Alan. "Archbishop Describes British as Children Fighting for Buns." *Sydney Morning Herald*, October 24, 1975.

———. "Countdown to Crusade." *Challenge Weekly* 37, no. 1 (March 23, 1979).

Glennon, Jim. *Your Healing is Within You: An Introduction to Christian Healing*. London: Hodder and Stoughton, 1978.

Goodhew, Richard Henry. "Evangelism Explosion." *Southern Cross*, February 1983, 6–7.

Graham, Billy. "Australia: A Spiritual Superpower." *Sunday Telegraph*, May 20, 1979.

———. "Foreword." In "Amsterdam '83: A Pictorial Report." *International Conference for Itinerant Evangelists*, 2.

"Graham Announces 1986 Evangelists' Conference." *World Evangelization*, June 1985, 16.

"Graham's Beliefs Still Intact." *Christianity Today*, January 13, 1978.

Guinness, Howard. "Ampol Trial." *SMH*, October 6, 1956.

Halls, Tom. "Advent: Jesus is Coming: Studies in Mark 12–13." *Southern Cross*, November 1985, 13.

Henry, Carl F. H. *The Uneasy Conscience of Modern Fundamentalism*. Grand Rapids: Eerdmans, 1947.

Hewetson, David. "Four Parables from Luke." *Southern Cross*, October 1985, 15–16, 21.

Hill, Michael. "The Theological Fabric of First Corinthians: Chs 1–3, 5–6, 8–9, 12–14." *Southern Cross*, November 1984, 13–15.

Howell, Deryck. "Isaiah, Prophet of the Holy One: Is 1–12." *Southern Cross*, December 1985, 16, 21–22.

Horsburgh, Michael. "High Politics." *The Bulletin*, May 1993, 10.

International Congress on World Evangelization (ICOWE). "Unprogrammed Session on Radical Discipleship," July 21, 1974. BGCA CN 53, Series II, Subseries D, Tapes 180–84.

Jensen, Peter. "Four Psalms." *Southern Cross*, April 1984, 13–14.

Kaye, Bruce. "Freedom and Maturity for Evangelicals." *CWN Series*, August 16, 1974, 9.

King, Gordon J. S. "Old Testament Heroes: Nehemiah—Greatheart." *Sydney Morning Herald*, November 3, 1956.

Kitchen, J. H. "Signs of Spiritual Awakening in Sydney." *The Christian*, Friday April 24, 1959, 1.

Knox, D. B. "The Church and the People of God in the Old Testament." In *Knox: Works II*, 9–17.

———. "Four Fatal Flaws in the Draft Constitution." *Australian Church Record*, February 14, 1957, 8.

———. "Undefined Comprehensiveness Will Destroy the Church." *Australian Church Record*, February 3, 1955, 2.

Knox, Ian. "Lausanne and After: Practical Outcomes of Congress on World Evangelization." *The Life of Faith*, August 3, 1974.
"Lausanne 1974 Notice." *Southern Cross*, April 1973, 10–11.
"Lausanne Call for Action by Alliance." *The Australian Evangelical*, September–October 1974, 3.
Loane, M. L. "Come, Drink." *Southern Cross*, August 1971, 15.
———. "The Everlasting Arms." *Southern Cross*, April 1970, 14–15.
———. "From the Archbishop." *Southern Cross* 8, no. 6 (June 1968) 1–2.
———. "The Graham Crusade: Background." *Southern Cross* 7, no. 12 (December 1967, 2).
———. "Judgement." *Southern Cross*, January 1973, 17.
———. "Objections Answered." *The Christian*, March 1, 1968, 9.
———. "The Power of God." *Southern Cross*, October 1974, 18–19.
———. "Ruth, A Daughter of Moab." *Southern Cross*, September 1972, 9.
———. "They Could Not Believe It." *Southern Cross*, October 1975, 18–19.
———. "What Shall I Render." *Southern Cross*, February 1971, 14.
———. "What the Spirit Saith." *Southern Cross*, June 1976, 36–37.
———. "Woe Lo Go." *Southern Cross*, February 1972, 16–17.
Lormer, R. "What Jesus Christ Means to Me." *Sydney Morning Herald*, July 4, 1959.
"The Lost Chord of Evangelism." *Christianity Today*, April 1, 1957.
McGavran, Donald A. *Understanding Church Growth*. Grand Rapids: Eerdmans, 1970.
Mears, Ian, ed. *The Christian and Social Concern: A Set of Ten Studies on a Biblical Basis for Social Involvement*. Sydney: The Board of Education, Diocese of Sydney, 1981.
Mitchell, Ralph W. "Sydney Crusade Stirs Entire City." *The Life of Faith*, April 30, 1959, 283.
Morris, Leon. "Lausanne '74." *EFAC Bulletin* 14 (January 1975) 1–11.
Nichols, Alan. "Australia Crusade Begins." *Christianity Today*, April 12, 1968.
———. "The Australian Archbishop and the Evangelist." *Christianity Today*, June 8, 1979, 58.
———. "The Cross Over Sydney." *Christianity Today*, May 24, 1969.
———. "Evangelism by Confusion." *Southern Cross* 10, no. 8 (August 1970) 5.
———. "Graham Crusade Lifts Down-Under Church." *Christianity Today*, June 29, 1979.
O'Berg, O. D. "The Call to Personal Service." *Sydney Morning Herald*, May 18, 1957.
O'Brien, Peter. "Freedom from Death: Romans 8." *Southern Cross*, March 1984, 15–17.
Oldfield, W. A. "The Last Test Series in England." *Sydney Morning Herald*, August 25, 1956.
Olsen, Warwick. "Congress Participants." *Southern Cross*, February 1974, 17.
"Only God Can Judge Crusade's Success." *Australian*, May 21, 1979.
Oliver, Philip. "Half Nights of Prayer." *BGEA News Release*, March 28, 1979.
———. "Studies in Titus." *Southern Cross*, August 1984, 13–16.
Olsen, Ted. "Amsterdam 2000 Called the Most Multinational Event Ever." *Christianity Today*, August 2, 2000.
Olsen, Warwick. "Sydney Crusade Report." *Southern Cross*, April 1968, 6–7.
Oram, Jim. "Can We Challenge Billy Graham?" *Everybody's*, April 24, 1968.
Pitt, E. A. "The Place of the Bible in the Life of the Nation." *Sydney Morning Herald*, August 25, 1956.

Powell, G. "Why Did Billy Graham Succeed?" *Sydney Morning Herald*, May 23, 1959, 16.
Prior, A. "Graham's Sydney Campaign." *Watchman Examiner*, May 7, 1959.
Raiter, Michael. "Years On—Lausanne 2004." *Australian Church Record*, November 1, 2004, 4.
Reid, J. R. "Boy Restored." *Southern Cross*, August 1972, 14.
———. "Learning from the Ephesians." *Southern Cross*, June 1984, 13–17.
———. "One Because of the Believer's Love." *Southern Cross*, June 1969, 27–28.
———. "One Because of the Son's Sacrifice." *Southern Cross*, April 1969, 8–9.
———. "One Because of the Spirit's Work." *Southern Cross*, May 1969, 12–13.
———. "Romans 8." *Southern Cross*, May 1975, 19–20.
———. "Water Turned into Wine." *Southern Cross*, July 1972, 8.
"A Response to Lausanne." *Free Slave* 2, no. 4 (November 1974) 4–5.
Robinson, D. W. B. "Gospel and Church." *Southern Cross*, May 1991, 10.
Simper, Errol. "E1 Evangelism." *Country*, April 23, 1979.
Stanway, Alfred, Rt. Rev. "Africa Today." *Sydney Morning Herald*, June 1, 1957.
"Sydney Crusade Preparation in Top Gear." *Southern Cross*, March 1967, 18–19.
"Sydney Preparations for Graham Crusade." *The New South Wales Presbyterian* 33, no. 7 (April 10, 1959) 1–2.
Turner, John. "Paul's Letter to the Philippians: 4 Studies." *Southern Cross*, September 1984, 15–18.
Vitnell, Les. "God's Actions, Man's Actions: Studies in Acts." *Southern Cross*, June 1985, 14–15.
Wagner, C. Peter. "Lausanne Twelve Months Later." *Christianity Today*, July 4, 1975, 7–9.
Walker, Alan, Rev. "Discoveries on Both Sides of the Iron Curtain." *Sydney Morning Herald*, February 1, 1958.
Wallace, Tom, and Ian Mears, eds. *Living Gospel, Changing World*. Sydney: Pilgrim International, 1980.
Webb, Barry. "The Wisdom of Proverbs: Part 1." *Southern Cross*, February 1988, 26.
———. "The Wisdom of Proverbs: Part 2." *Southern Cross*, March 1988, 26–27.
Wirt, S. E. "Amsterdam '83 in Historical Perspective." *Decision*, ICIE, November 1983, 9.
Woodhouse, John. "The Gigantic Mercy of God: Studies in Jonah." *Southern Cross*, February 1985, 15–17.
"Young and Old Brave Cold to Show Their Faith." Sunday Telegraph, May 20, 1979.

Historical Literary Sources

Augustine. *De Doctrina Christiana*. New York: Clarendon, 1995.
———. *On Christian Doctrine*. Nicene and Post-Nicene Fathers. First Set, vol. 2. Translated by J. F. Shaw. Grand Rapids: Eerdmans, 1979.
Breward, Ian, ed. *The Works of William Perkins*. Abingdon: Sutton and Courtenay, 1970.
Cicero. *Brutus. Orator*. Translated by G. L. Hendrickson and H. M. Hubbell. LCL 342. Cambridge, MA: Harvard University Press, 1939.
Didache. *The Apostolic Fathers*. Edited and translated by Kinsopp Lake. 2 vols. LCL. Cambridge: Harvard University Press, 1965.

Johnson, Richard. *An Address to the Inhabitants of the Colonies Established in New South Wales and Norfolk Island*. London: Paternoster Row, 1792.
Martyr, Justin. 1 *Apol*. 67. In Ante-Nicene Fathers, vol. 1. Buffalo: Christian Literature Publishing Company, 1885–96.
Quintilian. *Institutio Oratoria*. Books 4–6. Translated by D. A. Russell. Loeb Classical Library. Cambridge: Harvard University Press, 1921.

Secondary Sources

Dissertations and Theses

Autrey, J. Denny. "Jean Claude and His Influence on Homiletics." PhD diss., SBTS, 2013.
Ballantine-Jones, Bruce. "Changes in Policy and Practices in the Anglican Diocese of Sydney 1966–2013: The Political Factor." PhD diss., Macquarie University, 2013.
Chilton, Hugh. "Evangelicals and the End of Christian Australia: Nation and Religion in the Public Square 1959–1979." PhD diss., University of Sydney, 2014.
Egan, Paul. "The Development of, and Opposition to, Healing Ministries in the Anglican Diocese of Sydney, with Special Reference to the Healing Ministry at St. Andrew's Cathedral 1960–2010." PhD diss., Macquarie University, 2012.
Frith, Eric William. "The Role of the Laity in Anglican Evangelicalism with Particular Reference to the Diocese of Sydney 1960–1982." Master of Theology Thesis, Charles Sturt University, 2017.
Gray, John Reginald. "Evangelism in the Anglican Diocese of Sydney, 1959–1989." Master's Thesis, UNSW, 1994.
Judd, Stephen. "Defenders of Their Faith: Power and Party in the Anglican Diocese of Sydney, 1909–1938." PhD diss., University of Sydney, 1984.
Kuhn, Chase. "Ecclesiology of Donald Robinson and David Broughton Knox: A Presentation, Analysis and Theological Evaluation of Their Thought on the Nature of the Church." PhD diss., University of Western Sydney, 2014.
Lake, Meredith. "Such Spiritual Acres": Protestantism, the Land and the Colonization of Australia, 1788–1850. PhD diss., University of Sydney, 2008.
Le Couteur, Howard Philip. "Brisbane Anglicans, 1842–1875." PhD diss., Macquarie University, 2006.
McIntosh, John. "Anglican Evangelicalism in Sydney 1897–1953." PhD diss., University of NSW, 2014.
Medeiros, Elias. "'The Reformers' Commitment to the Propagation of the Gospel to all Nations from 1555 to 1654." PhD diss., Reformed Theological Seminary, Mississippi, 2009.
Pipa, Joseph. "William Perkins and the Development of Puritan Preaching." PhD diss., Westminster Theological Seminary, 1985.
Reid, Andrew. "Evangelical Hermeneutics and Old Testament Preaching: A Critical Analysis of Graeme Goldsworthy's Theory and Practice." PhD diss., Ridley College Melbourne, 2011.
Shiner, Rory. "Reading the New Testament in Australia: An Historical Account of the Origins, Development, and Influence of D. W. B. Robinson's Biblical Scholarship." PhD diss., Macquarie University, 2017.

Books and Articles

Adam, Peter. "Preaching of a Lively Kind—Calvin's Engaged Expository preaching." In *Engaging with Calvin: Aspects of the Reformer's Legacy for Today*, edited by Mark D. Thompson, 13–41. Nottingham, Apollos, 2009.

———. "Reflecting on Fifty Years of Expository Preaching in Australia (1965–2015)," May 12, 2016. https://australia.thegospelcoalition.org/article/celebrating-fifty-years-of-expository-preaching-in-australia.

———. *Speaking God's Words. A Practical Theology of Preaching*. Leicester: IVP, 1996.

Ahlstrom, Sydney E. "The Problem of the History of Religion in America." *Church History* 57 (1988) 136.

Alexander, Fred. *Four Bishops and Their See*. Perth: UWP, 1957.

Allen, Pauline. "The Sixth-Century Greek Homily." In *Preacher and Audience: Studies in Early Christian and Byzantine Homiletics*, edited by Mary B. Cunningham and Pauline Allen, 201–26. Leiden: Brill, 1998.

Amador, J. David Hester. *Academic Constraints in Rhetorical Criticism of the New Testament: An Introduction to a Rhetoric of Power*. Sheffield: Sheffield Academic Press, 1999.

Anderson, Allan Heaton. *An Introduction to Pentecostalism*. New York: Cambridge University Press, 2005.

———. "The Pentecostal and Charismatic Movements." In *The Cambridge History of Christianity: World Christianities c. 1914–c.2000*, edited by Hugh McLeod, 89–107. Cambridge: Cambridge University Press, 2006.

———. *To the Ends of the Earth: Pentecostalism and the Transformation of World Christianity*. Oxford: Oxford University Press, 2013.

Anderson, R. Dean. *Ancient Rhetorical Theory and Paul*. Kampen: Kok Pharos, 1996.

Appleby, Joyce, et al. *Telling the Truth About History*. New York: W. W. Norton, 1994.

Aston, Nigel. "Rationalism, The Enlightenment and Sermons." In *The Oxford Handbook of the British Sermon 1689–1901*, edited by Keith A. Francis and William Gibson, 390–405. Oxford: Clarendon, 2012.

Atherstone, Andrew. "Are Sydney Anglicans Fundamentalists?" *St Mark's Review* 226 (November 2013) 1–12.

———. "The Implications of Semper Reformanda." *Anvil* 26, no. 1 (2009) 31–42.

Atherstone, Andrew, and John Maiden. "Anglican Evangelicalism in the Twentieth Century: Identities and Contexts." In *Evangelicalism and the Church of England in the Twentieth Century: Reform, Resistance Renewal*, edited by Andrew Atherstone and John Maiden, 1–47. Suffolk: Boydell, 2014.

Atkinson, Alan. *The Commonwealth of Speech*. Melbourne: Australian Scholarly, 2002.

———. *The Europeans in Australia: A History. Volume One, The Beginning*. New York: Oxford University Press, 1997.

———. *The Europeans in Australia: A History. Volume Two, Democracy*. New York: Oxford University Press, 2004.

———. *The Europeans in Australia: A History. Volume Three, Nation*. Sydney: UNSW Press, 2014.

Avis, Paul. "Prayer Book Use and Conformity." In *The Oxford Handbook of Anglican Studies*, edited by Mark Chapman et al., 125–38. Oxford: Oxford University Press, 2015.

Babbage, Stuart Barton, and Ian Siggins. *Light Beneath the Cross: The Story of Billy Graham's Crusade*. New York: Doubleday, 1960.
Backsheider, Paula R. *Reflections on Biography*. Oxford: Oxford University Press, 2001.
Baird, Julia. "As the Brothers Huddle, the Sisters are Splintered in a Demoralising Dame Drain." *Sydney Morning Herald*, May 27, 2002.
Banks, Robert. "The Theology of D. B. Knox." In *God Who is Rich in Mercy: Essays Presented to Dr. D. B. Knox*, edited by Peter T. O'Brien and David G. Peterson, 377–404. Homebush: Lancer, 1986.
Barclay, Oliver. *Evangelicalism in Britain 1935–1995*. Leicester: IVP, 1997.
Barcan, Alan. *Two Centuries of Education in New South Wales*. Sydney: New South Wales University Press, 1988.
Barkhuizen, Jan H. "Proclus of Constantinople: A Popular Preacher in Fifth-Century Constantinople." In *Preacher and Audience: Studies in Early Christian and Byzantine Homiletics*, edited by Mary B. Cunningham and Pauline Allen, 179–93. Leiden: Brill, 1998.
Barnett, Paul W. "Paul, the Miraculous and Ministry." In *Signs and Wonders and Evangelicals. A Response to the Teaching of John Wimber*, edited by Robert Doyle, 73–100. Homebush West: Lancer, 1987.
Barnett, Paul, and Peter Jensen. *The Quest for Power. Neo-Pentecostals and the New Testament*. Sydney: Anzea, 1973.
Barry, Amanda, et al., eds. *Evangelists of Empire? Missions and Colonialism in Historical Perspective*. Melbourne: University of Melbourne e-Scholarship Research Centre, 2008.
Barth, Karl. *Church Dogmatics, Volume 2.1: The Doctrine of God*. London: T. & T. Clark, 1957.
Bashford, Alison, and Stuart Macintyre. "Introduction." In *The Cambridge History of Australia, Volume 2: The Commonwealth of Australia*, edited by Alison Bashford and Stuart Macintrye, 1–12. New York: Cambridge University Press, 2013.
Bayton, John. *Cross Over Carpentaria: A History of the Church of England in Northern Australia from 1865–1965*. Brisbane: Smith and Paterson, 1965.
Bebbington, David. "The Discipline of History and the Perspective of Faith Since 1900." In *Christ Across the Disciplines: Past, Present, Future*, edited by Roger Lundin, 20–24. Grand Rapids: Eerdmans, 2013.
———. "Evangelical Christianity and Modernism." *Crux* 26, no. 2 (1990) 1–8.
———. "Evangelical Christianity and Romanticism." *Crux* 26, no. 1 (1990) 9–15.
———. *Evangelicalism in Modern Britain*. London: Routledge, 1989.
———. *Victorian Religious Revivals: Culture and Piety in Local and Global Contexts*. Oxford: Oxford University Press, 2012.
Bebbington, David, and David Ceri Jones, eds. *Evangelicalism and Fundamentalism in the United Kingdom during the Twentieth Century*. Oxford: Oxford University Press, 2013.
Beck, James R., ed. *Two Views on Women in Ministry*. Grand Rapids: Zondervan, 2005.
Beckford, James A. *Social Theory and Religion*. Cambridge: Cambridge University Press, 2003.
Beilby, James K., and Paul R. Eddy, eds. *Divine Foreknowledge*. Downers Grove: IVP, 2001.

Berger, Peter L. "The Desecularization of the World: A Global Overview." In *The Desecularization of the World: Resurgent Religion and World Politics*, edited by Peter L. Berger, 1–18. Grand Rapids: Eerdmans, 1999.

———. *The Heretical Imperative: Contemporary Possibilities of Religious Affirmation*. Garden City: Doubleday, 1979.

———. *The Sacred Canopy: Elements of a Sociological Theory of Religion*. New York: Anchor, 1967.

Berger, Peter, et al. *Religious America, Secular Europe? A Theme and Variations*. Aldershot: Ashgate, 2008.

Betz, Hans Dieter. "The Problem of Rhetoric and Theology According to the Apostle Paul." In *L'Apotre Paul: Personalité, Style et Conception du Ministère*, edited by Albert Vanhoye, 127–31. Louvain: Louvain University Press, 1986.

Bevans, Stephen. "Models of Contextual Theology." *Missiology* 13, no. 2 (April 1985) 185–202.

———. *Models of Contextual Theology: Revised and Expanded Edition*. Maryknoll: Orbis, 2002.

Beyerhaus, Peter. "Evangelicals, Evangelism and Theology: An Assessment of the Lausanne Movement." *World Evangelization*, March 1987, 8.

"Billy Graham Activates a Global Electronic Pulpit." https://www.washingtonpost.com/archive/politics/1995/03/14/billy-graham-activates-a-global-electronic-pulpit/.

Birkett, Kirsten, ed. *D. Broughton Knox: Selected Works, Volume II, Church and Ministry*. Kingsford: Matthias, 2003.

Blanch, Allan. *From Strength to Strength: A Life of Marcus Loane*. Melbourne: AS, 2015.

Bleby, Martin. *A Quiet Revival: Geoffrey Bingham in Life and Ministry*. Blackwood: New Creation, 2012.

Bloesch, Donald G. "Karl Barth." In *New Dictionary of Christian Ethics and Pastoral Theology*, edited by David John Atkinson et al., 184–85. Downers Grove: IVP, 1995.

Bock, Darrell L. *Acts*. Grand Rapids: Baker, 2007.

Bollen, J. D., et al. "Australian Religious History, 1960–1980." *Journal of Religious History* 11, no. 1 (1980) 8–44.

Bolt, Peter G. *Thomas Moore of Liverpool: One of Our Oldest Colonists*. Camperdown: Bolt, 2007.

———. "Thomas Moore's Sermon Collection in Its Colonial Context." *St Mark's Review* 230 (December 2014) 14–30.

———. "Timeline: Towards Lay and Diaconal Administration in Sydney Diocese." In *The Lord's Supper in Human Hands. Who Should Administer?*, edited by Peter Bolt et al., 36–67. Camperdown: Australian Church Record, 2008.

———. *William Cowper (1778–1858) the Indispensable Parson: The Life and Influence of Australia's First Parish Clergyman*. Camperdown: Bolt, 2009.

Bolt, Peter G., and Mark D. Thompson, eds. *Donald Robinson: Selected Works. Volume 1, Assembling God's People*. Camperdown: Australian Church Record, 2008.

———. *Donald Robinson: Selected Works. Volume 2, Preaching God's Word*. Camperdown: Australian Church Record, 2008.

Bolton, Geoffrey. *The Oxford History of Australia. Volume 5, 1942–1988*. Melbourne: Oxford University Press, 1990.

Bongiorno, Frank. "Search for a Solution, 1923–39." In *The Cambridge History of Australia, Volume 2: The Commonwealth of Australia*, edited by Alison Bashford and Stuart Macintrye, 64–87. New York: Cambridge University Press, 2013.
Bosch, David J. *Transforming Mission: Paradigm Shifts in the Theology of Mission*. Maryknoll, NY: Orbis, 1991.
———. *Witness to the World: The Christian Mission in Theological Perspective*. Eugene, OR: Wipf & Stock, 2006.
Bouma, Gary. *Australian Soul: Religion and Spirituality in the Twenty-First Century*. Melbourne: Cambridge University Press, 2006.
———. "Religion and Other Ideologies." In *Religion After Secularization in Australia*, edited by Timothy Stanley, 211–20. New York: Palgrave, 2015.
Bradley, James E., and Richard A. Muller. *Church History: An Introduction to Research Methods and Resources*. Grand Rapids: Eerdmans, 2016.
Brady, I. A. "Jubilee of Sydney's Electric Trains." *Australian Railway Historical Bulletin* 27 (March 1976) 41–66.
Braga, Stuart. *A Century Preaching Christ. Katoomba Christian Convention 1903–2003*. Australia: Katoomba Christian Convention, 2003.
———. "Guinness, Howard Wyndham." In *Australian Dictionary of Evangelical Biography*, edited by Brian Dickey, 140–42. Sydney: Evangelical History Association, 1994.
Bray, Gerald. *Biblical Interpretation: Past and Present. Contours of Christian Theology*. Downers Grove: IVP Academic, 2000.
Brenneman, Todd M. "America's Pastor: Billy Graham and the Shaping of a Nation." *Religious Studies Review* 42, no. 2 (June 2016) 133.
Brett, Judith. "The Menzies Era, 1959–66." In *The Cambridge History of Australia, Volume 2: The Commonwealth of Australia*, edited by Alison Bashford and Stuart Macintyre, 112–35. New York: Cambridge University Press, 2013.
Breward, Ian. *A History of the Australian Churches*. St Leonards: Allen and Unwin, 2004.
———. *A History of the Churches in Australasia*. New York: Oxford University Press, 2001.
———. "Learning to Write History for Australian Christians: A Uniting Church Historian Reflects on His Craft." *Uniting Church Studies* 1, no. 1 (April 1995) 47–53.
———. *The Work of William Perkins*. Abingdon: Sutton Courtenay, 1970.
Bridge, Carl. "Australia, Britain and the British Commonwealth." In *The Cambridge History of Australia, Volume 2: The Commonwealth of Australia*, edited by Alison Bashford and Stuart Macintrye, 518–36. New York: Cambridge University Press, 2013.
Broughton, Geoffrey. "The Significance of Biblical Theology." *St Mark's Review* 226 (November 2013) 13–24.
Brower, Kent E. "Eschatology." In *New Dictionary of Biblical Theology*, edited by T. Desmond Alexander and B. S. Rosner, 459–64. Downers Grove: IVP, 2020.
Brown, Callum G. *The Death of Christian Britain: Understanding Secularization 1800–2000*. London: Routledge, 2001.
———. "A Revisionist Approach to Religious Change." In *Religion and Modernization: Sociologists and Historians Debate the Secularization Thesis*, edited by Steve Bruce, 31–58. New York: Oxford University Press, 1992.

———. "What Was the Religious Crisis of the 1960s?" *Journal of Religious History* 34, no. 4 (December 2010) 468–79.

Brown, Callum G., and Michael Snape. "Introduction." In *Secularization in the Christian World: Essays in Honor of Hugh McLeod*, edited by Callum G. Brown and Michael Snape, 1–12. Surrey: Ashgate, 2010.

Brown, Judith M. *Augustus Short*. Adelaide: Hodge, 1974.

Brown, Stewart J. *Thomas Chalmers and the Godly Commonwealth in Scotland*. Oxford: Oxford University Press, 1982.

Bruce, F. F. "Eschatology." In *Evangelical Dictionary of Theology*, edited by Walter A. Elwell, 362–65. Grand Rapids: Baker, 1984.

Bruce, Steve. *God is Dead: Secularization in the West*. Oxford: Blackwell, 2002.

———. "History, Sociology, and Secularization." In *Secularization: New Historical Perspectives*, edited by Christopher Hartney, 190–213. Newcastle Upon Tyne: Scholars, 2014.

———. *Secularization: In Defense of an Unfashionable Theory*. Oxford: Oxford University Press, 2011.

———. "Secularization in the UK and the USA." In *Secularization in the Christian World: Essays in Honor of Hugh McLeod*, edited by Callum G. Brown and Michael Snape, 205–18. Surrey: Ashgate, 2010.

Bruce, Steve, ed. *Religion and Modernization: Sociologists and Historians Debate the Secularization Thesis*. New York: Oxford University Press, 1992.

Brunner, Emil. *The Word and the World*. London: SCM, 1931.

Burgess, Stanley M. "Antecedents of Pentecostalism." In *Encyclopedia of Pentecostal and Charismatic Christianity*, edited by Stanley M. Burgess, 30–33. New York: Routledge, 2006.

Burke, Kelly. "Archbishop Has a New House of God in His Hands." *Sydney Morning Herald*, Saturday June 30, 2001, 7.

Burstein, Miriam Elizabeth. "Anti-Catholic Sermons in Victorian Britain." In *A New History of the Sermon: The Nineteenth Century*, edited by Robert H. Ellison, 233–68. Leiden: Brill, 2010.

Calhoun, Craig, et al., eds. *Rethinking Secularism*. Oxford: Oxford University Press, 2011.

Calvin, John. *Calvin's Sermons on Timothy and Titus*. Edinburgh: Banner of Truth, 1983.

———. *Commentary on the Acts of the Apostles*. Edited by Henry Beveridge. Grand Rapids: Baker, 2009.

———. *Commentary on the Book of the Prophet Isaiah*. Translated by William Pringle. Grand Rapids: Baker, 2009.

———. *Commentary on the Gospel of John*. Edited by Henry Beveridge. Grand Rapids: Baker, 2009.

———. *Commentaries on Timothy, Titus and Philemon*. Translated by William Pringle. Eugene, OR: Wipf & Stock, 2006.

———. *Institutes*. 2 vols. Edited by John T. McNeill and translated by Ford Lewis Battles. 4th ed. Philadelphia: Westminster, 1960.

Cameron, Andrew. *Joined Up Life: A Christian Account of How Ethics Works*. Nottingham: IVP, 2001.

Cameron, Marcia. *An Enigmatic Life: David Broughton Knox, Father of Contemporary Sydney Anglicanism*. Brunswick East: Acorn, 2006.

———. *Phenomenal Sydney: Anglicans in a Time of Change, 1945–2013*. Eugene, OR: Wipf & Stock, 2016.
Carey, Hilary. "An Historical Outline of Religion in Australia." In *The Encyclopedia of Religion in Australia*, edited by James Jupp, 5–21. Cambridge: Cambridge University Press, 2009.
———. *Believing in Australia*. St Leonards: Allen and Unwin, 1996.
———. "Secularism Versus Christianity in Australian History." In *Secularization: New Historical Perspectives*, edited by Christopher Hartney, 8–33. Newcastle Upon Tyne: Scholars, 2014.
Carey, Hilary et al. "Australian Religion Review, 1980–2000." *Journal of Religious History* 24, no. 3 (2000) 302–6.
———. "Australian Religion Review, 1980–2000, Part 1: Surveys, Bibliographies and Religions Other Than Christianity." *Journal of Religious History* 24, no. 3 (2000) 296–313.
———. "Australian Religion Review, 1980–2000, Part 2: Christian Denominations." *Journal of Religious History* 25, no. 1 (2001) 56–82.
Carey, Peter. *Oscar and Lucinda*. St Lucia: University of Queensland Press, 2001.
Carnley Peter. *Reflections in Glass: Trends and Tensions in the Contemporary Anglican Church*. Pymble: Harper Collins, 2004.
Carson, D. A. *Christ and Culture Revisited*. Grand Rapids: Eerdmans, 2008.
———. *The Cross and Christian Ministry: Leadership Lessons from 1 Corinthians*. Grand Rapids: Baker, 2004.
Carson, D. A., and Timothy Keller. "Gospel-Centered Ministry." In *The Gospel As Center: Renewing Our Faith and Reforming Our Ministry Practices*, edited by D. A. Carson and Timothy Keller, 11–23. Wheaton: Crossway, 2012.
Carter, David, and Bridget Griffen-Foley. "Culture and Media." In *The Cambridge History of Australia, Volume 2: The Commonwealth of Australia*, edited by Alison Bashford and Stuart Macintrye, 237–62. New York: Cambridge University Press, 2013.
Cartledge, Mark J. "Charismatic Theology: Approaches and Themes." *Journal of Beliefs and Values* 25, no. 2 (2004) 177–90.
Castagno, Adele Monaci. "Origen the Scholar and Preacher." In *Preacher and Audience: Studies in Early Christian and Byzantine Homiletics*, edited by Mary B. Cunningham and Pauline Allen, 65–88. Leiden: Brill, 1998.
Chan, Sam. *Evangelism in a Skeptical World*. Grand Rapids: Zondervan, 2018.
Chant, Barry. "The Nineteenth and Early Twentieth Century Origins of the Australian Pentecostal Movement." In *Reviving Australia: Essays on the History and Experience of Revival and Revivalism in Australian Christianity*, edited by Mark Hutchinson et al., 97–122. Sydney: Centre for the Study of Australian Christianity, 1994.
Chapel, Bryan. *Christ-Centered Preaching: Redeeming the Expository Sermon*. 2nd ed. Grand Rapids: Baker Academic, 2005.
Chapman, Alister. "Evangelical International Relations in the Post-Colonial World: The Lausanne Movement and the Challenge of Diversity, 1974–89." *Missiology* 37, no. 3 (July 2009) 355–68.
———. *Godly Ambition: John Stott and the Evangelical Movement*. Oxford: Oxford University Press, 2012.

———. "Intellectual History and Religion in Modern Britain." In *Seeing Things Their Way: Intellectual History and the Return of Religion*, edited by Alister Chapman et al., 226–39. Notre Dame: University of Notre Dame Press, 2009.

———. "What Anglican Evangelicals in England Learned from the World, 1945–2000." In *Evangelicalism and the Church of England in the Twentieth Century: Reform, Resistance Renewal*, edited by Andrew Atherstone and John Maiden, 248–67. Suffolk: Boydell, 2014.

Chapman, John. "About the GOZpel! Southern Cross talks with John Chapman about Evangelising Australia." *Southern Cross*, September 1987, 12–14.

———. Director's Commentary on Matthew 28:18–20. *Preaching Christ Newsletter*, November 1989–January 1990, 1–2.

———. "Evangelism Every Sunday". *Evangelical Minister's Assembly 1991*, London England. https://www.proctrust.org.uk/resources/.

———. "Evangelism Today." *Southern Cross*, November 1972, 11.

———. "Evangelism: What? Why? How?" *Christ Cares 1972 Study* 4, 3–4.

———. "Forum on Church Growth." *Southern Cross*, April 1990, 13.

———. *A Foot in Two Worlds*. Kingsford: Matthias, 2009.

———. *A Fresh Start*. Matthias: Kingsford, 2003.

———. *Know and Tell the Gospel*. Matthias: Kingsford, 1998.

———. "Lay Presidency at the Holy Communion." In *Agenda for a Biblical Church: Volume 2, Debates and Issues from the National Evangelical Anglican Congress*, 103–9. Sydney: Anglican Information Office, 1981.

———. *Making the Most of the Bible*. Matthias: Kingsford, 2012.

———. *Making the Most of the Cross*. Matthias: Kingsford, 2011.

———. *Making the Most of the Rest of Your Life*. Kingsford: Matthias, 2007.

———. "Preaching That Converts the World." In *When God's Voice is Heard: Essays on Preaching Presented to Dick Lucas*, edited by Christopher Green and David Jackman, 161–74. Leicester: IVP, 1995.

———. "Regional Evangelism: The Gospel Rubber Hits the Road." *Southern Cross*, December 1984, 11.

———. "Repentance and Faith Every Sunday." *Evangelical Minister's Assembly 1991*, London England. https://www.proctrust.org.uk/resources/.

———. *Setting Hearts on Fire*. Kingsford: Matthias, 1999.

———. *A Sinner's Guide to Holiness*. Kingsford: Matthias, 2005.

———. *St. Helen's School of Evangelism*, 1991. Session 2 "What Should We Do?" http://www.st-helens.org.uk/resources/media-library/src/talk/3376/title/2-what-should-we-do.

Chartier, Roger. *Cultural History: Between Practices and Representations*. Cambridge: Polity, 1988.

Chaves, Mark. *American Religion: Contemporary Trends*. Princeton: Princeton University Press, 2017.

Chavura, Stephen. "'. . . But in Its Proper Place . . .' Religion, Enlightenment, and Australia's Secular Heritage: The Case of Robert Lowe in Colonial NSW 1842–1850." *Journal of Religious History* 38, no. 3 (September 2014) 356–76.

———. "The Secularization Thesis and the Secular State: Reflections with Special Attention to Debates in Australia." In *Religion and the State*, edited by Jack Barbalet et al., 65–92. London: Anthem, 2011.

Chavura, Stephen, and Ian Tregenza. "Introduction: Rethinking Secularism in Australia (and Beyond)." *Journal of Religious History* 38, no. 3 (2014) 299–306.

———. "A Political History of the Secular in Australia, 1788–1945." In *Religion After Secularization in Australia*, edited by Timothy Stanley, 3–26. New York: Palgrave, 2015.

Chester, Tim. *Awakening to a World in Need: The Recovery of Evangelical Social Concern*. Leicester: IVP, 1993.

———. "Social Involvement and Evangelism (Part I): Two Strong Cases." *The Briefing*, January 1, 2005.

Chester, Tim, and Tony Payne. "Social Involvement and Evangelism (Part II): How They Relate." *The Briefing*, February 1, 2005.

Childs, Brevard S. *Biblical Theology in Crisis*. Philadelphia: Westminster, 1970.

———. *The New Testament as Canon*. Philadelphia: Fortress, 1984.

Christie, Nancy, and Michael Gauvreau. "Introduction: 'Even the Hippies Were Only Slowly Going Secular': Dechristianization and the Culture of Individualism in North America and Western Europe." In *The Sixties and Beyond: Dechristianization in North America and Western Europe, 1945–2000*, edited by Nancy Christie and Michael Gauvreau, 3–38. Toronto: University of Toronto Press, 2013.

Christie, Nancy, and Michael Gauvreau, eds. *Sixties and Beyond: Dechristianization in North America and Western Europe, 1945–2000*. Toronto: University of Toronto Press, 2013.

Clark, C. M. H. "Faith." In *Australian Civilization: A Symposium*, edited by Peter Coleman, 78–79. Melbourne: F. W. Cheshire, 1962.

———. *A History of Australia, Volume 1: From the Earliest Times to the Age of Macquarie*. Melbourne: Melbourne University Press, 1962.

———. *A History of Australia Volume 6: The Old Dead Tree and the Young Tree Green 1916–1935*. Melbourne: Melbourne University Press, 1987.

Classen, Carl Joachim. *Rhetorical Criticism of the New Testament*. Tübingen: Mohr Siebeck, 2000.

Clelland, Donald A., et al. "In the Company of the Converted: Characteristics of a Billy Graham Crusade Audience." *Sociology of Religion* 35, no. 1 (1974) 47–49.

Clouse, Robert G. "Views of the Millennium." In *Evangelical Dictionary of Theology*, edited by W. A. Elwell, 714–18. Grand Rapids: Baker, 1984.

Coe, Shoki. "In Search of Renewal in Theological Education." *Theological Education* 9, no. 4 (Summer 1973) 237.

———. *Ministry in Context*. Bromley: Theological Education Fund, 1972.

Coffey, John. "Quentin Skinner and the Religious Dimensions of Early Modern Political Thought." In *Seeing Things Their Way: Intellectual History and the Return of Religion*, edited by Alister Chapman et al., 46–74. Notre Dame: University of Notre Dame Press, 2009.

Cole, Graham. "The Doctrine of Church: Towards Conceptual Clarification." In *Church, Worship and the Local Congregation*, edited by Barry G. Webb, 3–17. Sydney: Lancer, 1987.

Cole, Keith. *A History of the Church Missionary Society of Australia*. Melbourne: Church Missionary Historical, 1971.

———. *History of the Diocese of Bendigo*. Bendigo: Cole, 1991.

Colley, Linda. *Britons. Forging the Nation 1707–1837*. New Haven: Yale University Press, 2005.

Collingwood, Robin George. *An Autobiography*. London: Oxford University Press, 1939.
Collins, John N. *Diakonia Studies: Critical Issues in Ministry*. New York: Oxford University Press, 2014.
Conn, Harvey M. "Contextualization: Where Do We Begin." In *Evangelicals and Liberation*, edited by Carl E. Armerding, 90–119. New Jersey: Presbyterian and Reformed, 1977.
Coote, Robert T. "Lausanne II and World Evangelization." *International Bulletin of Missionary Research* 14, no. 1 (1990) 10–17.
Costas, Orlando. "Depth in Evangelism—An Interpretation of "In-Depth Evangelism" around the World." In *Let the Earth Hear His Voice: International Congress on World Evangelization, Lausanne, Switzerland, Official Reference Volume*, edited by J. D. Douglas, 675–94. Minneapolis: World Wide Publications, 1975.
Cox, Jeffrey. "The Master Narrative of Long-Term Religious Change." In *The Decline of Christendom in Western Europe 1730–2000*, edited by Hugh McLeod and Werner Ustorf, 201–17. Cambridge: Cambridge University Press, 2003.
———. "Towards Eliminating the Concept of Secularization: A Progress Report." In *Secularization in the Christian World: Essays in Honor of Hugh McLeod*, edited by Callum G. Brown and Michael Snape, 13–26. Surrey: Ashgate, 2010.
Craig, William Lane. "Middle Knowledge. A Calvinist-Arminian Rapprochement?" In *The Grace of God, the Will of Man*, edited by Clark H. Pinnock, 141–64. Grand Rapids: Zondervan, 1989.
———. *Reasonable Faith: Christian Truth and Apologetics*. 3rd ed. Crossway: Wheaton, 2008.
Cruickshank, Joanna. "The Sermon in the British Colonies." In *The Oxford Handbook of the British Sermon 1689–1901*, edited by Keith A. Francis et al., 513–29. Oxford: Clarendon, 2012.
Cunningham, Mary B., and Pauline Allen, eds. *Preacher and Audience: Studies in Early Christian and Byzantine Homiletics*. Leiden: Brill, 1998.
Curthoys, Ann, and John Docker. *Is History Fiction?* Sydney: UNSW Press, 2010.
Curthoys, Ann, and Ann McGrath. *How to Write History That People Want to Read*. Sydney: UNSW Press, 2009.
Dallimore, Arnold A. *George Whitefield*. Wheaton: Crossway, 1990.
Damousi, Joy. *Colonial Voices: A Cultural History of English in Australia 1840–1940*. Cambridge: Cambridge University Press, 2010.
Darian-Smith, Kate. "World War 2 and Post-War Reconstruction, 1939–49." In *The Cambridge History of Australia, Volume 2: The Commonwealth of Australia*, edited by Alison Bashford and Stuart Macintrye, 88–111. New York: Cambridge University Press, 2013.
Dargan, Edwin Charles. *A History of Preaching: From the Apostolic Fathers to the Great Reformers A.D. 70–1572*. Vol. 1. Harvard: Armstrong, 1905.
———. *A History of Preaching: From the Close of the Reformation Period to the End of the Nineteenth Century 1572–1900*. Vol. 2. Harvard: Armstrong, 1954.
Davie, Grace. *Europe: The Exceptional Case, Parameters of Faith in the Modern World*. London: Longman and Todd, 2002.
———. "Thinking Broadly and Thinking Deeply: Two Examples of the Study of Religion in the Modern World." In *Secularization in the Christian World: Essays in*

Honor of Hugh McLeod, edited by Callum G. Brown and Michael Snape, 219–31. Surrey: Ashgate, 2010.

Davies, Glenn. "The Authorisation of a Deacon to Administer the Holy Communion." In *The Lord's Supper in Human Hands: Who Should Administer?*, edited by Peter Bolt et al., 68–76. Camperdown: Australian Church Record, 2008.

———. "Dialogue Evangelism." *Southern Cross*, November 1993, 35.

Davies, Horton. *Like Angels from a Cloud: The Metaphysical Preachers, 1588–1645*. Eugene, OR: Wipf & Stock, 2004.

———. *Varieties of English Preaching 1900–1960*. London: SCM, 1963.

———. *Worship and Theology in England, Volume 1: From Cranmer to Hooker 1534–1603*. Grand Rapids: Eerdmans, 1996.

———. *Worship and Theology in England, Volume 2: 1603–1690*. Grand Rapids: Eerdmans, 1996.

Davis, John. *Australian Anglicans and Their Constitutions*. Canberra: Acorn, 1993.

Davison, Graeme. *Narrating the Nation in Australia*. Menzies Lecture, 2009. London: Menzies Centre for Australian Studies, University of London, 2010.

———. "Religion." In *The Cambridge History of Australia, Volume 2: The Commonwealth of Australia*, edited by Alison Bashford and Stuart Macintyre, 215–36. New York: Cambridge University Press, 2013.

De Koster, Lester. *Light for the City: Calvin's Preaching, Source of Life and Liberty*. Grand Rapids: Eerdmans, 2004.

De Quetteville Robin, Arthur. *Charles Perry, Bishop of Melbourne: The Challenges of a Colonial Episcopate, 1847–76*. Perth: UWAP, 1967.

Deconinck-Brossard, Françoise. "The Art of Preaching." In *Preaching, Sermon and Cultural Change in the Long Eighteenth Century*, edited by Joris van Eijnatten, 95–132. Leiden, Boston, 2009.

Dickey, Brian. "Delbridge, Graham." In *Australian Dictionary of Evangelical Biography*, edited by Brian Dickey, 92–93. Sydney: Evangelical History Association, 1994.

———. "Evangelical Anglicans Compared: Australia and Britain." In *Amazing Grace: Evangelicalism in Australia, Britain, Canada and the United States*, edited by George A. Rawlyk and Mark A. Noll, 215–40. Grand Rapids: Baker, 1993.

———. "Knox, David Broughton (1916–1994)." In *Australian Dictionary of Evangelical Biography*, edited by Brian Dickey, 206–7. Sydney: Evangelical History Association, 1994.

———. "Knox, David James (1875–1960)." In *Australian Dictionary of Evangelical Biography*, edited by Brian Dickey, 205–6. Sydney: Evangelical History Association, 1994.

———. *No Charity There: A Short History of Social Welfare in Australia*. Sydney: Allen & Unwin, 1987.

Dickson, John. "Players in God's Passion." *Southern Cross*, March 1998, 21–23.

———. *Promoting the Gospel: A Practical Guide to the Biblical Art of Sharing Your Faith*. Sydney: Bluebottle, 2005.

———. *Simply Christianity*. Kingsford: Matthias, 1998.

Dickson, John P. "Gospel as News: εὐαγγέλ—From Aristophanes to the Apostle Paul." *New Testament Studies* 51, no. 2 (2005) 212–30.

———. *Mission-Commitment in Ancient Judaism and in the Pauline Communities*. Tübingen: Mohr Siebeck, 2003.

Dodd, C. H. *The Apostolic Preaching and Its Developments*. New York: Harper, 1936.

Douglas, J. D. "Christian Socialism." In *Evangelical Dictionary of Theology*, edited by Walter A. Elwell, 1029. Grand Rapids: Baker, 1984.
Doyle, Robert. "A Response to Graham Cole's Paper." In *Church, Worship and the Local Congregation*, edited by Barry G. Webb, 19–25. Sydney: Lancer, 1987.
Doyle, Robert C. *Eschatology and the Shape of Christian Belief*. Carlisle: Paternoster, 1999.
Drummond, Lewis A. *The Evangelist: The Worldwide Impact of Billy Graham*. Nashville: Word, 2001.
Dudley-Smith, Timothy. *John Stott: A Global Ministry*. Leicester: Inter-Varsity, 2001.
———. *John Stott: Making of a Leader*. Leicester: Inter-Varsity, 1999.
Duffecy, James A. "Field, Edward Percy (1855–1928)." *Australian Dictionary of Biography*. National Centre of Biography, Australian National University. http://adb.anu.edu.au/biography/field-edward-percy-6167.
Dulles, Avery. *A History of Apologetics*. San Francisco: Ignatius, 2005.
Durston, Christopher, and Jacqueline Eales. "The Puritan Ethos 1560–1700." In *The Culture of English Puritanism 1560–1700*, edited by Christopher Durston and Jacqueline Eales, 9–13. London: Macmillan, 1996.
Eddison, John. "Introduction." In *Bash: A Study in Spiritual Power*, edited by John Eddison, vii–ix. Basingstoke: Iwerne Trust, 1982.
Edwards, David L., and John R. W Stott. *Evangelical Essentials: A Liberal-Evangelical Dialogue*. Downers Grove: Intervarsity, 1988.
Edwards, O. C., Jr. *A History of Preaching*. Nashville: Abingdon, 2004.
———. "Varieties of Sermon: A Survey." In *Preaching, Sermon and Cultural Change in the Long Eighteenth Century*, edited by Joris Van Eijnatten, 3–57. Leiden: Brill, 2009.
Edwards, Trevor. "Responding to 'The Romance of Preaching the Sydney Sermon.'" *St Mark's Review* 226 (November 2013) 36–47.
Eijnatten, Joris van, ed. *Preaching, Sermon and Cultural Change in the Long Eighteenth Century*. Leiden: Brill, 2009.
Elkin, Adolphus Peter. *The Diocese of Newcastle: A History*. Newcastle: Australian Medical, 1955.
Ellis, David. *Literary Lives. Biography and the Search for Understanding*. 2nd ed. New York: Routledge, 2002.
Ellis, E. Earle. "Paul and His Co-Workers." In *Prophecy and Hermeneutic in Early Christianity*, 3–22. Grand Rapids: Eerdmans, 1978.
———. *Prophecy and Hermeneutic in Early Christianity*. Grand Rapids: Eerdmans, 1978.
Ellison, Robert H. "Introduction." In *A New History of the Sermon: The Nineteenth Century*, edited by Robert H. Ellison, 1–14. Leiden: Brill, 2010.
———. *A New History of the Sermon: The Nineteenth Century*. Leiden: Brill, 2010.
Ely, Richard. "'Anglican' Religious Culture and 'Anglo-Australian' Religious Culture: A Comment on David Hilliard's Paper." *Australian Cultural History* (1988) 82–85.
———. "The Forgotten Nationalism." *Journal of Australian Studies* 20 (May 1987) 59–67.
———. "Now You See It: Now You Don't! Issues of Secularity and Secularization in Publicly Funded Elementary Schools in the Australian Colonies during the Middle Third of the Nineteenth Century." *Journal of Religious History* 38, no. 3 (September 2014) 377–97.

―――. "Secularization and the Sacred in Australian History." *Historical Studies* 19, no. 77 (1981) 553–56.

Emery, Ossie, et al. *The Delbridge Years: Youth Work in the Anglican Diocese of Sydney from 1942–1952*. Sydney South: Anglican Press Australia, 2012.

Erdozain, Dominic. "'Cause is Not Quite What it Used to Be': The Return of Secularization." *English Historical Review* 127, no. 525 (2012) 377–400.

―――. "Godly Ambition: John Stott and the Evangelical Movement." *The Journal of Ecclesiastical History* 64 (2013) 668–69.

Erickson, Millard J. *Christian Theology*. 2nd ed. Grand Rapids: Baker, 1998.

Escobar, Samuel. "Evangelism and Man's Search for Freedom, Justice and Fulfilment." In *Let the Earth Hear His Voice: International Congress on World Evangelization, Lausanne, Switzerland, Official Reference Volume*, edited by J. D. Douglas, 303–26. Minneapolis: World Wide Publications, 1975.

Evans, Richard J. *In Defence of History*. London: Granta, 1997.

Fee, Gordon D. *Paul's Letter to the Philippians*. Grand Rapids: Eerdmans, 1995.

Fee, Gordon D., and Douglas Stuart. *How to Read the Bible for All its Worth*. Grand Rapids: Zondervan, 2014.

Fenn, Richard K. *Beyond Idols*. Oxford: Oxford University Press, 2001.

Finke, Roger, and Rodney Stark. *The Churching of America, 1776–2005: Winners and Losers in our Religious Economy*. New Brunswick: Rutgers University Press, 2005.

Fitzgerald, Thomas E. *The Ecumenical Movement. An Introductory History*. Westport: Greenwood, 2004.

Fitzmyer, Joseph A. *The Acts of the Apostles*. Anchor. New Haven: Yale University Press, 1998.

Fitzpatrick, Martin. "Latitudinarianism at the Parting of the Ways." In *The Church of England c.1689–c.1833: From Toleration to Tractarianism*, edited by John Walsh, 209–27. Cambridge: Cambridge University Press, 1993.

Fletcher, Brian H. "The Anglican Ascendancy 1788–1835." In *Anglicanism in Australia: A History*, edited by Bruce Kaye, 7–30. Carlton: Melbourne University Press, 2002.

―――. "Anglicanism and Nationalism in Australia, 1901–1962." *Journal of Religious History* 23, no. 2 (1999) 215–33.

―――. "Christianity and Free Society in NSW, 1788–1840." *Journal of the Royal Australian Historical Society* 86 (2000) 93–113.

―――. "The Diocese of Sydney and the Shaping of Australian Anglicanism: 1900–1962." In *Making History for God*, edited by Geoffrey R. Treloar and Robert D. Linder, 111–32. Sydney: Robert Menzies, 2004.

Ford, James Thomas. "Preaching in the Reformed Tradition." In *Preachers and People in the Reformations and Early Modern Period*, edited by Larissa Taylor, 65–88. Leiden: Brill, 2003.

Forrester, Duncan. "Wealth and Poverty." In *The Cambridge History of Christianity: World Christianities c. 1914–c.2000*, edited by Hugh McLeod, 514–33. Cambridge: Cambridge University Press, 2006.

Forsyth, Robert. "Are Sydney Anglicans Actually Anglicans?" *St Mark's Review* 226, no. 4 (November 2013) 59–70.

Foster, Tim. *The Suburban Captivity of the Church: Contextualizing the Gospel for Post-Christian Australia*. Moreland: Acorn, 2014.

Foucault, Michel. "Nietzsche, Genealogy, History." In *The Foucault Reader*, edited by Paul Rabinow. London: Penguin, 1991.

Foulkes, Francis. "The Church and Evangelism: A Rejoinder." *Interchange* 17 (1975) 26–33.

Frame, John M. *Apologetics: A Justification of Christian Belief.* 2nd ed. Phillipsburg: P&R, 2015.

Frame, Tom. "Anglicans: Anglican History, Beliefs and Practices." In *The Encyclopedia of Religion in Australia*, edited by James Jupp, 120–28. Cambridge: Cambridge University Press, 2009.

———. *Anglicans in Australia.* Sydney: UNSW Press, 2007.

———. *A Church for a Nation: The History of the Anglican Diocese of Canberra and Goulburn.* Alexandria: Hale and Iremonger, 2000.

———. *Losing My Religion: Unbelief in Australia.* Sydney: UNSW Press, 2009.

———. "Preaching on National Commemorations." *St Mark's Review* 227 (February 2014) 16–20.

Frame, Tom, and Geoff Treloar, eds. *Agendas for Australian Anglicanism.* Adelaide: ATF, 2006.

France, Peter, and William St. Clair. "Introduction." In *Mapping Lives. The Uses of Biography*, edited by Peter France and William St. Clair, 1–5. Oxford: Oxford University Press, 2002.

France, Peter, and William St. Clair, eds. *Mapping Lives. The Uses of Biography.* Oxford: Oxford University Press, 2002.

Francis, Keith A. "Nineteenth-Century British Sermons on Evolution and The Origin of Species: The Dog That Didn't Bark?" In *A New History of the Sermon: The Nineteenth Century*, edited by Robert H. Ellison, 269–308. Leiden: Brill, 2010.

———. "Paley to Darwin: Natural Theology Versus Science in Victorian Sermons." In *The Oxford Handbook of the British Sermon 1689–1901*, edited by Keith A. Francis and William Gibson, 445–59. Oxford: Clarendon, 2012.

———. "Sermon Studies: Major Issues and Future Directions." In *The Oxford Handbook of the British Sermon 1689–1901*, edited by Keith A. Francis and William Gibson, 611–30. Oxford: Clarendon, 2012.

———. "Sermons: Themes and Developments." In *The Oxford Handbook of the British Sermon 1689–1901*, edited by Keith A. Francis and William Gibson, 31–46. Oxford: Clarendon, 2012.

Francis, Keith A., and Robert J. Surridge. "Sermons for End Times: Evangelicalism, Romanticism, and Apocalypse in Britain." In *The Oxford Handbook of the British Sermon 1689–1901*, edited by Keith A. Francis and William Gibson, 374–85. Oxford: Clarendon, 2012.

Frappell, Ruth. "Imperial Fervor and Anglican Loyalty 1901–1929." In *Anglicanism in Australia: A History*, edited by Bruce Kaye, 76–99. Carlton: Melbourne University Press, 2002.

Frappell, Samantha. "Post-War Revivalism in Australia: The Mission to the Nation, 1953–1957." In *Reviving Australia: Essays on the History and Experience of Revival and Revivalism in Australian Christianity*, edited by Mark Hutchinson et. al, 249–61. Sydney: Centre for the Study of Australian Christianity, 1994.

Gaden, John. "An Australian Theology?" *Bulletin of Australian Studies* 2 (1985) 22–23.

Garton, Stephen, and Peter Stanley. "The Great War and Its Aftermath, 1914–22." In *The Cambridge History of Australia, Volume 2: The Commonwealth of Australia*, edited by Alison Bashford and Stuart Macintrye, 39–63. New York: Cambridge University Press, 2013.

Gascoigne, John. *The Enlightenment and the Origins of European Australia.* Cambridge: Cambridge University Press, 2002.

———. "Introduction: Religion and Empire, an Historiographical Perspective." *Journal of Religious History* 32, no. 2 (2008) 159–78.

———. "The Unity of Church and State Challenged: Responses to Hooker from the Restoration to the Nineteenth Century Age of Reform." *Journal of Religious History* 21, no. 1 (February 1997) 60–79.

Gascoigne, John, and Hilary M. Carey. "Introduction." In *Church and State in Old and New Worlds*, edited by Hilary M. Carey and John Gascoigne, 1–30. Leiden: Brill, 2011.

George, Timothy. *Theology of the Reformers.* Nashville: Broadman, 1988.

Gibson, William. "The British Sermon 1689–1901: Quantities, Performance, and Culture." In *The Oxford Handbook of the British Sermon 1689–1901*, edited by Keith A. Francis and William Gibson, 3–31. Oxford: Clarendon, 2012.

Giles, Kevin. "Michael Jensen and the Bible as Propositional Revelation Only." *St Mark's Review* 226 (November 2013) 25–35.

Gilliland, Dean S. "Appendix: Contextualization Models." In *The Word Among Us: Contextualizing Theology for Mission Today*, edited by Dean S. Gilliland, 313–17. Dallas: Word, 1989.

Gilliland, Dean S., ed. *The Word Among Us: Contextualizing Theology for Today.* Dallas: Word, 1989.

Gladwin, Michael. *Anglican Clergy in Australia, 1788–1850: Building a British World.* Woodbridge: Royal Historical Society & Boydel, 2015.

———. "Editorial." *St Mark's Review* 230 (December 2014) v–x.

———. "The Journalist in the Rectory: Anglican Clergymen and Australian Intellectual Life, 1788–1850." *History Australia* 7 (2010) 1–28.

———. "Mission and Colonialism." In *The Oxford Handbook of Nineteenth-Century Christian Thought*, edited by Joel D. S. Rasmussen et al., 282–304. Oxford: Oxford University Press, 2017.

———. "Preaching and Australian Public Life: 1788–1914." *St Mark's Review* 227 (February 2014) 1–14.

Glasser, Arthur. "Salvation Today and the Kingdom." In *Crucial Issues in Mission Tomorrow*, edited by Donald McGavran, 33–53. Chicago: Moody, 1972.

Glennon, Jim. *Your Healing is Within You: An Introduction to Christian Healing.* London: Hodder and Stoughton, 1978.

Goldman, Lawrence. "Contemporary and Historical Biography: The Oxford Dictionary of National Biography 2004–14: A Ten-Year Review." *Historian* 121 (Spring 2014) 14–18.

Goldsworthy, Graeme. *Christ-Centered Biblical Theology: Hermeneutical Foundations and Principles.* Downers Grove: IVP, 2012.

———. *The Goldsworthy Trilogy.* Carlisle: Paternoster, 2003.

———. *Gospel-Centered Hermeneutics: Biblical-Theological Foundations.* Nottingham: Apollos, 2006.

———. *Preaching the Whole Bible as Christian Scripture: The Application of Biblical Theology to Expository Preaching.* Leicester: IVP, 2000.

Gordon, Colin, ed. *Michel Foucault, Power/Knowledge: Selected Interviews and Other Writings 1972–1977.* New York: Pantheon, 1980.

Graham, Billy. "Why Lausanne?" In *Let the Earth Hear His Voice: International Congress on World Evangelization, Lausanne, Switzerland, Official Reference Volume*, edited by J. D. Douglas, 22–36. Minneapolis: World Wide Publications, 1975.

Grant, James. *Episcopally Led and Synodically Governed: Anglicans in Victoria, 1803-1997*. Melbourne: ASP, 2010.

Green, Christopher. "Preaching that Shapes a Ministry." In *When God's Voice is Heard: Essays on Preaching Presented to Dick Lucas*, edited by Christopher Green and David Jackman, 11–23. Leicester: IVP, 1995.

Green, Ian. "Preaching in the Parishes." In *The Oxford Handbook of The Early Modern Sermon*, edited by Peter McCullough et al. 137–54. Oxford: Oxford University Press, 2011.

———. *Print and Protestantism in Early Modern England*. Oxford: Oxford University Press, 2000.

Green, Michael. "Methods and Strategy in the Evangelism of the Early Church." In *Let the Earth Hear His Voice: International Congress on World Evangelization, Lausanne, Switzerland, Official Reference Volume*, edited by J. D. Douglas, 159–80. Minneapolis: World Wide Publications, 1975.

Greenwood, Gordon. *Australia: A Social and Political History*. Sydney: Angus and Robertson, 1972.

Greidanus, Sidney. *The Modern Preacher and the Ancient Text*. Leicester: IVP, 1988.

Grenz, Stanley J., and Denise Muir Kjesbo, eds. *Women in the Church: A Biblical Theology of Women in Ministry*. Downers Grove: IVP, 1995.

Grider, J. Kenneth. "Arminianism." In *Evangelical Dictionary of Theology*, edited by Walter A. Elwell, 79–81. Grand Rapids: Baker, 1984.

Grimshaw, Patricia et al. *Creating a Nation: 1788-1990*. Melbourne: McPhee Gribble, 1994.

Gunson, Neil. "Preaching in Victoria's Congregational Churches in the Early 20th Century." *St Mark's Review* 230 (December 2014) 51–59.

Halsall, Guy. *Barbarian Migrations and the Roman West, 376-568*. Cambridge: Cambridge University Press, 2007.

Hammond, T. C. *In Understanding Be Men*. Leicester: IVP, 1968.

Hansen, Collin. "Stott Life Portrait: A New Biography Portrays Both the Evangelist's Triumphs and His Frustrations." *Christianity Today* (February 1, 2012) 47–49.

Harris, Bruce. "Gospel and Church: A Response." *Southern Cross*, July 1991, 10, 25.

Harris, Rex, et al. "Memories of the Delbridge Years." In *The Delbridge Years: Youth Work in the Anglican Diocese of Sydney from 1942-1952*, 43–60. Sydney South: Anglican Press Australia, 2012.

Hartney, Christopher. "States of Ultimacy and the Cult of the Dead Soldier: The Anzac Tradition, the Secularization Paradigm, the Charisma of Materiality, and Civil Religion as It Is Embodied in the Australian War Memorial, Canberra." In *Secularization: New Historical Perspectives*, edited by Christopher Hartney, 214–50. Newcastle Upon Tyne: Scholars, 2014.

Hay, J. R. "The Institute of Public Affairs and Social Policy in World War II." *Historical Studies* 20, no. 79 (2008) 198–216.

Heath, Malcolm. "Codifications of Rhetoric." In *The Cambridge Companion to Ancient Rhetoric*, edited by Erik Gunderson, 59–76. Cambridge: Cambridge University Press, 2009.

Hedlund, Roger E. *Roots of the Great Debate in Mission*. Bangalore: TBT, 1993.

Hein, Jennifer. "'Decently and in Good Order': The Salvation Army in Nineteenth Century South Australia as an Example of the Interface Between Religion and Secular Society." In *Secularization: New Historical Perspectives*, edited by Christopher Hartney, 58–67. Newcastle Upon Tyne: Scholars, 2014.

Hemer, Colin J. "The Speeches of Acts: II. The Areopagus Address." *Tyndale Bulletin* 40 (1989) 239–59.

Hempton, David. "Protestant Migrations: Narratives of the Rise and Decline of Religion in the North Atlantic World c. 1650–1950." In *Secularization in the Christian World: Essays in Honor of Hugh McLeod*, edited by Callum G. Brown and Michael Snape, 41–56. Surrey: Ashgate, 2010.

Hengel, Martin. *The Pre-Christian Paul*. Valley Forge: Trinity International, 1991.

Hesselgrave, David J. "The Contextualization Continuum." *Gospel in Context* 2, no. 3 (July 1979) 4–11.

———. *Paradigms in Conflict: 10 Key Questions in Christian Missions Today*. Grand Rapids: Kregel, 2005.

Hesselgrave, David J., and Ed Rommen, eds. *Contextualization: Meanings, Methods, and Models*. Leicester: IVP, 1989.

Hewetson, D. "Not Shepherds but Coaches. The Consecration of Rt. Rev. Kenneth H. Short, 1 April 1975." *Southern Cross*, May 1975, 12–13.

Hewitt, Martin. "Preaching from the Platform." In *The Oxford Handbook of the British Sermon 1689–1901*, edited by Keith A. Francis and William Gibson, 78–98. Oxford: Clarendon, 2012.

Hilliard, David. "Anglicanism." In *Australian Cultural History*, edited by F. Smith and S. Goldberg, 15–32. Melbourne: Cambridge University Press, 1988.

———. "Anglicans: Church of England in Australia." In *The Encyclopedia of Religion in Australia*, edited by James Jupp, 128–40. Cambridge: Cambridge University Press, 2009.

———. "Australia: Towards Secularization and One Step Back." In *Secularization in the Christian World: Essays in Honor of Hugh McLeod*, edited by Callum G. Brown and Michael Snape, 75–92. Surrey: Ashgate, 2010.

———. "'God in the Suburbs': The Religious Culture of Australian Cities in the 1950s." *Australian Historical Studies* 24, no. 97 (1991) 399–419.

———. *Godliness and Good Order: A History of the Anglican Church in South Australia*. Adelaide: Wakefield, 1986.

———. "Pluralism and New Alignments in Society and Church 1967 to the Present." In *Anglicanism in Australia: A History*, edited by Bruce Kaye, 124–48. Melbourne: MUP, 2002.

———. "The Religious Crisis of the 1960s: The Experience of the Australian Churches." *Journal of Religious History* 21, no. 2 (June 1997) 209–27.

———. "Round the Churches with Quiz." *St Mark's Review* 230 (December 2014) 1–13.

Himmelfarb, Gertrude. *The New History and the Old: Critical Essays and Reappraisals*. 2nd ed. Cambridge: Harvard University Press, 2004.

Hocken, Peter D. "Charismatic Movement." In *The New International Dictionary of Pentecostal and Charismatic Movements*, edited by Stanley M. Burgess, 477–519. Grand Rapids: Zondervan, 2002.

Hoekema, Anthony A. *The Bible and the Future*. Grand Rapids: Eerdmans, 1994.

———. *Saved By Grace*. Grand Rapids: Eerdmans, 1991.

Holden, Colin, ed., *People of the Past? The Culture of Melbourne Anglicanism and Anglicanism in Melbourne's Culture, 1847-1997*. Melbourne: University of Melbourne, 2000.

Holland, Tom. *Dominion. The Making of the Western Mind*. London: Little Brown, 2019.

Hollenweger, Walter J. *Pentecostalism. Origins and Development Worldwide*. Peabody: Hendrickson, 1997.

Hollow, Matthew. "Introducing the Historian to History: Autobiographical Performances in Historical Texts." *Rethinking History* 13, no. 1 (2009) 43-52.

Holmes, Richard. "The Proper Study?" In *Mapping Lives. The Uses of Biography*, edited by Peter France and William St. Clair, 7-8. Oxford: Oxford University Press, 2002.

Hölscher, Lucian. "Europe in the Age of Secularization." In *Secularization in the Christian World: Essays in Honor of Hugh McLeod*, edited by Callum G. Brown and Michael Snape, 197-204. Surrey: Ashgate, 2010.

Holt, Jonathan. "The Emergence of Expository Preaching in Sydney Anglican Churches." *St Mark's Review* 230 (December 2014) 72-83.

Hoover, A. J. "Apologetics." In *Evangelical Dictionary of Theology*, edited by Walter A. Elwell, 69-70. Grand Rapids: Baker, 1984.

Horsburgh, Michael. "Government and Social Welfare." *Interchange* 43 (1988): 41-46.

Horner, David. "Australia in 1942: A Pivotal Year." In *Australia 1942: In the Shadow of War*, edited by Peter J. Dean, 11-31. Cambridge: Cambridge University Press, 2013.

Howard, Donald. "Blood, Sweat and Tears." In *Preach or Perish: Reaching the Hearts and Minds of the World Today*, edited by Donald Howard, 131-41. Camden: Kingsgrove, 2008.

Hudson, Wayne. *Australian Religious Thought*. Clayton: Monash University Publishing, 2016.

Hughes, Frank Witt. *Early Christian Rhetoric and 2 Thessalonians*. Sheffield: Sheffield Academic, 1989.

Hunt, Arnold. "Preaching the Elizabethan Settlement." In *The Oxford Handbook of The Early Modern Sermon*, edited by Peter McCullough et al. 366-86. Oxford: Oxford University Press, 2011.

Hunt, Keith, and Gladys Hunt. "A Double Portion of Language Skills." In *John Stott: A Portrait by His Friends*, edited by Chris Wright, 89-91, Leicester: IVP, 2011.

Hunt, Lynn. "French History in the Last Twenty Years: The Rise and Fall of the *Annales* Paradigm." *Journal of Contemporary History* 21 (1986) 209-24.

Hunt, Robert A. "The History of the Lausanne Movement, 1974-2010." *International Bulletin of Missionary Research* 35, no. 2 (2011) 81-84.

Hutch, Richard A. *Biography, Autobiography, and the Spiritual Quest*. London: Continuum, 2000.

Hutchison, Mark. "Australia." In *New International Dictionary of Pentecostal and Charismatic Movements*, edited by Stanley M. Burgess, 26-29. Grand Rapids: Zondervan, 2002.

———. "Dain, Arthur John 'Jack' (1912-2003)." ADEB Online, www.webjournals.ac.edu.au.

———. "Pentecostals." In *The Encyclopedia of Religion in Australia*, edited by James Jupp, 517-23. Cambridge: Cambridge University Press, 2009.

Hutchinson Mark, and John Wolffe. *A Short History of Global Evangelicalism*. Cambridge: Cambridge University Press, 2012.

Ihalainen, Pasi. "The Enlightenment Sermon: Towards Practical Religion and a Sacred National Community." In *Preaching, Sermon and Cultural Change in the Long Eighteenth Century*, edited by Joris Van Eijnatten, 219–62. Leiden: Brill, 2009.
Inglis, Ken. *Speechmaking in Australian History*. Canberra: Allan Martin Lecture, 2007.
Israel, Kali. "Changing the Place of Narrative in Biography: From Form to Method." *Life Writing* 7, no. 1 (April 2010) 5–14.
Jackson, Hugh. *Australians and the Christian God*. Melbourne: Mosaic, 2013.
———. "White Man Got No Dreaming: Religious Feeling in Australian History." *Journal of Religious History* 15, no. 1 (1988) 1–11.
Jarrott, Reginald E. "Australasia." In *One Race, One Gospel, One Task: World Congress on Evangelism, Berlin 1966, Official Reference Volumes, Volume 1*, edited by Carl Henry and W. Stanley Mooneyham, 236–38. Minneapolis: World Wide Publications, 1967.
Jenkins, Keith, ed. *The Postmodern History Reader*. London: Routledge, 1997.
Jenkins, Philip. *The Next Christendom: The Coming of Global Christianity*. 3rd ed. Oxford: Oxford University Press, 2011.
Jensen, Michael. "Sydney Anglicanism: A Response." *St Mark's Review* 226 (November 2013) 112–26.
Jensen, Michael P. *Sydney Anglicanism: An Apology*. Eugene, OR: Wipf & Stock, 2012.
Jensen, Peter. *The Revelation of God*. Leicester: IVP, 2002.
———. "True Spirituality." https://phillipjensen.com/sermons/true-spirituality.
Jensen, Peter F. "Broughton Knox on Training for the Ministry." In *D. Broughton Knox: Selected Works, Volume 1, The Doctrine of God*, edited by Tony Payne, 21–36. Kingsford: Matthias, 2000.
Jensen, Phillip, and Sam Freney. "Majoring on the Majors: Phillip Jensen on John Chapman." Interview, March 25, 2013. http://matthiasmedia.com/briefing/2013/03/interview-majoring-on-the-majors/.
Johnson, Norris R., et al. "Attendance at a Billy Graham Crusade: A Resource Mobilization Approach." *Sociology of Religion* 45, no. 4 (1984) 300–309.
Judd, Stephen. "Church Politics and the Anglican Church League." *St Mark's Review* 226 (November 2013) 102–11.
———. "Robert Brodribb Hammond." In *Australian Dictionary of Evangelical Biography*, edited by Brian Dickey, 148–50. Sydney: Evangelical History Association, 1994.
Judd, Stephen, and Kenneth Cable. *Sydney Anglicans: A History of the Diocese*. Sydney: Anglican Information Office, 1987.
Judd, Stephen, and Brian Dickey. "Wright, John Charles (1861–1935)." In *Australian Dictionary of Evangelical Biography*, edited by Brian Dickey, 412–13. Sydney: Evangelical History Association, 1994.
Judge, Edwin Arthur. "Paul's Boasting in Relation to Contemporary Professional Practice." *Australian Biblical Review* 16 (1968) 37–50.
———. "The Religion of the Secularists." *Journal of Religious History* 38, no. 3 (September 2014) 307–19.
Judge, Edwin Arthur, and David M. Scholer. *Social Distinctives of the Christians in the First Century*. Grand Rapids: Baker, 2008.
Julian, Ruth. "Ground Level Contextualization." In *Local Theology for the Global Church: Principles for an Evangelical Approach to Contextualization*, edited by Matthew Cook et al., 57–75. Pasadena: World Evangelical Alliance, 2010.

Jupp, James. "Anglican Catholic Church." In *The Encyclopedia of Religion in Australia*, edited by James Jupp, 118–19. Cambridge: Cambridge University Press, 2009.

———. "Introduction." In *The Encyclopaedia of Religion in Australia*, edited by James Jupp, 1–4. Cambridge: Cambridge University Press, 2009.

———. "The Social Role of Religion." In *The Encyclopedia of Religion in Australia*, edited by James Jupp, 28–40. Cambridge: Cambridge University Press, 2009.

———. "Time, Place and Social Status." In *The Encyclopedia of Religion in Australia*, edited by James Jupp, 41–52. Cambridge: Cambridge University Press, 2009.

Kärkkäinen, Veli-Matti. *An Introduction to Ecclesiology: Ecumenical, Historical and Global Perspectives*. Downers Grove: IVP, 2009.

Kato, Byang H. "The Gospel, Contextualization and Syncretism." In *Let the Earth Hear His Voice: International Congress on World Evangelization, Lausanne, Switzerland, Official Reference Volume*, edited by J. D. Douglas, 1216–24. Minneapolis: World Wide Publications, 1975.

Kaye, Bruce. *A Church Without Walls*. Blackburn, Victoria: Dove, 1995.

———. "The Emergence and Character of Australian Anglican Identity." In *Anglicanism in Australia: A History*, edited by Bruce Kaye, 154–76. Carlton: Melbourne University Press, 2002.

Kaye, Bruce, ed. *Anglicanism in Australia: A History*. Carlton South: Melbourne University Press, 2002.

Keats-Rohan, K. S. B., ed. *Prosopography Approaches and Applications: A Handbook*. Oxford: Prosopographica et Genealogica, 2007.

Keller, Timothy. *Center Church*. Grand Rapids: Zondervan, 2012.

———. *Preaching: Communicating Faith in an Age of Skepticism*. London: Hodder and Stoughton, 2015.

Kelly, J. N. D. *Golden Mouth: The Story of John Chrysostom: Ascetic, Preacher, Bishop*. Ithaca, NY: Cornell University Press, 1995.

Kennedy, George A. *The Art of Persuasion in Greece*. New Jersey: Princeton University Press, 1963.

———. *Classical Rhetoric and Its Christian and Secular Tradition from Ancient to Modern Times*. 2nd ed. Chapel Hill: North Carolina University Press, 1999.

———. *Greek Rhetoric Under Christian Emperors*. Princeton: Princeton University Press, 1983.

———. "Historical Survey of Rhetoric." In *Handbook of Classical Rhetoric in the Hellenistic Period 330 B.C.–A.D. 400*, edited by Stanley E. Porter, 3–41. Leiden: Brill, 1997.

———. *A New History of Classical Rhetoric*. New Jersey: Princeton University Press, 1994.

———. *New Testament Interpretation Through Rhetorical Criticism*. Chapel Hill: University of North Carolina Press, 1984.

Kim, Seyoon. "Paul as an Eschatological Herald." In *Paul as Missionary: Identity, Activity, Theology, and Practice*, edited by Trevor J. Burke and Brian S. Rosner, 9–24. London: T. & T. Clark, 2011.

Kinzig, Wolfram. "The Greek Christian Writers." In *Handbook of Classical Rhetoric in the Hellenistic Period 330 B.C.–A.D. 400*, edited by Stanley E. Porter, 633–70. Leiden: Brill, 1997.

Kneidel, Greg. "Ars Praedicandi: Theories and Practice." In *The Oxford Handbook of The Early Modern Sermon*, edited by Peter McCullough et al., 3–20. Oxford: Oxford University Press, 2011.
Knight, George W. *The Pastoral Epistles*. Grand Rapids: Eerdmans, 1992.
Knox, D. B. "Christian Unity." In *D. Broughton Knox Selected Works, Vol II: Church and Ministry*, edited by Kirsten Birkett, 35–36. Kingsford: Matthias, 2004.
———. "Biblical Concept of Fellowship." In *D. Broughton Knox Selected Works, Vol II: Church and Ministry*, edited by Kirsten Birkett, 57–84. Kingsford: Matthias, 2004.
———. "The Church and the Denominations." *RTR* 13 (1964) 44–53.
———. "Church, the Churches and the Denominations of the Churches." In *D. Broughton Knox Selected Works, Vol II: Church and Ministry*, edited by Kirsten Birkett, 85–98. Kingsford: Matthias, 2004.
———. "De-Mythologizing the Church." In *D. Broughton Knox Selected Works, Vol II: Church and Ministry*, edited by Kirsten Birkett, 23–31. Kingsford: Matthias, 2004.
———. "Holy Spirit," In *D. Broughton Knox: Selected Works Volume III, The Christian Life*, edited by Tony Payne and Karen Beilharz, 109–14. Kingsford: Matthias, 2006.
———. "The Message of the Gospel." In *D. Broughton Knox: Selected Works Volume III, The Christian Life*, edited by Tony Payne and Karen Beilharz, 25–46. Kingsford: Matthias, 2006.
Köstenberger, Andreas, and Peter T. O'Brien, eds. *Salvation to the Ends of the Earth: A Biblical Theology of Mission*. Downers: IVP, 2001.
Kreitzer, Beth. "The Lutheran Sermon." In *Preachers and People in the Reformations and Early Modern Period*, ed. Larissa Taylor, 35–64. Leiden: Brill, 2003.
Lake, Meredith. *Faith in Action: HammondCare*. Sydney: New South Publishing, 2013.
———. "Samuel Marsden's Work and the Limits of Evangelical Humanitarianism." *History Australia* 7 (2010) 1–23.
Lane, Adrian. "Learning from the Legacy of John Charles Chapman." *St Mark's Review* 230 (December 2014) 84–102.
Latourette, K. S. "Ecumenical Bearings of the Missionary Movement and the International Missionary Council." In *A History of the Ecumenical Movement, Volume 1, 1517–1948*, edited by Ruth Rouse and Stephen Charles Neill, 353–402. 3rd ed. Geneva: WCC, 1986.
Lawton, William James. *The Better Time to Be: The Kingdom of God and Social Reform. Anglicans and the Diocese of Sydney 1885 to 1914*. PhD diss., University of New South Wales, 1985.
———. "'That Woman Jezebel'—Moore College After 25 Years." The Moore College Library Lecture, Sydney, 1981, 4–12.
Le Couteur, Howard. "Anglican High Churchmen and the Expansion of Empire." *Journal of Religious History* 32, no. 2 (2008) 193–215.
———. "Where Are All the Men?: An Attempt by the Anglican Church in Australia to Counter Secularization at the Beginning of the Twentieth Century." In *Secularization: New Historical Perspectives*, edited by Christopher Hartney, 68–89. Newcastle Upon Tyne: Scholars, 2014.
Lewis, Donald M., ed. "Introduction." In *Christianity Reborn: The Global Expansion of Evangelicalism in the Twentieth Century*, 1–8. Grand Rapids: Eerdmans, 2004.
Lindberg, Carter. *The European Reformations*. Oxford: Blackwell, 1996.
Lloyd-Jones, Martyn D. *Preaching and Preachers*. London: Hodder and Stoughton, 1971.

Loane, Ed. "The Church." *St Mark's Review* 226 (November 2013) 48–58.
Loane, Marcus L. *Archbishop Mowll: The Biography of Howard West Kilvinton Mowll, Archbishop of Sydney and Primate of Australia.* London: Hodder & Stoughton, 1960.
———. "The Art of Preaching." *Southern Cross*, November 1974, 11–12.
———. *A Centenary History of Moore Theological College.* Sydney: Angus and Robertson, 1955.
———. "David Broughton Knox." In *Broughton Knox: Principal of Moore College, 1959-1985.* Newtown: Moore Theological College, 1994.
———. "Foreword." In *Preach or Perish: Reaching the Hearts and Minds of the World Today,* edited by Donald Howard, v–vi. Camden: Kingsgrove, 2008.
———. *Hewn From the Rock: Origins and Traditions of the Church in Sydney.* Sydney: Anglican Information Office, 1976.
———. *Makers of Our Heritage: A Study of Four Evangelical Leaders.* London: Hodder and Stoughton, 1967.
———. *Mark These Men.* Kambah, ACT: Acorn, 1985.
———. *Masters of the English Reformation.* Edinburgh: Banner of Truth, 2005.
———. *Men to Remember.* Canberra: Acorn, 1987.
———. "Mowll, Howard West Kilvinton (1890–1958)." In *Australian Dictionary of Evangelical Biography,* edited by Brian Dickey, 272–78. Sydney: Evangelical History Association, 1994.
———. "Reaching Out to Touch the Ends of the Earth for God." In *John Stott: A Portrait by His Friends,* edited by Chris Wright, 89–91. Leicester: IVP, 2011.
———. "The True Position of Evangelicals in the Church of England." *The Australian Church Record: The National Church of England Newspaper,* October 7, 1971, 5.
Long, Thomas G. "Preaching the Good Always." In *The Legacy of Billy Graham: Critical Reflections on America's Greatest Evangelist,* edited by Michael G. Long. Louisville: Westminster John Knox, 2008.
Loos, Noel. "The Australian Board of Missions, the Anglican Church and the Aborigines, 1850–1900." *Journal of Religious History* 17 (1992) 194–209.
Lucas, Dick. "Helpless with Laughter at the Hookses." In *John Stott: A Portrait by His Friends,* edited by Chris Wright, 45–52, Leicester: IVP, 2011.
Lucas, Richard, Rev. Rector Emeritus, St Helen's Bishopsgate, Service of Thanksgiving for John Chapman, March 1, 2013. http://www.st-helens.org.uk/resources/media-library/src/talk/53263/title/tribute-reading-address-and-prayers.
MacBride, Tim. *Preaching the New Testament as Rhetoric: The Promise of Rhetorical Criticism for Expository Preaching.* ACT Monograph Series. Kindle Ed. Eugene, OR: Wipf & Stock, 2014.
MacCulloch, Diarmaid. *The Reformation: A History.* New York: Penguin, 2005.
———. *Thomas Cranmer: A Life.* New Haven: Yale University Press, 1996.
Macintosh, Neil K. *Richard Johnson, Chaplain to the Colony of NSW.* Sydney: Library of Australian History, 1978.
———. "Richard Johnson." In *Australian Dictionary of Evangelical Biography,* edited by Brian Dickey,187–89. Sydney: Evangelical History Association, 1994.
Macintyre, Stuart. *A Concise History of Australia.* Cambridge: Cambridge University Press, 2004.
Mack, Burton L. *Rhetoric and the New Testament.* Minneapolis: Fortress, 1990.

Mack, Peter. *A History of Renaissance Rhetoric 1380–1620*. Oxford: Oxford University Press, 2011.

———. "Rediscoveries of Classical Rhetoric." In *The Cambridge Companion to Ancient Rhetoric*, edited by Erik Gunderson, 261–77. Cambridge: Cambridge University Press, 2009.

MacLeod, Christine, and Alessandro Nuvolari. "The Pitfalls of Prosopography." *Technology and Culture* 47, no. 4 (October 2006) 757–76.

Maddox, Marion. "Hillsong and the Mega-Churches." In *The Encyclopedia of Religion in Australia*, edited by James Jupp, 325–29. Cambridge: Cambridge University Press, 2009.

Maddison, Angus. *The World Economy, Volume Two: Historical Statistics*. Paris: Organisation for Economic Co-operation and Development, 2006.

Magnuson, Norris A. "The Social Gospel." In *Evangelical Dictionary of Theology*, edited by Walter A. Elwell, 1027–29. Grand Rapids: Baker, 1984.

Malherbe, Abraham J. *Paul and the Popular Philosophers*. Minneapolis: Fortress, 1989.

Manchester, Simon. "The Preaching of John Chapman." *The Briefing*, March 11, 2013. http://matthiasmedia.com/briefing/2013/03/the-preaching-of-john-chapman.

Mansfield, David. "Are We All Evangelists?" *Southern Cross*, February 1998, 17.

———. *The Chappo Collection: Life, Laughter, Leadership, Love in the Lord Jesus Christ*. Sydney: Grace Abounding, 2017.

———. "The Privilege and the Responsibility of the Gospel." *Southern Cross*, April 1998, 17–18.

Mansfield, Joan. "The Social Gospel and the Church of England in New South Wales in the 1930s." *Journal of Religious History* 13, no. 4 (1985) 411–33.

Maple, G. S. "Barker, Frederic." In *Australian Dictionary of Evangelical Biography*, edited by Brian Dickey, 24–26. Sydney: Evangelical History Association, 1994.

Marsden, George M. *Reforming Fundamentalism: Fuller Seminary and the New Evangelicalism*. Grand Rapids: Eerdmans, 1987.

———. *Understanding Fundamentalism and Evangelicalism*. Grand Rapids: Eerdmans, 1991.

Martin, David. *A General Theory of Secularization*. Oxford: Blackwell, 1978.

———. *On Secularization: Towards a Revised General Theory*. Aldershot: Ashgate, 2005.

———. *A Sociology of English Religion*. London: SCM, 1967.

Martin, William C. *A Prophet with Honor: The Billy Graham Story*. New York: William Morrow, 1991.

Massam, Katharine. "Christian Churches in Australia, New Zealand and the Pacific, 1914–1970." In *The Cambridge History of Christianity: World Christianities c. 1914–c.2000*, edited by Hugh McLeod, 251–84. Cambridge: Cambridge University Press, 2006.

Matheson, Ann. "Preaching in the Churches of Scotland." In *The Oxford Handbook of the British Sermon 1689–1901*, edited by Keith A. Francis and William Gibson, 152–65. Oxford: Clarendon, 2012.

Maxwell-Stewart, Hamish, and Ian Duffield. "Skin Deep Devotions: Religious Tattoos and Convict Transportation to Australia." In *Written on the Body: The Tattoo in European and American History*, edited by Jane Caplan, 129–31. London: Reaktion, 2000.

McClymond, Michael J. "Issues and Explanations in the Study of North American Revivalism." In *Embodying the Spirit: New Perspectives on North American Revivalism*, edited by Michael J. McClymond, 1–46. Baltimore: Johns Hopkins University Press, 2004.

———. "Mission and Evangelism." In *The Oxford Handbook of Evangelical Theology*, edited by Gerald R. McDermott, 351–54. Oxford: Oxford University Press, 2010.

McDonald, David. "Chappo's Gain," November 16, 2012. https://macarisms.com/2012/11/16/chappos-gain/.

McGavran, Donald. "Dimensions of World Evangelisation." In *Let the Earth Hear His Voice: International Congress on World Evangelization, Lausanne, Switzerland, Official Reference Volume*, edited by J. D. Douglas, 94–107, 108–15. Minneapolis: World Wide Publications, 1975.

———. "Will Uppsala Betray the Two Billion?" *Church Growth Bulletin* 4, no. 5 (May 1968) 6–9.

McGillion, Christopher. *The Chosen Ones: The Politics of Salvation in the Anglican Church*. Crows Nest: Allen & Unwin, 2005.

McGrath, Alister. "Evangelical Anglicanism: A Contradiction in Terms?" In *Evangelical Anglicans: Their Role and Influence in the Church Today*, edited by R. T. France and Alister E. McGrath, 12–13. London: SPCK, 1993.

———. *Evangelicalism and the Future of Christianity*. Downers Grove: IVP, 1995.

McIntyre, C. T. "Vatican Council II." In *Evangelical Dictionary of Theology*, edited by Walter A. Elwell, 1135–37. Grand Rapids: Baker, 1984.

McKitterick, Rosamond. *The Frankish Church and the Carolingian Reforms, 789–895*. London: Royal Historical Society, 1977.

McLean, David. "From British Colony to American Satellite? Australia and the USA during the Cold War." *Australian Journal of Politics and History* 52, no. 1 (2006) 64–79.

McLeod, Hugh. "Being a Christian at the End of the Twentieth Century." In *The Cambridge History of Christianity: World Christianities c. 1914–c.2000*, edited by Hugh McLeod, 636–47. Cambridge: Cambridge University Press, 2006.

———. "The Crisis of Christianity in the West: Entering a Post-Christian Era?" In *The Cambridge History of Christianity: World Christianities c. 1914–c.2000*, edited by Hugh McLeod, 323–47. Cambridge: Cambridge University Press, 2006.

———. "Introduction." In *The Cambridge History of Christianity: World Christianities c. 1914–c.2000*, edited by Hugh McLeod, 1–14. Cambridge: Cambridge University Press, 2006.

———. "Reflections and New Perspectives." In *The Sixties and Beyond: Dechristianization in North America and Western Europe, 1945–2000*, edited by Nancy Christie and Michael Gauvreau, 453–68. Toronto: University of Toronto Press, 2013.

———. *The Religious Crisis of the 1960s*. Oxford: Oxford University Press, 2007.

McMullin, Ross. *Light on the Hill: The Australian Labor Party 1891–1991*. Melbourne: Oxford University Press, 1992.

Megill, Allan. "The Reception of Foucault by Historians." *Journal of the History of Ideas* 48 (1987) 117–34.

Melleuish, Gregory. "A Secular Australia? Ideas, Politics and the Search for Moral Order in Nineteenth and Early Twentieth Century Australia." *Journal of Religious History* 38, no. 3 (Sept 2014) 398–412.

Merrett, David, and Simon Philip Ville. "Tariffs, Subsidies, and Profits: A Re-Assessment of Structural Change in Australia in 1901–39." *Australian Economic History Review* 51, no. 1 (2011) 46–70.
Meuser, Fred W. *Luther the Preacher*. Minneapolis: Augsburg, 1983.
Mews, Stuart. "The Revival of Spiritual Healing in the Church of England 1920–26." In *The Church and Healing*, edited by W. J. Sheils. 299–332. EHS 19. Oxford: Blackwell, 1982.
Meyers, Elizabeth Lehman. "Synagogue." In *Anchor Bible Dictionary*, edited by David Noel Freedman et al. New York: Doubleday, 1992.
Michaels, J. Ramsey. "Gifts of the Spirit." In *Encyclopedia of Pentecostal and Charismatic Christianity*, edited by Stanley M. Burgess, 215–18. New York: Routledge, 2006.
Miley, Caroline. *The Suicidal Church: Can the Anglican Church Be Saved?* Annandale: Pluto, 2002.
Milikan, David. "Christianity and Australian Identity." In *The Shape of Belief in Australia*, edited by Dorothy Harris et al., 28–39. Sydney: Lancer, 1982.
———. *The Sunburnt Soul: Christianity in Search of an Australian Identity*. Homebush West: Anzea, 1981.
Miller, Donald E., et al., eds. *Spirit and Power: The Growth and Global Impact of Pentecostalism*. Oxford: Oxford University Press, 2013.
Miller, Donald E., and Tetsunao Yamamori. *Global Pentecostalism. The New Face of Christian Social Engagement*. Berkeley: University of California Press, 2007.
Miller, Donald G. *The Way to Biblical Preaching*. New York: Abingdon, 1957.
Miller, Perry. *The New England Mind: The Seventeenth Century*. Cambridge: Belknap, 1939.
Mitchell, William Fraser. *English Pulpit Oratory from Andrewes to Tillotson: A Study of its Literary Aspects*. London: SPCK, 1932.
Moberg, David O. *The Great Reversal: Evangelism Versus Social Concern*. Philadelphia: Lippincott, 1972.
Mol, Hans. "Australian Christianity Today: Some Reflections." *Interchange* 30 (1980): 65–70.
Moore, Gerard. "Baptism in Australia: Secularization, 'Civil Baptism' and the Social Miracle." In *Christian Worship in Australia: Inculturating the Liturgical Tradition*, edited by Stephen Burns and Anita Munro. Strathfield: St Paul's, 2009.
Moreau, A. Scott. "Contextualization That is Comprehensive." *Missiology: An International Review* 34, no. 3 (July 2006) 325–35.
———. "Evangelical Models of Contextualization." In *Local Theology for the Global Church: Principles for an Evangelical Approach to Contextualization*, edited by Matthew Cook et al., 165–95. Pasadena: World Evangelical Alliance, 2010.
Morgan, D. Densil. "Preaching in the Vernacular: The Welsh Sermon, 1689–1901." In *The Oxford Handbook of the British Sermon 1689–1901*, edited by Keith A. Francis and William Gibson, 199–214. Oxford: Clarendon, 2012.
Morgan, Patrick. "Realism and Documentary: Lowering One's Sights." In *The Penguin New Literary History of Australia*, edited by Laurie Hergenhan, 238–52. Australian Literary Series. Ringwood: Penguin, 1988.
Morgan-Guy, John. "Sermons in Wales in the Established Church." In *The Oxford Handbook of the British Sermon 1689–1901*, edited by Keith A. Francis and William Gibson, 183–98. Oxford: Clarendon, 2012.

Morley, Rachel. "Fighting Feeling: Re-Thinking Biographical Praxis." *Life Writing* 9, no.1 (2012) 77–95.
Morris, Jeremy. "Preaching the Oxford Movement." In *The Oxford Handbook of the British Sermon 1689–1901*, edited by Keith A. Francis et al., 406–27. Oxford: Clarendon, 2012.
Morris, Leon. *The Apostolic Preaching of the Cross*. London: Tyndale, 1955.
Moses, John A. "Canon David John Garland and the ANZAC Tradition." *St Mark's Review* 154 (1993) 12–21.
———. "David John Garland, Priest: A Triton among the Minnows." *St Mark's Review* 230 (December 2014) 60–71.
———. "Sydney Anglicanism: An Apology." *Journal of Religious History* 39, no. 4 (December 2015) 627–28.
Mueller, Charles S. *The Strategy of Evangelism*. St Louis: Concordia, 1965.
Munslow, Alun. "History and Biography: An Editorial Comment." *Rethinking History* 7, no. 1 (2003) 1–11.
Murphy, James J. *Rhetoric in the Middle Ages: A History of Rhetorical Theory from Saint Augustine to the Renaissance*. Berkeley: University of California Press, 1974.
Murray, Iain H. *Australian Christian Life from 1788. An Introduction and Anthology*. Edinburgh: Banner of Truth, 1988.
Murray, Stuart. *Post-Christendom*. Carlisle, UK: Paternoster, 2004.
Nelson, Warren. "Hammond, Thomas Chatteron (1877–1961)." In *Australian Dictionary of Evangelical Biography*, edited by Brian Dickey, 150–53. Sydney: Evangelical History Association, 1994.
Neusner, Jacob. *The Rabbinic Traditions About the Pharisees Before 70*. Atlanta: Scholars, 1999.
Neville, David J., ed. *The Bible, Justice and Public Theology*. Sheffield: Sheffield Phoenix, 2014.
Newbigin, Lesslie. *The Gospel in a Pluralistic Society*. Grand Rapids: Eerdmans, 1989.
Nichols, Alan. *David Penman: Bridge-Builder, Peacemaker, Fighter for Social Justice*. Sutherland: Albatross, 1991.
———. "Future World Leaders." *Southern Cross Magazine*, September 1974, 2–3.
Nicholls, Bruce J. *Contextualization: A Theology of Gospel Culture*. Downers Grove: IVP, 1979.
Noble, Thomas A. *Tyndale House Fellowship: The First Fifty Years*. Leicester: IVP, 2006.
Noll, Mark. *America's God: From Jonathan Edwards to Abraham Lincoln*. New York: Oxford University Press, 2002.
———. *American Evangelical Christianity: An Introduction*. Oxford: Blackwell, 2001.
———. *Between Faith and Criticism: Evangelicals, Scholarship and the Bible in America*. San Francisco: Harper, 1986.
———. *The New Shape of World Christianity*. Downers Grove: IVP, 2009.
Null, Ashley. "Official Tudor Homilies." In *The Oxford Handbook of The Early Modern Sermon*, edited by Peter McCullough et al. 348–65. Oxford: Oxford University Press, 2011.
Null, Ashley, and John W. Yates III. "A Manifesto for Reformation Anglicanism." In *Reformation Anglicanism: A Vision for Today's Communion*, edited by Ashley Null and John W. Yates III, 186–201. Wheaton, IL: Crossway, 2017.

O'Brien, Anne. "The Case of the 'Cultivated Man': Class, Gender and the Church of the Establishment in Interwar Australia." *Australian Historical Studies* 27, no. 107 (October 1996) 242–57.
———. *God's Willing Workers*. Sydney: UNSW Press, 2005.
———. "Moyes, John Stoward (1884–1972)." In *Australian Dictionary of Biography*. http://adb.anu.edu.au/biography/moyes-john-stoward-11190/text19945.
———. "Religion." In *The Cambridge History of Australia: Volume 1, Indigenous and Colonial Australia*, edited by Alison Bashford and Stuart Macintrye, 414–37. Melbourne: Cambridge University Press, 2013.
O'Brien, Peter T. "The Church as a Heavenly and Eschatological Entity." In *The Church in the Bible and the World: An International Study*, edited by D. A. Carson, 88–119. Grand Rapids: Baker, 1987.
———. *Consumed by Passion: Paul and the Dynamic of the Gospel*. Homebush: Anzea, 1993.
O'Brien, Susan. "A Transatlantic Community of Saints: The Great Awakening and the First Evangelical Network, 1735–1755." *American Historical Review* 91 (1986) 811–32.
O'Farrell, Patrick. "The Cultural Ambivalence of Australian Religion." In *Australian Cultural History*, edited by S. L. Goldberg and F. B. Smith, 7–14. Cambridge: Cambridge University Press, 1988.
———. "Writing the General History of Australian Religion." *Journal of Religious History* 9, no. 1 (1976) 65–73.
O'Neill, Michael. "Barth's Doctrine of Election." *Evangelical Quarterly* 76, no.4 (2004) 311–26.
Old, Hughes Oliphant. *The Reading and Preaching of the Scriptures in the Worship of the Christian Church, Volume 1: The Biblical Period*. Grand Rapids: Eerdmans, 2007.
———. *The Reading and Preaching of the Scriptures in the Worship of the Christian Church, Volume 2: The Patristic Age*. Grand Rapids: Eerdmans, 1998.
———. *The Reading and Preaching of the Scriptures in the Worship of the Christian Church, Volume 3: The Medieval Church*. Grand Rapids: Eerdmans, 1999.
———. *The Reading and Preaching of the Scriptures in the Worship of the Christian Church, Volume 4: The Reformation*. Grand Rapids: Eerdmans, 2002.
———. *The Reading and Preaching of the Scriptures in the Worship of the Christian Church, Volume 5: Moderatism, Pietism, and Awakening*. Grand Rapids: Eerdmans, 2004.
———. *The Reading and Preaching of the Scriptures in the Worship of the Christian Church, Volume 6: The Modern Age*. Grand Rapids: Eerdmans, 2007.
———. *The Reading and Preaching of the Scriptures in the Worship of the Christian Church, Volume 7: Our Own Time*. Grand Rapids: Eerdmans, 2010.
Oliphint, K. Scott. "A Primal and Simple Knowledge." In *Theological Guide to Calvin's Institutes*, edited by David W. Hall and Peter A. Lillback, 16–43. New Jersey: P&R, 2008.
Olivar, Alexander, O. S. B. "Reflections and Problems Raised by Early Christian Preaching." In *Preacher and Audience: Studies in Early Christian and Byzantine Homiletics*, edited by Mary B. Cunningham and Pauline Allen, 21–32. Leiden: Brill, 1998.
Olson, David T. *The American Church in Crisis*. Grand Rapids: Zondervan, 2008.

Olwa, Albert. "Festo Kivengere, a Ugandan Preacher in Australia." *St Mark's Review* 230 (December 2014)103–17.
Orpwood, Michael. *Chappo: For the Sake of the Gospel*. Kingsford: St. Matthias, 1995.
Packer, J. I. *Concise Theology*. Wheaton: Tyndale, 1993.
———. *Evangelism and the Sovereignty of God*. Nottingham: IVP, 1961.
———. *Fundamentalism and the Word of God*. Grand Rapids: Eerdmans, 1958.
———. "The Evangelical Anglican Identity Problem: An Analysis." In *Anglican Evangelical Identity: Yesterday and Today*, 25–72. London: Latimer Trust, 2008.
———. *Keep in Step with the Spirit: Finding Fullness in Our Walk with God*. Grand Rapids: Baker, 2005.
———. "Why Preach?" In *The Preacher and Preaching*, edited by Samuel T. Logan Jr., 1–30. New Jersey: Reformed, 1986.
Padilla, C. René. "Evangelism and the World." In *Let the Earth Hear His Voice: International Congress on World Evangelization, Lausanne, Switzerland, Official Reference Volume*, edited by J. D. Douglas, 116–33. Minneapolis: World Wide Publications, 1975.
———. "The Politics of the Kingdom and the Political Mission of the Church." In *Proclaiming Christ in Christ's Way*, edited by V. Samuel and A. Hauser, 180–98. Oxford: Regnum, 1989.
Palmer, Bryan D. *Descent into Discourse: The Reification of Language and the Writing of Social History*. Philadelphia: Temple University Press, 1990.
Parker, T. H. L. *Calvin's Preaching*. Edinburgh: T. & T. Clark, 1992.
Patterson, William Brown. *William Perkins and the Making of Protestant England*. Oxford: Oxford University Press, 2018.
Paulin, Roger. "Adding Stones to the Edifice: Patterns of German Biography." In *Mapping Lives: The Uses of Biography*, edited by Peter France and William St. Clair, 103–14. Oxford: Oxford University Press, 2002.
Payne, Tony. "Chappo and the Magic Potion," March 18, 2013. http://thebriefing.com.au/2013/03/chappo-and-the-magic-potion/.
———. "The Ethics of Everyday Evangelism." *The Briefing*, August 2, 2008.
Payne, Tony, ed. *D. Broughton Knox: Selected Works, Volume 1, The Doctrine of God*. Kingsford, NSW: Matthias, 2000.
Payne, Tony, and Karen Beilharz, eds. *D. Broughton Knox: Selected Works Volume III, The Christian Life*. Kingsford: Matthias, 2006.
Pecknold, C. C., and Tarmo Toom, eds. *T&T Clark Companion to Augustine and Modern Theology*. London: Bloomsbury, 2013.
Perkins, Gavin. "The Danger of Living the Gospel Without Speaking the Gospel." *The Briefing*, July 17, 2008.
Perkins, William. *Works*. Vols. 1 and 2. London: John Legatt, 1631.
Perszyk, Ken. *Molinism: The Contemporary Debate*. New York: Oxford University Press, 2011.
Peterson, David G. *The Acts of the Apostles*. PNTC. Grand Rapids: Eerdmans, 2009.
Petras, Michael. "Charles Haddon Spurgeon's Sermons in Australia." *St Mark's Review* 230 (December 2014) 31–39.
Pettett, David. "Charles Simeon's Influence on Samuel Marsden's Chaplaincy in New South Wales." In *From Cambridge to Colony: Charles Simeon's Enduring Influence on Christianity in Australia*, edited by Edward Loane, 25–37. London: Latimer Trust, 2016.

———. *Samuel Marsden: Preacher, Pastor, Magistrate and Missionary*. Camperdown: Bolt, 2016.

———. "The Sermons of Samuel Marsden: Evangelical Preaching in Early Colonial Australia." *St Mark's Review* 230 (December 2014) 40–50.

Pierard, Richard V. "*Pax Americana* and the Evangelical Missionary Advance." In *Earthen Vessels: American Evangelicals and Foreign Missions, 1880–1980*, edited by Joel A. Carpenter and Wilbert R. Shenk, 155–79. Grand Rapids: Eerdmans, 1990.

Piggin, Stuart. "The American and British Contributions to Evangelicalism in Australia." In *Evangelicalism: Comparative Studies of Popular Protestantism in North America, the British Isles, and Beyond, 1700–1990*, edited by Mark A. Noll et al., 290–309. Oxford: Oxford University Press, 1994.

———. *Billy Graham in Australia, 1959: Was It Revival?* North Ryde: Centre for the Study of Australian Christianity, 1989.

———. "The History of Revival in Australia." In *Re-Visioning Australian Colonial Christianity: New Essays in the Australian Christian Experience 1788–1900*, edited by Mark Hutchinson and Edmund Campion, 173–93. Sydney: Centre for the Study of Australian Christianity, 1994.

———. "Jesus in Australian History and Culture." In *Mapping the Landscape: Essays in Australian and New Zealand Christianity. Festschrift in Honor of Professor Ian Breward*, edited by Susan Emilsen and W. William Emilsen, 150–63. New York: Peter Lang, 2000.

———. "Power and Religion in a Modern State: Desecularization in Australian History." *Journal of Religious History* 38, no. 3 (September 2014) 320–40.

———. "The Properties of Concrete: Sydney Anglicanism and Its Recent Critics." *Meanjin* 65, no. 4 (2006) 184–93.

———. "Roman Catholicism." In *Evangelical Dictionary of Theology*, edited by Walter A. Elwell, 955–59. Grand Rapids: Baker, 1984.

———. *Spirit, Word and World: Evangelical Christianity in Australia*. Rev. ed. Melbourne: Oxford University Press, 2012.

Piggin, Stuart, and Robert D. Linder. *Attending to the National Soul: Evangelical Christians in Australian History 1914–2014*. Clayton: Monash, 2020.

———. *The Fountain of Public Prosperity: Evangelical Christians in Australian History 1740–1914*. Clayton: Monash, 2018.

Pinnock, Clark H. *Grace Unlimited*. Minneapolis: Bethany, 1975.

Pinnock, Clark H., et al., eds. *The Openness of God*. Downers Grove: IVP, 1994.

Plantinga, Alvin. *God, Freedom, and Evil*. Grand Rapids: Eerdmans, 1977.

———. *The Nature of Necessity*. New York: Oxford University Press, 1974.

Pollard, John. "The Papacy." In *The Cambridge History of Christianity: World Christianities c. 1914–c.2000*, edited by Hugh McLeod, 29–49. Cambridge: Cambridge University Press, 2006.

Pollock, John. *The Billy Graham Story*. Rev. and updated ed. Grand Rapids: Zondervan, 2003.

Pollon, Frances. *The Book of Sydney Suburbs*. Sydney: Angus and Robertson, 1990.

Porter, Andrew. "Cultural Imperialism and Protestant Missionary Enterprise, 1780–1914." *Journal of Imperial and Commonwealth History* 25, no. 3 (1997) 367–91.

———. *Religion Versus Empire? British Protestant Missionaries and Overseas Expansion, 1700–1914*. Manchester: Manchester University Press, 2004.

Porter, Brian, ed. *Melbourne Anglicans: The Diocese of Melbourne, 1847–1997*. Melbourne: Mitre, 1997.

Porter, Muriel. *Sydney Anglicanism and the Threat to World Anglicanism*. Surrey: Ashgate, 2011.

Porter, Stanley E., ed. *Handbook of Classical Rhetoric in the Hellenistic Period, 330 B.C.– A.D. 400*. Leiden: Brill, 2001.

Porter, Stanley E., and Thomas H. Olbricht, eds. *The Rhetorical Analysis of Scripture: Essays from the 1995 London Conference*. JSNT Supplement 146. Sheffield: Sheffield Academic, 1997.

Porter, Stanley E., and Dennis L. Stamps, eds. *The Rhetorical Interpretation of Scripture: Essays from the 1996 Malibu Conference*. JSNT Supplement 180. Sheffield: Sheffield Academic, 1999.

Potts, David. *The Myth of the Great Depression*. Melbourne: Scribe, 2006.

Powell, Graeme, and Stuart Macintyre. *Land of Opportunity: Australia's Post-War Reconstructionism*. Canberra: National Archives of Australia, 2015.

Prince, John, and Moyra Prince. *Out of the Tower*. Homebush: Anzea, 1987.

Rack, Henry D. "Doctors, Demons and Early Methodist Healing." In *The Church and Healing*, edited by W. J. Sheils, 137–52. Oxford: Blackwell, 1982.

Raiter, Michael. "Social Involvement and Evangelism (Part III): Some Final Reflections." *The Briefing*, February 1, 2005.

Randall, Ian M. "Conservative Constructionist: The Early Influence of Billy Graham in Britain." *Evangelical Quarterly* 67 (1995) 309–33.

Rawlyk, George A., and Mark A. Noll, eds. *Amazing Grace: Evangelicalism in Australia, Britain, Canada, and the United States*. Grand Rapids: Baker, 1993.

Rayner, Keith. *The History of the Church of England in Queensland*. Brisbane: University of Queensland, 1962.

Reid, John R. *Marcus L. Loane: A Biography*. Brunswick East: Acorn, 2004.

Retief, Frank. "More Thanks from South Africa for Chappo." http://acl.asn.au/more-thanks-from-south-africa-for-chappo/.

Reymond, Robert L. *A New Systematic Theology of the Christian Faith*. Nashville: Thomas Nelson, 1998.

"The Right Reverend Peter Chiswell 18 Feb 1934–6 Dec 2013." *The Link* (Summer 2013–14) 5.

Robert, Dana L. *Christian Mission: How Christianity Became a World Religion*. Chichester: Wiley-Blackwell, 2009.

Robin, Arthur de Quetteville. *Charles Perry, Bishop of Melbourne: The Challenges of a Colonial Episcopate, 1847–76*. Perth: University of Western Australia Press, 1967.

Robinson, D. W. B. "The Bishop as Evangelist." In *Donald Robinson: Selected Works. Volume 2, Preaching God's Word*, edited by Peter G. Bolt and Mark D. Thompson, 85–98.

———. "Charismatic Christianity." In *Donald Robinson: Selected Works. Volume 2, Preaching God's Word*, edited by Peter G. Bolt and Mark D. Thompson, 191–201.

———. "'The Church' Revisited. An Autobiographical Fragment." In *Donald Robinson: Selected Works. Volume 1, Assembling God's People*, edited by Peter G. Bolt and Mark D. Thompson 259–71.

———. "David Broughton Knox: An Appreciation." In *God Who is Rich in Mercy: Essays Presented to Dr. D. B. Knox*, edited by Peter T. O'Brien and David G. Peterson, xi–xvii. Homebush: Lancer, 1986.

———. "David Broughton Knox: What We Owe Him." http://acl.asn. au/?s=David+Broughton+Knox.

———. "The Gifts of the Spirit." In *Donald Robinson: Selected Works. Volume 2, Preaching God's Word*, edited by Peter G. Bolt and Mark D. Thompson, 172–83.

———. "Liturgical Patterns of Worship." In *Donald Robinson: Selected Works. Volume 1, Assembling God's People*, edited by Peter G. Bolt and Mark D. Thompson, 318–36. Camperdown: Australian Church Record, 2008.

———. "Origins and Unresolved Tensions." In *Interpreting God's Plan: Biblical Theology and the Pastor*, 1–17. Carlisle: Paternoster, 1998.

———. "Theology of Evangelism." In *Donald Robinson: Selected Works. Volume 2, Preaching God's Word*, edited by Peter G. Bolt and Mark D. Thompson, 99–102.

Robinson, Haddon. *Biblical Preaching. The Development and Delivery of Expository Messages.* 3rd ed. Grand Rapids: Baker Academic, 2014.

Rowland, Christopher C. "Liberation Theology." In *The Oxford Handbook of Systematic Theology*, edited by John Webster et al., 551–62. Oxford: Oxford University Press, 2007.

Russell, C. Allyn. "Donald G. Barnhouse: Fundamentalist Who Changed?" *Journal of Presbyterian History* 59 (1981) 33–57.

Ruthven, Jon Mark. "Cessationism." In *Encyclopedia of Pentecostal and Charismatic Christianity*, edited by Stanley M. Burgess, 84–86. New York: Routledge, 2006.

Ryken, Philip, et al., eds. *Give Praise to God: A Vision for Reforming Worship: Celebrating the Legacy of James Montgomery Boice.* Phillipsburg: P&R, 2003.

Rylaarsdam, David. *John Chrysostom on Divine Pedagogy: The Coherence of His Theology and Preaching.* Oxford: Oxford University Press, 2014.

Ryle, J. C. *Expository Thoughts on the Gospels—For Family and Private Use.* New York: Robert Carter & Brothers, 1859.

———. *Holiness: Its Nature, Hindrances, Difficulties and Roots.* Grange Close: Evangelical, 1879.

Sardica, José Miguel. "The Content and Form of 'Conventional' Historical Biography." *Rethinking History* 17, no. 3 (2013) 383–400.

Satterthwaite, Philip E. "The Latin Church Fathers." In *Handbook of Classical Rhetoric in the Hellenistic Period 330 B.C.–A.D. 400*, edited by Stanley E. Porter, 671–94. Leiden: Brill, 1997.

Satyavrata, Ivan M. "Globalization of Pentecostalism." In *Encyclopedia of Pentecostal and Charismatic Christianity*, edited by Stanley M. Burgess, 218–20. New York: Routledge, 2006.

Schreiter, Robert J. *Constructing Local Theologies.* London: SCM, 1985.

Schweiger, Hannes. "Global Subjects: The Transnationalization of Biography." *Life Writing* 9, no. 3 (September 2012) 249–58.

Seaver, Paul S. *The Puritan Lectureships: The Politics of Religious Dissent, 1560–1662.* London: Oxford University Press, 1970.

Seymour-Smith, Martin, ed. *The English Sermon, An Anthology, Volume 1.* Carcanet: Cheadle and Cheshire, 1976.

Siegert, Folker. "Homily and Panegyrical Sermon." In *Handbook of Classical Rhetoric in the Hellenistic Period 330 B.C.–A.D. 400*, edited by Stanley E. Porter, 421–44. Leiden: Brill, 1997.

Shaw, George P. *Patriarch and Prophet: William Grant Broughton, 1788–1853: Colonial Statesman and Ecclesiastic.* Melbourne: Melbourne University Press, 1978.

Sheetz-Nguyen, Jessica A. "Catholic Preaching in Victorian England, 1801–1901." In *A New History of the Sermon: The Nineteenth Century*, edited by Robert H. Ellison, 207–32. Leiden: Brill, 2010.

———. "'Go Ye Therefore and Teach All Nations.' Evangelical and Mission Sermons: The Imperial Period." In *The Oxford Handbook of The Early Modern Sermon*, edited by Peter McCullough et al., 548–64. Oxford: Oxford University Press, 2011.

Shenk, Wilbert R. "2004 Forum for World Evangelization." *International Bulletin of Missionary Research* 29 (January 2005) 31.

Shilton, Lance. "Aftermath of Lausanne: Evangelism in a Changing World." *New Life*, August 29, 1974, 5.

———. "Cathedral Sermon, at His Installation as Dean of St. Andrew's, 30 Nov 1973." *Southern Cross*, December 1973, 15–16.

Shiner, Rory. "An Appreciation of D. W. B. Robinson's New Testament Theology." In *Donald Robinson, Selected Works: Appreciation*, edited by Peter G. Bolt and Mark D. Thompson, 9–64. Camperdown: Australian Church Record, 2008.

Sidenvall, Erik. "A Classic Case of De-Christianization? Religious Change in Scandinavia c. 1750–2000." In *Secularization in the Christian World: Essays in Honor of Hugh McLeod*, edited by Callum G. Brown and Michael Snape, 110–30. Surrey: Ashgate, 2010.

Simeon, Charles. *Evangelical Preaching*. Portland, OR: Multnomah, 1986.

———. *Horae Homileticae*. Rev. ed. London: James Cornish, 1846.

Siriwardana, Mahinda. "The Causes of the Depression in Australia in the 1930s: A General Equilibrium Evaluation." *Explorations in Economic History* 32, no. 1 (1995) 51–81.

Smart, Simon, ed. *Public Christianity: Talking About Faith in a Post-Christian World*. North Sydney: Centre for Public Christianity, 2011.

Smith, Christian. *American Evangelicalism: Embattled and Thriving*. Chicago: University of Chicago Press, 1998.

Smyth, Charles. *The Art of Preaching: A Practical Survey of Preaching in the Church of England 747–1939*. New York: MacMillan, 1940.

Snape, Michael. "The Great War." In *The Cambridge History of Christianity: World Christianities c. 1914–c.2000*, edited by Hugh McLeod, 131–50. Cambridge: Cambridge University Press, 2006.

———. 'War, Religion and Revival: The United States, British and Canadian Armies during the Second World War." In *Secularization in the Christian World: Essays in Honor of Hugh McLeod*, edited by Callum G. Brown and Michael Snape, 135–50. Surrey: Ashgate, 2010.

Snowman, Daniel. "Historical Biography." *History Today* (November 2014) 55–56.

Spinks, Bryan D. "Liturgy." In *The Cambridge History of Christianity: World Christianities c. 1914–c.2000*, edited by Hugh McLeod, 471–82. Cambridge: Cambridge University Press, 2006.

Spooner, John. *The Golden See. The Diocese of Ballarat: The Anglican Church in Western Victoria*. Sydney: John Ferguson, 1989.

Spurgeon, C. H. *The Soul Winner*. New York: Fleming H. Revell Co., 1895.

Stanley, Brian. *The Bible and the Flag: Protestant Missions and British Imperialism in the Nineteenth and Twentieth centuries*. Leicester: IVP, 1990.

———. *The Global Diffusion of Evangelicalism*. Nottingham, England: IVP, 2013.

———. *Invading Australia: Japan and the Battle for Australia, 1942*. Melbourne: Viking, 2008.

———. "'Lausanne 1974': The Challenge from the Majority World to Northern-Hemisphere Evangelicalism." *Journal of Ecclesiastical History* 64, no. 3 (July 2013) 533–51.

Stark, Rodney. *The Rise of Christianity: How the Obscure, Marginal Jesus Movement Became the Dominant Religious Force in the Western World in a Few Centuries*. San Francisco: Harper Collins, 1997.

———. "Secularization RIP." *Sociology of Religion* 60, no. 3 (1999) 249–73.

Stark, Rodney, and Roger Finke. *Acts of Faith: Explaining the Human Side of Religion*. Berkeley: UCP, 2000.

Steel, Catherine. "Divisions of Speech." In *The Cambridge Companion to Ancient Rhetoric*, edited by Erik Gunderson, 77–91. Cambridge: Cambridge University Press, 2009.

Steele, Dominic. *Introducing God*. Course Manual. Annandale: Media Bible Fellowship, 2003.

Stephens, Geoffrey. *The Anglican Church in Tasmania: A Diocesan History to Mark the Sesquicentenary, 1992*. Hobart: Trustees of the Diocese, 1991.

Stockdale, R. I. H. "Youth Organisations and Prospects for the Future 1950." *Youth Report to the Diocese of Armidale*. Diocesan Registry Armidale.

Stoneman, David. "Richard Bourke: For the Honor of God and the Good of Man." *Journal of Religious History* 38, no. 3 (September 2014) 341–55.

Stott, John R. W. *Between Two Worlds: The Challenge of Preaching Today*. London: Hodder and Stoughton, 1982.

———. "The Biblical Basis." In *Let the Earth Hear His Voice: International Congress on World Evangelization, Lausanne, Switzerland, Official Reference Volume*, edited by J. D. Douglas, 65. Minneapolis: World Wide Publications, 1975.

———. *The Challenge of Preaching*. Grand Rapids: Eerdmans, 2013.

———. *The Contemporary Christian*. Leicester: IVP, 1992.

———. "Counsellor and Friend." In *Bash: A Study in Spiritual Power*, edited by John Eddison, 57–65. Basingstoke: Iwerne Trust, 1982.

———. *Evangelical Truth: A Personal Plea for Unity*. Leicester: IVP, 1999.

———. "Foreword." In *When God's Voice is Heard: Essays on Preaching Presented to Dick Lucas*, edited by Christopher Green and David Jackman, 9–10. Leicester: IVP, 1995.

———. *I Believe in Preaching*. London: Hodder and Stoughton, 1982.

———. *John Stott at Keswick: A Lifetime of Preaching*. Milton Keynes: Authentic Media, 2009.

———. *Preacher's Portrait*. Grand Rapids: Eerdmans, 1961.

———. "Twenty Years After Lausanne: Reflections." *International Bulletin of Missionary Research* (April 1995) 50–55.

Stout, Harry S. *The Divine Dramatist: George Whitefield and the Rise of Modern Evangelicalism*. Grand Rapids: Eerdmans, 1991.

Stowers, Stanley K. "Social Status, Public Speaking and Private Teaching: The Circumstances of Paul's Preaching Activity." *Novum Testamentum* 26 (1984) 59–82.

Strong, Rowan. "Eighteenth-Century Mission Sermons." In *The Oxford Handbook of the British Sermon 1689-1901*, edited by Keith A. Francis and William Gibson, 497-512. Oxford: Clarendon, 2012.

Sturch, R. L. "Reinhold Neibuhr." In *New Dictionary of Christian Ethics and Pastoral Theology*, edited by David J. Atkinson et al., 628-29. Downers Grove: IVP, 1995.

Sugden, C. M. "Social Gospel." In *New Dictionary of Christian Ethics and Pastoral Theology*, edited by David J. Atkinson et al., 799-800. Downers Grove: IVP, 1995.

Synan, Vinson. "The Pentecostal Movement in North America and Beyond." *Journal of Beliefs and Values* 25, no. 2 (August 2004) 153-54.

Taksa, Lucy. "'All a Matter of Timing': Managerial Innovation and Workplace Culture in the New South Wales Railways and Tramways Prior to 1921." *Australian Historical Studies* 29, no. 110 (2008) 1-26.

Tanner, Norman, S. J., ed. *Vatican II: The Essential Texts*. New York: Image, 2012.

Taylor, Charles. "Afterward: Apologia pro Libor suo." In *Varieties of Secularism in a Secular Age*, edited by Michael Warner et al., 300-24. Cambridge: Harvard University Press, 2010.

———. *A Secular Age*. Cambridge, MA: Belknap, 2007.

Taylor, Larissa, ed. *Preachers and People in the Reformations and Early Modern Period*. Boston: Brill Academic, 2003.

Taylor, William, and David Dargue. *Style or Substance: The Nature of True Christian Ministry*. Glasgow: Bell and Bain, 2016.

Teale, Ruth. "The 'Red Book' Case." *Journal of Religious History* 12 (June 1982) 74-89.

Tennant, Bob. "Missions, Slavery, and the Anglican Pulpit, 1780-1850." In *A New History of the Sermon: The Nineteenth Century*, edited by Robert H. Ellison 139-80. Leiden: Brill, 2010.

———. "The Sermons of the Eighteenth-Century Evangelicals." *A New History of the Sermon: The Nineteenth Century*, edited by Robert H. Ellison, 114-32. Leiden: Brill, 2010.

Terracini, Paul. "Bishop JS Moyes and the Attempt to Ban the Communist Party." *History Australia* 8, no. 2 (2011) 106-27.

———. *John Stoward Moyes and the Social Gospel: A Study in Christian Social Engagement*. Katoomba: Xlibris, 2015.

———. "Moyes, Menzies, and the Vietnam War: New Insights into the Public Correspondence Between the Prime Minister and the Bishops." *Journal of Religious History* 36, no.1 (March 2012) 70-88.

Tizon, Al. *Transformation after Lausanne*. Oxford: Regnum, 2008.

Thiselton, Anthony C. *The First Epistle to the Corinthians*. NIGTC. Grand Rapids: Eerdmans, 2000.

Thomas, Sherry L. "Perfection and Perfectionism." In *Encyclopedia of Pentecostal and Charismatic Christianity*, edited by Stanley M Burgess, 363-65. New York: Routledge, 2006.

Thompson, Mark. "Lay Administration: The Theological Considerations." In *The Lord's Supper in Human Hands: Who Should Administer?*, edited by Peter Bolt et al., 21-35. Camperdown: Australian Church Record, 2008.

———. "A Reflection," November 17, 2012. http://acl.asn.au/john-chapman-a-personal-reflection/.

Thompson, Roger C. *Religion in Australia*. Melbourne: Oxford University Press, 1994.

Thornhill, John. *Making Australia: Exploring Our National Conversation*. Newtown: Millennium, 1992.
Tice, Rico. *Christianity Explored*. New Malden: Good Book, 2011.
―――. *Honest Evangelism*. New Malden: Good Book, 2015.
Towns, Elmer L., and Gary L. McIntosh, eds. *Evaluating the Church Growth Movement: 5 Views*. Grand Rapids: Zondervan, 2004.
Tregenza, Ian. "Secularism, Myth, and History." In *Secularization: New Historical Perspectives*, edited by Christopher Hartney, 173–89. Newcastle Upon Tyne: Scholars, 2014.
Tridgell, Susan. *Understanding Our Selves: The Dangerous Art of Biography*. Bern: Peter Lang, 2004.
Trollinger, William Vance. "Godly Ambition: John Stott and the Evangelical Movement." *Church History* 82 (2013) 765–67.
Trueman, Carl. "Preachers and Medieval Renaissance Commentary." In *The Oxford Handbook of The Early Modern Sermon*, edited by Peter McCullough et al., 54–71. Oxford: Oxford University Press, 2011.
Turnbull, Richard. *Anglican and Evangelical?* London: Continuum, 2007.
Twelftree, Graham H. "Signs and Wonders." In *New Dictionary of Biblical Theology*, edited by T. Desmond Alexander and Brian S. Rosner, 775–81. Downers Grove: IVP, 2020.
Valentine, Thomas James. "The Causes of the Depression in Australia." *Explorations in Economic History* 24, no. 1 (1987) 43–62.
Van den Toren, Benno. *Christian Apologetics as Cross-Cultural Dialogue*. New York: T. & T. Clark, 2011.
Van Engen, Charles. "Five Perspectives of Contextually Appropriate Missional Theology." In *Appropriate Christianity*, edited by Charles Kraft, 183–202. Pasadena: William Carey Library, 2005.
Ville, Simon. "The Economy." In *The Cambridge History of Australia, Volume 2: The Commonwealth of Australia*, edited by Alison Bashford and Stuart Macintrye, 377–402. New York: Cambridge University Press, 2013.
Wacker, Grant. *America's Pastor: Billy Graham and the Shaping of a Nation*. Cambridge: Harvard University Press, 2014.
Wagner, Tamara S. "The Victorian Sermon Novel: Domesticated Spirituality and the Sermon's Sensationalization." In *A New History of the Sermon: The Nineteenth Century*, edited by Robert H. Ellison, 309–40. Leiden: Brill, 2010.
Wallace, Max, ed. *Realising Secularism: Australia and New Zealand*. Sydney: Australia New Zealand Secular Association, 2010.
Walls, Andrew F. "The American Dimension in the History of the Missionary Movement." In *Earthen Vessels: American Evangelicals and Foreign Missions, 1880–1980*, edited by Joel A. Carpenter and Wilbert R. Shenk, 1–28. Grand Rapids: Eerdmans, 1990.
―――. "The Eighteenth-Century Protestant Missionary Awakening in its European Context." In *Christian Missions and the Enlightenment*, edited by Brian Stanley, 30–34. Grand Rapids: Eerdmans, 2001.
―――. *The Missionary Movement in Christian History: Studies in the Transmission of Faith*. Maryknoll: Orbis, 2006.

Walsham, Alexandra. "Miracles in Post-Reformation England." In *Signs, Wonders, Miracles: Representations of Divine Power in The Life of the Church*, edited by Kate Cooper and Jeremy Gregory, 273–306. Suffolk: Boydell, 2005.

Walter, James. "Growth Resumed, 1983–2000." In *The Cambridge History of Australia, Volume 2: The Commonwealth of Australia*, edited by Alison Bashford and Stuart Macintyre, 162–86. Cambridge: Cambridge University Press, 2013.

Ward, Kevin. "Christianity, Colonialism and Missions." In *The Cambridge History of Christianity: World Christianities c. 1914–c.2000*, edited by Hugh McLeod, 71–89. Cambridge: Cambridge University Press, 2006.

Ward, Kevin, and Brian Stanley, eds. *The Church Mission Society and World Christianity, 1799–1999*. Grand Rapids: Eerdmans, 2000.

Ward, Kevin, and Emma Wild-Wood, eds. *The East African Revival: History and Legacies*. Surrey: Ashgate, 2012.

Ware, James P. *The Mission of the Church in Paul's Letter to the Philippians in the Context of Ancient Judaism*. Boston: Brill, 2005.

Warner, Rob. "Evangelical Bases of Faith and Fundamentalizing Tendencies." In *Evangelicalism and Fundamentalism in the United Kingdom during the Twentieth Century*, edited by David Bebbington and David Ceri-Jones, 328–47. Oxford: Oxford University Press, 2013.

———. *Reinventing English Evangelicalism, 1966–2001: A Theological and Sociological Study*. Milton Keyes: Paternoster, 2007.

———. *Secularization and Its Discontents*. London: Continuum, 2010.

Warren, Max, ed. *To Apply the Gospel: Selections from the Writings of Henry Venn*. Grand Rapids: Eerdmans, 1971.

Warrington, Keith. "Gifts of Healing." In *Encyclopedia of Pentecostal and Charismatic Christianity*, edited by Stanley M. Burgess, 232–34. New York: Routledge, 2006.

Watson, Duane F., ed. *Persuasive Artistry: Studies in New Testament Rhetoric in Honor of George A. Kennedy*. Sheffield: JSOT, 1991.

Webster, Peter, and Ian Jones. "New Music and the 'Evangelical Style' in the Church of England, c.1958–1991." In *British Evangelical Identities Past and Present*, edited by Mark Smith, 169–70. Milton Keynes: Paternoster, 2008.

Wells, David F. *Above All Earthly Powers: Christ in a Postmodern World*. Leicester: IVP, 2005.

Wenzel, Siegfried. "The Arts of Preaching." In *The Cambridge History of Literary Criticism, Volume 2*, edited by Alastair Minnis and Ian Johnson, 84–96. Cambridge: Cambridge University Press, 2005.

West, Janet. "Hilliard, William George (1887–1961)." In *Australian Dictionary of Evangelical Biography*, edited by Brian Dickey, 165–66. Sydney: Evangelical History Association, 1994.

White, Paul. *Alias Jungle Doctor: An Autobiography*. Carlisle: Paternoster, 1977.

Whiteman, Darrell L. "Contextualization: The Theory, the Gap, the Challenge." *International Bulletin of Missionary Research* 21 (January 1997) 2–7.

Williams, A. E. *West Anglican Way: The Growth of the Anglican Church in Western Australia*. Perth: Province of WA, 1989.

Williams, Graham, and Judy Robinson. "War in the Cloisters." *Sydney Morning Herald*, March 13, 1993, 39.

Williams, J. R. "Baptism in the Holy Spirit." In *New International Dictionary of Pentecostal and Charismatic Movements*, edited by Stanley M. Burgess, 359–60. Grand Rapids: Zondervan, 2002.

Wilson, Bryan R. *Religion in Secular Society: A Sociological Comment*. London: Watts, 1966.

———. *Religion in Sociological Perspective*. Oxford: Oxford University Press, 1982.

Windsor, Lionel. "Speech and Salvation 1: Are All Christians Commanded to Evangelise?" *The Briefing*, September 19, 2011.

Winter, Ralph. "The Highest Priority: Cross-Cultural Evangelism." In *Let the Earth Hear His Voice: International Congress on World Evangelization, Lausanne, Switzerland, Official Reference Volume*, edited by J. D. Douglas, 213–58. Minneapolis: World Wide Publications, 1975.

Witherington, Ben, III. *New Testament Rhetoric: An Introductory Guide to the Art of Persuasion in and of the New Testament*. Eugene: Cascade Books, 2009.

Withycombe, Robert S. M. "Francis Bertie Boyce." In *Australian Dictionary of Evangelical Biography*, edited by Brian Dickey, 46–47. Sydney: Evangelical History Association, 1994.

Wolffe, John. "Anglicanism, Presbyterianism and the Religious Identities of the United Kingdom." In *Cambridge History of Christianity, Volume 8: World Christianities, c.1815–c.1914*, edited by Sheridan Gilley and Brian Stanley, 301–23. Cambridge: Cambridge University Press, 2006.

———. "British Sermons on National Events." In *A New History of the Sermon: The Nineteenth Century*, edited by Robert H. Ellison, 181–206. Leiden: Brill, 2010.

———. "Evangelicals and Pentecostals: Indigenizing a Global Gospel." In *Global Religious Movements in Regional Context*, edited by John Wolffe. Milton Keynes: Aldershot, 2002.

Wolterstorff, Nicholas. "The Reformed Liturgy." In *Major Themes in the Reformed Tradition*, edited by Donald K. McKim, 273–304. Grand Rapids: Eerdmans, 1992.

Wood, Gordon S. *Purpose of the Past: Reflections on the Uses of History*. New York: Penguin, 2009.

———. "The Purpose of the Past: Reflections on the Uses of History." *Historically Speaking* 10, no. 1 (January 2009) 2–6.

Woodhouse, John. "Lay Administration of the Lord's Supper: A Change to Stay the Same." In *The Lord's Supper in Human Hands: Who Should Administer?*, edited by Peter Bolt et al., 7–20. Camperdown: Australian Church Record, 2008.

———. "Signs and Wonders and Evangelical Ministry." In *Signs and Wonders and Evangelicals: A Response to the Teaching of John Wimber*, edited by Robert Doyle, 7–59. Homebush West: Lancer, 1987.

Wright, Judith. *Preoccupations in Australian Poetry*. Melbourne: Oxford University Press, 1965.

Wuellner, Wilhelm. "Biblical Exegesis in the Light of the History and Historicity of Rhetoric and the Nature of the Rhetoric of Religion." In *Rhetoric and the New Testament: Essays from the 1992 Heidelberg Conference*, edited by Stanley E. Porter and Thomas H. Olbricht, 492–513. Sheffield: JSOT, 1993.

———. "Where is Rhetorical Criticism Taking Us?" *Catholic Biblical Quarterly* 49, no. 3 (1987) 448–63.

Yarwood, A. T. *Samuel Marsden*. Melbourne: MUP, 1977.

"Youth for the Church." *The Armidale Diocese News*, June 1951, 19.

Online Sources

Adam, Peter. "Reflecting on Fifty Years of Expository Preaching in Australia (1965–2015)." *The Gospel Coalition Australia*, May 12, 2016. https://australia.thegospelcoalition.org/article/celebrating-fifty-years-of-expository-preaching-in-australia.
AFES. "History." https://www.afes.org.au/about/history.
Anglican Aid. "Anglican Aid's Annual Report 2016–17." *Issuu*, November 22, 2017. https://issuu.com/anglicanaid/docs/aa_report_2017-18.
Anglican Church of Australia. "Sunday Services: A Contemporary Liturgical Resource." http://www.sundayservices.anglican.asn.au/index.html.
Anglican Church League. "Bishop Peter Chiswell 1934–2013." *ACL*, December 11, 2013. https://acl.asn.au/bishop-peter-chiswell/.
Anglican Diocese of Armidale. "About the Diocese." http://www.armidaleanglicandiocese.com/diocese/about.
Anglican Diocese of Sydney. "Conduct of the Business of Synod Ordinance 2000." https://www.sds.asn.au/sites/default/files/ords/2000/29conductofbusiness.pdf?doc_id=MzIxMg==.
———. "Social Issues Committee." http://socialissues.org.au/.
Anglicare. "2018 Annual Review." https://www.anglicare.org.au/media/4348/anglicareannualreview_2018.pdf.
Australian Bureau of Statistics. "2016 Census." https://www.abs.gov.au/websitedbs/censushome.nsf/home/2016.
Britannica. "Confession of Faith." https://www.britannica.com/topic/confession-of-faith-theology.
Charles Sturt University. "Centre for Public and Contextual Theology (PaCT)." http://www.csu.edu.au/pact.
City Bible Forum. https://citybibleforum.org/.
Cleary, John. "Sunday Nights With John Cleary: Peter Jensen, Anglican Archbishop of Sydney." *ABC*, July 30, 2001. http://www.abc.net.au/sundaynights/stories/s809830.htm.
Cook, David. "John Charles Chapman (Chappo)." *Presbyterian Church of Australia: Moderator's Comments*, May 18, 2016. http://presbyterian.org.au/index.php/resources/moderator-s-comments/107-john-charles-chapman-chappo.
Cru. "About Us." https://www.cru.org/us/en/about.
Ellmoos, Laila, and Lisa Murray. "Building the Sydney Harbour Bridge." *Dictionary of Sydney*, 2015. https://dictionaryofsydney.org/entry/building_the_sydney_harbour_bridge.
Forsyth, Rob. "Holy Spirit: The Communicator." *Barneys*, July 31, 2015. https://www.barneys.org.au/talks/holy-spirit-the-communicator-3/.
Freyne, Catherine. "Sydney Technical College." *Dictionary of Sydney*, 2010. https://dictionaryofsydney.org/entry/sydney_technical_college.
GAFCON, Global Anglicans. "History." https://www.gafcon.org/about/history.
Goodreads. "A Fresh Start." https://www.goodreads.com/book/show/3812967-a-fresh-start.
Goodstein, Laurie. "Billy Graham Activates a Global Electronic Pulpit." *The Washington Post*, March 14, 1995. https://www.washingtonpost.com/archive/

politics/1995/03/14/billy-graham-activates-a-global-electronic-pulpit/47752b5f-8e05-4f79-b52c-f62349f5e70a/.

The Gospel Coalition. "Foundation Documents." https://www.thegospelcoalition.org/about/foundation-documents/.

———. "Theological Vision for Ministry." www.thegospelcoalition.org/about/foundation-documents/#theological-vision-for-ministry.

Grant, Sandy. "John Chapman Interview." *The Briefing*, June 19, 2012. http://thebriefing.com.au/2012/06/john-chapman-interviewed/.

Interserve. "Remembering John Reid." May 20, 2016. https://interserve.org.au/story/208-remembering-john-reid/.

Jensen, Phillip. "True Spirituality." *St. Matthias*, March 12, 1995. https://phillipjensen.com/sermons/true-spirituality.

KCC, Katoomba Christian Convention. "Resources." https://www.kcc.org.au/resources.html.

Langham Partnership. "History." https://langham.org/who-we-are/history/.

Lausanne Movement. "Lausanne Occasional Paper 21: Evangelism and Social Responsibility: An Evangelical Commitment." https://www.lausanne.org/content/lop/lop-21.

———. "Leaders and Future Meetings." https://www.lausanne.org/about/leaders/.

Matthias Media. *The Briefing*. http://matthiasmedia.com/briefing.

———. "Setting Hearts on Fire." http://www.matthiasmedia.com.au/setting-hearts-on-fire.

MTS, Ministry Training Scheme. "What is MTS?" https://mts.com.au/about/.

Navigators. "Remembering Charlie Riggs: Lifelong Laborer." https://www.navigators.org/blog/charlie-riggs-lifelong-laborer/.

NCLS. "NCLS Research." http://www.ncls.org.au.

NSW Government. "History of New South Wales Government Schools: Examinations." https://education.nsw.gov.au/about-us/our-people-and-structure/history-of-government-schools/facts-and-figures/examinations.

Palmer, Hugh. "Romans 1:1–17. A Service of Thanksgiving for John Chapman." *St Helen's Bishopgate*, March 1, 2013. http://www.st-helens.org.uk/resources/medialibrary/src/talk/53263/title/tribute-reading-address-and-prayers.

Percy, Natasha. "Waiting for Their Connection." *Sydney Anglicans*, October 13, 2008. https://sydneyanglicans.net/news/waiting_for_their_connection/26760.

Poole, Gavin. "ACL President's Address—2013 Annual General Meeting." *Anglican Church League*, August 29, 2013. http://acl.asn.au/presidents-address-2013-acl.

The Proclamation Trust. "PT Resources." http://www.proctrust.org.uk/resources/conference/Evangelical+Ministry+Assembly+1985.

———. "Question Time with Phillip Jensen—EMA 1986." https://www.proctrust.org.uk/resources/talk/385.

Reserve Bank of Australia. "Inflation Calculator." https://www.rba.gov.au/calculator/annualDecimal.html.

———. "Pre-Decimal Inflation Calculator." https://www.rba.gov.au/calculator/annualPreDecimal.html.

Retief, Frank. " More Thanks from South Africa for Chappo." *Anglican Church League*, November 23, 2012. http://acl.asn.au/more-thanks-from-south-africa-for-chappo/.

Richardson, John. "AEJCC, the First Address." *The Ugley Vicar*, July 13, 2011. http://ugleyvicar.blogspot.com.au/2011/07/eajcc-first-address.html.

Roads and Traffic Authority. "Tom Ugly's Bridge: Maintenance Works." http://www.rms.nsw.gov.au/documents/projects/sydney-south/tom-uglys-bridge/tom-uglys-bridge-maintanance-works-display-jun2006.pdf.

The Salvation Army. "2018 Annual Report." https://www.salvationarmy.org.au/about-us/news-and-stories/publications-and-resources/2018-annual-report/.

Skidmore, David. "Lambeth Struggles Over Homosexuality in Emotional Plenary Session." *ACNS: Anglican Communion News Service*, August 7, 1998. https://www.anglicannews.org/news/1998/08/lambeth-struggles-over-homosexuality-in-emotional-plenary-session.aspx.

Sydney Diocesan Services. "Recognised Churches Ordinance 2000." https://www.sds.asn.au/sites/default/files/ords/adminord/O73-0081.pdf?doc_id=NTE2MTU=.

Sydney Technical High School. "School History." https://sydneytech-h.schools.nsw.gov.au/about-our-school/school-history.html.

T4G. "About Us." http://t4g.org/about/.

Thompson, Mark. "John Chapman—A Personal Reflection from Mark Thompson." *Anglican Church League*, November 17, 2012. http://acl.asn.au/john-chapman-a-personal-reflection/.

UCCF: The Christian Unions. "Uncover." https://www.uccf.org.uk/uncover/.

Wikipedia. "Charles Court." https://en.wikipedia.org/wiki/Charles_Court.

———. "Richard Court." https://en.wikipedia.org/wiki/Richard_Court.

The Word One to One. https://www.theword121.com/.

"Canon John 'Chappo' Chapman is remembered by many as a winsome and dedicated evangelist—good humored, down-to-earth, and relatable. But here is a first scholarly assessment of Chapman's extraordinary contribution to the development of an Australian evangelical approach to preaching, evangelism, and the reform and indigenization of Australian Anglicanism. . . . As we continue to engage contemporary challenges to gospel ministry and mission in secular Australia, there is much to be gained from this absorbing study."

—**Kanishka Raffel**, archbishop, Anglican Diocese of Sydney

"This finely observed and meticulously researched historical study reveals Canon John 'Chappo' Chapman as one of the most dynamic evangelists and preachers in Australian history. Through careful analysis of Chapman's evangelistic vision and preaching prowess, Stace shows how Chapman adapted—with wit, cultural sensitivity, and creativity—an unchanging gospel message to the rapidly changing, secularizing Australian and Western cultures of the post-1960s period. This book will be the definitive work on Chapman's life and legacy for decades to come."

—**Michael Gladwin**, Charles Sturt University

"Doctoral dissertations are not, I imagine, most people's chosen reading matter. But, for the contemporary Christian believer, Baden Stace's formidable skill in research and reportage on the life and ministry of John Chapman, 'Sydney's one special Evangelist,' will be a veritable feast of good things, whether hitherto known or unknown."

—**Richard Lucas**, former rector, St. Helen's Bishopsgate

"Readers who knew John Chapman will be enriched by this insightful exploration of his life and influence as an evangelist, preacher, and provocateur in the Diocese of Sydney for more than thirty years, while also having a significant impact around the world. Those who knew not 'Chappo,' will nonetheless be richly informed by this scholarly, yet very readable, explanation of the profound impact of his life and ministry upon generations of clergy and lay people in Australia and beyond."

—**Glenn Davies**, former archbishop, Anglican Diocese of Sydney

"Stace's account of the Sydney-based evangelist John Chapman takes the understanding of his life and work to a new level of historical understanding and critical appreciation. This outstanding historical biography of John Chapman will be rewarding reading for all who are interested in the history of the global evangelical movement and Christian responses to the modern world as it took shape in the final decades of the twentieth century."

—**Geoffrey R. Treloar**, Australian College of Theology

"This book is a banquet for anyone wanting to feed their mind and heart on the wisdom and power of God—seen through the life of the evangelist and godly provocateur, John Chapman. The work that Baden Stace has done is so comprehensive, so informative, and so revealing that the reader cannot help but grow in insight and gratitude. This book is a gift to be carefully devoured."

—**Simon Manchester**, former rector, St. Thomas's North Sydney

"Australian evangelicals are extremely well served by a wealth of first-rate biography. In this volume, Stace adds to this rich tradition with a meticulously researched and insightful treatment of Sydney evangelist John Chapman. For those wishing to grasp a key chapter in the shaping of contemporary Australian Evangelicalism this volume will repay close study. I highly recommend it."

—**Rory Shiner**, senior pastor, Providence City Church

"For each generation, the Lord gifts his people with some extraordinary servants. John Chapman was one such servant. In this meticulous work of biographical history, Stace captures the man and sets him in his context. The work opens a window for the reader into the stimulating world of twentieth-century Evangelicalism and recounts how the gospel was advanced in that era of challenge and change. It is a fine book and I commend it warmly."

—**Peter Jensen**, former archbishop, Anglican Diocese of Sydney

www.ingramcontent.com/pod-product-compliance
Lightning Source LLC
Chambersburg PA
CBHW052110010526
44111CB00036B/1619